ENTERPRISE RISK
MANAGEMENT

ENTERPRISE RISK MANAGEMENT

John Fraser
Betty J. Simkins

The Robert W. Kolb Series in Finance

John Wiley & Sons, Inc.

Published by John Wiley & Sons, Inc., Hoboken, New Jersey.
Published simultaneously in Canada.

For general information on our other products and services or for technical support,
please contact our Customer Care Department within the United States at (800) 762-2974,
outside the United States at (317) 572-3993 or fax (317) 572-4002.

Wiley also publishes its books in a variety of electronic formats. Some content that
appears in print may not be available in electronic books. For more information about
Wiley products, visit our web site at www.wiley.com.

Library of Congress Cataloging-in-Publication Data:

Fraser, John, 1946–
   Enterprise risk management : today's leading research and best practices for
tomorrow's executives / John Fraser, Betty J. Simkins
       p. cm. – (The Robert W. Kolb series in finance)
   Includes index.
   ISBN 978-0-470-49908-5 (cloth)
 1. Risk management.   I. Simkins, Betty J., 1957–   II. Title.
   HD61.F74 2010
   658.15–dc22

Printed in the United States of America

Contents

10 How to Plan and Run a Risk Management Workshop   155

11 How to Prepare a Risk Profile   171

Foreword

I am pleased to welcome this important collection of authoritative papers on enterprise risk management. This subject has, unfortunately, operated below the visibility screen of most CEOs for many years. In the financial institutions, where regulations require a risk management process, most bank CEOs viewed it as a compliance process, much like internal audit and internal controls. They did not view risk management as a strategic process nor one that demanded much of their time and attention. As a consequence, most businesses have limited ability to assess its risk from rapid growth, increased complexity in financing and securitization, and globalization. Company executives have not been the only ones failing to pay sufficient attention to the topic. Few MBA, accounting, or finance programs departments featured courses and training in enterprise risk management.

The events of 2007–2009 have made the gaps in knowledge, training, and attention to risk management abundantly clear, albeit in a highly costly and tragic manner. Businesses, business schools, regulators, and the public are now scrambling to catch up with the emerging field of enterprise risk management. This subject must become a priority for students to study, executives to practice, and regulators to verify. Fraser and Simkins have produced an impressive contribution to the field, one that I believe will help to educate many. I hope this book, beyond its educational and attention-directing mission, will also stimulate the production of other articles and books so that a common body of knowledge can be developed for this vital profession. We are indebted to John Fraser and Betty Simkins for organizing the impressive author team and the editing of this book.

ROBERT S. KAPLAN
Baker Foundation Professor
Harvard University

ENTERPRISE RISK MANAGEMENT

PART I

Overview

CHAPTER 1

Enterprise Risk Management

An Introduction and Overview

JOHN R.S. FRASER
Vice President, Internal Audit & Chief Risk Officer, Hydro One Networks Inc.

BETTY J. SIMKINS
Williams Companies Professor of Business and Professor of Finance, Oklahoma State University

It's not the strongest of the species that survive, nor the most intelligent, but those that are the most responsive to change.

—Charles Darwin

WHAT IS ENTERPRISE RISK MANAGEMENT?

Enterprise risk management (ERM) can be viewed as a natural evolution of the process of risk management. The Committee of Sponsoring Organizations of the Treadway Commission (COSO) defines enterprise risk management as: "... a process, effected by an entity's board of directors, management and other personnel, applied in strategy setting and across the enterprise, designed to identify potential events that may affect the entity, and manage risk to be within its risk appetite, to provide reasonable assurance regarding the achievement of entity objectives." The COSO definition is intentionally broad and deals with risks and opportunities affecting value creation or preservation. Similarly, in this book, we take a broad view of ERM, or what we call—*a holistic approach to ERM.*

Some sources have referred to ERM as a new risk management paradigm. As in the past, many organizations continue to address risk in "silos," with the management of insurance, foreign exchange, operations, credit, and commodities each conducted as narrowly focused and fragmented activities. Under ERM, all risk areas would function as parts of an integrated, strategic, and enterprise-wide system. And while risk management is coordinated with senior-level oversight, employees at all levels of the organization using ERM are encouraged to view risk management as an integral and ongoing part of their jobs.

The purpose of this book is to provide a blend of academic and practical experience on ERM in order to educate practitioners and students alike about this evolving methodology. Furthermore, our goal is to provide a holistic coverage of ERM, and in this process, provide the "'what," "why," and "how" of ERM to assist firms with the successful implementation of ERM.

The chapters that follow are from some of the leading academics and practitioners of this new methodology, with the in-depth insights into what practitioners of this evolving business practice are actually doing, as well as anticipating what needs to be taught on this topic. The leading experts in this field clearly explain what enterprise risk management is and how you can teach, learn, or implement these leading practices within the context of your business activities.

Enterprise Risk Management introduces you to the wide range of concepts and techniques for managing risk in a holistic way, by correctly identifying risks and prioritizing the appropriate responses. It offers a broad overview of the different types of techniques: the role of the board, risk tolerances, risk profiles, risk workshops, and allocation of resources, while focusing on the principles that determine business success. This comprehensive resource also provides a thorough introduction to enterprise risk management as it relates to credit, market, and operational risks, and covers the evolving requirements of the rating agencies and their importance to the overall risk management in a corporate setting. As well, it offers a wealth of knowledge on the drivers, the techniques, the benefits, and the pitfalls to avoid, in successfully implementing enterprise risk management.

DRIVERS OF ENTERPRISE RISK MANAGEMENT

There are theoretical and practical arguments for the use of ERM. As outlined in Chapter 2 there has been an increasing consciousness in risk literature that a more holistic approach to managing risk makes good business sense.

External drivers for its implementation have been studies such as the Joint Australian/New Zealand Standard for Risk Management,[1] the Committee of Sponsoring Organizations of the Treadway Commission (COSO),[2] the Group of Thirty Report in the United States (following derivatives disasters in the early 1990s),[3] CoCo (the Criteria of Control model developed by the Canadian Institute of Chartered Accountants),[4] the Toronto Stock Exchange Dey Report in Canada following major bankruptcies,[5] and the Cadbury report in the United Kingdom.[6]

Major legal developments such as the New York Stock Exchange Listing Standards and the interpretation of the recent Delaware case law on fiduciary duties, among others, have provided an additional force for ERM.[7] In addition, large pension funds have become more vocal about the need for improved corporate governance, including risk management, and have stated their willingness to pay premiums for stocks of firms with strong independent board governance.[8] ERM has also increased in importance due to the Sarbanes-Oxley Act of 2002—which places greater responsibility on the board of directors to understand and monitor an organization's risks.

Finally, it is important to note that ERM can increase firm value.[9] Security rating agencies such as Moody's and Standard & Poor's include whether a company has an ERM system as a factor in their ratings methodology for insurance, banking, and nonfinancial firms.

SUMMARY OF THE BOOK CHAPTERS

As mentioned earlier, the purpose of this book is to provide a blend of academic and practical experience on ERM in order to educate practitioners and students alike about this evolving methodology. Furthermore, our goal is to provide a holistic coverage of ERM, and in this process, provide the what, why, and how of ERM to assist firms with the successful implementation of ERM. To achieve this goal, the book is organized into the following sections.

> Overview
> ERM Management, Culture, and Control
> ERM Tools and Techniques
> Types of Risks
> Survey Evidence and Academic Research
> Special Topics and Case Studies

A brief description of the author(s) and the chapters is provided below.

Overview

In Chapter 2, "A Brief History of Risk Management," we ask Felix Kloman—retired risk management consultant, conceptual thinker, and lover of sailing—to provide the background and history of risk management and the evolution of enterprise risk management. Felix was ideally suited to do this as someone who has dedicated more than 30 years to sharing stories, raising interesting risk concepts, and generally enjoying the challenges of this entire field. There is no one we know who is better suited or knows more about this topic. He takes us right back literally to some of the earliest recorded thinking on risk management and brings us through the ages to current thinking. Felix goes back to the basic questions of "What is risk management? When and where did we begin applying its precepts? Who were the first to use it?" He provides a highly personal study of this discipline's past and present. It spans the millennia of human history and concludes with a detailed list of contributions in the past century. This is an ideal starting point for anyone new to the topic of risk management or the older scholars who wish to revisit this easy-to-read summary of risk. Felix is adamant in his view that risk must consider opportunities as well as threats.

"ERM and Its Role in Strategic Planning and Strategy Execution" is presented in Chapter 3 by Mark L. Frigo (Director, the Center for Strategy, Execution, and Valuation and Ledger & Quill Alumni Foundation, Distinguished Professor of Strategy and Leadership at the DePaul University Kellstadt Graduate School of Business and School of Accountancy, Chicago) and Mark S. Beasley (Deloitte Professor of Enterprise Risk Management and Professor of Accounting in the College of Management at North Carolina State University, and Director of North Carolina State's Enterprise Risk Management Initiative). The authors have captured the essence of leading ERM and strategic risk management initiatives at their universities as well as their work with hundreds of practice leaders in enterprise risk management. They recognize that one of the major challenges in ensuring that risk management is adding value is to incorporate ERM in business and strategic planning of organizations. They explain how focusing on strategic risks serves as a filter for management and boards of directors to reduce the breadth of the risk playing field and ensure that they are focused on the right risks. These insights should help respond to the numerous calls following the recent credit crisis for improvements in overall risk oversight, with a particular emphasis on strategic risk management.

In Chapter 4, "The Role of the Board of Directors and Senior Management in Enterprise Risk Management," Bruce Branson (Professor and Associate Director, Enterprise Risk Management Initiative, North Carolina State College of Management) explains that the oversight of the enterprise risk management process employed by an organization is one of the most important and challenging functions of a corporation's board of directors. He notes that a failure to adequately acknowledge and effectively manage risks associated with decisions being made throughout the organization can and often do lead to potentially catastrophic results. Bruce explains the shared responsibility between the members of the board and the senior management team to nurture a risk aware culture in the organization that embraces prudent risk taking within an appetite for risk that aligns with the organization's strategic plan. He identifies the legal and regulatory framework that drives the risk oversight responsibilities of the board. He also clarifies the separate roles of the board and its committees vis-à-vis senior management in the development, approval, and implementation of an enterprise-wide approach to risk management. Finally, the chapter explores optimal board structures to best discharge their risk oversight responsibilities.

ERM Management, Culture, and Control

Anette Mikes (Assistant Professor of Business Administration at Harvard Business School) provides insights into the types of roles that CROs play, based on her personal research in Chapter 5, "Becoming the Lamp Bearer: The Emerging Roles of the Chief Risk Officer." Anette gained her PhD in enterprise risk management from the London School of Economics, and is setting up a program at Harvard Business School with Robert Kaplan to teach ERM. Anette describes the role of chief risk officers (CRO) and different types of ERM methodologies that she sees in practice. She draws on the existing practitioner and academic literature on the role of chief risk officers, and a number of case studies from her ongoing research program on the evolution of the role of the CRO. Anette describes the origins and rise of the CRO, and outlines four major roles that senior risk officers may fulfill: (1) the compliance champion; (2) the modeling expert; (3) the strategic advisor; and (4) the strategic controller. She demonstrates how chief risk officers could improve business decision making and incorporate both good risk analytics and expert judgment, as well as influence risk-taking behavior in the business lines. As she explains: "The art of successful risk management is in getting the executive team to see the light and value the lamp-bearer." This chapter will be of great interest to all CROs and those organizations thinking about how to implement ERM.

"Creating a Risk-Aware Culture" is discussed in Chapter 6 by Doug Brooks (President and CEO, Aegon Canada Inc.). The author draws on his actuarial training and business insights to provide the methods to create a positive culture for risk management in any organization. The actuarial profession has for several years recognized and been a leading advocate for the research and expansion of ERM into their organizations. Actuaries are by training and experience well versed in managing risks and have expanded into additional areas such as investments and know how best to apply ERM concepts. We wanted to ensure the actuarial profession was included in this book and were delighted when we approached Doug Brooks that he suggested writing about the role of culture in risk management. Doug has been one of the early pioneers in ERM and this has likely added to his continued professional success, as he was recently appointed President and CEO of Aegon Canada Inc. Doug observes that an organization could possess world-class technical capabilities and strong processes for collecting and reporting information, but still have a bankrupt culture so that no value was added through ERM efforts. He considers that there is nothing more crucial to the success of ERM efforts in an organization than an informed and supportive culture. He points out that culture is not merely an intangible concept, but that its elements can be defined and progress in moving toward a desired culture can be measured. He notes that to be successful in risk management, organizations must recognize the importance of encouraging and rewarding disciplined behaviors, as well as openness in communication. Culture is key to ERM and this chapter is helpful to all practitioners who are implementing ERM.

Chapter 7, "ERM Frameworks," is authored by one of the leading authorities on risk frameworks, Professor Emeritus John Shortreed of the University of Waterloo, Canada. Professor Shortreed provides a forward-looking view at the forthcoming international framework for risk management. He is the Canadian representative on the committee that has developed the new ISO 31000 Risk Management Standard (due to be published around the same time as this book). This chapter is a great "companion" for those using the new ISO 31000 standard. Historically, ERM has been molded by the Australian/New Zealand Risk Standard 4360, by COSO's 2004 publication, and recent pronouncements of rating agencies such as Standard & Poor's; however, this new ISO standard is expected to have greater international acceptance in years to come. This chapter describes the new ISO risk management framework, which incorporates best practice from COSO, PMI (Project Management Institute), the Australian and New Zealand Standard (AS/NZS 4360:2004) and other leading international risk management standards. John notes that an ERM framework can often be implemented in a step-by-step way and this approach will assist in building acceptance of ERM and in encouraging a risk culture, particularly if potentially successful areas are selected for the first steps. As the risk management culture matures in the organization there should be noticeable improvements in the ability to discuss risks easily, decision making under uncertainty, comfort levels with risk situations, and achievement of objectives.

Susan Hwang (Associate Partner, Deloitte, Toronto, Canada) provides some original views on the role of Key Risk Indicators (KRIs) in Chapter 8 "Identifying and Communicating Key Risk Indicators." Since 2000 when Hydro One first began practicing ERM, there have not been a lot of new concepts introduced, despite the numerous publications on the topic. A year or two ago, John Fraser was at a presentation made by Susan Hwang on the topic of KRIs and realized that she was describing a concept that we had not seen before. She demonstrated how to use metrics, or what were often packaged among Key Performance Indicators, as a means of identifying evolving risks that might arise or increase in the future. This is a seemingly simple concept but one that we thought to be important to identifying future key risks. We found that virtually nothing had been written on the topic before, so we asked Susan to write this chapter and share her findings and views. Susan notes that the formal use of KRIs as an ERM tool is an emerging practice. Although many organizations have developed key performance indicators as a measure of progress against the achievement of business goals and strategies, this differs from using KRIs to support risk management and strategic and operational performance. In this chapter, Susan clarifies what KRIs are and demonstrates their practical applications and value to an organization. She outlines the guiding principles for designing KRIs, and discusses implementation and sustainability. The key message she shares is that there are lots of metrics and performance measures in any organization, but the art of ERM is identifying the key ones that will help identify future risks.

ERM Tools and Techniques

"How to Create and Use Corporate Risk Tolerance" is presented in Chapter 9 by Ken Mylrea (Director, Corporate Risk, Canada Deposit Insurance Corporation) and Joshua Lattimore (Policy and Research Advisor, Canada Deposit Insurance Corporation). The authors explore and provide practical examples of the role of risk tolerances. John first learned of Canada Deposit Insurance Corporation (CDIC) in the early 1990s when CDIC issued expectations about the business and financial practices of its member institutions. These principle-based standards were developed by Ken Mylrea and focus on enterprise-wide governance and management. Their underlying premise was that well-managed institutions are less likely to encounter difficulties that could result in CDIC having to pay the claims of depositors. A key feature of the standards was the requirement that institutions' management and board of directors perform a self-assessment against the CDIC control criteria and report the results to the CDIC. In setting the context for this chapter, Ken and Joshua pose the following questions: What is risk tolerance? Why is setting risk tolerance important? What are the factors to consider in setting risk tolerance? And how can you make risk tolerance useful in managing risk? They describe risk tolerance as the risk exposure an organization determines appropriate to take or avoid taking, that is, risk tolerance is about taking calculated risks—namely, taking risks within clearly defined and communicated parameters set by the organization.

In Chapter 10, "How to Plan and Run a Risk Management Workshop," Rob Quail (Outsourcing Program Manager at Hydro One Networks Inc.) provides hard-hitting practical advice on how to actually design and run a risk workshop. Rob was a major reason for the success of ERM at Hydro One and its sustainability to date. He has run more than 200 risk workshops at all levels, including facilitating meetings of up to 800 staff! When we were designing this book we realized that there was nothing we could find documented elsewhere on how to design and run a risk workshop. Rob describes in an easy step-by-step fashion how to design workshops based on the objectives to be achieved, for example, how important is team building versus specific action planning? Rob explains that risk workshops play a vital role in ERM by helping engage executive managers and staff in understanding the corporate objectives and the risks to achieving these within given tolerances. He goes on to show how workshops not only help identify and address critical risks, but also provide opportunities for participants to learn about organizational objectives, risks, and mitigants. He makes it clear that one size does not fit all and each workshop has to be designed carefully depending on the circumstances and desired outcomes.

In Chapter 11, "How to Prepare a Risk Profile," John Fraser (Vice President, Internal Audit & Chief Risk Officer at Hydro One) provides practical advice on how to prepare a risk profile for executive management and the board of directors. We wanted to have a chapter on risk profiles, and while there is a lot written about risk maps, heat maps, and risk identification, we could not find anything specific about how to actually conduct structured interviews and prepare a risk profile. As a result, we decided to document the Hydro One model, which we have been using since 1999, and which has been proven to be simple and effective. This methodology is based primarily on interviews with executives and risk specialists and complements the results captured by risk workshops. Ideally the results of workshops and interviews (or surveys) should be consolidated and reconciled. It is our hope that these step-by-step instructions will give confidence to risk managers implementing ERM on how best to conduct these interviews effectively. As Sir Graham Day, who was an early champion of ERM at Hydro One, told John "ERM obviously works in practice but can you make it work in theory?"

Chapter 12, "How to Allocate Resources Based on Risk," by Joe Toneguzzo (Director—Implementation & Approvals, Power System Planning, Ontario Power Authority) outlines a business framework for prioritizing resources based on risks, as part of the business planning process. Soon after we began implementing ERM at Hydro One, Joe Toneguzzo—who was responsible for obtaining funding and allocating resources for asset management—worked with the Hydro One Corporate Risk Management Group to determine how best to do so utilizing a risk-based approach. (Joe is now with another organization.) A methodology and supporting business process was developed that has served Hydro One well and is regarded as a leading asset management resource allocation model, as validated in international forums on this subject area. The concept involves identifying the critical business risks and the expenditures proposals available to mitigate them. This is followed by rating all the expenditure proposals in a consistent manner based on the risks that will be mitigated per unit of cost. The expenditures proposals are then dispatched on a priority basis, based on cost/benefit scores (where the benefit is measured in terms of reduced risk) until the resources are exhausted. The advantages of the methodology developed are that it is transparent, consistent, and easy to justify to stakeholders such as regulators, boards of directors, and others. Joe takes us through the theory and practice in an easy-to-follow manner.

John Hargreaves (Managing Director, Hargreaves Risk & Strategy, London, England) explores and provides guidance on the popular topic of quantifying risks in Chapter 13, "Quantitative Risk Assessment in ERM." John Hargreaves has seen his ideas and expertise implemented in various major organizations in England and brings an easy-to-understand introduction to what can become complex theories. John enjoyed a successful career in the real world of finance with major organizations, including being responsible for introducing risk management systems in a major bank following the last U.K. depression. Over the last 10 years, he has helped implement risk management systems in about 60 organizations. This chapter explains the complex world of quantification of risks in progressive steps to help those who are new to ERM. John provides descriptions of four differing approaches to the quantification of individual risks. Statistical methods for calculating and reporting a company's total corporate risk are described and illustrated by a simple example and he also shows how quantified risks may be incorporated in the business planning process. Note that specialized methods to quantify risks in financial institutions are not covered here. His chapter is a must-read for anyone interested in the theory of practical and workable methods for quantifying risks.

Types of Risks

In Chapter 14, "Market Risk Management and Common Elements with Credit Risk Management," Rick Nason (Partner, RSD Solutions, and Associate Professor of Finance, Dalhousie University, Nova Scotia) explains very sophisticated trading and market risk concepts and risk management methods in an easy-to-understand format. Rick left the exciting world of derivatives trading at a major Canadian bank to join the even more exciting world of academia where he is sharing his experiences through his teaching and consulting activities. Although comfortable with the complex models and math for market risk and derivatives, Rick decided to write this chapter for the general practitioner who wants to learn about market risk management and how it relates to credit risk management. In this chapter, Rick describes how to consider these risks and a framework that provides a focus on market risk. Rick points out that market risk management requires not only an understanding of the tools and techniques, but also of the underlying business in order to successfully implement the market risk function within the enterprise risk management framework of the organization.

Continuing his discussion from the previous chapter, Rick Nason provides the basic elements of credit risk management as well as the more sophisticated concepts every credit risk manager should understand in Chapter 15, "Credit Risk Management." Each year, Rick runs a credit competition at the university, as well as consulting with major banks on ERM and credit risk management. Rick explains that when conducting credit analysis, it is important to remember that, unlike market risk, credit risk is almost always a downside risk; that is, unexpected credit events are almost always negative events and only rarely positive surprises. He also reminds the reader that no one extends credit to a customer, or executes a loan to a counterparty, expecting that it will not be repaid. Rick has crafted this chapter for the general practitioner who wants to learn about credit risk management and for the more experienced credit managers seeking to validate their approach.

Diana Del Bel Belluz (President, Risk Wise Inc.) explains operational risk concepts and methods in an easy-to-read format that will be essential to any student of ERM and helpful to more experienced readers in Chapter 16, "Operational Risk Management." Diana has taught risk management since 1992 and has a background in decision science. With her broad experience from her consulting practice, she understands the challenges of a wide variety of organizations in getting a handle on this multifaceted topic. In this chapter, Diana explains the fundamentals of risk management in an operational setting and how operational risk management can be used to capture the full performance potential of an organization. She explores what is meant by operational risk and why it is important. She frames her explanations around questions such as: How do you align operational risk management with enterprise risk management? How do you assess operational risks? Why do you need to define risk tolerance for aligned decision making? What can you do to manage operational risk? How do you encourage a culture of risk management at the operational level? This chapter provides a well-rounded introduction to a topic that is becoming of increasing interest.

In Chapter 17, "Risk Management: Techniques in Search of a Strategy," Joseph V. Rizzi (Senior Investment Strategist, CapGen Financial Group, New York) explores the reasons for the losses that triggered massive shareholder value destruction resulting in dilutive recapitalizations, replacement of whole management teams, the failure of numerous institutions, and the adoption of the $700 billion TARP rescue program, and what can be done to avoid this in future. He suggests that risk management needs to move away from a technical, specialist control function with limited linkage to shareholder value creation. This can be achieved by firms and risk decisions moving from an internal egocentric focus to an external systems approach incorporating the firm within a market context. Further, he states that we need to move beyond risk measurement to risk management that integrates risk into strategic planning, capital management, and governance. Joseph draws on Warren Buffett's principles and numerous practical examples (including Long Term Capital Management) to explain, using charts and models, how governance and ERM can address many of the pitfalls we have seen.

Daniel A. Rogers (Associate Professor of Finance, School of Business Administration, Portland State University) provides in Chapter 18, "Managing Financial Risk and Its Interaction with Enterprise Risk Management," a useful background on financial risk management, namely corporate strategies of employing financial transactions to eliminate or reduce measurable risks. He includes possible definitions and examples of industry applications of financial hedging. He then moves on to a basic review of the theoretical rationales for managing (financial) risk and explores the potential for the interaction of financial hedging with other areas of risk management (such as operational, strategic). He also discusses the lessons that can be applied to ERM from the knowledge base about financial hedging. He points out that active board involvement and buy-in are critical to the implementation of a successful ERM program, and that boards that better understand financial risks are likely to be more receptive to conversations about other significant risks that could negatively affect company performance.

Benton E. Gup (Robert Hunt Cochrane/Alabama Bankers Association Chair of Banking at the University of Alabama) traces the evolution of bank capital requirements in Chapter 19, "Bank Capital Regulation and Enterprise Risk Management," from the 1800s to the complex models used in Basel I and II. He points out that the recent subprime crisis makes it clear that our largest banks and financial institutions do not have adequate risk management as evidenced by problems with major banks and that the models employing economic capital can be subject to large errors. He goes on to introduce enterprise risk management and economic capital, which he believes represent the future of bank capital. He notes that enterprise risk management uses a "building block" approach to aggregate the risks from all lines of business, and that economic capital must be "forward looking," and based on expected scenarios instead of recent history.

In "Legal Risk Post-SOX and the Subprime Fiasco: Back to the Drawing Board" (Chapter 20), Steven Ramirez (Director, Business & Corporate Governance Law Center, Loyola University, Chicago) notes that legal risk should be managed in accordance with basic notions of risk management generally. He points out that it should not exist within a risk silo, but should be managed with a view toward the firm's overall risk tolerance and through coordinated efforts of senior management, as well as the board. Professor Ramirez explains in a "no holds barred" way how the rules of professional responsibility governing lawyers were flawed, corporate law was stunted, whistle-blowing was not encouraged, codes of conduct were wholly optional, and there was insufficient regulation of the audit function. This chapter reviews the most developed framework governing legal and reputational risk (SOX) and suggests innovative and proactive ways that controls could be improved and risk can be reduced in the future.

"Financial Reporting and Disclosure Risk Management" is discussed extensively by Susan Hume, Assistant Professor of Finance and International Business, School of Business, the College of New Jersey) in Chapter 21. The author boils down the key requirements of the extensive regulations for financial reporting and disclosure into an easy-to-understand chapter. Key topics such as reporting on internal controls under Sarbanes-Oxley, accounting for derivatives, and fair value accounting are discussed and explained. Susan explains how ERM reporting and disclosure provides the forum to discuss the key vulnerabilities and risks of the firm and strengthens management accountability. It is for the board and senior management to set the risk policy, establish the key levels of acceptable risk exposure, and communicate these policies to managers and other employees. Implementation and reporting then flows up from the bottom to senior management and to the risk management committee, which may be a subcommittee of the board in the ideal structure. This chapter will be an ideal place to gain an introduction to these complex requirements as well as add helpful insights for the more experienced reader.

Survey Evidence and Academic Research

John Fraser and Betty Simkins (co-editors of this book) teamed with Karen Schoening-Thiessen (Senior Manager of Executive Networks in the Governance and Corporate Responsibility Group at the Conference Board of Canada) to develop and analyze the first survey evidence of risk executives working in the area of ERM about the literature they find most effective in assisting and facilitating the successful implementation of ERM. The study in Chapter 22, "Who Reads What Most Often?" highlights crucial areas of need on ERM, and it is hoped that these will be a starting point to encourage and stimulate more advances in the research and practice of ERM. It highlights excellent opportunities for academics to closely collaborate with practitioners to conduct research in these key areas of need. The chapter also discusses problems and challenges risk executives have encountered that were not addressed in the literature. Detailed listings are provided of the top readings of articles (i.e., surveys, academic studies, and practitioner articles), books, and research reports. This chapter was originally published in the Spring/Summer 2008 issue of the *Journal of Applied Finance*.

Chapter 23, "Academic Research on Enterprise Risk Management," by Subbu Iyer (PhD student, Oklahoma State University), Daniel A. Rogers (Associate Professor, Portland State University), and Betty Simkins (Williams Companies Professor of Finance, Oklahoma State University), provides a summary to date of research on enterprise risk management. To conduct the review, they searched academic journals and other databases of academic research and limited their focus to papers that can be classified as either academic research or case studies that would be appropriate for a classroom setting. After a thorough search of ERM literature, the authors located 10 research studies and 5 case studies to synthesize. Overall, the authors find little in the way of consistent results about ERM. In addition, they find that more case studies on enterprise risk management are needed so that risk executives can learn from the experiences of others who have successfully implemented it.

In Chapter 24 "Enterprise Risk Management: Lessons from the Field," we have the benefit of the knowledge from a trio of experienced ERM experts, namely: William G. Shenkir (William Stamps Farish Professor Emeritus, University of Virginia's McIntire School of Commerce), Thomas L. Barton (Kathryn and Richard Kip Professor of Accounting, University of North Florida) and Paul L. Walker (Associate Professor of Accounting, University of Virginia). The authors of this chapter have been involved in the area of ERM since 1996. They have taught ERM at the undergraduate and graduate levels and for businesses and executives worldwide as well as consulting on ERM implementation. They point out that one of the early lessons that companies glean from ERM is that many layers of the company, including senior management, operating managers, and regular employees do not know or understand the strategies and objectives of the organization and how these, in turn, relate to their daily job and tasks. ERM compels companies to identify and focus on the organization's strategies and objectives. This chapter is illustrated with numerous real-life examples and provides a wonderful lesson in what enterprise risk management is like in real life.

Special Topics and Case Studies

In Chapter 25, "Rating Agencies Impact on Enterprise Risk Management," Mike Moody (Managing Director, Strategic Risk Financing Inc.) provides the history and current published thinking of the major rating agencies. This is an area that we expect will expand and become more established as time goes on. Mike has an MBA in finance, is the Managing Director of a risk consulting firm, and was a risk manager of a Fortune 500 company. He has a broad view of the risk universe and what is happening due to the activities of the rating agencies. The interest taken by the agencies, especially Standard & Poor's (S&P) in recent years, has focused boards and senior management on the need for and the advantages of ERM. Mike notes that one of the primary reasons for the movement of rating agencies into ERM is that they believe companies with an enterprise-wide view of risks, such as that offered by ERM, are better managed. Several have also noted that ERM provides an objective view of hard-to-measure aspects such as management capabilities, strategic rigor, and ability to manage in changing circumstances. He explains that the view of S&P is that positive or negative changes in ERM programs are considered as leading indicators that show up long before they could be seen in a company's published financial data. This chapter provides a sound base for understanding the background and role of rating agencies in ERM, a story that is likely still evolving.

"Enterprise Risk Management: Current Initiatives and Issues" (Chapter 26), contains a roundtable discussion sponsored and published by the *Journal of Applied Finance,* which includes an expert group of academics and practitioners in the area of risk management. The discussants consisted of Bruce Branson (Associate Director of the Enterprise Risk Management Initiative and Professor in the Department of Accounting at North Carolina State University), Pat Concessi (Partner in Global Energy Markets with Deloitte and Touche, Toronto, Canada), John R.S. Fraser (Chief Risk Officer and Vice President of Internal Audit at Hydro One Inc. in Toronto), Michael Hofmann (Vice President and Chief Risk Officer at Koch Industries, Inc. in Wichita, Kansas), Robert (Bob) Kolb (Frank W. Considine Chair in Applied Ethics at Loyola University Chicago), Todd Perkins (Director of Enterprise Risk at Southern Company, Inc. in Atlanta, Georgia), Joe Rizzi (Senior Investment Strategist at CapGen Financial in New York, but at the time of the roundtable discussion, he was the Managing Director of Enterprise Risk Management at Bank of America and La Salle Bank in Chicago, Illinois), and the moderator Betty J. Simkins (Williams Companies Professor of Business and Associate Professor of Finance in the Spears School of Business at Oklahoma State University). This roundtable explored many avenues, concerns, and possible solutions in this evolving arena of risk management.

Demir Yener, Senior Advisor at Deloitte Consulting, Emerging Markets (Washington D.C.), discusses enterprise risk management applications suitable for, and as they exist in, a number of emerging market corporations in Chapter 27, "Establishing ERM Systems in Emerging Countries." He notes that there is a growing interest in improving corporate governance practices in emerging markets. Following the financial crises in the Far East and Russia, which impacted many other emerging markets in 1997–1998, there was a realization that corporate governance practices had to be improved along with the financial sector infrastructure. The Financial Stability Forum was convened, as a result of which the OECD (Organisation for Economic Co-operation and Development) Principles of Corporate Governance were developed in 1999. Since then the principles have been revised in 2004, and other standards of business conduct had been introduced to provide guidance in a number of critical areas of global cooperation for business and finance among nations. The emerging countries in Demir's sample include Egypt, Jordan, Mongolia, Serbia, Turkey, and Ukraine. The ERM concept is still a new concept in these countries and it is likely to take a while to get the emerging country firms, given the legal and regulatory requirements, to reach the desirable level of risk management practices.

In Chapter 28, "The Rise and Evolution of the Chief Risk Officer: Enterprise Risk Management at Hydro One," Tom Aabo (Associate Professor, Aarhus School of Business, Denmark), John R.S. Fraser (Chief Risk Officer, Hydro One Inc.), and Betty J. Simkins (Williams Companies Professor of Business, Oklahoma State University) describe the successful implementation of enterprise risk management (ERM) at Hydro One Inc. over a five-year period. This chapter was first published in the *Journal of Applied Corporate Finance.* Hydro One is a Canadian electric utility company that has experienced significant changes in its industry and business. Hydro One has been at the forefront of ERM for many years, especially in utilizing a holistic approach to managing risks, and provides a best practices case study for other firms to follow. This chapter describes the process of implementation beginning with the creation of the chief risk officer position, the deployment of a pilot workshop, and the various tools and techniques critical to ERM (e.g., the Delphi Method, risk trends, risk maps, risk tolerances, risk profiles, and risk rankings).

As this brief overview indicates, the chapters in this book present an impressive coverage of crucial issues on enterprise risk management and are written by leading ERM experts globally. We believe that no other book on the market provides such a wide coverage of timely topics—such as ERM management, culture and control, ERM tools and techniques, types of risk from a holistic viewpoint, leading case studies, practitioner survey evidence, and academic research on ERM. The authors of these chapters and we, the editors, invite reader comments and suggestions.

FUTURE OF ERM AND UNRESOLVED ISSUES

As is generally recognized, ERM is still evolving with new techniques and research of best practices being studied and documented on almost a daily basis. Some of the issues that we feel deserve the attention of our readers and those interested in the future of ERM include:

- Why have some companies succeeded and others failed in the implementation of ERM?
- What do we predict for the future of ERM?
- What research issues remain?
- A comment on universities' ERM programs and education.
- What unresolved issues do we see?

The above issues all merit study and more attention than they have received to date. An entire chapter, if not book, could be written on the reasons for failure in the implementation of ERM. Often it appears to be caused in part by confusion over exactly what ERM is and undue expectations of management. Our observation is that too often the skills and techniques are not available and without support from the most senior ranks, ERM is destined to fail.

We expect ERM to continue to grow until, in looking back, future managers will ask "How could you have managed without these basic techniques?" Obviously there has to be more discussion and clarification on what ERM is and what it has to offer. While regulatory interest can force ERM into companies, if not done well, it can become another box-ticking exercise that adds little value.

As highlighted in Chapter 23, the opportunities to study ERM and assist in moving this new methodology forward are limitless and likely to continue. While some analysis can be done based on public information, it will require proactive visionary academics to go into the real world and study what is evolving in real business practices. This is a veritable goldmine for some intrepid academics and a minefield for the more timid.

NOTES

1. The Joint Australian/New Zealand Standard for Risk Management (AS/NSZ 4360: 2004), first edition published in 1995, is the first guide on enterprise risk management that provides practical information. This publication covers the establishment and implementation of the enterprise risk management process.

2. The Committee of Sponsoring Organizations of the Treadway Commission (COSO) (September 1992 and September 2004).

3. Group of Thirty, Derivatives: Practices and Principles (Washington, DC: 1993).

4. CoCo (Criteria of Control Board of the Canadian Institute of Chartered Accountants).

5. "Where Were the Directors"—Guidelines for Improved Corporate Governance in Canada, report of the Toronto Stock Exchange Committee on Corporate Governance in Canada (December 1994).

6. Committee on the Financial Aspects of Corporate Governance (Cadbury Committee, final report and Code of Best Practices issued December 1, 2002).

7. NYSE Corporate Governance Rules 7C(iii)(D) www.nyse.com/pdfs/finalcorpgovrules.pdf and Emerging Governance Practices in Enterprise Risk Management, the Conference Board (2007).

8. McKinsey & Company and Institutional Investor, 1996. "Corporate Boards: New Strategies for Adding Value at the Top."

9. Risk management in general has been shown to increase firm value. See Smithson, Charles W., and Betty J. Simkins, "Does Risk Management Add Value? A Survey of the Evidence," *Journal of Applied Corporate Finance* vol. 17, no. 3 (2005): 8–17.

ABOUT THE EDITORS

John Fraser is the Vice President, Internal Audit & Chief Risk Officer of Hydro One Networks Inc., one of North America's largest electricity transmission and distribution companies. He is an Ontario and Canadian Chartered Accountant, a Fellow of the Association of Chartered Certified Accountants (U.K.), a Certified Internal Auditor, and a Certified Information Systems Auditor. He has more than 30 years experience in the risk and control field mostly in the financial services sector, including areas such as finance, fraud, derivatives, safety, environmental, computers, and operations. He is currently Chair of the Advisory Committee of the Conference Board of Canada's Strategic Risk Council, a Practitioner Associate Editor of the *Journal of Applied Finance*, and a past member of the Risk Management and Governance Board of the Canadian Institute of Chartered Accountants. He is a recognized authority on enterprise risk management and has co-authored three academic papers on ERM—published in the *Journal of Applied Corporate Finance* and the *Journal of Applied Finance*.

Betty J. Simkins is Williams Companies Professor of Business and Professor of Finance at Oklahoma State University (OSU). She received her BS in Chemical Engineering from the University of Arkansas, her MBA from OSU, and her PhD from Case Western Reserve University. Betty is also active in the finance profession and currently serves as Vice-Chairman of the Trustees (previously President) of the Eastern Finance Association, on the board of directors for the Financial Management Association (FMA), as co-editor of the *Journal of Applied Finance,* and as Executive Editor of *FMA Online* (the online journal for the FMA). She has coauthored more than 30 journal articles in publications including the *Journal of Finance, Financial Management, Financial Review, Journal of International Business Studies, Journal of Futures Markets, Journal of Applied Corporate Finance,* and the *Journal of Financial Research* and has won a number of best paper awards at academic conferences.

CHAPTER 2

A Brief History of Risk Management

H. FELIX KLOMAN
President, Seawrack Press Inc.

INTRODUCTION

What *is* risk management (and its alternative title "enterprise risk management")? When and where did we begin applying its precepts? Who were the first to use it? This is a brief and highly personal study of this discipline's past and present. It is a description of some of its emotional and intellectual roots. It spans the millennia of human history and concludes with a detailed list of contributions in the past century.

RISK MANAGEMENT IN ANTIQUITY

Making good decisions in the face of uncertainty and risk probably began during the earliest human existence. Evolution favored those human creatures able to use their experience and minds to reduce the uncertainty of food, warmth, and protection. *Homo sapiens* survived by developing "an expression of an instinctive and constant drive for defense of an organism against the risks that are part of the uncertainty of existence."[1] This "genetic expression" can be construed as the beginning of risk management, a discipline for dealing with uncertainty.

As the millennia passed, our species developed other mechanisms for coping with each day's constant surprises. We invented a pantheon of divine creatures to blame for misfortune, praise for good luck, and to whom we offered sacrifices to mitigate the worst. These gods and goddesses, the personification of heavenly bodies, high mountains, and the deepest seas, led to a dependence on human oracles, soothsayers, priests, priestesses, and astrologers, to predict the future. We created a written language (Mesopotamia, Sumeria, Egypt, Phoenicia) in order to pass knowledge to the future. As our species used language, experience, memory, and deduction to explain random uncertainty, we created an alternative and backup explanatory system.

The classical world of the Greeks and Romans demonstrates the development of written language, providing a significant advantage over oral recitation. At first, Greek memories passed on information from the past. Their written language extrapolated it into more rational predictions. Homer, capturing memory, sang of Zeus, Hera, Athena, Apollo, and the corps of divinities responsible for the victory at Troy as well as the misadventures of Odysseus on his return home. But by 585 BC, the Greek philosopher Thales used his observations, written data, and deductions to predict an eclipse of the sun, even though he continued to profess a belief in these gods.[2] A century later Herodotus used intelligent "enquiry" to write "history," but he too persisted with the power of divinities. It was finally Thucydides, in the early 400s BC, who proposed a "new penetrating realism," one that "removed the gods as explanations of the course of events." Thucydides was "fascinated by the gap between expectation and outcome, intention and event."[3] Perhaps he should be called the father of risk management.

A few philosophers in classical Greece tried to emphasize observation, deduction, and prediction, but they inevitably collided with the inertia of belief in the long-standing system of divine intervention as the explanation for misfortune as well as good luck. With the growth and dominance of the new monotheistic religions in the Middle East and Mediterranean, it would take another millennium before the ideas Thucydides first advanced grew into the solid body of scientific knowledge to replace myth and superstition.

AFTER THE MIDDLE AGES

Jump ahead another 1,000 years to the emergence of the Renaissance and Enlightenment. Two changes encouraged the idea that we could actually think intelligently about the future. Peter Bernstein described the first, in his *Against the Gods*: "The idea of risk management emerges only when people believe they are to some degree free agents."[4] The second was our growing fascination with numbers. Our increasing disenchantment with the explanation that a "superior power" ordained everything became coupled with the capability of manipulating experience and data into numbers and thence probabilities. We could predict alternative futures! Peter Bernstein's book is a joyful and often lyrical exploration of development of the concept of risk as both threat and opportunity. We became capable of "scrutinizing the past" to suggest future possibilities. He describes those men who first advanced the ideas of probability measurement, introducing us to familiar and unfamiliar names from the Renaissance onward:

Leonardo Pisano (who introduced Arabic numerals)
Luca Paccioli (double-entry bookkeeping)
Girolamo Cardano (measuring the probability of dice)
Blaise Pascal ("fear of harm ought to be proportional not merely to the gravity of the harm, but also to the probability of the event")
John Graunt (who calculated statistical tables)
Daniel Bernoulli (the concept of utility)
Jacob Bernoulli (the "law of large numbers")
Abraham de Moivre (the "bell" curve and standard deviation)
Thomas Bayes (statistical inference)
Francis Galton (regression to the mean)
Jeremy Bentham (the law of supply and demand)

Today's risk management rests, for better or for worse, on these and other fascinating characters.

Where once philosophers and theologians attributed fortune or misfortune to the whims of gods, the efforts of those early thinkers described in Bernstein's book, "have transformed the perception of risk from chance of loss into opportunity for gain, from FATE and ORIGINAL DESIGN to sophisticated, probability-based forecasts of the future, and from helplessness to choice."[5]

Bernstein contrasts the development of more rigorous quantitative approaches to probabilities with recent attempts to understand why "people yield to inconsistencies, myopia, and other forms of distortion throughout the process of decision-making." His story of risk and risk management is one of rationality and human nature, fighting with each other and then cooperating, to provide a better understanding of uncertainty and how to deal with it. "... Any decision relating to risk involves two distinct yet inseparable elements: the objective facts and a subjective view about the desirability of what is to be gained, or lost, by the decision. Both objective measurement and subjective degrees of belief are essential; neither is sufficient by itself."

"The essence of risk management," Bernstein concludes, "lies in maximizing the areas where we have some control over the outcome while minimizing the areas where we have absolutely no control over the outcome and the linkage between effect and cause is hidden from us."

THE PAST 100 YEARS

Experience and new information allowed us to think intelligently about the future and plan for potential unexpected outcomes. Many millennia contributed to our growing ability to distill and use information, but the developments since 1900 are more apparent and useful. Here is a synopsis of these critical events.

The twentieth century began with euphoria, new wealth, relative peace, and industrialization, only to descend into chaotic regional and worldwide wars. These and other catastrophes crushed illusions about the perfectibility of society and our species, leaving us less idealistic and more appreciative of the continuing uncertainty of our future.

Ideas drove change in this century. Stephen Lagerfeld cogently summed it up:[6] "Apart from the almost accidental tragedy of World War I, the great clashings of our bloody century have not been provoked by the hunger for land, or riches, or other traditional sources of national desire, but by *ideas*—about the value of individual dignity and freedom, about the proper organization of society, and ultimately about the possibility of human perfection."

Risk management is one of those ideas that a logical, consistent, and disciplined approach to the future's uncertainties will allow us to live more prudently and productively, avoiding unnecessary waste of resources. It goes beyond faith and luck, the former twin pillars of managing the future, before we learned to measure probability. As Peter Bernstein wrote, "If everything is a matter of luck, risk management is a meaningless exercise. Invoking luck obscures truth, because it separates an event from its cause."[7]

If risk management is an extension of human nature, I should list the most notable political, economic, military, scientific, and technological events of the past

100 years. The major wars (from the Russo-Japanese, World Wars I and II, Korea, the Balkan, the first Gulf War and Iraq, to the numerous regional conflicts) and the advent of the automobile, radio, television, computer and Internet, the Great Depression, global warming, the atom bomb and nuclear power, the rise and fall of communism, housing, the dot-com, derivative, and lending bubbles, and the entire environmental movement affected the development of risk management. Major catastrophes did so more directly: the Titanic (the "unsinkable" ship sinks), the Triangle Shirtwaist fire (the failure to allow sufficient exits), Minimata Bay (mercury poisoning in Japan), Seveso (chemical poisoning of the community in Italy), Bhopal (chemical poisoning in India), Chernobyl (Russian nuclear meltdown), Three Mile Island (potential U.S. nuclear disaster that was contained), *Challenger* (U.S. space shuttle break up), Piper Alpha (North Sea oil production platform explosion and fire), Exxon Valdez (Alaskan ship grounding and oil contamination), to cite some of the more obvious. Earthquakes, tsunamis, typhoons, cyclones, and hurricanes continue to devastate populous regions, and their increasing frequency and severity stimulate new studies on causes, effects, and prediction, all part of the evolution of risk management.

[handwritten margin note: Natural Disaster]

The most significant milestones, in my opinion, are more personal: the new ideas, books, and actions of *individuals* and their *groups* all of whom stimulated the discipline. Here's my list:

1914 Credit and lending officers in the United States create Robert Morris Associates in Philadelphia. By 2000 it changes its name to the Risk Management Association and continues to focus on credit risk in financial institutions. In 2008 it counted 3,000 institutional and 36,000 associate members.[8]

1915 Friedrich Leitner publishes *Die Unternehmensrisiken* in Berlin (Enzelwirt. Abhan. Heft 3), a dissertation on risk and some of its responses, including insurance.

1921 Frank Knight publishes *Risk, Uncertainty and Profit,* a book that becomes a keystone in the risk management library. Knight separates uncertainty, which is not measurable, from risk, which is. He celebrates the prevalence of "surprise" and he cautions against over-reliance on extrapolating past frequencies into the future.[9]

1921 *A Treatise on Probability,* by John Maynard Keynes, appears. He too scorns dependence on the "Law of Great Numbers," emphasizing the importance of relative perception and judgment when determining probabilities.[10]

1928 John von Neumann presents his first paper on a theory of games and strategy at the University of Göttingen, "Zur Theorie der Gesellschaftsspiele," *Mathematische Annalen,* suggesting that the goal of not losing may be superior to that of winning. Later, in 1944, he and Oskar Morgenstern publish *The Theory of Games and Economic Behavior* (Princeton University Press, Princeton, NJ).

The U.S. Congress passes the Glass-Steagall Act, prohibiting common ownership of banks, investment banks, and insurance companies. This Act, finally revoked in late 1999, arguably acted as a brake on the development of financial institutions in the United States and led the risk management discipline in many ways to be more fragmented than integrated. The financial disasters after 2000 cause some to question the wisdom of revocation.

1945 Congress passes the McCarran-Ferguson Act, delegating the regulation of insurance to the various states, rather than to the federal government, even as business became more national and international. This was another needless brake on risk management, as it hamstrung the ability of the insurance industry to become more responsive to the broader risks of its commercial customers.

1952 The *Journal of Finance* (No. 7–, 77–91) publishes "Portfolio Selection," by Dr. Harry Markowitz, who later wins the Nobel Prize in 1990. It explores aspects of return and variance in an investment portfolio, leading to many of the sophisticated measures of financial risk in use today.[11]

1956 The *Harvard Business Review* publishes "Risk Management: A New Phase of Cost Control," by Russell Gallagher, then the insurance manager of Philco Corporation in Philadelphia. This city is the focal point for new "risk management" thinking, from Dr. Wayne Snider, then of the University of Pennsylvania, who suggested in November 1955 that "the professional insurance manager should be a risk manager," to Dr. Herbert Denenberg, another University of Pennsylvania professor who began exploring the idea of risk management using some early writings of Henri Fayol.

1962 In Toronto, Douglas Barlow, the insurance risk manager at Massey Ferguson, develops the idea of "cost-of-risk," comparing the sum of self-funded losses, insurance premiums, loss control costs, and administrative costs to revenues, assets, and equity. This moves insurance risk management thinking away from insurance, but it still fails to cover all forms of financial and political risk.

That same year Rachel Carson's *The Silent Spring* challenges the public to consider seriously the degradation to our air, water, and ground from both inadvertent and deliberate pollution. Her work leads directly to the creation of the Environmental Protection Agency in the United States in 1970, the plethora of today's environmental regulations, and the global Green movement so active today.[12]

1965 The Corvair unmasked! Ralph Nader's *Unsafe at Any Speed* appears and gives birth to the consumer movement, first in the United States and later moving throughout the world, in which *caveat vendor* replaces the old precept of *caveat emptor*. The ensuing wave of litigation and regulation leads to stiffer product, occupational safety, and security regulations in most developed nations. Public outrage at corporate misbehavior also leads to the rise of litigation and the application of punitive damages in U.S. courts.[13]

1966 The Insurance Institute of America develops a set of three examinations that lead to the designation "Associate in Risk Management" (ARM), the first such certification. While heavily oriented toward corporate insurance management, its texts feature a broader risk management concept and are revised continuously, keeping the ARM curriculum up-to-date.[14]

1972 Dr. Kenneth Arrow wins the Nobel Memorial Prize in Economic Science, along with Sir John Hicks. Arrow imagines a perfect world in which every uncertainty is "insurable," a world in which the Law of Large Numbers works without fail. He then points out that our knowledge is always incomplete—it "comes trailing clouds of vagueness"—and that we are best prepared for risk by accepting its potential as both a stimulant and penalty.

1973 In 1971, a group of insurance company executives meet in Paris to create the International Association for the Study of Insurance Economics. Two years later, the Geneva Association, its more familiar name, holds its first Constitutive Assembly and begins linking risk management, insurance, and economics. Under its first Secretary General and Director, Orio Giarini, the Geneva Association provides intellectual stimulus for the developing discipline.[15]

That same year, Myron Scholes and Fischer Black publish their paper on option valuation in the *Journal of Political Economy* and we begin to learn about derivatives.[16]

1974 Gustav Hamilton, the risk manager for Sweden's Statsforetag, creates a "risk management circle," graphically describing the interaction of all elements of the process, from assessment and control to financing and communication.

1975 In the United States, the American Society of Insurance Management changes its name to the Risk & Insurance Management Society (RIMS), acknowledging the shift toward risk management first suggested by Gallagher, Snider, and Denenberg in Philadelphia 20 years earlier. By 2008, RIMS has almost 11,000 members and a wide range of educational programs and services aimed primarily at insurance risk managers in North America. It links with sister associations in many other countries around the world through IFRIMA, the International Federation of Risk & Insurance Management Associations.[17]

With the support of RIMS, *Fortune* magazine publishes a special article entitled "The Risk Management Revolution." It suggests the coordination of formerly unconnected risk management functions within an organization and acceptance by the board of responsibility for preparing an organizational policy and oversight of the function. Twenty years lapse before many of the ideas in this paper gain general acceptance.

1979 Daniel Kahneman and Amos Tversky publish their "prospect theory," demonstrating that human nature can be perversely irrational, especially in the face of risk, and that the fear of loss often trumps the hope of gain. Three years later they and Paul Slovic write *Judgment Under Uncertainty: Heuristics and Biases,* published by Cambridge University Press. Kahneman wins the Nobel Prize in Economics in 2002.

1980 Public policy, academic and environmental risk management advocates form the Society for Risk Analysis (SRA) in Washington. *Risk Analysis,* its quarterly journal, appears the same year. By 2008, SRA has more than 2,500 members worldwide and active subgroups in Europe and Japan. Through its efforts, the terms risk assessment and risk management are familiar in North American and European legislatures.[18]

1983 William Ruckelshaus delivers his speech on "Science, Risk and Public Policy" to the National Academy of Sciences, launching the risk management idea in public policy. Ruckelshaus had been the first director of the Environmental Protection Agency, from 1970 to 1973, and returned in 1983 to lead EPA into a more principled framework for environmental policy. Risk management reaches the national political agenda.[19]

1986 The Institute for Risk Management begins in London. Several years later, under the guidance of Dr. Gordon Dickson, it begins an international set of examinations leading to the designation, "Fellow of the Institute of Risk Management," the first continuing education program looking at risk management in all its facets. This program is expanded in 2007–2008 for its 2,500 members.[20]

That same year the U.S. Congress passes a revision to the Risk Retention Act of 1982, substantially broadening its application, in light of an insurance cost and availability crisis. By 1999, some 73 "risk retention groups," effectively captive insurance companies under a federal mandate, account for close to $750 million in premiums.

1987 "Black Monday," October 19, 1987, hits the U.S. stock market. Its shock waves are global, reminding all investors of the market's inherent risk and volatility.

That same year Dr. Vernon Grose, a physicist, student of systems methodology, and former member of the National Transportation Safety Board, publishes *Managing Risk: Systematic Loss Prevention for Executives,* a book that remains one of the clearest primers on risk assessment and management.[21]

1990 The United Nations Secretariat authorizes the start of IDNDR, the International Decade for Natural Disaster Reduction, a 10-year effort to study the nature and the effects of natural disasters, particularly on the less-developed areas of the world, and to build a global mitigation effort. IDNDR concludes in 1999 but continues under a new title, ISDR, the International Strategy for Disaster Reduction. Much of its work is detailed in *Natural Disaster Management,* a 319-page synopsis on the nature of hazards, social and community vulnerability, risk assessment, forecasting, emergency management, prevention, science, communication, politics, financial investment, partnerships, and the challenges for the twenty-first century.[22]

1992 The Cadbury Committee issues its report in the United Kingdom, suggesting that governing boards are responsible for setting risk management policy, assuring that the organization understands all its risks, and accepting oversight for the entire process. Its successor committees (Hempel and Turnbull), and similar work in Canada, the United States, South Africa, Germany, and France, establish a new and broader mandate for organizational risk management.[23]

In 1992, British Petroleum turns conventional insurance risk financing topsy-turvy with its decision, based on an academic study by Neil Doherty of the University of Pennsylvania and Clifford Smith of the University of Rochester, to dispense with any commercial insurance on its operations in excess of $10 million. Other large, diversified, transnational corporations immediately study the BP approach.[24]

The Bank for International Settlements issues its Basel I Accord to help financial institutions measure their credit and market risks and set capital accordingly.

The title "Chief Risk Officer" is first used by James Lam at GE Capital to describe a function to manage "all aspects of risk," including risk management, back-office operations, and business and financial planning.

1994 Bankers Trust, in New York, publishes a paper by its CEO, Charles Sanford, entitled "The Risk Management Revolution," from a lecture at MIT. It identifies the discipline as a keystone for financial institution management.[25]

1995 A multidisciplinary task force of Standards Australia and Standards New Zealand publishes the first Risk Management Standard, AS/NZS 4360:1995 (since revised in 1999 and 2004), bringing together for the first time several of the different subdisciplines. This standard is followed by similar efforts in Canada, Japan, and the United Kingdom. While some observers think the effort premature, because of the constantly evolving nature of risk management, most hail it as an important first step toward a common global frame of reference.[26]

That same year Nick Leeson, a trader for Barings Bank, operating in Singapore, finds himself disastrously overextended and manages to topple the bank. This unfortunate event, a combination of greed, hubris, and inexcusable control failures, receives world headlines and becomes the "poster child" for fresh interest in operational risk management.

1996 The Global Association of Risk Professionals (GARP), representing credit, currency, interest rate, and investment risk managers, starts in New York and London. By 2008, it has more than 74,000 members, plus an extensive global certification examination program.[27]

Risk and risk management make the best-seller lists in North America and Europe with the publication of Peter Bernstein's *Against the Gods: The Remarkable Story of Risk*. Bernstein's book, while first a history of the development of the idea of risk and its management, is also, and perhaps more importantly, a warning about the overreliance on quantification: "The mathematically driven apparatus of modern risk management contains the seeds of a dehumanizing and self-destructive technology."[28] He makes a similar warning about the replacement of "old-world superstitions" with a "dangerous reliance on numbers," in "The New Religion of Risk Management," in the March–April 1996 issue of *The Harvard Business Review*.

1998 The collapse of Long-Term Capital Management, a four-year-old hedge fund, in Greenwich, Connecticut, and its bailout by the Federal Reserve, illustrate the failure of overreliance on supposedly sophisticated financial models.

2000 The widely heralded Y2K bug fails to materialize, in large measure because of billions spent to update software systems. It is considered a success for risk management.

The terrorism of September 11, 2001, and the collapse of Enron remind the world that nothing is too big for collapse. These catastrophes reinvigorate risk management.

PRMIA, the Professional Risk Manager's International Association, starts in the United States and United Kingdom. By 2008, it counts 2,500 paid and 48,000 associate members. It, too, sponsors a global certification examination program.[29]

In July, the U.S. Congress passes the Sarbanes-Oxley Act, in response to the Enron collapse and other financial scandals, to apply to all public companies. It is an impetus to combine risk management with governance and regulatory compliance. Opinion is mixed on this change. Some see this combination as a step backward, emphasizing only the negative side of risk, while others consider it a stimulus for risk management at the board level.

2004 The Basel Committee on Banking Supervision publishes the Basel II Accords, extending its global capital guidelines into operational risk (Basel I covered credit and market risks). Some observers argue that while worldwide adoption of these guidelines may reduce individual financial institution risk, it may increase systemic risk. These global accords may lead to similar guidelines for nonfinancial organizations.[30]

2005 The International Organization for Standardization creates an international working group to write a new global "guideline" for the definition, application, and practice of risk management, with a target date of 2009 for approval and publication.[31]

2007 Nassim Nicolas Taleb's *The Black Swan* is published by Random House in New York. It is a warning that "our world is dominated by the extreme, the unknown, and the very improbable ... while we spend our time engaged in small talk, focusing on the known and the repeated."[32] Taleb's 2001 book, *Fooled by Randomness* (Textere, New York) was an earlier paean to the importance of skepticism on models.

2008 The United States Federal Reserve bailout of Bear Stearns appears to many to be an admission of the failure of conventional risk management in financial institutions.

Perhaps Peter Bernstein's *Against the Gods* is a fitting end to this list of risk management milestones. It illustrates the importance of communication. Too often, new ideas have been unnecessarily restricted to the cognoscenti. Arcane mathematics, academic prose, and the secretiveness of current risk management "guilds," each protecting their own turf, discourage needed interdisciplinary discussion. Peter's lucid prose, compelling syntheses of difficult concepts, personal portraits of creative people, and particularly his warnings of the perils of excess quantification, bring us an appreciation of both the potential and perils of risk management. No matter what title we attach to this thinking process (risk management; enterprise risk management; strategic risk management; etc.), it will continue to be a part of the human experience.

None of this retrospection has any meaning or value unless it acts as a stimulant for a more prudent, intelligent, and optimistic use of the ideas and tools of past innovators.

Step out and create some new risk milestones.

Paradoxically, the very mortality that bears each of us along to a finite conclusion also gives us, through its unfolding, the means to repossess what we believe we have lost. It is in memory, given its true shape through the imagination, that we can truly possess our lives, if we will only strive to regain them.

—Louis D. Rubin Jr., *Small Craft Advisory*
Atlantic Monthly Press, New York, 1991

Risk and time are opposite sides of the same coin, for if there were no tomorrow there would be no risk. Time transforms risk, and the nature of risk is shaped by the time horizon: the future is the playing field.
—Peter Bernstein, *Against the Gods*, John Wiley & Sons, New York, 1996
(Revision September 2008. An earlier version of this brief history appeared in the December 1999 issue of *Risk Management Reports*.)

NOTES

1. Douglas Barlow, in letter to the author, January 8, 1998. Barlow was, for many years, the risk manager for Canada's Massey Ferguson Company.
2. Robin Lane Fox, *The Classical World* (New York: Basic Books, 2006) 49.
3. Ibid., 157.
4. Peter L. Bernstein, *Against the Gods* (New York: John Wiley & Sons, 1996) xxxv.
5. Ibid., 337.
6. Stephen Lagerfeld, "Editor's Comment," *Wilson Quarterly* (Autumn 1999).
7. Bernstein, op. cit., 197.
8. See www.rmahq.org for more information about RMA.
9. See 1985 reprint from the University of Chicago Press and first edition, 1921, Hart, Schaffner, and Marx, Boston.
10. See 1963 reprint from Macmillan.
11. See www.afajof.org.
12. See 1952 original and 2003 reprint from Houghton Mifflin, Boston.
13. See Grossman Publishers, New York, 1965.
14. See www.aicpcu.org.
15. See www.genevaassociation.org for more information on the Geneva Association.
16. See www.journals.uchicago.edu.
17. See www.rims.org for more information on RIMS.
18. See www.sra.org for more information about SRA.
19. See *Science*, vol. 221, no. 4615, September 9, 1983, and www.science.mag.org.
20. See www.theirm.org for more information about IRM.
21. Prentice-Hall, Englewood Cliffs, NJ, 1993.
22. See www.unisdr.org for more information on ISDR.
23. See www.archive.official-documents.co.uk.
24. See *Journal of Applied Corporate Finance*, vol. 6, no. 3 (Fall 1993) www.blackwell-synergy.com.
25. See www.terry.uga.edu/sanford/vita.html.
26. See www.standards.com.au.
27. See www.garp.org for more information about GARP.
28. Bernstein, op. cit., 7.
29. See www.prmia.org for more information about PRMIA.
30. See www.bis.org.
31. See www.iso.org.
32. Nassim Nicholas Taleb, *The Black Swan* (New York: Random House, 2007) xxvii.

ABOUT THE AUTHOR

Felix Kloman is President of Seawrack Press, Inc. and a retired principal of Towers Perrin, an international management consulting firm. His experience includes serving as Editor and Publisher of *Risk Management Reports* for 33 years, from 1974 to 2007, and more than 40 years in risk management consulting with Risk Planning Group (Darien, CT), Tillinghast (Stamford, CT), and Towers Perrin (Stamford, CT). He is the author of *Mumpsimus Revisited* (2005), and *The Fantods of Risk* (2008), both sets of essays on risk management. He is a Fellow of the Institute of Risk Management (London), a past director of the Nonprofit Risk Management Center, a past and founding director of the Public Entity Risk Institute, past chairman of the Risk Management & Insurance Committee for the U.S. Sailing Association, and a charter member of the Society for Risk Analysis. He received the Dorothy and Harry Goodell Award from the Risk & Insurance Management Society in 1994.

He is a graduate of Princeton University, 1955, with an AB in History.

CHAPTER 3

ERM and Its Role in Strategic Planning and Strategy Execution

MARK S. BEASLEY, PhD, CPA
Deloitte Professor of Enterprise Risk Management and Director of the ERM Initiative, College of Management, North Carolina State University

MARK L. FRIGO, PhD, CPA, CMA
Director, The Center for Strategy, Execution, and Valuation and Ledger & Quill Alumni Foundation Distinguished Professor of Strategy and Leadership at the DePaul University Kellstadt Graduate School of Business and School of Accountancy

Enterprise risk management (ERM) has rightfully become a top priority for directors and executive management. The current economic crisis highlights the disastrous results when risks associated with strategies are ignored or ineffectively managed. Coming out of the crisis are numerous calls for improvements in overall risk oversight, with a particular emphasis on strategic risk management.

One of the major challenges in ensuring that risk management is adding value is to incorporate ERM in business and strategic planning of organizations. The "silos" that separate risk management functions in organizations also create barriers that separate strategic planning from ERM. In many cases, risk management activities are not linked or integrated with strategic planning, and strategic risks can be overlooked, creating dangerous "blind spots" in strategy execution and risk management that can be catastrophic.

The challenge, as well as opportunity, for organizations is to embed risk thinking and risk management explicitly into the strategy development and strategy execution processes of an organization so that strategy and risk mindsets are one in the same. This chapter is based on articles, cases, and research by the authors in leading ERM and Strategic Risk Management initiatives at North Carolina State University and DePaul University, respectively, and their work with hundreds of practice leaders in enterprise risk management.

RISING EXPECTATIONS FOR STRATEGIC RISK MANAGEMENT

The expectations that boards of directors and senior executives are effectively managing risks facing an enterprise are at all-time highs.[1] Much of this shift in expectations was prompted initially by corporate scandals and resulting changes in corporate governance requirements, such as the Sarbanes-Oxley Act of 2002 (SOX) and the NYSE Corporate Governance Rules updated in 2004. Debt-rating agencies such as Standard & Poor's, Moody's, and Fitch now examine enterprise-wide risk management practices of institutions as part of their overall credit-rating assessment processes. Their particular focus is on understanding the risk management culture and the overall strategic risk management processes in place.[1]

The economic crisis that began in 2007 and still continues is now shining a huge spotlight on the board and senior management's enterprise-wide risk management processes. Reform proponents are pointing to failures in the overall risk oversight processes, including unaware boards, overreliance on sophisticated models, and underreliance on sound judgment. Critics argue that because returns on certain strategic initiatives were so great, risks that were present were either unknown or ignored.[2] Numerous calls are now arising for drastic improvements in risk management, with a specific call for more formal risk considerations in managing an organization's deployment of specific strategic initiatives.

This sentiment is evidenced by Federal Reserve Governor Randall S. Kroszner's October 2008 speech where he argued that financial institutions must improve the linkage between overall corporate strategy and risk management given that "survivability will hinge on such an integration." Governor Kroszner noted that many firms have forgotten the critical importance of undertaking an adequate assessment of risks associated with the overall corporate strategies.[3]

This shift toward greater expectations for effective enterprise-wide risk management oversight is complicated by the fact that the volume and complexities of risks affecting an enterprise are increasing as well. Rapid changes in information technologies, the explosion of globalization and outsourcing, the sophistication of business transactions, and increased competition make it that much more difficult for boards and senior executives to effectively oversee the constantly evolving complex portfolio of risks.

Even before the recent financial crisis, board members believed that risks were increasing. Ernst & Young's 2006 report, "Board Members on Risk," found that 72 percent of board members surveyed believed that the overall level of risk that companies face has increased in the past two years, with 41 percent indicating that overall levels of risk have increased significantly.[4] Given recent events, that concern is only heightened. Similarly, management has a comparable observation. IBM's 2008 "Global CFO Study" reported that 62 percent of enterprises with revenues greater than $5 billion encountered a major risk event that substantially affected operations or results in the last three years and nearly half (42 percent) stated that they were not adequately prepared.[5]

Many of the risks threatening an enterprise are difficult to see and manage, given their systemic nature. However, while many risks may be unknown, they often have a similar impact. Management and boards of directors are increasingly being held accountable for considering the probabilities and impact of various possible risk scenarios tied to their overall business strategies, even for risk events that may not be foreseeable. For example, the events of 9/11 and the catastrophic impact of Hurricane Katrina, although "unknown" by most, had similar impacts: loss of employees, destroyed operations, damaged IT infrastructure, lack of cash flow, and so on. Management and boards are not expected to predict the next 9/11–type event, but they are expected to consider and be proactive about thinking of responses to events (whatever the cause) that might have a similar impact. That is, management should have a plan for any significant scenario that might lead to consequences that might be detrimental to its core strategy, such as a loss of employees, destroyed operations, damaged IT infrastructure, lack of cash flow, drastic shift in regulations, and so on.

The rise in the volume and complexities of risks is complicated by the fact that many of the techniques used by boards and senior executives are dated, lack sophistication, and are often ad hoc. Few boards and senior executives have robust key risk indicators that provide adequate data to recognize shifts in risks patterns within and external to their organizations, resulting in an inability to proactively alter strategic initiatives in advance of risk events occurring. This has created an "expectations gap" between what stakeholders expect boards and senior executives to do regarding enterprise-wide risk management and what they actually are doing.

In response to these changing trends, organizations are embracing ERM because it emphasizes a top-down, holistic approach to effective risk management for the entire enterprise. The goal of ERM is to increase the likelihood that an organization will achieve its objectives by managing risks to be within the stakeholders' appetite for risk. ERM done correctly should ultimately not only protect but also create stakeholder value.

ERM Positioned as Value-Adding

ERM differs from a traditional risk management approach, frequently referred to as a "silo" or "stovepipe" approach, where risks are often managed in isolation. In those environments, risks are managed by business unit leaders with minimal oversight or communication of how particular risk management responses might affect other risk aspects of the enterprise, including strategic risks. Instead, ERM seeks to strategically consider the interactive effects of various risk events with the goal of balancing an enterprise's portfolio of risks to be within the stakeholders' appetite for risk. The ultimate objective is to increase the likelihood that strategic objectives are realized and value is preserved and enhanced.

Several conceptual frameworks have been developed in recent years that provide an overview of the core principles for effective ERM processes. In 2004, the Committee of Sponsoring Organizations of the Treadway Commission (COSO) issued its "Enterprise Risk Management—Integrated Framework," with this definition of ERM (see www.coso.org):

> *Enterprise risk management is a process, effected by the entity's board of directors, management, and other personnel, applied in strategy setting and across the enterprise, designed to identify potential events that may affect the entity, and manage risk to be within the risk appetite, to provide reasonable assurance regarding the achievement of entity objectives.*

Note that ERM is directly related to "strategy setting." For ERM to be value creating, it must be embedded in and connected directly to the enterprise's strategy. Another part of this definition refers to the goal of ERM, which is to help the enterprise achieve its core objectives. So, to be effective, ERM must be part of the strategic planning process and strategy execution processes.

The Conference Board's 2007 research study, "Emerging Governance Practices in Enterprise Risk Management," notes that while many organizations are engaging in some form of ERM, only a few have full-fledged ERM program infrastructures.[6] Many of these organizations initially launched their ERM efforts out of a compliance function, such as compliance with SOX, emerging privacy legislation, and environmental regulations. More boards and senior executives are now working to shift their ERM approach from a compliance orientation to a *strategic orientation*, consistent with the view that an enterprise-wide approach to risk management should be value enhancing. A 2008 survey, "The 2008 Financial Crisis: A Wake-Up Call for Enterprise Risk Management," by the Risk and Insurance Management Society (RIMS) found that about 65 percent of the businesses surveyed have begun or plan to implement a strategic risk management system.[7]

Board Demands for More Strategic Risk Management

Boards are feeling an increasing pressure to strengthen their overall oversight of the enterprise's risk management processes, with a stronger emphasis on strategic risk management. Recent reports, such as the Conference Board's "Overseeing Risk Management and Executive Compensation" report issued in December 2008, note that while companies report some progress in developing an enterprise-wide risk management program, it has yet to be adequately embedded in strategy execution and entity culture.[8]

Boards are becoming more aggressive at pushing management to reassess vulnerabilities in existing risk management processes and to begin strengthening the soundness of its risk management analysis to the company's strategic setting activities. Benchmarking surveys about the state of ERM consistently find that the launch of ERM is often tied to the board's (more specifically the audit committee's) demand for more robust risk management processes. Boards are now asking management about their risk oversight processes and they are adding formal risk discussions to their agendas on a regular basis.[9] Boards are also seeking to take a strategic view of Governance, Risk and Compliance (GRC) by setting and articulating the organization's "Enterprise Risk Policy and Appetite" and the role of each GRC function.[10] Despite these emerging trends, board members still believe they need to have a better handle around issues affecting *strategic risk*.

INTEGRATING RISK INTO STRATEGIC PLANNING

Successful deployments of ERM in strategic planning seek to maximize value when setting strategic goals by finding an optimal balance between performance goals and targets and related risks. As management evaluates various strategic alternatives designed to reach performance goals, it includes related risks across each alternative in that evaluation process to determine whether the potential returns are commensurate with the associated risks that each alternative brings. It also considers how one strategic initiative might introduce risks that are counterproductive to goals associated with another strategy. At that point, management is in a better position to evaluate various strategic alternatives to ensure that the combined risks that the entity might take on are within the stakeholders' appetite for risk and that they collectively support the strategic direction desired.

Considering risk during strategy planning also creates an ability to seize risk opportunities. Again, the goal of ERM is to preserve and enhance value. In some situations, ERM may reveal areas where the enterprise is being too risk averse or is ineffectively responding to similar risks that exist across multiple silos of the enterprise. In other situations, ERM may identify risk opportunities that may create potential increased returns to the enterprise. If risks are ignored in strategy, risk opportunities may be overlooked.

A consumer products company's experience illustrates the advantage of connecting strategy and risks. As part of its sales strategy, the company sought to increase revenues by strategically aligning with a key distributor customer through electronic reordering systems. As part of this alliance, the consumer products company entered into contracts requiring the automatic shipment of products to the retail customer's distribution warehouses within two-hour increments upon receipt of the customer's electronic reorder purchase request.

As the consumer products company began to launch its ERM processes, senior management quickly discovered a huge potential threat to this strategic arrangement with the retail customer. The company's information technology (IT) disaster recovery processes were set to be within acceptable tolerance limits established by the IT group. In an effort to balance costs with perceived IT needs, the IT group had put recovery procedures in place to fully restore IT-based sales systems within a two-day (not two-hour) period. When core sales executives learned about this recovery time frame, they quickly partnered with IT to reduce recovery thresholds to shorter windows of time. Had they not linked IT's disaster recovery response risks with the sales strategies to fulfill customer orders within two-hour increments, a looming IT disaster could have significantly affected their ability to achieve sales goals, thus compromising the enterprise's ability to achieve strategic goals. Needless to say, this discovery also prevented other risks that might have been triggered by a disaster, including legal risks tied to contract violations, cash flow losses due to idle sales functions, and reputation risks that could have been realized given the large size and visibility of both the consumer products company and retailer customer.

Recognizing Strategic Business Risk

Strategic risk management can help companies avoid the problem of not recognizing risks soon enough and can help management take swift action to deal with those risks that do occur. What initially appeared to be a minor disruption in the value chain for Nokia and Ericsson in March 2000 turned out to be a critical event for both companies. On Friday, March 17, 2000, a line of thunderstorms appeared in Albuquerque, New Mexico. A lightning bolt struck a Philips semiconductor plant, causing a fire in a plant that made chips for both Nokia and Ericsson and presented similar risks to both companies. The fire was minor, lasting only 10 minutes, and the damage at first appeared to be limited, so Philips expected to be back in operation within a week. As it turns out, the disruption to the plant was months rather than weeks, and the impact on production was significant.

Nokia quickly noticed the problem with the supply of the parts even before Philips told them there was a real problem. They took fast action to address the situation once they determined that the potential impact of the disruption in the supply of chips from the Philips plant could translate into an inability to produce 4 million handsets, representing 5 percent of the company's sales at the time.

In contrast, Ericsson responded slowly and didn't have alternative sourcing options. By the time management realized the extent of the problem, they had nowhere else to turn for several key parts. This partly stemmed from the company's strategy in the mid-1990s, when it simplified its supply chain to cut costs and in the process weakened its supply backup. One manager at Ericsson said: "We did not have a Plan B." Underestimating the risk of the disruption in supply from the Philips plant and being unable to manage the problem were major factors that led to Ericsson exiting the phone headset production market in 2001.[11]

What lessons do these contrasting cases offer about integrating strategies and risk management surrounding the supply chain?[12]

- Link the potential impact of supply chain disruptions to revenue and earnings to prioritize and manage risk.
- Build in the necessary levels of redundancy and backup and maintain supply chain intelligence and relationships.
- Continuously monitor supply chain performance measures to quickly identify problems so that countermeasures can be taken.
- Share information and foster communication at the first instance of a problem.

Evaluating Strategic Business Risk

The first step in strategic risk management is finding a way to systematically evaluate a company's strategic business risk. That has to begin with first making sure that management and the board understand the entity's key strategies that are designed to preserve and create stakeholder value. For a for-profit entity, key strategies are generally linked to increasing shareholder value through initiatives designed to boost revenues, to maintain or reduce costs, or to pursue growth through mergers and acquisitions. A thorough understanding of specific drivers of shareholder value that management and the board are pursuing is necessary before risks surrounding those drivers can be accurately and completely considered. And, that understanding of specific strategy drivers has to permeate leadership across the organization if risks are to be managed effectively.

The next step to strategic risk management surrounds defining the entity's use of the term "risk." Michael Porter's definition in his landmark book, *Competitive Advantage*, is useful: "Risk is a function of how poorly a strategy will perform if the 'wrong' scenario occurs."[13] Thus, strategic risk management begins by identifying and evaluating how a wide range of possible events and scenarios will impact a business's strategy execution, including the ultimate impact on the valuation of the company.

Before management can effectively manage risks that might be identified by various scenario analyses, they need to define an overriding risk management goal.

Risk appetites can vary across industries and entities. Without an understanding of stakeholder appetites for risks, neither management nor the board know what strategic risks are to be managed and what risks are to be accepted.

The Return Driven Strategy framework is an effective tool for integrating strategic goals and risk management goals. The framework is the result of more than a decade of research and application, involving the study of thousands of companies and the identification of strategic activities that separate the best performers from the worst. The Return Driven Strategy framework describes the hierarchy of strategic activities of best performing companies in terms of financial impact and shareholder value.

The Return Driven Strategy is comprised of 11 core tenets and 3 foundations that together form a hierarchy of interrelated activities that companies must perform to deliver superior financial performance. These tenets and foundations summarize the common activities of high-performance companies and identify flawed strategies of marginal performers. Here is a list of the 11 tenets and 3 foundations of Return Driven Strategy.[14]

11 Tenets of the Return Driven Framework

The Commitment Tenet

1. Ethically maximize wealth.

 Management must understand, define, and then align all activities toward the shareholder wealth creation objectives and ensure that the business operates within the ethical parameters set by its communities.

Two Goal Tenets

2. Fulfill otherwise unmet customer needs.
3. Target and dominate appropriate customer groups.

 To avoid commoditization, management must focus on fulfilling otherwise unmet customer needs. The path to business success is through the customer—sufficiently large enough groups of customers. This means targeting economically profitable customer groups that have sufficient size and growth opportunities while fulfilling otherwise unmet needs which are not commoditized.

Three Competency Tenets

4. Deliver offerings.
5. Innovate offerings.
6. Brand offerings.

 Through synchronization of these three competency tenets, offerings are created that target customer needs. Management needs to consider the *executability* of plans at the outset, with the three higher tenets as primary goals. Continuous innovation of the entirety of the offerings to develop offerings designed to enhance needs currently unfulfilled. Branding of the offerings to bridge the customer's explicitly understood need to the offering that uniquely fulfills it.

Five Supporting Tenets

7. Partner deliberately.
8. Map and redesign processes.
9. Engage employees and others.

10. Balance focus and options.
11. Communicate holistically.
    The supporting activities are done to support the achievement of the higher
        level tenets: the competency tenet, goal tenet, and commitment tenet.

There are three foundations that are critical to the Return Driven Strategy:

1. Genuine assets.
   The 11 tenets are the "verbs" of strategy. Genuine assets are the "nouns."
       Genuine assets are the building blocks of sustainable competitive ad-
       vantage. Activities are copied by competitors, leading to price com-
       petition and reduced cash flow returns. This can be defended only by
       leveraging unique assets to create unique offerings that cannot be copied
       (patents, brands, scale and scope, etc.).
2. Vigilance to forces of change.
   The ability and agility to capitalize on opportunities and avoid threats is
       foundational. Management must take advantage of opportunities and
       avoid threats in each of the three tenets arising from (1) government,
       legal, and other regulatory change, (2) demographic and cultural shifts,
       (3) scientific and technological breakthroughs.
3. Disciplined performance measurement and valuation.
   A discipline that links strategy to ultimate financial results is necessary for
       measuring the achievement of strategic goals. Performance measures
       must be in place to support the achievement of the strategy and its
       resulting value creation.

This framework describes how an enterprise's strategy can be aligned with
the ultimate objective to "Ethically Maximize Shareholder Wealth." This is a valid
goal for a business entity: to create shareholder wealth, to strive to maximize
it, and to do so while adhering to the ethical parameters of stakeholders and
communities.[15]

That ultimate strategic goal can work simultaneously as the entity's risk management goal as well. That is, management must understand, define, and then align
risk management activities toward ethical shareholder wealth creation objectives.
In doing so, risk management activities must be justified in terms of shareholder
wealth creation. If wealth preservation or creation isn't linked to risk management
activities, then particular risk management activities should be challenged.

We believe that, to be effective, a framework for strategic risk management
needs to include these three characteristics:

1. Alignment with a commitment to ethically create shareholder wealth. Risk
   management must have a strong alignment with protecting and creating
   shareholder value. Rule No. 1 of strategic risk management should read:
   "First, don't destroy shareholder value." But to add value, strategic risk
   management should be firmly aligned with the creation of shareholder
   wealth and have a focus on risk opportunities (e.g., the "upside" of risk). Of
   course, shareholder wealth should be created within the ethical parameters
   of the constituents and the communities in which the company operates.

Any framework for strategic risk management should have the ability to make the connection among the strategy of the organization, its execution and related risk management, and the valuation of the entity.[16]

2. Holistic. Strategic risk management should be holistic and broad enough to encompass the spectrum of entity-wide activities needed to achieve an organization's strategy. A framework for strategic risk management needs to be integrated so that various facets of strategic business risk can be linked with the overall goals of the business. This is where an ERM approach to risk management helps provide value through its emphasis on viewing risk-related scenarios using a top-down, holistic portfolio approach to determining how various silo risk events might interact to limit or destroy value. A holistic approach to strategic risk management helps connect various business unit goals and objectives and related risks to the overall goal of maximizing shareholder wealth. Without a holistic view, strategic activities within one aspect of the enterprise may be creating strategic risks for another part of the business.

For example, Harley Davidson's recent letter to shareholders describes one of its strategic goals to expand into international markets, particularly China and Japan. The letter also describes another strategic goal to enhance its "H.O.G." brand mystique and motorcycling lifestyle. In this case, the strategic desire to expand into Asian cultures, if left unmanaged, has the potential to create risks associated with its strategic desire to expand the Harley mystique if changes are made to Harley products to satisfy the motorcycling preferences of riders in different cultures. To effectively manage strategic risks, management needs to monitor how each strategic initiative might be throwing off counterproductive risks impeding other strategic objectives.[17]

3. Capable of identifying and evaluating events and forces of change. Strategic risk management has to be an ongoing, continual process. It can't be an activity that happens only occasionally. Risks are constantly evolving, which means an organization's strategies may need to evolve as well, so effective strategic business risk management must be capable of regularly identifying and evaluating how events, scenarios, and forces of change will impact the business strategy and its performance. Management's dashboard of key performance metrics should also include key risk indicators that provide leading information about changing risk conditions so that management is better prepared to adjust strategies ahead of the risk curve in a proactive manner, rather than be blindsided by shifting risk conditions that are realized too late to adjust deployments of key strategies, such as the situation at Ericsson. Robust management scorecard-reporting systems that include key strategy and risk management metrics can help strengthen management's effectiveness at staying on top of key changes that may impact the entity's strategic goals.

Using a Framework to Build a Strategic Risk Management Mindset

Executive teams have used the Return Driven Strategy as a holistic framework to set, evaluate, refine, and execute strategy. It also has been integrated into strategic planning processes and used as a way to evaluate the impact of events and scenarios, including merger-and-acquisition scenarios, on a strategy's performance. As directors and management have used the framework to evaluate the business strategy, they have been able to hone in on key risks that could destroy shareholder value while considering the upside of risk in terms of the opportunities, thereby using it as a strategic risk management framework.

CREATING A STRATEGIC RISK MINDSET AND CULTURE

How risky is our strategy? What events and risk scenarios could ruin our business? Do we have the right countermeasures and risk management strategies in place? These are just some of the questions on the minds of executives and board members today.

A Strategic Risk Management Mindset

A strategic risk management mindset focuses on examining how well a business strategy will perform under different scenarios and events. It encourages and supports thinking about scenarios where the strategy could perform so poorly that it could potentially result in significant losses, destruction of shareholder value, or a damaged corporate reputation. For example, management at Fidelity Investments knows that their strategy of providing investment services to an investor base all across the globe creates unbelievable demand for resiliency in its information technology functions. The tolerance for information systems outages or lack of access to pricing information approaches zero. They know that customers have little appetite for Fidelity to say their "systems are down." Thus, one of the key areas of focus of Fidelity's Risk Advisory Services Group is to oversee the business continuity planning processes at Fidelity.

A strategic risk mindset should also consider the "upside" of risk.[18] For example, the Target Corporation sidestepped the competitive threat from Wal-Mart by focusing on a customer segment different from Wal-Mart's and achieved profitable growth opportunities in the process. As another example, Samsung, confronted with serious brand erosion and commoditization risk, turned its attention to build on product innovation, speed to market, and a strong brand to turn a position of weakness into a position of market strength.

Risk can include loss of tangible assets, and it can also mean the potential loss of one of the company's most valuable assets—its reputation.[19] The H.J. Heinz Company has centered its enterprise risk management function on supporting an ultimate goal of protecting the Heinz reputation. In fact, its ERM program is formally known within as "Enterprise Reputation and Risk Management (or ER^{2}M)." Heinz's ER^{2}M helps the company meet two primary reputation related goals: (1) to further support doing the common thing uncommonly well, and (2) to help Heinz become the most trusted packaged food company. To help management see the importance of thinking about risk and reputation, Heinz defines risks as "anything that can prevent the company from achieving its objectives." They recognize that any event that affects the Heinz reputation in the food industry will directly impact its ability to achieve its objectives.

Ultimately, strategic risk management and ERM need to be connected with the potential impact on shareholder value. Effective strategic risk management should provide a way for identifying and evaluating how a wide range of possible events and scenarios will impact a business's strategy execution, including the impact on the assets and shareholder value of the company. That's how risk management is positioned at the Dow Chemical Company. The objective of effective enterprise risk management at Dow is to improve management's ability to run its business with the view that if they can manage risks better, they can be more competitive. Management and the board realize they have the responsibility to pursue opportunities, which will require the assumption of risks. They seek to assume those risks in a well-managed, controlled manner that recognizes the reality that as new strategies are created, new risks arise that need to be managed.

The Return Driven Strategy framework provides a way to evaluate the strategic risks of a company from the perspectives of shareholder value risk, financial reporting risk, governance risk, customer and market risk, operations risk, innovation risk, brand risk, partnering risk, supply chain risk, employee engagement risk, R&D risk, and communications risk. It also provides a useful framework for understanding the cause-and-effect linkages in critical risk scenarios and explains how those scenarios would play out in the business strategy and impact profitability, growth, and shareholder value.[20]

The framework encourages thinking around these risk categories:

- *Shareholder value risk* provides a high-level overview of risk and is driven by future growth and return on investment as reflected in the plans of the company and the company's perceived ability to execute on them. Anything that will impede growth and returns, including the risk of unethical activities of the company, should be considered in assessing shareholder value risk using the first tenet of Return Driven Strategy, "Ethically Maximize Wealth."
- *Financial reporting risk* is driven by reporting irregularities in areas such as revenue recognition, which can result in restatements of financial reports and be devastating to shareholder value.
- *Governance risk* is driven by factors such as controls and governance capabilities, including the need for compliance with laws and regulations.
- *Customer and market risk* is driven fundamentally by the extent to which a company's offerings fulfill otherwise unmet needs, and this provides protection against competition.
- *Operations risk* can be driven by any part of the value chain and often surfaces with the inability to deliver offerings, which is at the heart of Return Driven Strategy.
- *Innovation risk* is driven by the inability to change or create offerings that fulfill customer needs better than your competitors do.
- *Brand risk* includes the risk of brand erosion and damage to a company's reputation.
- *Partnering risk* is driven by the activities of your partners, from vendors to joint ventures, to other associations, including counterparty risks.

- *Supply chain risk* focuses on the increasing risk in outsourcing and global supply chains.
- *Employee engagement risk* is driven by the employment practices of the company.
- *R&D risk* is driven by the processes and pipeline of options for new offerings for future growth.
- *Communications risk* is driven by how well your company communicates internally and externally.

Recognizing Value of Strategic Risk Management at High-Performance Companies

Research on high-performance companies can provide valuable insights about risk management. High-performance companies are vigilant to forces of change, and they manage risks and opportunities better than other companies. By better understanding how the success or failure of a business is driven by its plans and actions, we can improve how we value companies—and run our businesses.

Research about high-performance companies highlights that one of the challenges facing management teams is how to link business plans and enterprise risk management. There are three approaches for effective strategic risk management to consider: (1) a strategic risk assessment process, (2) a process to identify and protect Genuine Assets that are at risk, and (3) strategic risk monitoring and performance measurement.

BUILDING A STRATEGIC RISK ASSESSMENT PROCESS

A simple process for strategic risk assessment involves four steps:[21]

1. **Risk assessment of plans.** Strategic risk assessment can begin by conducting an overall risk assessment of strategic plans, including an understanding of how they drive value and the key assumptions those plans are based on. This assessment includes scenario analysis of various iterations of changing assumptions surrounding drivers of the strategy.
2. **Identify critical risk scenarios.** The next step is to identify and describe "critical risk scenarios" considering the severity and likelihood of the events and scenarios that might occur, especially those outside management's control, such as systemic risks. At this stage, management and the board need to define their overall appetite for these critical risk scenarios.
3. **Identify countermeasures.** Next, management would identify possible countermeasures for managing the critical risk scenarios and would consider the cost/benefit of the countermeasures.
4. **Establish a process for continuous monitoring.** Management would establish a process for continuous monitoring of the risk profile of the company, including the use of key risk indicators (KRIs) and best practices of performance measurement and performance management such as the Balanced Scorecard.[22]

Here are some questions to address during a strategic risk assessment process:

- What events or scenarios could create significant downside risk in your business strategy and plans?
- What key assumptions have been made about the viability of specific strategic initiatives and what ranges of possible scenarios exist surrounding the variability inherent in these assumptions?
- What is our appetite surrounding certain strategies and their associated ranges of key risk exposures? What is the worst case scenario surrounding each strategy and would the entity be able to survive certain risk events?
- What countermeasures have been developed to address these risk scenarios and events?
- Has the company considered the upside of risk and how it plans to realize the opportunities?
- What are the roles of the CFO, general counsel, chief risk officer (CRO), internal audit, and others in assessing and managing the threats and opportunities in your plans and business strategy?
- How is enterprise risk management incorporated and embedded in your plans and business strategy?
- What performance measures and key risk indicators are you monitoring to continuously assess and manage strategic business risk?

Strategic Risk Management Processes

There are several approaches to building a strategic risk management process. Several are described next.

Risk assessments. One approach is to regularly assess strategic risks from three perspectives: risks, opportunities, and capabilities (ROC). *Risks* are about risk of loss—the downside of risk, such as loss of revenue or loss of assets. *Opportunities* are about the upside of risk, such as opportunities for gains in revenue, profitability, and shareholder value. *Capabilities* are about distinctive strengths of an organization that can be used to manage the risks and opportunities.

Tools for risk assessment. There are many tools that can be useful in strategic risk assessment, including brainstorming, analysis of loss data, self-assessments, facilitated workshops, SWOT (strengths, weaknesses, opportunities, threats) analysis, risk questionnaires and surveys, scenario analysis, and other tools.

Competitive intelligence. The area of competitive intelligence (CI) can be a valuable part of strategic risk management. CI is an integral component of fact-based strategic planning processes. It should definitely be part of strategic risk management and ERM. "The ethical collection and analysis of CI can reduce the risk associated with strategic decision making," says Gary Plaster of the Landmark Group and a founding member of the Society of Competitive Intelligence Professionals. Around 400 BC, Sun-tzu in *The Art of War* wrote "Keep your friends close and your enemies closer," which is one way of thinking about CI. For example, pharmaceutical companies are vigilant about being at trade shows and scientific meetings, and they monitor clinical trials in the industry. "War games" are used at pharmaceutical companies like Wyeth to develop plans to counter potential market moves by competitors.[23] Competitive intelligence is an asset that can be used to manage customer and market risks.

Corporate sustainability risk. One of the areas often overlooked in risk management is related to corporate sustainability and corporate social responsibility (CSR). Connecting strategy and CSR is a challenge for executive teams, as Debby Bielak, Sheila Bonini, and Jeremy Oppenheim wrote in their October 2007 article, "CEOs on Strategy and Social Issues," in the *McKinsey Quarterly.* The risks and opportunities facing companies in the area of corporate sustainability are more complex and have greater potential impact than ever before, and senior executives, board members, and managers are seeking better ways to manage these challenges and opportunities. In his book *Making Sustainability Work,* Marc Epstein presents a definition for corporate sustainability that's useful in strategic risk management. He focuses on nine principles of sustainability: (1) ethics, (2) governance, (3) transparency, (4) business relationships, (5) financial return, (6) community involvement/economic development, (7) value of products and services, (8) employment practices, and (9) protection of the environment. Each of these areas can be assessed as part of strategic risk management. For example, changes in environmental regulations and expectation of environmental standards for companies in a global business environment should be considered in risk assessment and risk management strategies.

Risk transfer and retention strategies. One of the basic countermeasures for managing and mitigating risk involves risk transfer and retention strategies. After identifying critical risk scenarios, which include the potential effect on company assets and shareholder value, management must determine how much should be retained or transferred. The risk management strategy should consider whether to protect corporate assets by purchasing insurance, self-insuring, or creating a captive. This assessment requires a deep understanding of the types and limits of insurance and consideration of emerging legal, regulatory, and political trends; damage awards; geographic locations; available insurance products; and options as well as coverage law.

Focus on Genuine Assets at Risk

Some of the most valuable assets of an organization aren't on the balance sheet. Genuine assets include the most valuable tangible and intangible resources and capabilities of an organization and must be protected because some of them may be at risk.[24] Companies routinely insure tangible assets on the balance sheet to protect against loss. But what about protecting the genuine assets?

Genuine assets are the tangible and intangible resources, capabilities, and traits that make an organization and its offerings unique, such as employee expertise, brand, reputation, and so on. As mentioned, some genuine assets appear on the balance sheet, but many don't. As the "building blocks" of strategy, genuine assets form the basis for creating sustainable competitive advantages. And only through these advantages can you plan and execute business strategy that leads to higher returns, higher growth, and, ultimately, increased market value.

When identifying these assets, management should be very specific as to what the genuine asset is. They should think specifically about how it allows the company to accomplish its strategy in ways other firms couldn't, thereby leading to higher performance. How difficult would it be for another firm to develop a similar genuine asset, allowing it to copy the activity that led to high performance? How long would it take? How much money would it cost?

To help identify and manage the risks to genuine assets, management should ask three questions:

1. What are the *most valuable* and *unique* capabilities and resources (genuine assets) of the company?
2. What scenarios and events could put the most valuable genuine assets at risk?
3. What countermeasures can be developed to protect these assets?

Examples of genuine assets to consider in a risk assessment would include corporate reputation, customer information, competitor intelligence, vendor intelligence, specialized processes and capabilities, existing patents and trademarks, and intellectual property that should be protected with patents, trademarks, and other means.

Customer information is an example of a genuine asset that must be protected. Information security is a big issue at most companies, yet breaches occur, sometimes with significant potential impact. For example, the British government recently announced that government workers lost two computer disks containing names, addresses, dates of birth, national insurance numbers, and banking information for approximately 25 million residents of the United Kingdom, almost half its population. Effective risk management in the area of data security requires the right mindset and attitude toward information security among employees. It requires an understanding and awareness that the information on a $20 storage device or a $1,000 laptop, if not protected, could result in potential loss of customers, corporate reputation, and shareholder value.

Some genuine assets can support and be part of an effective risk management strategy and can help protect a company against risks. For example, having a "Plan B" in place for potential disruptions in critical parts of the supply chain is an example of a genuine asset for effective strategic risk management. Another example is employees having a risk mindset and risk attitude that support the organization's strategy and risk appetite.

Strategic Risk Management and Performance Measurement

Many people believe that the recent financial crisis is largely attributable to the failure to link performance incentives with the risk management activities within the enterprise. Many of the executive compensation packages provide numerous unintended incentives for management to assume excessive amounts of risk exposures to achieve specific performance compensation targets.

Compensation incentives are typically designed to encourage executives to achieve strategic goals and initiatives and boards have typically evaluated those executives on whether they successfully achieve specific targets. Unfortunately, for many, risks associated with those compensation packages are overlooked. Boards are sometimes unaware of the nature of all risk exposures to the organization created by the executives. As long as the expected returns are achieved, few questions about the amount and types of risks being assumed are voiced.

The recent crisis is now placing greater light on the risks inherent in these executive compensation packages, and regulations are now being established to shed more insight into the risks associated with performance incentives. For example, the U.S. Treasury Department announced in January 2009 a new requirement for the chief executive officer (CEO) of financial institutions that receive federal funding under the Troubled Asset Relief Program's (TARP) Capital Purchase Program. For those entities, the CEO must certify within 120 days of receiving the funding that the entity's compensation committee has reviewed the senior executive's incentive compensation arrangements with the senior risk officers to ensure that these arrangements do not encourage senior executives to "take unnecessary and excessive risks that could threaten the value of the financial institution."

Effective strategic risk management should be a continual process that includes metrics for continuous monitoring of risk. An organization's key risk indicators and metrics should link to the potential impact of risk on shareholder value. Holistic performance management systems such as the Balanced Scorecard give organizations an unprecedented opportunity to align strategy and performance measures with risk management—and to achieve integrated, strategic risk management.

The Balanced Scorecard focuses on strategy and accountability and fosters a continuous process for risk assessment and risk management. The Balanced Scorecard framework can help management develop and use these risk metrics. With its focus on strategy and accountability, the Balanced Scorecard can foster a continuous process for risk assessment and risk management.

Strategy maps also can provide a useful way to understand the cause-and-effect relationships in critical risk scenarios and can suggest risk metrics that would be valuable in effective risk management. Risk dashboards can also provide a way to monitor key metrics and trends.

Kaplan and Norton's closed-loop management system (the Execution Premium model) provides another useful platform for a systematic approach to strategic risk management that integrates with overall management.[25] The Strategic Risk Management Lab at DePaul University has been working with management teams to help them embed strategic risk management into each stage of the management system.

- In Stage 1, "Develop the Strategy" involves defining mission, vision and values; conducting strategic analysis and formulating strategy. This stage is where companies can conduct strategic risk assessments and formulate strategic risk management plans as part of their strategy. This can be done using a variety of tools and frameworks including the Return Driven Strategy framework.
- In Stage 2, "Translate the Strategy" involves defining strategic objectives and themes; selecting measures, targets and strategic initiatives. In this stage,

management can identify strategic risk management objectives and measures that could be included in Balanced Scorecards. Risk management objectives can be incorporated in the financial perspective and internal process perspective of Balanced Scorecards and Strategy Maps. They can also use strategy maps to identify the cause-and-effect linkages and root causes of key strategic risks.

- In Stage 4, "Monitor and Learn" involves holding strategy reviews and operational reviews. In this stage management teams can hold strategic risk management reviews.
- And in Stage 5, "Test and Adapt" management conducts strategic risk analysis.

These are just a few examples of using the closed-loop management system to drive better strategic risk management.

Critical Steps for Value-Added Strategic Risk Management

Strategic risk management is increasingly being viewed as a core competency at both the management and board levels. In fact, board members are increasingly focused on strategic risk management, asking executives such questions as "Of the top five strategic business risks the company faces, which ones are you looking at, and what countermeasures are you devising?" The Strategic Risk Management Lab in the Center for Strategy, Execution, and Valuation at DePaul University is sharing with management teams and boards emerging best practices gleaned from its research. Consider the following list of 10 practices worth striving toward.[26]

1. Communicate and share information across business and risk functions—and externally. This is considered by some to be the ultimate risk management "best practice."
2. Break down risk management silos. Establish interdisciplinary risk management teams, so that each functional area can understand where it fits into the entire company strategy and how it affects other areas.
3. Identify and, where possible, quantify strategic risks in terms of their impact on revenue, earnings, reputation, and shareholder value.
4. Make strategic risk assessments part of the process of developing strategy, strategic plans, and strategic objectives. Again, this requires a combination of skills that can be achieved by creating interdisciplinary teams.
5. Monitor and manage risk through the organization's performance measurement and management system, including its Balanced Scorecard.
6. Account for strategic risk and embed it within the strategic plan and strategic plan management process. Wherever scenario planning is included in developing the strategic plan, there should also be a discussion of countermeasures in the event that a risk event occurs.
7. Use a common language of risk throughout your organization. Everyone must understand the organization's particular drivers of risk, its risk appetite, and what management considers acceptable risk levels.
8. Make strategic risk management, like strategy management itself, a continual process. Risk is inherently dynamic, so risk management and

assessment must evolve from being an event to being a process—and must include regular analysis and critical risk information refreshes. Strategic risk management reviews should be conducted as part of regular strategy reviews.

9. Develop key risk indicators (KRIs) to continuously monitor the company's risk profile. Like the Balanced Scorecard with its measures, targets, and initiatives, the risk management system should include KRIs, thresholds and trigger points, and countermeasures to mitigate or manage the risk.

10. Integrate ERM into Strategy Execution Systems. This means integrating ERM into the entire management system. This will require strategic risk management as a core competency in organizations and a commitment to continuously monitor and manage risk in the strategy and its execution.

CONCLUSION

The need to connect strategy and enterprise risk management couldn't be more relevant than it is in the current economic climate. Effective strategic risk management is likely to make the difference between survivability and demise for many. Designed effectively, the connection of ERM and strategy should be value-adding, allowing the enterprise to be more proactive and flexible in managing uncertainties tied to strategies as they unfold.

The key to successful strategic risk management is the ability to identify those risks embedded in the organization's business strategy that are potentially the most consequential. Focusing on strategic risks serves as a filter for management and boards of directors to reduce the breadth of the risk-playing field and ensure that they are focused on the right risks.

NOTES

1. For example, see Standard & Poor's "Enterprise Risk Management: Standard & Poor's To Apply Enterprise Risk Analysis to Corporate Ratings," (May 2008) New York. www.standardandpoors.com.

2. For example, see the *New York Times* magazine "Risk MisManagement" January 4, 2009, feature story that was highly critical of the short comings of risk oversight processes at many of the failed financial services institutions.

3. Federal Reserve Governor Randall S. Kroszner's speech, "Strategic Risk Management in an Interconnected World," October 20, 2008, Baltimore, Maryland. www.federalreserve.gov.

4. Ernst & Young 2006 report, "Board Members on Risk." www.ey.com.

5. IBM Global Business Survey's "Balancing Risk and Performance with an Integrated Finance Organization: The 2008 Global CFO Study" (2008).

6. The Conference Board's 2007 research study, "Emerging Governance Practices in Enterprise Risk Management."

7. "The 2008 Financial Crisis: A Wake-Up Call for Enterprise Risk Management," by the Risk and Insurance Management Society (RIMS).

8. The Conference Board's "Overseeing Risk Management and Executive Compensation" report (December 2008).

9. See the article by Mark Beasley, Bruce Branson, and Bonnie Hancock, titled "Rising Expectations: Audit Committee Oversight of Enterprise Risk Management," *Journal of Accountancy* (April 2008) 44–51.

10. See the article by Mark L. Frigo and Richard J. Anderson, "A Strategic Framework for Governance, Risk and Compliance" *Strategic Finance* (February 2009).

11. For more about this example, see "Trial by Fire: A Blaze in Albuquerque Sets Off Major Crisis for Cell-Phone Giants" in the January 29, 2001, issue of the *Wall Street Journal*.

12. See article by Mark L. Frigo, "Strategic Risk Management: The New Core Competency" *Balanced Scorecard Report* (January–February 2009).

13. Porter, Michael E. *Competitive Advantage* (New York: Free Press, 1985), 476.

14. Frigo, Mark L., and Joel Litman, *Driven: Business Strategy, Human Actions and the Creation of Wealth* (Chicago, IL: Strategy and Execution, 2008).

15. For more, see Mark L. Frigo and Joel Litman, *Driven: Business Strategy, Human Actions and the Creation of Wealth* (Chicago, IL: Strategy and Execution, 2008); "What Is Return Driven Strategy?" by Mark Frigo and Joel Litman in the February 2002 issue of *Strategic Finance*; and "Performance Measures That Drive the First Tenet of Business Strategy" by Mark Frigo in the September 2003 issue of *Strategic Finance*.

16. For more about this, see "When Strategy and Valuation Meet: Five Lessons from Return Driven Strategy" by Joel Litman and Mark Frigo in the August 2004 issue of *Strategic Finance*.

17. For more discussion of Harley-Davidson and strategic risk management, see Chapter 14, "Co-Creating Risk Management, Governance, and Transformational Change," in *Co-Creating the Future: Engaging Customers, Employees and All Stakeholders to Co-Create Mutual Value* by Venkat Ramaswamy and Francis Gouillart (2009); Frigo, Mark L. and Venkat Ramaswamy, *Co-Creating Wealth: A New Risk-Return Paradigm of Value Co-Creation* (2009); and Frigo, Mark L. and Venkat Ramaswamy, "Co-Creating Risk-Return" Working Paper (2009).

18. See Slywotzky, Adrian, "The Upside of Risk: The 7 Strategies for Turning Big Threats Into Growth Breakthroughs," *Crown Business* (2007).

19. For a discussion on the importance of reputation risk management, see the article by Robert Eccles, Scott Newquist, and Roland Schatz titled "Reputation and Its Risks," *Harvard Business Review* (February 2007).

20. For more about Return Driven Strategy, see Mark L. Frigo and Joel Litman, *Driven: Business Strategy, Human Actions and the Creation of Wealth* (Chicago, IL: Strategy and Execution, 2008).

21. See article by Mark L. Frigo, "When Strategy and ERM Meet," *Strategic Finance* (January 2008).

22. See Robert S. Kaplan and David P. Norton, "The Balanced Scorecard: Measures That Drive Strategic Performance," *Harvard Business Review* (January–February 1992) 71–79.

23. See "Corporate Covertness: More Firms Use 'CI' Analysts to Gather Data on Rivals, But It's Mostly Hugh-Hush" *Chicago Tribune*, December 10, 2007; and "The Intelligence Diaries: Here's Your Study Guide To What the Industry Once Knew—And Lost," *Pharmaceutical Executive*, November 2007.

24. For a discussion on genuine assets, see Chapter 12 "Genuine Assets" in Mark L. Frigo and Joel Litman, *Driven: Business Strategy, Human Actions and the Creation of Wealth* (Chicago, IL: Strategy and Execution, 2008).

25. Kaplan, Robert S., and David P. Norton, "Mastering the Management System," *Harvard Business Review* (January 2008), and Kaplan, Robert S., and David P. Norton, *Execution Premium: Linking Strategy to Operations for Competitive Advantage* (Boston, MA: Harvard Business School Press, 2008).

26. See article by Mark L. Frigo "Strategic Risk Management: The New Core Competency," *Balanced Scorecard Report* (January–February 2009).

ABOUT THE AUTHORS

Mark S. Beasley, PhD, CPA, is Deloitte Professor of Enterprise Risk Management and Professor of Accounting in the College of Management at North Carolina State University. He is the Director of NC State's Enterprise Risk Management (ERM) Initiative (www.erm.ncsu.edu), which provides leadership about ERM practices and their integration with strategy and corporate governance. Mark currently is serving on the board for the Committee of Sponsoring Organizations of the Treadway Commission (widely known at COSO). He has previously served on several national task forces and working groups, including the Auditing Standards Board SAS No. 99 Fraud Task Force and the advisory board for the Conference Board's research about board of director responsibility for ERM. He is the author of textbooks, casebooks, and continuing education materials and has published extensively in business and academic journals. Mark is also a frequent speaker at national and international conferences on ERM, internal controls, and corporate governance, including audit committee practices. He received a BS in accounting from Auburn University and a PhD from Michigan State University.

Mark L. Frigo, PhD, CPA, CMA is Director of the Center for Strategy, Execution, and Valuation and the Strategic Risk Management Lab in the Kellstadt Graduate School of Business at DePaul, and Ledger & Quill Alumni Foundation Distinguished Professor of Strategy and Leadership in the School of Accountancy at DePaul University. He is a leading expert in Strategic Risk Management. The author of 6 books and more than 80 articles, his work is published in leading business journals including *Harvard Business Review*. He is the editor of the Strategic Management section of *Strategy Finance* and lectures frequently at universities and conferences in Europe. He is the co-author with Joel Litman of the book *Driven: Business Strategy, Human Actions and the Creation of Wealth* (www.returndriven.com). He received his BS in Accountancy from the University of Illinois, an MBA from Northern Illinois University and completed postgraduate studies in the Kellogg Graduate School of Management at Northwestern University. He is a CPA in the State of Illinois and a Certified Management Accountant. Dr. Frigo received his PhD in Economics and Econometrics. Dr. Frigo serves as an advisor to executive teams and boards of directors in the area of Strategic Risk Management.

CHAPTER 4

The Role of the Board of Directors and Senior Management in Enterprise Risk Management

BRUCE C. BRANSON
Professor of Accounting and Associate Director, North Carolina State University
Enterprise Risk Management Initiative

INTRODUCTION

The oversight of the enterprise risk management (ERM) process employed by an organization is one of the most important and challenging functions of a corporation's board of directors. In concert with senior management of the company, the board must establish the appropriate "tone at the top" to ensure that risk and risk management considerations remain at the forefront of strategic and operating decisions made within the business. The 2008–2009 global financial crisis and the rapidly deteriorating global economy has created a context in which companies now face risks that are more complex, more interconnected, and potentially more devastating than ever before. Failure to adequately acknowledge and effectively manage risks associated with decisions being made throughout the organization can and often do lead to potentially catastrophic results.

We need look no further than to the current status of the financial services sector to observe the devastation associated with poorly monitored and managed risk taking. Risks associated with credit quality, liquidity, market disruptions, and reputation have all contributed to unprecedented bankruptcies, bank failures, federal government intervention, and rapid (and forced) consolidation within the industry. The fallout from this financial cataclysm spread quickly to the broader economy, as companies in almost every industry have suffered from the effects of a global credit freeze, dramatic reductions in consumer demand, and extreme volatility in commodity, currency, and equity markets.

The perception that aggressive and unchecked risk taking has been central to the breakdown of the financial and credit markets has led to increased legislative and regulatory focus on risk management and risk prevention. In this environment, boards and companies must be aware that regulators and the legal system may apply new standards of conduct, or reinterpret existing standards, to increase board responsibility for risk management. Boards cannot and should not be involved in the actual day-to-day *management* of risks encountered by the companies they serve. The role of the board is to ensure that the risk management processes designed and implemented by senior executives and risk management professionals employed by the company act in concert with the organization's strategic vision, as articulated by the board and executed by senior management. As well, the board must exercise significant oversight to be confident that risk management processes are functioning as designed and that adequate attention is paid to the development of a culture of risk-aware decision making throughout the organization.

By actively exercising its oversight role, the board sends an important signal to the company's senior management and its employees that corporate risk management activities are not roadblocks to the conduct of business nor a mere "check-the-box" activity. Executed properly, ERM can and should become an integral component of the firm's corporate strategy, culture, and value-creation process. The board can provide direction and support for the ERM effort, but without one or more risk champions within the executive leadership, most ERM programs are destined to fail. Thus, there is a shared responsibility between the members of the board and the senior management team to nurture a risk-aware culture in the organization that embraces prudent risk taking within an appetite for risk that aligns with the organization's strategic plan.

The company's ERM system should function to bring to the board's attention the company's most significant risks and allow the board to understand and evaluate how these risks may be correlated, the manner in which they may affect the company and management's mitigation or response strategies. It is critically important for board members to have the experience, training, and intimate knowledge of the business required in order to make meaningful assessments of the risks that the company encounters. The board must also consider the best organizational structure to give risk oversight sufficient attention at the board level. In some companies, this has driven the creation of a separate risk management committee of the board. For other organizations, it may be reasonable for these discussions of risk to occur as a regular agenda item for an existing committee such as the audit committee, enhanced by periodic review at the full board level. No one size fits all, but it is vitally important that risk management oversight be a board priority.

This chapter addresses the proper role of the board of directors in corporate risk management. It identifies the legal and regulatory framework that drives the risk oversight responsibilities of the board. It also clarifies the separate roles of the board and its committees vis-à-vis senior management in the development, approval, and implementation of an enterprise-wide approach to risk management. Finally, the chapter explores optimal board structures to best discharge their risk oversight responsibilities.

GOVERNANCE EXPECTATIONS FOR BOARD OVERSIGHT OF RISK MANAGEMENT

The risk oversight responsibility of boards of directors is driven by a variety of factors. These factors include the fiduciary duty owed to corporate shareholders, which is a function of state law; U.S. and foreign laws and regulations such as the recently enacted Emergency Economic Stabilization Act of 2008 (EESA) and the Sarbanes-Oxley Act; New York Stock Exchange (NYSE) listing requirements; and certain established corporate best practices. As well, the risk of damage to corporate reputation from shareholder activism or adverse media coverage for companies believed or found to possess inadequate risk management capabilities also strongly contributes to the desirability of sound risk oversight by corporate boards.

The Delaware courts (which serve to establish law for a wide swath of corporate America) have developed guidelines for board oversight responsibilities through a series of court cases that have dealt with purported violations of the fiduciary duties of care and loyalty that are owed to the company by members of the board. The Delaware Chancery Court has stated[1] that director liability for a failure of board oversight requires a "sustained or systemic failure of the board to exercise oversight—such as an utter failure to assure a reasonable information and reporting system exists." To avoid liability, boards should ensure that their organizations have implemented comprehensive monitoring systems tailored to each category of risk. The board should periodically review these monitoring systems and make inquiries of management as to their robustness. The board should also consider retaining outside consultants for an independent assessment of the adequacy of the methodology that has been implemented. The company's general counsel may also be utilized to provide an assessment as to whether the board has effectively fulfilled their oversight responsibility for the ERM program.

The board should be especially sensitive to so-called "red flags," or violations of existing risk limits established by the risk management team. These violations must be investigated by the board or delegated to the appropriate manager for investigation, and the board should document their actions in minutes that accurately convey the time and effort spent by the board in reviewing the deviation from established policies. To preserve their liability shield, boards must ensure that the monitoring system in place includes reports on significant regulatory matters (such as fines that have been levied against the company), that may be used as evidence in shareholder litigation. The board should treat such a report as a red flag and investigate appropriately.

Corporate risk management issues have recently appeared in two important examples of federal regulatory oversight—the EESA and the Sarbanes-Oxley Act. Also, companies with foreign operations must be cognizant of the legal requirements in each of the locales in which they do business. Whether or not a particular piece of legislative rule making that relates to risk management directly applies to the company and board, such laws and regulations will undoubtedly influence the activities that a company undertakes. Given the current environment and enhanced focus on risk management and risk oversight, a failure by the board to adequately oversee a system of compliance with legal requirements can raise issues under state law with respect to the board's fiduciary duties, but also can provide opportunities for litigators to highlight such failures in other claims against the company and board, such as tort liability or even criminal liability. It is imperative that the board is aware of all material legal requirements applicable to the company, and the company should take care to include these risks in the development of their ERM program.

The most recent example of federal legislation that includes an explicit focus on risk management is the Troubled Asset Relief Program (TARP) contained in the EESA. The act requires that boards of financial institutions participating in the TARP Capital Purchase Program (CPP) institute certain restrictions on executive compensation that relate to corporate risk taking. Specifically, participants in the TARP CPP must comply with the requirements illustrated in Box 4.1. Although these requirements apply only to financial institutions participating in the CPP, they do provide insight into federal concern over the issue of how compensation programs may contribute to excessive risk taking. Because of this concern, companies that are not directly affected by these requirements should still consider reviewing their compensation plans to determine whether the compensation structure encourages excessive risk taking. To the extent that incentive compensation is externally viewed as a source of inappropriate risk, the interaction between compensation and risk may inevitably find its way into other legislative and regulatory responses and/or become a focus of shareholder activism and undesirable media attention.

Box 4.1   Executive Pay Requirements under the Troubled Asset Relief Program Capital Purchase Program*

In order to comply with Section 111(b)(2)(A) of EESA for purposes of participation in the program, a financial institution must comply with the following three rules:

(1) Promptly, and in no case more than 90 days, after the purchase under the program, the financial institution's compensation committee, or a committee acting in a similar capacity, must review the [senior executive officer (SEO)] incentive compensation arrangements with such financial institution's *senior risk officers*, or other personnel acting in a similar capacity, to ensure that the SEO incentive compensation arrangements do not encourage SEO's to take *unnecessary and excessive risks* that threaten the value of the financial institution.

(2) Thereafter, the compensation committee, or a committee acting in a similar capacity, must meet at least annually with senior risk officers, or individuals acting in a similar capacity, to discuss and review the relationship between the financial institution's risk management policies and practices and the SEO incentive compensation arrangements.

(3) The compensation committee, or a committee acting in a similar capacity, must certify that it has completed the reviews of the SEO incentive compensation arrangements required under (1) and (2) above. These rules apply while the Treasury holds an equity or debt position acquired under the program.

---

*Excerpted from Treasury Department Notice 2008-PSSFI.

The Sarbanes-Oxley Act of 2002 imposes significant requirements on companies and their boards, including audit committee oversight of internal and external auditors, certification of quarterly and annual financial statements and periodic reports by the chief executive officer and chief financial officer, maintenance of well-functioning financial reporting and disclosure controls, enhanced disclosure of financial measures not based on generally accepted accounting principles (GAAP), and a ban on personal loans to directors and officers. Although not directly tied to the risk oversight responsibilities of boards, compliance with Sarbanes-Oxley requirements involves risk management issues. As an example, in determining the effectiveness of controls over financial reporting, or in the financial statement certification process, the company should focus on whether material risks are identified and disclosed. In their review of the company's compliance with Sarbanes-Oxley requirements, the board should make inquiries as to whether these risk management issues have been acknowledged.

The New York Stock Exchange (NYSE) imposes specific risk oversight obligations on the audit committee of an NYSE-listed company. These NYSE rules require that an audit committee "discuss policies with respect to risk assessment and risk management."[2] Box 4.2 provides an excerpt from the NYSE corporate governance rules germane to this requirement. These discussions should address major financial risk exposures and the steps the board has taken to monitor and

Box 4.2   Excerpt from the NYSE's 2004 Final Corporate Governance Rules*

Among numerous other responsibilities, duties, and responsibilities of the audit committee include:

(D) Discuss policies with respect to risk assessment and risk management;
Commentary: While it is the job of the CEO and senior management to assess and manage the company's exposure to risk, the audit committee must discuss guidelines and policies to govern the process by which this is handled. The audit committee should discuss the company's major financial risk exposures and the steps management has taken to monitor and control such exposures. The audit committee is not required to be the sole body responsible for risk assessment and management, but, as stated above, the committee must discuss guidelines and policies to govern the process by which risk assessment and management is undertaken. Many companies, particularly financial companies, manage and assess their risk through mechanisms other than the audit committee. The processes these companies have in place should be reviewed in a general manner by the audit committee, but they need not be replaced by the audit committee.

*"Final Corporate Governance Rules," New York Stock Exchange (2004) www.nyse.com.

control these exposures, including a general review of the company's risk management programs. As the NYSE commentary indicates, the rules permit a company to create a separate committee or subcommittee (often a separate risk committee of the board) to be charged with the primary risk oversight responsibility. This is subject to the need for the risk oversight processes conducted by that separate committee or subcommittee to be reviewed in a general manner by the audit committee, and for the audit committee to continue to discuss policies with respect to risk assessment and management. As in our earlier discussion concerning the TARP certification requirements for those financial institutions participating in the CPP, these rules only apply to NYSE-listed firms. Yet, it seems prudent for all boards to acknowledge that they may be subject to "best practice" standards in the eyes of their shareholders and the general public.

Boards should also take advantage of industry-specific regulators (such as the Federal Reserve and the FDIC in the banking industry) and specialized risk management organizations that have published best practice guidance. The Committee of Sponsoring Organizations of the Treadway Commission (COSO), a private-sector organization sponsored by professional accounting associations and institutes, has developed an ERM framework that promotes an enterprise-wide perspective on risk management. That document emphasizes the role of the board in risk management in its definition of ERM:

> *Enterprise risk management is a process,* effected by the entity's board of directors, *management, and other personnel, applied in strategy setting and across the enterprise, designed to identify potential events that may affect the entity, and manage risk to be within the risk appetite, to provide reasonable assurance regarding the achievement of objectives.* (emphasis added)[3]

The COSO integrated framework provides a valuable benchmarking tool and offers detailed guidance on how a company may implement enterprise risk management procedures in its strategic planning efforts and across the entire organization. The COSO ERM framework presents eight interrelated components of risk management: (1) the internal environment (the tone of the organization), (2) objective-setting, (3) event identification, (4) risk assessment, (5) risk response, (6) control activities, (7) information and communications, and (8) monitoring. The COSO enterprise risk management framework has become well accepted as a development tool for organizations seeking to initiate and/or improve on an ERM program.

In 2007, Standard & Poor's (S&P) announced a major initiative to incorporate an explicit evaluation of ERM programs as part of their credit ratings analysis of companies. S&P has actively evaluated the ERM practices of financial institutions, insurance companies, and the trading operations of many large energy companies for some time. Beginning in late 2008, S&P extended this evaluation to nonfinancial issuers. Box 4.3 provides an excerpt from the S&P announcement that highlights their expectations for board involvement in risk management activities. It is clear that they expect active and engaged board-level participation in the establishment of the proper "tone at the top" as well as in the approval and monitoring of specific risk policies the firm develops.

Box 4.3   Excerpt from Standard & Poor's "PIM Framework for Assessing ERM Practices"*

In November 2007, Standard & Poor's issued a request for comment titled, *Criteria: Request For Comment: Enterprise Risk Management Analysis For Credit Ratings Of Nonfinancial Companies,* which announced S&P's proposal to expand its analysis of ERM processes as part of its credit-rating assessments into 17 different industries.** S&P has developed an ERM assessment framework—the "PIM Framework" denoting policies, infrastructure, and methodology—to assess the robustness of enterprise risk management practices within an entity as part of the credit evaluation process. Within the PIM framework, S&P views "risk governance" as the foundation of the evaluation structure. Several components of risk governance include activities involving the board of directors:

- In consultation with the business, the institution has established risk policies that would be approved by the board's risk committee.
- The institution ensures that periodic dialogue takes place among the board, business heads, and group risk management on the appropriateness and relevance of the various key financial and nonfinancial risk metrics.
- Ensure that the board is well engaged with ERM initiatives within the organization and is to some degree setting the tone.

---

*"Assessing Enterprise Risk Management Practices of Financial Institutions," Standard & Poor's (2006). www.standardandpoors.com.
**"Criteria: Request for Comment: Enterprise Risk Management Analysis For Credit Ratings on Nonfinancial Companies," Standard & Poor's (2007). www.standardandpoors .com.

Reputational damage resulting from the lack of adequate risk oversight is present even without mandated requirements to adhere to specific risk management–related laws, regulations, stock exchange listing rules, and best practices. Even absent any actual legal exposure, the board of a company whose excessive risk taking leads to a crisis or poor financial and/or operating performance will likely face significant criticism in the press and from shareholders. In these circumstances, the board may also be faced with proxy contests, either from a competing slate of directors standing for election or through other shareholder resolution campaigns. Proxy attacks against directors viewed as responsible for failures of risk oversight have become more and more common. The business press has also highlighted and targeted directors that they view as underperforming. With the enhanced attention being paid to risk oversight and management, one can expect increased pressure on companies perceived to have taken on excessive levels of risk or who have been found to lack robust risk oversight capabilities.

DELEGATION OF RISK OVERSIGHT
TO BOARD COMMITTEES

Many boards find it helpful to assign primary risk oversight responsibility to a committee of the full board. This committee is charged with directly overseeing the risk management function and should receive regular reports on the status of the ERM process from those members of senior management responsible for risk management for the enterprise. This committee, in turn, should make regular reports to the full board to ensure that the board as a whole has an understanding of the risk profile of the entity and can then engage in strategic, risk-informed decision making appropriate to their leadership role.

In many instances, boards delegate primary responsibility for risk oversight to the audit committee, in spite of the audit committee's seemingly overwhelming list of responsibilities related to financial reporting and the internal/external audit function. Audit committees are the most common board committee to be charged with performance of oversight duties over management's risk policies and guidelines, and they are being asked to discuss with management the enterprise's key risk exposures—including risk exposures beyond financial reporting related risks. A recent Conference Board study of audit committee charters of Fortune 100 companies reported that 66 percent of these companies place primary risk oversight responsibility on the audit committee, using language similar to the examples illustrated in Box 4.4 for the Coca-Cola Company, Wal-Mart Stores, and Apple.[4]

Audit committees (or other board committees) that have been charged with this responsibility for risk oversight are increasing their demands on management for more information about risk management processes and for up-to-date information about management's assessment of key risk exposures. Within senior management, it is often the chief financial officer (CFO) or chief audit executive (CAE) who has been asked to take the lead in risk management efforts for the organization. The 2006 Conference Board report, "The Role of U.S. Corporate Boards in Enterprise Risk Management," reports that the executive most frequently cited by directors as responsible for informing the board on risk issues is the CFO—with more than 70 percent reporting this relationship. However, in growing numbers, organizations are creating Chief Risk Officer (CRO) positions to serve as the risk leader or "champion," while others are creating executive-level risk committees comprised of the CFO, CRO, general counsel, executives in charge of strategy and internal audit, and/or other key business unit leaders to lead the ERM effort.

FORMALIZING RISK MANAGEMENT PROCESSES

The complexity and sheer number of risks affecting organizations has expanded at a rapid pace over the past decade. Boards and senior executives are increasingly feeling the pressure to respond to these increased demands on their time and expertise. A 2007 study, "Board Members on Risk,"[5] reports that 72 percent of board members who participated in the survey believe that the overall level of risk that the organizations they serve currently faces has increased in the past two to three years, with 41 percent indicating that the overall level of risk has increased significantly. Senior executives and their boards are realizing that the practice of

---

Box 4.4   Illustrative Language from Audit Committee Charters

---

Below are excerpts from three audit committee charters that provide examples of audit committee involvement in risk oversight:

1. The Coca-Cola Company's *Audit Committee Charter* states that one of the 14 responsibilities of the Audit Committee of the Board of Directors includes:

    Risk Assessment and Risk Management. The committee will review and discuss with management, the internal auditors, and the independent auditors the company's policies and procedures with respect to risk assessment and risk management.

2. Wal-Mart Stores includes the following language in their *Audit Committee Charter*:

    Discuss with management the company's major financial risk exposures and the steps management has taken to monitor and control such exposures, including the company's risk assessment and risk management policies.

3. The *Audit and Finance Committee Charter* of Apple states that one of the responsibilities of the committee is:

    Review and discuss with Management (i) Management's financial risk assessment and risk management policies, (ii) the Corporation's major financial risk exposures and the steps Management has taken to monitor and control such exposures.

---

managing risk informally or on an ad hoc basis is no longer tolerable and that, in many instances, current processes have proved inadequate in today's rapidly evolving business world.

To address these concerns, many boards have adopted ERM as a process to develop a more robust and holistic top-down view of key risks facing the organization. Although the adoption of ERM is largely in response to emerging expectations for greater risk oversight, recent data shows that entities that outperform their peers are more likely to have developed a more formal risk management process.[6] Proponents of ERM stress that the goal of effective ERM is not to lower risk. Rather, ERM is designed to more effectively manage risks on an enterprise-wide basis so that stakeholder value is at least preserved, but hopefully enhanced. Said differently, ERM allows management and the board to make better, more "risk-intelligent," strategic decisions. Recent evidence, cited above, seems to support this notion.

An ERM focus is assisting boards and senior executives to think about risks more holistically. This is far different than traditional approaches to risk where management has historically assigned risk oversight responsibilities to individual functions or business units (these are often referred to as "silos" or "stove-pipes" of the business in the language of ERM). The common result of a stove-pipe approach to risk management is that risks are often managed inconsistently or within each individual risk manager's personal tolerance for risk. More importantly, these risks may be effectively managed within an individual business unit to acceptable levels, but the risk responses or treatments selected by the manager may unknowingly create or add to risks for other units within the organization. Furthermore, traditional silo-based approaches to risk management often fail to anticipate that certain risk events may be correlated with other risk events, triggering a cascading series of risk exposures. Often the net result when risks are managed in this manner is an increase (rather than reduction) in the overall risk exposure for the enterprise.

SENIOR EXECUTIVE LEADERSHIP IN RISK MANAGEMENT

An ERM approach to risk management requires a top-down view of risks faced by the organization. Visible leadership from and embrace by the senior executive team is a critical component to an effective ERM process. Those organizations that have started down the ERM path attest to the reality that the adoption of a holistic view of risks, which requires that risk information be shared transparently across silos within the organization, requires a significant change in the corporate culture or mindset of management at all levels within the enterprise. As employees across the organization are held accountable for the ownership of risks within their areas of responsibility, senior executive leadership is needed to reinforce the importance of this movement toward a more transparent, enterprise-wide view of risk management.

The CFOs are uniquely positioned to lead the overall enterprise risk management effort. CFOs are already intricately involved in providing an overall view of the organization from a financial risk perspective, which gives them an enterprise-wide understanding of the key activities that drive performance. CFOs also have an existing relationship with the audit committee. Thus, as audit committees turn to management to strengthen the enterprise's approach to risk management, they are naturally turning to CFOs to kick-start the process.

CFOs have responded to these new challenges by designing basic structures for identifying and assessing risks across the enterprise. For many, this begins by defining risk terminology or developing common definitions of key risk concepts so that risk management approaches are implemented consistently across the enterprise. Providing a clear definition of risk terms (including a discussion of whether "risk" represents both risky opportunities and downside risks) is often the required first step. Once risk is defined, senior management can then survey the organization to identify potential risk drivers and risk events through questionnaires, interviews, risk workshops, and external risk scanning to generate an inventory of risks that may pose potential threats and/or opportunities for the enterprise.

Leadership is needed to ensure that risks are assessed consistently across the organization. Risk champions at the senior executive level must develop procedures to govern how risks are to be assessed, not only from a likelihood or probability perspective, but also from an impact perspective in order to prioritize those risks most important for senior executive and board oversight. Based on risk rankings, reflecting probability and impact assessments, management is now in a position to identify those risks with the greatest need for the development of an appropriate risk response. Senior executives should then identify key risk indicators that can be included in management information reports to allow for proactive management of these risks on an ongoing basis.

The above discussion provides an abbreviated overview of the core elements of an ERM approach, and also illustrates the nature of risk management leadership that the audit committee and board are expecting from the senior executive team. Later chapters are devoted to a thorough discussion of tools and techniques that identify and assess risks and that develop appropriate treatment strategies tailored to the specific risks encountered.

THE ROLE OF THE INTERNAL AUDIT FUNCTION IN ERM

The CFO and other senior executives formally lead the ERM effort, but internal audit plays a major role in supporting the risk management process. In many cases, audit executives who lead the internal audit function have often initiated the ERM launch within their organizations. Although internal audit is naturally involved in risk management activities, there are specific roles the internal audit function should and should not assume throughout the ERM process. Internal audit should provide an assurance service on risk management processes, giving assurance that risks are evaluated correctly, evaluating risk management processes, evaluating the reporting of key risks, and reviewing the management of key risks. However, internal audit should not be involved in developing the risk management process for board approval, imposing risk management processes, making decisions on risk responses, managing identified risks, or establishing the enterprise's risk appetite. The internal audit's role should be to monitor the effectiveness of ERM processes designed and implemented by senior management. Direct reporting of the internal audit function's monitoring activities puts audit committees in a position to be more objectively informed about the effectiveness of management's risk management processes, including the accuracy and completeness of risk information they receive directly from senior management.

EXTERNAL AUDIT AS AN INDEPENDENT SOURCE OF KEY RISK IDENTIFICATION

Audit committees also exert pressure on their external auditors to share risk information they glean from audits of financial statements and, for publicly traded entities, the audit of internal controls over financial reporting required by the Sarbanes-Oxley Act. In the process of understanding the entity and its environment (a requirement for financial statement audits to be conducted in conformance with auditing standards), external auditors are likely to identify key business risks affecting the enterprise. Auditors of publicly traded companies may also identify deficiencies in risk responses as they assess the effectiveness of internal controls surrounding core business processes that affect financial reporting. Proactive audit committees recognize that the external auditor can serve as a rich source of risk information that can assist the audit committee in challenging the completeness of risk inventories prepared by management. External auditors recognize that this contribution is a value-added activity for their clients and respond with greater dialogue about key risks when participating in executive sessions with the audit committee.

While boards and senior executives are strengthening their risk oversight processes at a rapid pace, few entities are currently able to claim that they have fully developed ERM processes in place. Most recognize that the implementation of ERM is an evolutionary process, whereby risk oversight improves over time. Most ERM proponents believe there is no "one size fits all" approach to enterprise risk management. As boards and senior management strive to make real progress toward developing ERM processes into more mature business operating models, they will need to be patient. Immediate success is rare—ERM must be viewed as a long-term cultural change and realistic expectations must be established for its implementation.

ERM IMPLEMENTATION STRATEGIES

In fulfilling its obligation to exercise oversight over risk management, the board or board committee charged with the primary responsibility for oversight should focus on the adequacy of the organization's enterprise risk management system. Risk management must be tailored to the specific entity, but in general an effective ERM process will identify the significant risks that the organization faces in a timely manner, implement appropriate risk management strategies that are in concert with the company's risk appetite and specific risk exposures, integrate the consideration of risk and risk management into strategic decision making throughout the company, and feature explicit policies and procedures that adequately transmit necessary information with respect to significant risks to senior management and, as appropriate, to the board or relevant committee. To accomplish these objectives, there are certain implementation strategies that can help the board and the senior executives delegate responsibility for the ERM program in designing and modifying the risk management function. The sections that follow discuss the following strategies:

- Role of the audit committee
- Role of the board
- Training
- Board composition
- Reporting
- Compliance
- Culture

Role of the Audit Committee

As discussed earlier in the chapter, most boards delegate primary oversight of risk management to the audit committee, which is consistent with the NYSE corporate governance rules illustrated in Box 4.2. That rule requires the audit committee to discuss policies with respect to risk assessment and risk management. For many companies, however, the scope and complexity of enterprise risk management may dictate consideration of establishing a dedicated risk management committee of the board in order to force increased attention at the board level on risk management and oversight. The NYSE listing requirement permits boards to so delegate the primary risk oversight function to a different board committee, subject to limited continuing audit committee oversight.

The audit committee may not always be the best choice for providing direct oversight of the ERM program at the board level. Given the significant responsibilities specifically mandated or delegated to it by the Sarbanes-Oxley Act, the audit committee typically has a crowded meeting agenda and may not have sufficient time and resources to devote to the optimal level of risk oversight. In addition, the audit committee's focus on compliance with financial reporting rules and auditing standards is not necessarily the best approach for understanding the broad array of risks faced by their organization. In fact, it may be argued that an intense focus on compliance may hinder certain risk awareness because once satisfaction is reached that a standard has been correctly followed, it is natural to then turn to new issues rather than to continue spending scarce time on an issue seemingly resolved. A recent example of this phenomenon may be found in the banking industry, where the creation of off-balance sheet entities (structured investment vehicles and trusts) conformed to applicable accounting guidance but, in hindsight, clearly contributed to the catastrophic escalation of risk that has led to financial ruin for many financial institutions.

If primary responsibility for risk oversight remains with the audit committee instead of a newly constituted risk committee, the audit committee should explicitly include dedicated agenda time for the periodic review of risk management policies and the status of key risks apart from its review of the financial statements and compliance issues. Although this will undoubtedly further burden the audit committee, it is critical to allocate necessary time and attention to the risk oversight role specifically. The goal should be to facilitate serious and thoughtful board-level discussion of the organization's ERM process, the trends in the key risks the company encounters, and the robustness of the company's policies, procedures, and actions designed to respond to and treat these risks.

Role of the Board

The primary board-level risk oversight role is typically delegated to a committee, but the full board is ultimately responsible for monitoring the ERM program. Hence, the board should devote meeting time to discuss and analyze information about the entity's ERM program and the most significant risks impacting the company's ability to achieve its strategic objectives. This can be accomplished through reports delivered by the committee charged with risk management oversight and by appropriately summarized versions of the materials provided by senior management and advisors to that committee. Risk management issues also commonly arise in the context of the work of other committees. For example, the compensation committee is charged with approval and oversight of the incentive compensation arrangements for senior management personnel. These compensation agreements must be carefully structured to ensure that they do not create incentives for the senior management team to take on risky projects (that breach the board-approved risk tolerance or appetite of the organization) in an attempt to maximize bonus compensation. Specialized committees may also be charged with specific areas of risk exposure. Within financial institutions, for example, credit, market, and asset/liability management committees are common, while some boards of energy and manufacturing companies have committees largely devoted to environmental and safety issues.

Training

In-depth knowledge of the organization's fundamental operations is required for understanding the implications of the key risks a company is exposed to and then assessing the company's planned responses to these risks. Director orientation and training programs should be reviewed to ensure they provide enough substance for directors to develop an understanding of the company's businesses. These programs should also discuss the company's risk inventory and provide an overview of the ERM process employed by the entity. In addition to orientation programs for new directors, a company should consider the development of continuing education materials for directors on an ongoing basis, to supplement board and committee meetings. Participation in workshops offered through various organizations can help keep directors abreast of current industry and company-specific developments and specialized issues. Site visits by directors, either within the framework of the board meeting schedule or as part of a continuing education program, can be valuable for companies where a physical inspection is important for appreciating the business-unit risks that the company faces. These visits should allow directors to assess firsthand some of the health and safety, operational, and other risks facing the company much better than a prepared presentation or written communication.

Director training should be tailored to the issues most relevant and important to the particular company and its business. For example, investment banks that issue and trade complex securities and derivatives generally monitor their financial exposure to market risk through daily value at risk (VaR) calculations. Workshops or Web-based presentations to inform bank board members about the underlying assumptions and the approach to calculating the VaR statistic can be critical for understanding the risks the bank faces. Most business decisions are made in the context of the economic and political environments in which the various business units operate, and presentations that illuminate key aspects of these differences across the company will be useful to the board's understanding of the company's operations. Although there are presently no legal requirements that mandate continuing education for the board, these efforts can be extremely valuable in helping directors to discharge their duties and to avoid negative media attention that may follow announcements of bad news events.

Board Composition

Recent changes to corporate governance requirements and best practices guidance have led many companies to enhance the independence and diversity of their boards. There has also been a downward trend in the participation of senior executives on boards of unaffiliated entities. Because of this, companies are often confronted with the fact that a significant portion of their boards may lack detailed knowledge of the industry in which the company operates. Under these conditions, the importance of well-designed and executed orientation programs for new directors and the creation of opportunities for continuing education for all members of the board are critical. As a function of this new environment, boards should pay particular attention to the background and experience of the individual board members asked to serve on the committee charged with oversight of the ERM function.

As seats on the board open up due to retirements or the creation of additional directorships, the board should aggressively recruit new members with relevant industry expertise and, if possible, with a background that includes risk management experience. For boards on which the CEO serves as the sole representative of the senior management team, it may be prudent to consider adding a second or third management representative, such as the COO, CFO, or chief risk officer (if a separate CRO position has been established), to provide an additional source of information in the boardroom on the company's business, operations, and risk profile. Direct lines of communication between non-CEO executives and the board or relevant board committee should already be present. Actual membership on the board is likely to allow for more consistent and timely input from these senior executives to the board.

The board's ability to perform its oversight role effectively is largely dependent on the flow of information that occurs among the directors, senior management, and the risk management executives in the organization. If the board is unsure whether they are receiving sufficient information to discharge their responsibilities, they need to be aggressive in their requests for that data. Directors must have adequate knowledge of such information as:

- The external and internal risk environment faced by the firm.
- The key material risk exposures affecting the company.
- The methodology employed to assess and prioritize risks.
- Treatment strategies for key risks.
- Status of implementation efforts for risk management procedures and infrastructure.
- The strengths and weaknesses of the overall ERM program.

Reporting

If the board has delegated primary risk oversight responsibility to a committee of the board, that committee should meet in executive sessions with the designated ERM leader in a manner analogous to the audit committee and its regular sessions with the company's internal auditor, and with senior management in connection with CEO and CFO certifications of the financial statements. Senior risk managers and the senior executive team need to be comfortable in informing the board or relevant committee of rapidly emerging risk exposures that require the immediate attention of the board. These reporting channels must be open at all times as a complement to regular reporting procedures. As previously discussed, the committee charged with risk oversight should make regular reports to the full board to keep them apprised of important changes in the organization's risk profile and/or exposure to key risks.

Compliance

Senior management should also provide the board with a comprehensive review of the company's legal compliance programs and how they affect the company's risk profile. There are a number of principles to consider when assessing the adequacy of compliance efforts. There should be a strong and visible "tone at the top" emanating from both the board and senior management that emphasizes that noncompliance with corporate policy will not be tolerated. Actions of the board and the senior executive team should provide an unambiguous signal to the organization that policies and procedures are to be followed scrupulously. The compliance program should be designed by individuals with the appropriate level of expertise and will typically include workshops and written materials. The full board should review compliance policies periodically in order to assess their effectiveness and to make any revisions deemed prudent or necessary to conform to changes in applicable laws. To ensure that policies are respected, it is essential that there be consistency in enforcement through appropriate disciplinary measures. Finally, there should be a clear reporting system in place so that employees understand when and to whom they should report suspected violations.

Culture

In addition to the formal compliance program, the board must also encourage management to promote a corporate culture that understands the business case for risk management and incorporates it into its overall corporate strategy and day-to-day business operations. The enterprise risk management function cannot be viewed as a drag on the achievement of corporate objectives or isolated as a specialized corporate function, but instead should be established as an integral part of everyday decision making within the business units. Companies must incur risk in order to run their businesses and maximize returns for stakeholders. The board must recognize that there can be significant danger in excessive risk aversion, just as there is danger in unchecked risk taking. But the assessment of risk, the accurate weighing of risks versus rewards, and the informed response to risk exposures should be incorporated into all business decision making.

The company's enterprise risk management structure should enable ongoing efforts to assess and analyze the most likely areas of future risk for the company. This process, often referred to as environmental scanning, is a key element of avoiding or successfully mitigating those risks before they become crises. In their review of the organization's risk management processes, the board should ask senior management directing the ERM program to discuss with them the most likely sources of significant far-horizon risks and how the company is planning for any significant potential vulnerability.

CONCLUSION

As stated at the opening of this chapter, the oversight of the enterprise risk management (ERM) processes employed by an organization is one of the most important and challenging functions of a corporation's board of directors. It is the board's responsibility to work in concert with senior management of the company to establish the appropriate "tone at the top" to ensure that risk and risk management remain at the forefront of strategic and operating decisions made within the business. As a simple survey of the financial press would indicate, we find ourselves today in an environment in which companies face risk exposures that are more complex, more interconnected, and potentially more devastating than ever before. To ensure that they are faithfully discharging their fiduciary duties, boards must adequately acknowledge and manage risks associated with decisions being made throughout the organization and operate with the understanding that these risks can and often do lead to potentially catastrophic results.

NOTES

1. In re Caremark International Inc. Derivative Litigation, 698 A.2d 959, 971.
2. "Final Corporate Governance Rules," New York Stock Exchange (2004) www.nyse.com.
3. Committee of Sponsoring Organizations of the Treadway Commission (COSO), Enterprise Risk Management – Integrated Framework, September 2004, www.coso.org, New York, NY.
4. "The Role of U.S. Corporate Boards in Enterprise Risk Management," the Conference Board (2006).
5. "Board Members on Risk," Ernst & Young (2007).
6. See "Balancing Risk and Performance with an Integrated Finance Organization – The Global CFO Study 2008," IBM Global Business Services.

PART II

ERM Management, Culture, and Control

CHAPTER 5

Becoming the Lamp Bearer

The Emerging Roles of the Chief Risk Officer

ANETTE MIKES
Assistant Professor of Business Administration, Harvard Business School

One of the greatest contributions of risk managers—arguably the single greatest—is just carrying a torch around and providing transparency.
—Chief Risk Officer, interviewed on November 17, 2006

Opinion has a significance proportioned to the sources that sustain it.
—Benjamin Cardozo (1870–1938)

Despite the widespread adoption of enterprise risk management (ERM) in the financial services industry, banks suffered hundreds of billions of dollars of losses during 2007–2008, stemming from risks that few executives had understood (Treasury Committee 2007a, 2007b). Under the shock of the first subprime-related loss disclosures, industry observers raised the question: "Where were the risk managers?" (Bookstaber 2007). In February 2008, a joint study by the Senior Supervisors Group—representatives of eight banking supervisory bodies—noted that, while "some firms recognized the emerging additional risks and took deliberate actions to limit or mitigate them ... other firms did not fully recognize the risks in time to mitigate them adequately" (Senior Supervisors Group 2008, 2). The group emphasized significant differences in firms' approaches to risk management, particularly in the design and scope of risk assessment and reporting practices.

Further, regulators and industry observers continue to call for the appointment of executives who are exclusively devoted to the role of enterprise-wide risk oversight, particularly since one early victim of the subprime credit debacle, Merrill Lynch, lacked a chief risk officer and another, Citigroup, was immediately blamed for its ineffective risk oversight (*American Banker* 2008). Going forward, many argue that the role of the chief risk officer is going to be further emphasized in corporate governance. As Peter Raskind, National City Bank's chief executive officer, argued in an interview in the pages of the *American Banker* toward the end of the first year of the subprime credit crisis: "This environment has absolutely underscored the need for that person. But it's not just credit risk. It's operational risk, reputation risk, and so on."[1]

Risk management in banks is a relatively recent function. Under the leadership of chief risk officers, risk-management staff groups are currently carving out their territory in response to uncertainties ranging from adverse asset-price movements to borrower defaults and threats to the financial health of the enterprise. The visibility of risk management and, in particular, of the Chief Risk Officer (CRO) has increased outside the banking industry, too. In a 2008 survey, consulting firm McKinsey tracked the diffusion of CRO appointments by industry in the United States (Winokur 2009). McKinsey found that 43 percent of insurance companies had appointed a senior risk officer with enterprise-wide risk oversight, in contrast to 19 percent in 2002. Other industries with a significant number of CRO appointments include energy and utilities (50 percent of companies had a CRO in 2008), health care, and metals and mining (20 percent to 25 percent of companies were reported to have a CRO). Furthermore, it is widely expected that rating agencies will assess the quality and scope of ERM as part of their rating process going forward (Standard & Poor's 2008; Ernst & Young 2008).

Enterprise risk management, under the leadership of CROs, has the promise to bring enterprise-wide risks, which threaten the achievement of the firm's strategic objectives, into the open and under control. Its organizational significance is that, by providing a process to identify, measure, monitor, and manage uncertainty in strategic decision making, strategic planning, performance management, and deal-approval processes, it enables top management to maintain or alter patterns in risk taking.

This chapter addresses the question: How may chief risk officers realize that organizational significance? I draw on the existing practitioner and academic literature on the role of chief risk officers and on a number of case studies from my ongoing research program on the evolution of the role of the CRO. The first section deals with the origins and rise of the CRO and outlines four major roles that senior risk officers may fulfill. The following sections discuss and illustrate those roles.

THE ORIGINS OF THE CRO

In 1956, *Harvard Business Review* published "Risk Management: A New Phase of Cost Control," in which Russell Gallagher called for a "workable program for 'risk management' . . . putting it under one executive, who in a large company might be a full-time 'risk manager.'" The article proposed that, in the face of increasingly expensive insurance premiums, the "postwar battle for tighter cost controls" required a "concerted method of attack" on the management of risks and hazards—namely, the appointment of a professional insurance manager. So began the saga of the chief risk officer in the world of insurance. Indeed, until recently, most nonfinancial firms considered buying insurance to be the core task of the risk-management function (Butterworth 2001).

The seeds of a more strategic role for the chief risk officer were sown in the 1970s. The publication of the Black-Scholes options-pricing model in 1973 triggered the staggering rise of derivatives markets (Buehler et al. 2008) by enabling more effective pricing and mitigation of risk. Over the next three decades, the world of risk management in the financial services sector changed profoundly as banks and securities houses created a "gigantic clearinghouse for packaging, trading and transferring risks" (Buehler et al. 2008). Financial firms both created and took advantage of many important innovations to contain financial risks; the arsenal of risk management was no longer limited to insurance policies. Increasing financial sophistication resulted in two new risk-management strategies: (1) portfolio diversification, and (2) hedging. Energy companies, food producers, and other firms followed suit in widening their risk-management toolkits as markets opened for the trading of various industry-specific risks. However, as Merton observed, top executives in most industries persistently regarded the application of derivatives and other risk-management tools as essentially tactical and therefore delegated the management of financial risk to a host of in-house financial experts such as insurance managers and corporate treasurers (Merton 2005). The dangers of delegation and the resultant "silo" approach have been ruthlessly exposed by a number of corporate scandals over the last two decades and during the credit crisis of 2007–2008, as it became clear that many firms had taken large risks without an appropriate understanding of the long-term, firm-wide consequences, which, by 2009, had spread far beyond their organizations onto millions of stunned stakeholders and innocent bystanders.

The creation of the CRO role with a dedicated risk-management unit occurred intermittently at first; some of the earliest attempts took place in large financial services firms, often as a reaction to excessive investment losses. In 1987, Merrill Lynch, having suffered large losses on mortgage-backed securities in March of that year, appointed Mark Lawrence, a senior executive, to establish a dedicated risk-management unit. But because there was, as yet, no pressure to institutionalize this new organizational function, the role of CRO lacked credibility (Wood 2002) and the unit gradually lost power (Power 2005). GE Capital's risk-management unit was an exception. James Lam, appointed chief risk officer in 1993, became the first to hold the role of integrated risk oversight with that title (Lam 2000). His unit, designed as an integral part of GE's finance function, displayed a "rigorous process approach," allocating risk-based approval authority down the business lines, applying data-driven analytics to identify and monitor risk, and strictly enforcing risk limits.[2] In the early 2000s, Deutsche Bank created the position of CRO (Hugo Banziger) with the mandate to make the risk and profit implications of business-line decisions transparent. By then, the concept of a risk-management head had evolved from a defensive administrative "cop" to—at least in aspiration—a business partner and advisor in risk taking (Power 2005, 134; Wood 2002). This shifted the risk-management model (and the CRO) out of the back office and into the front line with a more strategic role. As the new risk-based capital adequacy reform (Basel II) gathered momentum, calls for assembling risk-management practices under the umbrella of a dedicated risk organization and under the oversight of a high-level executive intensified.

The rise of the CRO was not confined to the financial sector: Sulzer Medica appointed a CRO in 2001, following legal losses, and Delta Airlines employed a CRO in 2002 in response to the heightened concern for risks in the airline industry following the 9/11 terrorist attacks (Power 2005).

Nevertheless, it was the increasing codification of enterprise risk management into various risk-management standards that accelerated the appointment of senior risk officers with an enterprise-wide risk oversight. Multi-disciplinary task forces in Australia and New Zealand published the first Risk Management Standard in 1995 (revised in 1999 and 2004) and other standard-setters followed suit (Ferma 2002; COSO 2003), successfully spreading the notion that enterprise risk management was good management. Several companies aspiring to be best-practice organizations adopted enterprise risk management and appointed chief risk officers to oversee its implementation (Aabo et al. 2005). McKinsey's 2008 survey found that 10 percent of nonfinancial firms had CROs, up from 4 percent in 2002 (Winokur 2009).

In tandem with the rise of the chief risk officer and the dedicated risk-management function, the internal auditing profession also staked a claim on the risk-management domain (Koleman 2003). The Institute of Internal Auditors, an international professional association of certified internal auditors, included risk management as part of the audit profession's competencies and stimulated the development of control risk self-assessment as the bedrock of enterprise risk management. Furthermore, external auditors had reinvented the financial audit to be more perceptive of the client's business risk and associated risks, offering business-risk assessments simultaneously as an audit-planning tool and as an advisory mechanism. Overall, the shape of a risk-management services industry had become visible, with risk professionals, internal auditors, and external auditors competing to design and service the internal risk-management space of corporations (Power 2000).

Not surprisingly, CROs come from many walks of life, including internal audit, external audit, financial management, business management, and consulting. Industry surveys (PricewaterhouseCoopers 2007; Deloitte 2007; IBM 2005) show that CROs fulfill a variety of roles that nevertheless fall into two categories: (1) a compliance and control function on one hand, and (2) a more strategic "business partner" role on the other hand. Much of the industry debate prior to the subprime-credit crisis focused on how CROs ought to balance their *compliance champion* role with that of an active participant in business decision making. The credit crisis directed attention to a series of risk-management failures (Stulz 2009), particularly the gaps in financial institutions' internal risk-assessment practices. Indeed, there is wide variation in the usefulness and reliability of the risk models used by various financial institutions (Tett 2008). My recent research indicates that firms' risk-modeling initiatives vary in style and quantitative sophistication and that senior risk officers exercise a large degree of discretion in determining the use and mix of quantitative and qualitative risk-management tools (Mikes 2005, 2007b). This finding highlights the role of the CRO as a *modeling expert* who deploys a certain degree of quantitative enthusiasm or quantitative skepticism in the management of different risk categories (Mikes 2008b). Further, different CROs interpret their "business partner" roles differently. In a study of 15 chief risk officers, I found that some CROs strive to grasp the key strategic uncertainties affecting their organizations (whether measurable or not) and proactively help top management anticipate emerging strategic risks; these CROs play the role of *strategic advisor*. Other CROs confine their attention to the measurable risk universe and the production of "catch-all" metrics for aggregate risk taking and risk-adjusted performance; they enact the role of the *strategic controller*.

In sum, the role of the chief risk officer is not only multifaceted but also varies according to the industry, the emphasis the risk function places on compliance with regulatory and risk-management standards, and the extent and sophistication of the firm's risk modeling. The next four sections turn in detail to the four major CRO roles, namely (1) compliance champion, (2) modeling expert, (3) strategic controller, and (4) strategic advisor.

THE CRO AS COMPLIANCE CHAMPION

The role of compliance champion entails advocating and policing compliance with pressing stakeholder requirements and keeping up with new regulations and standards affecting the design and roles of the risk-management function. Many CROs initiate a "risk policy framework"—a determination of what risks need to be addressed and by whom—on which the board and a senior executive then sign off.

The risk policy framework fulfills several roles:

First, it sets the boundaries of acceptable risk taking by ensuring that the appropriate standards and controls are in place. As one senior risk officer put it, the framework tells the business lines "the rules of engagement, making sure that the do's and the don'ts are sufficiently clear."[3] It is now widely recognized in risk-management circles that "both Barings's and Société Générale's losses were created by employees not following the processes."[4] Research on so-called man-made disasters has long established that complex organizations (in any industry) generate "normal accidents" (Perrow 1984) and routine errors that are suited to—and, indeed, called for—the creation of a specialist CRO role (Power 2004, 141). In such settings, CROs are pressure points in the border territory between risk controlling and risk taking; "the risk officer is not necessarily responsible for each risk type, but is responsible to ensure each risk-type owner has set appropriate standards."[5] Although the CRO supports and enhances the management of risk, detailed risk management remains the responsibility of line management.

Second, the risk policy framework advocates a shared understanding of the spectrum of risks the organization cares about; naturally, this spectrum changes over time. Some chief risk officers consider the creation of this shared understanding to be the key benefit of their work because it reinforces the company's shared understanding of its strategic priorities. Hydro One's chief risk officer, John Fraser, is a case in point. He maintains that enterprise risk management starts with top management agreeing about strategic objectives; then they develop a shared understanding of the principal risks (Mikes 2008a). Fraser acknowledges that his role was "not to give the answers" to the problems of the business but to facilitate the emergence of a shared understanding among managers. He achieved this in interactive risk workshops:

> Enterprise risk management is a contact sport. Success comes from making contact with people. Magic occurs in risk workshops. People enjoy them. Some say, "I have always worried about this topic, and now I am less worried, because I see that someone else is dealing with it, or I have learned it is a low probability event." Other people said, "I could put forward my point and get people to agree that it is something we should be spending more time on, because it is a high risk."[6]

Third, the risk policy framework gives chief risk officers a plan, a language, and the authority with which to oversee the development of risk-measurement and monitoring tools for each risk type. At a basic level, every risk function operates a host of templates with which to collect risk information, establish risk-assessment guidelines, and construct risk models that collect loss and other risk-related data to track the firm's evolving risk profile. But there is a plethora of tools and practices for measuring and communicating risk and wide variation in their application even within a particular industry.

THE CRO AS MODELING EXPERT

In general, chief risk officers play a powerful role in selecting the people, processes, and systems that will define the scope of risk measurement and control in their organizations. The infrastructure of most modern risk-management functions contains a wide variety of risk models, processes, and information systems, the design of which requires the CRO to play the role of the modeling expert.

Deutsche Bank's CRO, Hugo Banziger, recalled his early experiences with system-building:

> I ... had to build an entirely new organization from scratch. We designed a dedicated credit process; hired and trained credit staff, as there were no credit people with derivatives know-how in the market; built credit-risk engines with the help of traders; and created our own Potential Future Exposure model, using Monte Carlo simulations and stress-testing portfolios. After that, we had to build a credit system that could integrate all these functions and aggregate our derivative counterparty exposure globally. These were six very challenging years.[7]

Banziger is one of several chief risk officers who emphasize risk aggregation as well as risk measurement. As they see it, the creation of an aggregate view of quantified risks is the key benefit of implementing firm-wide risk models. Aggregating risk exposures had been a challenge to risk practitioners for a long time, largely due to the variety of risk measures applied to the different risk types and insufficient knowledge of the correlations between risk exposures, the diversification benefits, and the concentration penalties. The recent development of economic capital as a common-denominator measure for market, credit, and operational risks enables firms to aggregate their quantifiable risks into a total risk estimate.[8] Indeed, Wood (2002) argues that the key role of the CRO is to fine-tune the calculation of economic capital for organizational-control purposes. Accordingly, recent works in the risk-management literature advocate risk-based internal capital allocations (measured by economic capital) for performance measurement and control. The ideal of introducing risk-based performance measurement in banks has emerged in tandem with developments in risk quantification and, importantly, risk aggregation.

Risk aggregation requires a high degree of modeling expertise on the part of the risk-management function; it entails the extension of risk analytics to uncertainties with explicable (but not yet known) properties and the adjustment of the measurement approaches as further data become available.

In a recent study, however, CROs voiced divergent opinions on the benefits and limitations of the available menu of risk-modeling initiatives (Mikes 2008b, 2009).

One group of CROs took a skeptical view, emphasizing that risk models were useful tools for managing a narrow set of risks, such as those that lend themselves to conventional statistical analysis (e.g., credit-card risks in a given geography and consumer segment). Due to the homogeneity of such risk profiles and the large number of data points, decisions in such areas could be automated. But these CROs felt that, in less homogeneous business segments, such as lending to both small enterprises and large corporations, risk models were intrinsically less reliable (*quantitative skepticism*) and the judgment of veteran experts was essential. They did not consider risk modeling accurate enough to produce an objective picture of the underlying risk profiles, only to indicate the underlying trends.

Another group of CROs, however, were committed to extensive risk modeling and fostered a culture in which risk models were regarded as robust and relevant tools in decision making (*quantitative enthusiasm*), particularly in strategic planning and performance management. In these banks, risk experts gradually expanded the modeling infrastructure to uncover the natures and distributions of hitherto unknown uncertainties (including such risks as lending to small and medium-size enterprises), classifying and measuring these as part of the economic-capital framework. They quantified many operational risks as well, in order to make the aggregate risk profile more comprehensive. These additional risk assessments, once aggregated into the total risk profile, influenced the calculation of economic capital for control purposes. However, linking these risk calculations to planning and performance measurement was not automatic. Several senior risk officers were aware that simply wielding aggregate risk numbers would not convince business lines to change the way they did business. As one senior risk officer explained: "There is still an argument that the methodology and data underlying the quantification measurements themselves are not sufficiently reliable.... An aggregate view has to evolve. We have to be more confident in the quality of it. I wouldn't like to run the business on the aggregate view as we see it today."[9]

THE CRO AS STRATEGIC CONTROLLER

The evolution of the aggregate view has paved the way for the role of the CRO as *strategic controller*. This role assumes that the risk function, having built firm-wide risk models, enables the company to operate a formal risk-adjusted performance management system. Chief risk officers in this category preside over the close integration of risk and performance measurement and ensure that risk-adjusted metrics are deemed reliable and are relied on. They advise top management on the absolute and relative risk-return performance of various businesses and influence how capital and investments are committed.

A senior risk officer who fulfilled this role described the risk-adjusted planning process as follows: "We obviously get involved with risk appetite. The businesses put forward their proposals, having linked in with [the group risk-management department]. They generate appropriate figures upon which we make the choices about where to bet the bank. The calculations are done by the businesses initially. They work it through with the risk department."[10]

Another CRO emphasized the importance of risk-adjusted performance measurement as a way of making business managers accountable for risk taking: "If we align the incentives correctly, then I don't have a job. The aim is getting the business units accountable for risk and the risk correctly charged and visible."[11]

The strategic controller role requires a legitimate risk-modeling capability, which is foundational to risk-based performance management. However, the construction of risk-adjusted performance measurement is inherently political. Risk-adjusted performance measures do not work by themselves; they have to be made to work. The CRO needs to be aware that a new, risk-adjusted view of performance will inherently affect resource and reward allocations; internal jurisdictions may therefore resist it.

For both political and theoretical reasons, CROs must also be modest in their claims of "objectivity." There can be no genuine objectivity in the measurement or management of that which has not yet happened and may never happen; other parts of the organization will easily recognize this as the soft underbelly of the risk-management function. Field studies on CROs in action show that, time and again, distrust of risk numbers and critique from other organizational groups require the CRO and the risk-management function to reconstitute and revise risk-adjusted performance metrics. Such objectivity as these calculations can achieve may well be the result of an organizational consensus, emerging from the process of challenge and revision. On the other hand, it has been shown that, in the face of challenge and critique from well-established organizational control groups, chief risk officers' "dreams of measurement" for control purposes may turn out to be just that (Mikes 2005, 2009; Power 2004).

THE CRO AS STRATEGIC ADVISOR

In the role of *strategic advisor*, senior risk officers command board-level visibility and influence, predominantly as a result of their grasp of emerging risks and nonquantifiable strategic and operational uncertainties. They bring judgment into high-level risk decisions, challenge the assumptions underlying business plans, and use traditional risk controls and lending constraints to alter the risk profiles of particular businesses.

Many senior risk officers aspiring to this role do not regard risk modeling as sufficiently accurate to produce an objective picture of the underlying risk profiles; they rely on risk calculations mainly to indicate underlying trends (*quantitative skepticism*). They are therefore reluctant to link risk measurements to planning and performance management, leaving these control practices to their traditional realm, the finance function. Instead, they seek to mobilize their own experience with other expert views from the organization to help decision makers understand emerging risks, the nature of which is not explicable by modeling. As one such senior risk officer explained: "The key decisions you make are not based on what you put in the model and what gets spat out. . . . The way I think of it: Risk is chemistry, it's not particle physics. You cannot separate the risks."[12]

Key to the strategic advisor role is the CRO's ability to create processes that channel risk information to key decision makers and thus prevent "risk incubation." While acknowledging that this role is new to them, several CROs are now championing practices of risk anticipation such as risk-based scenario planning and devil's-advocate systems. Looking beyond the risk silos and "taking a 30,000-foot view of the world,"[13] these CROs conduct forecasts and assessments in order to find vulnerabilities and problem areas and alert the executive and supervisory boards.

Risk anticipation often surfaces multiple and conflicting views. As one senior risk officer explained with a hint of self-mockery, the role of the senior risk manager is like that of the "medieval licensed jester, allowed to be more skeptical about what is going on, constantly challenging existing assumptions and views, and scrutinizing strategic decisions before they are made. The difficulty is to challenge without causing offence" (Mikes 2009).

This role requires the senior risk officer to build a track record and credibility; as Hydro One's CRO, John Fraser, put it, "You have to earn your spurs."[14] Some senior risk officers in banks who came through the ranks of line management believe they are better positioned to play the role of the strategic advisor than their risk-specialist peers. Having earned the trust and respect of line management, they can negotiate the conditions of good business by understanding both viewpoints, that of the target-focused business originator and that of the risk-conscious controller. As one senior risk officer explained:

> *You need to know the business generators well enough to know ... that their own stance and emotion and the fervor for a deal will impair their judgment. Most people, most very successful deal-doers, will always push the envelope. The issue is to understand how they operate within their values. So not only do you understand where they're likely to over-egg it because the rewards are there, but also you know how to approach them when you want to slow them down. One, they have to trust you. And two, they have to respect your judgment. But you don't achieve that overnight. You generally get it by being encouraging of what you believe is good business.[15]*

The development of the strategic advisor role is partially driven by governance demands for organizational resilience and the management of extreme events, such as fundamental surprises, sudden losses of meaning (sudden events that make no sense to the people involved), and events that are inconceivable, hidden, or incomprehensible (Weick 1993). The specter of "black swan events" (Taleb 2007) raises fundamental questions about the role of risk management and that of the CRO: Should low-probability events be understood under the rubric of risk modeling or rather as fundamental surprise (Power 2007)? The shift in focus from probabilities and statistical loss distributions to facilitating organizational resilience and sense-making under stress marks the difference between the role of the CRO as strategic controller and that of the CRO as strategic advisor.

WHICH CRO ROLE TO PLAY?

The compliance role tends to be well-defined by the environment; within an industry, there is not much room for variation in that role. The modeling role, however, presents risk functions with a practical choice of processes and models and a philosophical choice of where to draw the line between what can be reliably measured and modeled and what must be placed in the hands of qualitative judgment. It is this line that divides (although never absolutely) the role of strategic controller from the role of strategic advisor (see Exhibit 5.1 for a summary of the strategic CRO roles).

Both assume a high degree of path dependency; the requisite resources and capabilities can only be obtained over time (recall Deutsche Bank's six-year effort).

Exhibit 5.1 Summary of the Business-Partner Roles of the CRO

	Strategic controller	Strategic advisor
Modeling capabilities		
Primary objective of risk modeling	Measuring the aggregate risk profile of products and business lines	Anticipating changes in the risk environment
The role of judgment in risk modeling	Model design contains the modeler's judgment of complex relationships between variables	Model design is deliberately simple. Managerial judgment is exercised to adjust model implications to reflect additional complexities
Strategic capabilities		
Span of risk control	Quantifiable risks	Quantifiable and nonquantifiable risks
The essence of the business partner role	The integration of risk management with planning and performance management	The risk function's ability to influence discretionary strategic decisions and to articulate to line managers the long-term risk-implications of their decisions
	The CRO as the advocate of risk-adjusted performance	The CRO as a seasoned business executive and "devil's advocate"
Modeling attitudes		
Calculative culture	Quantitative enthusiasm: Risk numbers are deemed representative of the underlying economic reality	Quantitative skepticism: Risk numbers are taken as trend indicators
	Emphasis on the "robust" and "hard" nature of modeling	Emphasis on learning about the underlying risk profile from the trend signals
	Risk-adjusted performance measures are recognized	Risk-adjusted performance measures are discussed, but are open to challenge

Source: Mikes (2008b).

The strategic advisory role requires an intimate knowledge of the business and what can go wrong—experience that risk officers can only gain by having lived through many organizational successes, losses, and crises. The strategic controller role, on the other hand, calls for building a sophisticated risk-modeling capability, which is foundational to risk-based performance management. But risk-adjusted performance measures do not work by themselves—they must be made to work. To make risk numbers count in planning and performance management requires leadership, political flair, communication, and well-chosen allies—all of which can only be developed over time.

It is possible that some CROs may develop the strategic advisor and the strategic controller roles successively if they can negotiate the path dependencies involved. Once models are tasked with accounting for risk-adjusted performance, the room for managerial judgment shrinks as that judgment is built into the model design up front. Quantitative skeptics are presently reluctant to delegate their understanding of risk-adjusted performance to models. However, some of them recognize that, over time, much of their judgment may be fed into the model design and that careful organizational positioning and packaging will eventually make risk-adjusted performance metrics legitimate and acceptable for control purposes.

Although quantitative enthusiasts maintain that models are capable of accommodating complex relationships between numerous variables, these risk officers also face important judgment calls; they must anticipate when even the most advanced of risk models will cease to be accurate as a result of major shifts in the environment. Given that most risk models in use at the time of this study had been developed in an unusually favorable credit environment (1998–2007), modeling experts whose career trajectory spans several "prolonged stress events" are hard to come by.

CONCLUSION

Chief risk officers, no matter what type of calculative culture they foster, are balancing at least two conflicting objectives: (1) to produce an aggregate view of risks, and (2) to retain case-by-case business knowledge and model familiarity with which to inform expert judgment. Striking the right balance remains a challenge for all CROs and their choice must be congruent with their organizations' decision making, risk taking, and modeling cultures.

With a new regulatory era and a severe and protracted financial crisis upon us, senior risk officers are under pressure to demonstrate how they are realizing the risk-oversight potential of their function. No professional realm can operate indefinitely if it clashes with the requirements of stakeholders (Gardner et al. 2001). As a professional group, chief risk officers need to accommodate the demands of a wide diversity of stakeholders—including regulators, corporate executives, shareholders, debt holders, and the general public—which in turn requires that the risk function have a clear, well-defined position in the organizational governance process. Senior risk officers increasingly consider the CEO and the board to be their primary customers. However, many risk functions have been caught by the credit crisis in a work-in-progress compliance-champion mode, while others have been in transition toward their particular understanding of the business-partner role. The ideas and practices of risk management, unlike those of long-established professions, have not yet been codified into a unified domain, leaving chief risk officers with a fuzzy role in corporate governance.

But lack of codification is an opportunity for definition. This fuzziness is a historic opportunity for the profession to improve business decision making by defining and amalgamating the strengths of the compliance-champion, modeling expert, strategic-advisor, and strategic-controller roles and by incorporating both good risk analytics and expert judgment. Yet the ultimate test remains the ability of risk managers to influence risk-taking behavior in the business lines. As one CRO participant, quoted at the outset of this chapter, remarked: "One of the greatest contributions of risk managers—arguably the single greatest—is just carrying a torch around and providing transparency."[16] The art of successful risk management is in getting the executive team to see the light and value the lamp bearer.

NOTES

1. Risk Chiefs: "As the Bar Rises, So Does Demand." *American Banker* (January 31, 2008) 48.

2. Author's interview on September 9, 2008. The identity of the interviewee is disguised for confidentiality reasons.

3. Author's interview on August 31, 2008. The identity of the interviewee is disguised for confidentiality reasons.

4. Private communication to the author, received October 16, 2008. The identity of the source is disguised for confidentiality reasons.

5. Private communication to the author, received November 11, 2008. The identity of the source is disguised for confidentiality reasons.

6. Mikes, A. "Enterprise Risk Management at Hydro One." Harvard Business School Case No. 9-109-001. (2008).

7. Hayes, N. "People, processes, systems: Deutsche Bank's Hugo Banziger knows it takes all three." *RMA Journal* (December 2002). Available on http://findarticles.com/p/articles/mi_m0ITW/is_4_85/ai_n14897213/pg_2?tag=artBody;col1.

8. Economic capital is a statistically estimated amount of capital that could cover all liabilities in a worst-case scenario, be it an unexpected market, credit, or operational loss. For risk practitioners and regulators, the conceptual appeal of economic-capital methods is that "they can provide a single metric along which all types of risks can be measured." (Bank for International Settlements, 2003, 6).

9. Author's interview on March 3, 2008. The identity of the interviewee is disguised for confidentiality reasons.

10. Mikes (2005, 170).

11. Author's interview on November 17, 2006. The identity of the interviewee is disguised for confidentiality reasons.

12. Author's interview on August 17, 2006. The identity of the interviewee is disguised for confidentiality reasons.

13. Mikes (2005, 205).

14. Mariga, Vanessa. "Moving into the C-Suite." *Canadian Underwriter* (March 2008) 10–16.

15. Author's interview on 22 November 2007. The identity of the interviewee is disguised for confidentiality reasons.

16. Author's interview on November 17, 2006. The identity of the interviewee is disguised for confidentiality reasons.

REFERENCES

Aabo et al. 2005. The rise and evolution of the chief risk officer: Enterprise risk management at Hydro One. *Journal of Applied Corporate Finance*, 17, 62–75.

American Banker. 2008. Risk Chiefs: As the bar raises, so does demand. Publication date: January 31.

Bank for International Settlements (BIS) Joint Forum. 2003. Trends in risk integration and aggregation. (August). Accessed on www.bis.org on May 13, 2004.

Bookstaber, R. 2007. Where were the risk managers? Accessed October 17, 2007, on http://blogs.wsj.com/economics/2007/10/16/bookstaber-asks-where-were-the-risk-managers/.

Buehler, K., Freeman, A., and Hulme, R. 2008. The new arsenal of risk management. *Harvard Business Review* (September).

Butterworth, M. 2001. The emerging role of the risk manager. In Pickford, J. (ed.), *Mastering Risk*, vol. 1: Concepts. (London, UK: Financial Times-Prentice Hall.

COSO. 2003. Committee of Sponsoring Organizations of the Treadway Commission, Enterprise Risk Management Framework.

Crouhy, M., Galai, D., and Mark, R. 2000. *Risk management*. New York: McGraw-Hill.

Deloitte, 2007. Global risk management survey: Accelerating risk management practices. 5th ed. Available on www.deloitte.com/dtt/research/0,1015,cid%253D151389,00.html.

Drzik, J., Nakada P., and Schuermann, T. 2004. Risk capital measurement in financial institutions–Part one. (May 14). Accessed on www.Erisk.com.

Economist Intelligence Unit. 2005. Global Risk Briefing.

Ernst & Young. 2008. Making a difference: Rating enterprise risk management. Accessed on www.ey.com on September 10, 2008.

Federation of European Risk Management Associations (FERMA). 2002. A risk management standard. (Brussels).

Gallagher, R.B. 1956. Risk management: New phase of cost control. *Harvard Business Review*.

Gardner, H., Csikszentmihalyi, M., and Damon, W. 2001. *Good work: When excellence and ethics meet*. New York: Basic Books.

Garside, T., and Nakada, P. 1999. Enhancing risk measurement capabilities. Available on www.erisk.com. Previously published in *Balance Sheet*, vol. 8, no. 3, 12–17.

Hayes, N. People, processes, systems: Deutsche Bank's Hugo Banziger knows it takes all three. *RMA Journal*, December 2002. Available on http://findarticles.com/p/articles/mi_m0ITW/is_4_85/ai_n14897213/pg_2?tag=artBody;col1.

IBM Business Consulting Services. 2005. The clairvoyant CRO. Available on www.ibm.com/industries/financialservices/doc/content/bin/fss_clairvoyant_cro.pdf.

Knight, Frank H. 1921. *Risk, uncertainty, and profit*. Mineola, NY: Dover Publications.

Kloman, H.F. 2003. Enterprise risk management: Past, present and future. Reprinted in Kloman, H.F., *Mumpsimus revisited: Essays on risk management*. Lyme, CT: Seawrack Press.

Lam, J. 2000. Enterprise-wide risk management and the role of the chief risk officer. Accessed on www.erisk.com on May 14, 2004.

Liebenberg, A.P., and Hoyt, R.E. 2003. The determinants of enterprise risk management: Evidence from the appointment of chief risk officers. *Risk Management and Insurance Review*, 37–52.

Lore, M., and Borodovsky, L. 2000. *The professional's handbook of financial risk management*. New York: Butterworth-Heinemann Finance.

Marrison, C. 2002. *The fundamentals of risk measurement*. New York: McGraw-Hill.

Marshall, C. 2001. *Measuring and managing operational risks in financial institutions: Tools, techniques and other resources*. New York: John Wiley & Sons.

Merton, R.C. 2005. You have more capital than you think. *Harvard Business Review* (November).

Mikes, A. 2005. Enterprise risk management in action. PhD Thesis, London School of Economics.

Mikes, A. 2007a. Convictions, conventions and the operational risk maze—The Cases of three financial services institutions. *International Journal of Risk Assessment and Management 7*, no. 8: 1027–1056.

Mikes, A., and Townsend, D. 2007b. Beyond compliance: The maturation of CROs and other senior risk executives. *GARP Risk Review*, 39 (November–December): 12–18.

Mikes, A. 2008a. Enterprise risk management at Hydro One. Harvard Business School Case 9-109-001.

Mikes, A. 2008b. Chief risk officers at crunch time: Compliance champions or business partners? *Journal of Risk Management in Financial Institutions*, 2, no. 1 (November–December): 7–24.

Mikes, A. 2009. Risk management and calculative cultures. *Management Accounting Research*, 20: 18–40.

Perrow, C. 1984. *Normal accidents: Living with high risk technologies*. New York: Basic Books.

Power, M.K. 2000. The audit implosion: regulating risk from the inside. The Institute of Chartered Accountants in England and Wales.

Power, M.K. 2003. The invention of operational risk. London: London School of Economics and Political Science, ESCR Centre for the Analysis of Risk and Regulation, Discussion Paper, no. 16.

Power, M.K. 2004. Counting, control and calculation: Reflections on measuring and management. *Human Relations*, 765–783.

Power, M.K. 2005. Organizational responses to risk: The rise of the chief risk officer. In B. Hutter, and M.K. Power. *Organizational encounters with risk*. Cambridge, UK: Cambridge University Press.

Power, M.K. 2007. *Organized uncertainty – Designing a world of risk management*. Oxford, UK: Oxford University Press.

PricewaterhouseCoopers. 2007. Creating value: Effective risk management in financial services.

Risk Management. 2007. A view from the top. (September). Online publication, accessed in October 2008 on www.allbusiness.com/company-activities-management/management-risk/8911274-1.html.

Standard & Poor's. 2008. Enterprise risk management: Standard & Poor's to apply enterprise risk analysis to corporate ratings. *Ratings Direct*, (May).

Stulz, R. 2009. Six ways companies mismanage risk. *Harvard Business Review*, (March).

Taleb, N.N. 2007. *The black swan*. London, UK: Penguin.

Tett, G. 2008. Cindarella role moves to the centre of attention. *Financial Times*, (April 28).

Treasury Committee (of the United Kingdom Parliament House of Commons). 2007a. Minutes of Evidence Taken before Treasury Committee, Tuesday, December 4, 2007 (Uncorrected transcript of Oral Evidence given by Mr. E. Gerald Corrigan, Managing Director and Co-Chair of the Firmwide Risk Management Committee, Goldman Sachs; Lord Charles Aldington, Chairman, Deutsche Bank; Mr. Jeremy Palmer, Chairman and CEO, Europe, Middle East and Africa, UBS; and Mr. William Mills, Chairman and Chief Executive of City Markets and Banking, Europe, Middle East and Africa, Citigroup). Accessed on www.publications.parliament.uk/pa/cm/cmtreasy.htm on January 10, 2008.

Treasury Committee (of the United Kingdom Parliament House of Commons). 2007b. Minutes of Evidence Taken before Treasury Committee, Tuesday, October 16, 2007 (Corrected transcript of Oral Evidence given by Dr. Matt Ridley, Chairman, Mr. Adam Applegarth, Chief Executive, Sir Ian Gibson, Senior Non-Executive Director, and Sir Derek Wanless, Non-Executive Director, Northern Rock). Accessed on www.publications.parliament.uk/pa/cm200607/cmselect/cmtreasy/cmtreasy.htm on January 10, 2008.

Weick, K. 1993. The collapse of sensemaking in organizations: The Mann Gulch disaster. *Administrative Science Quarterly*, 38: 628–652.

Winokur, L.A. 2009. The rise of the risk executive. *Risk Professional*, (February) 10–17.

Wood, D. 2002. From cop to CRO. Accessed on www.erisk.com on May 14, 2004.

ACKNOWLEDGMENTS

I am grateful to Robert Kaplan, John Fraser, and Betty Simkins for their comments on earlier drafts of this chapter. I am also indebted to Roxanna Myhrum, David Newman, and John Elder for their enthusiasm, perceptive questions, and thorough editing work.

ABOUT THE AUTHOR

Anette Mikes received her PhD from the London School of Economics in 2006. Her thesis "Enterprise Risk Management in Action" is the first field-based research study on risk management in financial institutions. She holds an MSc in Economics and Finance from the Budapest University of Economics and an MSc in Accounting and Finance (with distinction) from the London School of Economics. She held a Tutorial Fellowship at the London School of Economics (2004–2005) and was an Associate (Executive Education) at London Business School (2002–2005).

Having spent 18 months as an Advisor to the Group Risk function at Standard Chartered Bank, Mikes instigated and directs the Risk Futures research initiative. With the cooperation of a number of senior risk officers contributing to the British Bankers' Association's Risk Advisory Panel, this ongoing research program investigates evolving directions in risk management and the emerging roles of senior risk officers.

Mikes has spoken at numerous international conferences and published research papers in the *International Journal of Risk Assessment and Management*, the *Journal of Risk Management in Financial Institutions*, and *Management Accounting Research*.

Her current work focuses on risk governance and the role of risk management in strategy formulation.

CHAPTER 6

Creating a Risk-Aware Culture

DOUGLAS W. BROOKS
President and Chief Executive Officer of AEGON Canada, Transamerica Life Canada
and AEGON Fund Management, and Chairman of AEGON Capital Management

THE IMPORTANCE OF CULTURE

There is nothing more crucial to the success of enterprise risk management (ERM)
efforts in an organization than an informed and supportive culture. Furthermore,
culture is not merely an intangible concept—its elements can be defined and
progress in moving toward a desired culture can be measured.

Information, technical skills, and processes are important, and some processes
are necessary to assist in developing an appropriate culture. However, an organization could possess world-class technical capabilities and strong processes for
collecting and reporting information, but still have a bankrupt culture so that no
value was added through ERM efforts.

Defining Culture

The definition of culture used for this chapter is based on a question: "What
determines how decisions are made in an organization?" The key to culture, in
the context of ERM, is the impact it has on business decisions. A strong culture
is one in which decisions are made in a disciplined way, taking into account
considerations of risk and reward on an informed basis. This decision-making
culture extends throughout the organization, from the largest strategic decisions
to the most routine day-to-day business decisions.

Note that "disciplined decision making" in an ERM context does not mean
that no risk is taken, or that risk is minimized. Rather, it means that decisions that
create undue risk—either because they take the organization out of its defined risk
appetite, or because the reward is not sufficient for the risk taken—are avoided.
That does not mean that mistakes or misjudgments may not occur, but it means
that the process ensured the consideration of the correct elements with the goal of
optimizing the risk-return profile of the organization.

The Goals of Culture

The goal of a risk-aware culture is to ensure that all business decision makers
understand and behave, recognizing:

- The importance of identifying and assessing risks in current and potential business activities.
- The importance of communicating current and potential risks.
- The importance of taking risk and reward into account in business decisions.

Again, it is worth stating that the goal is to ensure that decisions taken throughout the organization are taken with these goals in mind. That means that the risk-aware culture must extend throughout the organization, and not be limited to a group either outside of—or even senior to—the individuals responsible for making business decisions for the organization.

The Importance of Culture

If one accepts that the goal of ERM is to ensure that business decisions are made to optimize stakeholder value through optimizing risk and reward, then a strong risk-aware culture is a necessary condition for success in ERM. If any elements are missing, then:

- Not all relevant risks may be identified and assessed.
- Decision makers may not be aware of some risks as decisions are being made.
- Decisions may be made ignoring certain risks.

Clearly, if these circumstances were to occur, then the organization cannot be sure that good risk-adjusted business decisions were consistently being made. Therefore, the organization cannot have a strong ERM framework.

When the Chips Are Down

Culture can be observed in a positive sense—that is, a decision-making process may be mapped out that reflects considerations about risk: risks involved with the business decision are identified, and sound risk-adjusted decisions that add value may be observed. This kind of process may, and often does, occur in almost every organization, either deliberately as the result of the creation of a risk-aware culture (whether explicitly recognized as such), or simply because organizations must have some processes that involve disciplined approaches.

However, the telling point occurs when there is pressure to make a decision that involves trade-offs between short-term gains and long-term risk-adjusted value. Short-term gains may involve sales—meeting or exceeding sales targets and market expectations; accounting gains resulting from transactions that create accounting earnings; or even personal incentive targets. If there is significant pressure to relax the organization's risk requirements, and the organization makes a decision that is clearly counter to the risk policies and desired risk profile of the organization, it cannot have a strong risk culture.

This may occur at any level of an organization. It may occur at the top of an organization if an acquisition is being considered, and considerations of risk fall victim to the ego of the participants. They may be put aside because the participants in the transaction have "fallen in love with the deal," and cannot bear the thought of backing out of the transaction given the work that has been put into it and the potential benefits of the transaction. These benefits may already be crystallizing in individuals' minds as they contemplate the shape of the post-transaction business. Rewards may also incent this type of behavior. These may be tangible rewards—bonuses and salary increases—or they may be intangible because the participants in successful transactions are those recognized in the organization, given higher profiles and promotions.

At lower levels of an organization, incentives may also play a part in rewarding behaviors that involve undue risk. Individuals seeking to maximize their bonuses may take risks, particularly if their bonus is based on immediate results and down-plays long-term profitability and risk. For example, a sales manager whose bonus is entirely or largely based on sales results alone has no motivation to look at risk and reward. In fact, the organization is implicitly telling the sales manager that it is sales results that are important to the organization and that by achieving and exceeding his sales targets, he has every right to believe that he is adding value to the organization.

For example, in the insurance industry certain products have substantially more risk than other products. They may also have significantly different profitability profiles. However, the commission to the agent or distributor may be the same. The message to the agent is that sales of the different products are equally valuable to the organization. This may be completely false, but it is not the distributor's role to question the organization with respect to its products. If the sales manager's income is based on an override of the commissions that the agents receive for selling the products, then the message to him or her is the same.

Naturally, there is a point at which simplicity of compensation structures and comparative structures within an industry must be recognized. However, organizations must have the information to determine what the consequences of their compensation structures are likely to be. In the insurance example, it may not be practical or realistic for the company to offer lower commissions on its riskier or less-profitable products to the selling agent. However, the sales managers should certainly be compensated based on the risk-adjusted profitability of the business. That again implies that the organization has and uses the information to measure the risk-adjusted profitability of the business.

Other motivations for poor risk taking may be externally driven. Competitor organizations may—apparently successfully—be taking risk. Stock analysts and other commentators may give these companies credit for this business, and their stock values may increase as a result. Additionally, just because an inappropriate risk is taken does not mean that it will not pay off. It is annoying to see poor decisions lead to good results! Nevertheless, an organization that wishes to create a strong risk culture must continue to be disciplined in the face of these pressures. That will necessarily entail strong internal and external communications—identifying why decisions that appear successful are not being taken.

There is much discussion about the cause of the subprime mortgage lending crisis and the associated and widespread market disruptions that have occurred. This is not an attempt to provide a comprehensive view of the causes of the crisis. However, at its core, the crisis resulted from plain and simple bad business. This business should not have been done in disciplined organizations. Making loans to individuals who do not have the resources to pay the true costs of the loan, and who are inappropriately leveraging their assets is fundamentally bad business. As organizations experienced success with this model (as property values increased, hiding the degree of exposure and leverage), other organizations were pressured to enter the game by the short-term thinking of the financial markets, which reward short-term business growth at the expense of long-term value and risk.

Financial and risk management models, rating agencies, regulators, and many others may take, and may legitimately share in some of the blame for the crisis, but the underlying causes were related to bad business motivated by short-term gains that were rewarded in the financial markets. How does an organization stay disciplined in the face of the market pressures that exist? It is extremely difficult to stand firm in the face of these pressures, particularly when an organization is public, and the markets determine who is deemed successful using inappropriate criteria.

Organizations must communicate effectively, both within the organization and to external stakeholders, the reasons for decisions to avoid businesses that are determined to be poor risks. Internally, this can be reinforced through compensation systems that reward long-term risk-adjusted value.

Culture Can Discourage Good Risk Taking

Culture may also result in suboptimization by discouraging appropriate risk taking. This can occur by punishing people for taking risks that do not work out, whether or not they were correct to make the decision to take the risk.

A well-known example of this in a sports context took place during the 1980 baseball playoffs between the New York Yankees and the Kansas City Royals. The Yankees had a speedy runner (Willie Randolph) on first base representing the run that would tie the game. There were two outs in the eighth inning. A ball was hit to the corner of the outfield, and the runner on first base got a good start. The third base coach recognized that the runner was a strong runner, and that the fielder who was fielding the ball was a weak thrower. The fielder would have to throw the ball to another fielder who would then relay the ball to the catcher to try to tag out the runner. Given that there were two outs, the chances of another hitter being successful in hitting safely and scoring the runner were he to stop at third were much less than 50 percent. In other words, the third base coach made a good risk-based decision to send the runner around third base toward home plate to try to score. However, in the actual event, the fielder made a good throw to the infielder who made a perfect relay to the catcher, just tagging out the runner before he would have scored. The result was that the third base coach was fired the next day. Clearly, this type of good risk-based decision making was not encouraged in the New York Yankees organization.

Similar instances occur in business. For example, decisions taken to hedge exposures to certain risks may be criticized when the risk does not materialize, particularly if other companies have taken the risk and been rewarded for doing so. This may lead to inappropriate risk taking to avoid the criticism of having spent time and resources on hedging.

Good risk-taking organizations recognize that not all well-thought-out risks will succeed. Farson and Keyes (*Harvard Business Review*, August 2002) refer to leaders in organizations that encourage strong risk taking as "failure-tolerant" leaders. Such leaders recognize that good decisions based on disciplined approaches are the right decisions, whether they work out, while sloppy, undisciplined decisions are wrong regardless of whether they result in profit.

ELEMENTS OF A RISK-AWARE CULTURE

An organization wishing to have a risk-aware culture must encourage certain behaviors and reward them, as well as putting various processes into place. Culture is all about behavior. Processes are necessary to encourage and reinforce desired behaviors.

Behavioral Elements

Actions speak louder than words. This is a simple but profound expression, and it applies directly in the area of organizational culture. Processes that exist on paper, but are not applied in practice, will be viewed as unimportant within an organization. It is only when a process is taken seriously that it actually reinforces the desired culture.

Organizations must expect the results that are encouraged both explicitly and implicitly through behaviors that are rewarded. If, for example, bonuses and promotions result from achieving sales targets at the expense of organizational risk, then the implicit message to staff is that the risk discipline of the organization is second to sales results, and the company must expect that staff will behave in a way consistent with the results that are rewarded, regardless of what may exist on paper with respect to risk discipline. In order to create and sustain a strong risk-aware culture, it is important to be deliberate and explicit about the behaviors that are expected in the organization.

Process Elements

Having stated above that behavioral elements are primary, it is vital to create robust processes that encourage the defined behaviors. These processes include measurement, monitoring, reporting, and governance.

HOW TO CREATE A RISK-AWARE CULTURE

Creating a risk-aware culture requires a deliberate approach. It will not happen by accident. The following steps and approaches are suggested to accomplish the introduction of a strong risk-aware culture.

Defining the Elements

The first step to creating a risk-aware culture is to know what elements that culture should contain. There have been attempts to define the elements of a risk-aware culture. *Risk Manager* magazine (Issue 3, February 2004) contained the following list of characteristics:

- Strong leadership within the organization and its projects.
- Devolving risk management to the workplace.

- Participative management style.
- Utilizing knowledge of all staff and team members.
- Encouraging staff to be accountable for their actions.
- Enabling capture of risk at all levels of the organization or area/project chosen for the risk assessment.
- Determining controls before risks occur.
- Improving communication and teamwork.
- Encouraging risk awareness across the organization.

This list describes some of the attributes of an organization that has a risk-aware culture. Another approach is to define the elements of a culture that should result in these desirable characteristics. The following is a list of elements developed as part of an ERM framework in one organization that the author of this chapter worked in:

- Acting with integrity.
- Understanding impacts on customers.
- Embedded risk management—discipline.
- Full and transparent communication.
- Collaborative decision making.
- Alignment of incentives and rewards.

It is important that an organization develop cultural elements that it believes will lead to sound decision making and that it is willing to commit to encouraging and rewarding within the organization.

Measuring and Monitoring

Results in most business endeavors are achieved by having measures of success and monitoring progress toward goals using these measures. The same can be true for progress toward cultural goals as well as financial objectives or the implementation of operational objectives. Measurement can be based on nonfinancial information, and on information that is not in the organization's financial accounts. For example, if a defined element of an organization's risk culture is "participative management style," or "collaborative decision making," there is likely no source of information available except to ask people within the organization about how decisions are made.

The structure and handling of a survey to glean information about such processes in an organization is critical to its success. The survey must be nonthreatening—individuals must be free to give honest answers to questions without fear of reprisal. Guaranteed anonymity is an important characteristic of a successful survey. The survey must also be repeatable—that is, consistent responses producing reliable trends should be generated when the survey is repeated. To measure progress, it is necessary to perform the survey periodically. The survey must also pose questions that are designed to get at the heart of the cultural elements that it is designed to identify and measure. It is beyond the scope of this chapter to determine how to best structure a survey to get the desired objective results. However, such expertise is available, and should be sought to ensure valid results.

Involvement and Buy-In

Implementing a strong risk-aware culture requires the buy-in of those in the organization. A step that can significantly increase the success of the buy-in process is the involvement of the organization, or at least key people within the organization, in the definition of the desired culture. Involvement in the creation of an objective is one of the best ways to create buy-in for any goal. People will generally develop ownership of goals and objectives that they work to create.

Openness

A strong risk culture cannot exist in an organization that discourages open communication. Full and transparent communication is an integral part of a risk-aware culture. Ideas and questions must be encouraged, and not explicitly or implicitly discouraged. Negative behavior can occur in many ways:

- Individuals, particularly senior-level ones, may dominate discussions with the implication that other points of view are discouraged.
- There may be topics that are "taboo" in organizations, discouraging openness in questioning business models or approaches.
- Models may be seen as "unquestionable," or answers about their functioning and use may be brushed off by technical specialists.
- Organizations may get tunnel vision as a result of the overly homogeneous composition of decision-making groups, when it is often a question from a different perspective that causes an "ah ha" in understanding.
- Shooting the messenger is an obvious way of discouraging people from bringing issues to the fore.
- Decisions may be made based on emotion, or pleasing senior-level people, rather than based on facts—clearly discussions should not be closed without fact-based evidence.

Strong organizations will display the opposites of these approaches, encouraging the raising of issues and questioning from differing perspectives on any topics, and basing decisions as far as possible on fact.

Tone from the Top

Virtually every organizational change objective will identify "tone from the top" as a key element. With culture, tone is critical, and the support must be behavioral as well as simply providing funding or resources. It is up to leadership to effectively define the culture of the organization by encouraging, discouraging, and exhibiting certain behaviors.

Alignment of Incentives and Rewards—Walking the Talk

Incentives and rewards, and the importance of their alignment with corporate objectives, cannot be overemphasized. Employees will exhibit behaviors that are rewarded and/or that minimize stress in the workplace. Incentive compensation systems implicitly put value on certain results. Employees have every right to assume that the goals identified in the incentive compensation system are those that the employer wishes them to achieve to add value to the organization. If these goals do not include proper recognition of risk and reward, then the organization will reap what it sows, and take on inappropriate risk.

Rewards cannot always be in the form of compensation. Organizations reward behaviors through promotions and recognition. While an organization may give lip service to risk, and to risk-based decision making, the stronger messages are given by those behaviors that are actually rewarded within the organization.

WHAT DOES RISK MANAGEMENT HAVE TO DO?

The risk management function bears some of the responsibility for developing an appropriate risk-aware culture within an organization. This goes beyond defining the elements of the culture, monitoring them, and determining new initiatives and directions intended to promote the desired characteristics of the culture. It has to do with the risk management area's own behaviors.

Those within risk management departments in organizations, particularly in technical and financial industries, will be strong technicians. Training has been largely technical, and rewarded behaviors have been largely technically oriented. However, communication and even marketing skills are also important attributes for those in risk management functions. Risk managers must be able to provide rationale for their decisions and input to business decisions. It may be necessary to veto a new product, if it does not satisfy the organization's risk-weighted return objectives, or if it involves risks that the company is not capable of taking on and managing effectively. However, in doing so, the risk manager must be able to clearly explain the reasons for the recommendation, as well as show empathy for the business personnel who may have invested significant time in the project. Involving risk management early in development processes is another key characteristic of a risk-aware organization.

Those in risk management areas must also appreciate the business that they are in. Business managers will respect the opinions of risk managers and others outside their businesses if those individuals demonstrate an understanding of the business and its objectives. People who have no experience in business will lack credibility and will be dismissed by business leaders.

Solid and reliable data is another requirement to gaining credibility within an organization. Data that is suspect, or that can be challenged, will be ignored and conclusions drawn from it will rightly be disregarded. Therefore, a risk management function must do its own diligence on its information.

Risk management areas must also be wary of being perceived as "crying wolf." The issues raised must be real issues, and of sufficient importance to warrant changes to business plans and projects. Again, understanding the business will assist in determining the relevance and magnitude of issues, as well as the ability to communicate their importance to those making the business decisions. Not all issues that are raised as potential risks will actually play out as real risks. The market or other conditions that may lead to a risk materializing may not occur, which does not mean that the risk identified and raised was not appropriate. However, it is a challenge that risk management areas must overcome.

Risk management should not run the organization. It is the function of the risk management area to provide information, analysis, and processes to management that will allow good risk-based decision making. This was the approach taken at Hydro One, where the Corporate Risk Management Group received the Sir Graham Day Award for Excellence in Culture Change in 2002 as a result of helping to embed enterprise risk management throughout the organization.

CONCLUSION

To be successful in risk management, organizations must recognize the importance of encouraging and rewarding disciplined behaviors, as well as openness in communication. In his book *Strategic Risk Taking: A Framework for Risk Management*, Aswath Damodaran concludes in Chapter 12 with a number of principles that affect the success of risk management. It is no surprise that several of these principles speak directly to culture:

- Managing risk well is the essence of good business practice and is everyone's responsibility.
- To succeed at risk management, you have to embed it in the organization through its structure and culture and get the right people.

REFERENCES

Damodaran, Aswath. 2008. *Strategic risk taking: A framework for risk management*. (Upper Saddle River, NJ: Wharton School Publishing).

ABOUT THE AUTHOR

Doug Brooks was appointed President and CEO of AEGON Canada, Transamerica Life Canada, and AEGON Fund Management, and Chairman of AEGON Capital Management on September 24, 2008. Mr. Brooks has extensive experience in the life insurance industry. From 2002 to 2006, Mr. Brooks was Chief Risk Officer of Sun Life Financial. A graduate of the University of Waterloo in mathematics and actuarial science, Mr. Brooks has been active in the insurance industry and served in numerous leadership positions, particularly the Society of Actuaries and the Canadian Institute of Actuaries, where he is a past member of the board of directors. He was chair of the Joint Risk Management Section of the Canadian Institute of Actuaries, Casualty Actuarial Society, and Society of Actuaries in 2006–2007. Mr. Brooks is a Fellow of the Society of Actuaries (FSA), a Chartered Enterprise Risk Analyst (CERA), a Fellow of the Canadian Institute of Actuaries (FCIA) and a Member of the American Academy of Actuaries (MAAA).

CHAPTER 7

ERM Frameworks

JOHN SHORTREED, PhD
Professor Emeritus, Civil Engineering, University of Waterloo

INTRODUCTION

Enterprise risk management (ERM) is equivalent to the ISO definition of "risk management framework." The ISO definition of a risk management framework, and thus an ERM framework is:

> **risk management framework:** *set of components that provide the foundations and organizational arrangements for designing, implementing, **monitoring**, reviewing and continually improving **risk management** throughout the organization. (ISO Guide 73 "Risk Management—Vocabulary" 2009, Geneva)*

In the ISO definition, the foundations include the policy, objectives, mandate, and commitment to manage risk and the arrangements include plans, resources, processes, relationships, accountabilities, and activities.

An organization's risk management framework exists only to facilitate the Risk Management Process (RMP), which should be used for any decision in the organization. The RMP identifies the associated risks, assesses the risks, treats the risks within an appropriate context, and is supported by risk communication and consultation as well as monitoring and review.

The ERM framework is integrated into the organization's overall strategic and operational policies and practices. There is one ERM framework at the organizational level and as many RMPs as there are decision/management positions—hundreds or even thousands. RMP is specified by the ERM framework and is the key risk management process.

Introduction to the ISO Risk Management Framework

The importance of risk management is recognized by the publication in 2009 of an International Standards guide, *ISO 31000 Risk Management—Principles and Guidelines*, developed by a work group of international experts from more than 30 countries. The same working group also revised *ISO Guide 73* (2002) in 2009, and it provides definitions for risk management.

This chapter is based on the ISO risk management framework rather than attempting a comprehensive historical review and development of a state-of-the-art ERM framework. The ISO framework is current best practice for risk management frameworks. It incorporates best practice from COSO, PMI (Project Management Institute), the Australian and New Zealand Standard (AS/NZS 4360:2004) and other leading international risk management standards.

While ISO 31000 leaves some latitude to the organization for the specific framework and associated risk management process, it is expected that the generic ISO framework would be followed and the organization's ERM framework would be easily recognized as an ISO 31000 framework. This is necessary in order to realize the benefits of common understanding based on standard terminology and processes.

The overarching concept of the ISO ERM framework is that the risk management in an organization is fully integrated into the management and direction of the organization, risk management is just one aspect of management and is just one more tool available to managers besides tools for: operations, finance, planning, human resources, and so forth. Risk according to ISO's general definition is "effects of uncertainty on objectives." It is expected that any decision will involve a routine and appropriate consideration of the associated risks and their possible treatment along with consideration of impacts on objectives, which are not uncertain. Risk management is not an add-on step but rather is fully integrated and embedded in all decision processes.

Uncertainty in risk may involve uncertainty of objectives and their measures, effectiveness of controls, the nature of events and their consequences, stakeholders' views, or uncertainty of any sort. Risk management seeks to enhance the likelihood of positive consequences and reduce the likelihood of negative consequences as defined by the organization's objectives.

Any decision by any manager can have either positive or negative effects on the organization's objectives. The uncertain consequences of a decision, positive and/or negative, are inextricably bound to each other and cannot be separated. Expressions such as "run a risk," "take a risk," "faint heart ne'er fair maiden won," "take a chance," all describe the uncertainty of a decision outcome. "You pay your money and take your choice." Then you wait for the future to unfold and add up the positive and negative consequences, to see if according to your objectives, it was a good choice or not.

An "opportunity" is a situation where, on balance of probabilities, the net expectation is a favorable decision outcome A "threat" is a situation when, on balance of probabilities, the net expectation is an unfavorable outcome. Both opportunities and threats have associated risks.

The organization first examines the external and internal context in which it operates. Then the organization reviews its objectives, including any risk-specific objectives. Risk criteria that are used to determine the acceptability or tolerability of a risk, in deciding either to pursue an opportunity or respond to a threat, are based on the objectives.

The ISO framework can accommodate profit-seeking organizations as well as regulators who exist only to protect the public from harm. The later organizations may focus primarily on negative consequences although it is recommended that they consider also positive consequences such as trust of public, cost-effectiveness of controls, and so on. The reason for this flexibility in application is because the risk framework is driven by objectives and those objectives can accommodate any goals, purposes, limitations, zero tolerance criteria, absolute priorities, and so on.

The ISO standard's risk management process can be applied to the whole organization, to part of the organization, to particular types of risk in isolation, or to a specific asset, project, or activity. The standard recognizes that management of risk is more effective if it is conducted in a consistent manner across an organization as defined by the ERM framework.

Principles of Risk Management and Excellence in Risk Management

The ISO framework is principle-based rather than prescriptive. It provides a general framework for ERM with the expectation that individual countries, industrial sectors, and organizations will craft their own detailed and specific frameworks to their own unique situations. The principles have their own chapter in the ISO standard and are expanded in an annex on excellence in risk management.

The overarching ISO principle is that risk management should have net value to the organization. Risk management should make money, enhance reputation, contribute to public safety, improve sustainability, generally enhance benefits, and reduce harm. It does this by improving the decision makers' understanding of the effects of uncertainty on objectives, devising risk treatments that are objective-effective, and doing monitoring, review, and improvement of risks and controls.

To illustrate the issue of uncertainty/risk and value, consider a study of dams constructed by the U.S. Bureau of Reclamation. The study compared planning estimates prior to construction with data for the projects once built and in operation. The study found that if in the planning period the Benefit to Cost ratio was 1.0 there was only a 17 percent chance the actual project would break even. A prior Benefit to Cost ratio of 4.0 (benefits exceeding costs by 300 percent) was needed to achieve a 95 percent probability of achieving a Benefit to Cost Ratio of 1.0 or break even. The benefits were systematically overestimated and the costs were systematically underestimated (James and Lee 1971). Effective risk management should reduce these biases and improve the estimates of actual value.

Based on a comprehensive analysis of existing principles for risk management the ISO Working Group identified 10 principles for risk management (after ISO 31000, clause 4):

1. Creates value for objectives of health, reputation, profits, compliance, and so on, less the costs of risk management.
2. Is an integral part of organizational processes including project management, strategic planning, auditing, and all other processes.
3. Is part of decision making through analysis and evaluation to understand risk and determine its acceptability as treated.
4. Explicitly addresses uncertainty and how it can be modified.
5. Is systematic, structured and timely and produces repeatable and verifiable outcomes and decisions.
6. Is based on the best available information including historical data, expert opinion, stakeholder concerns, and so forth, tempered with the quality and availability of the information.
7. Is tailored to the organization, its objectives, its risks, and its capabilities.

8. Takes human and cultural factors into account in addition to technical and other "hard" factors that impact the likelihood of consequences.
9. Is transparent and inclusive so that communication and consultation with stakeholders and others keeps the risk management and risk criteria current and relevant.
10. Is dynamic, iterative and responsive within a "continuous improvement" environment that responds to changes in context, trends, risk factors and other internal and external factors.

These principles provide the basic attributes for an ERM, however, as the organization implements an ERM framework it will exhibit characteristics of "risk maturity" in addition to adherence to the principles. In ISO 3100, Annex A describes the excellence characteristics and evidence for their existence and change in an organization. The excellence characteristics are:

- Continuous improvement in the framework using a formal process.
- Accountability for risks with readily available lists of risk owners.
- Use of the RMP in all decision making with documentation as appropriate.
- Constant communications about risk, risk controls, and other "of possible interest" aspects of RMP.
- High profile for risk management as a core commitment in the organization.

ELEMENTS OF AN ERM FRAMEWORK

The first steps to implementing ERM is to have a list of components that provide a comprehensive specification for the framework. Then these components must be designed and the associated implementation plan developed. Most ERM frameworks, including ISO 31000, do not specify these components but rather give conceptual guidance on the framework and its relational structure. In this section a set of seven main components and their subcomponents for the ISO framework are introduced after a short conceptual outline of the ISO framework.

ERM Framework: Concept and Elements

The underlying concept in ISO 31000 for an ERM framework is a quality management approach using the Deming paradigm of Plan-Do-Check-Act (PDCA) (Deming 1986). The quality of decision making in an organization is enhanced through continuous improvement of the risk management framework. The framework is designed, implemented, monitored, and continuously improved following the PDCA approach.

The ERM framework in an organization supports the risk management process for decision making in the organization. The framework also aggregates information on risks, risk management, and performance of risk controls in the organization. The Risk Management Process (RMP) is the key element of the ERM framework. The RMP ensures that risk management and the operation of risk controls will increase good consequences and reduce bad consequences within a continuous improvement cycle.

The framework has to be practical. Managers are usually overworked and one extra responsibility for which they are accountable needs to be manageable if it is to be done effectively. Overly prescriptive approaches, while comprehensive and detailed, may be too onerous and counterproductive. Therefore a principle-based approach is used and adopted to the circumstances. Successful frameworks are usually simple to understand and to implement yet allow for sophistication and subtlety in their application and continuous improvement. As a general rule efforts in risk management should be proportional to the magnitude of the risk and/or the benefits of the risk controls including impacts on stakeholders.

The framework and RMP should use standard terminology and processes. Where possible, *ISO Guide 73* terminology should be used and if other terms are used then a link should be made to ISO terminology. For example, if "environmental scan" is used then it should be linked to the ISO term "external context" so the relationship to the framework is clear. Many shortcomings of current risk management are due to the use of nonstandard terminology and the resulting ineffective communication, lack of understanding, and less innovation.

An ERM framework has seven components:
1. Mandate and commitment to the ERM framework.
    a. Agreement in principle to proceed with ERM.
    b. Gap analysis.
    c. Context for framework.
    d. Design of framework.
    e. Implementation plan.
2. Risk management policy
    a. Policies for the ERM framework, its processes and procedures.
    b. Policies for risk management decisions:
        • Risk appetite.
        • Risk criteria.
        • Internal risk reporting.
3. Integration of ERM in the organization.
4. Risk Management Process (RMP).
    a. Context.
    b. Risk assessment (identification, analysis, and evaluation).
    c. Risk treatment.
    d. Monitoring, review, and actions.
    e. Communications and consultation.
5. Communications and reporting.
6. Accountability.
    a. Risk ownership and risk register.
    b. Managers' performance evaluation.
7. Monitoring, review, and continuous improvement.
    a. Responsibility for maintaining and improving ERM framework.
    b. Approach to risk maturity and continuous improvement of ERM framework.

Exhibit 7.1 illustrates a typical framework for an organization to implemented ERM according to ISO 31000 (Broadleaf 2008). It shows in addition to the main components of an ERM framework, other processes and functions necessary for implementation and continuous improvement. It is expected that each organization will customize the ISO framework to suit their organization's structure, roles, and responsibilities, with a view to making integration of risk management easier and more effective.

In Exhibit 7.1 the outer set of four boxes is a "Plan-Do-Check-Act" (PDCA) format modified for implementing an ERM framework in an organization, namely: "Commit & Mandate" (Act); "Communicate & Train" (Do); "Structure & Accountability" (Do); and "Review & Improve" (Check and Act). The plan step is not shown directly but it results in the framework design shown in Exhibit 7.1.

The inner set of five boxes in Exhibit 7.1 is the RMP from ISO 31000. It is used for any decision in the organization. RMP has tasks or activities of "Establish context," "Risk assessment," "Treat risks," "Communicate and consult," and "Monitor and review." Exhibit 7.1 illustrates the relationship between the ERM framework and the RMP, which is a component of the ERM framework. There is also an administrative activity shown: "Management Information System," which provides the interface between the organization's overall risk management framework and the hundreds or thousands of RMPs within the organization. The risk management information system acts to roll up all the risks in the organization for purposes of risk appetite, as well as roll down the framework to the individual risk and control owners for purposes of local risk criteria.

RISK MANAGEMENT PROCESS (RMP)

This section describes the ISO RMP as shown in the inner boxes of Exhibit 7.1. Exhibit 7.1 illustrates the traditional set of risk management tasks to support and assist decision making by any manager anywhere in the organization. *Context* sets the stage for the decision or activity requiring risk management; *risk assessment* identifies, analyzes, and evaluates the risks; *risk treatment* enhances the likelihood of positive consequences and reduces the likelihood of negative consequences to acceptable or tolerable levels; *monitoring and review* keeps close watch over the risk and the controls implemented to modify the risk; and *communication and consultation* is continuous to ensure that the stakeholders are engaged and contribute to the management of risks.

The RMP is the first framework component presented because it is used for all decisions in the organization. RMP is a method to modify risks to create value. The ERM framework exists primarily to facilitate application of the RMP everywhere in the organization.

The RMP in Exhibit 7.1 is not a flow chart but a relational diagram that must be tailored to the individual organization before implementation as a process flow chart. The tailored implementation ensures that risk management is both practical and aligned with the organization's structures, processes, and objectives.

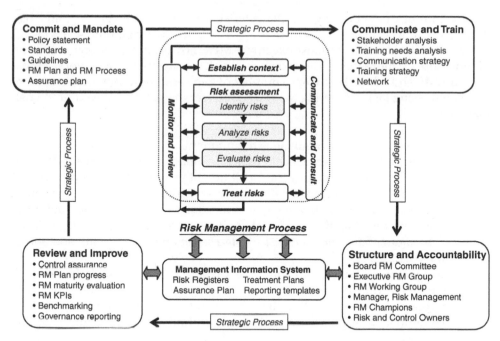

Exhibit 7.1 An ISO 31000 Compatible Framework for Implementing ERM Including the Risk Management Process

Source: © Broadleaf Capital International Pty Ltd., 2008, www.Broadleaf.com.au. Used with permission of Broadleaf Capital International—adapted from a presentation at IRR workshop on Implementing Risk Management ISO 31000 style; Toronto (2008), see www.IRR-NERAM.ca.

There is a range of approaches to RMP that reflects the context of the risk. For example, the risk context may vary at one extreme from:

- Routine operations where risks are well known from historical data, associated processes are relatively straightforward, mistakes are expensive and avoidable, controls are well known and standard, and so forth. Examples include consumer loans and installing electrical networks. A prescriptive approach with checklists, close supervision, audits, retraining as needed, and other traditional methods of quality control and assurance are appropriate; to
- Strategic planning decisions where risks are not well known, data is limited, risk assessments are difficult and subjective, risk treatments are speculative, mistakes can be catastrophic, and in general, decision making is done under extreme uncertainty. General approaches are used, including sampling of expert opinion, checks such as Delphi techniques to ensure opinions are well considered and as informed as possible, "what if" scenario analysis to help understand the risk, and extensive review of options, their risks, and the effectiveness of possible treatments. A risk matrix is often used to structure the risk assessment.

In spite of the wide range of characteristics of risks, risk contexts, and risk management decisions, the ISO RMP is applicable to any situation. The ISO RMP is functionally identical to most existing RMPs. For example, in one study the author mapped more than 50 environmental risk management frameworks onto a similar RMP and while there were a number of gaps with tasks not included, there were no missing tasks. Tailoring the RMP to reflect the specific context of the risk may include:

- Legal and regulatory compliance requirements.
- Need for a nested hierarchical risk assessment and treatment procedures. For example, if simple pass/fail risk acceptance criteria are not met and there is a chance that more detailed analysis will change the result, then more detail assessment and treatment activities take place. For many "political" decisions the iterative cycle of *risk assessment-risk treatment options-communication and consultation with stakeholders* may take years and sometimes decades.
- Recognition of known-unknown risks where the emphasis is less on risk assessment (not possible) and more on the risk financing and other contingency controls as well as the application of policies on risk appetite, precautionary approaches, resilience, flexibility, and robustness of the organization.
- Due diligence dictated by the body of common law that indicates for a specific situation what a minimal level of risk controls and risk management is required for both the upside and downside risks.
- Focus of most resources on one task such as risk communication and consultation when it is known, for example, that stakeholder support is critical and perceptions may be contrary to the view of the organization or existing data.
- Focus on risk assessment as in the benefit/safety of chemicals where the "true" answer is unknown or unknowable based on historical studies.
- Use of Monte Carlo and other gaming methods where risk factors such as the general global economy will impact sales of a product and these methods may help with the decision on how many products to produce—not too many and not too few.
- The availability of data and the costs to obtain it.
- The available knowledge in the organization and capacity to assess and treat risks. For example, operations in developing countries, in war zones, and so forth.

This chapter does not provide a comprehensive look at the five activities in the RMP but rather gives an overview and understanding of each activity. It is noted that any organization will have a number of RMPs already existing based on history, regulation, and industry norms. The alignment of these existing RMPs into the ERM framework and the organization's policy RMP is an additional challenge in the "tailoring" exercise that is not covered in this chapter.

Before considering the five risk management tasks it is helpful to consider the characteristics of controls and the associated decision-making task. In the RMP, decision making is not shown explicitly because it is implicit in the organization's structure and the roles and responsibilities assigned to each decision maker. Decisions are influenced by risk management but the risk management process is only one part of the decision process.

There are six different options or approaches to risk treatment and control. All should be considered and often they are used in combination:

1. Make a conscious decision either to avoid or pursue a risk, often as a first step in a decision process. Is this something to be involved in or not? If so, to what extent and with what level of risk management?
2. Remove or isolate the risk source by changing materials, using a different supplier, modifying the operational process, or other methods of removing the source of risk.
3. Change the nature and magnitude of the likelihood through redundancy, training, simplification of operations, bonuses for good performance, incentives, or otherwise modifying likelihood.
4. Change the nature and magnitude of the consequences through protective equipment, improved design and appearance to change behavior, leverage desirable outcomes through financial incentives, or otherwise mitigate the consequences.
5. Share the risk with another party or parties often in partnerships or through insurance, which does not reduce the total risk but reduces the risks, both positive and negative, to the organization.
6. Retain the risk, as treated, by choice or default if no explicit decision is made on the acceptability of the risk. Retaining the risk may include identification of possible contingency plans and the provision of capital reserves.

Risk Management Process: Context

The context for the risk management process is a relatively new risk management activity, first introduced in the 2004 New Zealand and Australia Risk Management Standard. It builds on the framework-context for the organization where the organization-wide risk appetite is formulated and the risk management environment of the organization is defined. The context looks at the laws, market, economy, culture, regulations, technology, natural environment, stakeholders' needs, issues, and concerns, and basically anything that could impact the objectives, risk criteria, or other risk management activities.

The main output of context is the risk criteria to be used to determine the acceptability of the risks. A second output of the context activity may be the specification of the other risk management activities, such as communication and consultation and risk assessment.

The risk criteria is used to evaluate the significance of the risk by comparisons against the risk with existing controls or the risk with proposed treatments. If the comparison leads to the decision that the risk is not acceptable then further risk treatments are considered. In some cases the risk cannot be modified to make it acceptable and in this case the risk criteria is shifted from acceptance mode to tolerability by posing the question "Is there some possible level of risk that while not acceptable can be tolerated?" In the case of negative consequences this may be

ALARA (As Low As Reasonably Achievable), BAT (Best Available Technology), and other approaches to determine the tolerability of risks.

The context may be organized into three categories:

1. The external context—anything outside the organization that must be taken into account in risk management, including stakeholders, regulations, contracts, trends in business drivers, local culture and social norms, employment situations, and competition.
2. The internal context—anything inside the organization that must be considered in the RMP, including capabilities, resources, people and their skills, systems and technologies, information flows, decision-making processes (formal and informal), internal stakeholders, policies and strategies within the organization, and other constraints and objectives.
3. The risk management context—any activity in the RMP that requires attention in seeking to find the appropriate level of risk and associated risk treatments, controls, monitoring, and review. This includes responsibility for the risk, scope of the RMP, linkages of the product or service to other products and services in the organization, risk assessment methods to use (may be specified by regulations, industry norms, stakeholder requirements such as business plan formats, etc.), the time available for the RMP, background studies that may be needed, coordination with communication and consultation task as well as the monitoring and review task, and other processes and procedure matters.

The context as with other RMP tasks must be practical and within the value-added parameters of the organization. This may involve the standardization of RMP tasks including boiler plate context and checklists, with brainstorming for additional items. In many cases guidance will be found from best practice, industry norms, conferences, special software tools, and other opportunities for discovering "good" approaches.

Risk Management Process: Risk Assessment

Risk assessment involves three tasks. It is not possible here to do more than describe in very general terms the objectives of each task and possible approaches to these tasks. For instance for business and finance organizations, nongovernment organizations, or for agricultural organizations there are whole books dedicated to methods for the three tasks:

1. Risk identification. Risks associated with any decision must be identified and placed in a risk register or risk log before they can be treated, even if it is later determined that the risk levels with existing controls are acceptable. It should be assumed that not all risks will be identified and like any of the RMP activities there needs to be provision for monitoring and review to add risks to the register. Risk identification may use historical data, often categorized in terms of credit risks, operation risks, market risks, technological risks, human behavior risks, country risks, and other convenient mutually exclusive categories that assist in risk identification. Risk names may

help stakeholders relate to the risks and have the potential to improve the effectiveness of controls. In many cases risks will be described in aggregate terms representing hundreds or more subrisks. Risk identification may use brainstorming, "what if" methods, scenario analysis or other methods for helping people identify risks, particularly infrequent risks, "black swan" risk situations (Taleb 2007) and other search techniques. One set of risk identification techniques is tree methods, either leading up to an event (tree roots) or following an initial event (tree branches), sometimes structured in terms of decision trees.

2. Risk analysis. The purpose of risk analysis is to provide the decision maker with sufficient understanding of the risk, that they are satisfied they have the appropriate level of knowledge about the risk to make decisions on risk treatment and acceptance. Risk analysis methods can vary from quantitative mathematical models to qualitative expressions of expert opinions or even organized and structured gut feelings. Risk analysis may be organized into estimates of likelihood of events, estimates of consequences of events, and estimates of the combined effect of likelihood and consequences according to the risk criteria. Risk analysis may be organized into multiple outcomes and their likelihoods in the form of a probability distribution. Risk analysis may include separate determination of risk factors that identify special vulnerabilities or opportunities for success associated with particular markets, people, products, and so forth. Risk factors are usually determined by industry-wide or population-wide studies, such as the tendency for higher credit defaults with lower credit ratings to give a rather obvious example.

   Root cause analysis of risks is both a useful and potentially confounding concept. The basic idea is to carry the analysis to the point where there is a cause of the risk that is fundamental in that if the root cause is treated then the risk consequences and/or likelihood will be modified. For example, accident analysis or debriefing of successful programs can benefit from root cause analysis. Was it the actions of the sales person, the advertising program, the design of the product, or the follow-up service that resulted in the success? Root cause analysis can be confounding, for example, when cause is inappropriately assigned to operators rather than the design of the system and specification of job tasks.

3. Risk evaluation. Each risk, if identified and analyzed, is evaluated by comparing the residual risk after risk treatment (or with existing controls) against the risk criteria. The risk is then accepted as treated or not accepted and subjected to risk treatment. The risks associated with controls and their implementations are also considered in the risk evaluation and the risk analysis. Risk controls may not work as estimated, some controls such as those involving counter parties will have additional risks of failure of the counter parties, or with partners that do not meet their contractual obligations, or the controls fail for any reason.

   If it is not possible to find a risk treatment that is acceptable then the risk is revisited and it is determined if there is any way to make the risk tolerable usually with more extensive controls.

   Risk evaluation methods are numerous and can include multidimensional objectives, risk matrices, voting, subjective ratings, testing by focus groups, statistical analysis models, market testing, and evaluation gaming. Care must be taken that the risk evaluation method and results are accurately communicated to the decision maker and other stakeholders so limitations and uncertainties are known. Note that if the risk analysis is not quantitative then the risk evaluation must be qualitative.

In many situations the risk assessment is not done as three separate tasks but with methods that combine the tasks. In some well-established methods such as HAZOP (HAZard Analysis and OPerability study) (Crawley and Preston 2008) and FMEA (Failure Mode and Effects Analysis) (Wikipedia 2009a) not only are identification, analysis, and evaluation included in the method but also risk treatment since the team doing the analysis of the system usually selects risk controls until the risk criteria are met.

The risk matrix is a combined risk assessment method that is widely used for strategic risks and other risks that require subjective analysis and evaluation. It is used when quantitative methods are not available and a knowledgeable and experienced team that collectively can provide an acceptable and comprehensive understanding of the risk is available to do risk identification, analysis, and evaluation. The team first identifies the risk and places it in the risk register. Then the team produces a subjective rating on a 3–5 point scale for both the likelihood and the consequences of the risk. The two ratings are plotted on the risk matrix using the subjective ratings. Then the team identifies the acceptable risk levels and/or the level of risk by identifying cells in the matrix that have say high, medium, or low risks or alternatively risks that require treatment or not, the result is sometimes called a "heat map" when high medium and low negative risks are shown in red, yellow, and green. Although popular, risk matrix methods should be used with caution because of the following characteristics:

- The matrix helps the team compare one risk to other risks as the question is asked: Should these two risks be in the same risk cell? Often Delphi techniques and other cyclical reevaluation methods are used to ensure consistency.
- The team should clarify if the likelihood is an expected value or an extreme value.
- The team needs to understand what controls are in place in the evaluation, for instance, while not desirable for other reasons, some of the team members may be thinking of "inherent" risks or the risk without any controls, including even human behavior (e.g., operator actions are often the treatment of last chance).
- The team can be swayed by dominant and persuasive personalities, including the facilitator, and checks should be in place including secret ballots, rules for interventions, and so on.
- Often arithmetic is done on the ratings, which is not mathematically sound, for example the rating for likelihood is incorrectly multiplied by the rating for consequences and the product referred to as the level of risk. This is why risk definitions more generally and accurately refer to "level of risk being some combination of likelihood and consequence."

- Risks descriptions may be interpreted by team members differently. Care must be taken to make sure the risk and risk treatment can be unequivocally related to the risk being considered.

Risk Management Process: Risk Treatment

Treatment, like medical treatments, may be either vitamins to enhance well-being or therapy to reduce undesired consequences. Risk treatment includes the identification of control options, selection of a control option, and implementation of the selected control. The medical analogy, including wellness criteria is useful to appreciate the complexity of the tasks in risk treatment, particularly since there is uncertainty at every step in the process. This is reflected in the ISO standard by the fact that about 8 percent of the standard is dedicated to risk treatment, including preparation of treatment implementation plans, strategies for evaluating treatment options, and the key role for monitoring of treatment implementation and performance of controls.

Risk Management Process: Monitoring and Review

Monitoring and review along with risk communication and consultation are two RMP activities that are applied to the three "line" activities of context, assessment, and treatment. Monitoring and review are key to the continuous improvement of risk management. For example, most approaches to risk maturity examine how monitoring and review leads to actions and then to observable improvements. Every aspect of RMP needs to be monitored and reviewed including:

- Has the risk changed in character due to trends? Are there new risks evolving or emerging?
- Has the context for the risk management changed, as for example after events such as the October 2008 financial crisis?
- Is the risk treatment plan being implemented? As planned?
- Are controls effective?
- What is the appropriate frequency of monitoring?
- Should monitoring be done by internal audit, third party, or self-assessment?
- Based on actual outcomes for objectives was the risk assessment accurate?
- Can monitoring be improved by identifying better key performance indicators?

Risk Management Process: Communication and Consultation

Because risk is uncertainty about effects on objectives there is a strong incentive for communication and consultation. For example, many exercises in strategic planning are "team" exercises, which grapple with uncertainty about future markets, what the competition is doing, technological innovations, the state of the economy, the accuracy of cost estimates, and the probability of war. There must be extensive communications among team members, and consultations with other experts in the organization to ensure the accuracy and effectiveness of activities in the RMP.

There have been extensive studies of risk communication that focus on how risks are perceived, including by team members doing the risk management. People's perception of risks changes with the frequency of the risk, natural versus man-made risks, the uncertainty of the risk and other factors (Standards Australia 2009). In addition, people are notoriously bad at doing mental arithmetic on likelihoods such that even the simplest methods of ensuring accurate calculations of probabilities and frequencies will reap considerable benefits.

Some recognized prophets in risk management (Kloman 2008) go so far as to argue that if you don't get risk communication right then you can't do effective risk management. Consider the risks associated with assets backed by subprime mortgages, which led in part to the October 2008 financial crisis. Might the crisis have been avoided if there had been improved communication and consultation, to explore questions such as "What is the risk associated with this asset? Are there any common root causes? What additional risks are associated with failure of controls? What is best lending practice?"

Like monitoring and reviewing, communication and consultation is a part of all the other tasks in the RMP. As captured in the expression "the more you tell the more you sell" communication improves the effectiveness of risk management for positive consequences as well as negative consequences. Communication and consultation are also key to success in risk assessment, treatment, and evaluation activities. In many risk management processes communication and consultation can account for more than 50 percent of the resources required. Consider, for example, the importance of communication and consultation in winning elections where the outcome is always uncertain.

Risk Management Process: Recording the Risk Management Process

Risk management activities should be recorded. This is standard policy for any important activities in any organization and this task is illustrated in Exhibit 7.1 as a "Management Information System" that links the RMP to the risk management framework. Records created as an integral part of the RMP provide for traceability of decisions, continuous improvement in risk management, data for other management activities, legal and regulatory requirements, and so forth. Systems for record keeping, storage, protection, retrieval, and disposal need to be carefully designed, implemented, monitored, and reviewed.

MANDATE AND COMMITMENT TO THE ERM FRAMEWORK

Risk management should be fully integrated into the management of the organization. This integration requires a mandate and commitment from the board and senior management. This mandate is either for a new ERM framework or for the improvement of an existing framework. There are three steps in the organization's mandate and commitment, which may be done in an iterative and/or interactive way.

1. Decision to undertake a review of the risk management framework, assignment of a champion, and resources.
2. Champion conducts and reports on:
   a. Gap analysis of existing ERM framework and other risk management processes in the organization, usually against ISO 31000, industry norms, and other benchmarks.
   b. Context for risk management in the organization.
   c. Design of a (revised) ERM framework, and recommendations for implementation.
3. Approval of the ERM framework, and the implementation plan including IT system, alignment of the risk management and organizational processes, changes in evaluation of managers to reflect risk management performance, measures of framework performance and monitoring, and review of the framework in a continuous improvement cycle.

The commitment to ERM must be continuous so that the framework will not only be implemented but maintained and sustained. It is an ongoing commitment.

Rationale for Commitment to ERM

ERM benefits to the organization have been identified as including:

- Proactive rather than reactive management of risk resulting in more successes, fewer setbacks, and more effective operations and controls.
- More effective and structured approach to opportunities and threats by managing the associated risks in effective and efficient ways.
- Better compliance with regulations and other requirements, including employee moral, enhanced health and safety, and crisis management.
- Improved stakeholder trust and confidence in the organization.
- Better corporate governance through improved understanding of risks, their control, and general resilience and robustness of the organization.

If the organization believes in these benefits of risk management for their organization they will appoint a champion to do a gap analysis, conduct a context for the ERM framework, and design an appropriate ERM.

Gap Analysis for ERM

The first step in developing (or revising) an ERM framework is a gap analysis of existing processes against a benchmark such as ISO 31000 to provide a baseline for the design of the framework as well as to confirm the potential benefits.

The gap analysis will consider a checklist of elements of the framework such as in the section above. Each element will be described, including its function and operation. For every element, the gap analysis will evaluate its existence or not, its criticality to the organization, and its effectiveness. The result will be a template for the design of the framework.

The gap analysis is complicated by the existence in organizations of hundreds or more existing risk management activities each with its own unique terminology and processes. These "historical" risk management activities will be for health and safety, environmental protection, process safety, fraud detection, validation checks, "what if" analysis of strategic initiatives, procedures for collecting receivables, validation of stakeholder analysis, among other activities. Existing risk management activities may have gaps when compared to modern risk management frameworks and processes. For the ERM framework to integrate and incorporate existing activities it will be necessary to specify some basic principles, standard terminology, and a method of translating them into a common RMP. This is not easy due to inertia and resistance to change as well as the volatility in many organizational structures and associated roles and responsibilities. Use of dual terminology for an interim period may be necessary.

Context for ERM Framework

The organization must review the context in which it operates, starting with the external context that includes market conditions, competition, technology trends, legislative requirements, weather and climate impacts, country risks, political environment, globalization factors, key drivers of profitability and sustainability, including financing and other resources, external stakeholders' needs issues and concerns, and any other factors that influence threats or opportunities and their associated risks.

The internal context will include the complexity of the organization in terms of size, number of locations, number of countries, degree of vertical integration, existing regulatory and legal requirements, key internal drivers of the organization, the objectives of the organization, stakeholders and their perceptions, capabilities of the organization, existing strategies and organizational structure of the organization, and any other internal factors that will impact risks or risk management.

The combination of the external and internal context will help to set parameters and objectives for the design of the ERM framework. The context will determine:

- The characteristics of risks faced by the organization and the benefits of risk management.
- The resources needed for risk management including the need for a chief risk officer.
- Combined with the gap analysis, the possible emphasis needed for the various components of the ERM framework and the risk management process.

Design, Decision, and Implementation of the ERM Framework

The elements of the ERM framework will be designed to suit the framework context and follow the elements of frameworks as described in this chapter.

Once designed, the ERM framework, its implementation plan, and process for continuous improvement must be approved by the organization then implemented. Exhibit 7.1 provides an example of one ERM framework design.

RISK MANAGEMENT POLICY

Risk management policy for ERM frameworks can be considered in three groups:

1. Policies for the ERM framework and its processes and procedures.
2. Policies for risk management decisions.
   a. Risk appetite.
   b. Risk criteria.
   c. Internal risk reporting.
3. Commitment, responsibility, and timing for monitoring, and review of policies.

Policies for the ERM Framework

The policies should be presented in a short (usually public) document that outlines the context for the organization risk management framework, perhaps including the gap analysis, the organization's approach to risk management, the standard terminology and risk management processes to be followed, the procedures for continuous improvement of the framework, the accountability for risk and risk management, and how the organization will monitor and review risk management and the performance of controls. These ERM policies for processes and procedures are equivalent to the framework structure illustrated in Exhibit 7.1.

Policies for Risk Management Decisions

The ERM framework should provide overarching policies that are applied in the RMP through risk criteria and risk evaluation.

Policies for Risk Management Decisions: Risk Appetite

The relationship between threats (a situation with predominantly risks with expected negative consequences) and opportunities (a situation with predominantly risks with expected positive consequences) is reinforced by our modern market economy. Even in fairy tales where "faint heart ne'er fair maiden won" it always seems that the two elder sons lost out before the younger succeeded. Enhanced achievement of objectives invariably leads to higher levels of risk. The organization has to decide on its risk appetite or how much risk it needs to take to achieve its objectives and those of its shareholders and stakeholders. Risk appetite is "amount and type of risk an organization is prepared to pursue or take" (*ISO Guide 73*).

The organization must "take a risk," or "run a risk," in order to achieve objectives of growth, return, sustainability, enhanced reputation and trust, avoidance of decline, and so forth. Risk management tries to ensure that the organization selects a risk appetite in an informed and predictable way. Risk appetite will be expressed in risk criteria in each RMP and risk criteria are used in risk evaluation to determine the treatment needed for acceptable risk.

Risk appetite has two dimensions, one that focuses on the average or expected situation and one that focuses on the extreme or worst case situation:

1. The risk appetite dimension for expected outcomes of risk consequences. This is the normal situation that is expected when there is no recession, no new "killer" technology, no innovations by competitors, and generally business as usual. In some fields such as perhaps mining this "average all things considered" situation may never exist.
2. The risk appetite dimension for unexpected or "worst case" outcomes of risk consequences. This is the survival dimension of strategic initiatives and is usually expressed in terms of resilience and robustness of the organization to the slings and arrows of outrageous fortune. It is noted that some worst cases are the product of wildly successful initiatives that place the organization in a position where it fails because it cannot cope with that much success.

Consider a simple example of risk appetite for the average or "business as usual all things being equal" situation. The organization expects, all things considered, that objectives will be achieved within reasonable variance about the average. For example, publicly traded companies will provide guidance on this expectation in terms of a range of quarterly performance values. The second dimension of risk appetite in this analogy is concerned with "surprises" or outcomes outside the guidance levels. Surprises, if large enough, can render the organization unable to cope. This inability to cope may be either on the low side with insufficient revenues and profit or on the high side with unexpected increase in demands for products that strain supply lines, lead to shortages, unhappy customers, loss of reputation, and in some cases take over by other organizations.

The two dimensions of risk appetite together provide the basis for risk criteria that set out what risks the organization will take and what risks it will not take. The risk criteria provide for each decision in the organization guidance on acceptable risk levels. This "risk criteria" guidance must recognize the average and frequent situation as well as the infrequent extreme situation. Setting the risk criteria is risky business. How extreme a situation should be considered? 90 percent, 95 percent, or 99 percent? What assumptions should be made about the performance of individual decision makers to respect the organization-wide risk criteria when they formulate their local risk criteria? How effective are the controls to prevent "rogue decisions" and failures to escalate decisions? Are the quality assurance methods for operational risks and their controls sufficient? What is the importance of cumulative risks and common cause risks? Controls for risk appetite can include, for example, "one ship one organization."

The risk appetite for the average dimension is usually calculated by Monte Carlo methods or even by simple use of averages from historical records. Care should be taken to validate the parameters chosen and to have a monitoring and review process to detect and correct for poor estimates as well as for trends that change historical values.

The risk appetite "worst case" dimension for the simple financial situation might be estimated by considering the maximum monetary loss (or gain) that can be tolerated based on capital reserves, income potential, capabilities of the organization, capabilities of suppliers, information technology limitations, and other basic resources. This simplest worst-case dimension of risk appetite is often prescribed by regulators in the case of banks as the required reserve capital, or by the marketplace based on assessments by investors determining the stock price.

The world is not simple. Risk appetite for nonmonetary situations is still concerned with the likelihood of surprises or deviations from the expected, including the worst case. Conceptually it is exactly the same as the simple financial example. However, it usually is not possible to adequately calculate risk levels, determine with some certainty the capacity of the organization's reserves, robustness, and resilience, and determine the risk appetite. While the three estimation processes are the same, the lack of measurements for risk and the capacity of reserves and resilience mean that subjective methods must be used.

Determination of risk appetite "worst case" may be done as follows:

- Extreme values of risks are aggregated for the organization where they are "named" described and estimated, by quantitative methods if possible.
- Requirements for resilience, robustness, and reserve capacity to manage some reasonable and plausible likelihood of extreme risk consequences is calculated.
- Estimate of available resilience, robustness, and reserve capacity from step 2 is compared to the requirements from step 1 and the risk appetite is set by specifying in some way the limits on risks that can be accepted by the organization. This is a messy process to say the least.
- Risk appetite is refined continuously as risk criteria are applied to actual risk management activities in the organization at various levels in the organizational structure. Events such as precedence-setting court cases, catastrophic failures, and other "black swan" events will lead to review of the risk appetite, but there should also be routine periodic monitoring and evaluation.
- Risk appetite "average" can be calculated by the same analysis procedure and it is recommended that the same process be used for each dimension. This will allow for a consistent approach to the setting of the risk criteria to meet both the business case objectives as well as the survival objectives.

Organizations face many different categories or "silos" of risks such as reputation risks, financial risks, health risks, market risks, and so forth. The equivalencies of levels of risk between these silos must be estimated for purposes of risk appetite. This may be done by using a four or five interval rating scale, with appropriate descriptors such as "level 1 (negative) reputation risk is being on the front page for three days" or "level 3 (positive) competitive market risk is 40 percent above target sales." Often an organization uses a workshop process to determine the risk appetite equivalencies.

For some categories, such as financial resilience of the organization, the interval scale can be anchored in historical data such as the stock market and other measures of the health of organizations subject to shocks of different magnitudes. For risks with no quantitative measures it may still be possible to anchor qualitative estimates to previous historical situations and outcomes.

Risk appetite is applied throughout the organization in the RMP through the risk criteria. The risk criteria often include limits or checklists for decisions. If these limits are exceeded then the decision gets escalated to the next higher level. While the aggregation of risks can in some situations be quantitatively assessed through Monte Carlo and other simulation methods, in general this is not possible and like much of risk management the only recourse is to subjective methods of risk assessment with rigor and checks provided through various techniques. One well-known technique borrowed from the justice system is cross-examination of evidence (or devil's advocate methods) to illuminate the plausible range of likelihood for specific events.

Policies for Risk Management Decisions: Risk Criteria

Risk criteria are based on the objectives of the organization as well as the risk appetite and the risk management context. The organization's objectives may consider ethical and moral positions, existing laws, treatment of employees, clients, suppliers, and customers, climate change, and environmental impacts. In general, the policy will be to accept these as minimums to be exceeded so they are never violated. These policies usually specify how they will be monitored and reviewed for corrective action where needed.

For policies on sustainability of community, historical artifacts and heritage, health, climate change, environmental improvement, and so forth, organizations may select targets using accepted indicators such as carbon footprint, emissions, frequency of violations, and so forth. Targets are published in the organization's annual report along with past performance.

The new approach to safety and other risks with negative consequences is that while social, ethical, and moral considerations are paramount this does not preclude a pursuit of other objectives such as profits. Indeed, often the controls for safety can also provide competitive advantage and other positive objectives as well for the same level of safety achieved in a different way. For example, in the 1970s Jaguar achieved air pollution standards by redesigning the engines and at the same time achieved more power and improved fuel economy, while others used add-on devices that increased fuel usage and lowered power.

At the organization level there may also be policy positions on expansion of the organization, leadership in sector, sustainability, reputation, excellence, or creation of employment, and other social goals.

The risk criteria are established at the level of the individual decision making. At the framework level the organization will establish the risk appetite and the associated guidance for risk criteria. Risk criteria should include anything and everything the organization values, has committed to, and that is reflected in its objectives. Risk criteria may be limits, optimization criteria, conditional, or almost anything. Risk criteria, while set prior to decision making, should be subjected to periodic review and may even in unusual situations be reviewed during specific risk management processes.

Policies for Risk Management Decisions: Risk Reporting

Integration with the organization's structure and reporting require that risks be aggregated both vertically and horizontally and similarly risk appetite disaggregated to the individual manager's level of interest. The problem is typically defined by the structure of the organization chart and the lines of reporting and direction between components of the organization chart.

This is a policy issue because there are many different ways to do the aggregation and disaggregation. In some cases, such as use of resources, profits, revenues, and so forth, standard accounting procedures can be used. Even in these cases methods for modeling uncertainty may not usually be specified. For example, in Basel II the method to be used for the value at risk is left to the individual organization and is not specified.

The policy-setting task is complicated by the shift from predominance of qualitative measures at the strategic level to predominantly quantitative measures at the local manager's level such as numbers of units, percentage of the budget, number of employees, value of sales, and cost of insurance. The issue is how to compare these numerical values to the risk appetite. There is much scope for risk in the reporting function and the impact on risk appetite, for example, should be managed in some way.

Review of Policies

Policies can be poorly implemented and their effectiveness degrades over time. A key dimension of an ERM framework is to have policies that are simple to understand, work, and can be reviewed over time to ensure they are sustained and continuously improved. Every day newspapers provide examples of organizations that fail because policies were not followed.

For example, Nick Leeson at Barings Bank (Wikipedia 2009b) was provided with funds in excess of his organization's policy limits within the month he lost all his funds and bankrupted the organization. Similarly, inquiries into the October 2008 financial disaster will uncover hundreds of these failures of policy implementation leading to the collapse of many organizations.

Simplicity is essential. Many years ago I observed the setting of key performance indicators for transit services in London, England. In an exemplary way the list of key performance indicators were reduced from more than 100 to just 1; that is, "passenger miles per pound." Everyone could understand the indicator, it could be calculated from existing data, and it drove the organization in the direction of its key objectives—to produce riders and to save money. Moreover it played a key role in setting risk appetite and in structuring risk criteria as managers at all levels could relate the current value of the performance indicator to their own activities and risks.

There is a need for the review of organizational successes and failures using root cause analysis and other methods to determine the role of policies, policy maintenance, and application of policies.

In the initial stages of implementing a framework for ERM much of the risk management activity will concern integration of existing risk management processes. This can provide an opportunity to review policies because they will be integrated into the ERM framework one by one. The review of associated historical data on risk management decisions also provides a unique opportunity to review risk appetite and risk criteria policies. In workshops using evidence on costs of risk management, effectiveness of controls, and so forth, the organization can refine policy but also gain internal credibility about the value of the ERM framework. Typically, once a recommendation comes out of this process people come forward and say "I always thought it should be that way."

Last but not least the ERM framework should itself be reviewed. Are risks reduced or enhanced by controls? Does risk management produce value through reduction of uncertainty? Are better decisions made and strategic planning improved? Too often, "number of inspections," "coordinating meetings held," "risk priority ratings," and other irrelevant and intermediate process statistics find their way into monitoring and review of risk management frameworks. Indicators that measure objectives are more difficult to develop but are the only meaningful measures of the success of ERM.

INTEGRATION OF RISK MANAGEMENT AND RESOURCES FOR ERM

ERM is not stand-alone but is fully integrated with the organization's management, reporting, roles and responsibilities, right down to taking out the garbage—everything works as one. It is for this reason that ISO emphasizes not being certifiable. Since ERM is intended to be aligned and integrated with the organization's management structure and since the organization's management structure is not certifiable as right or wrong (in fact, the flavor of the month is expressed by the current popular "how to" business book from management by objectives and in search of excellence), then it follows that ERM is not certifiable.

Integration of ERM is made possible since risk relates to uncertainty of achieving objectives and the goal of the general management of an organization is to achieve objectives. Objectives provide the glue for integration of ERM into the organization processes. Although the name is no longer popular, "management by objectives" is still a defining characteristic of organizational management.

There are two keys to making ERM integrated: (1) the top down key and (2) the bottom up key. If senior management makes it clear that ERM will be done and then adjust their own processes to explicitly consider risk in all their decisions, then the signal will be loud and clear and other managers will see the advantage of implementing ERM and including risk considerations in all decisions. In one large organization, once it became clear that the central organization was using ERM then there was a big demand for the one-person risk department (they have about 35,000 employees) to help the various divisions with implementing ERM—there was a $1^1/_2$–year backlog for resources to facilitate workshops to initiate ERM in suborganization units (personal communication, name withheld on request).

The second key to integrating ERM is found in incorporating existing risk management processes into the framework. Existing processes for credit risk, site remediation, health and safety, operational risks, HR procurement and firing, maintenance, achieving sales targets, and so forth, are integrated one by one into the framework. This will require considerable effort since regulations and/or industry or professional norms may require alternative terminology and processes.

One approach to the bottom-up issue is to construct dual-labeled diagrams to show both ISO and the existing regulations and/or industry or professional terminology. It is also likely that many existing risk management approaches will be revisited and revised to be ISO compatible. For example, Australia has adopted a guideline for audit and assurance planning based on the ISO 31000 risk management process. Also the standard for medical devices was recently revised and is aligned with the ISO 31000 approach to risk management. (For example, see ISO 14971 2007, "Medical Devices—Application of Risk Management to Medical Devices," 2nd ed.).

Integration of ERM, particularly the risk management process of Exhibit 7.1 is facilitated by the fact that most organizations are structured around a natural set of processes and tasks that reflect how they produce their products, goods, or services. For example, a company that produces widgets has a supply purchasing department, a production department, a sales department, a storage facility, a shipping department, a customer service department, a legal department, internal audit, and so on—a set of departments that mirror the flow of tasks for producing and selling widgets. The risks also tend to be characterized by the same departmental structure. For all these reasons the ERM framework has a natural integration structure given by the existing organizational structure.

In larger organizations, full integration of ERM will likely take from three to five years once ERM is initiated. This is because of delays in moving from level to level in the organization (often meeting in the middle if a start is made from the bottom up and the top down), to allow time for one or two continuous improvement cycles, and the need for extensive change management to overcome inherent inertia. For example, BHP Billiton, a large mining firm with about 200,000 employees, the process took about four years and this was considered record time.

The implementation plan, created as a part of implementing the framework, should be used as the basis for monitoring the implementation of risk management in the organization and adjusting the plan where necessary. Issues of change management, strategic planning, and business processes should be reviewed to ensure effective integration of ERM.

One dimension of integration of ERM is the provision of resources, including funds and expertise to ensure that managers have the resources for ERM. This could be done on annually and be included in the general budgeting process rather than a separate process for ERM. In most cases, internal resources, particularly for training and other roll-out activities illustrated in Exhibit 7.1, may need to be supplemented by external resources.

Integration is greatly assisted by communications, accountability, and continuous improvement, the next three components of the framework.

COMMUNICATIONS, CONSULTATION, AND REPORTING

Communication and consultation—"continual and iterative processes that an organization conducts to provide, share or obtain information and to participate in dialogue with **stakeholders** *(3.3.1.1) and others regarding the management of* **risk***."*
—ISO Guide 73

The information can relate to the existence, nature, form, likelihood, severity, evaluation, acceptability, treatment, or other aspects of the risk management. Consultation is a process of informed communication between an organization and its stakeholders on an issue prior to making a decision or determining a direction on a particular issue. Consultation is a process not an outcome, which impacts on a decision through influence rather than power; and about inputs to decision making, not joint decision making. Internal communication and consultation should be appropriately recorded.

Communication about the framework and its elements is needed both for internal and external stakeholders. This is to inform and to be informed. Internal communications during the implementation of ERM are important to ensure that everyone in the organization knows what the ERM framework is and what is expected of them.

The framework should identify the responsibilities for risk communications and the role for managers as to what information they should provide about their operations, decisions, risks, and so forth. These responsibilities normally will include communication about both the risk and the risk controls on a periodic basis. The risk communications will utilize performance indicators for the risks and risk management, but also may have their own performance indicators to allow for monitoring and review of risk communications. The latter may include measures of stakeholder satisfaction with communications and consultation.

Of particular importance is communications during crisis situations and the execution of business contingency plans after a crisis. Communication policies would speak to questions such as: What is a crisis? Who is in charge? Who is authorized to be the official organization spokesperson? What should employees do? What steps should be taken? Who should communicate to customers? What communication principles and guidelines should be followed? (e.g., tell the truth, indicate what has happened, say what the organization is doing, tell others what actions they should do, do not promise things that cannot be delivered, speak only about things in your area of responsibility, partner with respected organizations, test messages) (Leiss 2009).

As reflected in the ISO definition above, consultation is a critical component in the ERM framework. Although decision making is the prerogative of the organization and managers in the organization, information from stakeholders can help inform decisions and assist with the continuous improvement of ERM. Consultation about communication is also needed. The external communication framework should pay particular attention to legal, regulatory, and governance requirements.

ACCOUNTABILITY

The ERM framework should specify or have a process that will specify who is accountable for every identified risk in the organization as well as who is responsible for controls to treat the risk. Managers should have the authority for managing the risks or controls they are accountable for and their performance should be evaluated and appropriately rewarded. Continuous improvement of the controls and the risk management process is also part of ownership.

Everyone in the organization should know who "owns" each risk or risk control and this is usually contained in a (risk) management information system consisting of a collection of risk registers, treatment plans, reporting templates, and assurance plans. The management information system can contain as many as 100,000 risks in large organizations and to be practical it should be aggregated into risk registers levels corresponding to the levels in the organization. Since ERM is integrated into the organization the levels of aggregation of risks will naturally follow the regular organization roles and responsibilities, so no additional organizational structure should be needed.

The ERM framework itself should have an owner who is accountable for the implementation of ERM in the organization and for its continuous improvement. This owner may also have the responsibility for communication and consultation for ERM as per above.

CONTINUOUS IMPROVEMENT

ERM frameworks are always a work in progress. In the initial years of implementation ERM may be limited to areas with high benefits and ease of implementation. Even after a number of years of implementation the framework will be in a state of change, albeit at a lower rate. This is because of "continuous improvement" in the framework.

The risk management performance of individual managers is usually monitored and continuously improved through a hierarchy of four review processes:

1. Self-evaluation by the individual manager, perhaps with cooperative assistance from other managers in a mutual mentoring situation.
2. Internal audit of the manager's department, including the functioning of ERM, particularly the risk management process component of ERM (Standards Australia 2005).
3. External audit of critical risks and controls (usually auditing process and performance rather than prescriptive check lists), often as a regulatory activity, for example, to ensure public safety.
4. External review of risk management through participation by the organization in standards organizations, industry-wide user groups, and so forth. This activity contributes to excellence in risk management.

The ERM framework should specify a set of rules for determining the appropriate degree of oversight needed for individual risk or risk control owners.

Monitoring and review of the framework on a periodic basis should look at the framework and the risk culture in the organization: Is the framework implemented? Are the framework policies still appropriate? Do managers accept the framework as the norm? Are risk treatments reducing the effect of uncertainty on objectives? Do external stakeholders have an enhanced appreciation of the organization and trust it to manage risks that impact them? Is the ERM framework "Goldilocks" with just the right level of effort?

Monitoring activities for continuous improvement of the framework may result in a measure of the risk management maturity of the organization: How far along the road to excellence in risk management is the ERM framework? Is there a demonstrated capacity to maximize the organization's opportunities and minimize their threats? The basic elements of risk management maturity for an ERM framework are given in Annex A, "Attributes of Enhanced Risk Management" of ISO 31000, under five attributes:

1. Continual improvement in risk management through the setting of organizational performance goals, measurement, review and the subsequent modification of processes, systems, resources, capability, and skills. Risk management should use key performance indicators designed to measure success in meeting the organization's objectives.
2. Accountabilities for risk management should be assigned to qualified individuals who are adequately resourced.
3. Explicit evidence of risk management processes both in management processes and in decision making.
4. Effective external and internal risk management communications is essential. Comprehensive and frequent internal and external reporting on both significant risks and on risk management performance contributes substantially to effective governance within an organization as well as trust by stakeholders.
5. Risk management is embraced and embedded into management processes by all levels of management as integral to achieving the organizational objectives.

CONCLUSION

ISO 31000 provides an internationally recognized benchmark for the design and implementation of ERM framework for risk management. The ISO 31000 approach for developing and implementing ERM is similar to and compatible with other approaches but is the first standard to provide a complete and practical solution. It will be published in 2009.

The components of this comprehensive and practical ERM framework are outlined in this chapter. Each organization must determine from its own context how the components of the ISO ERM framework should be integrated into their organization to achieve an ERM framework that will be both comprehensive in scope and practical for the organization.

An ERM framework can often be implemented advantageously in a step-by-step way with considerable learning done along the way. Vertical committees can provide design and validation of key parts of the framework such as the risk management process. This approach will also assist in building acceptance of ERM and encouraging a risk culture, particularly if potentially successful areas are selected for the first steps.

As the risk management culture matures in the organization there should be noticeable improvements in the ability to discuss risks easily, decision making under uncertainty, comfort levels with risk situations, and achievement of objectives.

REFERENCES

Broadleaf Capital International. 2008. Home page, www.broadleaf.com.au/index.html.
Crawley, F., and Preston, M. 2008. *HAZOP: Guide to best practice*, London: Institution of Chemical Engineers.

Deming, W.E. 1986. *Out of the crisis*. Cambridge, MA, MIT Press.

ISO 2007. ISO 14971. *Medical devices—Application of risk management to medical devices* (2nd ed.), Geneva.

ISO 2009. ISO 31000. *Risk management—Principles and guidelines*, Geneva.

ISO 2009. ISO/IEC. *Guide 73, risk management—Vocabulary*, Geneva.

James, L.D., and Lee, R.R. 1971. *Economics of water resources planning*. New York: McGraw-Hill.

Kloman, F. 2008. Mumpsimus revisited: Essay on risk management," Chapter 8. *Risk Communication*. Lyme, CT, Seawrack Press, Inc./Xlibris Corporation.

Leiss, W. 2009. Home page for risk communication. McLaughlin Center for Health Risk Assessment, University of Ottawa, Canada. www.leiss.ca/index.php?option=com_content&task=view&id=75&Itemid=55.

Standards Australia. 2005. HB 254. Governance, risk management and control assurance. Sydney, Australia.

Taleb, N.N. 2007. *The black swan: The impact of the highly improbable*. New York: Random House.

Wikipedia 2009a. Failure mode and effects analysis (FMEA). http://en.wikipedia.org/wiki/Failure_mode_and_effects_analysis.

Wikipedia 2009b. Nick Leeson and the failure of Barrings Bank. http://en.wikipedia.org/wiki/Barings_Bank.

ABOUT THE AUTHOR

John Shortreed recently retired as Director of the Institute for Risk Research (www.irr-neram.ca) after 28 years of risk research, including hazardous materials, blood systems, emergency response, air quality and health, all modes of transportation, land use, criteria for public safety, pharmaceutical drugs, risk frameworks, and standards development. He is a member for Canada of ISO 31000 (2009) working group and was also the Canadian representative for *ISO Guide 73* (2002). He has participated for 15 years in the development of risk standards in Canada, with particular attention to frameworks for risk management for both public and private organizations. He is a jack of all risk management trades and master of none. He continues with risk research activities, particularly into the changes that will be required in response to the ISO 31000 risk management standard. ISO 31000 requires integrated organization-wide ERM with specified risk ownership accountability, as well as allowing for positive consequences for risks. For example, these changes will require extensive changes in risk assessment methods and implementation of risk management in organizations.

CHAPTER 8

Identifying and Communicating Key Risk Indicators

SUSAN HWANG
Associate Partner, Deloitte & Touche LLP

> *... Key risk indicators—if I can use a fighter pilot analogy—is really the heads up display [to see] where my risks are going to come from. If we can achieve that using key risk indicators, it becomes a very useful tool in any organization.*
> —Garth Hinton, Director of Operational Risk for EMEA, Citigroup

INTRODUCTION

The formal use of key risk indicators (KRIs) as an enterprise risk management (ERM) tool is an emerging practice. Although many organizations have developed key performance indicators (KPIs) as a measure of progress against the achievement of business goals and strategies, this differs from using KRIs to support risk management and strategic and operational performance.

The current risk management landscape suggests that organizations are increasingly acknowledging the need to manage significant risks of all types and from all sources proactively. There is additional recognition that risk can be best managed using a variety of tools. KRI is one of several risk management tools and can complement other techniques in an ERM toolkit. For example, many financial institutions are developing a sophisticated system of KRIs for operational risk management. At the same time, these institutions use other risk management techniques such as risk and control self-assessments (RCSAs), loss event information, and scenario analyses to manage operational risks.

However, there are challenges associated with developing and implementing a KRI framework. Apart from the reality that there are no observable best practices for designing KRIs, some organizations fail to see the incremental value of using this technique. As with many ERM practices, there are also challenges in implementing and sustaining a KRI framework. The road to maximizing the value of KRIs has not been easy, but there are encouraging signs of increasing adoption and the evolving use of KRIs.

In this chapter, we clarify what KRIs are and demonstrate their practical applications and value to an organization. We then outline guiding principles for designing KRIs, and discuss considerations for implementation and sustainability. The information contained in this chapter is drawn from the broad experience the author gained while providing consulting services to a large variety of client organizations and represents her personal view and perspective. Insofar as possible, empirical information on current practices is included.

WHAT IS A KEY RISK INDICATOR?

Definition

A KRI is a measure to indicate the potential presence, level, or trend of a risk. A KRI is first and foremost a measurement tool. It can indicate whether a risk has occurred or is emerging, a sense of the level of the risk exposure, the trending of and/or changes in risk exposure. Note that KRIs provide information about a risk situation that may or may not exist and as such serves as a signal for further action. Based on the measurement, KRIs help to focus action by providing a direction to follow. A KRI can be equated to a thermometer that measures the temperature of a patient. The reading encourages the physician to delve more deeply into the condition of the patient and the reason for the high temperature.

KRIs measure the risk of the "well-being" of an organization. When effectively designed and used, KRIs have predictive value and can act as early warning signals on the possible changes in an organization's risk profile.

Examples of KRIs

The reality is that organizations are not short of KRIs, although many times these are not identified as such. In fact, one of the challenges is that organizations have too many KRIs, resulting in the unmanageable situation of not being able to focus on the most significant ones. For example, for deposit-taking institutions such as banks in the United States and Canada, the Risk Management Association (RMA) is offering a library of KRIs consisting of thousands of KRIs relating to operational risks to their members. There is a clear need to select the ones that are most relevant to the risk being monitored and that reflect the uniqueness of the organization or business area.

Exhibit 8.1 provides some examples of KRIs. In addition to illustrating the breadth of KRIs, these measures can also exist at different levels of granularity. An example is provided in Exhibit 8.2.

The decisions on both the selection of KRIs and the level of granularity depend on the intended audience and what kinds of decisions will be driven by KRI reporting. In the above example, the top level (i.e., aggregated or generic/common) KRIs can be very useful to a Chief Compliance Officer to gain a bird's-eye view of the compliance risk trends of an organization, while the drilled-down measures (KRIs that are specific to business units) provide more meaningful information for the Privacy Officer or Anti-Money Laundering (AML) Officer for developing tactical risk management actions.

Human Resource	Information Technology	Finance
• Average time to fill vacant positions • Staff absenteeism/sickness rates • Percentage of staff appraisals below "satisfactory"	• Systems usage versus capacity • Number of system upgrades/version releases • Number of help desk calls	• Daily profit and loss adjustments (number, amount) • Reporting deadlines missed (number) • Incomplete profit and loss sign-offs (number, aged)
Legal/Compliance	**Audit**	**Risk Management**
• Outstanding litigation cases (number, amount) • Compliance investigations (number) • Customer complaints (number)	• Outstanding high-risk issues (number, aged) • Audit findings (number, severity) • Revised management action target dates (number)	• Management overrides • Credit defaults (number, amount) • Limit breaches (number, amount)

Exhibit 8.1 Examples of KRIs
Source: Used with permission of Deloitte.

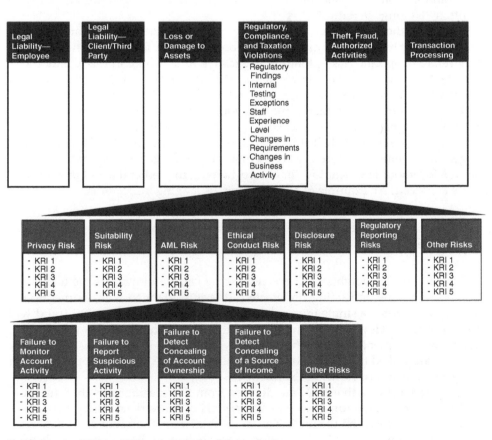

Exhibit 8.2 KRIs at Different Levels of Granularity
Source: Used with permission of Deloitte.

KRI reporting, therefore, serves to provide useful management information. Common KRIs are frequently aggregated for senior management reporting; some examples include measures related to audit, compliance, staff turnover, information technology, and business continuity. On the other hand, KRIs for specific risks may just be reported at the function/business unit level. This is not to suggest that specific KRIs, without being aggregated, are never reported to senior management. On the contrary, these KRIs may be escalated to senior management's attention when the measure meets preset criteria, in other words, trigger levels or thresholds.

Differentiation from Key Performance Indicators

Although some key performance indicators (KPIs) often serve as KRIs, it is important to understand the difference between the two types of measures. KPIs are measures that are focused on performance targets and are based on a wide range of strategic, tactical, and operational objectives. Some examples of these objectives relate to volume of business, revenue, or profitability goals, market share, and customer satisfaction. KPIs measure actual performance and as such are often "lagging" in nature.

KRIs, on the other hand, are measures that help monitor risk and involve thresholds that may warrant mitigation actions once these thresholds are triggered. They relate to specific risk(s) that are suggestive of a change in the likelihood or impact of the risk event(s) occurring. KRIs can also show the level of stress or strain under which current risk management activities may be operating. Therefore, these are measures of risk that in turn may affect performance, that is, the failure to achieve targets. Instead of focusing on achieving targets, they often involve defining threshold levels. KRIs that exceed preestablished threshold levels should trigger management attention for potential risk management actions. As such, useful KRIs should be "leading" in nature, helping to predict if a KPI may or may not be achieved. An example of a leading versus lagging indicator is:

- Lagging: Number of staff-related fraudulent incidents.
- Leading: Percentage of staff taking no vacation.

Staff in key/vulnerable positions not taking vacation increases the likelihood of fraud occurring and going undetected. It is important to note, as mentioned later in this chapter, a single measure is not a conclusive indicator that fraud will or has occurred. However, when a preestablished threshold level is exceeded, it triggers management action for further analysis.

KRIs are linked to risk, performance, and strategy. A pictorial representation of this relationship is shown in Exhibit 8.3.

Exhibit 8.3 shows that KRIs are derived from the specific risks that the organization wants to monitor, as well as the drivers of those risks. Risks themselves are determined based on the organization's strategies and objectives. When managed ineffectively, risk can lead to performance challenges. In summary, KRIs need to be linked to strategy, objectives, and target performance levels, with a good understanding of the sources of risk (i.e., risk drivers).

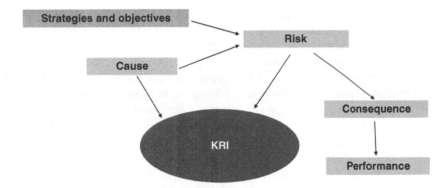

Exhibit 8.3   KRIs Are Linked to Risk, Performance, and Strategy
Source: Used with permission of Deloitte.

PRACTICAL APPLICATIONS

The most commonly understood and used application of KRIs is to help monitor risk. In fact, KRIs can be used for a wide variety of other reasons. From an implementation standpoint, it is important to identify which of these applications resonate most with management so that a stronger case can be made to implement a KRI framework.

KRIs can support strategy and performance in the following ways:

- Validate organizational planning and monitor performance.
- Enhance operational efficiency and effectiveness.
- Clarify risk-taking expectations.
- Monitor risk exposures.
- Measure risk.

The following section reviews each of these applications in more detail.

Validate Organizational Planning and Monitor Performance

Given that business strategies and objectives define performance goals and targets, and that KRIs are best derived from performance goals and targets, the development of KRIs help to better define, and at times challenge, performance targets and business strategies and objectives. Deep analysis of the drivers to risk in the process of defining KRIs provides the opportunity to validate how realistic goals and plans are. As well, through monitoring KRIs, an organization is better equipped to monitor performance and its strategic plan.

With regard to an example of practical application, an organization can define KRIs as part of its strategic planning process, aligning the KRIs to its performance goals. This can also be done at the business unit level where KRIs are aligned with tactical operational goals. Monitoring KRIs enables the organization to better monitor performance through the enhanced ability to predict what may impact performance. KRIs can be included in management reporting through a scorecard tracking progress against plan.

A Canadian telecom company embarked on a KRI initiative several years ago where the project's mandate was to identify existing metrics that could provide a forward-looking view to help better manage the business. As can be expected of a typical telecom company, it is not short of performance metrics especially ones that are system-generated. One of the areas that the company delved into was around customer churning, which was identified to have a significant impact on profitability of the business. The project team analyzed cases where subscribers left the company by reviewing customer complaints, network availability and downtimes, and events brought to the attention of senior management regarding customer dissatisfaction. They came to the conclusion that the level of customer satisfaction, or in reality dissatisfaction, was a key driver for subscribers leaving the company. In particular, they have noticed those customers who have phoned into the call center to complain two times or more are the most likely to leave the company. Once this linkage was established, this company started to tag second calls from subscribers and monitor the related metrics as an input to efforts aimed at improving customer satisfaction and financial results.

Note that in reality KPIs are frequently developed/reviewed annually based on updated strategic and/or business plans, while KRIs are developed as part of an organization's risk management program. As such, the development of KPIs and KRIs has historically not been a coordinated process. Given an enhanced level of understanding of the application of KRIs to an organization's planning and performance processes, there is increased potential that these measures are aligned with the strategic direction of the organization.

Enhance Operational Efficiency and Effectiveness

One of the most critical decisions of an organization is where to allocate its scarce resources to get the highest risk-adjusted return. KRIs can support operational efficiency and effectiveness by serving as an important input to resource allocation decisions. This is typically achieved through being part of a larger risk identification and assessment process used to prioritize workload such that focus is directed to areas of higher risk. See Exhibit 8.4.

Exhibit 8.4 illustrates this process. A typical risk prioritization tool consists of two conceptual components:

1. KRIs—leading risk indicators indicative of the level of risk.
2. Risk prioritization rules—reflecting how KRIs should be risk scored. Components include weightings assigned to the KRIs and decision rules around aggregating risk scores.

The output from the risk tool (i.e., the risk scores) helps to prioritize workload so that resources are dedicated to the highest risk areas.

Many organizations use risk prioritization tools, which comprise KRIs as indicated above. These include:

- Internal audit departments and compliance functions use risk models to prioritize audits or examinations.

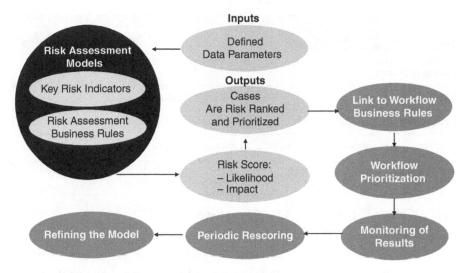

Outcome: Enhanced Operational Efficiency and Effectiveness

Exhibit 8.4   KRI Is a Component of a Larger Risk Assessment Process
Source: Used with permission of Deloitte.

- Health care, tax revenue agencies, and other public services use similar tools to prioritize cases and applications received.
- Financial services regulators use risk prioritization tools to prioritize their focus on supervising regulated entities.

To illustrate the use of KRIs by a financial services regulator, consider a regulatory organization that focuses on the securities industry. This organization regulates and supervises more than 200 entities and has been developing risk assessment models for each of its key departments to help guide the allocation of scarce compliance resources. These models, which include risk indicators to help predict solvency of, and business and trade conduct appropriateness at, the regulated entities, help to determine the frequency and coverage of examination efforts. Results have proven that fewer compliance resources are now needed and, more importantly, there is a higher level of confidence that this regulator is more focused on the higher risk areas within the securities industry.

Clarify Risk-Taking Expectations

Since KRIs are measurable, they help to communicate and reinforce expectations and accountability for risk management. By ensuring that KRIs are aligned with the most significant risks, an organization further clarifies the critical performance areas that need to be monitored. In addition, thresholds and escalation levels relating to KRIs reflect what is acceptable and not acceptable to management and reflect an organization's risk appetite. KRIs, however, are not the only means to communicate risk-taking expectations. Formal articulation of risk appetite and tolerances and risk management policies are other important means to communicate

KRIs Help to Communicate	An Example—Percentage Change in Sales
Who is responsible for monitoring the specific risk	Sales Department
What is acceptable	5% drop in sales
When to escalate issue	>6% drop in sales
Whom the issue should be reported to	District Sales Director
How the risk should be addressed	Increase marketing program, promotional discounts

Exhibit 8.5   KRIs Help to Clarify Risk-Taking Expectations
Source: Used with permission of Deloitte.

risk-taking requirements and boundaries set up by management and the board of directors.

An example of how KRIs help to clarify risk-taking expectations is illustrated in Exhibit 8.5.

Monitor Risk Exposures

A more widely used application is to use KRIs to proactively assess and address shifts in risk exposure. KRIs highlight, on a more real-time basis, current risk levels, and trends and changes in risk levels over time to enable more timely actions. They provide early warning signals to trigger actions that would help to prevent or minimize material losses or incidents. In this application, KRIs are typically used in conjunction with risk and control self-assessments (RCSAs) and other risk identification and assessment tools to support the timely identification of risks.

KRIs are used by many global financial institutions to help identify and manage operational risk. A European-based insurance group initially developed 14 generic KRIs, which are reported consistently around the world. These KRIs were developed by the central risk management function at the global head office, with input from the business executives. These KRIs represent high-level risk metrics that are applied across all country units and business units and are intended to cover major operational risks. This organization sees generic KRIs as a tool to monitor and compare the risk profiles of different entities within the group. A second phase of the initiative involved developing specific KRIs that are most applicable to the different divisions and countries. As a result, the project enabled local entities and business units to monitor their own risk profiles more effectively. The central risk management function also manages the development and implementation of the specific KRIs and will independently monitor the risk profiles. Most recently, this global insurance group embarked on the initiative involving the determination of thresholds to guide escalation decisions.

The determination of threshold levels should be aligned with the organization's risk tolerance. Frequently, thresholds are based on industry averages,

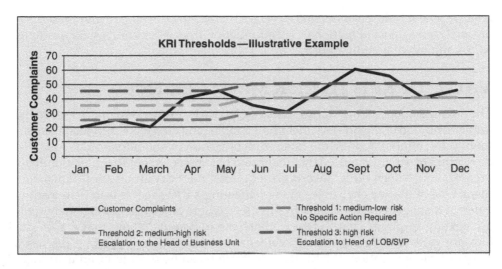

Exhibit 8.6   KRIs Provide Tangible Measures to Trigger Action
Source: Used with permission of Deloitte.

historical averages, service level agreement (SLA) requirements, and management expectations. Thresholds provide tangible triggers for management action as illustrated in Exhibit 8.6. In this example, monitoring trends in customer complaints would enable an organization to better understand whether there are risks evolving that could impact the organization's sales objectives. Different thresholds set for customer complaints will require different management actions.

Measure Risk

The use of KRIs to calibrate economic capital models is more applicable to the larger financial institutions, especially those that are required to meet risk-based regulatory capital requirements. These institutions, mostly global banks and insurance companies, are required to maintain a risk measurement system that supports the calculation of minimum regulatory capital. Factors that are forward looking and reflect the quality of the institution's control and operating environments, for example, meaningful drivers of risk, need to be considered in estimating risk and capital. Beyond minimum regulatory requirements, financial institutions are looking to maintain the appropriate level of economic capital to protect them from "unexpected losses." These are losses above and beyond the expected level and estimated up to a predetermined confidence level. Economic capital, therefore, represents a common measurement of risk. For these institutions, KRIs are among the inputs to calibrate capital models.

Global banks are more advanced in this area than other types of financial institutions and the use of KRIs is focused on operational risk management. KRIs are often used to adjust economic capital qualitatively (i.e., using management judgment rather than through quantitative means). For several financial institutions, enterprise-level and business unit–level KRIs are being developed and these KRIs are analyzed against operational risk information from other sources, for example, RCSA and internal audit reports.

VALUE OF KRIs TO RISK MANAGEMENT

The identification of the appropriate set of KRIs to be used, and the actual implementation of the process (including establishing data feeds and management monitoring efforts), require the dedication of resources and attention. Frequently, development activities are led by a dedicated risk management function within the organization. Nonetheless, the process requires the active participation of management. One of the key challenges in implementing a KRI process is to demonstrate value to management, especially in situations where other risk management tools are already in place. This section outlines the *incremental* value that a KRI system brings to the organization. Together, with the section above that discusses the practical application of KRI, the information can be used to build a stronger business case to management for the purpose of soliciting their active support and involvement in developing and sustaining a KRI process.

The incremental value of KRIs to risk management is summarized as follows:

- Risk appetite—Through the setting of threshold levels and escalation levels, KRIs support and validate the risk appetite and risk tolerance levels of an organization.
- Risk identification—Compared with RCSAs and scenario analysis, KRI is a more objective way of identifying risk. More practically, unlike other risk management tools that are conducted on a periodic basis (e.g., annually), KRIs can be set at a continuous operational mode and can therefore help identify risk on a more timely basis. In addition, KRIs are typically at a more granular level thus providing information on more specific areas of concern.
- Risk mitigation—A KRI system involves triggering investigative and/or corrective action and supports day-to-day management of the business. Thresholds serve as controls in constraining activities within limits.
- Risk culture—Through defining the critical business areas associated with KRIs that need to be monitored, and related threshold and escalation levels, the system helps focus the organization on what is important. The clarity in direction drives organizational behavior and desired outcome.
- Risk measurement and reporting—KRIs provide objective and quantitative risk information. They can be tracked against policy limits and performance standards to enable the evaluation of risk levels and trends. KRIs can be incorporated with other risk information in management and board of director reporting that collectively provides a holistic picture of the organization's risk well-being.
- Regulatory compliance—For organizations that include KRIs in their risk and capital measurement systems, data from established KRIs can be used as one of the inputs into operational risk capital calculations. In this case, capital relief is a strong incentive to implement a KRI system. For global financial institutions that are required to satisfy regulators' requirements on risk based capital, the implementation of a KRI system is mandatory.

DESIGN PRINCIPLES

A set of high-quality KRIs should possess some minimum design characteristics that typically relate to performance measures. These characteristics include being specific and clear, measurable, accurate and reliable, comparable, based on recent data, and cost-effective to implement. Note that at the time of writing, there are no specific regulatory and professional standards regarding the approach to developing KRIs. Nonetheless, designing effective KRIs should follow best practice guiding principles, as outlined below.

Keep the Stakeholders and Objectives in Mind

The overriding principle for a KRI system, and, in fact, for any risk management system, is that it has to add value to the key stakeholders. These stakeholders can be both internal and external to an organization. Identifying who the stakeholders are, their needs and specific requirements, and what the KRIs will be used for (refer to the different applications discussed earlier in the chapter) is a first step toward developing a KRI framework. The specific set of KRIs and the depth of these KRIs as discussed earlier in the chapter should be aligned with stakeholders' needs. A good indication of the degree of alignment is to ask the questions: "What decisions are to be made by the stakeholders from the organization's risk management system?" "Do the KRIs help them make these decisions?" Keeping the stakeholders and their objectives in mind not only ensures that the selected KRIs are relevant, but that the stakeholders will be more willing to support the development and sustainability of a KRI framework.

Leverage Management Insight and Existing Metrics

As mentioned earlier, organizations typically have in place many KPIs, and likely KRIs, that they are already monitoring. Organizations should try to keep their KRI development process cost-effective by assessing the usability of existing performance metrics in a KRI system, and leverage the insight of management regarding business strategies, objectives, and performance goals in the selection of the specific set of KRIs. Engaging management in the evaluation process has the additional benefit of promoting buy-in to the use of KRIs and driving the appropriate risk culture.

However, caution should be exercised when it comes to selecting KRIs as there is inherent bias on the part of management to choose KRIs that are already in place. As such, the independent risk management function should filter the input provided by management and ensure that the KRIs chosen represent the most appropriate indicators of risks.

Have a Good Basic Understanding of the Risks

Build on the foundation of the organization's risk management program to develop the KRI system. As an example, significant risks would typically be identified through existing processes, for example, through RCSAs. Select KRIs based on the most significant risks that have already been identified.

KRIs need to be relevant to the risk being monitored. This typically requires an analysis of the risk and its drivers to ensure there is a causal relationship between the KRI and the risk. Correlation between causes and risk events must exist and, ideally, be validated through statistical analysis, assessment of impact, and influence based on experience and expert judgment, and back-testing with empirical data.

Limit Indicators to Those That Are Most Representative

Focus on the most important risks and KRIs that have the strongest causal relationship. As mentioned earlier, the reality is that organizations often have too many performance and risk measures in place. ERM is about managing the most significant risks. A cost-effective process requires filtering through these measures to find the set that is most representative of the significant risks. The KRI framework should involve a manageable process.

Ensure Clarity in What Is Being Measured

Ensure that there is clear understanding and documentation of the definition of the selected KRIs and how exactly they are being measured. The consistency in the definition and calculation method is critical to ensuring comparability and proper aggregation. For example, when staff turnover rate is measured, there needs to be clarity on the treatment of part-time and temporary staff, shared resources, and people who are on extended leave, and so on.

Focus More on Objective Measures

Consider sources of information and, to the extent practical, select measures that are more objectively measured and that come from an external or independent source. An external or independent source does not necessarily mean that the measures have to be supplied from a third party outside of the organization. A source internal within the organization that is independent of the area being measured also has a high degree of reliability. The lowest level of objectivity will be measures derived from the judgment of individuals involved in managing the risk.

Consider the Wider Set of KRIs

The nature of KRI is such that, when used in isolation, a single KRI may not act as confirmation on the specific level and trending of risk. The main reason is that there are few, if any, leading indicators that perfectly correlate with specific risks. Therefore, meaningful analysis should involve studying several KRIs at the same time, and ensuring interpretation is put in the right context. Collectively they tell a better story about the risk being monitored.

Consider the Relative Importance of KRIs

Not all KRIs are created equal, given differences in the significance of the associated risk and the strength of correlation to the risk. After selecting the most appropriate

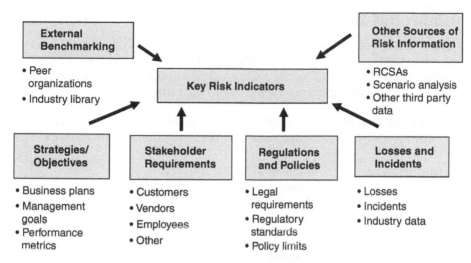

Exhibit 8.7   Sources of Information to Designing KRIs
Source: Used with permission of Deloitte.

set of KRIs, one can use threshold levels and weightings (if needed) to differentiate the degree of their relevance to the overall risk analysis.

Monitor for Continual Usefulness

Implement a dynamic process to validate the usefulness of the selected KRIs over time and make changes where appropriate. As the performance focus and risk profile of the organization change over time, KRIs currently being monitored will diminish in relevance and new KRIs will need to be identified and monitored. A process should be established to continuously review and assess KRIs being monitored.

Think Longer Term

To reduce implementation efforts, organizations may be tempted to choose KRIs based solely on the fact that they are already available or are easy to collect. Do not let short-term data constraints restrict which KRIs to use. Identify indicators that may have future value as part of a phased approach to KRI development.

Finally, it is important to look to internal and external sources to design effective "forward-looking" predictive KRIs. Exhibit 8.7 outlines some of the useful sources.

IMPLEMENTATION CONSIDERATIONS

The implementation of a KRI framework requires effort and resources and should therefore be planned and managed carefully. The following lists some key implementation considerations.

Obtaining Buy-In

It is important to understand and to communicate to the stakeholders the benefits to be gained through KRIs. Position KRIs as part of the overall ERM program and emphasize their incremental value and practical applications. When making the case for KRIs, the following examples of arguments can be made:

- Financial benefit: The use of KRIs can result in improved profitability, reduced losses or earnings volatility, additional recoveries and/or capital relief.
- Improved quality: The use of KRIs can positively impact service delivery, social responsibility, customer service, and/or reputation.
- Satisfied people: The use of KRIs can lead to better alignment of resources and skills, and more balanced workload.

Lack of Resources and Skills

Organizations may find that they lack the resources and skills to develop and implement a KRI framework and that there is no accountability for KRI implementation.

Organizations should leverage internal knowledge and engage management who understands the business and the risks, as well as technical experts in the area of risk management and KRIs, to help identify KRIs. In addition, establish clear accountability for designing, monitoring and actioning KRIs. Exhibit 8.8 lays out accountability in these areas.

Data and Technology Challenges

The effectiveness of using specific KRIs is dependent on the availability and integrity of data needed to provide the trend analyses. Consider the reliability

Business Area	Risk Management	Internal Audit
• Identify KRIs	• Provide guidance and challenge the selection of KRIs and thresholds	• Validate and provide independent assurance on the KRI process
• Set thresholds	• Report on breaches	• Incorporate outputs into audit plan
• Monitor against targets/limits	• Report to senior management and the board of directors	
• Escalate breaches	• Identify trends	

Exhibit 8.8 Accountability for KRIs
Source: Used with permission of Deloitte.

of the internal and external data source and any limitations these have. Designing reports on the different levels of KRIs to meet the needs of the stakeholders is another consideration. Note that reporting on exceptions, rather than each selected KRI, provides a sharper focus for management action. In addition, the analysis of the KRIs (groupings rather than individual measures) and with other risk information is an important component of meaningful risk analyses and reporting.

Assess the need for a tool to collect, calculate, monitor, and maintain KRIs for cost-effectiveness purposes. The decision whether to automate the process depends on a number of factors, including the volume of KRIs, data sources, frequency of computation, complexity of calculations, the need for correlation analysis, and linkage to workflow and business tasks.

Integration with Business Activities

From a practical standpoint, integrate the use of KRIs into the organization's business activities and overall risk management program. Ensure that the process is linked to strategy formulation, performance management, risk appetite determination, and organizational culture fostering processes. KRIs complement the other risk management tools, so analysis and reporting should be performed on an integrated basis.

Sustainability of the KRI Framework

KRIs need to be continuously reviewed to provide ongoing value. Changes in the environment, the organization's business and operations, risks and data sources can change the relevance of specific KRIs at any point in time. It is therefore necessary to define a process and assign accountability for reviewing and updating KRIs and to conduct external benchmarking analysis where needed. In addition, it is important that business management takes ownership for monitoring and taking action on KRI information to ensure sustainability of KRI implementation.

CONCLUSION

The formal use of KRIs as one of several risk management tools is an emerging practice. Organizations with a history of managing their performance through the use of performance (and risk) metrics, and those that need to develop a KRI framework to meet regulatory requirement,[1] tend to have more mature KRI processes in place. KRIs act as an early warning tool and bring incremental value to the overall risk management system. When developed and implemented properly, KRIs can provide significant insight into changes in the risk profile and bring strategic and operational value to an organization.

NOTE

1. International Convergence of Capital Measurement and Capital Standards (Basel II Framework) by the Bank for International Settlements (BIS). (June 2006).

ACKNOWLEDGMENT

Intellectual input from Kamal Nijjar, a colleague at Deloitte & Touche LLP, who co-developed presentation material on which information in this chapter is based, is gratefully acknowledged by the author.

ABOUT THE AUTHOR

Susan Hwang is an Associate Partner in Deloitte's Enterprise Risk practice and is the national leader of the firm's risk management practice in Canada. Susan is highly experienced in providing assistance to many organizations on enterprise risk management (ERM) implementation and other risk management projects. Previous experience in ERM includes developing strategies and plans for ERM implementation, facilitating the establishment of needed infrastructure and supporting culture for ERM implementation, and designing methodologies for specific ERM program components. Her broader experience in the field of risk management includes evaluating the effectiveness of corporate governance, conducting risk and internal control assessments, and advising on risk-based strategic initiatives. Susan's clients are from a broad range of industry sectors, including financial services, higher education, technology, the public sector, manufacturing and consumer business. Susan earned a BSc Honours degree from the London School of Economics and Political Science. In addition to holding several other professional designations, she is also an MBA from the Kellogg School of Management (International Program) and a Certified Risk Professional (CRP) from the Bankers Administration Institute (BAI). Susan is a frequent speaker at various conferences on the topic of risk management, and chairs a bi-monthly ERM Roundtable attended by senior risk officers of various organizations.

PART III

ERM Tools and Techniques

CHAPTER 9

How to Create and Use Corporate Risk Tolerance

KEN MYLREA
Director, Corporate Risk, Canada Deposit Insurance Corporation

JOSHUA LATTIMORE
Policy and Research Advisor, Canada Deposit Insurance Corporation

> *Take calculated risks. That is quite different from being rash.*
> —General George S. Patton (1885–1945)

INTRODUCTION

The objective of this chapter is to enable you, the reader, to understand and use risk tolerance.[1] To do so, we answer these questions: What is risk tolerance? Why is setting risk tolerance important? What are the factors to consider in setting risk tolerance? And, once determined, how can you make risk tolerance useful in managing risk?

Given this objective, the approach and principles set out in this chapter are practical rather than academic.[2] Moreover, in applying them, it is important to remember that risk tolerance is but one topic to consider in implementing enterprise risk management (ERM). ERM, stripped to its bare essence, is all about an organization ensuring and demonstrating that it is identifying and managing the significant risks to which it is exposed. ERM also is but one component of a broader framework that brings together corporate governance,[3] strategic management,[4] and risk management[5]—all supported by an organization's control environment.[6] These components are interconnected and they must work together in order for an organization to purport that it is "well managed."[7] Risk tolerance is a topic that underlies each of the four components of this overall framework—and is a key element of ERM. Setting risk tolerance ensures an organization makes risk decisions and manages risk exposures according to established expectations.

WHAT IS RISK TOLERANCE?

Risk tolerance is the risk exposure an organization determines appropriate to take or avoid taking. This definition is simple. But three key concepts are important to understanding and implementing it.

The first is "risk." Risk is commonly referred to as the chance, possibility, or uncertainty of outcome or consequences. Risks stem from every activity an organization undertakes. Risks include those directly related to the organization's principal business activities (i.e., the risks that are unique to those business activities) as well as risks stemming from the operations supporting those principal activities (e.g., operational risks). These risks exist continuously, whether you have identified them or not. But a risk event first must happen before it can have a risk impact, and such risk impacts can be positive or negative. You should not always view risks as bad things. It is only if you do not identify, understand, and manage risks that consequences can be bad.

This leads us to our second key concept: risk exposures. As the term implies, risk exposures are simply the extent to which you are exposed to a risk (or a portfolio of risks). Risk exposures are a function of the potential impact of a risk event and its probability of occurrence. Potential risk events can impact an organization's financial position, its ability to achieve its goals (which can be financial or other goals), and its reputation. In the past, organizations have been concerned mostly with the material financial impact of a risk event. But as risk events in recent years have shown us, we also must consider two other factors: (1) the potential reputational impact of a risk event, and (2) the potential impact a risk event could have on an organization's ability to carry out its goals. The potential impact of a risk event can range from insignificant to high. You also need to think about the likelihood of a risk event happening. The probability that a risk event will occur can range from highly unlikely to highly likely.

Finally, you need to understand the concept of "appropriate." Determining what is appropriate requires applying judgment. You must apply judgment while individually and collectively considering your risk attitude, goals, operational capability, and capacity to take risk and the cost/benefit of managing the risk—factors that will be addressed later in this chapter. This is true even for organizations that model their risk positions using portfolio theory. These models require judgment about the key assumptions used in the models. An organization's judgment about the appropriateness of its risk exposures needs to be able to withstand the scrutiny of persons who are independent of the organization, objective in terms of their perspective, and knowledgeable about the specific risk under review. To be considered appropriate, a knowledgeable outsider giving careful consideration to the nature, magnitude, complexity, and implications of the risk should be able to come to substantially the same conclusion as to the risk exposure as does the organization.

WHY IS SETTING RISK TOLERANCE IMPORTANT?

Setting risk tolerance clarifies what is (and what is not) an acceptable risk exposure. Clarity enables an organization to know with certainty what risk exposures it can take and what risk exposures it must avoid.

Establishing risk tolerance also allows an organization to compare actual risk exposures against authorized risk exposures. Comparing helps an organization determine whether it is undermanaging—or conversely—overmanaging a given risk. It answers the question: Do we need to do more, or less, to manage this risk?

Determining risk tolerance also helps an organization skirt the risk intolerance trap (i.e., running for the hills whenever a risk creeps out of the bushes). Without a common understanding that "risk" is not always a "four-letter word," an organization could default to trying to eliminate its risks (i.e., following a "better safe than sorry" risk management strategy). There is potential upside and downside to taking risks. Trying to dodge risks altogether—rather than managing and leveraging them—could harm an organization in the long run. Remember what Jawalarlal Nehru, the first Prime Minister of India, once said: "The policy of being too cautious is the greatest risk of all."[8]

WHAT ARE THE FACTORS TO CONSIDER IN SETTING RISK TOLERANCE?

First weigh the considerations, then take the risks.[9]
—Field Marshal General Helmuth von Moltke

There is no magic quantitative formula for establishing risk tolerance. But, there are five questions an organization needs to ask itself when it comes to establishing risk tolerance.

1. What is my organization's attitude toward risk?
2. What are the goals of my organization?
3. How capable is my organization of managing risk?
4. Does my organization have the capacity to absorb a potential loss related to taking the risk?
5. What are the costs and benefits of managing the risk?

In summary, risk attitude relates to a person's willingness to take risk.[10] It depicts whether the person is inherently a risk taker or a risk avoider. Goals, risk management capability, and risk management capacity relate to the amount of risk that would seem appropriate irrespective of a person's willingness to take risk. In turn, the cost/benefit of managing a risk provides a reality check as to whether seeking to manage a risk within a certain risk tolerance makes sense from a strictly dollars and cents perspective. It is necessary to consider each factor individually, then collectively—reflecting that, at the end of the day, you must be in a position to manage appropriately the risks to which your organization is exposed in pursuing its goals.

Now let us look at these factors in more detail.

Attitude About Risk

Risk attitude[11] is a person's propensity to take risk. Simply, is a person a risk taker, risk-averse, or risk-neutral? The following example is often used to show how a person's risk attitude can be determined.

Assume you are given the chance to place a bet based on the outcome of the flip of a coin. "Heads" you win $1. "Tails" you receive nothing. Knowing that there is an equal probability of turning up heads or tails—and that under the laws of very large numbers, you should expect to "win" 50 cents on average—how much would you be willing to pay to place this bet? If you are willing to pay more than 50 cents, you are a risk taker. That is, you are willing to risk more than the expected average payoff of 50 cents for the chance to win the dollar. If you are willing to pay less than 50 cents, you are a risk avoider. And if you are willing only to pay 50 cents, you are risk neutral.

Although you would think people typically would only place this bet if the cost of the bet were less than 50 cents, the popularity of casinos shows this is not always the case. In short, some people (and some organizations) are willing to take more risk than others.

Goals

Goals set the target to which an organization directs its resources. This is important from a risk-tolerance perspective. Because goals incent risk-taking behavior, differing goals can lead to differing risk tolerances. Let us show this by comparing "for-profit" private-sector organizations (i.e., private-sector organizations set up with the primary goal of maximizing owner value) with "public-policy mandated" public-sector organizations (i.e., organizations governments create to fulfill a defined public-policy mandate). For illustrative purposes, let us ignore other forms of private- and public-sector organizations such as "not-for-profit" private-sector organizations (i.e., private-sector organizations set up to achieve a defined nonfinancial goal) and "commercial" public-sector organizations (i.e., organizations governments create to deliver a service for the government on a commercial "for-profit" basis—though usually with some public-policy constraints).

Exhibit 9.1 sets out the key differences.

These differences might appear few and minor. But their implications are important for several reasons.

Exhibit 9.1   Private-Sector Organization versus Public-Sector Organization

Difference	"For-Profit" Private-Sector Organization	"Public-Policy Mandated" Public-Sector Organization
Ownership	Private owners	Public owners (i.e., government on behalf of taxpayers)
Goals/objectives	Maximize owner value	Fulfill public policy mandate
Performance measures	Return on investment	Mandate fulfillment

First, public- and private-sector organizations can have different goals because of the expectations of their "owners." This is important because risks stem from the activities and operations an organization undertakes in pursuing its goals. Exhibit 9.2 illustrates this point using our simple example. As the table shows, public- and private-sector organizations face different risks. Some risks (e.g., strategic risk) exist for private-sector organizations but not for public-sector organizations. Other risks (e.g., liquidity risk) take on a different nature for public-sector organizations than for private-sector organizations. This is due to the existence of an explicit or implied financial government guarantee. Finally, some risks (e.g., reputation risk) impact public-sector organizations differently than private-sector organizations—again because of the explicit or implied government backstop and the impact on public (i.e., voter) opinion.

More importantly—given our focus on risk tolerance—an organization's goals (driven by its ownership and performance measures) dictate how it sees and reacts to its risks. This perception creates incentives regarding the tolerance and management of these risks.

Continuing with our simple example, "for-profit" private-sector organizations view risks as opportunities that have upside and downside potential for adding value. They assess opportunities as to their risk/reward probability and manage those opportunities to achieve the expectations of owners. Those expectations typically reflect a defined level of return on investment. And, at the end of the day, investors will judge the success of a private-sector organization on its ability to create value for its owners. In pursuing value, private-sector organizations also can choose their risks by choosing what business activities to undertake. Similarly, they can avoid unacceptable risks by exiting the business activity from which the risk stems or by reinsuring or otherwise sharing risks with third parties.

On the other hand, public-sector organizations are created to fulfill public policy mandates. As such, they must accept and manage the risks to which they are exposed in fulfilling their mandates. To avoid these risks would clearly seem contrary to the rationale for creating a public-sector organization in the first place. Also, the performance of such organizations usually is measured in terms of whether or not they are fulfilling their mandates. Not fulfilling its mandate (which implicitly could mean fulfilling it at any cost) is not an option. Given these circumstances, public-sector organizations tend to be concerned about potential adverse risk outcomes (particularly any adverse impact on the reputation of the organization and/or its political masters). Certainly, risks can impact public-sector organizations in positive ways. But these organizations usually focus on risks' downside implications—that is, threats to the fulfillment of public-policy mandates. Accordingly, public-sector organizations tend to be less tolerant of risk. It is better to avoid adverse risk events, they would say, than to have to deal with them in public.

In summary, goals (driven by owner expectations) create powerful incentives influencing risk tolerance and risk management.

Capability to Manage Risk

In determining risk tolerance, you also have to consider an organization's risk management capability. By this we mean the ability to manage risk exposures

Exhibit 9.2   Risks for Private-Sector versus Public-Sector Organizations

Risk	Private-Sector Organization	Public-Sector Organization
Strategic Risk (i.e., the risk that the organization does not engage in activities that enable it to fulfill its goals).	Yes. A business must make a choice as to which activities to pursue to create shareholder value.	No. The government dictates business activities in a prescribed public-policy mandate.
Business Risks (i.e., the risks that are unique to the business activity).	Yes. The risks that stem from the chosen business activities.	Yes. The risks that stem from the public-policy mandate.
Financial Risks (i.e., the organization's exposure to liquidity, credit, and market risks).	Yes. The extent of these risks depends on the nature and extent of business activities.	Yes. But liquidity risk often is reduced because the government owns the organization. The extent of credit and market risks depends on the nature and extent of business activities.
Solvency/Capital Risk (i.e., the risk that the organization's capital is not sufficient to support current and planned operations).	Yes. The quantity and quality of capital needed to support current and planned operations reflect the risks to which the organization is exposed and any regulatory capital requirements.	Yes. But solvency risk usually is reduced because of government ownership, which may provide an explicit or implicit government guarantee.
Operational Risks (i.e., the people, information, technology, process, and other risks related to running the organization).	Yes. The nature and extent of these risks depend on the nature and extent of business activities.	Yes. The nature and extent of these risks depend on the nature and extent of business activities.
Reputation Risk (i.e., the risk of a loss of credibility).	Yes. Impaired credibility could impair shareholder value and, in the worst case scenario, bankrupt the organization.	Yes. But government ownership enhances credibility that the public-policy mandate will be fulfilled. In the worst case, impaired credibility could topple a government in power and/or result in a change in the public-policy mandate, a change in the organization responsible for administering the mandate and/or a change in the people in the organization administering the mandate.

within desired risk tolerance ranges. "Capability" differs from an organization's "capacity" to manage risk, which we will discuss later in this chapter.

Several elements combine to provide risk management capability:

- The organization's understanding of its risk: Does the organization understand the potential risk events that could result in the occurrence of a risk and the potential impact and likelihood of these events?
- The organization's risk measurement: Does the organization have risk measurement models that see risk beyond the typical approach of predicting future risk exposures based solely on historical information?
- The organization's human resources: Does the organization have sufficient, qualified, and experienced people to manage the risk?
- The organization's risk management practices: Does the organization have appropriate and effective risk management practices in place to manage the risk?
- The organization's risk management controls and oversight: Does the organization have appropriate and effective controls and oversight in place to ensure that risk management practices are working?
- The organization's risk management control environment (e.g., proper tone at the top, good communications about risk, an organization structure aligned with decision-making authorities, code of conduct). Does the organization's risk management environment support or impede the management of its risks?

Take it from the Oracle of Omaha, "Risk comes from not knowing what you're doing."[12] An organization must have the capability to manage its risks within its risk tolerance ranges.

Capacity to Take Risk

Determining risk tolerance also requires consideration of an organization's ability to assume the impact of an adverse risk event.

As noted earlier, risk events can adversely impact an organization in three ways: (1) they can cause material financial loss; (2) they can impede an organization's ability to achieve its goals; and, (3) they can impair an organization's reputation. So, in setting risk tolerance, an organization needs to consider the following:

- Its financial capacity to absorb a loss related to an adverse risk event. Does the organization have sufficient sustainable earnings to cover expected losses and sufficient unencumbered capital to cover unexpected losses? Thus, to paraphrase the former U.S. Secretary of Defense, Donald Rumsfeld: Is your organization equipped to deal with both "known unknowns" and "unknown unknowns"?[13]
- The potential impact of an adverse risk event on the achievement of the organization's goals. What is the likelihood that an adverse risk event could impede the organization in achieving its goals?

- The potential impact of an adverse risk event on an organization's reputation. As Benjamin Franklin warned us: "It takes many good deeds to build a good reputation, and only one bad one to lose it."[14] Could an adverse occurrence of a risk event cause a sustained adverse impact to the organization's reputation?

In summary, being in a position of wanting to take risk and having the ability to manage such risk might not be enough. An organization also must have the capacity (financial and other) to absorb the adverse affects of risk events should they occur.

Cost/Benefit of Managing Risk

In addition to considering risk attitudes, goals, risk management capability, and risk-taking capacity, determining risk tolerance also requires that you carefully consider whether the benefits of managing each risk exposure exceeds the costs of doing so. All things being equal, it normally would not be practical to buy a $10 safe to hold a $5 bill.

HOW CAN YOUR ORGANIZATION MAKE RISK TOLERANCE USEFUL IN MANAGING RISK?

So, after considering the key risk tolerance factors and applying sound judgment, your organization should be in a position to determine appropriate risk tolerances. Now, how can your organization make these useful in application?

The easy answer to this question is to set risk policies that formalize expectations about the management of each major source or category of risk. But more difficult questions arise: What guidance should the policies contain? When should your organization enact the policies? What should your organization do with the policies? The answers depend on who will be making the risk management decision.

We suggest that an organization's board of directors or similar governing body (referred to as the "board") should make all policies respecting significant risks.[15] This reflects the importance of risk management as a governance tool.

In many—but not necessarily all—situations, an organization's board will direct its management to make risk decisions about significant risks. In other situations, the board will decide to retain discretionary decision-making responsibility.

In each situation, board risk policies should set out:

- What risk management decisions to make.
- Who is authorized to make these decisions.

In situations in which the board has delegated decision-making responsibility to management, such policies also should clarify:

- The risk tolerance (i.e., parameters) within which the board expects management to manage the risk.

- The information management should provide the board about the management of the risk, so that the board can carry out its oversight responsibilities.

Where the board retains discretionary decision-making responsibility, it is usually not helpful for the board to fetter its discretion by establishing risk tolerance decision-making criteria through a board policy. Where the board retains decision-making responsibility, the critical governance principle is to put the board in a position to act with due care in making the decision. This is not a matter about decision-making criteria. Rather, it is a matter of governance process. Accordingly, the issue is not what criteria the board will apply—but rather, what information, analysis, and opinion it wants to have in hand so that it can reach its decision with due care. In these situations, the policies should clarify what recommendations and supporting rationale the board expects to get from management before making its decisions.

This leads us to the next question: When should board policies be made?

The board could set risk tolerance up front. The logic to that is simple. Risk management is all about managing risks within defined parameters. And risk tolerance is all about formalizing these expectations. So, to ensure the organization manages its risks within expectations it would be ideal, in a perfect world, to set risk tolerances up front—before the organization begins taking risks (including before engaging in new activities that expose the organization to new risks).

But setting risk tolerance requires a board to obtain a solid understanding of the risks being considered. For *de novo* organizations (or types of business), this means providing the board with a theoretical description of the risks, potential risk events, and the potential impact and likelihood of such events. But, most organizations are implementing ERM (and formalizing risk tolerance) well after they have engaged in business activities and started taking risks. In these cases, management should give the board a more practical description of the organization's actual risks—which includes management's assessment of the organization's actual exposure to each risk.

But what should the organization do with these policies once they have been formalized by the organization's board? This is simple. Once the board has approved the policies, management should communicate them to each person who is in a position to expose the organization to risk. That way everybody understands the board's expectations. The board also needs to put strong incentives in place to ensure management pays close attention to the policies. For example, the board should require management to advise the board about any policy breaches. And the board should demand an annual formal ERM sign-off from management attesting, among other things, that the organization has an effective ERM process—and that by using this process, it has ensured that significant risks were identified and are being managed in accordance with board risk policies.

Formalized risk tolerances also provide a useful reference point against which you can gauge risks and risk exposures when communicating with external stakeholders. In this regard, an organization's annual report provides an opportunity to report on risk and risk management. In addition to describing risk governance and management practices, it can report on whether risk exposures fall within the organization's accepted range of tolerance. And if they do not, it can explain why this is the case and what the organization is doing to correct the situation.

CONCLUSION

Risk tolerance describes the risk exposures that are appropriate for your organization to take or not to take. It is an important component of risk management in that it clarifies what risk exposures are acceptable to take and what exposures are to be avoided. However, it is but one topic to consider in implementing enterprise risk management, which in turn is but one component of a broader framework that brings together corporate governance, strategic management, and risk management—all supported by an organization's control environment.

Determining risk tolerance involves applying judgment giving careful consideration to five key factors:

1. Your organization's *attitude* toward taking risk.
2. Your organization's *goals*.
3. Your organization's *capability* to manage the risk.
4. Your organization's *capacity* to absorb the impact of potential loss related to taking the risk.
5. The *cost/benefit* of managing the risk.

Each factor must be considered *individually* and *collectively*—reflecting ultimately that your organization must be in a position to demonstrate that it is appropriately managing the risks to which it is exposed in pursuing its goals.

An important way of formalizing and communicating risk tolerance is through policies. When risks could be important to an organization's financial position, achievement of its goals and/or reputation, the organization's board of directors should establish policies respecting those risks. Such policies should set out the risk management decisions to be made and who should make these decisions. Where the board of directors has delegated decision-making responsibility to management, policies should also clarify:

- The risk tolerance (i.e., parameters) within which the board expects management to manage the risk.
- The information that management should provide to the board about the management of the risk, so that the board can carry out its oversight responsibilities.

But, where the board retains decision-making responsibility, it is usually not helpful for the board to fetter its discretion by establishing risk tolerance decision-making criteria through a board policy.

In theory, an organization should establish risk policies before conducting business activities. In practice, most organizations implement ERM (and formalize risk tolerance) well after they have engaged in business activities and started taking risks. In such situations, organizations set risk tolerance policies once they have a better understanding of their actual risk exposures.

The board and management should communicate risk policies to everyone who is in a position to expose the organization to risk, so that those people know the organization's expectations. The board and management should put the right incentives in place so that policy breaches get identified and reported.

An organization's performance against established risk tolerances provides a useful reference point against which an organization can report on its risk and risk management to its external stakeholders. In addition to describing risk governance and management practices, organizations should consider reporting on whether risk exposures fall within the organization's accepted range of tolerance. And if they do not, organizations should explain why this is the case and what they are doing to correct the situation.

In sum, risk tolerance is about taking calculated risks—that is, taking risks within clearly defined and communicated parameters set by the organization.

NOTES

1. For the purpose of simplicity, we have used tolerance in its singular rather than plural form. In practice, organizations typically set a tolerance for each of its significant risks.

2. The views expressed in this chapter are those of the authors and do not necessarily reflect those of Canada Deposit Insurance Corporation.

3. The direction and oversight the governing body provides for the organization.

4. The process for deciding on a strategy, executing the strategy, and reviewing the results to determine whether the results match expectations (and if not, adjusting the strategy or implementing the strategy differently).

5. The activity of identifying, assessing, managing, monitoring, and reporting risks.

6. The organization's working environment, which results from factors such as its tone at the top, the alignment of its organizational structure with its decision-making authority, its sufficiency of financial and other resources, its communications style, and the conduct of its personnel.

7. The state or condition wherein: (a) an organization's operations are subject to effective governance by its governing body, are being managed in accordance with ongoing, appropriate, and effective strategic and risk management processes, and are being conducted in an appropriate control environment; and (b) any significant weakness or breakdowns related to those areas are being identified and appropriate and timely action being taken to address them.

8. Jawalarlal Nehru (November 14, 1889–May 27, 1964). Indian politician and the first Prime Minister of the Republic of India.

9. Helmuth Karl Bernhard Graf von Moltke, (October 26, 1800–April 24, 1891). Prussian Army Field Marshal General and widely regarded as one of the great military strategists of the latter half of the 1800s.

10. The term "person" should be read to include an individual, group of individuals, or an organization.

11. Some literature may refer to risk attitude as risk appetite—that is, the inclination or desire to take risk. Risk attitude (or risk appetite if you prefer) should not be confused with risk tolerance, which as defined earlier in this chapter, is the risk exposure an organization determines appropriate to take or avoid taking.

12. Warren Buffett, (August 30, 1930–). American investor, businessman, and philanthropist regarded as one of the world's greatest stock market investors.

13. Donald Henry Rumsfeld, (July 9, 1932–). U.S. Secretary of Defense under President George W. Bush (2001–2006).

14. Benjamin Franklin (January 17, 1706–April 17, 1790), politician, statesman, and diplomat, one of the Founding Fathers of the United States, scientist, philosopher, printer, writer, and inventor.

15. A significant risk (or combination of risks) is important for the board to identify because of its probability of occurrence, severity of impact, or both, on the organization's financial position, its ability to achieve its goals (which can be financial or other goals), and its reputation.

ABOUT THE AUTHORS

Ken Mylrea is Director, Corporate Risk for Canada Deposit Insurance Corporation (CDIC). He is responsible for putting enterprise risk management (ERM) in place at CDIC. Ken also has helped other organizations in Canada and abroad implement ERM and has spoken about ERM implementation issues at governance and risk management conferences.

Ken has more than 30 years experience in the financial services sector. Prior to taking on his current role, he worked in the public sector in the areas of bank analysis, bank examinations, and public policy. Among his accomplishments include the development of governance, strategic management, risk management, and control standards for financial institutions, as well as the development and implementation of bank accounting standards, board governance policies, and risk assessment and rating methodologies, including deposit insurance premiums systems.

Joshua Lattimore is Policy and Research Advisor at Canada Deposit Insurance Corporation. His areas of knowledge relate to corporate governance, enterprise risk management, and public policy. He is currently coordinator of a subcommittee at the International Association of Deposit Insurers for developing guidance for governance of deposit insurers and coordinator of a subcommittee for developing research on risk management. Joshua has a master's degree in international affairs from Carleton University in Ottawa, Canada, and a bachelor's degree in international relations from the University of Toronto.

CHAPTER 10

How to Plan and Run a Risk Management Workshop

ROB QUAIL, BASc
Outsourcing Program Manager, Hydro One Networks Inc.

INTRODUCTION

The guidelines and advice in this chapter are based on the author's experience facilitating more than 200 risk workshops of various forms, with the number of participants ranging from 8 to 800. It is not intended to be a comprehensive guide to facilitation techniques, but assumes the reader has some basic understanding of how to facilitate a management meeting.

WHAT IS A RISK WORKSHOP?

A risk workshop is a *structured, large-group conversation* about *future* uncertainties.

- The workshop is *structured* to yield specific results within a specific agenda: decisions, learning, and commitment to action. Therefore, there is a set agenda and a facilitator, whose responsibility is to ensure that the conversation takes a specific form aligned with the workshop's objectives.
- The workshop involves a *large group*. Large, in this sense, means more than seven or eight participants—more people than could normally have a satisfactory, efficient conversation about a complex topic on their own in a single pass, without leadership or guidance, and achieve an effective outcome or result.
- The workshop is a *conversation*. The emphasis in a risk workshop is on enabling an open and frank discussion among people with knowledge or authority over the subject risks, and on encouraging contrary views and perspectives.
- The workshop is *about the future*. It concerns future events and uncertainty; it attempts to gather all the known, relevant facts, assumptions, suppositions and uncertainties about a future set of events or situations, predict how those events or situations might affect the organization's shared goals, and predict how the organization would or should handle that scenario.

WHY USE WORKSHOPS?

It is tempting to think of workshops as merely a data gathering exercise; after all, from the risk manager's perspective, the workshop provides access to a whole roomful of experts for a specified period of time. It gets results much more quickly than data mining of similar scope, and certainly is much quicker than surveys or individual interviews.

However, the benefits of risk management workshops go far beyond the convenience for the risk manager:

- Learning opportunity: A well-structured workshop allows participants to examine risks from a range of perspectives, and learn from other experts and leaders in the room. Participants will inevitably emerge from the workshop understanding their business better and with heightened awareness of corporate objectives, and the landscape of internal and external risk environments. If the workshop agenda includes discussion of current, committed, and contemplated mitigants, they will also gain a greater understanding of how other parts of the organization are mitigating risk, and how these mitigants might fit together.
- Team building: Risk workshops are an excellent tool for promoting team building. A risk workshop provides a "safe" environment to share perspectives and ideas and ensures equal opportunity for participation. It is a great "get to know you" exercise for a recently established management team.
- Efficient use of time: Risk workshops can be an effective way for a management team to cover a large amount of ground very quickly. The focus on a defined agenda and use of facilitation techniques and risk management tools ensure that the discussion sticks to the highest-priority issues.
- Risk management education: Risk workshops provide a "live" demonstration of risk management techniques and approaches. As such, they are an excellent vehicle for educating participants on the theory and application of risk management to specific business problems.
- Continuous improvement: Risk workshops provide the risk manager with an environment for continuously improving the quality of tools and techniques. By repeated exposure and use by managers from a variety of levels and backgrounds, a program of workshops will effectively validate such tools as risk tolerances and voting guides.

HOW TO CONDUCT A RISK WORKSHOP

The following sections provide a general model for planning and executing a typical risk workshop. The entire process is depicted in Exhibit 10.1.

PREPARATION

A smoothly run and successful workshop that results in usable outcomes depends on adequate preparation; an effective workshop on risks is never the result of "winging it." Regardless of the objectives and nature of the workshop, the greater the extent of preparation, the greater the likelihood there will be of a successful outcome.

	Step
Workshop Preparation	Identify the sponsor.
	Set the workshop objectives.
	Set the scope. • Organizational objectives • Risk universe • Time horizon
	Assemble reference materials. • Risk magnitude scale • Probability scale • Strength of mitigants scale
	Set the agenda.
	Decide on attendees.
	Arrange venue.
Workshop Execution	Facilitate the workshop. For each risk: • Introduce the risk • Assess magnitude • Assess strength of mitigants • Assess probability • Decide on tolerability
	Record the results.

Exhibit 10.1   How to Conduct a Risk Workshop

Identify the Sponsor

Given the use of tools such as "anonymous" voting and facilitated discussion, a risk workshop has the appearance of being a democratic process. It is *not*. It is a consultation and should be conducted under the leadership of a specific decision maker. Therefore, all risk workshops must have an executive sponsor who is ultimately accountable for the scope of the risks under discussion; someone who is "in charge"; someone who ultimately "owns" the risks. This person is *not* the risk manager. The role of the sponsor for a risk workshop is to set the context for the workshop, provide a view of their tolerance for risk taking, to pass ultimate judgment, on behalf of the broader organization, on the tolerability of risk exposures, and ultimately be able to present the results to those to whom the sponsor is accountable.

As described throughout the following sections, the sponsor will make decisions concerning the planning and design of the workshop, he or she will play a critical role in setting the context and tone of the workshop itself, and he or she will ultimately assume responsibility for the outputs of the workshop and ensuring that agreed-to actions are completed. Although the risk manager will do all the "heavy lifting" in terms of planning and executing the workshop, the sponsor will need to make key decisions before, during, and after the workshop and together these decisions will be the ultimate determinant of the workshop's success.

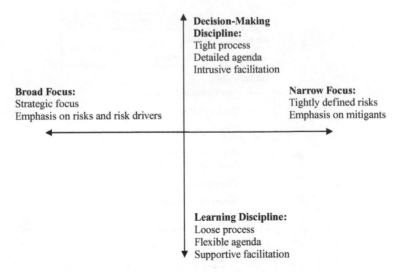

**Decision-Making
Discipline:**
Tight process
Detailed agenda
Intrusive facilitation

Broad Focus:
Strategic focus
Emphasis on risks and risk drivers

Narrow Focus:
Tightly defined risks
Emphasis on mitigants

Learning Discipline:
Loose process
Flexible agenda
Supportive facilitation

Exhibit 10.2   Setting Workshop Objectives

Set the Objectives of the Workshop

It is imperative, in designing a risk workshop, that the facilitator gets a clear understanding of the sponsor's objectives for the workshop, as this will have implications for most other aspects of workshop design. A useful model for understanding these objectives is illustrated in Exhibit 10.2.

The vertical axis of this figure represents the desired discipline of the workshop. Learning Discipline workshops, at the bottom of this scale, place the emphasis on discussion and casual discourse on the subject risk areas, to enhance individual and collective understanding of the risks, rather than driving toward decision making. The process is loosely defined, there is a lot of scheduled "slack" in the agenda, and the facilitator is relatively hands-off in allowing the discussion to follow the apparent interest of the participants. Learning workshops are well suited to new problems and new risk areas, with relatively cohesive management teams and no real imperative for immediate decision making. Because workshops can be excellent team-building forums, they can also be well-suited to new teams, so long as the goals of the workshop do not include driving to immediate decision making on a specified list of risks and issues.

At the opposite extreme of the vertical axis, Decision-Making Discipline workshops are results-oriented. The agenda is highly prescriptive right down to the minute, the process is highly scripted, and the facilitator keeps the process strictly on-topic and on-schedule. Decision-Making workshops are, as the name implies, called for when a management team must make a decision immediately on the significance of risks and the adequacy of controls. A high degree of trust in the facilitator is required, because the facilitator will play a highly intrusive role in keeping the discussions on-topic and on-schedule.

The horizontal axis of Exhibit 10.2 depicts the focus of the workshop. Broad Focus risk workshops explore arrays or groups of risks at the strategic level. The emphasis is on identifying, understanding, and measuring risks, rather than evaluating the adequacy of mitigants, as the high-level depiction of risks may not lend itself to the discrete evaluation of mitigants to the point where a judgment of adequacy is possible. The agenda of these workshops will allow for greater understanding of the risk environment and the interplay of internal and external factors on the risks. Such workshops are useful for executive teams at the start of a strategic planning exercise. They are also useful at the commencement of large projects or programs (the "storming" stage).

At the opposite end of the horizontal scale in Exhibit 10.2, Narrow Focus risk workshops are targeted at risks that are depicted and understood to a high degree of specificity. Such workshops will normally make use of performance or other indicator data, and may require the participation of functional or technical experts. Narrow workshops also allow for a greater emphasis on the evaluation of controls and mitigants for each risk. These workshops are best suited for technical groups and detailed planning exercises, such as annual departmental business planning.

Note that it is not an either-or decision. The facilitator must get an understanding of where among these four extremes the sponsor's preference lies. This can be gleaned by asking questions such as:

- How essential is it that we get through all of the risks on the agenda?
- Do you expect that decisions will be made in the room?
- What is the level of understanding of the participants of the risks that are on the agenda? How important is it to you that they understand them all?
- Do you need to develop a detailed understanding of specific elements of these risks and how we are mitigating them, or are you looking for more of a high level of understanding of the risks as a suite?
- What is the level of trust and cohesiveness of this group?

Set the Scope

The scope of the risk workshop will consist of three elements: (1) the Organizational Objectives, (2) the Risk Universe, and (3) the Time Horizon.

1. Organizational Objectives. Specifying the organizational objectives is an important activity because it helps define the scope of the session, it will assist in clarifying which risks will be selected for detailed scrutiny during the workshop, and it forms the basis of reference materials to be used by participants in evaluating risk magnitude. What are the stated objectives of the broader organization, and more specifically the objectives or results for which the sponsor is accountable? Depending on the emphasis on formal objective-setting in the organization, these may be readily obtained (for example, from a Balanced Scorecard or some other formal statement of goals) or may need to be articulated as a step in workshop preparation. Objectives might be defined in areas such as financial results, reputation, customer relationship, operational efficiency, corporate stewardship, safety, and so on.

2. Risk Universe. The risks selected for discussion at a workshop should be drawn from a broader "risk universe." The facilitator should help the sponsor produce the list of risks in the "universe" that are relevant to the sponsor's organizational objectives and known to be of possible concern. A risk may be selected for discussion because either it is considered to be

a serious threat to one or more of the organizational objectives, or because it is the responsibility of the sponsor to mitigate that risk on behalf of the broader organization.

3. Time Horizon. The sponsor and facilitator set a limit for how far into the future the workshop will look in examining risks. Ordinarily, risk workshops will have a horizon of somewhere between three and seven years. The horizon will be a function of the scope of the organization (more senior-level workshops will tend to have longer horizons), the timeline of the organizational objectives (if the objectives are expressed relative to a specific time horizon, that might be a useful reference point), and the volatility of the business (if the business environment is extremely uncertain then looking forward more than a few years may not yield very reliable results).

Assemble Reference Materials

In order to have an efficient workshop, easy-to-use reference materials are important. The following should be assembled prior to the session.

- Risk Magnitude Scale. An essential tool for any risk workshop is a common framework that participants will use to gauge the magnitude of the risk. Risk magnitude should *always* be expressed in terms of impact on the organizational objectives. Thus, a magnitude scale will consist of a matrix very much like the one depicted in Exhibit 10.3, with the objectives listed down the left-hand column and a range of potential outcomes laid out under a numerical scale that represents varying degrees of "badness." Experience has shown that a 1–5 scale provides enough gradations for most workshops. See Box 10.1.

Box 10.1 A Word on Risk Tolerances and Magnitude Scales

If the broader organization has a set of established and documented Risk Tolerances, these are extremely valuable for setting Magnitude Scales. As described elsewhere in this text, Risk Tolerances are expressed in terms of deviation from the broader Organizational Objectives. Therefore, the ideal Magnitude Scales are those that are designed to express the corporate attitude toward a range of outcomes corresponding to each Corporate Objective. So for example, if a Magnitude scale in the form of Exhibit 10.3 has a 1–5 scale, the outcomes for each objective can be pegged to a specific point on that scale (such as "4 – Severe") to represent what the tolerances describe as" highly intolerable" outcomes or losses.

- Probability Scale. Participants will also need a reference to allow consistent ratings of probabilities. Again, a 1–5 scale is recommended, with the

Objective	Attribute	Event	5 Worst Case	4 Severe	3 Major	2 Moderate	1 Minor
Financial	Net income	Net income shortfall (after tax, in one year)	>$100M	$50M–$100M	$25M–$50M	$5M–$25M	<$5M
	Creditworthiness	Change in financial ratios or risk	Event of default; unable to raise any capital due to credit rating	Credit rating downgrade to below "investment grade"; unable to raise full amount requ red capital	Credit rating downgrade	Put on credit "watch"	Credit rating agencies and bondholders express concern
Reputation	Public profile	Negative media attention; opinion leader and public criticism	National media attention; opinion leaders/customers nearly unanimous in public criticism	Provincial/state media attention; most opinion leaders/customers publicly critical	Significant local attention; severe opinion leaders/customers publicly critical	Letter(s) to board of directors or CEO	Letter(s) to senior management
	Employee confidence	Employee dissatisfaction	Widespread departures of key staff with scarce skills or knowledge	Sharp, sustained drop in employee survey results; departures of key staff with scarce skills or knowledge.	Sharp decline in employee survey results; sharp increase in grievances.	Modest decline in employee survey results; modest increase in grievances	Less than planned improvements in employee survey results.
Competitiveness	Unit cost reduction	Failure to reduce unit costs	Unit costs increase by >25%	Unit costs increase by 15%–25%	Unit costs increase by 10%–15%	Unit costs increase by 5%–10%	Unit costs not reduced
	Work program accomplishment	Work program shortfall	>10 Critical projects late or; <50% of noncritical work completed	6–10 Critical projects late or; 50%–69% of noncritical work completed	3–5 Critical projects late or; 70%–84% of noncritical work completed	1 or 2 Critical projects late or; 85–94% of noncritical work completed	No critical projects late; >95% of noncritical work completed
Safety and Environment	Employee: workforce availability/safety	Employee injury	Employee fatality or major permanent disability	Employee critical injury	LTI frequency > 50% above target	LTI frequency > 25% above target	LTI/AS above target
	Environmental performance	Adverse environment impact	Widespread offsite impacts (eg.; regional or municipal water supply)	Multiple local offsite impacts (eg.; multiple residential properties or private water supplies)	Significant local offsite impact (eg.; a public thoroughfare);	Minor local offsite impact (eg.; a single residential property or private water supply)	Minor impact on corporate property only

Exhibit 10.3 Sample Risk Magnitude Scale

Exhibit 10.4 Sample Probability Scale

Rating	Likelihood Scale	Probability in Planning Period (5 years)
5	Very Likely	> 95%
4	Likely	95% to 65%
3	Medium	65% to 25%
2	Unlikely	25% to 5%
1	Remote	< 5%

midpoint representing a 50/50 chance of occurring at least once over the workshop time horizon. An example is shown in Exhibit 10.4.

- Strength of Mitigants Scale. A step in the process is to allow participants to express their degree of confidence in the mitigants and internal controls in place to manage the risk. Once again a 1–5 scale provides a reasonable degree of granularity. A sample Mitigants Strength scale (in this case with a strong emphasis on internal controls) is shown in Exhibit 10.5.

Set the Agenda

Once the objectives for the workshop have been set, the next task is to set the agenda. An obvious question is how much time is available and how many risks can be covered in the available time? There are no hard-and-fast rules, but as general guidelines:

- An entire day of risk discussions can be exhausting, and after working through eight or so risks, the process will start to seem stilted and formulaic to the participants. Allow adequate time for breaks and do not try to extend a risk workshop beyond eight hours in total. Half-day workshops are more likely to yield a positive experience for participants, even if it means breaking up the workshop over two or more days. Remember, a risk workshop should seem to participants like a stimulating and efficient conversation, not drudgery.
- For a workshop with a reasonable balance between learning and decision making, 40 minutes per risk is the minimum time that should be allotted.
- Some extra time should be allowed for the first few risks until the participants get familiar with the workshop process and tools.

The method for choosing (from the Risk Universe) the risks for discussion is another decision that is primarily up to the sponsor. Alternatives include:

- The sponsor chooses the risks alone. Although this approach is simple and quickly done, it does not allow consultation beyond whatever awareness of the risk profile the sponsor has already. This may cause key or emerging risks to go undiscussed.
- Advance polling, using e-mail, interviews, and so on, to involve the participants in choosing the risks from the Risk Universe in advance of the workshop date. This approach has the principal advantage of broad involvement in the process and a sense of ownership in the agenda among

Score	Rating	Description
5	Full mitigants; prescriptive; senior mgmt/CEO oversight	**Full controls established (see Full mitigants below), <u>Plus:</u>** ❏ Objectives, policies, plans, and measures all formally approved by senior management/CEO and clearly documented ❏ Authorities, responsibilities, and accountabilities tightly defined ❏ Formal coordination of decisions of different parts of the organization ❏ Prescriptive/detailed procedures exist ❏ Close, frequent monitoring of performance ❏ Overall controls are subject to formal and/or independent review
4	Full mitigants	**All elements fully implemented and complete**
3	Substantial mitigants	**Only one or two elements are missing/incomplete**
2	Partial mitigants	**A significant number of missing/incomplete elements**
1	Few mitigants	**Almost no elements in place**

Full mitigants consist of:

❏ Business objectives communicated to all levels
❏ Policies established and communicated so that people understand expectations
❏ Plans have been established and communicated
❏ Measurable performance targets set
❏ Authorities, responsibilities, and accountabilities established
❏ People have the necessary knowledge and skills
❏ People have the necessary resources and tools, including appropriate computer systems
❏ Adequate, timely communication/coordination to allow people to perform their responsibilities
❏ Control activities such as procedures in place and appropriately scaled to risk
❏ Performance is monitored against targets; assumptions are challenged periodically
❏ Follow-up to ensure effective change
❏ Overall control is periodically assessed
❏ Residual risks accepted on a cost-benefit basis

Exhibit 10.5   Sample "Strength of Mitigants" Scale

participants. However, it can be more costly and requires considerably more lead time.

• The sponsor and facilitator together arrive at a "best-efforts" list of risks and the participants modify and choose from that list as an early item on the workshop agenda. Anonymous voting techniques may be employed to involve the group in the selection of the risks for discussion at the workshop. This approach represents a reasonable compromise between the above approaches.

Decide on Attendees

For most risk workshops, as a general rule, the target number of active participants should range from about 8 to 16. Smaller groups usually do not offer the variety of perspectives or require formalized facilitation of the type described in this chapter. Larger groups can be unwieldy and there are special challenges in controlling group dynamics and giving everyone a sense that they have had a fair amount of "air time." Large groups can be accommodated but require additional detailed planning and more experienced facilitators; see the section "Tough Spots."

The decision on who attends will ultimately be left to the sponsor. The list of attendees will depend very much on which risks are on the agenda for discussion, assuming these are known in advance: the attendee list should allow for full exploration of the risks on the agenda, and, if applicable, decision making on the actions to be taken. This means that the workshop should include functional or technical experts and key management stakeholders and decision makers. Another useful rule is to ensure that any person or group that might reasonably be expected to carry an action item out of the workshop is represented.

Other considerations:

- If the workshop concerns the key risks to the success of a department or business unit within an organization, you will want to ensure that all the key groups within that unit are represented.
- If the workshop concerns key risks to a large project, in addition to the technical experts or "leads" for various facets of the project plan, ensure that the project management office or other key project governance roles are represented.
- If a purpose of the workshop is "team building," this will be a factor in selecting attendees as well; excluding members of the "team" will have negative consequences on team cohesion and compromise "team building."
- Consider inviting attendees from other organizations or companies, such as partners or service providers, where the objectives or mitigants are shared or jointly resourced.

To facilitate a risk workshop, the author recommends a two-person facilitation "team." One person, the "facilitator," will focus on running the meeting and guiding the discussion. The other person, the "record keeper," will ensure that what is said or decided at the meeting is recorded. Although it is possible for the facilitator to assume both roles, experience has shown that the workshop can be run more efficiently and produce better documented results if there is a separate record keeper assisting the facilitator. Note: The record keeper role is not just a "recording" function. The record keeper must have the ability to listen to and understand the discussion and boil it all down to a few key points to be recorded and simultaneously displayed to participants (i.e., on to a screen by a projector).

Arrange Venue

Normally a U-shaped seating configuration is preferred as it allows for face-to-face contact, simultaneous reading of displayed materials, and a central position from which the facilitator can direct the discussion and keep everyone engaged. The ideal layout for the room will have two computers and two projectors and screens set up at the front of the room where all participants can see them: one screen for displaying context information and/or voting results (assuming anonymous voting is used) and the other screen for recording the key discussion points. It is also worthwhile to have one or more flipcharts for recording "parked items" and other items that may come up, but are not central to the agenda.

Often it can be helpful to hold the workshop away from the normal place of business, to avoid the temptation for people to sneak back to their desks. To further limit interruptions, the author has in the past deliberately chosen workshop venues where blackberry and cellular service is not available.

EXECUTION

Assuming the preparation is complete and thorough, the execution of the workshop is focused mostly on maintaining or controlling the discussion, properly recording what is said and decided, and reporting the results.

Facilitate the Workshop

The purpose of this section is to describe the basic elements common to most or all risk workshops, not to provide a detailed explanation of meeting facilitation techniques. More facilitation "tips and tricks" are provided in the next section. (Note: This section assumes the use of anonymous voting, which the author considers an essential tool for efficient risk workshop execution.)

Although the workshop will be customized based on its specific objectives and focus, each risk discussion will have the following components. For each risk:

- **Introduce the risk.** Ensure all participants have a common understanding of what is meant by the subject risk. An effective way to do this is to ask participants to briefly describe, as a simple scenario, how this risk might come to pass; what triggering event or condition would signify that the risk has occurred; and what might be experienced by the organization as a result. Record the key discussion points and display these using an overhead projector. Have the group brainstorm several of these brief scenarios; record them all.

- **Magnitude.** Have the participants assign a magnitude to the "worst credible" impact of the risk using the Risk Magnitude Scale. Introduce the vote with an instruction like this: "Review the scenarios that have just been described, and decide in your own mind which of these represents a credible scenario that is the most harmful. Then decide which of the objectives is most threatened by this scenario and find a point on the Risk Magnitude Scale corresponding to that objective that most closely resembles this impact. The risk score associated with that impact will be your vote."

  The voting is followed by a conversation to explore the rationale behind responses and probe into the reasons behind diversity of opinion. To encourage a complete discussion, the facilitator should ask questions like, "Which objective did you feel was most threatened by this risk?" and "Please describe the mental journey you took in evaluating the risk and deciding how to vote." The facilitator should record the key perspectives of participants.

The primary objective of this discussion is not necessarily to "force" consensus on the magnitude of the risk (although this is of course preferable), but to ensure that all perspectives get communicated and are understood by all participants, especially the sponsor.

This portion of the workshop can involve one or more revotes and rounds of discussion. The facilitator should introduce a revote by saying something like: "Now we have heard a range of perspective and arguments on the potential magnitude of this risk. Let's see how many of you have changed your minds as a result." It may take multiple iterations of "vote—discuss—vote—discuss" to complete this part of the agenda. It is important to remember that the role of the facilitator is to get all views on the table and encourage constructive debate.

- **Strength of Mitigants.** Using the Strength of Mitigants Scale, have participants assign an overall rating to the current and committed mitigants of the risk. This can be introduced by saying, "Consider all the activities that you are aware of to prevent this risk from occurring or hurting our organization. Decide for yourself how complete this set of activities is, relative to the kinds of things described in the voting guide." Once the vote is complete, the facilitator should then ask participants to list for the rest of the group the mitigants they were considering in their vote, and describe and record the key strengths and gaps/weaknesses in current mitigants. If the discussion is lively and results in significant learning by participants, have a revote following the discussion.

- **Probability.** Using the Probability Scale, have participants assign a probability of the risk coming to pass with an impact as large as was assigned in the second step above, in light of their view of the likelihood of the initiating events or conditions and their degree of confidence in the mitigants. Discuss the results and accompanying rationale and, if necessary, revote if there was significant deviation on the initial vote.

- **Tolerability.** At this point the facilitator should summarize the results of the discussion, including the voted scores and the discussion notes. In consultation with participants, the sponsor should then declare whether in their view the current level of risk exposure is tolerable to the organization. If the answer is that the risk is tolerable, no more discussion is required. If the answer is that it is intolerable, then normally the group will review the controls or other options needed and suggested to mitigate the risk down to a tolerable level, and discuss and assign additional actions needed.

It is important that the discussion on actions not become too detailed, or it will derail the discussion and put the agenda at risk. The author has found it useful to categorize actions into two types:

- *Quick hits,* which are relatively simple, well understood actions that can be implemented with minimal resources and planning. Quick hits can be assigned to an individual to ensure they are done by a specific date.

- *Big ideas,* which are expressions of potential actions that require more thought and analysis. Big ideas are best assigned to a "Champion," who will take responsibility for further evaluation and consultation, and bring a more fully formed action plan back to the sponsor or group at a later, specified date for approval.

Risk:

Description

Scenarios
• ×

Magnitude and Probability

| • × |

	Risk Score	Control Strength	Gap	Tolerable Risk?
Risk Rating				

Controls	
Working:	**Gaps/Needs:**
+	−

Initiatives

Name	Description	Responsible	Due
	• ×		

Exhibit 10.6   Sample Record-Keeping Template

Record the Results

As mentioned in an earlier section, it is best to have a dedicated record keeper in the room, recording what gets said and displaying it for all to see. This can be most conveniently done by typing key points into a computer and simultaneously projecting them on a screen so all participants can refer to what was said and know that the key points are being properly recorded. The intent is not to record every word that gets said, but the highlights of the discussion in point form. Also any decisions, conclusions, or actions need to be clearly noted. It is recommended that the record keeper prepare a template in advance that follows the workshop agenda (see Exhibit 10.6). Throughout the workshop, the facilitator must keep an eye on the note-taking screen to ensure that the record keeper is able to keep up with the discussion and capture the key aspects of what is said.

Prepare the Final Report

One of the advantages of having a real-time record keeper is that a report of the workshop, showing the risk map and discussion points and actions, can be finalized and distributed to the sponsor and participants as required within a matter of hours. The report should include as a minimum:

- A graphical or tabular summary of the results of the workshop (e.g., a risk map), showing the results of the voting and the conclusions on which risks are tolerable or intolerable with current mitigants.
- A summary of committed actions, in a "who-what-by-when" format.

It is best to schedule a debrief meeting with the sponsor to walk through the highlights of the report and make sure they are clear on the next steps for following up on assigned actions.

TECHNIQUES FOR PLANNING AND FACILITATING EFFECTIVE RISK WORKSHOPS

The facilitator of a risk workshop is responsible for guiding the workshop participants through the process and ensuring effective and efficient discussions on the subject risks. This section provides some useful general advice and tips for workshop facilitators.

"Anonymous" Voting

The author has used so-called "anonymous" voting tools (wireless keypad transmitters and receivers) for more than 200 risk workshops over a nine year period, to great effect. These systems allow the facilitator to pose a question, displayed for the group to see, along with a range of numerical responses (corresponding to the scales described in the previous section) and obtain and feedback to participants a quick, real-time poll of the views of participants. These systems have the following advantages:

- They ensure full participation. Every participant is forced to go through the mental exercise of thinking individually through the question posed by the facilitator and deciding for themselves on an appropriate response. This enables subsequent full participation in the discussion.
- They are efficient. In a matter of seconds the entire room can get feedback on the views of all participants concerning the question being posed, and get an instant read of the degree of consensus or disagreement. If, in the initial round, there is a narrow distribution of votes, indicating that consensus already exists, this is a signal to the facilitator that the discussion can be short and merely focused on quickly obtaining the "reasons why." This can save time in a tight agenda and leave more time for topics where there is a broader range of views.
- They stimulate discussion. The facilitator can probe for arguments supporting each response. If there is broad disagreement (shown by a broad distribution of votes), the facilitator can immediately probe into the reasons why and stimulate a healthy debate.
- They reduce the opportunity for individuals to dominate the discussion. In the absence of the voting tools, more senior people in the room can (often unwittingly) influence others' views and dominate the discussion. Several years ago, the author sat in on a two-day workshop where anonymous voting was not employed, and instead participants held up cards indicating their own vote. In this session, other participants fell into a pattern of waiting to see how the "boss" voted before holding up their cards. Obviously, such a dynamic is not conducive to thorough discussion of all critical aspects of an issue on its own merits.

Useful Facilitation Tips

What follows are some useful ideas to help ensure successful, stimulating risk workshops.

- Inquire. Ask open-ended questions, such as "Why?" Ask participants to speak not just on behalf of themselves but what they think others might be thinking. Ask for the contrary view ... "What are some of the arguments against this?" Ask for evidence. "How do you know?"
- Restate. Summarize or paraphrase what you have just heard. Summarize the key points and then ask someone to add to them or comment on them or contradict them.
- Provoke. State extreme views that you might have heard or imagined on the subject of discussion. Encourage healthy debate.
- Use silence. After asking a question that gets no immediate response, it is extremely tempting to fill the silence by talking more or restating the question. Don't. Wait through the silence. If you wait long enough, someone will speak.
- Get out of the way. If a good animated discussion starts to happen that is directly on topic, and there is available time, try to "blend in with the furniture." Walk to the side of the room or sit down. Let them run with it. Wait for the discussion to peter out or drift off topic before again making your presence felt.
- Don't over-explain. The author's experience is that the more participation (and less explanation or lecturing) there is in a workshop agenda, the more engaged the participants will be. Avoid lengthy descriptions of the steps to be taken or the underlying theory. Tell them the bare bones of what they need to do for the next step in the process, and then let them learn by doing.

Tough Spots

- *Nonparticipation.* It is the author's opinion that the duty of the facilitator is to create the *conditions* for an open discussion, and the duty of the attendees at a workshop to actually participate. Therefore, the author does not believe that the facilitator should go to greater lengths (beyond the provision of anonymous voting systems) to ensure that all attendees fulfill their duty to participate. That being said, if an attendee is not participating in the discussion, there are options to encourage that person to speak up, such as making a point of asking them by name what they think, when there is a pause in the discussion. Care must be taken not to intervene in this fashion too often, however, or the facilitator will start to assume the "crutch" role of drawing-out all silent attendees. It is better to make it clear at the start of the workshop that all attendees are expected to contribute to the best of their ability.
- *Dominators.* If a member is dominating the discussion, say, "Let's find out what other people think on this. Anyone else?" If the dominator is also the sponsor, the best approach is to call a brief recess and take the sponsor aside

and discretely coach them to withhold their views to allow them to gain the benefit of others' perspectives.

- *Large groups.* If you are successful in building enthusiasm for risk workshops, you may be asked to try to do something with a much larger group. (Note: The author's largest group was 800 participants.) Obviously the goals in large group sessions are different than those for smaller groups. It is a practical impossibility to make everyone feel like a full participant in the entire discussion. Instead you may choose to have the discussion in subgroups, and then have each subgroup appoint a spokesperson to summarize the discussion and share it with the larger group. Or, if interactive discussion is not a key objective of the meeting you may use anonymous voting to gather the entire group's views on the risks or issues and then have "experts" or people in a position of authority stand up and provide commentary on or reactions to the voted results.

CONCLUSION

We have shown how to plan, organize, and facilitate a risk workshop. Risk workshops play a vital role in ERM by helping engage executive managers and staff in understanding the corporate objectives and the risks to achieving these within given tolerances. As such, not only do workshops help identify and address critical risks, they also provide excellent opportunities for participants to learn about organizational objectives, risks, and mitigants.

ABOUT THE AUTHOR

Rob Quail holds a BASc in Industrial Engineering at the University of Toronto. Rob has an extensive background in the risk and control field, including Environmental Management, Occupational Safety, and Internal Audit. Since 1999 he has designed and facilitated more than 200 management workshops on risk and control at Hydro One. Rob has successfully applied Enterprise Risk Management to a disparate range of business problems and decisions, including annual business and investment planning, major transformational, infrastructure, and technology projects, acquisitions, partnerships, divestitures, downsizing, and outsourcing. Hydro One was so successful in integrating risk management into the core management processes and attitudes in the company, that late in 2003 Rob recommended that the group be dissolved as a full-time work group. Since then Rob has worked in the areas of customer care, project management, and outsourcer management, and provided risk management services to Hydro One's senior executive on an as-needed basis. He continues to be a popular speaker at risk management conferences, and performs as a musician in clubs in the Toronto area in his spare time.

CHAPTER 11

How to Prepare a Risk Profile

JOHN R.S. FRASER

Vice President, Internal Audit & Chief Risk Officer, Hydro One Networks Inc.

INTRODUCTION

One of the key building blocks of enterprise risk management (ERM) is the preparation and sharing of a corporate risk profile.[1] One might even go so far as to state that where there is no corporate risk profile there is no ERM. How a profile is prepared, how frequently it is prepared, and with whom it is shared are all subject to different treatments in each organization. However, a good guiding principle to follow is to keep it simple. Tools and methodologies should follow suit and not become overly bureaucratic or complex.

This chapter will hopefully assist organizations in choosing the most effective type of risk profile for their needs and provide guidance in preparing and communicating it to management and boards. The following descriptions of alternative methods will assist students of ERM to understand how and why profiles assist management and boards, and how these may be done most effectively in varying situations.

The chapter is organized into two parts. In the first part, readers are provided with background information on the definition, purpose, use, and types of risk profiles along with the advantages and disadvantages of the various methodologies used to gather the information needed to prepare a risk profile. It also covers how and why profiles assist management and boards and how these may be done most effectively in varying situations. The second part of the chapter is dedicated to how to prepare the simplest type of profile—the "top 10." It uses Hydro One as a case study.[2] Since 1999 and over tumultuous periods of high risk, the top 10 method has proven its value to Hydro One's management and board. The success of this type of profile is a result of its simple preparation and effectiveness of purpose.

DEFINITION AND USES OF A CORPORATE RISK PROFILE

A corporate risk profile is a periodic documentation of the key risks to an organization to achieving its stated business objectives over a specified future time period.[3] For some businesses that are subject to great volatility it may be helpful to prepare these more frequently and, conversely, less frequently for static industries or organizations.

The primary purpose of a risk profile is to assist the CEO and management team in communicating with the board. This means that the risk profile is prepared as a service to the CEO and should reflect the CEO's understanding and tone. Where a risk profile is prepared at lower levels of the organization, for example, at a division or subsidiary, it should be viewed as a management tool for the head of that division or subsidiary. The corporate risk profile can also be used by the management team for other purposes such as strategic and business planning, resource allocation and action plans.

A corporate risk profile should be prepared for use by the management of an organization as part of the ERM process. It is important to note, however, that it differs in many respects from risk descriptions included in filings for purely regulatory purposes. Typical differences include:

- Duration: The time horizon for a corporate risk profile should typically be in the range of three to five years, whereas regulatory filings are usually for a much longer term or in perpetuity. For example, matters for which lawsuits could be brought by investors in the future.
- Types of risks: Regulatory filings are usually restricted to financial matters, that is, those areas that would be of interest to an investor. By contrast, where an organization sets a corporate target for safety and has risks of achieving this target it is unlikely to be of much interest to investors.
- Purpose: Corporate risk profiles are prepared to assist in better managing the company. Regulatory filings are usually prepared with both promotional and legal protection motives. Although these two types of risk descriptions can and should be reconciled, they have different purposes. Yet arguably, they should remain mutually exclusive.

The term "risk profile" has been used in a number of ways by different disciplines and these may not reflect the meaning used in ERM. For instance, investment analysts prepare risk profiles to assess whether an organization is a sound investment and, likewise, rating agencies prepare them to decide how credit worthy an organization is. Such profiles take into account the industry, the demand for products and services, the quality of management, the competition, and the financial structure and strength of an organization. These are valid methodologies but have special purposes and define risk in terms of the users of that profile. In these cases, the investors or lenders. They are not risk profiles as used in ERM.

One also hears about developing a risk profile or a risk forecast of what an organization may look like at a future date. This may envision an organization's capital structure or target market. This again, however, is more of a useful strategic planning and visioning exercise.

Preparing a risk profile is truly generic. The same principles and methodologies apply whether an organization is public or private stock, not-for-profit, or government. Even a home environment interested in preparing one, could follow the same principles and methodologies. A true ERM risk profile should be holistic and reflect *all* risks to the organization's business objectives.

COMMON TYPES OF CORPORATE RISK PROFILES

Different types of corporate risk profiles are used to demonstrate and communicate key risk information. Each type serves a purpose best suited to an organization's needs and has features that help focus the attention of senior management and the board. For each type of risk profile, there are strengths and weaknesses just as there are advantages and disadvantages to the methodologies applied in gathering information for these profiles. The next section highlights three different types of commonly used corporate risk profiles: the top 10 list, the risk map, and the heat map.

The "Top 10" List

The simplest method of identifying, ranking, and sharing the top risks facing an organization is often referred to as a "top 10" list. The term "top 10" is familiar, easily understood, and denotes a short yet important list of risks. It is successfully used because it is not an exhaustive list that confuses and often becomes unmanageable. The secret lies in keeping it simple and easy to communicate.

Simply put, a top 10 risk profile provides a ranked listing of the most significant risks facing an organization and likely to impact the organization's ability to meet its stated objectives. A top 10 list should also provide trending information, such as whether a risk is getting more or less risky and a comparative rating of the risks at previous periods. (Special attention is given on how to prepare a top 10 list later.)

The Risk Map

A risk map (see Exhibit 11.1) is one of the most widely described ways to present the largest risks facing an organization. It is visually appealing, and easy to understand and describe. It usually consists of two axis: the vertical axis showing the potential impact of the risk and the horizontal axis showing the estimated likelihood of the

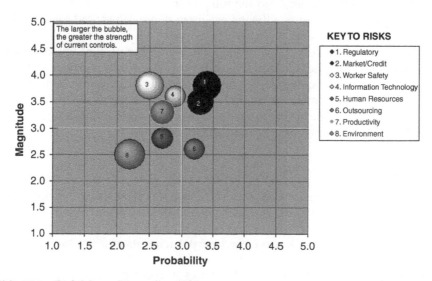

Exhibit 11.1 Risk Map—December 2006

risk occurring, both usually on a scale from 1 (low) to 5 (high). The map is often divided into four quadrants[4] —for analysis purposes—as follows:

1. High Impact/Low Likelihood: Risks falling into this quadrant (see upper left quadrant) are often of a crisis nature (e.g., ice storms, earthquakes) or described as "fat tail" events when applying "value at risk" thinking. Such events, because of their unpredictability, are often mitigated by use of insurance or disaster recovery planning.
2. Low Impact/Low Likelihood: Risks falling into this quadrant (see lower left quadrant) are typical of business as usual events that are not critical to the business but need to be either accepted or managed by normal operational means.
3. High Impact/High Likelihood: Risks falling into this quadrant (see upper right quadrant) are urgent and require the extensive attention of the board and management. Complete focus should be exercised until these have been mitigated to an acceptable level.
4. Low Impact/High Likelihood: Risks falling into this quadrant (see lower right quadrant) are often foreseeable or transactional type errors that need to be mitigated through procedural type controls to an acceptable cost/benefit level.

Risk maps are ideally best prepared during a risk workshop using voting technology.

Features that can be added to a risk map include:

- Mitigants: The adequacy of mitigants over each risk can be shown, for example, by the color or the size of the symbol (e.g., a bubble as shown in Exhibit 11.1) used for each risk, where small symbols show low levels of mitigation and large symbols show high levels of mitigation. This helps the reader to better understand the full picture.
- Trends: Arrows showing the increasing or decreasing trend for each risk can be helpful to readers.
- Risk versus controls chart: Risks can also be later plotted on another chart, reflecting both the magnitude and probability on the vertical axis and the adequacy of mitigants on the horizontal axis. This demonstrates whether there is an alignment of the mitigants with the severity of the risks. The chart helps ensure appropriate use of resources by identifying risks that are overcontrolled and those that are undercontrolled.

The Heat Map

A heat map is usually color-coded to show the levels of risks and mitigants[5] in a matrix format. Descriptions of the levels and format used can vary but would generally consist of a matrix of the risk sources and the organizational units. Heat maps are well suited for risk surveys where participants assign a rating or color to the risks.

A risk source heat map typically shows a generic list of risks, sometimes grouped by categories such as strategic, operational, and systemic with columns to the right showing the ratings for the severity of each risk and the adequacy of the related mitigants.

An organization heat map can list the organizational entities such as departments, locations, or product lines in the first column while, next to each entity, are color-coded squares identifying the level of each risk. High risk is usually denoted by red, medium risk by yellow, and low risk by green.

A more sophisticated application of this type of heat map could be used by a worldwide trading operation. The map may be designed to show the trading desk locations across the columns on the page with the various product risks listed down the side (see the example in Exhibit 11.2). Such an application is ideal for an online computerized reporting risk management system. In this instance, the CEO or head trader, can look at the computer screen showing a real-time heat map and then double click on any yellow or red square to show greater detail as to what is causing the color. If the CEO clicked on New York's precious metals' red square it would bring up a more detailed view of the New York operation and reveal that traders' desk profits have not been reconciled with the back office within the permitted time; hence, triggering a red flag to be turned on by the staff who are accountable as part of their duties.

Global Trading Risk Profile (Heat Map)

	London	New York	Toronto	Sydney
Bonds	Medium			
Equities			Medium	
Foreign exchange			Medium	
Interest rate		Medium		Medium
Precious metals		High		

New York Precious Metals Operations

	Traders	Middle Office	Back Office
Personnel			
Settlements			Medium
Reconciliations	High	Medium	High
Compliance			

Exhibit 11.2   Heat Map

Exhibit 11.3   Risk Information Gathering Alternatives

	Advantages	Disadvantages
Risk Workshop	Popular with participants due to efficient use of time and learning/sharing opportunities Can target groups of people Immediate results Often described as "magical" due to the enriched discussions and information shared*	High level of facilitation skills required Voting technology required Limited by geography Must have sufficient expertise and knowledge among the participants in the room
Structured Interview	Creates conversations Efficient use of interviewee time Face-to-face contact promotes and strengthens relationships, enhancing ERM for a risk-aware culture	Limited by geography High level of interview skills required, including familiarity with a wide variety of risk types No opportunity for dialogue among fellow decision makers Requires sufficient time to schedule and conduct interviews
Formal Survey	Can cover a larger number of participants** Consistent structure Well documented	Quality of responses may be an issue No conversations, no learning opportunity for respondents Sufficient preparation time is needed to compose questions Subject to delays

*As described in detail during an interview in an article titled "Q&A With Hydro One's Chief Risk Officer," by Matt Kelly in *Compliance Week*, January 25, 2005.
**For geographically dispersed organizations, surveys can be submitted to and consolidated electronically at head office, or be conducted locally using a single off-the-shelf risk management application that rolls up the results automatically electronically to the corporate computer system.

ADVANTAGES AND DISADVANTAGES OF INFORMATION-GATHERING METHODOLOGIES

There are a variety of ways to gather the information required to prepare risk profiles, as well as various advantages and disadvantages for each type of information gathering methodology used. Although the above comparative chart (Exhibit 11.3) depicts these, it is by no means exhaustive. Organizations should consider each methodology against their needs, resources, and capabilities.

HOW TO PREPARE A "TOP 10" RISK PROFILE—HYDRO ONE'S EXPERIENCE

In the first half of this chapter, we defined the purpose and uses of corporate risk profiles. Furthermore, we identified the most common types and the alternative methodologies for gathering information used in these risk profiles. This background knowledge is needed to proceed to the next part of this chapter, which focuses on how to prepare a top 10 risk profile and track its accuracy and usefulness. This section will cover in more detail significant aspects of what is involved in the preparation, consolidation, and documentation of this type of profile. Specifically, these aspects, in sequential order, include:

- Scheduling interviews and gathering background information.
- Preparing interview tools such as obtaining corporate business objectives, scanning events, listing potential risks, providing a list of prior risks, and compiling written notes.
- Summarizing the interview findings.
- Summarizing the risk ratings and trends.
- Drafting the top 10 risk profile.
- Reviewing the draft risk profile.
- Communicating the risk profile with the board or board committee.
- Tracking the results.

Step 1: Schedule Interviews and Gather Background Information

It is essential to develop a plan of action before embarking on the actual interviews. The duration, the resource requirements, and the level of detail all need to be considered in order to be most effective.

How Often Should a Top 10 Profile Be Prepared?

This is a key decision to ensure positive cooperation and feedback from organizational executives. For most organizations an annual profile may be too infrequent given the fluctuating changes in the marketplace and within the organization itself. On the other hand, a profile every quarter may be excessive, especially for organizations just starting ERM. A semi-annual profile is the most expedient interval to start. It can then be adjusted after some experimentation.

Who Should Be Interviewed and How Should Interviews Be Scheduled?

Hydro One's experience has shown that interviewing the top 40 executives and risk specialists,[6] draws the most efficient and balanced range of responses for an average-sized organization.[7] Ideally, interviews are conducted by two members of the ERM team, one who is facilitating the interview and the other who is taking detailed notes.

Scheduling a half-hour interview can be more easily accommodated than an hour-long interview. As well, all interviews should be scheduled within a set time period. A three-week time period is practical and provides a picture at a point in time without becoming blurred unless events affecting the organization change dramatically during the process (e.g., market collapse, earthquake, hostile takeover attempt).

What to Consider When Interviewing the CEO?

Since the CEO is the sponsor,[8] care is required in approaching interviews and sessions involving the CEO as his or her views need to be reflected in the product, while still leaving the opportunity to make further refinements based on consultation with other members of the management team and other sources of information. Thus, it may be appropriate to interview the CEO for thoughts on various risks but caution the CEO that once this information is consolidated with other interviews and sources a different risk profile may emerge. Ultimately, however, the CEO should be prepared to review and discuss the report with the executive team before it is finalized and shared with the board.

What Background Information Needs to Be Gathered?

At this point, key background information that can influence the risk profile should be gathered. This could include benchmarking information, performance measures, and other trend analyses that might be used as key risk indicators (see Chapter 8 on Key Risk Indicators), internal and external audit reports and results of risk workshops, both at the senior and line management levels.

In an ERM environment the interviews with senior management and risk specialists should be validated against other ERM information. Such other information ideally would include divisional risk assessments prepared as part of the annual business planning process, and risk assessments (e.g., from risk workshops) as part of major projects and initiatives throughout the year. The results of these divisional and project risk assessments should be consolidated and used as critical input to the corporate risk profile. Altogether, these significant sources of information should complement and validate each other with any significant differences investigated as to their cause.

Step 2: Prepare the Interview Tools

As with undertaking any kind of major project or new initiative, preparation is essential. Crafting a corporate risk profile is no different. The bulk of the work is in preparing the interview tools. Here, the Hydro One experience is used to explain what they are, how they are developed, and why they are needed.

Obtaining Corporate Business Objectives

Before proceeding with ERM, and the eventual top 10 list, clearly articulated corporate business objectives must be identified. Surprisingly, this information is not always readily available in some organizations, where major business objectives may be understood but are not officially documented. They could be manifested by the large sums of money spent on certain initiatives, buried in annual reports and other disclosures, or scattered throughout business planning documents. Hence, it is imperative to first compile and get executive agreement on a list of the top 8 or 10 corporate business objectives over the next few years. These objectives should be stated in measurable terms such as growing sales by 20 percent, achieving certain profit levels, expanding overseas to certain countries, and reaching specific safety or customer satisfaction targets. These are, however, not to be confused with key performance indicators (performance measures), which all too often are prepared on an annual basis only. Business objectives must not only be articulated in terms of stretch targets or new initiatives but also in terms of preserving shareholder value, corporate reputation, employee morale, and an organization's customer base.

For the remainder of the chapter, all further discussions about ERM and creating a top 10 profile will be framed in terms of risks to achieving corporate business objectives. In fact, the first matter raised at each interview should be to inform the interviewee that discussions will be focused on the risks to meeting the business objectives over the next few years.

Scanning of Events

One of the key inputs into preparing a corporate risk profile is having a good understanding of what external events have happened recently or might happen to impact the organization. This is sometimes referred to as an "environmental scan." A simple way to prepare this is to compile an ongoing file of newspaper clippings, research reports, articles, and other items depicting events that have happened that could impact the organization or its stakeholders.[9] Examples of these events include changes in governments, proposed and actual regulatory changes, stock market anomalies (e.g., inverted yield curves), surprising and relevant law suits raised or settled with similar businesses, disasters or crises. Compiled regularly, the file becomes a comprehensive compendium, which then needs to be summarized into one or two pages of the most impactful events or potential risk issues. It is subsequently distributed, in advance, to the interviewees or presented at the start of the interview with a qualifying statement that the summary is intended to remind the interviewees of what has happened since the last interview and get them thinking about what external events could impact the organization. Many interviewees find the summary informative and look forward to receiving it. It also provides them with an opportunity to identify, discuss, and even add additional events or items that may have been inadvertently omitted.

Prepare a List of Potential Risks

In many real-life examples of ERM, management is provided with and asked to rate, either a static list of risks, or to discuss risks without any prompts from the interviewer. As a result, interviewees do not always consider risks not already identified on the list provided or may not be responsive to general questions like "What keeps you awake at night?" At Hydro One, the practice is to bridge these two approaches and provide the interviewees with a list of past and potential risks at the start of the interview, urge them to be anticipatory in their thinking, and through gentle probing and discussion explore scenarios that could materialize into or create new risks.

What Is Presented in the List of Potential Risks? The list at Hydro One consists of brief descriptions of risks grouped into categories such as safety, regulatory and customer expectations. Each risk that was mentioned in the last risk profile is highlighted in the color denoting the previous risk rating. For example, red denotes high risks and yellow denotes medium risks. Risks that were not mentioned, because they were rated as low or are still evolving, are left uncolored and are referred to as "white spaces." Examples include pandemic risks, regulatory changes, and pending environmental legislation.

What Is the Objective of the List? All of the risks are listed in three columns on a large sheet of paper, which allows interviewees to quickly scan and focus on their areas of interest. Some interviewees spend most of the interview process just on their area of accountability or specialty. Others may choose to discuss the risks that are of particular concern to them. The objective to presenting these risks is to solicit opinions as to whether the risks are likely to impact the business and in what time frame. It requires skill on behalf of the interviewer to work with the various personality types, gain the interviewee's confidence, and retrieve accurate and appropriate information to prepare a valid risk profile.

Provide a Prior List of Top Risks   In addition, interviewees should be provided—at the onset of the interview—with a matrix of the prior list of top risks and their respective ratings as identified in the previous risk profile. (See Exhibit 11.4.) This matrix has additional blank columns for recording the interviewee's current ratings of risks, if different, and the expected trending, be it flat, upward, or downward. The interviewees are encouraged to provide their opinion prior to the end of the interview as to whether each rating should be adjusted and where they feel the trend is going. They are also asked whether any other risks should be included in the top 10 risks. A final column on the sheet is used for making brief comments by the interviewer.

Date			Executive/Risk Specialist Interviewed	
Risk Source	**Previous Risk Rating**	**Trend ↑Upward Downward↓**	**Current Rating (If Different)**	**Comments**
Customer expectations	**Very high**			
Condition of assets	**Very high**			
Government policy uncertainty	**High**			
Regulatory uncertainty	**High**			
Human resources	**High**			
Adequate electricity supply	**Medium**			
Employee accidents	**Medium**			
Cost reduction	**Medium**			
Other:				
Other:				

Exhibit 11.4   Risk Profile—Interview Sheet

Hydro One's experience shows that some interviewees like this format and proceed to provide their assessments of each risk and add any new ones. Other interviewees prefer not to provide an opinion on the ratings and trending of these risks, but will speak knowledgeably about the risks and the relevant mitigants and provide valuable qualitative data and perspectives. Hydro One caters to these differences and does not impose a single expectation of each interviewee. This is where ERM may be considered as much an art as a science.

Written Notes   With most interviews there can be a generous amount of discussion and information collected. It can be a challenge, therefore, to facilitate an interview while also taking copious notes. Ideally, then, there should be two interviewers from the ERM group, one team member leading the interview and the other team member taking detailed notes.

Feedback from the Interviewees on the Interview Process   For several years now, Hydro One has been conducting these interviews. During that time, there has been positive feedback from the interviewees on the process involved. Overall, the interviewees have commented on learning more about the risks to the organization as a whole and thinking about them more on a practical level. The interviewers have also found the dialogue to be nondefensive, allowing the interview to play a key role in ensuring the business objectives are well understood throughout the broader management team.

Step 3: Summarize the Interview Findings

Once all of the interviews have been completed it is time to summarize the findings. Often there is a tight deadline in order to present the results to the management team, and subsequently to a board level committee or the board itself. In a centralized organization only a few people may be conducting or summarizing the interviews, while in a large worldwide organization it may be done by local champions who then provide summarized documentation for consolidation at the head office by the ERM group.

Helpful Tips When Summarizing
A helpful method used at Hydro One is to prepare individual sheets for each major risk with two columns:

1. The first identifies the sources of risk and causes for any increases in risk.
2. The second denotes the mitigation efforts and causes for any decreases in risk.

Each comment listed in either of the above two columns is annotated with the initials of the interviewee for quick reference and follow-up if required to any specific issue. Although all interviews are treated confidentially and sources are never revealed, the practice is to maintain documentation of the original interview notes and to occasionally follow up with the interviewee for further clarification as required.

These individual risk sheets, when completed, become a summary of the key facts and descriptions, thus providing the basis for compiling or updating the risk profile. If there are conflicting views on any risks, they would need to be explored and validated.

Step 4: Summarize the Risk Ratings and Trends

Wherever interviewees have provided new ratings and/or trends for a risk these need to be recorded and tallied on a spreadsheet to determine whether the overall ratings or trends should indeed be changed.

The decision to add a risk or change a risk rating comes from one or more of the following:

- The key issues from the summarized interview findings.
- Risk ratings collected from the interviewees.
- Trends indicated by the interviewees.

Sometimes the ERM group may have to draft descriptions of evolving risks on a pro forma basis to be discussed with the executive team for inclusion in the profile. This is because the ERM group may believe that the risks, which have not been prioritized before, are escalating. In describing these new risks the ERM group needs to substantiate the escalation with findings from the interviews and other evidence.

Step 5: Draft the Top 10 Risk Profile

Once the interviews have been conducted and the results summarized, the risk manager is faced with deciding how best to communicate the profile. The following section provides some helpful principles to guide the crafting of the document and any related presentations.

Keep It Simple
When drafting the corporate risk profile, Hydro One follows some basic principles and best practices. First, the document is relatively simple and easy to understand. This goes back to the guiding principle of keeping ERM simple. Second, the document is a combination of descriptions and an easy-to-understand chart. One of its attractions is that it is written in plain lay English rather than legalese.

Key Foundational Elements
The document itself is divided into three parts. The first part focuses on foundational information such as the process followed, the number of interviews completed, the time frame for the assessment (e.g., three years forward), and the risks that have been removed from or added to the profile since the last one. The second part consists of a matrix (see Exhibit 11.5). This matrix lists the top risks, shows the current ratings, trends, and previous ratings for comparison, and references the risk descriptions on subsequent pages. The third part consists of a half-page narrative for each risk. Each narrative describes the sources of the risk, the business objectives impacted, and the mitigants in place or planned.

Risk Source	Page	Trend	Risk Rating July 2003	Risk Rating January 2003	Risk Rating January 2002
Adequate electricity supply	3	↗	Very High	Very High	High
Performance, productivity, and people ("Getting the Work Done")	4	↗	Very High	Very High	Medium High
Government policy uncertainty	5	→	Very High	High	High
Regulatory uncertainty	5	↘	High	Very High	Very High
Employee accidents	6	→	High	High	Very High
Capacity of transmission network	7	↗	High	Medium High	Medium
Condition of transmission network	8	↘	Medium High	Medium High	Medium
Information technology	8	↗	Medium High	Medium	Low
Condition of distribution assets	9	↘	Medium	Medium High	High
Customer expectations	9	↘	Medium	Medium High	High
Environment	10	↘	Medium	Medium	Medium

Exhibit 11.5 Risk Profile Matrix

Hydro One evaluates and describes risks as "residual risks," in other words, after taking into account ＿＿ent and planned mitigating actions. It does not use the term "inherent ris＿ ＿＿ ＿n rare cases such as the weather.[10]

Tips to Cons＿ ＿itial Draft
Great ca＿ ＿ e initial profile as it may be the first such docume＿ ＿＿. Recognizing Hydro One's experience in using t＿ ＿uidelines and tips follow:

- Assess ＿ ＿he management style, the CEO's known preferences a＿ ＿ any sensitive areas and issues. This knowledge may help g＿ ＿＿ter of the profile as to how risks should be described in light of the ＿＿umstances and personalities involved.
- "Take Baby Steps." Describe the essence of the risks in a broad enough manner so readers can relate rather than having to dive into overly detailed descriptions that may not be as universal in understanding and application.
- Use the corporate vernacular. Play back corporate terms and examples that will resonate and be easily understood by management and the board.

- Portray the corporate risk profile in a palatable fashion. Practically speaking, the profile should be viewed as a reflection of management's understanding of the key risks faced by the enterprise and the mitigants underway or planned to manage them. This is not to say that risks should be downplayed or sugar-coated. Rather they can be expressed as a realistic "roadmap" or opportunity for improvement. Trying to cover too much detail, or to be too stark in the initial depiction of risks, is likely to threaten not only future exercises in risk profiling, but the entire ERM process.
- Capture and describe any wide divergent views of risk. It is often defined as uncertainty about future events. Therefore, where it is apparent that there is a wide divergence of views on the impact, probability, or adequacy of the mitigation of the risks, it is important to capture and describe this uncertainty in the profile. Avoid suggesting a level of precision about a rating or number that may not reflect reality. The reason is that mathematical formulae may portray exact numbers and therefore imply greater certainty than may be appropriate.
- Refrain from using strict predefined categories or descriptions of risk. In practice risks evolve, get addressed, and often diminish either due to management's mitigation strategies, changes in strategic objectives, or due to external factors. Hydro One's risk descriptions are customized and continue to evolve, split, and regroup much like amoeba in a Petri dish. By opting to customize categories and descriptions, the profile is a more accurate reflection of the evolving environment. It does, however, require greater skill and knowledge of the business.

An Example of Hydro One's Evolving Risk Categories

For illustrative purposes, we provide an example of how a risk at Hydro One evolved as did the related risk profile descriptions. Several years ago, Hydro One labeled a risk as "asset condition" to reflect the potential impact on its objectives in the event of asset failures. It became evident later on that there were fundamental distinguishing risk characteristics between its transmission assets and its distribution assets. As a result, Hydro One split this risk grouping and gave each type of asset its own risk category and rating. As the electricity generation and demand locations started to shift in the province of Ontario, Hydro One then split the transmission asset risk into two separate parts. This split currently reflects the risks due to those from the existing condition of these assets versus those associated with not having sufficient assets in the right physical locations to meet growing shifts in generation and demand. More recently, distributed generation (e.g., windmills) has mushroomed and will require a multimillion dollar upgrade of the distribution grid. This has resulted in a new risk category being formed. Exhibit 11.6 shows the evolution of the single initial risk category, asset condition, into four discrete risk categories.

Step 6: Review the Draft Risk Profile

Once the risk profile has been prepared or updated by the ERM group, it is then presented to a management committee. Refinements are made and, in some cases, additional research may be required to resolve any questions of fact that are noted.

Risk Category	2002	2004	2006	2008
Asset condition[a]	X			
Transmission assets—condition[b]		X	X	X
Transmission assets—capacity[c]			X	X
Distribution assets—condition[d]		X	X	X
Distribution assets—generation connections[e]				X

Notes:

a. Risk arising from aging asset base and lack of current asset information.

b. and d. Split of (a) into separate asset classes for transmission and distribution assets.

c. Increasing risk due to geographic shifts in demand and generation locations.

d. Distribution assets—condition split out from (a) above.

e. Risk due to need to significantly change design of assets to accommodate new sources of widely distributed renewable energy (e.g., windmills).

Exhibit 11.6   The Evolution of Asset Risks

The management committee, led by the CEO, takes ownership of the profile (by accepting or approving it).

Step 7: Communicate the Risk Profile with the Board or Board Committee

As mentioned earlier in the chapter, the primary purpose of the corporate risk profile is to share the key risks facing the organization with the board. The risk profile should then be shared with the full board at least annually. The profile should be presented to the board or a delegated board committee by the Chief Risk Officer or another member of senior management on behalf of the CEO and the management team. This is the practice at Hydro One. As part of good corporate governance, the board should also insist on viewing updated profiles on a periodic basis or requesting interim updates during a crisis.

A board subcommittee may also be charged as the designated forum for championing and monitoring ERM. Often it falls to the overburdened audit committee, but hopefully in the future more boards will appoint a specific risk committee to monitor ERM and ensure the oversight of all major risks. Such a committee would ideally be comprised of the chairs of all other board subcommittees.

The secondary purpose of the profile is to provide an important base for strategic planning. The profile reminds executive management and the board of the risks they currently face under the existing strategic plan. Thus, future deliberations as to changes in the board's and management's vision, and the undertaking of new initiatives and exploration of opportunities, can be framed in terms of how the existing risks might then be affected by new strategic directions.

Step 8: Track the Results

There are a number of ways in which the accuracy and usefulness of the corporate risk profile can be monitored. The most obvious is the passage of time. Are unforeseen risks manifested over time and are organizations surprised by a risk that was not identified, discussed, evaluated, and mitigated to the extent deemed appropriate by management and the board? Should a major previously unidentified risk surface after a risk profile was prepared, management and the board must review and understand how this happened. More to the point, what was missed in the process that allowed such a risk to go undetected or unreported?

Another way to monitor the usefulness of the corporate risk profile is to compare how money and resources are allocated relative to the top 10 risks identified. For instance, is the board presented with proposals to approve expenditures that do not align with the risk profile? If resources and management attention are not allocated according to the risk profile the board should probe into whether the profile was inaccurate or why the need for additional resources was not thoroughly thought through.

CONCLUSION

In this chapter, we have seen how vital the corporate risk profile is to the overall ERM process. A distinction was drawn between a risk profile prepared for ERM as a practical management and governance tool and other types of risk profiles prepared for different purposes either within the organization or by others about the organization. Although there are varying levels of sophistication and effort that can be expended on preparing risk profiles, the chapter described a proven methodology that can be used by organizations getting started in ERM or those that are having difficulty implementing it. In essence, a corporate risk profile:

- Helps to align the understanding of business objectives and related risks between the board, executive management, and line management.
- Helps to ensure significant risks are understood in a structured and consistent framework.
- Plays an integral part in strategic planning and resource allocation.
- Assists in marketing the value of ERM by demonstrating how the process works and how it adds value.

NOTES

1. ISO defines a risk profile as "a description of a set of risks" and risk as "the effect of uncertainty on objectives" (ISO/IEC CD 2 *Guide 73* as of April 1, 2008).
   HM Treasury's The Orange Book: Management of Risk Principles and Concepts (October 2004) defines a Risk Profile as "the documented and prioritized overall assessment of the range of specific risks faced by an organization."

The *2002 Risk Management Standard* produced by the Institute of Risk Management (UK) and the Institute of Insurance and Risk Managers (UK) defines a Risk Profile thus in section 4.5: "The result of the risk analysis process can be used to produce a risk profile which gives a significance rating to each risk and provides a tool for prioritizing risk treatment efforts. This ranks each identified risk so as to give a view of the relative importance."

2. Hydro One Inc. is the largest electricity transmission and distribution company in Ontario, Canada. It has total assets of about Can\$13.8 billion and has 1.3 million customers. It has been preparing semi-annual risk profiles since 1999 based on interviews with executives and risk specialists (Note 8). These profiles are validated periodically by comparison with the results from risk workshops.

3. A specific number of years forward (i.e., more than just one, unless a crisis is being evaluated) should be used for consistency. Hydro One uses three years.

4. James DeLoach in his 2000 book *Enterprise-Wide Risk Management: Strategies for linking risk and opportunity* provides an excellent analysis of the actions to be taken to address each of these quadrants (135–137).

5. Mitigants may be defined as all of the actions taken by an organization to reduce risks, including such actions as internal controls, insurance, and lobbying. The term "control" is often used by auditors in referring to risk management. However, mitigants encompass a much broader range of initiatives and actions than just controls.

6. Risk specialists have roles in specialized areas such as safety, environment, treasury, insurance, finance, marketing, public relations, and customer care.

7. This conclusion is based on our experience over a four year period (2000–2003) at Hydro One, with approximately 5,000 employees, where the bottom-up risk workshop data from approximately 40 workshops per year (involving about 400 staff) was compared to the data gathered from the top 40 executives and risks specialists.

8. Sponsor: At Hydro One, the role of the Chief Risk Officer has been positioned as a facilitation and support function. Accordingly, risk workshops and risk profiles are always positioned as providing assistance to a "sponsor." The sponsor is held accountable for providing leadership for the assignment and is usually identified as the most senior executive involved in the assignment. For a corporate risk profile the CEO is identified as the sponsor.

9. Stakeholders include customers, suppliers, shareholders, regulators, the public, and employees.

10. See "Mistake #1: Inherent Risk is a Workable Basis for ERM" in "Ten Common Misconceptions About Enterprise Risk Management" by John R.S. Fraser, Hydro One, and Betty J. Simkins, Oklahoma State University, *Journal of Applied Corporate Finance*, vol. 19, Fall 2007.

REFERENCES

DeLoach, James W. 2000. *Enterprise-wide risk management: Strategies for linking risk and opportunity*. Upper Saddle River, NJ: Prentice Hall.

Fraser, John R.S., and Betty J. Simkins. 2007. Ten common misconceptions about enterprise risk management. *Journal of Applied Corporate Finance*.

HM Treasury. 2004. *The orange book: Management of risk principles and concepts*.

The Institute of Risk Management (UK) and the Institute of Insurance and Risk Managers (UK). 2002. *The Risk Management Standard*.

ISO/IEC CD 2. 2008. *Guide 73* (April 1).

Kelly, Matt. 2005. Q&A with Hydro One's chief risk officer. *Compliance Week* (January 25).

ABOUT THE AUTHOR

John Fraser is the Vice President, Internal Audit & Chief Risk Officer of Hydro One Networks Inc., one of Canada's largest electricity transmission and distribution companies. He is an Ontario and Canadian Chartered Accountant, a Fellow of the Association of Chartered Certified Accountants (UK), a Certified Internal Auditor, and a Certified Information Systems Auditor. He has more than 30 years' experience in the risk and control field mostly in the financial services sector, including areas such as finance, fraud, derivatives, safety, environmental, computers, and operations. He is currently the Chair of the Advisory Committee of the Conference Board of Canada's Strategic Risk Council, a Practitioner Associate Editor of the *Journal of Applied Finance*, and a past member of the Risk Management and Governance Board of the Canadian Institute of Chartered Accountants. He is a recognized authority on enterprise risk management and has co-authored three academic papers on ERM—published in the *Journal of Applied Corporate Finance* and the *Journal of Applied Finance*.

CHAPTER 12

How to Allocate Resources Based on Risk

JOSEPH P. TONEGUZZO
Director—Implementation & Approvals, Power System Planning,
Ontario Power Authority

INTRODUCTION

Optimal allocation of resources to maximize the probability of achieving the business objectives of an enterprise is a key deliverable of the business planning process undertaken annually by leading companies. This chapter describes a practical business framework for allocating resources, assumed in this chapter to be company expenditures, based on managing risks that jeopardize the successful achievement of company objectives. Resource allocation based on identifying and managing risks is a common business practice for enterprises that own, operate, maintain, and replace a portfolio of industrial or civil assets, such as energy, transportation, and hospitality sector companies and government entities responsible for managing public infrastructure. Although the discussion is focused on the optimal allocation of resources based on risk, the concepts have also been applied in businesses that focus on opportunities or a combination of opportunities and risks.

The Risk Focused Resource Allocation Framework (RFRAF) described is based on about a decade of best practice learning of this specific subject area by the electric power industry. This business sector has been studying, developing, implementing, operating, and improving risk-focused resource allocation processes to improve business performance, as part of the evolution of the industry toward competition. During the past 10 years, the regulated vertically integrated (generation, transmission, and distribution) businesses historically dominating this industry were unbundled in many global jurisdictions. The primary purpose of moving to this new business model was to stimulate competition between generators and drive efficiencies from the natural monopoly-based transmission and distribution functions, through more focused regulation in the sector. These changes in the business environment resulted in the electric power industry embarking on a series of international studies[1] to establish and improve business models for the optimal allocation of resources to deliver the improved business performance demanded by the shareholders, regulators, and other stakeholders involved in this industry. To streamline the regulatory process, the regulated transmission and distribution businesses within this sector developed resource allocation frameworks having a high degree of transparency, consistency of results, and efficiency of execution. These attributes of transparency, consistency, and efficiency should be valued within the business planning model used by any enterprise. The international effort to study, develop, implement, and improve these business models and supporting decision-making frameworks is expected to be of value to any industry that must optimally dispatch finite resources to achieve company objectives.

The business framework discussed has been developed and refined by the electric power industry after considerable analysis of similar frameworks used in other large-scale regulated and competitive businesses. The elements of the framework are generic in nature and have been utilized in many competitive and regulated businesses to develop annual business plans that require the prioritization of expenditures to deal with:

- Growth in demand for products or services.
- Ongoing operating and maintenance (O&M) work to sustain the business or its facilities.
- Work associated with replacing end-of-life facilities.
- Efficiency improvements to lower costs and/or improve performance.

Examples of such businesses include the oil and gas industry, facilities management, the hospitality sector, infrastructure services, fleet management, the airline and aerospace industry, the shipping industry, and a range of other businesses.

The chapter focuses on the key design elements of an effective RFRAF and includes a discussion of some key lessons learned while developing, implementing, operating, and improving the framework.

To facilitate the discussion, this chapter has been structured in accordance with the following six key components of the framework:

1. Risk policy and a center of excellence for risk management.
2. Translating strategic objectives into risk-based concepts.
3. Risk-based business processes and organizational considerations.
4. Concepts, methods, and models enabling risk identification, evaluation, mitigation, prioritization, and management.
5. Information requirements and challenges.
6. Measures of effectiveness for continuous improvement.

Also included are some practical lessons and best practices for managing the interdependencies between these key operational elements. Understanding these interdependencies is critical to the overall effectiveness of the RFRAF.

The RFRAF, which is discussed within this chapter, is a subset of both the higher level Enterprise Risk Management Framework (ERMF) and the corporate level Business Planning Framework (BPF). The ERMF is a corporate-wide, continuous process encompassing all aspects of the business, including the processes necessary for the ongoing management of risk in real time. The ERMF is therefore at a higher level than the RFRAF described in this chapter. The BPF is also a corporate-wide process that is typically conducted on an annual basis and includes setting the basic business assumptions to be used in all business evaluations within the company (such as cost of capital, inflation, external cost escalation factors, relevant

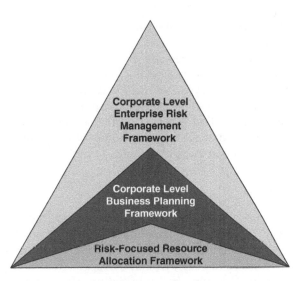

Exhibit 12.1 Major Business Frameworks for Achieving Business Objectives

exchange rates, growth projections, effects of competition, productivity targets, benchmarking).

Exhibit 12.1 shows the relationship between these major business frameworks and the RFRAF, which underpins these major corporate level business processes.

Risk management is the process whereby an organization systematically identifies, assesses, evaluates, manages, reports, and monitors risks on an ongoing basis to ensure that barriers to achieving the strategic objectives of the business are identified and managed, as necessary. The typical steps within a comprehensive risk management process are well documented within the literature on this subject.[2]

RISK POLICY AND A CENTER OF EXCELLENCE FOR RISK MANAGEMENT

Two fundamental ingredients for the successful development and implementation of a RFRAF are:

1. The existence of a corporate level risk management policy outlining the overall risk management strategy and objectives.
2. The establishment of a center of excellence (COE) within the company, comprised of senior management and working level staff interested in championing the development, implementation, operation, and continuous improvement of the required business processes and related concepts.

Key Policy Elements

In addition to outlining the overall risk management strategy and objectives, the corporate level risk management policy should also document the various risk-based definitions and the roles, responsibilities, accountabilities and authorities necessary to achieve the objectives of risk management. Risk has been defined as "the combination of the probability of an event and its consequence."[3]

Based on this generally accepted definition, risk can therefore be considered a two-dimensional concept requiring an understanding of the *probability* of an undesirable event occurring and the expected *consequence* should the event occur. The corporate level risk management policy and the related policy implementation processes, procedures, and concepts must build on this definition and develop risk identification, assessment, evaluation, mitigation, and resource allocation methods and tools that are consistent with this definition. Subsequent sections in this chapter describe methods and tools that are founded on the basis of this important definition, which must be understood by all staff involved in the business planning effort.

Center of Excellence

Championing, developing, implementing, operating, and improving a RFRAF requires a substantial and sustained effort within the company. A critical first step in the development and implementation phase is the identification of staff from the senior management, middle management, and professional ranks of the company who are committed to participating in this initiative. The existence of a core group of staff from these various levels interested in championing and developing the required policies with the board of directors and executives of the company and developing/implementing the required enabling business processes is critical to the successful establishment of the RFRAF. Experience has shown that the COE does not need to be a specific organizational unit dedicated to this initiative. Given the need to spread the principles and knowledge of risk-based concepts throughout the company and the multidisciplined nature of risk assessments, the COE is most effective when it is comprised of staff who hold regular positions within the various line units. The members of the COE-Team must, however, allocate sufficient time to take on the additional responsibilities for overseeing the development, implementation, operation, and continuous improvement of the RFRAF. This dispersed COE-Team should also be formally constituted and meet regularly to develop and monitor the progress of implementation initiatives and to help overcome operational challenges or barriers associated with improvement initiatives. The COE-Team should also be involved in specific strategic and operational process steps, within the framework, such as updating the key decision factors used within the RFRAF, as the business environment changes. These key decision factors will be defined and discussed in more detail in the following sections. Experience has shown that this dispersed team, embedded within the various line units, can effectively act as champions and change agents for new processes and methods. Members of the COE-Team are also in a good position to identify new opportunities for improvement, train senior staff across the company, and promote new processes, methods, and models to senior management and working level professional staff.

Translating Strategic Objectives into Risk-Based Concepts

The effective allocation of resources based on risk requires company staff responsible for business planning to understand the relationship between the business objectives of the company, the operational and strategic risks that may jeopardize the achievement of those objectives, and the risk-based concepts that enable the systematic identification, evaluation, and prioritization of the various risks. A primary design element of a RFRAF is a methodology that establishes the relationship between the strategic objectives, the operational and strategic risks of the business, and the risk-based concepts that enable identifying, quantifying, comparing, and organizing the various risks in order of importance.

The methodology typically used to establish these relationships is to involve the company leadership team in a workshop designed to develop the correlation between the strategic business objectives (SBOs), the detailed measures of success or key performance indicators (KPIs), and the degree of tolerance within the company for deviations from the KPIs, termed risk tolerances (RTs). This workshop is also used to inform the business leaders of the risk based concepts utilized within the RFRAF. Having a common understanding at the leadership level of the risk-based concepts is critical to the successful development of the framework. Experience has shown that utilizing a top-down process for establishing the degree of risk tolerance to shortfalls in attaining each specific KPI is an effective approach for determining the appetite for risk inherent within the company. The final product of the workshop is an information source that identifies and consolidates the relationships between the SBOs, KPIs, RTs, and the risk-based concepts. This product, termed the corporate risk matrix (CRM), provides critical risk-based information and indicators to facilitate identifying risks, conducting detailed risk assessments, and developing evaluation methods and models. The CRM also serves as an effective guideline enabling the consistent evaluation and prioritization of risks and is an excellent communication tool for use with line staff involved in business planning. Utilities in the electric power industry use products of this nature as an integral part of business planning.[4]

As indicated in the previous section, risk is "the combination of the probability of an event and its consequence." The approach for establishing the relationships between the SBOs, KPIs, RTs, and risk-based concepts must therefore deal with these two domains of event consequences and probabilities.

THE CONSEQUENCE DOMAIN

Establishing KPIs linked to the SBOs has been a common business practice for effectively managing companies for many years. However, in order to effectively allocate resources based on risk, having the KPIs is not sufficient. It is also necessary to determine the degree of tolerance that the leadership team of the company has for deviations from each specific KPI. The higher the tolerance for deviations from KPIs the more the company may profit by avoiding expenditures and keeping costs low. However, inadequate expenditures in critical business areas increase the likelihood of missing KPI targets and the related SBOs critical to the mid-term to long-term success of the company. Therefore establishing the degree of tolerance to deviations from the KPIs, through the development of formal RTs, is a fundamental design element of the framework. See Exhibit 12.2.

Exhibit 12.2 SBO/KPI/RT Hierarchy

As an example, the power industry described in the introduction may have the following five SBOs within the five-year business planning period:

1. Become a first quartile performer in delivering reliable service to the customer base.
2. Maintain a high level of customer satisfaction and retain electrical load (revenue) by keeping rates to customers at existing levels.
3. Increase net income by x%.
4. Maintain high standards of public and employee safety.
5. Maintain good corporate reputation.

These strategic objectives would need to be translated into specific reliability, efficiency, and profitability targets. These specific targets must be meaningful to the line staff responsible for assessing business risks in the operational time frame and identifying the work and expenditures required to mitigate unacceptable risks during business planning.

Exhibit 12.3 provides a sample breakdown of the linkages between the SBOs and the KPIs.

The RTs associated with each KPI are categorized into a number of consequence levels from minor to catastrophic. A good practice in developing the planning consequence levels is to use a five-point scale. Practical application of the framework has shown that using the five-point scale provides sufficient granularity of analysis and allows for adequate degree of freedom when describing the implications of each tolerance level and the related response required by the company under each situation, as follows:

1. **Minor**—Noticeable disruption to the achievement of results. This outcome would result in response from departmental professional and trades staff accountable for the issue, usually under routine procedures.
2. **Moderate**—Material deterioration in the achievement of results. This outcome would result in response from departmental management staff and the potential for establishing a dedicated working level, multidisciplined team to resolve.
3. **Major**—Significant deterioration in achievement of results. This outcome would result in response from divisional management staff and may require the formulation of interdepartmental working level teams, with management oversight to resolve.
4. **Severe**—Fundamental threat to operating results. This outcome would result in immediate senior management attention and the formulation of a dedicated management team and working teams to identify and resolve the underlying issues.
5. **Catastrophic/Worst Case**—Results threaten the survival of the company in its current form. This outcome would result in full-time senior management attention and the formation of dedicated full-time management teams and working level teams to identify and resolve the underlying issues.

Exhibit 12.4 outlines some representative RTs for three KPIs associated with Exhibit 12.3.

Exhibit 12.3 Strategic Business Objectives and Key Performance Indicator Relationship

Strategic Business Objective	Key Success Factor	Key Performance Indicator
First Quartile Reliability	Improve overall system reliability by a% over the business planning period.	Reduce frequency of system outages by b% in Northern Service Areas and c% in Southern Service Areas.
No Increase in Customer Rates	Improve productivity by d%, exceeding inflationary expectations with sufficient margin to meet net income targets.	Unit cost reduction e%/yr for all work programs. Work program accomplishment 100%.
Increase Net Income by x%	Obtain regulatory approval for increased Return on Equity (ROE), based on benchmark studies of ROE in other jurisdictions and providing regulator with assurance of no rate increases. Reduce O&M expenditures by f% within 3 years.	Successful regulatory filing for increased return on equity within next 2 years. 70% of O&M savings from consolidation of operations centers, work centers, and warehouses and 30% of savings from a maintenance optimization program to be implemented for all key asset groups over next 2 years.
Maintain Public and Employee Safety	Stay within good historic safety levels experienced by the company.	Historical levels of frequency and severity of public and employee safety incidents do not degrade.
Maintain Good Corporate Reputation	Public Profile—Positive industry, national, state, and local media attention on high level of service reliability, low rates, and good environmental performance. Employee satisfaction high; skills and competencies align with company requirements.	At least one article per year in major industry publication, national, state, and local newspapers outlining high quality of industry performance in the areas of service reliability, low cost, and safety and environmental performance. Maintain satisfaction scores at high levels and all required employee training completed.

The CRM is used by all staff involved in the business planning effort to assist in identifying risk events that may adversely impact the KPIs under a scenario where no incremental risk treatment is applied to the identified event. This is termed the "do-nothing" scenario. The CRM is also useful in assessing the adequacy and cost-effectiveness of risk mitigation alternatives/initiatives.

Experience with the application of the CRM indicates that some of the corporate level KPIs and related RTs do not always correlate well with the risks experienced by line staff responsible for the daily operation or annual planning of the business. In these cases, it has been found useful to develop another level of

Exhibit 12.4   Key Performance Indicators and Risk Tolerance Relationships

Key Performance Indicator	Risk Tolerance (Planning Consequences)
Reduce frequency of system outages by b% in Northern Service Areas and c% in Southern Service Areas	Minor—Improvement only 75% of expectation Moderate—Improvement only 50% of expectation Major—No improvement from recent history Severe—Degrades below recent historical levels Catastrophic—Degrades below regulatory compliance level
Unit Cost Reduction d%/yr for all work programs	Minor—Achieve 75% of expectation Moderate—Achieve 50% of expectation Major—No reduction from recent history Severe—Increases 5% above recent history Catastrophic—Increases 10% above recent history
Work Program Accomplishment 100%	Minor—Achieve 90% of target Moderate—Achieve 80% of target Major—Achieve 70% of target Severe—Achieve 60% of target Catastrophic—Achieve 50% of target

detail below the KPIs. These more detailed indicators termed planning indicators (PIs) provide working level staff with detailed measures that can be directly related to local or departmental level risks and understood by the operations or planning staff. In the utility example, the SBO for achieving first quartile reliability and the related KPI for improving overall service area reliability may not be meaningful to working level operations and planning staff. These staff members are only capable of identifying, assessing, and mitigating risks at the local area (subservice area) level. In these cases the KPI, developed by the top-down process, should be cascaded to a more detailed level to provide guidance for staff directly involved in the risk identification and mitigation effort. The following Exhibit 12.5 provides an example of how a KPI can be cascaded to a more detailed level.

It should be noted that this more detailed level requires the availability of a reliability methodology, capable of establishing the required reliability contribution from local areas to the overall service area.

The SBOs, KPIs, PIs, and RTs should be reviewed annually as part of the routine initiation of the business planning process or whenever the business objectives are modified. Given that the RTs can be sensitive to changes in the business environment, it is also a good practice to review the RTs whenever a change to the operational or strategic business environment is identified by one of the lines of business. In the following electric utility example, if specific equipment failure rates began to increase (thereby effecting system reliability) and/or the regulator were to increase penalties for noncompliance of reliability performance, the RTs and PIs would need to be reviewed by the COE-Team.

Another good practice within this portion of the framework is to utilize the KPIs as part of the regular business reporting process. This ensures staff members involved in the process recognize that the risks they identify and manage within the framework directly influence the performance of the company. In addition,

Exhibit 12.5 Key Performance Indicator/Planning Indicator/Risk Tolerance Relationship

Key Performance Indicator	Planning Indicator	Risk Tolerance (Planning Consequences)
Improve frequency of system outages by b% in Northern Service Area and c% in Southern Service Area	Improve frequency of system outages by b% in Northern Service Area by improving the five local areas as follows: Local Area 1—20% Local Area 2—10% Local Area 3—20% Local Area 4—30% Local Area 5—20%	Minor—Improvement only 75% of expectation Moderate—Improvement only 50% of expectation Major—No improvement from recent history Severe—Degrades below recent historical levels Catastrophic—Degrades below regulatory compliance level
	Improve frequency of system outages by c% in Southern Service Area by improving the four local areas as follows: Local Area 1—25% Local Area 2—10% Local Area 3—25% Local Area 4—40%	Minor—Improvement only 75% of expectation Moderate—Improvement only 50% of expectation Major—No improvement from recent history Severe—Degrades below recent historical levels Catastrophic—Degrades below regulatory compliance level

when company performance results in underachievement for specific KPIs, the corrective actions should be consistent with the threshold levels identified by the CRM. Maintaining this consistency and communicating it to staff validates the importance of the KPIs, PIs, RTs, and the framework to company staff. The consistent application of the risk framework also ensures resources are regularly adjusted to achieve the required performance results.

The Probability Domain

Risk analysis includes identifying events in the internal or external business environment, which could compromise the achievement of one or more business objectives. It is not sufficient however to simply identify undesirable events and the related business consequences. Risk analysis also requires determining the probability (or likelihood) of the event actually occurring within the discrete time frame being assessed. For the purpose of this discussion, the time frame of interest is the business planning period, typically between one and five years.

Exhibit 12.6 provides the categories and related probability levels typically used in business planning and risk prioritization processes. The probability scale

Exhibit 12.6 Representative Categories and Probability Levels for Assigning Probabilities to Risk Events

Probability Categories	Expectation of Event Frequency in years	Probability in Any Given Year	Probability in Planning Period (5 years)
Very Likely	> 1 in 2	> 0.45	> 95%
Likely	1 in 2 to 1 in 5	0.45 *to* 0.19	95% *to* 65%
Medium	1 in 5 *to* 1 in 20	0.19 *to* 0.05	65% *to* 25%
Unlikely	1 in 20 *to* 1 in 100	0.05 *to* 0.011	25% *to* 5%
Remote	< 1 in 100	< 0.011	< 5%

for evaluating the likelihood of undesirable events occurring should provide both a sufficient range of probability categories and adequate distinction between the various categories. Experience and evaluation of good practices has determined that developing five categories of probability ranging from "Remote" to "Very Likely" provides a good range for segmenting undesirable events for the purpose of identifying, evaluating, controlling, and optimizing risks over the business planning period. Experience and evaluation of good practices has also established that the probability levels should range from less than 1 percent for the Remote category to about 90 percent for the Very Likely category.

The Integration of Business Objectives/Risk Events/Risk Concepts

Consolidating the consequence and probability concepts described in the above sections results in identifying a two-dimensional "risk space" with event consequence represented on one axis and probability (or likelihood) represented on the other, as shown in Exhibit 12.7.

The policy discussed earlier should identify senior management as responsible for determining the level of unacceptable risk for each specific corporate level KPI. This is represented by the red (unacceptable risk) zone in Exhibit 12.7. Experience with the framework has shown that having senior management establish the unacceptable region of risk, and the actions that must be taken for intermediate risk levels, in advance of the development of the business plan is necessary for effective risk identification and analysis. Once the unacceptable region of risk is identified, any internal operational or external business events determined to be within this unacceptable region must be effectively controlled. The least cost risk mitigation alternative for effectively controlling "unacceptable events" will be scheduled as a nondiscretionary expenditure, within the associated expenditure prioritization process. Examples of unacceptable risks could include severe safety events, violations of mandatory regulatory requirements, and events resulting in catastrophic financial consequences.

It should be noted that the effectiveness of the overall framework is only as good as the accuracy of the methods and models used to quantify the likelihood and consequence of the various undesirable events and relating them to the KPIs. Given that some of the assessments may require the application of expert judgment, it is

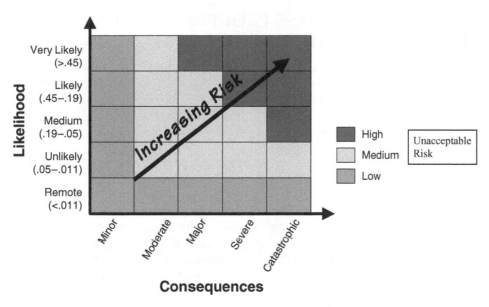

Exhibit 12.7   Risk Space Concept for Identifying Business Risks

advisable to develop independent methods to validate the results of the bottom-up risk identification, mitigation, and prioritization process. The development of alternate methods to assist in validating the results of the detailed bottom-up risk identification, mitigation, and prioritization process will be discussed later in this section.

The overall purpose of the framework is to establish a prioritized list of expenditure plans that minimize the overall risk of the enterprise falling short of meeting its key goals and objectives. The development, sustainment, and continuous improvement of the CRM significantly contributes to the success of the RFRAF. The CRM provides:

- A single source of information linking the SBOs, KPIs, PIs, RTs, and risk concepts.
- Top-down direction on the appetite for risk within the company.
- A useful method of communicating what constitutes risk in relation to the SBOs.
- A top-down guide for use by all staff levels within the company to identify bottom-up operational and strategic risks that are candidates for mitigation through the development of investment proposals (IPs). An IP describes/ specifies the technical and/or process based solution/work necessary to effectively mitigate unacceptable risk events. This includes identifying the cost of the mitigating solution and the change in risk profile compared to the "do-nothing" option.
- Consistent treatment of risk across the enterprise.
- A consistent information source for assessing the overall effectiveness of the bottom-up solutions/IPs.

RISK-BASED BUSINESS PROCESSES AND ORGANIZATIONAL CONSIDERATIONS

As mentioned in the introduction, the RFRAF is a subset of the broader business planning framework and therefore must provide information required by this higher level business process.

Risk-Based Business Processes

The main process steps that must be completed as part of the RFRAF are outlined in the following seven steps:

1. Identify business risks and assess/evaluate their impact on the SBOs, KPIs, and PIs under a "do-nothing" scenario. The assessment must investigate both strategic risks and routine operational risks. Strategic risks are typically assessed by senior and middle management staff within workshops comprised of several related disciplines across the organization. The operational risks are typically assessed by the various departmental and regional experts involved in the business planning effort. The results of both assessments are documented on a consistent risk evaluation template. At a minimum, the risk evaluation template requires a description of the risk event, the KPIs or PIs impacted by the event, and the expected probability and consequence for each impacted KPI. The probability and consequence associated with the "do-nothing" scenario on each KPI should be quantified to the extent possible, using appropriate methods and models. Experience over a number of years of application has shown that it is preferable to assess these risks over at least two specific time periods used within business planning. For each risk event the level of risk should initially be assessed over the first two-year period of the business plan. This is to be followed by an assessment of the risk event over the entire business planning period (typically five years) or beyond. This information is of importance for prioritizing work. Urgent and important risk events having significant impacts in the first two-year period are given priority over those that materialize over a longer period of time. It is useful in executing the process to provide an estimate of the time requirements for establishing the risk mitigation options for each risk event. Including this information on the risk evaluation template at this point in the process facilitates the identification of potential resource constraints in performing the next phase of the process, outlined in Step 2 below.
2. Establish the key risks requiring treatment (or mitigation) based on the probability and consequence information developed in Step 1. If the analysis shows that there are constraints on the resources available to develop the risk mitigation options, only the events that represent the largest risks to the business will be evaluated and mitigated.
3. For each of the risk events requiring treatment, a series of risk-mitigation alternatives is developed. For the strategic risks identified in the management level multidisciplined workshop mentioned in Step 1, a dedicated group of management staff develops the mitigation alternatives. For the operational

risks the various departmental and regional experts develop the mitigation alternatives. Each alternative is assessed in relation to a prioritization index calculated as follows:

$$\text{Prioritization Index} = \frac{\text{Total Risk Reduction Benefit to SBOs}}{\text{Expenditure Level}}$$

The preferred alternative is selected for mitigating each risk event based on the highest Prioritization Index. These preferred alternatives become the Investment Proposals (IPs), which must be prioritized as part of the overall RFRAF, based on the highest risk-reduction impact to the SBOs per expenditure level.

4. All high-priority risk events identified within Steps 1 to 3 are prioritized through the use of a prioritization model. The prioritization model is designed to incorporate the input from all submitted IPs and uses the Prioritization Index to sequence the proposals in an optimum manner to achieve the greatest risk reduction for the least cost. The resulting portfolio of preferred IPs represents the optimal scenario for achieving the SBOs in a least cost manner.

5. Given the importance of the decision to proceed with this portfolio of preferred IPs, the next step in the process involves conducting a validation review through the application of a series of validation tests on the optimal scenario developed by the prioritization model. These validation tests are conducted prior to approving the implementation of the portfolio of preferred IPs for the purpose of providing the approval authorities with supplemental information related to:

   a. Sensitivity of the optimal scenario to the prioritization criteria.
   b. Compatibility to historical business performance.
   c. Ability to implement the portfolio of preferred IPs given possible resource constraints. This includes availability of equipment, material, staff skills and competencies, outages, and/or other related business constraints.
   d. Comparability to other independent strategic assessments, which can be used to validate the overall level of expenditures and/or the expected level of business performance in the various business areas.

Further details on the validation review and related tests are provided below:

Sensitivity of the optimal scenario to the prioritization criteria—Conducting sensitivity analysis on the weighting factors used for prioritization provides approval authorities with valuable information related to the stability of the portfolio of preferred IPs. A good practice in this area involves predetermining alternative weighting factors within a senior management workshop and reviewing program changes produced by the prioritization model. IPs consistently ranking high under various reasonable alternative weighting factors can proceed with a high degree of confidence. Experience has shown that conducting a sensitivity analysis for only the factors that can be quantified also provides a good alternate source of information in deciding on final programs, as this eliminates the impact of qualitative or subjective assessments. In a utility environment this sensitivity test could mean only using the cost and reliability based KPIs, assuming critical safety events are nondiscretionary.

Compatibility to historical business performance—Comparing the portfolio of preferred IPs and forecasted KPI performance to the historical portfolio of expenditure programs and the historical performance of comparable KPIs provides valuable information based on actual results. This type of comparison is effective in long-standing companies such as electric utilities that have information sources going back many decades. Changes from history should be explained based on either a change in the SBOs or a change in risk profile associated with a specific area of the business. Companies without a long history or that have experienced significant changes in the products and services delivered will need to find other means of performing such comparisons. This may include using benchmarking methods to establish cost and service/product performance in relation to comparable organizations or competitors.

Ability to implement—Conducting comparisons between the portfolio of preferred IPs and the resources (capital, human, materials, equipment, etc.) available to finance and perform the work, provides information related to the ability to complete the program in the allotted time. This is a critical check in an era of constrained capital, professional and trades expertise, and uncertain availability of necessary equipment and materials. Another concern in the industrial business environment is the availability to obtain the required equipment outages (i.e., downtime) to perform the work while still delivering on commitments to customers and/or contributions to the bottom line.[5]

Comparability to independent strategic assessments—Many businesses perform macro-level strategic assessments to forecast the overall mid-term or long-term capital or O&M requirements of the business based on factors such as growth projections, infrastructure replacement rates, and/or asset aging rates. If the results of these independent forecasts can be reconciled with the portfolio of preferred IPs developed by the risk-based process described previously, the confidence level of the approval authorities can be significantly increased. Experience with the process has shown that conducting such comparisons typically requires grouping the expenditures associated with the portfolio of preferred IPs into higher level categories of assets, regions, services, deliverables, and/or accounting designations (capital and O&M), depending on the nature of the business and the strategic assessments. Given the importance of the decision (approving the details of a work program that is expected to achieve the SBOs of the company) the effort required to perform this comparison is worth the increase in confidence gained when two independent methods identify similar requirements.

In the electric utility industry, for example, models[6] have been developed to establish long-term capital requirements based on assets reaching end-of-life and requiring replacement with equivalent facilities. The models use probability density functions to represent expected end-of-life ages for various asset groups. When these probability density functions are applied to the demographic profile of the asset base the expected level of asset replacement can be generated. Assuming like-for-like replacement and typical unit replacement costs enables the generation of mid-term to long-term forecasted capital requirements for specific asset groups. Conducting macro-level, long-term studies of this nature can also assist in identifying the risk to certain KPIs such as degradation in levels of system reliability as the system ages and equipment begins to fail. These types of assessments provide long-term forecasts of both the expected level of capital expenditures and the risk of delivery performance, using a completely separate long-term/top-down type of analysis. Comparing the results of strategic assessments of this nature to the results of the bottom-up annual risk analysis described earlier provides a valuable cross-check on the results. If the results of the two independent assessments can be reconciled, confidence in both approaches is increased. If the results do not reconcile, further investigation is warranted, including comparisons to the other validation tests mentioned earlier.

6. The next step in the process involves reviewing all the available information in a workshop with the approval authorities and approving the preferred portfolio of IPs. This preferred portfolio of IPs represents the optimal work program for achieving the SBOs. The business planning process will use this optimal work program to allocate costs and resources to various business units depending on the approach used within the company.

7. The final step in the process involves establishing the necessary work program performance measures and monitoring processes to ensure effective, efficient, and timely delivery of the portfolio of preferred IPs.

Exhibits 12.8 and 12.9 summarize the main elements in the process.

Experience with operating the process indicates that major efficiency gains can be obtained by identifying typical risk events and standardizing the consequence

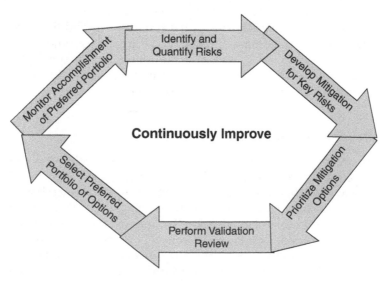

Exhibit 12.8 Key Process Steps of the RFRAF

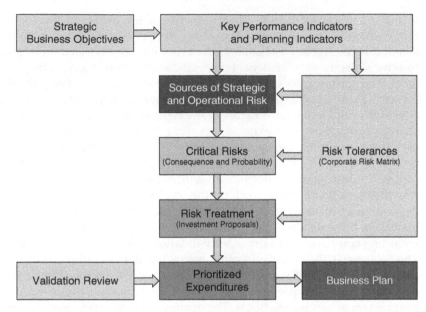

Exhibit 12.9 Key Elements and Products of the Risk-Based Business Processes

and likelihood assessments through the development of pick lists based on specific criteria, which can be selected by operations staff. In the electric power utility example for evaluating KPI risks associated with the frequency of system outages, it was found that a major reduction in evaluation effort could be achieved by correlating the frequency of system outages to standard equipment failure rates and certain generic system configurations. These correlations were observed from the initial risk assessments and resulted in the development of simple pick lists for the consequence and likelihood assessments, associated with the KPI for frequency of system outages. A major reduction in evaluation effort was achieved by providing Operations staff with simple pick lists for the consequence and likelihood assessments based on these correlations. This obviated the need for unique assessments for each occurrence of this risk event across the company. As experience is gained with the RFRAF, efficiencies of this nature begin to emerge, reducing the overall effort while improving the accuracy of the assessments.

Organizational Considerations

A dedicated organizational unit should be established within the company to manage the routine operation of the business processes within the RFRAF. It should be noted that this formal organizational unit is distinct from the COE-Team mentioned earlier. The primary functions of the COE-Team are to develop the RFRAF, promote and launch the related implementation initiatives, oversee successful implementation, develop and monitor performance measures, and help develop and promote improvements. The purpose of the dedicated organizational unit is to operate the detailed processes, including establishing an information system and developing the required guidelines and procedures necessary for effective functioning of the annual process. The leader of this dedicated organizational unit should be a member of the COE-Team. Experience has shown that this dedicated organizational unit should be located within a business unit that does not have a stake in the outcome of the prioritization process. Examples of best locations include the finance function or a dedicated Investment Planning or risk function within the company. The dedicated organizational unit should be responsible for:

- Establishing the processes necessary to identify and manage risks.
- Obtaining models capable of prioritizing the investment proposals.
- Developing information systems and templates to ensure the transparency, consistency, and continuity necessary for process effectiveness and efficiency is in place.
- Conducting detailed training sessions to ensure staff involved in the processes have the necessary knowledge.
- Conducting macro-level studies, scenario analysis, and validation tests to ensure the outputs of the prioritization process are reasonable and robust.
- Implementing effective internal controls to provide oversight on all IPs to ensure evaluation accuracy and consistency within and between organizational units.
- Arranging, facilitating, and documenting the results of the senior management workshops necessary to obtain the required approvals.
- Updating the process elements and assumptions on an annual basis.
- Developing process measures to provide the monitoring necessary to ensure the process is effective and efficient and continuously improve the processes, models, tools, and information systems.
- Manage the implementation of the approved portfolio of IPs and make in-year adjustments as new risk information becomes available.

Experience in operating these processes indicates that the organizational hierarchy should be leveraged to ensure consistency in the identification of risk events and in the evaluation of their impacts on the SBOs, KPIs, and PIs. This is also the case for the development of the IPs designed to manage unacceptable risks. Having the managers and directors of the business units review and approve the risk evaluation templates and IPs developed by their expert staff serves to maintain some consistency in the identification and evaluation of risks between organizational units and/or geographic locations. This is a good practice, prior to submitting the risk-evaluation templates and IPs to the centralized business unit responsible for final prioritization. The centralized business unit responsible for prioritization should also develop a high-level expert responsible for reviewing risk scores submitted on all risk evaluation templates and IPs, in relation to historic evaluations and actual results from previous or similar evaluations. This practice ensures consistency across all business units within the company.

Exhibit 12.10 shows the typical business functions involved in the business planning processes, the span of the RFRAF, and the roles typically undertaken by the various organizational functions. Experience has shown that the process management role for the RFRAF should either be in the finance or investment planning functions.

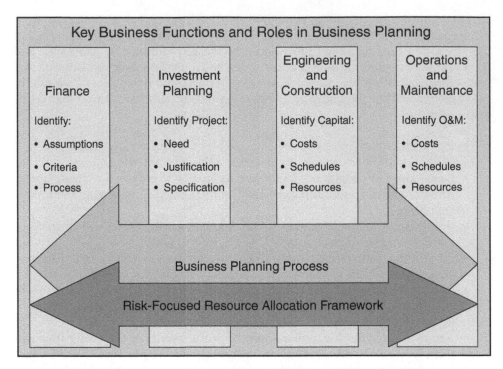

Exhibit 12.10   Business Functions Typically Involved in Business Planning and Risk Assessments

CONCEPTS, METHODS, AND MODELS ENABLING RISK IDENTIFICATION, EVALUATION, MITIGATION, PRIORITIZATION, AND MANAGEMENT

This section describes the generic concepts, methods, and models that are used within the RFRAF to identify, evaluate, mitigate, prioritize, and manage risks.

The Concept of Evaluation Time Frames

As mentioned earlier, both operational and strategic risks must be evaluated by knowledgeable staff within the organization when identifying events with potential for unacceptable impacts (consequences and the related probabilities of occurrence) on the SBOs of the business. Operational risks are typically evaluated by expert front-line staff responsible for operating and managing the business. This includes maintenance, operations, and customer account staff who deal with daily/weekly/monthly issues in the management of the business. These resources are responsible for executing the near-term elements of the business plan (defined as the first two years of the business plan) and have knowledge of factors such as immediate maintenance requirements, demand exceeding the capability of systems to deliver, and/or customer satisfaction issues. Experience has shown that most long-standing companies have the required knowledgeable resources, detailed business processes, and supporting information systems necessary to conduct the near-term risk assessments that are an integral part of the RFRAF.

Strategic risks typically span a longer time period and are also likely to span the responsibilities of several organizations or disciplines within the company. Uncovering risks of this nature is important because it may be necessary to invest in controlling these risks within the period of the business plan to ensure the SBOs can be realized over the planning period. Experience with the framework has shown that middle- and senior-management staff members typically possess the multidisciplined knowledge and work in time frames consistent with these strategic risks. Therefore, this group of staff members are in the best position to identify these risks and the related mitigation alternatives. Many companies have also established an organizational unit responsible for proactively identifying, evaluating, and managing strategic risks. In the electric utility industry several regulatory jurisdictions have recognized the importance of managing strategic risks and the regulatory authorities require utilities to establish and formally submit long-term plans to ensure the prudent management of this critical public infrastructure.[7] These long-term plans typically span about 10 years in recognition of the long lead times required to obtain approvals for new infrastructure and/or order and install major equipment. These plans also typically deal with risks associated with the aging of various fleets of similar assets, rather than the maintenance and replacement of specific assets, as is the case in the near-term evaluation mentioned earlier. Strategic risk evaluations of this nature can identify events that must be managed in the near-term (one to two years) or mid-term (three to five years) to prevent jeopardizing the achievement of SBOs over a much longer time frame (such as 10 years). The IPs developed to manage strategic risks must utilize the same template (and provide the same consequence and probability information for affected KPIs) as the operational risks and are subjected to the same prioritization process.

To effectively conduct a comprehensive risk evaluation, experience with the RFRAF indicates that it is useful to evaluate undesirable events in up to three distinct time frames: The near-term (defined as the first two years of the business plan); the mid-term (defined as years three to five of the business plan) and the long-term (defined as the period beyond five years). This should be accomplished utilizing company staff with specific knowledge of potential risks in these various time periods. As mentioned above, many companies also develop long-term strategic plans that contain information useful to the risk identification and evaluation process. Exhibit 12.11 illustrates the time frames of interest, the type of information provided for risk analysis and business planning, the basis for the risk information, and the level of analysis typically conducted in each time frame. It should also be noted that risk information in one time frame can be used to validate the risk assessments in an adjacent time frame or as a minimum inform the risk assessors of changing business circumstances and the effects on risk profiles over time. See Exhibit 12.11.

Methods and Models to Quantify the Impact of Risk Events

The overall risk-based process outlined earlier identified the importance of quantifying the probability and consequence imposed by critical risk events on each

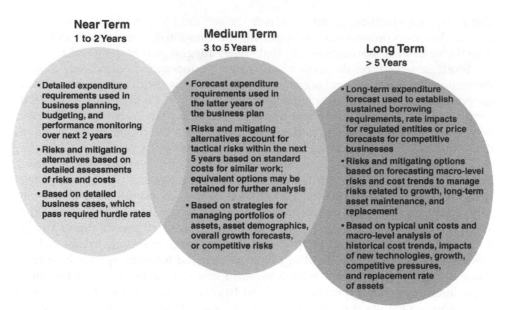

Exhibit 12.11   Time Frames and Information Contributions to Risk Assessments

impacted KPI. Quantification of risk-event impacts on KPIs, through the use of appropriate methods and models is far more desirable than the use of qualitative or subjective approaches, which may be a combination of judgment and specu-lation. The accuracy of the methods and models used to quantify the probability and consequence impacts on the KPIs is a determinative factor in the overall ef-fectiveness of the risk evaluation and mitigation process and possibly the success of the business. For this reason, significant effort should be focused on developing a portfolio of methods and models that enable the quantification of risk events in terms of each specific KPI or PI, to the extent practical.

These methods and models should be designed to enable quantification of KPI impacts associated with the "do-nothing" scenario for each risk event. They should also be capable of evaluating the KPI impacts for the risk-mitigation alternatives for the purpose of generating IPs. The electric power industry example discussed earlier identified the reduced frequency of unplanned system outages as a KPI for achieving the SBO of first-quartile reliability. To effectively quantify and manage risk a methodology and model should be put in place to quantify the impact on the frequency of system outages under a "do-nothing" scenario in the service ter-ritories. This method and model would also be used to identify the effectiveness of mitigation alternatives on the frequency of system outages in the service territo-ries. The mitigation options that provide the required reduction in the frequency of system outages at the lowest cost will be submitted to the prioritization process described in the following section.

Experience with the RFRAF in the electric power sector indicates that a large portfolio of such methods and models must be developed to quantify the risk impacts on all critical KPIs. This includes methods and models for conducting op-erational risk assessments affecting the near-term (such as asset condition methods

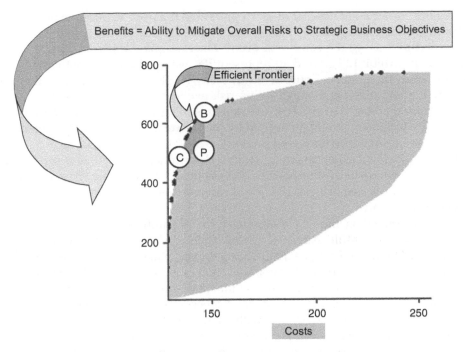

Exhibit 12.12   Graphical Representation of Prioritization Model Output

and models to evaluate the near-term risk of equipment failure) and strategic risk assessments impacting KPIs in the mid-term or long-term. The portfolio of methods and models must be capable of assessing a wide variety of risk factors (reliability, safety, environmental impacts, regulatory compliance, etc.) and deal with both technical and financial concepts.

Prioritization of Investment Proposals

As mentioned earlier, the prioritization model is designed to incorporate the input from all submitted IPs for the purpose of sequencing the proposals in an optimum manner to achieve the greatest risk reduction for the least relative cost. The resulting portfolio of preferred IPs represents the optimal scenario for achieving the SBOs in a least cost manner. A graphical representation of the output for a typical prioritization model appears in Exhibit 12.12. The model treats all IPs on a consistent basis and sequences the IPs from highest benefit to cost ratio to lowest. This approach enables the identification of what is known in the literature as the efficient frontier.

The IPs capable of producing the highest overall reduction in risk to the SBOs for the least overall cost would appear on the steep upward slope on the left portion of the graph. IPs of lower value would appear on the right portion of the graph where at the extreme end it may be observed that significant increases in expenditures produce little change in benefit. Output results of this nature are effective for establishing the cut-off points for projects (IPs) when expenditure constraints have been determined. The IP labeled "B" in Exhibit 12.12 would just make the cut-off point if a cost of 150 represented the upper limit of expenditures. The graphical representation also enables comparisons between alternative IPs designed to manage the same risk event. For example the IPs labeled "P," "C," and "B" in Exhibit 12.12 could all represent IPs designed to manage the same risk event. From the graphical output it can easily be observed that IP-P is the least effective alternative for managing this risk event, since IP-B can deliver higher benefits for the same cost and IP-C can deliver similar benefits at lower cost. In this example a judgment would be needed by the approval authorities to determine if the risk event should be mitigated under IP-B or IP-C. It should also be noted from this example that if expenditure constraints determined that IP-B was just beyond the level of affordability, this specific risk event would continue to be within the portfolio of preferred IPs (as IP-C) and receive funding for mitigation under a lower level of cost.

All prioritization models use some form of multicriteria decision analysis methodology (i.e., Multi-Attribute Utility Theory, Multi-Attribute Value Theory, Analytical Hierarchy Process) as the basis for the evaluation of inputs and there are many models available on the market.[8] Care must be taken to select a model that is consistent with the information and competencies available within the company. Once a model is selected the related input process must be established.

The detailed theory associated with such models is beyond the scope of this framework-based discussion. However, there are several good in-depth papers on project prioritization and project portfolio management.[9] In addition, regulatory authorities responsible for approving cost of service applications recognize the importance of prioritization methods and models in establishing the expenditure requirements of the utilities they regulate. They also value the transparency and consistency provided by these methods and models. As a result, regulatory authorities often require the submission of detailed information related to the prioritization approaches used by utilities. These submissions provide an excellent source of information related to the application of these business processes in a complex business environment.[10]

Overall, the prioritization model and supporting process must possess the following core capabilities:

- Be capable of accurately solving an optimization problem (maximizing the value of the portfolio of IPs) for multiple decision criteria.
- Create a level playing field for all IPs.
- Deal with IPs having different impacts on multiple decision criteria.
- Manage large numbers of IPs.
- Be capable of dealing with both capital and O&M expenditures.
- Provide a transparent and auditable analysis.
- Produce outputs that clearly identify the efficient frontier, the impact of expenditure constraints, and trade-offs between IPs designed to mitigate the same risk event or similar risk events.

Selection and implementation of a prioritization model and supporting methodology, which is compatible with the optimization problem and the information and competencies available within the company, is critical to the success of the initiative. Obtaining professional guidance from knowledgeable experts may be a prudent course of action given the complex nature of decision theory.

Management of the Portfolio of Preferred Investment Proposals

Once the portfolio of preferred IPs has been approved for implementation the dedicated organizational unit responsible for the RFRAF must oversee the successful implementation. This includes making adjustments to the approved portfolio should unforeseen higher priority risks materialize or expenditure constraints change throughout the year. This requires:

- Establishing performance measures associated with the approved portfolio of IPs.
- Developing a redirection process for managing in-year changes to the approved portfolio of IPs.
- Reporting on portfolio progress to senior management and regulatory authorities.

INFORMATION REQUIREMENTS AND CHALLENGES

Experience with implementing and operating a RFRAF indicates that overall the framework requires the development, processing, and storage of a considerable degree of new information. This includes information associated with the following products and related assessments:

- A corporate risk matrix and supporting governance framework, user guide, and catalog summarizing the rationale for selected KPIs.
- Generic templates for describing the risk events and IPs for managing critical risks. This includes related guidelines and procedures for their completion.
- Detailed risk-based input information to enable assessments for each risk event and IP to establish the impacts on KPIs. This information is derived from a new family of methods, models, and tools designed to provide new quantitative and qualitative information associated with risk events and the IPs, developed to mitigate the risk events.
- Completed templates identifying risk events and IPs for mitigating the critical risks. The completed templates include the related consequence and likelihood impacts on the KPIs with supporting business case information for the IPs. The information contained within these templates is used as input to the prioritization model.
- The portfolio of preferred IPs, developed by the prioritization model.
- Scenario and sensitivity studies associated with the validation review and related validation tests to facilitate the approval of the portfolio of preferred IPs. This may include the need for new risk-based input and output information associated with strategic tools, such as the Asset Retirement Model mentioned earlier (refer footnote 6).
- The approved portfolio of IPs, which forms the basis for the business plan.

- The development of a risk register, containing the history of risk events and related mitigating actions. The risk register can be of use in finding future efficiencies through the standardized assessment of certain common risks.
- Redirection plans and related performance measures and instructions to manage changes within the year.

As mentioned above, detailed information for the RFRAF requires the provision of consequence and likelihood information for various risk events and mitigation plans, in relation to the KPIs. The incremental information required for the RFRAF varies significantly depending on the type of risk assessments under consideration.

Operational risk assessments and strategic risk assessments impose different incremental information requirements on the business.

Operational Risk Assessment Information

Experience with implementing the RFRAF indicates that the consequence information associated with operational risk assessments is typically the easiest to obtain within the company. These assessments typically involve identifying and mitigating risk events associated with the failure of a business process, asset, or supplier to deliver the required business result. These types of failure events, and the related causes, are usually well understood by operations staff within the company. They are therefore capable of describing the failure outcome in terms of the consequence impact on the KPIs or PIs. Operations-based staff are also good at identifying typical mitigation measures for managing the risk and how this will change the consequences from the "do-nothing" alternative. The challenge for operational risk assessments is to identify the probability or likelihood of occurrence. This usually requires reviewing failure rate and cause information from historical records and forecasting the expected probability of occurrence in the future. This imposes a more complex level of analysis on the historical information and the generation of new information related to quantifying the probability domain.

Strategic Risk Assessments

If strategic risk assessments are normally conducted within the business the incremental information requirements are typically similar to those for operational risk assessments, where again establishing the probability domain is the biggest challenge.

If strategic risk assessments are not normally conducted within the business or new strategic risk assessments are required, the incremental information requirements are likely to be materially increased. The new strategic risk assessments may require detailed new financial and business performance information.

The RFRAF requires planning for a new family of input and output information within the company. The input information is needed to conduct risk assessments performed by a portfolio of new methods, models, and processes that enable the identification, quantification, and mitigation of operational and strategic risks to the SBOs of the company. The output information of these new methods, models, and processes includes a variety of new information that must all be stored to

maintain an effective audit trail for these critical business decisions. Output information includes probability and consequence information for each risk in relation
to the KPIs, financial evaluations for establishing least cost IPs, validation that
appropriate internal controls have been followed within and between organizational units, the portfolio of preferred IPs generated by the prioritization model,
results of the validation review, documentation from any related workshops, and
the approved portfolio of IPs, with supporting rationale.

Overall the implementation of a RFRAF can significantly increase the information requirements of a company and the COE-Team should therefore include
a senior-level expert from the information technology field to ensure that these
requirements are appropriately understood and accounted for while developing
information technology plans.

MEASURES OF EFFECTIVENESS FOR CONTINUOUS IMPROVEMENT

Given the importance of the RFRAF products, and the significant resource requirements necessary for the successful completion of the process steps, performance
measures should be established to ensure the effectives of the framework and
to identify areas requiring improvement. Some critical measures, which assist in
managing the overall performance of the framework and identify areas needing
improvement include:

- Percentage of KPIs having methods and models for quantifying risk impacts.
- Percentage of staff having completed the necessary training programs.
- Number of identified risk events evaluated under standardized pick lists for
  consequence and likelihood assessments.
- Accuracy of estimated resource requirements versus actual for completing
  the templates.
- Total hours of senior management time required in strategic risk workshops
  and approvals based workshops.
- Number of iterations required to achieve final approval of the portfolio of
  preferred IPs.
- Number of unforeseen events and in-year adjustments required by the redi-
  rection process.
- Percentage of work completed relative to plan.
- Actual versus forecasted budget.

Monitoring and managing to these performance measures facilitates the effective operation of the processes and the identification of process inefficiencies.
Identifying the root causes for poor performance under these measures followed
by the development of the corrective actions necessary to improve performance
will continuously improve the effectiveness and efficiency of the RFRAF.

CONCLUSION

The allocation of resources based on risk requires the development, implementation, operation, and continuous improvement of a comprehensive business

framework. This framework integrates critical knowledge, expertise, experience, and information available across the organization within a corporate-wide process, spanning all the major functions of the business. The development and implementation of the framework should be overseen by a COE-Team comprised of senior management staff from across all the major business functions involved in business planning and having an interest in the discipline of risk management.

The development and implementation phases require the establishment of SBOs, KPIs, RTs, and risk concepts. The framework also requires the development of methods and models for quantifying risk events to the best extent practicable. Where possible, industry-accepted methods and models should be utilized to enhance the credibility of the analysis. This is especially the case for regulated enterprises.

The effective functioning of the processes require the involvement of everyone from experienced senior management, having knowledge of the strategic business risks, to experts in the various line disciplines, who can identify and quantify the likelihood and consequences of credible operational risk events and determine the reasonable mitigation options. The successful operation of the process also requires the utilization of middle management, who possesses the knowledge and experience needed to provide a third-party opinion on the accuracy of the IPs submitted by their staff. This process step provides a critical control ensuring the projects are properly scored on a relative basis, prior to being subjected to the prioritization step.

The routine operation of the related business processes should fall under a dedicated organizational unit and the leader of this business unit should be a member of the COE-Team. The dedicated organizational unit and the COE-Team are collectively accountable for the success of the RFRAF and its continuous improvement.

The framework enables the integration of risk management and business planning bringing transparency, consistency, and traceability to the overall process. This combination of factors enhances the overall credibility of decision making within the company and regulated enterprises have seen success in defending revenue requirements when such a framework is in place.

The allocation of resources based on risk requires the implementation of a comprehensive integrated framework linking the SBOs to the strategic and operational risk events jeopardizing those objectives. The RFRAF facilitates the systematic identification and management of those risks by allocating limited resources where they provide the highest value. The framework represents a significant investment in resources, models, and information systems. However, if managed properly, the payback is nothing less than the long term success of the business.

NOTES

1. This work is part of an industry review of best practices in the area of Utility Asset Management conducted by the International Council on Large Electric Systems (CIGRE—Conseil International des Grands Réseaux Électriques). The work falls under CIGRE Study Committee C1—System Development and Economics. The information is

published within technical brochures designed as Best Practice Guides on Utility Asset Management for the Electric Utility Industry.

2. A good high-level description of the process is documented within the reference document entitled "A Risk Management Standard © AIRMIC, ALARM, IRM: 2002" at www.theirm.org/publications/documents/Risk_Management_Standard_030820.pdf. Structured approaches to risk management are also contained within certain risk standards published by government bodies such as the Canadian Risk Management Standard available at www.tbs-sct.gc.ca/pubs_pol/dcgpubs/RiskManagement/guide10-eng.asp, and the Australian/New Zealand Standard on Risk Management available www.riskmanagement.com.au/.

3. Reference—ISO/IEC *Guide 73* Risk Management—Vocabulary—Guidelines for use in standards. ISO stands for the "International Organization for Standardization" and is the world's largest developer of standards used by industrial-based businesses. IEC stands for the "International Electrotechnical Commission" and is the leading global organization that prepares and publishes international standards for all electrical, electronic, and related technologies.

4. An excellent example of such a product has been publically submitted to the British Columbia Utilities Commission by the British Columbia Transmission Corporation (BCTC) as part of their Transmission System Capital Plan for 2009 to 2018. For convenience, Appendix 12.A within this chapter contains the BCTC Corporate Risk Matrix. The BCTC–CRM is provided as Appendix D within the BCTC Transmission System Capital Plan for 2009 to 2018 (F2009 Capital Plan). This publically available document can be found at www.bctc.com/regulatory_filings/capital_plan/current_capital_plans/F2009+to+F2018+Transmission+System+Capital+Plan.htm.

5. The author is aware of one company that uses a two-day workshop to obtain commitments by service groups responsible for delivering the work specified within the portfolio of preferred IPs. The workshop involves the review and evaluation of all priority IPs by senior management through the use of face-to-face meetings with the line of business experts who are responsible for defending their risk scores and related budgetary needs. The priority IPs are not approved until the services groups responsible for delivering the work specified within the IPs provide assurance that the work can be delivered.

6. Refer to paper entitled "The Asset Retirement Model" presented to the North American Transmission & Distribution Conference & Expo, May 9–11, 2005. This paper describes how independent strategic assessments can be used during a validation review and is available at www.hydroonenetworks.com/en/customers/LDCs_and_Tx/downloads/ARM_Paper_2005_NATD_Conference.pdf.

7. See British Columbia Transmission Corporation—Transmission System Capital Plan for 2009 to 2018 (F2009 Capital Plan). This publically available document can be found at www.bctc.com/regulatory_filings/capital_plan/current_capital_plans/F2009+to+F2018+Transmission+System+Capital+Plan.htm.

8. See the web site reference to commercial products: www.prioritysystem.com/tools.html.

9. In-depth papers on project prioritization and project portfolio management available on www.prioritysystem.com/papers.html.

10. Reference—British Columbia Transmission Corporation—Transmission System Capital Plan for 2009 to 2018 (F2009 Capital Plan). Refer Section 4 of document and Appendix J. This publically available document can be found at www.bctc.com/regulatory_filings/capital_plan/current_capital_plans/F2009+to+F2018+Transmission+System+Capital+Plan.htm.

ABOUT THE AUTHOR

Joseph Toneguzzo is the Director of the Implementation and Approvals Division, within the Power System Planning Group of the Ontario Power Authority, the government agency responsible for establishing and evolving the long term integrated plan for the electric power system within the Province of Ontario. He has been a Professional Engineer within the Province of Ontario since 1980 and has over 30 years of experience within the electricity industry. His career included working for Ontario Hydro and Hydro One holding professional and/or management positions within the operations, planning, asset management, and regulatory affairs functions. He worked on several provincial, national, and international industry task groups involved in system planning, asset management, sector development, and regulatory affairs, including representing Canada in these areas within the International Council on Large Electric Systems (CIGRE—Conseil International des Grands Réseaux Électriques) from 2004 to 2008. He has co-authored many industry publications in the areas of System Planning, Integrated Resource Planning and Asset Management/Risk Management, which have been published in various electricity industry publications including CIGRE, the Institute of Electrical and Electronics Engineers—IEEE Transactions on Power Systems, the Electric Power Research Institute, and the Canadian Electricity Association.

BCTC Corporate Risk Matrix

Enterprise Risk Management (ERM) at BCTC

ERM is a common process for everyone in the organization to make use of when making decisions. The framework below describes the main ERM phases. Prior to using this Risk Matrix you should have identified the relevant risks in the identify phase. This Risk Matrix forms part of the "Assess" phase. The phases in the ERM framework are described below.

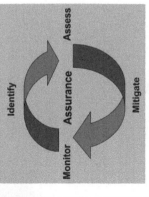

Identify all potential risks (threats) and opportunities related to achievement of organizational and departmental level business objectives.

Assess risks in terms of impact and likelihood. **In this phase you analyze the risk impact by utilizing the accompanying Corporate Risk Matrix.**

Mitigate risks with control activities and insurance programs. Identify control activities in place to manage risk and identify gaps requiring improvement action plans.

Monitor risk profile of inherent and residual risks, impact of changes to risk profile and risk appetite.

Provide **assurance** that control activities are effective through either management self-assessment or internal audit program.

LIKELIHOOD GUIDELINES		LIKELIHOOD OF OCCURRENCE
90%	5	(9 in 10) or greater likelihood that event will occur within next year.
50%	4	(1 in 2) or greater likelihood that event will occur within next year.
10%	3	(1 in 10) or greater likelihood that event will occur within next year.
1%	2	(1 in 100) or greater likelihood that event will occur within next year.
<1%	1	<1% (1 in 100) likelihood that event will occur within next year.

Likelihood vs. Impact colour matrix:

	1	2	3	4	5
5	Moderate	Moderate	High	Extreme	Extreme
4	Guarded	Moderate	High	Extreme	Extreme
3	Guarded	Moderate	Moderate	High	Extreme
2	Low	Guarded	Moderate	Moderate	High
1	Low	Low	Guarded	Guarded	High

IMPACT CRITERIA:

	1	2	3	4	5
Safety	First aid injury/illness	Medical aid injury/illness	Lost time injury/ temporary disability	Permanent disability	Fatality (ies)
Financial	Impact totaling < $500,000	Impact totaling $500,000 - $1 million	Impact totaling $1 million - $5 million	Impact totaling $5 million - $10 million	Impact totaling ≥ $10 million
Reliability	One of: < 250,000 customers hrs lost or < 2 GWh of energy not served or delivered.	One of: 250,000 – 1 million customers hrs lost or 2 - 7 GWh of energy not served or delivered.	One of: 1 - 3 million customer hrs lost or 7 - 20 GWh of energy not served or delivered.	One of: 3 million - 7 million customer hrs lost or 20 - 50 GWh of energy not served or delivered.	One of: ≥ 7 million customer hrs lost or ≥ 50 GWh of energy not served or delivered.
Market Efficiency	Customers and rate payers lodge complaints to BCTC	BCTC customers and rate payers lodge complaint to Government or the Utilities commission	Government or BCUC enquiry conducted into BCTC practices and policies	Government or BCUC impose strategic and operational changes upon BCTC	Failure to deliver required level of service resulting in loss of license to operate
Relationships	External opposition resulting in short term delays or minor modifications to work plans.	External opposition affecting BCTC's ability to implement its work plans is constrained and/or substantive modifications of its work plans are required.	External opposition resulting in increased regulatory oversight; shareholder scrutiny and/or restricted access to work sites.	External opposition resulting in increased regulatory/ legislative/court action or government intervention resulting in a loss of responsibilities impacting BCTC's corporate mandate, including restricted access to major project sites.	External opposition resulting in loss of license to operate and/or imposed corporate restructuring
Organization & People	Negligible impact on service delivery and staff.	Impacts the efficiency or effectiveness of some services, but would be dealt with internally.	Portions of the organization experience unexpected attrition or reduced attraction factors.	The ability to achieve the corporate goals is threatened or there is a significant increase in the cost of service.	Unexpected loss of multiple critical staff including senior leadership and the ability to deliver critical services.
Environment	Non-reportable environmental incident	Reportable environmental incident with short term mitigation (< 1 year)	Reportable environmental incident with long term mitigation (> 1 year)	Reportable environmental incident with regulatory fines and mitigation possible.	Reportable environmental incident with regulatory prosecution and/or uncertain mitigation.

Severity Classification

Extreme	Must be managed through a detailed plan by an executive.
High	Detailed research and planning required at senior management; executive attention is required.
Moderate	Management responsibility must be specified; managed by specific monitoring or response procedures.
Guarded	Managed by routine procedures; regular monitoring required.
Low	Managed by routine procedures.

Appendix 12.A   BCTC Corporate Risk Matrix

CHAPTER 13

Quantitative Risk Assessment in ERM

JOHN HARGREAVES
Managing Director, Hargreaves Risk & Strategy

First weigh the considerations, then take the risks.

—Helmuth von Moltke (1800–1891)

INTRODUCTION

The German military strategist Helmuth von Moltke advised that risks should be assessed before they are taken. This chapter discusses how risk assessment and risk quantification can best be achieved in a commercial or governmental enterprise.

Most companies have completed surveys of the risks they face, and have adopted systems to control some of the risks they have found. The depth of this analysis has varied from one company to another, depending on local factors. Not least among these factors would be the assessment by the management team and board members of the benefits that may be obtained from the risk-management approach.

However, many regulators, stock exchanges, and professional bodies have encouraged companies to improve the quality of their risk measurement, and have issued guidance, so there is considerable institutional conformance pressure (e.g., COSO 2004, Australia Standards 2004).

Some insights can be gained from the COSO definition of enterprise risk management, which reads as:

> *Enterprise risk management is a process, effected by an entity's board of directors, management and other personnel, applied in strategy setting and across the enterprise, designed to identify potential events that may affect the entity, and manage risk to be within its risk appetite, to provide reasonable assurance regarding the achievement of entity objectives. (COSO 2004)*

Many people are involved, so we need a structured method for assessing individual risks, but also we need to be able to look at the picture from an enterprise point of view in order to be able to assure ourselves that the total risk being taken is within our risk appetite.

This chapter examines how risks may be quantified. After a consideration of general principles, four differing approaches to the quantification of individual risks are explained and evaluated. Statistical methods for calculating and reporting a company's total corporate risk are described and illustrated by a simple example. Finally we consider how quantified risks may be incorporated in the business-planning process. We do not cover the specialist methods used to quantify risks in financial institutions.[1]

In this chapter, it is postulated that there is no single best way of evaluating and prioritizing risks. Different organizations will find different and equally valid solutions. Over time, these solutions evolve in response to changing circumstances and in the light of experience. The aim of this chapter is to provide organizations with some further ideas that contribute to the ongoing evolution and refinement of their risk-management practices.

We start by asking a simple question: Why do we need to quantify a particular risk? There are four main reasons: First, we need to be able to decide which risks we should concentrate on and which ones are not so important. There are large differences in magnitude between risks, as Box 13.1 illustrates. It is much more beneficial to life expectancy to cut down on smoking than to stop drinking coffee. So it is useful to be able to put risks into classes of relative importance. Second, we need to be able to decide whether to spend money on controlling the risk. We can estimate how much a new control will cost, but before implementing it we need to know whether the control will justify itself through reducing the risk. Third, the presence of risk will reduce the economic value of the corresponding activity, and may be sufficient to cancel out any financial contribution being made. Fourth, we need to be able to estimate how much a particular risk is contributing to the total risk being run by the organization.

Box 13.1   Differences in Risk Magnitudes—An Example

For a U.S. male aged 55, the life expectancy lost from:

• Regular coffee drinking	6 days
• Fires	14 days
• Accidents in the home	90 days
• Motor vehicle accidents	195 days
• Being 30% overweight	3.5 years
• More than 20 cigarettes/day	7 years
• Being unmarried	9.5 years

Source: Cohen and Lee, 1979.

In achieving the above we need to take account of William of Ockham's insight, which is just as valid now as it was 700 years ago. This is illustrated in Box 13.2.

Box 13.2 William's Insight

Dico ergo ad qõnem q
qz pluralitas
non est ponenda sine necessitate τ non
ē necessitas quare ocbeat poni tpus oi'
scretum mensuras motum angeli. naz

William of Ockham's Razor, often paraphrased as
All other things being equal,
the simplest solution is the best.

Source: William of Ockham 1288–1348.

It is instructive to examine a typical situation under which risks are initially identified and analyzed. We usually become aware of a risk either through an internal brainstorming session or analytical paper, or through a report of an external development. Initially the risk may be loosely defined and there may be conflicting opinions as to its importance.

Moving on from this initial stage, we try to discover more about the risk. We become more knowledgeable about the processes that can cause the risk to happen, and be better placed to make an estimate of the probability that the risk will materialize within our planning period. Sometimes probability estimates can be based on statistical frequency data. For example, data is available regarding the frequency of IT problems of various degrees of severity, and we can inform our probability estimates using this data, adjusting where necessary to reflect whether our situation differs from average. Also, we become more knowledgeable about the consequences of the risk materializing. Sometimes these are clear and defined, but often there are a number of different possible types of consequences. We need to consider what mix of these occurs, and judge the relative importance of them. Refer to Box 13.3 for a list of these consequences.

Box 13.3   Types of Consequences

- Financial
- Reputation
- Strategic
- Legal or regulatory
- For staff or suppliers
- For customers

The consideration of these consequences is necessary because it allows us to make an estimate of the possible impact of the risk on the organization.

Exhibit 13.1   Impact Range Probability Distribution

Impact range ($)	Probability	Typical value ($)
0 to 4,999	95%	1,000
5,000 to 49,999	4%	20,000
50,000 to 249,999	0.9%	100,000
Above 250,000	0.1%	1,000,000

Sometimes it is sufficient to take a typical outcome as the basis for our further work, but often it is necessary to consider two or more levels of intensity for the risk, each with its corresponding causal circumstances. For example, the cost of a fire in an office can be as little as a scorch mark on a table or it could be large enough to cause a company to go bankrupt. If we decide to use a complex methodology to model our risk, we might represent the relationship between probability and impact as a probability distribution. However, if we are using a simpler methodology we might estimate probabilities of an out-turn within each of a range of impacts. The example in Exhibit 13.1 illustrates this concept. In this example, we might consider the smaller risks to be operational issues, but the small-probability large-impact combinations could be of concern at the company level.

Note that at this stage of our work, we will probably become aware of the controls that are currently in place in relation to the risk, and we may also find out about other possible controls and actions that might be implemented to reduce its impact or reduce the probability of it happening. For a "new" risk, some of these actions may be clearly necessary, perhaps with a good risk reduction benefit for a small cost outlay. Others may be rather expensive to implement or may have a lesser result in terms of risk reduction, so it may not be clear as to whether to implement these or not.

RISK ASSESSMENT: FOUR ALTERNATIVE APPROACHES

When deciding the most appropriate method of evaluating an organization's risks, there is a choice between several broad alternative approaches. These are illustrated in Exhibit 13.2. The appropriate choice between them depends on cultural and environmental considerations, and on the industry concerned. In this chapter, we consider mainly strategic risks and managerial situations where financial risks are not dominant. Methods for quantification of financial risks in the financial services and energy sectors are covered in other chapters.

It is worthwhile to examine the four main alternative methods for the assessment of strategic risks, and to consider issues that contribute to the choice between them. These four methods are described next.

Method 1: Active Management of the Largest Risks

Chief executives will often maintain that they are already aware of the main risks facing their organizations. In view of this, they would maintain that the most important risk-management task is to manage these risks well. This attitude is

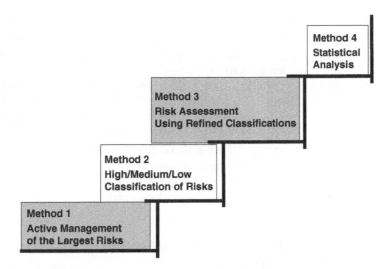

Exhibit 13.2 Methods of Quantifying Risk

justified by the fact that about 80 percent of the total risk facing an organization is usually concentrated in the top dozen risks.

In organizations that are beginning the implementation of risk management, and in those going through crisis situations, the resources available to control risk may be limited. In such circumstances it may be best to concentrate initially on the effective management of key risks. This avoids spreading the management effort too thinly and less effectively.

As illustrated previously, there are large differences between the impacts of different risks. Our example was drawn from ordinary life, but the point applies to company risks as well.

There are large differences, too, in risk probabilities. Some risks occur rarely and others happen quite frequently. Nevertheless, to uncover the top dozen risks with confidence it is usually necessary to consider at least twice that number of risks. This analysis often reveals a couple of large risks that have been underestimated by management.

It is sensible to take advantage of the effect of large differences in risk impact and probability through the adoption of an "Active" style of risk management (Box 13.4). It is certainly better to actively manage the top 12 risks than to make a long list of risks and do little about any of them!

Box 13.4 The Need to Attack Top Risks First

Probability	Impact	Action
High	High	Immediate
High	Low	Consider steps to take
Low	High	Consider steps to take and produce a contingency plan
Low	Low	Keep under review

The idea of concentrating on the top risks is good as a first approach to risk evaluation. Often it is also appropriate in a transitory situation where an organization is going through a process of rapid change. However, it is not an adequate basis for confident risk management in the medium term.

Active management of the top risks suffers from the drawback that it is not comprehensive. The business world is littered with examples of infrequently occurring risks that have led to the downfall of organizations. Sector regulators seek to ensure that companies do not overlook any risks that may have significant adverse impacts, but recent experience tells us that this is difficult to achieve in practice. However, favorable experience of the savings or risk reductions made by good management of the important risks indicates the benefits of extending management attention to the less significant risks as well.

Method 2: "High/Medium/Low" Classification of Risks: The Two-Dimensional Risk Map

A more complete coverage of risks may be obtained by using the two-dimensional risk map approach illustrated in Exhibit 13.3. Following this approach, a detailed list of risks is drawn together that, as far as possible, covers all the company's activities. For each risk, estimates of the probability of the risk occurring and the impact of the risk are made. These estimates are expressed in terms of High/Medium/Low categories and plotted on a risk map to illustrate graphically the relative rankings of their respective probabilities and impacts.[2]

It is common in this sort of approach to use traffic-light color highlights (i.e., red, amber, and green), in reports to distinguish high, medium, and low risks. Noncritical risks that are being managed satisfactorily are signified by a "Green Light" signal, and conversely high-risk situations that are causing concern are indicated by a "Red Light" signal.

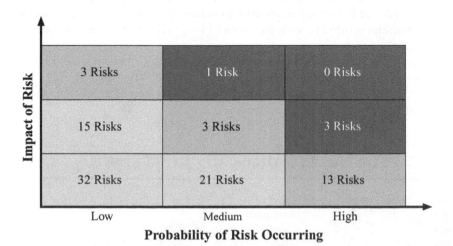

Exhibit 13.3   An Example of a Two-Dimensional Risk Map

The High/Medium/Low approach can work quite well if the risk analysis is done mainly by one person. However, if the risks are to be tackled at all levels of the organization, a number of people will need to be involved and there will be different views of specific risks. Often the definitions of the terms "high," "medium," and "low" are not exact and this can cause practical problems. Local managers, for example, may consider a specific risk in their projects to be high. This is because the projects they deal with represent the complete spectrum of their experience of the company. A board member or senior manager might only rate the risk as medium in light of a full knowledge of the company's risk map. Thus, classification bands need to be clearly defined so that all members of staff can participate in risk assessment.

The High/Medium/Low classification suffers from the deficiency that it is a crude yardstick. It does not register graduations of risk other than within the three-fold classification. So, if management expends effort to reduce a particular risk, it may well continue to register as "high." Thus, a system with only three graduations may be difficult to use for control purposes and at lower levels of the organization most risks would be classified as low. Thus, although this methodology meets the needs of some standards and regulators, we do not recommend it since, for a relatively small additional effort, a slightly more sophisticated methodology on the lines of Method 3 described below will be much more effective.

Method 3: Risk Assessment Using Refined Classifications: Refining the Classification

A possible solution to a simple but more effective risk management methodology is to employ a more refined classification of probabilities and impacts. For example, the graduations may be increased to five classifications such as Very High, High, Medium, Low, and Very Low, as recommended in the Australian and New Zealand Standards (Australian Standards 2004).

Defining Detailed Scales

If we have more scale graduations, it is more important to define exactly what we mean by each one. In order to achieve uniformity, numeric bands are established both for impact and probability. Thus, for a medium-sized company we might define a very high financial impact to mean an impact of more than say $10 million. Managers may not initially feel confident in making quantified probability estimates. However, in practice they are usually happy to estimate a probability using the probability scale as shown in Exhibit 13.4. In this scale, there is an approximate tripling of probability between one level and the next—this level of accuracy works well for many risk-management purposes, except for the most important risks that may need to be examined in detail.

In a situation where a risk is present with an associated set of controls, the question arises as to which probabilities we should assess. In particular, we normally assume that the existing controls are in place, and assess the probability that the risk will occur either in the following year or over the course of a short planning

Exhibit 13.4 An Example of a Probability Scale

Probability Score	Description	Range
5	Very High	More than 90%
4	High	31% to 90%
3	Medium	11% to 30%
2	Low	3% to 10%
1	Very Low	Less than 3%

period. Some practitioners, in particular those with an internal audit background, try to estimate also the probability that the risk would occur without the controls in place. This provides information on the value of the existing controls.

Similarly, managers are usually able to make a rough estimate of a financial impact, to the level of accuracy required by a system of scales, without too much effort. However, managers tend to be confused when faced with a situation where a risk has several types of impact, and their task is considerably simplified if they are supplied with a clear set of definitions such as those shown in Exhibit 13.5.

When using the scale shown in Exhibit 13.5 to assess a risk, managers should decide which has the highest type of impact and make the assessment based on this type. If a risk has mainly staff impact, and more than 50 staff are significantly affected, then the risk would be recorded as impact score 4. Similarly if there was major reputational damage, the score would be 4. However, if there were two or more types of impact at the same level, then the score would be one degree higher (i.e., a score of 5 in the above case).

Risk Perception Biases

It is known that estimates of impact or probability are prone to estimation bias, whether in quantified form or expressed as High/Medium/Low. There is a body of research work by Slovic, Tverski, Kahneman, and others on risk perception biases, mainly in the area of safety assessment. This research is now being applied to commercial risks (see Box 13.5). For a good summary of the development of the above theory, see the article on risk perception in Wikipedia.

A word of warning—care needs to be taken in using experts to assess risk. Paul Slovic found that experts are not necessarily any better at estimating probabilities than lay people. Experts are often overconfident in the exactness of their estimates, and put too much stock on small samples of data. When evaluating controls, you should guard against threshold bias. People prefer to move from uncertainty to certainty rather than making a similar gain that does not lead to full certainty. For example, most people would choose a control that reduces the incidence of a risk from 20 percent to 0 percent over one that reduces the incidence of the risk from 35 percent to 10 percent.

Documenting the Risk Appraisal

It is essential to keep good documentation of the causes of the risk that is being evaluated, and the assumptions being made as to how the company would be

Exhibit 13.5 An Example of an Impact Scale

Impact score	Description	Strategic	Financial % of turnover	Customers and staff	Reputational	Legal/Regulatory
5	Very High	Major impact on direction of business	Above 10%			Compulsory transfer of assets
4	High	Major impact on important business objective	3.1% to 10%	Significant impact on many (50-plus) customers or staff; Significant resource to rectify	Major adverse publicity and external interest with damage to reputation and/or long-term impact	Prosecution/ regulatory supervision
3	Medium	Noticeable impact but business still on course	1.1% to 3%	Noticeable Impact	Longer term adverse publicity, locally contained	Loss of regulatory approval
2	Low	Minor importance	0.3% to 1%	Minor or short-term problems	Short-term local adverse publicity	More serious breach but no long-term implications
1	Very Low		Less than 0.3%	Impact both minor and short-term	No adverse publicity	Minor breach of legal/regulatory requirements

Box 13.5   Risk perception

A desire for certainty is common in all people. Although we are risk averse to varying extents, one way to reduce the anxiety of confronting uncertainty is to deny it, leading to blind spots and the danger of unpleasant surprises. Probability and impact estimates can be biased by several effects:

- Availability bias: People tend to overestimate the probability of an event if instances of it are easy to recall or imagine.
- Illusion of control: In some circumstances people behave as if they were able to exact control when this is highly unlikely. Goal-focused leaders in stressful conditions are especially prone to this illusion.
- Confirmation bias: Having formed an opinion, people tend to pay more attention to information that confirms it and to ignore information that contradicts it.
- Group think: Reality testing can diminish as a result of group pressures to maintain unanimity and coherence.
- A feeling of dread: A dread risk elicits feelings of terror, uncontrollable catastrophe, and dislike of the unknown. The more a person dreads an activity, the higher its perceived risk, and the more that person wants the risk reduced.

affected. Clear documentation enables an analysis of the nature of a risk to be shared between managers, gives a basis for tracking risks over time, and helps in the removal of estimation biases. The scales methodology assigns a value to each probability or impact band as a representative value. Sometimes exact estimates rather than scale values are available, and in these cases the more accurate figures should be included. Managers should not forget to document their assumptions so that later revisions can be made.

Risk Databases

Many companies use spreadsheets to hold their risk information, but as their knowledge grows, and the number of controls increases, the spreadsheets become cumbersome. A best practice is to hold risk information in a relational database, together with all the other information regarding each risk. The database will typically contain specifications and control information in relation to all of the actions that are currently underway to reduce the risks that have been found and will also include risk reduction targets.

It is sometimes useful to differentiate in the database, for certain critical risks, between their short-term impact (i.e., their surprise element), and their medium-term effects. Risks whose impact is mainly short-term are likely to require different methods of management, and it is beneficial to be able to analyze the company's vulnerability to short-term shocks.

Method 4: Statistical Analysis

So far this chapter has discussed the use of bands or single "best guess" estimates of the impact and probability of each risk to represent its importance. However, this is a simplification of reality because in practice we may be uncertain of the probability estimates and the possible impact of the risk may vary continuously from almost zero to a high figure. Sometimes we may want to examine the impact of a number of risks together, for example, because their incidence is strongly interconnected.

In such cases we might be able to make some progress by examining a set of "what if" scenarios, making a range of assumptions for each risk. However, there may be too large a set of possibilities for this to be practical, in which case a more exact model can be created using Monte Carlo simulation techniques. This Monte Carlo approach is similar to the "what if" scenario method because it generates possible scenarios, but the number of scenarios examined is large and the variables used to generate the scenarios are weighted by the probability of their occurrence. Thus, each risk can be represented by a probability distribution rather than as a single value. The objective of the simulation model is to calculate the combined impact of the various uncertainties to obtain a probability distribution of the total outcome, perhaps at total-organization level. In practice this is easier to accomplish than one would think, because all the relevant technical aids are available in a spreadsheet-based form that is not difficult to use.

An example is shown in Exhibit 13.6 to demonstrate the logic of risk aggregation using two risks. In the example, the two risks lead to only four possible combined outcomes. In practice there will be a number of risks and each will have range of outcomes. Combining these together cannot be done manually, but cheap spreadsheet-based models are commercially available and these are not difficult to use.

Risks That Can Have Large Impacts

A company board of directors might ask whether any of the risks being considered by the risk managers might materialize in an extreme form, so that the existence of the organization was put at risk. Most risks have limited impact. For example, they may be limited by the value of the asset whose loss they represent; others can have a large impact, but with a correspondingly small probability. The extreme value parts of such risks tend to be risk-management blind spots and are often ignored because they might occur, say, once in 200 years or less. However, most companies will have a number of such risks, so that in aggregate they can be important, as many cases demonstrate. The problem in analyzing such risks revolves around the lack of data because there may have been no occurrences of the risk in living memory. However, a body of theoretical work has been done to analyze these situations statistically. This work was pioneered by Emil Gumbel, who in the 1950s showed that you can construct a statistical distribution (the Gumbel distribution) to represent the extreme-value "tail" of many risks (see Gumbel 1935, 1958). This was later generalized to include more risks by the introduction of the Generalized Extreme Value (GEV) distribution. This surprising result that all tails have similar shapes, and the intrinsic importance of the topic, has resulted in a body of research that is too mathematical to be covered here. A good introductory text in this area, giving many examples, is Reiss and Thomas (2001). Other references are Embrechts (1997) and Coles (2001).

See Box 13.6.

Box 13.6   Aggregating risks to a corporate total: A worked example

Risks do not "add up" in a straightforward manner, but can be aggregated using statistical techniques. This may be illustrated by the two-risk example set out below:

The example assumes two maintenance risks in a housing association's content. The two risks happen independently of one another.

Risk A. As a consequence of a lack of quality maintenance contractors there is a risk that maintenance may not be of suitable quality due to allocation of work to an incompetent contractor. The risk has an assessed probability of 25% per annum and impact of £30,000.

Risk B. There is a risk that taking legal proceedings against a maintenance contractor to achieve agreed performance may be disproportionately expensive due to slow court procedures. The risk has an assessed probability of 50% per annum and impact of £10,000.

In this way the average cost (often called the "expected loss") of each risk can be easily calculated. They can be simply added up to get the average cost for the whole organization.

AGGREGATING PROBABILITIES AND IMPACTS

In order to calculate what might happen in a particular year, say the next one, we need to enumerate the combinations of possibilities.

The table gives the distribution of combined impacts for the year. For example, there is a 12.5 percent probability of a combined loss of £40,000, but on the other hand a 37.5 percent probability of no loss at all. This illustrates that in practice it is more important to know the distribution of out-turns than it is to know the average cost of the risks.

Exhibit 13.6.A   Adding Expected Losses

Then the average cost of Risk A over a number of years will be 25% of £30,000 per year or	£7,500 per year
and the average cost of Risk B over a number of years will be 50% of £10,000 per year or	£5,000 per year
So the average cost of both risks together over a number of years will be	£12,500 per year

Exhibit 13.6.B   Calculating the Distribution of Combined Impacts

| | RISK A | | | RISK B | | | Combined Risks A and B | |
Happens?	Probability (%)	Impact (£)	Happens?	Probability (%)	Impact (£)		Probability	Impact (£)
Yes	25	30,000	Yes	50	10,000		12.5	40,000
Yes	25	30,000	No	50	—		12.5	30,000
No	75	—	Yes	50	—		37.5	10,000
No	75	—	No	50	—		37.5	—

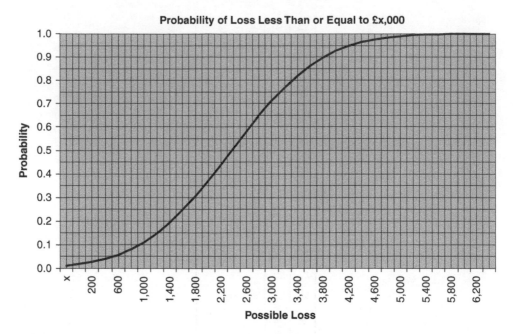

Exhibit 13.7 Medium-Term Total Corporate Risk of a Housing Association (Prior to Risk-Management Actions)

In practice there are many risks in an organization's risk profile and it would be impossible to do this analysis by hand.

TOTAL CORPORATE RISK: AN ILLUSTRATION

The total corporate risk faced by a company is not a single loss outcome. There is a wide possible range of outcomes that can be illustrated in the form of a distribution graph. This is also known as a cumulative probability distribution.

Exhibit 13.7 shows the risk distribution for a British housing association, calculated over a three-year planning period. By looking at the graph it can be seen that the median loss for the association, which maintains about 10,000 homes, is £2.4m over the planning period, as seen from the 50 percent (0.5) probability level on the graph. This justifies a vigorous program of risk management. It can be seen that there is an 80 percent chance that the association will have a loss of less than £3.3m over the planning period, and therefore a 20 percent chance the loss will be more than this. On the other hand, there is only a 20 percent chance that the association will have a loss of less than £1.4m over the planning period, so there is a large 80 percent probability that the loss will exceed this level.

Information of this type is crucial in setting the risk strategy and appetite for a company, and in deciding what level of contingency should be included in the business plan.

In the case concerned, a thorough risk-reduction program was implemented, and the total corporate risk was cut back by more than one-half.

INCORPORATING RISK QUANTIFICATION IN THE BUSINESS PLANNING PROCESS

It is good practice to use the business plan (excluding any general contingencies) as the basis for the evaluation of risks, so that the risk-management process can be integrated into the organization's normal planning and control mechanisms.

If the level of quantification in the risk-assessment process is based on the High/Medium/Low classification, it is not possible to aggregate the risks accurately. The consideration of risk in the business planning process must then be based on the analysis of individual risks using sensitivity analysis as explained further below.

On the other hand, if the quantification of an organization's top risks has been done accurately, for example by estimating probability distributions for each of these risks, paying due attention to the shapes of the tails of these distributions, and allowing for any correlations between them, then it is possible to aggregate the organization's risks into a total organization risk profile. If all the risks are measured against the baseline performance shown in the organization's business plan, then the above profile will represent the risk profile of the business plan.

This analysis can then be used as the basis for any general contingencies included in the plan. For example, the level of contingency might be chosen such that there is a 75 percent chance that the financial performance assumed in the plan will be met.

Similarly, the extremes of the distribution of a "Worst Case Financial Scenario" can be evaluated. The result can be compared with the company's financial covenants, and help in confirming its financial security.

These considerations will confirm the ability of a risk management action program to drive down the total corporate risk to lower levels.

It follows that a company's risk management strategy should be closely related to and consistent with its overall strategy. In particular, the overall strategy should not conflict with the risk appetite of the organization. The risk appetite might be set in the risk management strategy statement as limiting the total amount of risk taken so that it does not exceed agreed-upon quantified limits.

SENSITIVITIES AND SCENARIOS

As part of business-planning analysis, it is important for the management and the board of directors to understand the way in which the plan depends on critical assumptions. Many companies use the information collected in the risk management system to calculate the sensitivity of the plan to changes in individual key assumptions, both in financial terms and in terms of failure to meet other targets.

The results of the analysis are usually expressed as the effect of a unit change in an assumption (for example, a 1 percent increase in interest rates). This begs the question of just how likely it is that a 1 percent change will happen. It is helpful to supplement this information by taking a view as to how much the interest rates could increase, at a given level of probability, and to calculate the impact of this. For example, it may be the view of the financial markets that there is a 10 percent chance that the average interest rates over a company's business planning period could be more than, say, 1.5 percent than the rates assumed. The sensitivity calculation would show that if this happened, the impact on the company would be, say, £2m.

Once a set of sensitivities has been calculated for the key planning uncertainties, it is possible to combine them to calculate the robustness of the plan to particular self-consistent combinations of assumption changes, or scenarios. This process, though time-consuming, is useful in building up the confidence of management in the robustness of the plan. By making a careful choice of scenarios to be evaluated, the planning team can, at the same time, consider how they would adjust their plans in the eventuality that each of the scenarios materializes. Some possible plans might be more flexible than others and might be preferred for this reason.

Many organizations use spreadsheet models to hold their planning data. Often some of the key assumptions underlying the plan, for example those concerning inflation and interest rates, are represented explicitly in particular cells of the spreadsheet. By putting probability distributions rather than single values into these cells and then running a Monte Carlo simulation it is possible to obtain a probability distribution showing the sensitivity of the plan to likely combinations of these key planning assumptions.

It is also helpful to set up early warning systems to detect changes from plan assumptions (see Box 13.7).

Box 13.7   Early Warning Mechanisms

Business objectives and related plans need to include measurable performance targets and indicators. Key Performance Indicators can be useful early warning mechanisms. However, management's usual Key Performance Indicators may not be sufficient on their own for this purpose as they are generally designed to report past results. By the time Key Performance Indicators have shown a significant deterioration it may be too late to prevent losses or other adverse effects. Therefore, consider also the use of Key Risk Indicators.

Source: Excerpt from "Implementing Turnbull—A Boardroom Briefing," ICAEW.

To summarize, the reliability of the business-planning process can be significantly enhanced by the incorporation of risk quantification techniques.

CONCLUSION

This chapter discusses the four alternative approaches of an organization's quantification of risk. The choice depends on the organization's circumstances and capabilities. The chapter also presents a method for quantifying the total amount of risk in an organization's business plan. The members of the board need to feel that they have adequately assessed the risk and that the residual risk, after reduction measures and controls, is acceptable.

NOTES

1. For information on quantifying risks in financial institutions, see Marrison, 2002.
2. The British Risk Management Standard, published by IRM, Airmic, and Alarm, is based on this 3 by 3 matrix approach.

REFERENCES

Abbate D., Farkas, W., and Gourier, E. 2008. Operational risk quantification using extreme value theory and copulas: From theory to practice. *SSRN* (July).

Australia Standards. 2004. AS/NZS 4360 risk management.

Coles, S. 2001. *An introduction to statistical modeling of extreme values.* London, UK: Springer-Verlag.

Condamin L., Louisot, J-P., and Naim, P. 2006. *Risk quantification: Management, diagnosis and hedging.* New York: John Wiley & Sons.

COSO. 2004. Enterprise risk management—Integrated framework executive summary.

Embrechts P., Kluppelberg, C., and Mikosch, T. 1997. *Modelling extreme values for insurance and finance.* Berlin, Germany: Springer-Verlag.

Embrechts P., McNeil, A., and Straumann, D. 2002. Correlation and dependence in risk management properties and pitfalls. *Risk management: Value at risk and beyond*, M.A.H. Dempster, ed. (2002b). 176–223.

Garlick A. 2007. Estimating risk, a management approach. *Gower* (July).

Gumbel B. 1935. Les valeurs extrêmes des distributions statistiques. *Annales de l'Institut Henri Poincaré, 5*, 115–158.

Gumbel B. 1958. *Statistics of extremes.* New York: Columbia University Press.

Hargreaves J., and Mikes, A. 2001. The Quantification of Risk. *The Housing Corporation.*

Hubbard D. 2007. *How to measure anything: Finding the value of intangibles in business.* Hoboken, NJ: John Wiley & Sons.

Kahnerman D., Slovic, P., and Tversky, A. 1982. *Judgement under uncertainty: Heuristics and biases.* Cambridge, UK: Cambridge University Press.

Marrison C. 2002. *The fundamentals of risk measurement.* New York: McGraw-Hill.

Moeller R. 2007. *COSO enterprise risk management.* Hoboken, NJ: John Wiley & Sons.

Reiss, R-D., and Thomas, M. 2001. *Statistical analysis of extreme values.* 2nd ed. Basel, Switzerland: Birkhauser.

Slovic P., Ed. 2000. *The perception of risk.* London, UK: *EarthscanLtd.*

Slovic P., Fischhoff, B., and Lichtenstein, S. 1982. Why study risk perception? *Risk Analysis* 2 (2): 83–93.

Tversky A., and Kahneman, D. 1974. Judgment under uncertainty: Heuristics and biases. *Science 185* (4157) (September): 1124–1131.

ABOUT THE AUTHOR

Following a mathematics degree at Cambridge University and six years KPMG strategy consultancy experience, **John Hargreaves** took up a series of financial positions including periods as the Financial Controller of National Freight, a stint running Shell's central financial and management accounting and planning systems, and three years as the Finance Director of London Underground.

Since 1991 John has specialized in risk management, initially as Corporate Finance Director of Barclays Bank where he was responsible for introducing risk management systems following the last United Kingdom depression.

In 1996 he became Managing Director of Hargreaves Risk and Strategy, which has clients in the housing, banking, oil, and transport sectors. The consultancy has implemented risk management systems in about 60 organizations.

John is a leading expert on the quantification of risks. He has conducted research over a number of years on the risk profile of the U.K. social housing sector, initially through study of client risk maps but also through analysis of the risks that occurred in a sample of 41 companies. This knowledge was used in 2005 in the design of the sector's highly successful risk-related regulatory system.

John is also an authority on the relationship between risk management and strategy, and for 15 years has run a course on Strategic Management for an MSc program at the London School of Economics.

PART IV

Types of Risk

CHAPTER 14

Market Risk Management and Common Elements with Credit Risk Management

RICK NASON, PhD, CFA
Associate Professor Finance, Dalhousie University Principal, RSD Solutions

INTRODUCTION TO CREDIT RISK AND MARKET RISK

Credit risk is the potential for gain or loss due to changes in the credit worthiness of a customer or counterparty. Market risk is the potential for gain or loss due to changes in market conditions such as interest rates, commodity prices, exchanges rates, and other economic and financial variables such as stock prices or housing starts.

Credit and market risks differ from other risks such as operational risks in the sense that credit and market risks, as the name implies, are priced and observed in the capital markets. As such, tools and strategies exist to both measure and manage these risks while the measurement of most other types of risk are necessarily more subjective.

Due to their quantitative nature, along with the availability of data, credit, and market risk are probably the most studied and analyzed of the various risks that a manager needs to control. The availability of testable models, abundance of data, and the mathematical elegance of the field, however, mask the fact that credit and market risk management still remains as much of an art as it does a science. The lure of mathematical models for risk management is always strong, but the risk manager does well to remember that the only perfect hedge is in a Japanese Garden.

In this and the following chapter a framework for analyzing credit and market risk will be outlined. This chapter presents a common outline and taxonomy for considering these risks and proceeds to develop a framework that provides a focus on market risk. Chapter 15 continues the discussion with a focus on credit risk and a discussion of the factors behind the global credit crisis.

A Taxonomy of Market and Credit Risk

A wide variety of risks could ultimately be characterized, or linked to market risks. For the purposes of this chapter we utilize the following framework for considering these risks.

- Credit Risks
  - Customer credit risk: the risk that a customer cannot or will not pay an obligation or debt, whether it be through financial distress, dishonesty, or for legal reasons.
  - Sovereign risk: the risk that a sovereign, such as the government of a country, imposes an action, regulation, or law that effectively prevents an obligation from becoming fully payable in a timely fashion or else leads to an asset being expropriated in some shape or form.
  - Funding risk: the risk that the corporation itself cannot obtain sufficient funding in a timely fashion or at reasonable cost.
- Market Risks
  - Currency risk: the risk that changes in exchange rates impact the expected cash flows of an entity. Note that currency risk can have a direct effect such as the realized cash flows in the home currency differ from expectations, or indirectly in that expected sales are impacted due to competitive price changes related to exchange rates.
  - Interest rate risk: the risk that changes in interest rates impact the expected cash flows of an entity.
  - Commodity price risk: the risk that changes in commodity prices impact the expected cash flows of an entity.
  - Equity price risk: the risk that changes in equity prices impact the expected cash flows or operating strategies of an entity.
  - Economic risk: the risk that changes in various economic variables such as GDP growth, housing starts, or consumer confidence impact the expected cash flows or operating strategies of an entity.
  - Liquidity risk: the risk that changes in market liquidity dramatically impacts the ability of an organization to facilitate trades or trading strategies in an efficient manner and at reasonable costs due to shifts in market trading activity.

The combination of these risks has far-reaching implications beyond the impact on cash flows. Often the risks have significant correlations or feedback loops. Additionally their visible nature means that both competitors and customers are dealing with them simultaneously in unique or common ways, which can lead to market-wide feedback loops or cause conventional coping strategies to become more difficult to implement due to demand and market-wide liquidity issues.

Credit and market risks directly affect the broader economy and indeed the context of business. The simple perception (accurate or not) of significant changes in any of the above economic variables can have significant implications for a corporate entity as its creditors, shareholders, suppliers, and regulators have their own assessment of how the position of the entity has changed and thus react in their own ways accordingly. A dramatic example of this would be the impact of the credit crunch on the investment banking firm of Bear Stearns. The fears (real or perceived) that Bear Stearns would not be able to meet obligations or secure adequate funding led to customer withdrawal of activity with the firm and instigated the involvement of the Federal Reserve in proactively forcing a merger rescue.

Credit and Market Risk in an ERM Framework

As discussed, credit and market risks have impacts that reach far beyond the cash flows of an organization. Credit and market risks have an impact on the political, legal, and regulatory environment of business. They impact on business and consumer confidence. All of this results in implications for the marketing and operating strategies of an organization.

It is easy, but incorrect to dismiss these risks as a necessary and unavoidable part of doing business. While credit and market risks affect all firms to a greater or lesser extent, there are plenty of examples to illustrate how an organization's preparedness and response to these issues lead to competitive advantage. A clear example is that of Southwest Airlines, which by proactively and strategically hedging fuel costs, gained a significant cost advantage over competitors that for various reasons (some legitimate, and some dubious) consciously decided not to act on the risk of changing fuel prices.

As credit and market risk impact on the firm's business environment, relations with stakeholders (including creditors, shareholders, suppliers, employees, regulators, and customers), strategic plans and operating tactics, it is natural and imperative to include these risks into a company's ERM strategy. Although the nature and character of credit and market risk imply that it is simply the role of the CFO or treasurer to manage, (and indeed that is functionally where the strategies are most likely to be implemented), it is important to have credit and market risks considered, and the impacts on other risks taken into account within an ERM framework. Credit and market risks are not stand-alone risks. They impact on the other risks inherent in an organization, and likewise the specific credit and market risk of a firm are impacted by decisions made in managing the firm as a whole.

The financial risk philosophy of a firm has a direct link to the key strategies of the firm. For example, gold-mining companies tend to fall into two distinct groups: (1) those that hedge the price of gold for all of their expected future production, and (2) those that do not hedge any of their production. A gold company that hedges production is stating to its stakeholders that it is a company that is focusing on mining gold as efficiently as possible, and its success or failure will be based on this principle. A company that does not hedge its gold sales will have its success largely based on movements in the expected future price of gold. Obviously these two groups of companies appeal to very different shareholder groups. Shareholders who purchase gold stocks as a proxy for an investment in gold will prefer investing in those companies that do not hedge production, while investors who do not want gold price risk in their portfolios will prefer investing in companies that fully hedge production. A similar argument can be made for multinational companies that hedge, or do not hedge, their foreign currency exposures.

Credit risk management is also a strategic and an operating principle. For example, many car companies compete by offering generous credit terms. Alternatively, companies use their financing structure (and by implication their corporate credit risk) as a key part of their operating strategy. A low-debt, low-financial leverage policy tends to lead to a higher cost of capital, but with the advantage of decreasing the risk of bankruptcy and increasing financial flexibility, which can often be used to advantage in adverse economic conditions or tight credit market conditions.

It is important to note that credit and market risk decisions must be conscious strategic decisions. Financial theory does not give black-and-white answers to the correct response organizations should take to these risks. Credit and market risk management philosophies and strategies should be consciously decided on in an ERM framework that recognizes their strategic importance and their interrelatedness with other risks.

RESPONDING TO CREDIT AND MARKET RISK

Later in this chapter we discuss the specific actions that an entity can take in response to market risks. At this point, however, it is worthwhile to discuss the question of whether a firm should attempt to manage its market risks.

Before attempting to implement a risk management strategy it is first necessary to choose a risk philosophy. For publicly traded companies the following examples of risk philosophies as stated by two different corporate CEOs show two polar extremes that such risk philosophies might take:

1. "We have an absolute duty to our shareholders to mitigate those risks that are not mainstream to our business."
2. "Our shareholders do not expect or want normal economic relationships to be hedged away."

Where a corporation's philosophy of risk management lies between these two extremes depends on a variety of factors including:

- The competitive structure of the industry.
  - For example, can adverse commodity price changes be passed through to customers?
- The relative importance of cost as a competitive advantage.
- The tolerance of management and stakeholders for cash-flow volatility.
  - Does management get particularly nervous and spend an inordinate amount of time focusing on market risks to the detriment of the day-to-day management of the business?
  - Will creditors and potential customers be concerned about the viability of the business during times of adverse market conditions?
- The understanding by management of the tools and techniques of risk management.
  - Does management understand the basics of risk management instruments?
  - Does management feel comfortable in their understanding?
  - What is the comfort level of the board and major stakeholders in the use of risk management products?

- Management's perception of the wishes of shareholders.
  - What are the analysts writing about a company's risk management practices?
  - How do shareholders view the relative importance of risk management as a competitive advantage?
- The methods by which management's performance is measured and compensated.
  - Are managers significant shareholders in the firm?
  - Do managers have a significant portion of compensation that is performance-based? What are the performance measures used?
- Management's view of market direction and the strength of that view.
  - Does management have a positive or negative view of potential market price changes?
  - What is the strength of that view and what are the consequences of being wrong?

As the above points signify, there are several considerations, many of them often conflicting, to consider in the setting of a risk philosophy. As the following sections will argue, there are compelling arguments for and against aggressively managing market risk. One fact that is intuitively obvious is that a firm should be consistent in adhering to a stable risk philosophy.

The Case for Actively Managing Market Risk

There are many strong arguments for actively managing market risk. These arguments include: more predictable cash flows, reduction of financing costs, fiduciary responsibilities, to maintain focus on the core business strategy and operations, and avoidance of uncertainty.[1]

The main argument for actively managing market risks is to maintain predictability and consistency of cash flows. Predictability and consistency of cash flows are significant for a variety of reasons. To begin, shareholders and creditors prefer to have more predictable cash flows. Predictability of cash flows aids in operational planning, and forecasting. For companies that require ongoing research, development, or capital expenditures, the stability of cash flows helps to ensure that the necessary investments can be made regardless of economic conditions.

Stability of cash flows aids in the reduction of capital raising costs for two reasons. Not only do creditors and shareholders tend to reward more stable companies with lower costs of capital, but proactive management of market risk also reduces the probability of financial stress, which by itself leads to lower capital costs. Active risk management is also likely to open additional sources of financing such as securitizations, international financings, and structured financings as well as leading to a wider circle of potential investors and creditors, all of which increase liquidity for the firm and lower the cost of capital.

In certain instances the corporation may have an explicit or perceived fiduciary responsibility to manage market risk. Several different legal cases have been brought forward by shareholders claiming that the failure to disclose risk management policies was material information that needed to be disclosed. There have also been legal cases involving public corporations where management and directors were sued for failing to be proactive in market risk management. The basic result of these cases was that although it is not a requirement of management and directors to implement proactive market risk management, it is incumbent on them to make conscious and informed decisions regarding proactive market risk philosophies and strategies.

By proactively and properly managing market risk, management has one less thing to worry about. This allows the management team to focus on implementing core operational strategies without needing to be overly concerned about market events.

Finally, a major reason for market risk management is the certainty factor. Alternatively this could be called the "fear factor" or the "sleep factor." By knowing that market risk is actively managed, it means that management does not need to unnecessarily worry about market fluctuations.

The Case for Not Actively Managing Market Risk

Perhaps surprisingly there are many reasons for a corporation to not be proactive in managing market risk.[2] These reasons include: it is costly to do, it may not be in the shareholders' best interest, and it is difficult to do properly.

There is no debating that market risk management techniques can be costly. The direct costs are the fees (including spreads) that financial institutions charge for providing hedging instruments and strategies. Although forward-type transactions do not involve a premium, they involve a bid-ask spread on the forward price and they also can be costly in terms of upside risk that is foregone in the case of favorable market moves.[3] Option-type strategies involve an explicit upfront fee that many managers are reluctant to incur as the cost of the "insurance" is seen to outweigh the potential benefits of the hedge. A second cost of managing market risk is the need for information systems and professional risk managers to manage the positions of what has become an increasingly specialized field of expertise. Finally, a large-scale hedging program increases the complexity of the accounting and reporting requirements.

Reconsider for a moment the earlier example of gold companies that hedge all of their gold production. Investors who invest in gold-mining companies as a proxy for investing in gold do not want these companies to hedge the market price risk of gold. These investors want and expect the share price of these mining companies to fluctuate as gold prices fluctuate, which, of course, will not be the case if the company has hedged all of their gold production.

A related argument against corporate hedging of market risk is that savvy investors are in a better position to understand and manage their personal risk positions. Although this argument is perhaps true for sophisticated investors, it ignores the fact that few individual investors have the knowledge or time to conduct active risk management of their personal portfolios. Additionally it ignores the economies of scale that exist for a corporation in hedging their exposures. However, the argument is quite legitimate in the case of large institutional investors who may actively want to self-manage market risks and have the scale, technology, and capabilities to do so effectively.

The final argument against active risk management is that it is difficult to do properly and effectively. The well-known derivatives and hedging debacles are testament to this line of thinking. Most market risk management strategies involve derivatives that are difficult to understand and price. Additionally, even the simplest of derivatives can have subtle yet significant collateral effects, especially when market prices are volatile or the market is illiquid. As will be seen later in this chapter, there are a myriad number of factors that need to be taken into account and that are difficult to estimate, including the size and timing of the exposure. Ultimately, market risk management is as much an art as it is a science. The fact that market risk management is difficult, however, should not by itself be an excuse for not attempting to understand and manage these risks.

Natural Market Risk Management

Frequently, when market risk management is mentioned it is assumed that it involves the use of some sort of derivative or similarly complicated financial products. However, that does not necessarily need to be the case. Natural- or nonderivative-based risk management involves using operating, marketing, and/or financing strategies that minimize or potentially eliminate the need for a corporation to utilize complicated financial instruments.

The simplest way to hedge naturally is to diversify product lines, diversify geographically (both in terms of operations and in terms of product marketing), and to diversify funding sources as well as the countries of origin and types of funding.

For instance, a company with significant foreign currency exposure in its sales could mitigate some of the exchange exposure by funding in the country of their foreign sales. As foreign currency inflows drop due to currency fluctuations, so would the cash flows required to make interest payments in that same foreign currency. Likewise, increases in interest flows in the foreign currency would be offset somewhat by increased sales receipts due to the same currency changes.

Funding in a foreign country is particularly effective to hedge sovereign risk events such as expropriation. Assuming that debt contracts are appropriately cross-referenced to market disruption events such as currency controls or expropriation, a company can hedge a foreign capital investment in a country with significant sovereign risk by funding in that country. In the case of a sovereign event such as expropriation occurring, the company can at least (again assuming proper legal construction of funding contracts) walk away from its financial obligations. This obviously does not hedge or replace forgone future profits from the affected investment, but it does mean that the company does not suffer the double indignity of not only losing a capital investment but also having to repay the financing that went into it. The fact that a major foreign capital investment is funded with capital from the country of the investment may in some cases prevent an expropriation from occurring by making the sovereign think twice about the political fallout from targeting a company that has cross linkages with domestic investors.

Another simple way to mitigate exchange-rate risk is to diversify globally. Rarely do all currencies move in concert against a given developed country's currency. Marketing globally also generally opens up name recognition and thus funding potential with foreign investors. This increase in financial flexibility can be a competitive advantage in funding during times of tight market liquidity.

Other types of natural hedges involve passing on costs to customers through cost-plus contracts, as well as backward and forward integration on the supply and value chain. In fact the types of natural hedges available are limited only by the self-imposed operational constraints and management's willingness to engage in creative ideas.

The central issue with many natural hedges, however, is that they may drag the company out of its operational comfort zone. Additionally, natural hedges are seldom as well-fitted as financial-based hedges such as derivatives. It is wise to remember that financial hedges are never perfect as well.

Another issue with natural hedges is that they are long-term hedges. The time required to put them into place and to have them take effect is often over an entire business cycle—certainly not ideal for a management team that believes it needs to appease investors in each and every quarter.

MEASURING MARKET RISK

Before risk can be effectively managed, the nature and size of the risk must be measured. There are two distinct parts to measuring risk. The first part consists of uncovering what risks exist, while the second component is determining the size of the risk. Many different measures and techniques exist to calculate the size of a given risk; however, the determination of the existing risks rely on the experience, intuition, and creativeness of the risk manager.

To paraphrase a quote by Donald Rumsfeld, "there are known knowns, . . . known unknowns . . . and unknown unknowns. . . ."[4] In the context of market risk, the "known knowns" might, for example, be the fact that a company might know that its sales are related to the yen exchange rate. The "known unknown" might be that the company does not know how sensitive the relationship is. An "unknown unknown" might be the fact that the real driver of the company's sales is not the exchange rate of the yen, but the growth rate in China, which is the driver of the growth of its sales to suppliers in Japan who then forward sell to China.

It can be argued that the most significant risks that a company faces are the "unknown unknowns." The unfortunate aspect of this is that an organization is limited in what it can do to effectively manage a risk that it does not recognize as existing. For this reason it is incumbent on a risk management team to think creatively or in the "white spaces" when starting the exercise of measuring risk. An organization cannot plan for or mitigate all risks, but a creative team that focuses on what might be on the horizon can be a real asset to a firm. Additionally, by continually thinking creatively about what risks might occur, a firm will become better at recognizing the early stages of a shift that might lead to a unique risk coming into play.

There are a variety of techniques to compile the risks that a company faces. The first is to compile those risks that management and the employees are already aware of through focus groups and management debriefing sessions. The board of directors, with a broader mindset, and a more diverse set of backgrounds can be helpful in recognizing the risks on the horizon that management is missing due to its focus on the business. Of course, many of the risks will be a natural part of the day-to-day management of the business.

The Markets as Risk Indicators

The financial markets themselves provide many indications of risks on the horizon. Markets are efficient and effective indicators since they are composed of the collective judgment of a wide group of people who have a strong vested interest in the prices being accurate. Markets are composed of long-term investors, short-term speculators, consumers and suppliers of commodities and currencies, borrowers and lenders, as well as hedgers, central banks, and arbitragers. Each of these groups has a vested interest in profiting either directly or indirectly (through, for example, buying commodities and manufacturing them into higher value finished goods). Thus, the markets reflect the balance of the supply and demand for goods, currencies, and borrowing, the balance between the short- and long-term views of investors, and the actions of the arbitragers, regulators, and central banks that step in whenever the markets are perceived as out of balance.

The stock market is often quoted as a primary leading indicator of the future performance of the economy. Although major indices such as the S&P 500 give a broad indication of investors' projections for the future health of the economy, single stock prices can give indications of the future fortunes of an individual firm.

A second primary indicator in the markets is the publicly traded futures markets. Futures markets provide the prices at which investors, hedgers, and speculators are willing to trade commodities, interest rates, and currencies at a given time in the future. While futures prices are not perfect indicators of actual realized prices in the future, the quoted prices are generally considered to be one of the best indicators and are also considered to be unbiased in the sense that they will equally overstate and understate price changes.

Volatility of prices in the financial markets gives information about the level of uncertainty. The higher the volatility of the markets, the higher the level of uncertainty. A commonly followed index is the VIX, a daily index compiled and published by the Chicago Board of Options Exchange (CBOE). The VIX is an index that is composed by measuring the implied volatility that is implicit in the prices of equity options traded on the exchange. A high level of the VIX implied that investors are uncertain of the future direction of price changes.[5]

Volatility of market prices is measured by taking the standard deviation of market prices. A second related measure that is important for risk management is to measure the correlation of price changes. The correlation of price changes is just as important—if not more important—than the volatility in individual prices. Market prices are all interrelated to one extent or another. For example, oil prices tend to be correlated with equity prices and equity prices tend to be correlated with interest rates. Thus, examining risks in isolation can provide a distorted or even a misleading picture of the effect on an organization.

A frequently cited problem with using market data to calculate the potential impact of risks is that markets tend to be unstable. Indeed an examination of volatility levels and correlations can show large changes in relatively short periods of time.

A related technique that some companies use to measure the impact of outside forces comes from the developing field of prediction markets. Prediction markets have been in use for many years as a way to gauge elections. In a prediction market, participants buy "shares" in the future value or outcome of a variable. For example, a prediction market can be set up to predict the outcome of an election by having the shareholders who own shares in the winning candidate receive $1 for each share they own if that candidate wins. If the shares for candidate A sell for $0.63, and for candidates B and C for $0.22 and $0.15, respectively, then the prediction market is indicating that the probability of Candidate A winning is 63 percent, while the probabilities of candidates B and C winning are 22 percent and 15 percent, respectively.

A company can set up a prediction market to predict the demand for a given product by selling shares that represent various levels of demand in the future. The shares that trade among the participants at the highest prices are then taken as the most likely levels of demand to occur. Trading in a prediction market is allowed to take place at several different times. For instance, if a company wanted to predict the level of demand two years hence, it could issue "shares" with each share representing a different level of demand. Participants in the prediction market would then meet at a regular time (perhaps weekly) for a series of two months, with the market being considered closed at the end of the eight trading periods. The level of demand for which the shares were trading at the highest price would represent the most probable level of demand two years into the future. The company could then base its operational plans on this level of demand. Prediction markets have been shown to be surprisingly accurate, and generally better than using the predictions of experts, even when the participants in the prediction market are not all that well informed or knowledgeable about the field for which they are making a prediction.[6]

Measuring Potential Impact

Following the volatility and correlations of market prices and futures prices gives an indication of the direction of prices and how much they have the potential to change in a given period of time. The next step is to measure the effect of those price changes on the organization. It is key to determine whether the impact desired is the impact on earnings or the impact on cash flows, which may or may not be highly correlated to each other. Although financial theory suggests that cash flows are the more significant variable to manage, the publication of a firm's earnings are more widespread and, thus, the metric that is most closely followed by investors and the metric by which managers are most often compensated. Creditors, however, are more likely to be concerned about the impact of risks on cash flows.

A primary method to measure the impact on a firm is to run a regression of earnings against the price changes of various market variables. For instance, a company that has two commodity inputs and sells in two different currencies might run the following regression of quarterly earnings versus percent changes in each of the two currencies and percent changes in the two commodity prices:

$$E_t = A + CA_t + CB_t + FXA_t + FXB_t + \varepsilon_t \qquad (14.1)$$

In the above equation E_t is the percentage growth of earnings in time period t, while CA_t, CB_t, FXA_t, and FXB_t are the percentage changes in the price of commodity A, commodity B, exchange rate A, and exchange rate B for time period t respectively. (A and ε_t are an intercept and error term, respectively.)

When compiling the above equation one has to be careful because correlation among the variables can lead to inaccurate and misleading conclusions from the regression. For instance, a strong correlation may exist between a currency and a commodity in the regression. If the correlation is not accounted for, the regression results will be skewed, leading one to believe that one of the critical variables is not significant or vice versa. A second problem with performing a regression is the amount of data needed to get reliable results. Generally, upward of 10 years of quarterly data is needed before statistically significant results are obtained. Depending on the industry, economic relationships that existed 5 to 10 years ago may or may not still be relevant when looking at the next five years for risk management purposes.

Earnings at Risk

When the size of the potential move in market prices has been determined, and the effect of a move on market prices on the firm has also been calculated, then the two can be combined into a measure called Earnings at Risk. Earnings at Risk (EAR) is the corporate application of Value at Risk (VAR), which is used to measure potential losses in investment management and financial institutions. EAR is the most negative level of earnings that a corporation is expected to have with a given level of confidence. For instance, the EAR for a publicly traded company might be a negative $3.50 per share with 95 percent confidence. In other words, this EAR measure is saying that 95 percent of the time the earnings of the corporation will be better than a negative $3.50.

The full details of calculating the EAR are beyond the scope of this chapter. The basic process, however, is to measure the potential range of movements of market variables by measuring the standard deviation and correlations of market movements as described in the previous section. The impact of changes in market prices on the components of a firm's earnings, such as the impact on the firm's sales, expenses, interest expenses, and such is modeled. Then the firm's earnings are modeled using Monte Carlo simulation techniques and the distribution of the firm's potential earnings are calculated and usually presented in the form of a histogram as shown in Exhibit 14.1. The EAR is the value that corresponds to the leftmost area of the curve. The probability that the realized earnings of the company will be greater than the EAR is the area under the distribution to the right of the EAR level. Equivalently, we can state that the probability of the realized earnings of the company being below the EAR will be equal to the area under the curve in the "left-tail" of the distribution.

The EAR is a powerful and useful risk management tool. The management team can rerun the simulation, remodeling the firm assuming that certain risk management actions had been implemented so managers can compare the distribution of earnings given one risk management strategy versus a different strategy. A simulation obviously does not provide an answer to what will actually happen in the future, but it does provide a reasonable estimate of the range and the probabilities of possible outcomes.

There are also several drawbacks to utilizing Earnings at Risk. To begin, the technique is relatively complicated to calculate. Not only does it require knowledge of Monte Carlo simulation techniques, it also requires the firm to understand how

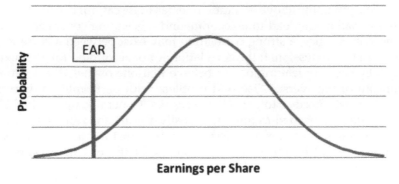

Exhibit 14.1 Histogram of Potential Earnings

each of the economic variables impacts the firm's results. These relationships are needed to build an accurate model. An inaccurate model will produce results that will not only be inaccurate but also misleading. It can also be argued that the insight gained from forcing the organization to understand how the income statement can be modeled from economic variables is a useful exercise in its own right for the management to carry out, whether or not it plans to conduct a Monte Carlo analysis for the purposes of calculating an EAR value.[7]

MARKET RISK MANAGEMENT WITH FORWARD-TYPE PRODUCTS

There are two main classes of derivatives that are used for managing market risk, namely forward-type products (forwards, futures, and swaps), and option-type products (calls, puts, captions, and swaptions). The characteristics of these two classes of hedging instruments are quite different and each implies a different set of risk philosophies of the firm.

Forwards are bi-lateral agreements to exchange an asset or a cash flow at a preset price and a preset time in the future. Forwards are over the counter (OTC) contracts traded between a corporate and a financial counterparty. Futures on the other hand are exchange-traded products. Economically the two products accomplish similar results, but the structural differences can be relatively significant.

The "buyer" of a forward (or futures) contract is agreeing to buy a preset amount of the underlying asset at a preset price and at a preset time in the future. Conversely, the "seller" of a forward contract is agreeing to sell the underlying asset at the same terms.

There is not an initial cash flow to enter into a forward contract (with the exception of margin or collateral, to be discussed later in this section). Instead, the price at which the transaction is to take place in the future is set so that it is a "fair" trade to both counterparties. After the forward price is set, economic conditions will change and thus the value of the contract will move in favor of either the buyer or seller of the forward contract.

Forwards and futures are available on a wide variety of financial indices, rates, and economic variables. For instance, futures are available on interest rates, stock and bond indices, government bonds (used as a proxy hedge for long-term interest rates), currencies, all sorts of commodities and variables such as temperature and rainfall.

Forward-type contracts "lock in" the price of the underlying commodity or rate at the maturity of the contract. For example, if a U.S.-domiciled company is expecting receipt of 200,000 euros in six months time it can enter into a forward contract today to sell those euros at a fixed price of 1 euro to 1.40 USD in six months. Note that if the value of Euros versus the U.S. dollar falls to, for example, 1 euro to 1.30 USD, then the company will benefit from the trade because it will still receive 280,000 USD, versus the current market value of 260,000 USD. Conversely, if the value of the euro increases relative to the U.S. dollar, for example, to 1 euro to 1.55 USD, then the company will have an opportunity cost since it will be obligated to sell the 200,000 euros at the lower preset exchange rate and receive only 280,000 USD instead of the current market value of 310,000 USD. An additional risk of using forwards to hedge occurs if the company does not receive the euros (if, for example, its client declares bankruptcy and cannot pay). In this situation, the company will still be forced to sell 200,000 euros to the forward counterparty at the preset forward price.

The same logic holds for multiperiod forward-type contracts such as interest rate swaps that "lock in" the effective interest rate. Although the locking-in feature of forward-type contracts reduces uncertainty in future asset and liability exposures, it does not allow the hedging company to profit from favorable moves in underlying prices and rates.

Hedging with forwards is quite straightforward assuming the size of the exposure has been accurately calculated. Since forward type strategies lock in the value and size of the hedge, it is imperative to have the hedge size properly calibrated. If the size of the exposure is uncertain, then it introduces another risk into the forward hedge, namely that the hedging company may be under-hedged if it underestimated the size of the exposure or over-hedged if it overestimated the size of the exposure. Return to the previous example of the company hedging an expected payment of 200,000 euros in six months, and locking it in with a forward contract to sell the euros for U.S. dollars at a rate of 1 euro to 1.40 USD. If the amount of receipts is actually only 170,000 euros and the euro appreciates to 1.60 USD, then the company will experience a loss on the excess hedge of 30,000 euros (which it will have to purchase at a price of 1.60 USD) and only receive 1.40 USD on these 30,000 extra euros. The loss will be 30,000 times 0.20 USD or 6,000 USD. The basis risk could work in favor of the company if the euro fell to 1.10 USD, on which it would receive an unexpected gain on the excess hedge of 30,000 euros times 0.30, which equals 9,000 USD.

In order to facilitate trading and create liquidity, futures are standardized forward products. Futures have standardized maturity dates, a standardized notional size for each contract, and a standardized underlying, or asset on which the contract is based (such as West Texas Intermediate Oil versus Brent Crude Oil, which are two different contracts that trade on different exchanges). The standardization of futures and the fact that they are traded on an exchange provide the advantages of liquidity and price transparency. Using exchange-traded futures provides a transparent way to value the hedging contract. Additionally, the company that uses futures knows that it can always easily adjust its hedge ratio by buying or selling more contracts.

There are also several disadvantages to trading futures versus forward contracts. To begin, the standardization of futures means that it is likely that the hedging company will have basis risk. Basis risk is the difference in price changes of the risk being hedged, and the price changes in the derivative instrument being used for the hedging. Basis risk with futures contracts will arise due to the timing of the maturity of the trade, the exact underlying commodity, and the notional size needed to hedge. For example, assume that a company needs to hedge a purchase of 30,000 gallons of jet fuel for a purchase to take place in Los Angeles in three months time on the 15th of the month. As there is not an exchange-traded futures contract on jet fuel, the hedging company may choose to use heating fuel futures contracts as a substitute (known as a cross-hedge). Obviously heating fuel may not move with 100 percent correlation to jet fuel and this introduces one source of basis risk. Furthermore, the heating fuel contract on the New York Mercantile Exchange (NYMEX) is for 42,000 gallons and this introduces a basis risk in the notional amount of the trade. Additionally, there is a timing imbalance as the futures contracts expire at the end of the month while the purchase of the jet fuel takes place mid-month. Finally, there is a basis risk in location as the NYMEX contract is based on the price for delivery in New York, while the company will be purchasing the jet fuel based on prices in Los Angeles. All of these factors introduce basis risk into the hedge. The basis risk can work either in the favor of, or against the company, but it is clearly desirable to reduce basis risk as much as possible.

A further complication of using futures to hedge is the margin requirements of the exchanges. At the inception of the trade both the buyer and seller of a futures contract need to post margin to ensure monies are available to settle contracts at expiry or settlement. Each day the futures exchanges calculate the gains or losses to each account based on the changes in values of the futures contracts. These changes in value are added or subtracted from each trader's portfolio of contracts. If the margin account falls below a certain level called the maintenance level then that account will receive a margin call and will have to post additional margin to bring its margin account up to the original margin level. The implication of this is that a company may be required to unexpectedly post additional margin to maintain its hedge. The benefit of the margin accounts is that it virtually eliminates counterparty credit risk issues.

A forward contract avoids many of the basis risks that are inherent in using futures. As previously stated, forwards are traded between a counterparty and a financial institution. Major financial institutions are willing to offer a variety of forward-type products and the range of underlying assets is even larger than that available on the exchanges. The main advantage of forward contracts is that they can be highly customized to the situation at hand. Although futures are standardized, each forward contract is specific as to the notional size, the specifics of the underlying, and the maturity date. Virtually all forward contracts are cash settled, meaning that the maturity value of the contract is exchanged and not the actual physical asset. This avoids complications with delivery options.

A disadvantage of a forward contract is that it incurs counterparty risk between the two parties. The counterparty risk of a bank failing is generally not a concern for a corporate hedging a position. However, the bank may be concerned about the counterparty risk of a corporate. To counter this risk, the two counterparties may set in place a collateral agreement that states if the value of the trade becomes imbalanced beyond a certain point then collateral must be posted with the other counterparty. In any case, the financial institution entering into a forward contract must set aside regulatory capital to offset the credit risk inherent in the trade. Additionally, the financial institution will set aside risk against the credit limit that it extends to the corporate client. Thus, if a corporation engages in a large number of forward contracts with a given counterparty it may impair or limit its ability to borrow from that same financial institution.

Another disadvantage of forwards is that they are not as liquid as futures contracts. Since forwards are highly customized, it generally implies that the best counterparty to unwind a trade would be with the financial institution with which the contract was originally entered. However, relying on one counterparty for a price implies that one may not always receive the best price. The standardization of futures contracts means that they can be unwound with a much larger number of potential counterparties who may already have positions or interest in the standardized contract.

Market Risk Management with Option-Type Products

An advantage of using options to hedge market risk exposure is that options allow the hedging company to profit from favorable moves in market prices or rates. There are two main types of options; call options provide the buyer of the option the right but not the obligation to buy at a preset price and at a preset time for a given notional amount, while a put option gives the option buyer the right but not the obligation to sell. Options are asymmetric instruments as the buyer of the option has the choice to transact, while the seller of the option must transact if the buyer chooses to do so. Therefore, the buyer of the option will only exercise his right to transact when market prices are at the buyer's advantage to do so. To have this right, the buyer of the option must pay a fee called the option premium to the seller of the option. Therefore, option transactions involve the payment of an upfront fee, and for this reason many companies prefer to hedge with futures that do not involve an upfront fee.

The premium paid for an option is a function of several variables, including the current spot price of the asset, the time to maturity of the option, the value of any benefits or costs of owning the underlying asset in the interim, the rate of interest, the price at which the buyer has the right to transact (called the strike price or exercise price), and finally the volatility of the underlying asset. Option pricing is complex, but there is a well-known formula called the Black-Scholes Option Pricing Model that is frequently used for pricing. All of the option-pricing variables are either part of the option contract (e.g., time to maturity, strike price), or easily observable or known in the market (the interest rate, costs, and benefits of owning the underlying asset). The only variable that is not known or easily observable is the volatility of the underlying asset. This volatility is technically the future volatility of the asset over the lifespan of the option. If the option price is known, the Black-Scholes Option Pricing Model can be solved for the "implied volatility" using the other known pricing variables. The implied volatility as calculated from observed market prices for options is a key method for determining the market's perception of the level of uncertainty in future market prices.

Options are also traded on exchanges and in the over-the-counter market. Options trade on virtually all of the asset classes that futures do. Additionally, options are available on individual stocks and bonds.

Although options involve an upfront premium, there are many advantages of using options. As previously mentioned, options allow the hedger to profit if market variables move in her favor. Return to the example of a company that needs to hedge the expected receipt of 200,000 euros in six months. The company could buy an option to sell the euros at a strike price of 1 Euro to 1.40 USD. The company would pay a premium for this, but it would be protected if the euro depreciated to 1 euro to 1.25 USD. The payoff from the option in this case would be 200,000 times 0.15 USD or 30,000 USD, which would compensate the company for the fall in value of the euro. However, if the euro appreciated to 1.74 USD, then the company would not exercise its option to sell euros at 1.40 USD, and instead would profit from selling the euros at the higher market price of 1.74.

A second advantage of using options is that the basis risk of being over-hedged or under-hedged, although not eliminated, is at least reduced. For example, if the company is over-hedged and it bought an option to sell 200,000 euros for USD, and it only received 170,000 euros, then it would not have to exercise the option and buy additional euros if the value of the euro appreciated. However, it would have paid more in extra premium for the larger size of the trade.

Multiperiod options such as caps, which provide a payout whenever the interest rate goes above the preset cap rate, work in much the same way. In other words, a company that hedges its interest rate payments with a cap will profit for those periods in which interest rates fall, but receive compensating cap payments for those periods where the interest rates go above the cap rate.

There is a large variety of options called exotic options. Exotic options are options that have specific payout functions. For example, Asian options are options where the payout is based on the average price over a period of time rather than the price at a specific point in time. Take, for instance, a company that purchases oil on the first day of every month. The company risk manager may decide to purchase an Asian option where the payout is based on the average of prices paid over the course of the year as the average yearly cost is more relevant than the cost at a given point in time.

Another type of exotic option is called a basket option. A basket option is an option that has a payout based on the average price of a basket of variables. A risk manager for a U.S.-domiciled company that sells in euros, yen, and pounds may structure a basket option where the payout is based on the average exchange rate achieved among the three currencies. Therefore, if two of the currencies decrease in value versus the USD, but the other currency increases, then the size of the payout will be reduced to the extent that the increasing currency offsets the two decreasing currencies. However, the cost of the premium will also be lower to reflect the probability of this occurrence.

There are many different types of exotic options. The general characteristic of exotic options is that they generally have lower premiums, but correspondingly their payouts tend to be lower as they relate to specific risk scenarios.[8] If the risk manager has a specific hedge he is trying to achieve (such as the average cost paid for fuel over the cycle of a year, or the net domestic currency proceeds received from a variety of foreign currencies) as in the above examples, then exotic options may be preferable to conventional option strategies. The disadvantage of exotic options is that they can be difficult to understand and difficult to price.

Trade-Offs Between Option Strategies and Forward Strategies

A constant concern of companies is deciding what the optimal strategy is when it comes to market-risk hedging. The short answer is that there is not an optimal strategy that with hindsight is always best. Consider the following simple example. Assume that a company needs to buy a single barrel of oil in three months' time and that the current price of oil is $100. Ignoring storage costs and the time value of money, we can also assume that the forward price of a three-month forward is also $100 a barrel. Finally, assume that the cost of a three-month call option on oil with a strike price of $100 is $15. If the price of oil in three months is above $100 a barrel, then the company will have preferred to have bought the forward contract. Conversely, if the price of oil is below $100 in three months then it would have preferred to do nothing and simply buy the oil in the spot market. Using a reference point of $100 per barrel, the following table gives the upside and downside for the three different strategies of (1) not hedging and waiting to buy in the spot market, (2) buying the forward contract at the forward price of $100, and (3) buying a call option with a strike price of $100 and a premium of $15.

For instance, if the price of oil falls to $75, the company will have a benefit of buying cheaper oil and saving $25 from the reference price of $100 if the company decided not to hedge and to buy in the spot market. Likewise, the company will be forced to buy at the higher price of $100 if it entered into the forward market and thus it will regret buying the forward by the amount of $25. If the company chose to hedge by buying a call option, it will save $25 on buying the oil in the spot market for $75, but since it paid $15 for the option the net advantage is $10. See Exhibit 14.2.

As Exhibit 14.2 shows, the "Do Nothing, Buy in the Spot Market" strategy has the same payoffs as the "Buy Forward" strategy except in reverse order depending on the realized future price of oil. The "Buy Call Option" strategy, however, is always the second best choice by the amount of the premium paid. The Buy Forward strategy locks in a price but does not allow the company to profit from favorable price moves, and thus carries a potential opportunity risk. The Do Nothing, Buy in Spot Market strategy allows the company to benefit from favorable price moves but does not protect against adverse market moves. The Buy Option Strategy protects the company against adverse price moves, and also allows the company to take advantage of favorable price moves but involves the payment of an upfront premium that could be costly if the price does not move significantly in either direction. Thus, the only conclusion that one can draw is that there is no optimal strategy when viewed with hindsight, but one can state that the option strategy will always be the same as the best strategy minus the cost of the premium paid.

Exhibit 14.2 Comparison of Spot, Forward, and
Option Hedging Strategies

	Buy in Spot Market	Buy Forward	Buy Call Option
70	30	−30	15
75	25	−25	10
80	20	−20	5
85	15	−15	0
90	10	−10	−5
95	5	−5	−10
100	0	0	−15
105	−5	5	−10
110	−10	10	−5
115	−15	15	0
120	−20	20	5
125	−25	25	10
130	−30	30	15

Operational Issues of Using Derivatives

There are a variety of operational issues that a company needs to be aware of when hedging a position with derivatives. Conceptually, derivatives are easy instruments to understand, although in practice things can be much more complicated. Derivatives are subtle instruments and are highly dependent on their specific structural features that are described in their documentation. Additionally, the valuation and accounting for derivatives is a specialized field requiring significant expertise.

A main operational issue with derivatives is the documentation and how it affects the relationship between the company and its financial institution counterparty. The documentation of derivatives is generally done under an International Swaps and Derivatives Association (ISDA) Master Agreement, as well as a Trade Confirmation.[9] The ISDA Master Agreement is a document that is negotiated between the legal representatives for the financial institution and the company. The ISDA Master Agreement specifies all of the terms that might come up in the life of a generic trade between the two counterparties. These issues would include how payments are to be handled and how day counts for calculating interest are to be defined. Additionally, it will contain definitions as to how payments are to be calculated and how issues such as the payments falling on a holiday are to be handled. When creating the documentation, it is wise to remember that derivatives are being used mainly for hedging purposes, and that the hedges are going to be most needed when extreme and unexpected market events happen. Thus, the documentation has to be valid, reasonable, and incorporate all known possible types of normal and extreme events. The ISDA Master Agreement is a standard template that has stood the test of time, and banks along with their corporate counterparties find it easiest to start with the standard ISDA template when negotiating their own contracts.

Once the ISDA Master Agreement has been completed between the two counterparties, each individual trade will be further documented with a Confirmation.

The Confirmation spells out the details for each individual transaction such as the notional size, time to maturity, and strike prices and will make reference to, and be governed under the Master Agreement. It is critical that the Confirmations be executed by someone who not only understands the legal language used, but also understands what the purpose of the trade is and how the trade is supposed to function in different market conditions. Frequently, derivative Confirmations are checked by legal departments that understand the legal language but do not always fully understand the underlying purpose of the trade. Conversely, the risk managers understand how the trade is supposed to work but do not always fully understand how that should be expressed in legal language. The problem is compounded by the fact that the documentation is usually drafted by the financial institution, which, of course, has a vested interest in making sure its interests are most strongly covered.

When choosing counterparties for hedging transactions, it is important to focus on more than just the price at which they are offering the trades. Although getting a fair price at inception of the trade is important, it is also important to have a counterparty that will provide fair prices and liquidity throughout the life of a transaction. Frequently, a company will wish to unwind a hedging transaction because of changes in its operations or changes in the nature of its activities. Therefore, it is essential that the company be able to unwind its hedges in a timely manner and at a reasonable value.

A company should also choose its hedge counterparties based on the quality and amount of advice that each of its counterparties provide. Financial institutions spend a lot of money and time hiring and training its derivatives personnel and counterparties should make use of that talent to the greatest extent possible.

One of the key services that financial institutions provide for its clients is periodic valuations. These valuations should be based on prices at which the financial institution would be willing to unwind the trade. These valuations are important for the company to know accurately. A comparison of the value of the hedge transactions versus the value of the risk exposure should be done on a regular basis to check the effectiveness of the hedging strategy and in order to change the hedging strategy if necessary.

When collecting valuations on existing trades, or for generating prices for potential transactions, it is wise to utilize a variety of sources to ensure fairness and independence of the valuations. A general rule is to secure quotes from three different financial institutions, and to check the reasonableness of each quote versus a similar exchange traded instrument. When soliciting quotes it is always best to ask for both the bid and the ask side of the trade (i.e., the price at which you could buy or sell the instrument). This prevents the pricing source from biasing the answer in order to increase their potential profit.

Governance and Oversight of Market Risk Management

The well-known debacles of companies getting into trouble with its risk management strategies and uses of derivatives highlights the need for companies to have strong and knowledgeable oversight of its risk management function and operations. Risk management and the use of derivatives can become quite complex. Often, organizations try to fine-tune its market risk management positions and in the process make them unnecessarily complex. This can rapidly lead to problems as inexperienced staff try to implement an overly complex and burdensome strategy. Another issue is that companies attempt to use its risk management practices as profit-generating activities. Although it is true that some companies have generated significant profits from taking positions using derivatives—in essence attempting to profit from over-hedging its market risk exposures—the use of this practice is highly questionable from a prudent risk management point of view. Unlike financial institutions, operating companies are not in business to profit from taking on market risk. The use of risk management techniques for trading profit has created significant concern from shareholders and has often prompted boards of directors (referred to as board) to take a knowledgeable and firm stance on the issue.

Many studies and publications have been produced to help shareholders and boards in their decisions regarding the implementation of market risk management strategies.[10] The central theme is that the board and management need to set the tone for risk management and strictly maintain oversight to ensure that policies and the spirit of those policies are followed.

At a minimum the board should set a risk philosophy that states clearly whether the firm will engage in hedging activities, and if so, if the firm will intentionally engage in hedging activities with an intention to profit from the trading. The board also needs to ensure that senior management and the risk management team have the knowledge and the necessary tools to successfully implement and maintain the given strategy. Additionally, the board needs to frequently assess the success of the risk management strategy and reaffirm that the necessary controls are in place.

Before implementing a specific hedging transaction involving derivatives, there are five questions that the risk manager should ask:

1. What risk does the product hedge?
   Although this sounds like a trivial question, it is quite often the case that a hedge will be put in place that does not directly correspond to a known or projected risk.
2. Will the hedge be effective?
   Again, this sounds like a fundamental question, but many of the more complex hedges that are implemented to reduce risks cease to become effective when extreme market events occur. Of course, this is when the effectiveness of the hedge is most necessary.
3. How will the hedge react when stress tested in different economic environments?
   This is of particular concern when cross hedges or correlations between hedges are involved.
4. Does the hedge transaction fit with your view of the markets and the corporate strategy?
   It is obviously important that the hedge strategy does not counteract the corporate strategy.
5. Is the hedge instrument manageable?
   Does the risk management team have the knowledge, the financial analysis tools and data necessary to properly evaluate and maintain the transaction?

Derivatives can aid a corporation greatly in the achievement of its goals. It is incumbent on management to utilize these financial tools in an effective and prudent manner. A poorly implemented risk management strategy will reflect poorly not only on the risk managers, but also on the senior management and the board of directors of the firm.

CONCLUSION

Credit and market risks are key elements of any organization's risk management plan. Although the tools and techniques for measuring and managing credit and market risk are among the most highly developed and quantitative of all the various classes of risk, it is still incumbent on the risk management team to use creativity, intuition, and common sense in managing these risks. Credit and market risk management requires not only an understanding of the tools and techniques, but also a comprehensive understanding of the underlying business in order to successfully implement the credit and market risk function within the enterprise risk management framework of the organization.

There are a variety of powerful tools such as derivatives that are available to the risk manager to deal with market risk. Used prudently derivatives facilitate the implementation of a wide variety of risk management tactics. The complexity of derivatives, however, requires careful and thoughtful oversight to ensure the intended risk management objectives are achieved.

NOTES

1. This section utilizes many of the arguments first put forward in *Managing Financial Risk: A Guide to Derivative Products, Financial Engineering, and Value Maximization*, 3rd ed., by Charles W. Smithson, McGraw-Hill, 1998.

2. This section relies heavily on the article "Caveat Emptor," *Risk* magazine, June 1995, 24–25, by D. Westby.

3. This point will be more fully examined later in this chapter in "Tradeoffs Between Option Strategies and Forward Strategies."

4. This quote was made by Donald Rumsfeld in June 2002 when he was Secretary of Defense for the United States. The full quote is: "There are things we know that we know. There are known unknowns; that is to say there are things that we now know we don't know. But there are also unknown unknowns. There are things we do not know we don't know."

5. More information about the VIX is available at the Chicago Board Options Exchange web site at www.cboe.com.

6. For more information about prediction markets see *The Wisdom of Crowds* by James Surowiecki, Anchor Books, 2005.

7. Another measure of risk similar to VAR and EAR is Cashflow at Risk (CAR). In other words, it is a measure of the risk that the cash flow will fall below some critical value. See Stulz 2003, among others, for more information.

8. Certain types of exotic options have much higher premiums; for example, Lookback options that have a payoff based on the highest price achieved during a given period.

9. Further information about ISDA and ISDA Master Agreements can be found at the International Swaps and Derivatives Organization's web site www.isda.org.

10. One of the better known and respected of these reports is "Derivatives: Practices and Principles," which was produced by the Group of Thirty Consultative Group on International Economic and Monetary Affairs Inc. in 1993, www.group30.org.

REFERENCES

Chicago Board Options Exchange, www.CBOE.com.

Group of Thirty Consultative Group on International Economic and Monetary Affairs Inc. 1993. *Derivatives: Practices and principles*, www.group30.org.

International Swaps and Derivatives Association, www.ISDA.org.

Smithson, Charles W. 1998. *Managing financial risk: A guide to derivative products, financial engineering, and value maximization*, 3rd ed. New York: McGraw-Hill.

Stulz, René M. 2003. *Risk management & derivatives*. Mason, OH: Thomson-Southwestern.

Surowiecki, J. 2005. *The wisdom of crowds*. Toronto, ONT: Anchor Books.

Westby, D. 1995. Caveat emptor. *Risk* (June) 24–25.

ABOUT THE AUTHOR

Rick Nason, PhD, CFA, has an extensive background in the capital markets and derivatives industry having worked in equity derivatives and exotics, credit derivatives, and capital markets training in a senior capacity at several different global financial institutions. Rick is a founding partner of RSD Solutions, a risk management consultancy that specializes in financial risk management consulting and training for corporations, investment funds, and banks.

Dr. Nason is also an Associate Professor of Finance at Dalhousie University in Halifax, Nova Scotia, where he teaches graduate classes in corporate finance, investments, enterprise risk management, and derivatives. He has been awarded several different teaching awards as well as being selected MBA Professor of the Year several times. His research interests are in financial risk management, enterprise risk management and complexity.

Rick has a MSc in Physics from the University of Pittsburgh and an MBA and a PhD in Finance from the Richard Ivey Business School at the University of Western Ontario. Additionally, he is a Chartered Financial Analyst charterholder. In his spare time he enjoys practicing risk management principles as he plays with his collection of pinball machines.

CHAPTER 15

Credit Risk Management

RICK NASON, PhD, CFA
Associate Professor Finance, Dalhousie University Principal, RSD Solutions

T he preceding chapter discussed the common elements of credit risk and market risk. Additionally, it covered some of the major principles of managing market risk. This chapter continues the discussion with a focus on credit risk, including an overview of the credit crisis that engulfed international capital markets.

CREDIT RISK ANALYSIS

The rise of credit instruments such as credit derivatives and collateralized debt obligations (CDOs) along with changes in the regulatory capital management rules for financial institutions has generated many new ideas, research, and analytical techniques for the management and trading of credit risk.[1] It is important when conducting credit analysis to remember that unlike market risk, credit risk is almost always a downside risk; that is, unexpected credit events are almost always negative events and are only rarely positive surprises. Second, it is imperative to remember that credit events are almost always unexpected. In other words, no one extends credit to a customer, or executes a loan to a counterparty, expecting that it will not be repaid.

Measuring credit risk is not a trivial task. The size of credit risk is composed of three parts: (1) the size of the potential exposure at the time of default, (2) the probability of a default or credit event occurring, and (3) the loss given that a credit event has occurred.

$$\text{Credit Risk} = \text{Exposure Size} \times \text{Probability of Default} \times \text{Loss Given Default}$$
$$(15.1)$$

Each of the terms in the above equation has a large amount of uncertainty in their measurement. Additionally, the measurement of each of the above terms, and in particular the probability of default and the exposure amount, are prone to large fluctuations through time.

Several different historical studies have been done of the Loss Given Default, which is also frequently known as one minus the Recovery Rate. The recovery rate is the percentage of the debt owed that the creditor receives when the affairs of the defaulted company are finally settled. Exhibit 15.1 shows the results of one such study by the credit rating agency Moody's and as reported in Hull.[2]

Exhibit 15.1   Recovery Rates on Corporate Bonds as
a Percentage of Face Value 1982–2003

Class of Security	Average Recovery Rate
Senior Secured	51.6
Senior Unsecured	36.1
Senior Subordinated	32.5
Subordinated	31.1
Junior Subordinated	24.5

It is important to note that there are wide deviations in the recovery rates based on the defaulting company's industry, and the nature of the circumstances that led to the company entering into financial distress. A rule of thumb is to assume that recovery will be 50 percent, or for a more conservative estimate to assume recovery of 40 percent, which would make the loss-given default factor 60 percent.

The potential exposure is the size of the credit outstanding at the time of a credit event occurring. For a straightforward instrument, such as a fixed coupon bullet bond, the exposure is simply the face value of the bond. However, if the bond has sinking fund or repayment features then it is obvious that the calculation of the exposure becomes more complicated. If the outstanding balance of the credit instrument can vary then the potential exposure amount is also a function of the credit event's timing. Calculating the extent of the potential exposure becomes progressively more complicated in a corporate setting where the size of the outstanding credit allowance or receivable is likely to fluctuate depending on the borrower's buying cycle or working capital cycle and any changes in credit policy of the creditor. Foreign currency fluctuations and changes in market value also add extenuating complications in the calculation of potential exposure.

To simplify the potential exposure calculation, many corporations adopt the policy of assuming that the exposure is the size of the maximum allowable credit limit granted to the counterparty. This conservative assumption is probably quite realistic because a customer in financial trouble is likely to maximize all available sources of financing, and this, of course, would include maximizing their accounts payable to their suppliers.

In the absence of a credit policy and credit limits, it is best to attempt to measure the peak exposure throughout the customer's buying or working capital cycle. In ideal circumstances this would be measured based on sales projections for each client, but the actual sales to the customer are likely to be correlated with their financial health. As a customer starts to worry about his financial health, he orders fewer goods, which, in turn, leads to stock outs or dated inventory, resulting in less customer satisfaction and sales, which, in turn, leads to worsening financial health, and the "credit death spiral" begins.

Measuring the probability of default at first glance appears to be an objective exercise and there are several well-established methods for measuring the probability of default. Simplistically, these methods can be divided into measures based on fundamental analysis, statistical analysis, and market-based methods. Each of these methods, however, tends to have large changes in value or measurement based on the period of analysis. Additionally, when using these methods, remember that all credit events are unexpected and tend to be caused by sudden and unforeseen changes in circumstances. It is conceptually and practically difficult for either a fundamental or a quantitative model to capture these unforeseen and unique events.

Fundamental Analysis of Credit Default Risk (Probability of Default)

The most basic method to assess the creditworthiness of a company has been the "Five Cs" of credit analysis: (1) capacity, (2) capital, (3) collateral, (4) conditions, and (5) character.

Capacity is the ability of the company to pay its obligations out of the cash flows generated by the business. Capacity is generally assessed by examining various accounting ratios such as the coverage ratio (which will be explained and discussed later in this section). Capital is the amount of cash that the company has on hand, while the collateral is based on the quality of the assets that can be sold in order to repay obligations if a credit event occurred. Conditions refer to the general business conditions that are specific to the company and its industry. Finally, character refers to the willingness of the company to pay its obligations in a timely manner. Basically character comes down to the reputation and integrity of the firm and its management.

Ability-to-pay measures are fundamental techniques based on accounting statements to assess creditworthiness. These accounting measures look at the short-term ability to cover exposures, longer term financial flexibility, and finally the safety buffer that the firm has in managing its cash flows.

Two frequently used accounting ratios to measure the short-term ability to pay are the Current Ratio and the Quick Ratio (also called the Acid Test).

$$\text{Current Ratio} = \frac{\text{Current Assets}}{\text{Current Liabilities}} \tag{15.2}$$

$$\text{Quick Ratio} = \frac{\text{Current Assets-Inventory}}{\text{Current Liabilities}} \tag{15.3}$$

These two ratios show the relative amount of assets that the firm could conceivably convert to cash quickly relative to the amount of liabilities that the firm is conceptually expected to pay in the short term. The Quick Ratio is a more conservative measure because it assumes that the value of the firm's inventory would not be available to turn into cash to pay liabilities in the times of a crisis. Additionally, if a firm is having financial difficulties it is reasonable to assume that the value of its inventory will be significantly impaired.

A third metric of short-term credit stability is the Burn Rate or the related measure Days Cash on Hand. The Burn Rate is the amount of expenses that the firm incurs on an average day and the Days Cash on Hand is the number of days that the firm can continue to pay its expenses without generating any sales.

$$\text{Burn Rate} = \frac{\text{Annual Expenses}}{365} \tag{15.4}$$

$$\text{Days Cash on Hand} = \frac{\text{Available Cash}}{\text{Burn Rate}} \tag{15.5}$$

These two measures are used to measure the credit risk of doing business with a new firm that is still in the product development stage and does not yet have a saleable product. The Days Cash on Hand provides the time period the firm has to either receive cash through developing a product and customer-related inflows or the number of days it has to raise an additional round of financing to continue operations.

The debt ratio is calculated to ascertain the long-term financial stability and flexibility of a firm. There are many different forms of the debt ratio, but the most common are as follows:

$$\text{Debt Ratio} = \frac{\text{Total Liabilities}}{\text{Total Assets}} \tag{15.6}$$

or

$$\text{Debt Ratio} = \frac{\text{Total Long-Term Debt}}{\text{Shareholder's Equity}} \tag{15.7}$$

These two ratios show the level of leverage and financial flexibility in the firm's capital and operating structure. It is important to realize that each industry will have different average debt ratios that are a function of the level of riskiness in that industry. Generally, companies that are in high capital-intensive industry with stable cash flows (for example, utility companies) tend to have higher debt ratios.

Another long-term measure of the credit risk of a company is the Coverage Ratio.

$$\text{Coverage Ratio} = \frac{\text{EBITDA} + \text{Lease Payments}}{\text{Interest} + \text{Principal Payments} + \text{Lease Payments}} \tag{15.8}$$

EBITDA is the earnings before interest and taxes, with depreciation and amortization added back. In essence, EBITDA is a proxy for the cash flow of the firm. The denominator of the above expression is the total contractual payments that a firm must make within the accounting period. Therefore, the Coverage Ratio is the ratio of the cash being generated by the firm divided by the amount of the contractual payments. A large Coverage Ratio implies that the firm has a large buffer of cash being generated to make its payments.

Accounting statements are historical in nature and it is usually several months before they become public. Therefore, when examining the credit risk it is important to pay as much attention to the trend of the ratio as it is to the value of any given ratio at a given point in time. Although the ratios are likely to fluctuate with both operating and business cycles, it is still possible to spot potential troubles early by examining changes in the ratios over time. For example, an increasing Debt Ratio and a declining Coverage Ratio would be signs of decreasing financial health and financial flexibility even though each of the numbers for the latest period by themselves might be within an acceptable range.

When examining accounting statements it is best to examine the ratios of a given company against its industry peers. This way trends in the industry can be separated out from trends in the financial health of the company. It is almost meaningless to judge the credit quality of a company by its accounting ratios on its own. It is only within the context of the industry and the trends through time that the changes in credit quality can be accurately evaluated.

A second and simplistic measure that is often used as an early warning sign of credit risk is to measure any significant and unexplained changes in the time it takes for a counterparty to repay. The stretching of payments by a customer could mean a change in their working capital policy, but more likely it is a sign that there are cash-flow problems that could escalate to a credit crisis.

A final method of fundamental analysis is to use credit ratings as published by the various credit-rating agencies such as Standard & Poor's, Moody's, or Fitch. These rating agencies are paid by the company being rated to conduct ongoing analysis of the firm's creditworthiness. The ratings themselves are widely available while company specific reports are available to subscribers.

Credit ratings by the various agencies are quick and easy to use. A key feature of using credit ratings is the ability to relate the rating to the large databases maintained by each of the rating agencies. These databases give the probability of default for a given period of time and also include transition matrices that show the probability of a credit "migrating" to a different rating. Exhibit 15.2 shows a Transition Matrix from Moody's as reported in Hull.[3]

As Exhibit 15.2 shows, a company that begins the year with a Baa rating has an 88.70 percent probability of finishing the year with a Baa rating, a 4.60 percent probability of finishing the year downgraded to a Ba rating, and a 0.19 percent probability of defaulting within a year.

Exhibit 15.2 One-Year Transition Matrix—Percentages Moody's 1970–2006

Initial Rating	Rating After One Year								
	Aaa	Aa	A	Baa	Ba	B	Caa	Ca-C	Default
Aaa	91.56	7.73	0.69	0.00	0.02	0.00	0.00	0.00	0.00
Aa	0.86	91.43	7.33	0.29	0.06	0.02	0.00	0.00	0.01
A	0.06	2.64	91.48	5.14	0.53	0.10	0.02	0.00	0.02
Baa	0.05	0.22	5.16	88.70	4.60	0.84	0.23	0.03	0.19
Ba	0.01	0.07	0.52	6.17	83.10	8.25	0.58	0.05	1.26
B	0.01	0.05	0.19	0.41	6.27	81.65	5.17	0.75	5.50
Caa	0.00	0.04	0.04	0.25	0.79	10.49	65.47	4.44	18.47
Ca-C	0.00	0.00	0.00	0.00	0.46	2.78	11.07	47.83	37.85
Default	0.00	0.00	0.00	0.00	0.00	0.00	0.00	0.00	100.00

A company that has a rating of Baa or better (BBB or better using the Standard & Poor's or Fitch rating systems) is considered to be an investment-grade credit, while companies with ratings Ba or BB and below are called interchangeably noninvestment grade, or high-yield, or junk bonds.

Although ratings are important in calculating the creditworthiness of a counterparty, it is also imperative for a company to maintain a keen focus on its own credit rating. The pricing of debt issuances (and by association the cost of debt) is closely correlated to the company's rating. A low rating will most certainly imply a higher cost of debt, and may result in the amount of financing available in either the debt or equity markets being limited.

Although easy to use, credit ratings are not without their drawbacks. Credit rating agencies have come under fire in recent years for not changing their ratings frequently enough to capture the changing dynamics of a given company. Rating agencies counter that they look at the credit risk of a company based on the whole business cycle, as opposed to just a point in time. Additionally, they examine the amount and quality of a company assets in an effort to assess recovery rate as part of their analysis. Thus, the rating should not be taken as strictly a moment-by-moment assessment of the default probability. A further component to the "stickiness" of the ratings is that the rating agencies wish to avoid unnecessary volatility in the bond trading of the companies they are rating. Many institutional investors have strict limits on their holdings of noninvestment grade bonds. A frequent flip-flop of a rating between investment and noninvestment grade would introduce a large amount of trading into and out of a company's bonds, which is obviously quite undesirable. To allow the market time to adjust in an orderly manner to a likely change of rating, the rating companies will issue rating warnings that signal that the company is under review for a positive or negative rating change.

Market-Based Analysis of Credit Default Probability

There are two main methods of measuring default risk using market-based measures. The first is to examine the yields to maturity on a corporation's debt issues, while the second method is to examine the price of a credit default swap based on the corporation.

The yield to maturity (or more accurately, the credit spread, which is the amount by which the yield to maturity of a risky corporate bond is above the yield to maturity of a similar risk-free Treasury bond that has an equivalent time to maturity) is the traditional measure of the market's perception of the probability of default of a company. The wider the credit spread the greater the perceived risk of the corporate bond suffering from financial distress. The yield to maturity is affected by the general level of interest rates, so it is quite important to look at the credit spread rather than simply the yield to maturity.

The yield to maturity and the credit spread will generally be affected by the structural features of the bond, or more specifically by any callable, put-able, convertibility, redeemable, extendable, or other embedded options in the bond. To account for the effects of embedded options on the bond's yield to maturity, a measure called the Option Adjusted Spread (OAS) is used. The OAS adjusts the yield to account for any embedded options and calculates a credit spread that would exist if the bond did not have any embedded option features. Using OAS allows one to compare spreads between conventional plain vanilla bonds and bonds with embedded option features.

The credit default swap market is a relatively new market. In a credit default swap, a counterparty to a trade, called the protection buyer, will pay a periodic fee (generally semi-annually), which is called the credit default swap spread, to the second party, which is called the credit protection seller. This fee is based on a notional amount. In return, the protection seller makes a payment to the protection buyer if and only if the underlying credit obligation (generally a publicly traded bond or a syndicated loan) suffers a credit event such as a bankruptcy or a failure to pay. The payment is generally based on the notional amount multiplied by one minus the recovery rate on the underlying credit obligation. In simple terms, the protection buyer is buying insurance against a credit risk event.[4]

There are a large numbers of hedgers, speculators, and market makers in the credit derivative market. The large volume of trading (larger even than the trading of the underlying bonds and loans) produces a dynamic market that provides instantaneous assessments by the market as to the credit quality of the underlying corporations that are traded. Since the payout of a credit default swap is directly related to a credit event, and, for instance, not related to interest rates, the credit default swap price is a direct reflection of the probability of a company's default. Credit default swaps are also one of the primary methods by which a company can hedge its credit risk exposure to other companies, which is a topic that will be covered later in this chapter.

Another market-based measure of assessing credit risk was developed by Moody's KMV.[5] This proprietary method, based on the Merton Model (an option-pricing model), models the equity of a firm as a call option written by the bondholders of the firm. To see why this is so, consider the case of a company that goes bankrupt. Although the equity holders lose all of the value that they had when they purchased the shares of the company, they are not responsible to make any more payments, and thus their downside is limited to the amount that they paid for their shares. On the upside, however, the value of the shares could rise if the fortunes of the company increase, and conceptually the profits accruing to the shareholders are unlimited. Thus, the payoff to the shareholder is similar to that of the payoff to the holder of a call option—the loss is limited to the amount of the premium paid, and the upside is conceptually unlimited.

Moody's KMV calculates an Expected Default Frequency (EDF) by utilizing the Merton Model of the firm. It calculates the asset volatility of the firm (implied by share prices) and the known market value (both equity market value and debt market value) of the firm. The asset volatility can be used to calculate the probability that the market value of the firm falls below the debt level of the firm. When that happens the firm is assumed to be bankrupt. These calculated levels of default are then correlated to empirically observed levels of default to create the EDF of the firm.[6]

The advantage of EDF measures are that they are dynamic, being based on the current market assessments of firm value and volatility. Additionally they are a forward-based measure as the market inputs are also forward-based.

Statistical-Based Models of Credit Risk

Credit scoring is a statistical-based method of estimating credit default risk. Credit scoring develops a set of factors from readily observed characteristics, each with a specific weighting that when added together provide a score by which to rank a company's creditworthiness. The most well-known credit scoring model is the Altman Z-Score, which is given by the following formula:

$$\text{Z-Score} = 1.2 \times F_1 + 1.4 \times F_2 + 3.3 \times F_3 + 0.6 \times F_4 + 0.999 \times F_5 \qquad (15.9)$$

Where:

$$F_1 = \frac{\text{Working Capital}}{\text{Total Assets}} \qquad (15.10)$$

$$F_2 = \frac{\text{Retained Earnings}}{\text{Total Assets}} \qquad (15.11)$$

$$F_3 = \frac{\text{Earnings Before Interest and Taxes}}{\text{Total Assets}} \qquad (15.12)$$

$$F_4 = \frac{\text{Market Value of Equity}}{\text{Book Value of Debt}} \qquad (15.13)$$

$$F_5 = \frac{\text{Sales}}{\text{Total Assets}} \qquad (15.14)$$

If the calculated Z-Score is below 1.80, then there is a high probability of the company encountering financial distress. If the Z-Score is above 2.99, then the company is considered to be a safe credit risk. Values of the Z-Score between 1.80 and 2.99 are considered to be in the gray zone.[7]

For different types of situations and different types of credits, different credit scoring models have been developed. For instance, for consumer credit, credit scores are calculated based on factors such as the length of time that the individual has been in their current employment, length of time in current residence, level of education, income, current debt levels, and past history of late payments.

The major drawback to credit scoring models is that they are dependent on a large amount of historical data. Without a large database, the statistical validity and reliability of a model is in serious question. An additional complication is that a credit scoring model assumes a large portfolio of credits under consideration. With a large portfolio of credits under examination, the statistical properties of a credit scoring model are more likely to be borne out. Since a credit scoring model is a quantitative model, it cannot account for company-specific effects or events, and thus relying on a model for a small portfolio of credit accounts may lead to misleading conclusions. This is why credit scoring is frequently used for securitizations of packages of credit cards or accounts receivables that involve a large number of credits.

Credit Risk Mitigation

As mentioned earlier there are three forms of credit risk: (1) customer credit risk, (2) sovereign risk, and (3) funding risk. Additionally, liquidity risk may be considered a special case of funding risk, as in, for example, the role of liquidity in the credit crisis that began in 2007. Mitigation of each of these risks will be discussed in turn.

Customer credit risk mitigation is based on setting policies such as the size of exposure to be taken with a given counterparty, the terms of repayment—including time to repay and any interest charges incurred, and whether collateral or partial prepayment will be required.

As mentioned earlier, extension of credit to customers is frequently used as part of a company's marketing package. The more liberal the credit terms offered to clients, the larger the expected sales, but also the larger the expected losses from credit risk. Additionally, there is an adverse selection aspect to extending liberal credit terms to customers because the clients with the most desperate credit situations are likely to take full advantage of credit. Therefore, the credit policy of a company toward clients is a major strategic risk decision that involves both the financial and marketing sides of the organization.

Generally companies will offer some form of credit to clients in order to facilitate sales and the practicalities of doing business. The most usual form is to offer a certain number of days to pay, with perhaps a set discount for early payment. However, if it is deemed upon analysis that the customer has a low likelihood of paying, or the customer has a poor track record of paying in a timely manner, then credit terms may be refused with cash on delivery being demanded, or even payment—full or partial—being required before an order is processed. Refusing a client credit may result in the loss of the client, which could lead to a competitor being stuck with credit losses to that client.

Another reason to reject credit to clients is that it is costly in its own right. A firm that extends credit has to secure additional financing to pay its own expenses that may need to be covered before the customers pay. A company needs to make sure that its extension of credit to customers does not impair its own working capital cycle, and by extension impair its own credit risk. Frequently, companies get into credit trouble on their own by extending favorable credit terms to customers, which in turn increases sales, but also increases the need for working capital. Thus, the firm gets into credit difficulty not through lack of sales, but through letting its credit policy dictate and dominate its working capital cycle and short-term financing flexibility.

There are a couple of techniques to manage credit receivables to clients besides tightening credit terms. If a company has sufficient receivables it can package the receivables into a structured note and sell it off to market investors in a securitization. This is the preferred method of receivables management by large national manufacturers that have a large and diverse group of customers who make credit purchases. Perhaps the best known examples of this are the financing arms of General Motors (General Motors Acceptance Corp., better known as GMAC) or Ford (Ford Motor Credit), which, on an ongoing basis, package auto loans into securitized notes. Note that in most cases a securitization will be without recourse, which means the risk of customer defaults is borne by the buyer of the securitization notes. Thus, the issuer of the note (for example, GMAC) not only receives financing by selling the loans, but also sheds the credit risk associated with the customer loans.

A second method is for the company to sell their receivables to a special purpose company called a factor company. A factor company essentially acts as an investor to buy the receivables of a company. A factoring transaction is much like a small-scale securitization that is bought by one investor, the factoring company. A company can sell its receivables with or without recourse. If the company sells its receivables with recourse, which means that the factoring company can come back to the company to recover any credit losses from defaulting customers, it will receive financing but will obviously not shed the credit risk of customers who default. Factoring, especially without recourse, is generally considered to be an expensive form of financing.

A second aspect of customer credit risk management is to decide in advance what actions will be taken if a customer fails to make timely payments. Will the company continually phone the customer, hire a collection agency, or start legal actions? What will be the sequence of actions, and what will be the level of outstanding credit that will trigger each set of responses? Setting a policy of when and how each of these actions will be taken in advance can save a lot of stress and management time when the inevitable event actually occurs—especially when a large number of customers and transactions are involved.

Another way to manage customer credit risk is through the use of credit derivatives. As stated earlier, in a credit derivative transaction the protection buyer pays a periodic fee called the credit default swap spread to a counterparty, which is generally a well-known financial institution. In return the financial institution makes a payment based on the recovery rate to the protection buyer if the underlying credit incurs a credit event, such as a default or bankruptcy. Credit derivatives are available on most well-known public companies that have outstanding bonds or syndicated loans. However, credit derivatives are generally not available on smaller or private companies.

Credit derivatives are conceptually simple products used to mitigate credit risk. However, on closer inspection, there are many difficult practicalities to using credit derivatives effectively. The first is the bulky nature of credit derivatives. Credit derivatives are generally sold in $10MM notional amounts, which means that their size is out of reach for all but the largest of customer credit accounts. The second aspect is that credit derivatives usually have a five-year maturity, which may be longer than a corporation wants to forecast its credit exposures going forward. An additional issue is that the outstanding credit risk to a customer is likely to fluctuate throughout the business cycle. This means that during parts of the credit cycle the hedging company is likely to be over-hedged, and at other times is likely to be under-hedged as the size of the credit exposure keeps changing. The final concern with using credit derivatives to hedge is that of structuring the credit derivative contract so that it matches the nature of the exposure in the event of a default. Most credit derivative contracts are based on the recovery rate of an outstanding bond. The recovery rate on a bond might be different than the recovery rate experienced by a corporation trying to recover monies owed on a receivable.

Assuming that the exposure is large enough, credit derivatives are useful tools to hedge the exposure to a sovereign. Credit derivatives are available on most sovereigns that corporations may be concerned about. Credit derivatives on sovereigns work the same as credit derivatives on corporations with the exception that additional events of credit risk, such as moratoriums and repudiation, which are more specific to sovereigns, are included in the clauses of default that trigger the payment on a transaction.

The technique of financing a large capital investment in a risky sovereign nation by financing the capital investment with monies from foreign nationals of the country was discussed earlier. This is a natural way to hedge an exposure, assuming that the corporation itself has enough name recognition in the foreign country to attract investors.

When dealing with the credit risk of foreign customers, letters of credit from a governmental agency such as the Export-Import Bank in the United States or the Economic Development Canada agency are used. These governmental agencies are set up to promote international trade by taking on many of the credit risks that are difficult for traditional financial institutions to assess and manage. These agencies provide letters of credit or credit insurance against the default of a foreign customer.

With all of the customer and sovereign credit risk mitigation techniques discussed so far there has been an explicit or an implicit cost involved. As with almost all types of risk management, there is a cost involved in reducing risk. By tightening credit terms, the firm reduces credit losses but also likely experiences a reduction in sales. By factoring receivables without recourse, the company will have to pay an implicit financing charge as well as a credit risk charge. By entering into credit derivatives companies will have to pay an explicit fee as well as carry significant risk in the transaction.

Hedging credit risk is a difficult management task. Effective credit risk management involves a host of trade-offs. The fact that credit risk is event-based makes it difficult to accurately track and efficiently protect oneself.

The final aspect of credit risk management is to ensure that one does not get into credit difficulties and that external financing is readily available at reasonable and competitive costs. This is what may be called the funding risk of a corporation.

The funding risk is a complex mix of the industry the company is in, the state of the capital markets in general, the name recognition of the company in both domestic and foreign markets, and both the perceived and actual financial health of the firm, which in turn is a function of the profitability, operating policies and capital structure of the firm.

The best way to mitigate funding risk is to operate as an efficient and profitable firm with large cash flows. In a competitive industry, however, that is obviously much easier said than done. A firm can mitigate its funding risk mainly by maintaining a conservative capital structure, maintaining a strong relationship with a portfolio of financial institutions, and by diversifying its funding both geographically and in the types of funding it seeks. Each of these elements, however, entails a trade-off in terms of time and or convenience. For example, a more conservative, less leveraged capital structure tends to be more expensive on an after-tax basis due to the tax efficiency of funding a corporation with debt. Partnerships with more banks lead to more complex relationships, and funding in different countries increases regulatory reporting requirements and costs.

Ultimately, successful funding risk management can lead to increased opportunities in both marketing opportunities and strategic opportunities—especially in times of economic downturns when funding is harder to find. Companies with financial flexibility can offer more generous credit terms than their competitors, can engage in more aggressive pricing policies, and can undertake more developmental opportunities for strategic gain if they have a funding advantage over their rivals. Indeed, funding imbalances among competitors during times of economic downturns often lead to acquisition activities with companies with the competitive funding advantages taking over their funding constrained competitors.

AN ANALYSIS OF THE CREDIT CRISIS

There are many proposed theories of the causes of the recent credit crunch, and several of the features leading to the collapse of the U.S. subprime lending market along with the market value of collateralized debt obligations (CDOs) hold many interesting and valuable lessons for students of risk management.

To understand the situation it is best to start with examining the U.S. credit, housing, and investment markets at the turn of the millennium. The U.S. housing market was by all anecdotal accounts a stable and growing market. House ownership was seen as a cornerstone of a prudent personal investment strategy. Demand for housing was strong and prices were steadily rising. Additionally, interest and mortgage rates in general were stable, consistently low, and falling as the Federal Reserve kept interest rates at historically low levels. A recurring strategy for individuals was to refinance their homes at each major lowering of interest rates. Furthermore, the lower interest rates, combined with rising housing prices, encouraged families to increase personal leverage and buy larger homes. The refinancing of homes at higher levels of leverage created liquidity because at each refinancing most homeowners would monetize the increase in their house values, as well as monetize their increasing level of leverage. This created a liquidity glut within the United States, which when combined with a matching global increase in liquidity, only reinforced the factors keeping interest rates low.

The low levels of interest rates were not a boon, however, for all, and in particular institutional investors such as pension funds, insurance companies, and endowment funds. These investors relied on relatively high interest rates on their fixed-income investments to be able to meet their future financial obligations. This created a demand for more highly structured instruments that held the promise of higher yields.

A final component to the context of this complex puzzle was the changing regulatory and competitive environment in the financial services sector. The international regulatory capital agreement known as Basel II was proposing changes in how much regulatory capital banks had to set aside as reserves in order to ensure their solvency. The essence of the proposed changes in the rules was that banks had a strong incentive to shed their credit risk by selling off credit risk in whatever form they felt best. An additional incentive of the regulatory reform was for the banks to learn how to better model credit and market risk. This in turn led to a flurry of research and development activity in mathematical models.

The environment was set for the introduction of CDOs. The structure of a basic CDO is shown in the following diagram. A CDO consists of an asset provider, generally a bank that has loan assets it wishes to shed. The bank sets up a special purpose vehicle (SPV). The sole job of the SPV is to act as a legal gateway between the bank and investors. The SPV either buys outright the package of loans from the bank, or more generally purchases the credit risk from the bank by utilizing a series of credit default swaps (CDS), or total return swaps (TRS) linked to each of the underlying credits in the portfolio of credits. The SPV in turn issues a series of structured notes to investors. The series of notes are issued so they create what is known as a "waterfall" structure, such that each tranche carries a different level of risk and a correspondingly different yield. The proceeds from the sale of the notes are generally invested by the SPV in risk-free Treasury Securities. See Exhibit 15.3.

At each period the bank collects the principal and interest payments from the loans in the portfolio, and pays the relevant CDS spread to the SPV. The SPV in turn makes any required payments on default to the bank. With the remaining CDS fees, and proceeds from interest on the Treasuries, the SPV makes payments to the note holders. Holders of the senior tranche (frequently called the Super-Senior as it was considered to be ultralow risk) have their promised yield paid first. Remaining monies are then used to pay the next tranche (generally an investment-grade tranche), and so on until any remaining proceeds are paid to the lowest tranche (which is considered to be equity because it was to receive any residual payments or value only after all other tranche holders received their full payments).

In the early days of these structures, there was strong demand for the high-grade tranches because they carried attractive yields and were considered to be low risk. The lower tranches, and in particular the equity tranches, were difficult to sell. In fact, the nickname for these tranches was "toxic waste" as they would be the first to suffer losses if any of the credits in the portfolio defaulted and the SPV had to make CDS default payments back to the bank. The banks could not readily sell the equity tranches, so they often had to keep them. In other words, the banks, in trying to reduce their risk, sold off that risk through the CDO, but they had to keep the worst of the credits (that is the first to default) for themselves. One positive effect of the banks keeping the equity tranche is that it gave investors

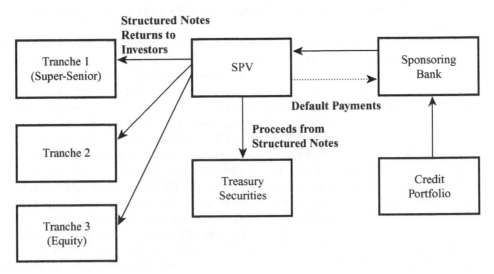

Exhibit 15.3 Structure of a CDO

confidence of the stability and safety of the more senior tranches. In other words, if the bank created a poor portfolio, they (the banks) would be the first to suffer losses due to their ownership of the equity piece.

The ironic history is that the default experience of companies in the early days of CDOs was incredibly benign. There was a lot of liquidity, and companies could easily borrow extra money and thus stay afloat. Indeed, the rise of CDOs made banks more willing to grant loans at more favorable terms and to weaker credits because they knew they were at least partially hedged through the increase in their credit risk management knowledge and in the use of instruments such as CDSs and CDOs. Since corporate defaults were low, this implied that the returns of the equity tranches of CDOs were much higher than expected.

The situation for the banks was that by creating CDOs, they were lowering their regulatory capital requirements by shedding credit risk, making large returns off their ownership of the equity tranches of the CDOs they created, satisfying their customers by creating higher yielding securities, and generating large issuance and service fees by creating these structures. This was the backdrop and context that created the credit crisis via interwoven systemic credit risks.

As the market for CDOs developed, the demand by institutional investors for higher yielding investments increased. To satisfy the demand for higher yielding assets, the banks sold lower rated tranches, including the equity tranches of the CDOs and also increased the risk characteristics of the underlying pool of assets. This introduced subprime mortgages into the pool of assets underlying the CDOs. Additionally, banks actively started taking on new sources of credit risk by selling protection via credit default swaps in order to increase their inventory of credit assets that they could repackage into CDOs.

Initially the subprime mortgages performed reasonably well, and this led to more aggressive assumptions when modeling the default history of these relatively new assets. Due to the strong investment performance of CDOs, and the increase in sophistication of the mathematical models underlying their valuation, investors became more comfortable with CDOs as assets, even though the valuation and structuring of them was complex and understood by only a small proportion of investors.

The start of the crisis began slowly and almost imperceptibly with an increase in the default rate of subprime mortgages. The housing market started to slow down in general, along with the general economy, which led to an increase in the number of defaults on conventional mortgages as well. The effect of this was to make the payment rates from the SPVs to the sponsoring banks increase in a number of the CDO structures. By itself this was not a problem because it only directly affected the lower tranches of these CDOs. However, even the investors in the higher tranches of CDOs began to question the valuations of their investments.

A catalyst for the crisis becoming full-blown was when two financial institutions had a dispute about the value of a specific CDO that was posted by one of them as collateral to the other bank. The bank holding the collateral demanded more collateral from its counterparty who countered that the value of the CDOs held was more than sufficient to satisfy the terms of their collateral agreement. The bank holding the collateral disagreed and threatened to sell the underlying CDOs to prove its point. This dispute, which was played out in the media, made several major institutional investors question the value of the CDOs that they held in their own portfolios. This was probably the first time that many of these investors had seriously tried to objectively price CDOs, and thus the first time that the complexity and sensitivity to assumptions in pricing were fully appreciated.

These exercises in valuation led to most of these investors deciding that it was prudent to significantly reduce their holdings of CDOs until they were better understood. The financial institutions were now holding significant portfolios of CDOs themselves, and significant holdings of credit risk in their inventories that they were planning to structure into new CDOs for the market. The dynamics of the market, and an effort to make their clients happy and defend the value of their credit inventories, forced many of the banks to create a market in the CDOs by agreeing to buy back the CDOs from their clients. These efforts to create liquidity and bolster the market did not work, and only led to the banks holding even larger amounts of credit assets that were falling rapidly in value and that proved to be nearly impossible to sell off at anything resembling a reasonable price. Ultimately, confidence was lost in the models for valuing and structuring CDOs, confidence was lost in the underlying assumptions, and the critical blow was that confidence was lost in the liquidity of these complex instruments.

There are many relevant lessons for the management of market and credit risk that can be gleaned from the credit debacle. The first and primary lesson is that of model risk. The world does not work by models. A model is at best a map, and just as a map is not the same as an actual highway, a model is not the same as the actual actions of traders. Models gain acceptance because they seem to work. Indeed the models for credit risk worked well as long as the credit risk in the markets were benign, which they were in the lead-up to the credit crisis. Although there were a couple of major credit incidents (Enron, WorldCom, Parmalat, and Delphi) in the years before the credit crisis, they were thought to be isolated and specific events, and thus did not interrupt the broader credit markets. Additionally, the level of personal bankruptcies was also relatively low as the U.S. economy prospered. However, when cracks in the default rate rose, and in particular mortgages, it showed that assumptions about default rates and recovery rates (the prices at which the foreclosed homes with defaulted mortgages would be sold) were seriously underestimated. Ultimately the lesson learned is that it is critical to understand how a model reacts in stress situations. A model may work fine when things are normal, but then again almost any model will work fine when the economic situation is positive and the volatility low. It is how the model works in times of uncertainty and stress that determines the success of a model.

The second lesson to learn from the credit crisis is that conditions change. Trends do not last forever, and eventually economic prices and rates may revert. Investors gained false confidence in falling interest rates, falling default rates, and high recovery rates on defaulted assets. Also, the uncertainty in the inputs to the model were not fully appreciated and understood, especially in the case of the subprime mortgages because it was such a new market.

A third lesson to learn is the need to understand the underlying dynamics of a model. The mathematics behind CDO and credit risk is complex and question-able at best. However, many investors took the mathematicians at their word even though the investors did not understand the components of the model or how the model components were put together. Investors abandoned their intuition about the markets for the mathematical rigor of the models. Conversely, the modelers who constructed the models for the most part did not fully incorporate real-life market dynamics and intuition into the model. Most of the modelers were mathematicians who had little to no trading experience. The investors who had the trading experience had little to no understanding of the mathematics.

A subtle but important effect that the credit risk and market models did not correctly incorporate was the correlation of default. A mathematical technique from the insurance industry called Copulas was used to model the correlation of default, which is a key component of valuing and trading CDOs. The Copula model, which is based on actuarial science, works well when a large number of investments are being made (such as a large number of life insurance policies being underwritten). However, in the case of CDOs, although the underlying package of credits was large, generally only a small number of CDOs were being purchased by any one investor. Second, it is not clear that the subtleties of default correlation are fully understood by either traders or mathematicians. For instance, if General Motors suffers a credit event, what does that imply about the change in the probability of default for Ford? One could argue that it implies an increase in the probability of default since the default of GM is obviously a sign that the car industry is in distress. Conversely, one could also argue that it implies that Ford's probability of default has gone down since one of its major competitors is hobbled by a default.

A related aspect to correlation risk is the presence of feedback loops. In the credit cycle, consumer confidence in housing prices increased, which led to the buying of more and larger homes. This increased prices, which in turn increased investors' confidence in lending money to home buyers. This created more credit, increased the incentives and availability of credit to buy larger homes, which in turn fed back into higher prices and the cycle continued upward. On the downside, as the economy started to turn, it become harder to refinance houses, and home buyers could no longer finance their increased leverage levels. This led to an increase in defaults, which led to investors pulling back from supplying credit to the housing market, which in turn led to lower prices, which led to more defaults until the cycle accelerated on the downside.

Although the market for CDOs was strong, liquidity in the market was high. This increased the confidence of even skeptical investors to enter the market as assurances of market liquidity provided an escape route if things went sour. However, at the exact moment that the need for liquidity was the greatest, the liquidity dried up as the market became a one-way market of sellers. Although several investment banks attempted to prop up the market through acting as market makers, this only increased their own risk and liquidity issues. As with models, it is likely that liquidity will always be there in normally functioning markets. However, when markets get distressed both liquidity and models tend to disintegrate, and indeed may negatively feed off each other. The practical lesson is that liquidity assumptions need to be aggressively stress-tested. The more complex or inexperienced the market is with a product, the more aggressive the stress-testing should be.

Ultimately, what crippled the market and created the crisis was the crisis of confidence. As investors became concerned about the valuation models and assumptions underlying their investments, they sold indiscriminately, which created a mini-panic in the market. The reliance on models and market liquidity may have gotten ahead of itself before the credit crisis, but an argument can be made that the pendulum has swung equally far in the opposite direction with an unwarranted extreme lack of confidence in risk management models becoming the norm.

CONCLUSION

Credit and market risk management must be an integral part of a firm's enterprise risk management strategy. Not only are credit and market risk important variables in the profitability of the firm, but they are also the risks for which well-developed methods of analysis and management exist. Despite the plurality of methods for managing these risks, it takes a combination of a clear strategy, a knowledge of the analytical tools, an understanding of the risk management instruments, responsible oversight and direction from senior management and the board, and perhaps most importantly, the ability to think clearly, creatively, and intuitively in order to balance the art and the science necessary for success in this branch of risk management.

NOTES

1. See, for example, de Serviguy and Renault (2004), Caouette et al. (2008), and Meissner, (2005).
2. *Options, Futures and Other Derivatives*, by John C. Hull, 7th ed., Pearson, Prentice Hall. (2008).
3. *Options, Futures and Other Derivatives*, by John C. Hull, 7th ed., Pearson, Prentice Hall. (2008).
4. In a generic insurance contract, the protection buyer must suffer a loss if the insured event occurs. In the case of a credit default swap, the protection buyer may be a speculator who does not own the underlying bonds or loans and does not suffer a loss as the result of the underlying company defaulting on its obligations. For this reason credit derivatives are technically and legally not insurance contracts.
5. Another similar source of credit risk, called CreditGrades, is offered by RiskMetrics. CreditGrades is also a company-specific risk measure that provides default probabilities and credit spreads.
6. More information about the Moody's KMV model is available at www.moodyskmv.com.
7. Edward Altman, "Financial Ratios, Discriminant Analysis and the Prediction of Corporate Bankruptcy," *Journal of Finance* (September 1968) 189–209.

REFERENCES

Altman, E. 1968. Financial ratios, discriminant analysis and the prediction of corporate bankruptcy. *Journal of Finance* (September) 189–209.
Caouette, J.B., Altman, E.I., Narayanan, P., and Nimmo, R. 2008. *Managing credit risk: The great challenge for global financial markets*, 2nd ed. Hoboken, NJ: John Wiley & Sons.
De Serviguy, A., and Renault, O. 2004. *The Standard & Poor's guide to measuring and managing credit risk*. New York: McGraw-Hill.
Hull, J.C. 2008. *Options, Futures and Other Derivatives*, 7th ed. Upper Saddle River, NJ: Prentice Hall.
Meissner, G. 2005. *Credit derivatives: Application, pricing, and risk management*. Hoboken, NJ: John Wiley & Sons.

ABOUT THE AUTHOR

Rick Nason, PhD, CFA, has an extensive background in the capital markets and derivatives industry having worked in equity derivatives and exotics, credit derivatives and capital markets training in a senior capacity at several different global financial institutions. Rick is a founding partner of RSD Solutions, a risk management consultancy that specializes in financial risk management consulting and training for corporations, investment funds, and banks.

Dr. Nason is also an Associate Professor of Finance at Dalhousie University in Halifax, Nova Scotia, where he teaches graduate classes in corporate finance, investments, enterprise risk management, and derivatives. He has been awarded several different teaching awards as well as being selected MBA Professor of the Year several times. His research interests are in financial risk management, enterprise risk management, and complexity.

Rick has an MSc in Physics from the University of Pittsburgh and an MBA and a PhD in Finance from the Richard Ivey Business School at the University of Western Ontario. He is a Chartered Financial Analyst charterholder. In his spare time he enjoys practicing risk management principles as he plays with his collection of pinball machines.

CHAPTER 16

Operational Risk Management

DIANA DEL BEL BELLUZ
President, Risk Wise Inc.

INTRODUCTION

A fable . . .

> When Richard Preston drove into work, a sick feeling of dread gnawed at his stomach. The morning paper had a front-page article on Steelbelt Corporation, the company where he had been working for the past 18 months. It was more bad news—a fiery crash that killed a young couple and their two children. The article said that a Steelbelt-500 tire on the crashed vehicle had failed. The journalist rehashed details from four other recent accidents involving Steelbelt tires. It raised questions about the quality of Steelbelt-500 tires, the same model that was manufactured at the plant where Richard worked. Now customers were afraid to buy Steelbelt's tires. Another article in the business section told of shareholders who were irate over a 50 percent drop in the value of the company's stock over the past two months. Rumors of layoffs and cost-cutting were circulating among Richard's co-workers. Two of Steelbelt's biggest customers were threatening to tear up their contracts to put the company's tires on 30 percent of their vehicles manufactured in North America and Europe.
>
> Steelbelt Corporation had been in business for more than 50 years and had grown from a single plant in Detroit to a multinational company. Richard had joined Steelbelt's internship program at the company's flagship plant right after completing his MBA. He had enjoyed his stints in production, purchasing, and finance. Sometimes, at lunch, he would hang out at the company's test track, watching the drivers and researchers from the lab. Richard loved working for Steelbelt—he loved the people, he loved the products, he loved the pioneering atmosphere. How could things have gone so terribly wrong?

Every organization exists to achieve its goals. A few organizations achieve their objectives flawlessly. Others fail miserably, to the point where the organization does not survive. And most organizations fall somewhere in between, achieving only lackluster results that are well below their performance potential. Why does this gap between potential and actual performance exist? It turns out that poor operational effectiveness is, in large part, caused by poor operational risk management (ORM).[1]

This chapter explores the fundamentals of risk management in an operational setting and how ORM can be used to capture the full performance potential of an organization. The Steelbelt fable is used throughout the chapter to illustrate the answers to fundamental questions, including:

- What is operational risk and why should you care about it?
- Is risk all bad?
- How do you assess operational risks, particularly in a dynamic business environment?
- Why do you need to define risk tolerance for aligned decision making?
- What can you do to manage operational risk?
- How do you encourage a culture of risk management at the operational level?
- How do you align operational risk management with enterprise risk management?

WHAT IS OPERATIONAL RISK AND WHY SHOULD YOU CARE ABOUT IT?

Every organization exists to achieve its goals. The nature of those goals can vary widely between organizations; for example, "profit" goals for shareholders (corporations), "serving citizens and protecting the public good" (government), or "support for worthy causes" (not-for-profits). Whatever its goals, to achieve them an organization needs to set objectives (*what* targets and milestones it will pursue on the path to its goals) and strategies (*how* it is going to accomplish its goals). Enterprise risk management (ERM) focuses on ensuring that an organization manages the uncertainty that exists around the achievement of its objectives. Operational risk management (ORM) is focused on managing the risks that appear during its day-to-day activities of actually executing the organization's strategy.

Thousands of decisions are made every day in every organization. A few are strategic decisions about *what* the organization wants to achieve in the future (i.e., its corporate objectives) and *how* it is going to achieve those objectives (i.e., its corporate strategy). These are corporate decisions, typically made infrequently and by the directing minds of the organization. Corporate decisions are about setting the destination and direction of the organization and defining the policies for how people will behave.

The central aim of operations is to perform, in other words, to effectively deliver on corporate objectives using corporate strategy. Failure to effectively and efficiently execute strategy is a major source of operational risk. The three main activities that executives must engage in to manage their operational risks are:

1. Establish clarity around objectives, roles, and responsibilities. This includes both a clear understanding by everyone of the corporate objectives that the organization as a whole is working toward and for each person a clear understanding of exactly how they will contribute and how that fits into the bigger picture. The organization's leadership needs to ensure that people know what the corporate strategy is so that they can *align* to it, pulling together to achieve the organization's goal and objectives.

For example, when NASA decides to land a spacecraft on the moon—that is a clear goal. To achieve it every single person in the organization needs to know exactly how he or she is expected to contribute to the achievement of that goal.

2. Align resources to deliver excellent performance. There is no excuse for mismanaging the factors that are within the organization's control. This includes amassing the right resources (people, business processes, and systems) and designing and applying effective and efficient processes that optimally configure and manage those resources toward the achievement of objectives, using the agreed strategy.

The ability to perform consistently and to deliver high quality results in a dynamic business environment doesn't just happen because of a perfect plan. That's because life is uncertain and not everything will go as expected. Managers who achieve excellent performance are proficient in adjusting their plans based on these capabilities:

- Understanding the factors within their control that drive performance (the interrelationships between people, business processes, and systems)
- Monitoring performance indicators to know which factors need to be adjusted to achieve the desired performance results
- Re-optimizing their resources toward the achievement of their objectives

The resource optimization process encompasses constant monitoring of progress and adjusting the operational plans and business practices required to maintain alignment to strategy and ultimately to deliver excellent performance.

Returning to the earlier example, NASA lands a spacecraft within a few yards of its target on the moon, which is 240,000 miles away from Earth. Although the NASA mission team starts with an excellent flight plan, they will spend 99 percent of their time during the flight monitoring the ship's position and the status of its systems and making course corrections to ensure that the ship is tracking for its ultimate destination.

3. Develop capabilities to handle unexpected or uncontrollable factors. For those risks that are outside of the expected range or are imposed on the organization by external forces, the management stance shifts from one of prevention and control to one of readiness and resilience. The three strategies for dealing with uncontrollable and unpredictable risks are:

1. Cultivating *awareness* of factors and trends in the external environment. It is only by keen monitoring of the environment that managers can anticipate and detect new risks.

2. Building *relationships* with external stakeholders. Positive relationships can help the organization to influence stakeholder decisions that could prevent or diminish the impact of negative external factors on the organization and enhance the impact of positive factors that contribute to success. Establishing rapport with stakeholders prior to a crisis occurring can be critical in managing through a crisis.

3. Developing *response* capabilities. This encompasses both the development of crisis management plans as well as the development of the capabilities to quickly realign the organization's resources so that it can respond with agility to massive or step changes or catastrophic events.

> To respond to events and conditions that are truly outside of the ordinary, a manager needs to be flexible, innovative, and improvising.

In the NASA example, this would mean identifying the expected conditions and factors that are beyond the organization's control (e.g., weather, meteorites, funding) and putting in place strategies and capabilities to deal with them (e.g., developing weather monitoring and forecasting systems to increase awareness of risks, developing meteorite avoidance systems to respond in a timely manner, and cultivating relationships with funding agencies and stakeholders to ensure the perceived value of NASA remains high). It also means putting in place capabilities for dealing with "unexpected" factors or events or conditions that are outside of the normal range.

To fully manage operational risk requires paying attention to all three activities together, that is, clarifying objectives, aligning resources, and developing capabilities to prepare for the unexpected. If any of those three actions are ignored, the organization will perform below its potential.

This assertion is validated by research conducted in 2004 by Mankins and Steele[2] in which they surveyed 197 companies worldwide with sales in excess of $500 million. They assessed the *actual performance* achieved for each company and compared it to the financial forecast in the company's business *plan*. On average, the companies were only achieving 63 percent of their objectives relating to financial performance. That amounts to an average performance loss of 37 percent.

Why does this 37 percent gap between potential and actual performance exist? The specific root causes that Mankins and Steele discovered are listed in Exhibit 16.1. Their research shows that poor operational performance is, in large part, caused by poor operational risk management. Note that the root causes they identified are all related to a failure to achieve one or more of the drivers of operational effectiveness:

- Establish clarity around objectives, roles, and responsibilities (15.8 percent of performance loss in the study is related to this ORM activity).
- Align resources to deliver quality in implementing strategy (15.4 percent of performance loss in the study is related to this ORM activity).
- Develop capabilities to handle unexpected or uncontrollable factors (6.3 percent of performance loss in the study is related to this ORM activity).

Based on the research, one can conclude that the core operational risk management activities are tightly aligned with performance drivers. If the research findings into financial performance shortfalls hold true for other organizational performance objectives, one can expect a tremendous cost associated with poor operational risk management in terms of the organization's ability to meet or exceed its performance targets. Executives and managers need to ask themselves, can they afford to leave 37 percent of the organization's performance potential on the table? If not, they need to care about and master operational risk management.

Returning to the Steelbelt fable, at the strategic level, the organization would have decided on its direction, for example, which markets to be in, which (and how much of each) products to make to meet market needs, and profit targets. At the operational level, those decisions would have been translated into sales,

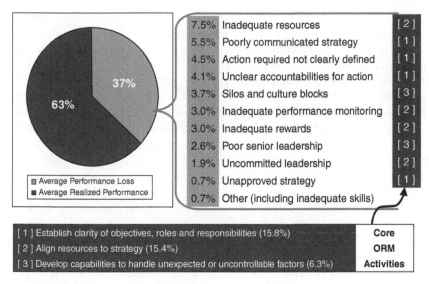

7.5%	Inadequate resources	[2]
5.5%	Poorly communicated strategy	[1]
4.5%	Action required not clearly defined	[1]
4.1%	Unclear accountabilities for action	[1]
3.7%	Silos and culture blocks	[3]
3.0%	Inadequate performance monitoring	[2]
3.0%	Inadequate rewards	[2]
2.6%	Poor senior leadership	[3]
1.9%	Uncommitted leadership	[2]
0.7%	Unapproved strategy	[1]
0.7%	Other (including inadequate skills)	

■ Average Performance Loss
■ Average Realized Performance

[1] Establish clarity of objectives, roles and responsibilities (15.8%)	**Core**
[2] Align resources to strategy (15.4%)	**ORM**
[3] Develop capabilities to handle unexpected or uncontrollable factors (6.3%)	**Activities**

Adapted from *Turning Great Strategy into Great Performance*, Mankins and Steele, Harvard Business Review August 2005

Exhibit 16.1 Where the Performance Goes
Source: Adapted from "Turning Great Strategy into Great Performance," Mankins and Steele, *Harvard Business Review*, August 2005.

production and cost targets. Included in the production targets would be targets for quality and safety to meet the expectations of customers, regulators, and other stakeholders.

The main character in the fable at the beginning of the chapter, Richard Preston wondered, "How could things have gone so wrong?" The fable contains a powerful example of what can happen when the ability to deliver high quality fails. In the fable it led to substandard tires, accidents, fatalities, and lawsuits that collectively damaged the company's reputation and threatened the survival of the organization. What could have led to that quality slip? The fable doesn't give us enough information to know. We can guess at the reason(s). Perhaps the objective of product safety was not clear or was in conflict with other priorities such as cost cutting. Perhaps resources (people, business processes, and systems) were not aligned to produce a high-quality product. Perhaps the company was unable to maintain alignment of its resources to its strategy because of unexpected factors such as a hurricane causing an oil price hike, causing softening in car sales, and causing pressure to lower costs to maintain market share and profit margins. Whatever the reason(s) for Steelbelt's predicament, the fable emphasizes the importance of appropriate management of operational risk and the impact it can have on the overall performance of an organization.

IS RISK ALL BAD?

For many people, the word "risk" has a negative connotation and is associated with losses or damages of some sort. But for some people, the word risk actually has a positive connotation. To them, risk is synonymous with the potential for benefit, reward, or a gain of some sort, in other words, an opportunity.

The fact is risk exists in all human endeavors. Risks (both threats and opportunities), benefits, and costs are inextricably linked. We take risks, not to avoid loss but to attain benefits. For people who see risk as something negative, the risk management mistake they most often make is to try to protect organizational value by avoiding, eliminating, or controlling all risk. This skews the distribution of resources toward value protection and away from value creation. The flaw in this risk-averse mindset is that in attempting to eradicate all threat of loss, the potential for gain is also diminished. But to take risks with no consideration or weighing of the possible losses can lead to unnecessary exposure to threats.

The trick is to find the level of responsible risk taking that avoids the extreme positions of reckless gambling and risk aversion. Taking responsible risks is a necessary part of business and life. In the words of Will Rogers "you've got to go out on a limb sometimes because that is where the fruit is." Robert Mittelstaedt,[3] business guru and Vice Dean and Director for Executive Education at the Wharton School, puts it this way "if you do not make any mistakes, you may not be taking enough risk, but failing to take any risks at all may be the most dangerous type of mistake that a business can make."

Since risks, benefits, and costs are all inextricably linked, how do you strike the right balance between them? Finding the balance is central to determining the organization's *risk tolerance*, which is covered in a later section. However, before discussing tolerance, the organization first must understand the magnitude of the risks it faces and what can be done about them.

Returning to the Steelbelt fable, there appears to be a classic risk (law suits and reputation damage triggered by lower quality) versus benefit (lower costs to protect market share and profit margin) tradeoff. The story doesn't tell us what led to the drop in quality. It does tell us that the company had a pioneering "atmosphere." Hindsight after a risk has materialized often makes it easy to forget how important that pioneering atmosphere would have been in fueling the company's growth for 50 years. Did they go too far with cost reductions this time? In the Steelbelt example, it would appear that the risk reward tradeoff might have been skewed toward reducing costs over maintaining quality.

HOW DO YOU ASSESS OPERATIONAL RISKS, PARTICULARLY IN A DYNAMIC BUSINESS ENVIRONMENT?

The reality of life is that every manager faces many, many risks in the course of a day but can only devote attention to the most significant few. To decide which risks are the "significant few" that merit attention, a manager can choose among several approaches, including: guessing; relying on gut feel based on intuition and experience; applying a disciplined approach to assessing the magnitude of the risks; or using some combination of these approaches. Regardless of the approach used to estimate the size of a risk exposure, at the end of the day, a value judgment must be made about whether the risk exposure is tolerable or if the organization needs to take on more risk or reduce its risk exposure to successfully meet its objectives and risk tolerance criteria.

Most operational environments are characterized by change. Change brings with it risks and crafting an appropriate response to change is a major aim of operational risk management. Some changes are within the organization's control, that is, those that emanate from within the internal environment (e.g., new or modified business processes, new systems, new people that bring new relationships, new leaders that bring new priorities). Other changes originate from the external business environment (e.g., new customers, new competitors, new regulations, changing demographics, changing economics, evolving stakeholder expectations, weather, climate). Although the organization can't control these external factors, it can control its response to and preparation for them.

In such a dynamic environment, how can one understand and appropriately assess operational risks? The key is to start with the objective that is to be achieved. The next steps are to identify the factors that drive performance and risk, to understand which of these factors are most likely to impact performance, and then to understand the size of the potential impact on the achievement of the objective(s). The simple definition of risk "more things can happen than will happen"[4] is a salient reminder of why it is good practice to consider the range of potential impacts rather than focusing on a single scenario or potential outcome. A simple way to accomplish this is to envisage both the *extreme* (or worst) case and the *typical* (or expected) case. Based on this analysis, a manager can decide which factors are most significant and concentrate his or her efforts on them. Finally, it is important to note the assumptions made in identifying, assessing, and selecting performance and risk factors.

Risk cannot be measured directly. It can only be estimated because it involves predicting a future outcome. Therefore, all risk estimates involve judgment. This is true whether they are based on quantitative assessment and well-established facts or strictly on intuition. Because there is no way to estimate a risk without making some assumptions, it is extremely important to clearly distinguish between assumptions and facts in the analysis. It is also wise to test assumptions to ensure they are still valid as changes occur in the business environment and as new information becomes available. If, over time, the assumptions prove to be incorrect or invalid, the entire analysis will need to be revisited.

The effort invested in risk assessment should be commensurate with the risk and with the information available. Large risks usually warrant a detailed risk assessment, perhaps even the construction of risk models. This is because large risks normally demand more resources for risk mitigation, and therefore it is advisable to gather enough information to make good resource allocation decisions. For smaller risks, managers generally rely on past experience and judgment because even if they are wrong, there is not a lot at stake. In cases where it is not possible or cost-justified to model the risk, it is necessary to rely on judgment.

To illustrate the principles of operational risk assessment, consider another chapter in the Steelbelt fable. When Richard Preston worked in the production department, he was responsible for reviewing and revising manufacturing procedures to ensure they were compatible with the company's new sustainability policy. Here are the seven steps Richard used to assess the operational risks associated with this task.

1. Clearly define the objective. In this case, Richard's objective is to ensure that manufacturing procedures are compatible with the company's new sustainability policy.
2. Understand the performance drivers. The achievement of this objective will be dependent on:
   - Richard's ability to gain accurate knowledge of the existing manufacturing procedures.
   - Richard's ability to develop a strong understanding of the expectations of the sustainability policy.
   - Richard's ability to put that knowledge together to make revisions to the written manufacturing procedures that reflect the new sustainability policy.
   - Richard's ability to update the manufacturing procedures such that the production unit can and wants to adopt them as part of their business practices.
3. Understand the risk drivers. What factors drive uncertainty around achieving objectives?
   - Richard's ability to gain accurate knowledge of the existing manufacturing procedures is dependent on his ability to gain the cooperation of the production department.
   - Richard's ability to develop a strong understanding of the expectations of the sustainability policy is dependent on his ability to educate himself and on the clarity of the policy.
   - Richard's ability to put that knowledge together to make revisions to the written manufacturing procedures that reflect the new sustainability policy is dependent on his ability to integrate and apply his knowledge.
   - Richard's ability to update the manufacturing procedures such that the production unit can and wants to adopt them as part of their business practices is dependent on his ability to work with the production department and understand the culture and other relevant factors that would motivate the business personnel.
4. Identify the factors most likely to impact objectives. Richard reviewed the performance and risk factors. He determined that the second and third risk factors above are within his control and he was confident in his ability to acquire and apply knowledge, so he decided that these two factors are not relevant. However, remaining risk factors are not entirely within his control. He quickly recognized that his ability to work collaboratively with the production department is key for both of those risk factors.
5. Estimate the size of the impact. The range of scenarios includes: full, partial, or no cooperation from the production department. Richard estimates that for the worst case scenario, that is, if the production department doesn't cooperate at all, he would be completely prevented from achieving his objective. The expected scenario is that the production team cooperates enough for him to be able to revise the written procedures but that they put up some resistance to applying the revisions in practice. With only partial cooperation Richard would only partially achieve his objective.

6. Select the significant few. Richard decided the most significant operational risk factor was obtaining the cooperation of the production department in actually adopting the revisions that introduce sustainability considerations into production procedures.
7. Identify the underlying assumptions. The key assumptions Richard made are:
   - That he will correctly understand and interpret the sustainability requirements.
   - That he can win the cooperation of the production department in the renewal process.
   - That his estimation of his ability to integrate and apply knowledge is accurate.
   - That the production department will adopt the changes if he communicates well.

This example of a simple risk assessment illustrates how one can quickly identify the key factors to focus on in order to effectively manage risk and ensure success in the pursuit of operational performance objectives.

WHY YOU NEED TO DEFINE RISK TOLERANCE FOR ALIGNED DECISION MAKING

Every decision or action carries within it both the potential for positive and negative effects on operational objectives and ultimately for the organization's corporate objectives. The challenge of effective management at both the enterprise and operational levels is to take decisions and actions that strike an *appropriate* balance between potential upside and downside effects. This balance is reflected in the organization's risk appetite and risk tolerance.

Risk appetite refers to how much risk an organization is willing to take on to ensure it has ample opportunity to achieve its objectives. When making a decision, managers and employees need to understand the organization's risk appetite in order to distinguish between which are the good risks and which are bad risks to take, in other words, where the organization will and will not go in the pursuit of its objectives. It is somewhat analogous to deciding if you want to go fishing on a small lake or the ocean. The larger body of water has more fish and therefore offers more opportunity than if you were to fish in a lake. But it also requires more equipment and has more perils. To use another sporting analogy, deciding the organization's risk appetite is akin to deciding in which baseball league you wish to play—pick-up, amateur, or professional. Each league has different expectations of players and also offers different potential benefits. A consumer analogy is deciding whether to shop at a store that offers deeply discounted prices but doesn't allow a refund versus a different store that has higher prices but provides a refund option.

Risk tolerance is used to communicate the appropriate level at which a risk must be managed to be considered acceptable. Risk tolerance is not defined as a single finite number, but rather as a tolerable zone or range of values where an operational risk is neither *under-managed* nor *over-managed*. When a risk is under-managed, existing management activities and practices around that risk do not produce enough certainty that operational objectives will be achieved. When a risk is over-managed, the amount of certainty produced by existing management activities and practices does not merit the investment of time, effort, and resources dedicated to the risk and would be better applied elsewhere. Employees and managers need to understand the organization's criteria for risk tolerance to ensure that their decisions lead to the most efficient and effective use of resources and balance potential upside and downside effects.

Risk appetite and risk tolerance are not usually derived empirically. They are statements of the organization's (and the decision maker's) values about what is appropriate, fair, and desirable behavior. An explicit understanding of risk appetite and risk tolerance is fundamental to enable an organization to implement systematic operational risk management. Yet many organizations (or more precisely their leaders) find it difficult to explicitly define and actively communicate about risk tolerance.

There are three common reasons that organizations fail to articulate their risk appetite and/or risk tolerance. The first reason is that many executives fall prey to the mistaken belief that articulating risk appetite or tolerance actually gives permission for risky behavior. The second reason is they don't know how to develop a reliable gauge of risk tolerance. The third challenge is that it is not always clear how to align risk tolerance and risk appetite with organizational objectives and strategies at the operational level. How does an organization overcome these barriers and define risk tolerance and appetite in a manner that sets out appropriate guidance for decision making and behavior?

The first step is to replace any vestiges of a risk-averse mindset with one that embraces risk management as the foundation of stewardship. For many people, risk is seen as negative, and any level of risk is seen as unacceptable, particularly when it comes to issues involving human health and safety. The rationale is that tolerance of any level of risk is not acceptable. However this frame of thinking is faulty. Of course, damage to humans, the environment, and society are all unacceptable. The job of risk management is not to decide how much damage can be sustained. Rather, it is to make the best use of resources. Stewardship is about deciding how to best allocate scarce resources (and attention) to ensure the achievement of objectives for performance while also meeting criteria for other valued outcomes such as employee health and safety, environmental sustainability, and corporate citizenship. Managers and employees cannot be expected to uphold the organization's values around risk appetite and risk tolerance if they are not clearly and explicitly communicated.

In order to communicate about risk appetite and tolerance, most organizations begin by gauging their *de facto* risk tolerance and appetite. The fact is that whether or not its leaders have formally articulated the organization's risk tolerance and risk appetite, they have done so tacitly in their decisions and in the business practices that they encourage and condone. Therefore, a logical way to measure risk appetite and tolerance is to estimate the level of risk that the organization is exposed to given its current objectives, strategies, and management practices. This is the de facto risk appetite and risk tolerance of the organization.

To illustrate, let's revisit the example of deciding whether to shop at a store that offers deeply discounted prices but doesn't allow a refund, versus a different store that has higher prices but provides a refund option. An organization might have a policy that for purchasing office supplies under a certain amount (say $500) employees can shop at the store with the discounted prices, but purchases of items that cost more than $500 must be made at a store that offers a refund. This policy shows that the de facto risk tolerance for office supply purchases is to put no more than $500 at risk to pursue the opportunity for savings. The threshold of $500 is an indication of the value the organization places on its cash. Upon reflection, executive management may decide that the threshold is too low, especially if it also considers the value of the time that employees would spend on returning items, particularly if the time spent on returning a purchase costs the organization more than $500.

Once senior leaders have an assessment of the organization's de facto risk appetite and risk tolerance, they can critically examine it to see if there are any gaps between the de facto, or *actual* values, and the *espoused* values. Actual values are how managers and employees *behave* based on the values that actually underpin the interpersonal dynamics of the organization.[5] Espoused values are what senior leaders *aspire to and communicate* both orally and in written form. If there are gaps between actual and espoused values, senior leaders may wish to make adjustments to bring them back into alignment. For example, as a result of assessing current risks and risk management practices, it is not uncommon for senior managers to be surprised to discover the high level of risks that some of their people are taking on behalf of the organization, or conversely, that their people are foregoing good opportunities because they are afraid to take on risk. As a result, senior leaders will typically seek to clarify policies and expectations around decision making by making risk appetite and risk tolerance explicit.

To improve the alignment of risk tolerance and risk appetite with organizational objectives and strategies, it is important to weave them into performance management and reporting systems. For instance, risk appetite can be worked into operational performance management by ensuring that performance targets encourage people to take on the amount of risk necessary to achieve the organization's objectives. Risk tolerance levels can be woven into the reporting system by using the boundaries of the tolerable zone as the triggers for escalating and reporting on problems and opportunities.

In the Steelbelt fable, we learn that Richard "loved the people, he loved the products, he loved the pioneering atmosphere." A pioneering atmosphere is a sign that the company had a healthy risk appetite. However, the risk tolerance is not clear in the case study. Was risk considered in the organization's cost-cutting measures? Were risk indicators around product quality established? Particularly at times of change, it is important to articulate how much risk the organization is willing to take on in order for employees to know how much latitude they have to innovate as they implement the change. It's also important to establish and monitor risk indicators that provide early warning signs that a risk is moving outside of the tolerable zone.

WHAT CAN YOU DO TO EFFECTIVELY MANAGE OPERATIONAL RISK?

All organizations manage operational risk to some degree or they would not survive. However, in many organizations risk management practices are ad hoc or patchy. This unnecessarily exposes the organization to unplanned risk and can have a negative impact on performance as described earlier. Whereas at the enterprise level, risk management is focused on *selection* of the best strategy, at the operational level the focus of risk management is on successful *execution* of strategy.

An earlier section provided some insight into how to systematically identify and assess risks. The previous section showed how to articulate risk appetite and tolerance. This section will address how to evaluate risk management effectiveness and how to develop effective risk response capabilities.

The systematic management of operational risk requires applying discipline to the tasks of:

- *Identifying and quantifying the risks associated with implementing a particular strategy*, so that the potential impact that these risks can have on operational objectives can be understood.
- *Evaluating the organization's risk management effectiveness* by assessing the ability of existing risk treatment efforts to maximize upside effects and minimize downside effects on objectives. If this evaluation reveals that the risk exposure is not within the bounds of the organization's risk tolerance, then the existing suite of risk treatments needs to be modified.
- *Developing an adaptive risk response capability* to bring the risk within the defined risk tolerance range and to keep it there when changes occur either in the level of risk (normally caused by changes in the internal or external business environment) or in the organization's risk tolerance.

To analyze the effectiveness of the organization's existing risk response, a good way to start is to inventory what is currently being done to treat each key risk identified. Next, the organization should compare the level of risk exposure under the existing risk treatments to the organization's risk tolerance. If the risk is tolerable, then no additional treatment is required. If the risk is under-managed, additional risk treatments are to be considered. If the risk is over-managed, then it may be advisable to reallocate some of the risk treatment resources to other more significant risks.

Typical risk response activities fall into one of two categories:

- *Monitoring* to detect changes in risk levels. This information is used to trigger risk treatment action.
- *Action* to change the potential likelihood of the risk (i.e., reduce or increase prevention activities) and/or the potential impact of the risk (i.e., reduce or increase mitigation activities).

For each risk that is either under- or over-managed, the person responsible needs to decide what can be done and how much needs to be done to bring the risk back within tolerance. Periodically, as changes are detected in either the level of risk exposure or the tolerance for risk, risk treatments will need to be reevaluated and if necessary modified to adapt to the new conditions.

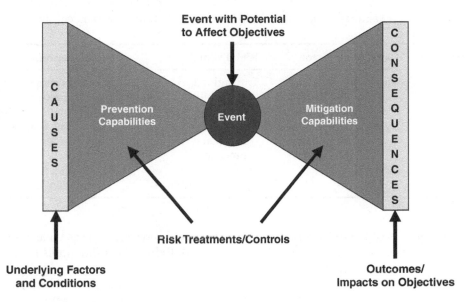

Exhibit 16.2 The Bowtie Model

Before launching into a description of how to manage risk, it is helpful to first understand the relationship between:

- A *risk factor* (also called a cause or issue or underlying condition), which is the precursor of a risk event.
- A *risk event* (also called a problem or opportunity) that occurs when a risk becomes manifest.
- A *consequence* (also called an outcome) that results when a risk transcends from possibility to actuality.

The Bowtie model shown in Exhibit 16.2 is used to map out the progression of a risk from underlying cause, to risk event, to consequence. In the middle, the knot of the bowtie represents an *event* with the potential to affect the achievement of objectives. The left half of the bow represents the underlying conditions or *causes* that trigger the event, including any *prevention capabilities* that are in place. Prevention capabilities (e.g., risk controls or risk treatments) focus on limiting the probability that a risk event will occur. The right half of the bow represents what unfolds after the event occurs, including any *mitigation capabilities* that are in place and the *consequences* of the event in terms of the ultimate impact on objectives. Mitigation capabilities (e.g., risk controls or risk treatments) focus on limiting the nature and extent of the effects that the event has on the achievement of objectives.

Exhibit 16.3 contains three illustrative examples of the relationship among cause, risk event, and consequence. In example #1, the risk event is an employee who trips and falls. The cause is a broken shoelace. The consequence of the event is the employee's wrist is sprained. To prevent falls, one would focus on eliminating the underlying cause, for example, avoiding broken shoelaces by monitoring shoelace wear and by making new shoelaces available. To mitigate the

Exhibit 16.3 Examples of the Relationship Between a Risk Factor, Risk Event, and Consequence

Example	Cause/Risk Factor	Risk Event	Consequence(s)
# 1	Broken shoelace	Trip and fall	Sprained wrist
# 2	Resistance to adopting sustainability enhancements to procedures	Sustainability principles not integrated into manufacturing practices	Company reputation and brand diminished in eyes of stakeholders
# 3	Cost reduction directives	Drop in quality standards of tires	Fatal vehicle accidents, brand damage

consequences of the risk event (i.e., falls), one could have employees wear protective equipment (e.g., wrist, elbow, or knee pads). Exhibit 16.4 illustrates how the Bowtie model is applied.

Example #2 in Exhibit 16.3 recasts the earlier Steelbelt example in which Richard Preston was charged with reviewing and revising manufacturing procedures to ensure they were compatible with the company's new sustainability policy. Recall the main risk factor that Richard identified was resistance by production personnel to adopting the sustainability enhancements to the manufacturing procedures. The potential risk event would be that sustainability principles are not integrated into manufacturing practices. The potential consequences are damage to the company's reputation as a good corporate citizen and an associated weakening of the Steelbelt brand. To prevent this risk event, Richard would need to

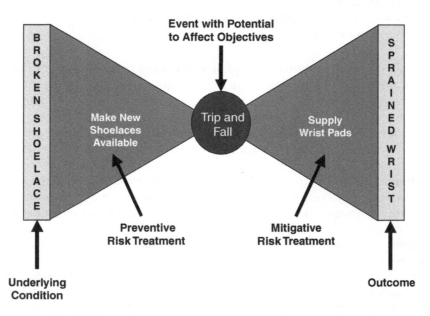

Exhibit 16.4 Bowtie Example

understand the root causes of the production department's resistance to change and design a response to overcome resistance.

The Bowtie model can be used in a *proactive* way to delineate the root causes that *may* lead to a risk event and the potential impacts the risk event *may* have on the achievement of objectives. The Bowtie structure makes it easy to list the existing risk prevention and mitigation capabilities. With an inventory of its current risk treatments in hand, the organization can evaluate if it is able to manage the most significant risks to a tolerable level. Through the lens of the Bowtie structure, gaps in existing risk treatments become immediately apparent. Further, because the Bowtie method is structured around the relationship between root causes, risk events, and potential consequences, the analysis pinpoints what elements of the existing risk treatments require enhancement.

The Bowtie method helps to draw the direct link from cause, to risk event, and to consequence. It is important to understand this progression because risk management efforts can either focus on *prevention* (i.e., eliminating or reducing the underlying cause thereby preventing the risk event from occurring) or on *mitigation* (i.e., eliminating or reducing the consequences *after* the risk event has happened).

The Bowtie approach can also be used as a learning tool *after* an incident—whether the event results in downside effects on objectives or is only a "near miss." The learning is gained by comparing the *expected* performance of the prevention and mitigation plans against their *actual* performance. This comparison will reveal risk treatments that are not effective and will also provide insight into how they might be enhanced to manage risk to a tolerable level.

In most cases, the risk response (or risk treatment) regimen will be some combination of prevention and mitigation measures. To make the most efficient use of resources, it is important that the risk treatment strategy should be tailored to the nature and magnitude of the risk. Exhibit 16.5 shows criteria for the selection of an appropriate combination of risk treatments based on level of risk.

- The upper-right quadrant represents risks that have both a high likelihood of occurring and potential for a large impact on objectives. For risks in

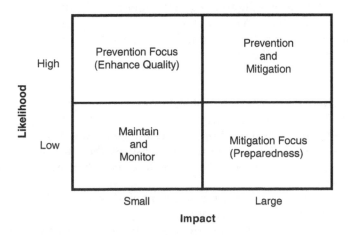

Exhibit 16.5   Risk Treatment Selection Criteria

the upper right quadrant, it is advisable to use both risk prevention and mitigation strategies.

- For risks in the lower-right quadrant where there is a low likelihood of occurrence but potential for large impact, it makes sense to steer any additional investment into risk mitigation, that is, to be prepared to respond if the risk event does happen. A preparedness stance is particularly important when the source of the risk is external to the organization, in which case the organization cannot prevent the risk event.

- For risks that fall into the upper-left quadrant, that is, where there is a high likelihood of occurrence but the potential impact is small, it makes sense to focus on preventing the risk event. Often operational risks in this quadrant are related to weaknesses in quality management and minimizing these risks will also lead to improvements in performance.

- Finally, risks in the bottom-left quadrant are either too small or sufficiently well managed that it usually unwarranted to implement additional risk treatments. Instead for risks in the bottom-left quadrant, it is prudent to maintain existing risk treatments and to monitor these risks to see if they are migrating toward one of the other quadrants. In addition, over-managed risks tend to be in the bottom left quadrant and they can represent a hidden supply of resources. By taking resources allocated to over-managed risks in the bottom-left quadrant and reassigning them to under-managed and significant risks in the three other quadrants, an organization can optimize its risk exposure and maximize the effectiveness of its resources.

Because prevention efforts are generally more cost-effective than mitigation efforts, it is wise to emphasize prevention where possible. To design effective prevention measures, it is necessary to uncover and address the underlying root causes. The "5 Whys" is a question-asking method that can be used to explore the cause-and-effect relationships underlying a particular risk event or problem. To use the 5 Whys method, one starts with the risk event and asks "*Why* did (or would) this happen?" and then repeats the question until the root cause(s) is revealed. It usually doesn't take much digging to get the root cause(s) of a risk event.

To illustrate how the 5 Whys method works, let's return to example #3 "cost reduction directives," which is found in Exhibit 16.3. The sequence from risk event to root cause might look like this:

- Fatal vehicle accidents (the problem).
- Why?—Tires failed (first why).
- Why?—Quality of tires not up to standard (second why).
- Why?—As a result of cost reduction measures, there was a switch to a lower cost supplier of materials, which led to a reduction in the quality of tires (third why).
- Why?—Changes to supply arrangement made exclusively on cost considerations, not on quality (fourth why).
- Why?—Risk not factored into quality assurance processes around new suppliers (fifth why).

The last answer reveals a systemic issue that would affect much more than just this particular supplier. If corrected, for example, by incorporating risk into quality assurance criteria, many other risk events would also be prevented.

The key with the 5 Whys method is to keep asking *Why* until you get to the underlying, root cause(s), which studies have shown is generally a combination of failures or weaknesses in the organization's system of management and business practices.[6] It may take from three to seven *Whys* to get to a systemic weakness. Typical management system weaknesses from an operational risk perspective are:

- No identification of risk.
- Insufficient resources allocated to manage the risk.
- Standard operating procedures not established or followed.
- Inadequate oversight of risk treatments (including communication and feedback).

Of course, no prevention program can guarantee that it will be 100 percent effective all of the time or that all underlying risk factors will be identified and controlled. Therefore, for risk events that have a large potential impact on objectives, it is wise to ensure that mitigation measures are in place. When used in a predictive way, the Bowtie model can help to identify risk events with major potential impacts on the achievement of objectives for which the organization is not adequately prepared. If existing risk mitigation capabilities would reduce the potential consequences to a tolerable level, then no additional risk mitigation treatments are needed. However, if the evaluation reveals that existing risk mitigation capabilities would not reduce the potential consequences to a tolerable level, the organization should improve its readiness to respond to and recover from the risk event should it occur.

In the Steelbelt fable, Richard asked, "How could things have gone so terribly wrong?" Inevitably, after any crisis, the next question that arises is: "Who is to blame?" In many organizations, the "culprit" is punished and things go back to normal. An organization with solid operational risk management will use the crisis as an opportunity to learn and enhance its risk management capabilities. For example, since most catastrophic losses are usually the result of failures in the system of management as opposed to an individual manager, the more useful questions from a learning perspective are:

- What gaps in our management system led to this negative outcome?
- What organizational blind spots prevented us from seeing this coming?
- How can we avoid a similar loss in future?

A variety of analytical methods (including the Bowtie model and the 5 Whys) can be used to answer these questions and learn from experience. Analyzing successes also provides an opportunity to learn from experience and to validate that the success is a result of careful management of the performance and risk factors versus sheer luck. Establishing a culture of learning is a key component in the drive for enhanced operational risk management and maximizing performance.

To summarize, the key concepts for the evaluation, selection, and design of an effective program of operational risk management treatments are:

- Determine if risk exposure is within tolerance limits. If not, adjust risk response activities.
- To determine how to best manage a risk, you need to first understand how it arises. The Bowtie method helps to map out the sequence from underlying cause, to risk event, and ultimately to consequences (i.e., impact on objectives).
- There are two main types of risk treatments: *Prevention* activities—aimed at reducing likelihood of occurrence of the risk event—and *Mitigation* activities—aimed at reducing magnitude of the impact should the risk event occur.
- Management of most operational risks consists of a combination of prevention and mitigation measures. In general, it is advisable to focus on prevention because it is more cost-effective. However, because no prevention regimen is perfect, for risk events with the potential for a significant impact on objectives, it is prudent to also put in place strong mitigation capabilities. Failures and successes need to be analyzed to identify opportunities for enhancing both individual risk treatments and the organization's ability to anticipate and manage risk.

HOW DO YOU ENCOURAGE A CULTURE OF RISK MANAGEMENT AT THE OPERATIONAL LEVEL?

To encourage a culture of risk management, leaders throughout the organization need to communicate about risk. The primary mode of communication required is *action*, that is, leadership by example. Spoken and written communication, while necessary, is secondary to action. This is because culture is primarily established through the actions of the leaders of the organization.

Specifically there are three ways leaders need to communicate to encourage a culture of risk management at the operational level:

1. Model good risk management behavior.
   Leaders must live risk management themselves. Statements of corporate values and ethics and business policies represent the organization's espoused risk management culture and are important tools in communicating what kind of culture the organization's leaders wish to instill. However, these written documents will be invalidated the instant that the organization's leaders act in a way that contradicts the espoused values.
2. Articulate expectations for risk management behavior.
   In particular, leaders need to communicate what constitutes good risk management behavior (i.e., what to strive for) versus poor behavior (i.e., what to avoid). These expectations need to be reflected in policy documents, procedures, and business practices. Most importantly, operational risk management expectations need to be integrated into performance management and reward systems. It is important to frequently reinforce written

expectations with spoken messages in both formal communications and informal conversations.

Rather than passively "pushing" risk management expectations on their people, leaders need to actively "pull" desired risk management behavior. This is accomplished by asking the people who report to them about how they are meeting risk management expectations. For example:

- How are they integrating risk thinking into their decision and management processes?
- What are the significant risks they face?
- What they are doing to manage risks to within a tolerable range?
- What risk indicators are they monitoring to ensure their most significant risks are under control?

3. Be clear about the consequences and follow through on them.

Human behavior is driven by consequences. People are motivated to act because they want to achieve positive consequences and/or avoid negative consequences. Therefore, it is important for leaders to "engineer" and clearly articulate both the positive consequences of meeting risk management expectations and the negative consequences of not doing so.

Then, leaders need to follow through with the consequences. This includes acknowledging good risk management behavior in others, particularly those who report to them. And it includes addressing situations where employees are not meeting risk management expectations. If poor risk management behavior is ignored, it will send a message that risk management is not important. The organization will pay twice for this. First, it will expose the organization to unnecessary risk; and second, it will demotivate those individuals who are making a genuine effort to meet risk management expectations.

Taken together, the above three actions communicate the "tone-from-the-top." Without strong and consistent leadership support, it is difficult, if not impossible to create a strong risk management culture.

HOW DO YOU ALIGN OPERATIONAL RISK MANAGEMENT WITH ENTERPRISE RISK MANAGEMENT?

At the enterprise level, decision makers are focused on *what* to achieve (strategic objectives) and *how* to get there (strategic direction). Therefore, executives must take a long-term perspective, looking out into the future to identify opportunities for sustaining or growing the organization. To do this, executives need to have a good read on the organization's current capabilities and capacity to execute. With a solid assessment of existing capabilities in hand, executives can identify the critical capabilities that the organization needs to develop (or acquire) to continue to meet its objectives and sustain the organization over the long term.

At the operational level, managers are focused on *execution* of strategy. Their focus is the present, the current planning and reporting cycle. To do this, managers need to focus on aligning their resources to effectively and efficiently deliver on their objectives.

Alignment of the enterprise and operational levels requires a translation of long-term enterprise objectives and strategies into short-term operational strategies and objectives. The key to aligning risk management at the operational and enterprise levels is to establish accountability through a clear line of sight between the enterprise and the operational levels. This line of sight is created by embedding risk management thinking into the organization's performance management and reporting systems.

The key performance management and reporting system elements that need to be clearly articulated for each person and coordinated across the organization are:

- Objective(s) or *what* it is that the person has to achieve. The concept of having a strategic goal for the organization and *measurable* objectives for each individual is fundamental to risk management. One can't begin to manage risk until one knows what is required to achieve each staff member's objective and the factors that create uncertainty around the achievement of that objective. In many public and private sector organizations, objectives are more like a list of hopes and dreams than they are meaningful and measurable targets that both inspire and hold people to account.
- Strategy or *how* the individual is to go about achieving each of their objectives. Strategy is sometimes referred to as a direction or path that the person is to pursue.
- Risk appetite or how much risk the organization is willing to take on to ensure the person has ample opportunity to achieve his or her objective. This may be incorporated into the strategy by defining which are the good risks and which are bad risks to take, that is, where the organization will and will not go in the pursuit of its objectives.
- *Performance measures and targets* that will be used to assess the individual's progress toward their operational objectives, and the organization's progress toward its strategic objectives.
- *Risk indicators and risk tolerance levels* that articulate the key conditions that will be monitored to provide an early warning that a significant risk event may be imminent or that a risk is about to move outside of the tolerable zone.

To systematically manage performance requires developing an understanding of the relationship between the drivers of performance and risk, including the development of measures to track risk factors and quantify their impact on performance. For example, imagine "knowledgeable staff" is a key performance driver for a specific objective and the associated risk factors are the ability to hire and train staff to the required level of knowledge. If the manager accountable for the performance driver notices a downward trend in the knowledge level of new recruits or that employees are completing training programs without achieving the level of knowledge required, that manager could intervene in a timely manner.

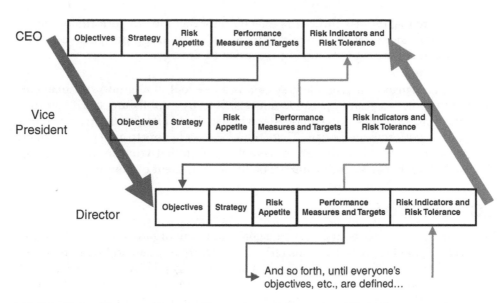

Exhibit 16.6 Alignment Between Enterprise and Operational Risk Management

But if he or she does not know about or turns a blind eye to the facts of reality, performance will inevitably suffer.

Exhibit 16.6 illustrates a mechanism for alignment between enterprise and operational levels. At the top level is the chief executive officer of the organization. The CEO's objectives are the enterprise objectives. His performance targets are translated into objectives for the people who report directly to him, that is, the vice president level. Then, each vice president translates his performance targets into objectives for his direct reports, that is, the director level. This translation of performance measures into objectives continues down the line and in doing so, enterprise objectives are translated into operational objectives. This creates a top-down mechanism for alignment.

Exhibit 16.6 also illustrates a bottom-up mechanism for alignment between operational and enterprise levels. Starting at the bottom of the figure, the performance measures of the director feed into the risk indicators for their vice president. In turn, each vice president will report his performance measures to the CEO who will monitor them as part of his suite of risk indicators. This creates a bottom-up mechanism for alignment.

To contribute to alignment, each person needs to do two things:

1. Ensure that each of their objectives corresponds to one of their boss's performance measures. This includes ensuring there is agreement on the desired risk appetite and risk tolerance around each of their objectives. This top-down perspective creates alignment through strategic and operational planning.

2. Ensure that the risk indicators they monitor include the performance measures of the people who report to them. This bottom-up perspective creates alignment during the ongoing execution of strategy.

The performance management system is a key tool in aligning risk management at the enterprise and operational levels. Start by establishing clarity around objectives and strategies. Next, understand how risk can affect your objectives and manage key performance drivers. Then, track key risk factors to give you adequate warning that a risk is reaching an intolerable level so that you can do something about it before if has a negative impact on the achievement of your objectives.

CONCLUSION

Every organization exists to achieve its goals. In many organizations, risks to the achievement of objectives are managed inconsistently or in an ad hoc fashion. As a result, many organizations experience a significant gap between their potential performance and their actual results. The aim of ORM is to manage the risks that emerge during the day-to-day activities of executing the organization's strategy thereby capturing the full performance potential of the organization. To do this, executives and managers need to do three things:

1. Establish clarity around objectives, roles, and responsibilities.
2. Align resources to deliver excellent performance.
3. Develop capabilities to handle unexpected or uncontrollable factors.

Risks (both threats and opportunities), benefits, and costs are inextricably linked. A key challenge for executives is articulating the organization's risk tolerance and appetite in a way that strikes the appropriate balance between potential upside and downside effects.

Effective ORM involves a systematic and disciplined approach to:

- Identifying and quantifying the risks associated with implementing a particular strategy.
- Evaluating and optimizing the organization's risk management effectiveness, including the selection of the appropriate mix of detection, prevention, and mitigation actions.
- Developing an adaptive risk response capability.

ORM is more than the development of risk management policy and the application of risk analysis tools. To be successful, it needs to become part of the organization's culture and seamlessly integrated into business practices. The culture of risk management can only be created through committed leadership on the part of the senior executive team.

The key to aligning risk management at the operational and enterprise levels is to establish accountability through a clear line of sight between the enterprise and executive levels. This line of sight is created by embedding risk management thinking into the organization's performance management and reporting systems.

Specifically the key drivers that represent the root causes of success and failure need to be identified, monitored, and managed to ensure that:

- Corporate and operational objectives are achieved.
- Resources are employed effectively and efficiently.
- The organization is ready to handle the risks that arise in the course of its day-to-day operations.
- People are accountable for their performance.

NOTES

1. See "Turning Great Strategy into Great Performance," Michael C. Mankins and Richard Steele, *Harvard Business Review*, July–August, 2005.

2. Ibid.

3. See Robert E. Mittelstaedt, *Will Your Next Business Mistake Be Fatal? Avoiding a Chain of Mistakes that Can Destroy Your Organization*, published by Wharton School Publishing, 2004.

4. Elroy Dimson of the London Business School is quoted by Peter L. Bernstein in "What Happens If We're Wrong?" *New York Times*, June 22, 2008.

5. See "Management may have never previously articulated these values and employees may never have identified them" in David Lapin, *Using Values & Ethics for Competitive Advantage*.

6. See James Reason, *Human Error*, published by Cambridge University Press, 1990.

ABOUT THE AUTHOR

Diana Del Bel Belluz is the President of Risk Wise Inc., a management consulting firm that helps executives and management teams implement systematic and sustainable risk management practices. Since 1990, Diana has been doing leading-edge risk management work for companies in a wide range of industries and for government organizations. Examples of client organizations that she has worked with are: Bombardier, British Columbia Safety Authority, Dofasco, Health Canada, the Nuclear Waste Management Authority, and the Toronto Transit Commission. In addition to helping individual organizations to enhance their operational risk management practices, Diana has advanced the field of risk management by serving on numerous industry committees, teaching university courses and management training seminars, speaking at conferences, and authoring publications on a wide range of risk management topics. She publishes the *Risk Management Made Simple* E-Zine, a free online newsletter (available at www.riskwise.ca) with tips on how to implement systematic risk management. She served as a core member of the founding faculty of the Centre of Excellence for Enterprise Risk Management at the Schulich School of Business at York University. She holds Bachelor's and Master's degrees in Systems Design Engineering from the University of Waterloo and is a Professional Engineer.

CHAPTER 17

Risk Management

Techniques in Search of a Strategy

JOE RIZZI
Senior Strategist, CapGen

INTRODUCTION

Spurred primarily by regulators, financial institutions invested significant resources in risk management over the last decade. An actuarial statistical approach to estimate future losses based on past experiences was used to create an illusion of improved control. Unfortunately, markets are not actuarial tables. The magnitude of the error became apparent once the 2007 credit crisis unfolded. For example, Merrill Lynch's one-day value at risk (VAR) at the end of 2007 was $154 million,[1] which was supposedly the maximum it could lose over a one-day period at the 99 percent confidence level. The undisclosed risk in the 1 percent beyond the confidence level was substantial, triggering its forced sale to Bank of America.[2] Other institutions with similar experiences include Citigroup, Wachovia, and Washington Mutual. These losses triggered massive shareholder value destruction resulting in dilutive recapitalizations, replacement of whole management teams, the failure of numerous institutions, and the adoption of the $700 billion TARP[3] rescue program. Clearly, something is wrong with the current state of risk management, which requires a rethinking of the activity.

Institutions, both large and small, assumed more risk to maintain income growth to offset challenging industry conditions and declining core profitability. As it turns out, the golden age of banking was not that golden. Large institutions increased risk through structured products. Smaller institutions used real estate concentrations in construction and development loans. They further increased the exposures by leveraging their position. Risk was deemed under control based on the twin illusions of liquidity and risk distribution. In fact, rather than distribute risk, institutions concentrated risk on both sides of their balance sheet. Liquidity evaporated once their leveraged positions began losing value.

This chapter explores why this occurred and what can be done to avoid this in future. Risk management needs to move away from a technical, specialist control function with limited linkage to shareholder value creation. Instead, we need to move beyond risk measurement to risk management that integrates risk into strategic planning, capital management, and governance. Enterprise risk management (ERM) provides a framework to integrate these functions. ERM incorporates the compounding impact of isolated risk decisions. Firms and risk decisions must move from an internal egocentric focus to an external systems approach that incorporates the firm within a market context.

CURRENT SITUATION

The financial services industry suffers from over capacity and product commoditization, which has pressured margins. Institutions increased risk exposure to enhance nominal returns without increasing shareholder value as reflected in Exhibit 17.1.

Exhibit 17.1 illustrates that not all risk increases enhance shareholder value. Opportunities to achieve true and lasting alpha like returns, "D," are difficult to find in the highly competitive financial services industry. Entry barriers are low and substitutes abound. Consequently, most risk increases involve systematic market, or beta risk, which shareholders can achieve on their own. Distinguishing between beta and alpha performance can be difficult.

This difficulty is especially true for new products with limited historical data. A strong and experienced governance system is needed to avoid paying alpha bonuses for beta returns. Movements along the curve represent changes in firm risk appetite. Changes in risk appetite have direct impact on capital requirements to maintain total risk levels.

Risk exposures can be increased on both sides of the balance sheets. Asset risk is increased by taking tail, downside, risk exposure inherent in many of the new products with option like payoffs. For example, Merrill Lynch's one-day VAR increased by almost five times from 2001 through 2007.[4]

Although VAR has its problems as a precise risk indicator, as a trend indicator it is useful. On the liabilities side of the balance sheet, leverage levels increased dramatically. This was accomplished by the large-scale use of off-balance sheet vehicles at banks and by raising debt to capital level at broker dealers.[5] In fact, the

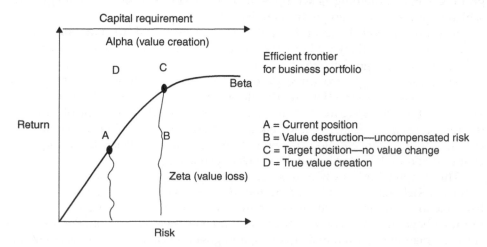

Exhibit 17.1 Value Implications of Risk Appetite Changes

large-scale capital raised by institutions served as a proxy for the undercapitalized or excessive leverage. In Merrill Lynch's case, that totaled almost $32 billion in the first half of 2008.[6] The consolidation of off-balance sheet vehicles by banks that were triggered once liquidity evaporated added billions of risk assets to already strained balance sheets.

Flawed risk models contributed to the problem. Overconfidence in the models created an illusion of adequate control. Profits were rising and the risk models did not indicate any undue concern. The models, however, failed in several respects. First, they mischaracterized the nature of risk by assuming risk to be exogenous to the system. Risk, however, is endogenous to markets caused by participant interactions similar to poker. Consequently, market behavioral changes were ignored or not adequately modeled.

Next, model risk is heavily dependent on data frequency and availability. Thus, for new products with a limited history, the models were inadequate. Finally, even if you have the data, models are based on experience, not exposures. Just because something has not yet occurred, the exposure may still exist. This is particularly true when dealing with large-scale event risks or "Black Swans." Risk models concentrated on the ordinary to the exclusion of infrequent extraordinary tail events by confusing history with science. This increased the incentives to take excessive remote risk based on overconfidence in the stability of observed patterns.[7]

Regulators compounded the problem by legitimizing the models. Basel II allowed institutions to rely on their own internal risk models to set capital levels without realizing the incentive for institutions to underestimate risk.[8] Furthermore, regulators increasingly relied on agency ratings. The agencies were using the same flawed models as the firms whose products they rated.

Decisions must be based on possibilities, not just history. History is just one possible scenario. Thus, not all risks are visible in historical returns. This is the basis of the peso problem where the extra yield, supposedly alpha, is merely compensation for an unseen risk, which may occur regardless of whether it has occurred in the past.[9]

The September 2008 collapse of independent investment banks illustrates the use of increased risk to compensate for a declining business model. Independent investment banks were largely artificial creations resulting from the Glass-Steagall separation of commercial and investment banking activities. They enjoyed a profitable existence up to the 1976 elimination of fixed commissions on stock trades. They then began searching for alternative revenue sources. Many, like Salomon Brothers, moved into higher risk—higher return activities like proprietary trading. The 1998 effective repeal of Glass-Steagall allowed commercial banks to enter agent-based underwriting and advisory businesses. This repeal had a predictable negative impact on investment banks.

Investment banks, once again, began searching for higher margin activities. This was clearly stated in the 2005 Goldman Sachs annual report. The business model outlined, subsequently known as the "Goldman Model," noted their traditional agency business had become a commodity. They now had to combine capital with advice. Goldman Sachs began moving into private equity, trading, and investing in structured products. Its initial success with this model caused considerable envy among its competitors who began copying the model.

The Goldman Model was essentially an asset-heavy hedge fund activity. It involved a variant of the carry trade or 5L strategy. The 5Ls are:

1. Long-term investments.
2. Large concentrated holdings.
3. Low-quality high-risk assets.
4. Leveraged positions.
5. (I)lliquid assets with liquidity funding mismatch.

The model worked in a bull market awash with liquidity and declining interest rates. The model also contained a potentially fatal flaw. The assets were funded short term, primarily in the overnight repo market. Thus, they used a toxic combination of high 30:1 leverage and short-term funding. Any change in the macroeconomic environment causing investors to change their risk appetite would cause liquidity challenges—just as in Long Term Capital Management (LTCM). Investment banking risk management failed in two key areas. First, they held insufficient capital to withstand the inevitable losses from holding higher risk assets. Second, they compounded the error by having inadequate liquidity to cover creditor concerns once portfolio losses began occurring.

Failure of the board to recognize and remedy the situation represents a governance breakdown. Frequently, directors were unaware of the risk implications of strategic initiatives, and confused short-term results with skill. For example, Merrill Lynch's strategy to match Goldman Sachs and become the structured finance market-share leader required assuming billions of additional warehouse asset risk. Essentially, they were making a franchise bet. This involved a large increase in risk appetite without adequate consideration of negative scenarios or capital structure implications. Next, incentive arrangements produced counterproductive behavioral changes. Strong managers began exploiting weak governance. Incentives became short-term oriented and based on nominal income with insufficient risk adjustments. Risk manager concerns, if raised at all, were presumably ignored or overruled, especially because the models, ratings, and regulators indicated that risk was under control.[10]

Even within risk management, organizational impediments exist. Individual risk functions tend to operate as independent "silos" with little or no strategic connection.[11] Additionally, there is limited consideration of business models and market states when evaluating transaction risks. Literally, it is failing to see the forest because of the trees. Market state changes are caused when an unstable market undergoes a rapid regime change. Herding causes the formation of "super portfolios" of overlapping positions. Once these positions reach a critical stage, a random trigger causes the unwinding of positions. Correlations change, diversification breaks down, and catastrophic losses occur over formerly diverse asset classes.[12]

Strategic risk, the major risk facing all organizations, was ignored. Strategic risk is the possibility of an event that impacts an organization's ability to achieve its business plan. The integration of risk into strategic planning, capital management, and performance measurement is needed.[13] This would combine business and risk considerations into a single, whole-firm view of value creation. See Box 17.1.

Box 17.1 Warren Buffett's Risk Management Lessons

Warren Buffett's Berkshire Hathaway 2001 and 2002 annual reports outline his risk management framework as follows:

- Accept only those risks you understand. (This requires guarding against the twin biases of overconfidence and the illusion of control.)
- Focus on impact not probability: Do not accept any single or group of risks which threaten solvency no matter how improbable. This requires a comparison of risk appetite to capital. Keep in mind risk is based not only on the experience of what has happened, but also on beyond the data exposures.
- Derivatives are dangerous because they create the incentive to cheat: They are opaque and imbedded with latent and potentially lethal dangers. Since their true nature does not manifest itself until later, track records are of little use. Thus, it becomes difficult to determine cheaters.
- Governance: Berkshire has a small number of interested, component directors who eat their own cooking.* They have a clearly stated risk appetite: $6 billion as of 2007 based on $120 billion shareholders' equity and are willing to sacrifice market share to stay within their risk appetite.

Like most of Buffett's principles, they appear deceptively simple. He had been roundly criticized during the credit boom for having lost his touch. His ability to ignore market pressure is in limited supply at most firms, and reflects the strong governance at Berkshire.

*Governance problems can exist at even closely held firms. Mid-level employees can exploit information asymmetries to limit senior management's ability to understand and control risk exposures.

RISK STRATEGY FRAMEWORK

Value is created on the asset side of the balance sheet through investment decisions. The value of risk management is to ensure funding of the investment plan by maintaining capital market access under all conditions. This entails maintaining a total risk profile consistent with rating targets. Consequently, balancing asset portfolio risk with capital structure is required. Failure to do so can undermine an institution's strategic position and independence.

Questionable strategic growth initiatives that were inappropriately funded underlie the problems at many financial institutions.[14] Bankers believed that growth added value. Unfortunately, growth can destroy value when the returns are less than their cost of capital. This is illustrated here:

Value = Cash flow + Investment (Return on Assets − Cost of Capital) T

Cost of capital cost of capital   (17.1)(17.2)

Source: Adapted from Modigliani and Miller (1961).

Exhibit 17.2   Gross Leverage Levels (Total assets divided by total shareholders' equity)

	1Q04	1Q07
Bear Stearns	28	34
Morgan Stanley	25	34
Lehman Bros.	25	32
Merrill Lynch	19	28
Goldman Sachs	20	28

Source: SEC filings and Kara Scannell, "SEC faulted for missing red flags at Bear Stearns," *Wall Street Journal*, September 27, 2008, A3.

Term (17.1) represents the value created by assets already in place, while term (17.2) is the value created by growth. T, the competitive advantage period, represents the number of years the firm enjoys the opportunity to invest in profitable projects. Growth can destroy value when an institution invests in projects earning less than their cost of capital. Value creation can also be impacted through poor risk management, which causes the disruption of a firm's investment program due to inadequate capital and liquidity positions to absorb unexpected events.

Insufficient returns from growth initiatives can strain capital structures and dividends. Maintaining such growth, absent a dividend cut, requires either a dilutive equity issuance or increased leverage. Rather than potentially upsetting shareholders, many institutions chose to increase leverage levels as reflected in Exhibit 17.2.

Surprisingly, even with the leverage increases, returns on equity for many institutions stayed in the low to mid-20 percent range. This was largely due to compensation levels exceeding 50 percent of revenues and compressed spreads. The leverage strategy left little room for error if conditions deteriorated.

Risk management includes a capital structure decision process linking strategy and capital levels. Risk management needs to support the institution's corporate strategy, which determines the risk universe faced by the bank organization as outlined in Exhibit 17.3. Firms can change the nature of risks retained by using risk management.

As Exhibit 17.3 highlights, the cash-flow volatility of current and future investments combined with the strategic investment plan drives the value of risk management. Low volatility, low-growth firms with limited investment needs have lower risk management needs than rapidly growing firms. Financial institutions have an additional demand for flexibility reflected in high investment-grade rating targets, that is, A and above. This is due to their liability sensitivity. Their customers are also creditors concerned with deposit and trading products. Thus, such ratings are necessary to maintain customers.

Traditional underwriting, mitigation, and transfer risk management techniques can be used to select those risks that the institution is competitively advantaged to own and eliminate the rest. For example, community banks have an informational advantage regarding local clients. Thus, they should retain such risk up to prudent concentration levels. Alternatively, market risks, like interest rate risk, should not be held unless the institution possesses special information or

Exhibit 17.3   Drivers of Risk Management Strategy
Source: Adapted from T. Oliver Leautier, *Corporate Risk Management for Value Creation* (Risk Books, 2007).

they are perceived to be mispriced. The retained risk should be covered by capital consistent with a ratings goal to ensure capital market access sufficient to fund the investment plan. Viewed in this light, risk management and capital can be seen as interchangeable with capital being the cost of retained risk. In fact, risk management is essentially tax-deductible synthetic equity. The key is to avoid a mismatch between the assets and liabilities and equity of the balance sheet. Too little capital relative to asset risk reduces flexibility, while excess capital depresses returns.

The overall institutional risk level is dependent on the board's risk appetite—the level of risk the organization is willing to assume on both sides of their balance sheet in pursuit of its strategy. Risk appetite is a relative term among stakeholders. Usually aligned, there are instances when management and stakeholder appetites differ. Management's risk appetite is best expressed as a continuum reflected in Exhibit 17.4 (adapted from Oliver Wyman 2007).

Obviously, no one consciously plans on accepting the risk of replacement, regulatory action, or failure. Rather, these situations result from the failure to consider adequately the probability of ruin in rare bad states. These strategies involve bets against randomness and an acceptance of peso risk. The 20-plus year financial bull market lulled management, directors, regulators, and shareholders into a false sense of security. They simply ignored these rare but possible negative states by assuming large risk positions relative to their capital.[15] Risk strategies that are successful except for rare events are like having an airbag that works except when there is a crash.

Risk appetite decisions involve determining how much of the firm's value is at risk should the worst case materialize, whether this is tolerable, and if not, how much additional capital is needed to self-insure. Exhibit 17.4 illustrates the apparent internal risk appetite continuum of many financial institutions as demonstrated by recent history. The skewed compensation systems that allowed managers to exit with huge payouts, and keep prior year bonuses, exacerbates this concern. It

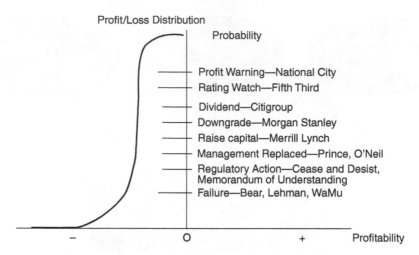

Exhibit 17.4   Risk Appetite Continuum

encourages managers to "roll the dice" in a "heads I win/tails you lose" situation. Senior management's interests were misaligned by their compensation systems. Consequently, they acted in a predictable and rational manner at the expense of their shareholders.

The risk appetite conflict between internal and external stakeholders is highlighted in Exhibit 17.5 (adapted from P. Laurin 2006).

Unresolved conflicts between internal and external risk appetite have underlined problems at many institutions. Management had undertaken new higher risk strategies with capital structures incapable of absorbing the inevitable losses in pursuit of maximizing their bonuses. Complicating matters is the pro-cyclical nature of risk appetite. As a bull market ages, income increases and vigilance declines. Institutions extrapolate, and assume short-term trends will continue. Eventually, absent strong governance, they move farther out on the risk curve by confusing a bull market with skill. This results in an overexposed position once the inevitable correction occurs.

Risk models contributed to increasing risk appetite. Individuals chose to maintain a given level of risk. Perceived risk declines trigger behavioral changes as we increase our risk exposure to return to our original risk level as if we had a risk thermostat. Institutions mistakenly believed risk management had reduced risk, and compensated by increasing their risk exposures.[16] This leads to the paradoxical conclusion that risk mitigation does not reduce risk—rather it redistributes it.

Additionally, many financial firms held large amounts of risk in which they had limited competitive advantages. They had effectively shifted from an "originate to distribute" to an "originate to hold" business model. This market risk, beta, while increasing nominal income, failed to create shareholder value. Even worse, they failed to compensate for their increased risk exposure. The current situation represents an amplified system-wide version of the LTCM collapse, which can be seen as the blueprint for the current crisis. Both situations involved large, leveraged, and illiquid concentration bets in tail risk options like assets based on models

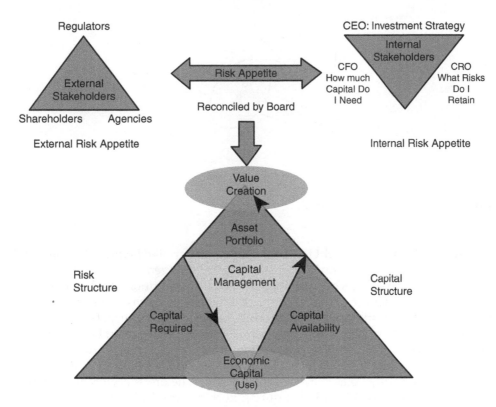

Exhibit 17.5   Risk Appetite and Value Creation

that underestimated risk.[17] The short put option exposure of LTCM was replaced by stealth-like structured finance products to exploit "blind spot" weaknesses in risk management systems. Structured finance products are the perfect moral hazard products to exploit the risk and compensation systems.[18] The legitimacy of structured products was enhanced by the high, often AAA ratings awarded to such products, which provided the appearance of liquidity.[19]

It is important to distinguish liquidity from solvency. Liquidity concerns the composition of the balance sheet. Specifically, it focuses on having enough cash to withstand a run of bad events. Liquidity allows you to survive long enough to succeed. Solvency relates to the overall collateralization of liabilities with asset values.

In a market crisis state, the key concern is liquidity. Yet surprisingly, both the regulators in BIS II and the rating agencies had expressed little concern on this issue. Asset prices become volatile during a liquidity crisis. Again, this was highlighted in LTCM. Their trades eventually worked, but since they had insufficient liquidity, they were forced out before they could realize the gains. This is illustrated below in Exhibit 17.6.

The size of the bid/offer spread during the panic stage complicates the conversion of assets into cash without loss. The inability to convert long-term assets to

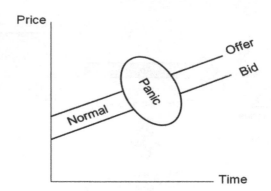

Exhibit 17.6   Asset Price Liquidity

cash to match short-term debt maturities, caused firms like Lehman Brothers and Bear Stearns to fail even though they were arguably solvent.

There are two sources of liquidity. Traditionally, institutions held cash or cash-like liquidity buffers to cover asset price liquidity concerns. This is, however, expensive. Many institutions switched to liability-based liquidity. This was based on the ability to have debt access on reasonable terms. Investment banks typically used short-term, frequently overnight funding to support long-term asset positions because it was less expensive. Unfortunately, this availability is fragile and subject to potentially volatile market conditions.[20] The presumption of the ability to borrow is state-specific. It holds during normal periods, but is invalid during panic states when price declines generate more sellers than buyers, thus creating a liquidity black hole.[21] Credit-based liquidity is illusory. The combination of leverage without liquidity is deadly regardless of the quality of a firm's assets. Asset problems eventually impact a firm's ability to access funding, which leads to a liquidity crisis.

GOVERNANCE

A key, but often neglected, component of risk management is governance. As Rene Stulz rightfully points out, risk managers are not solely responsible for the current credit crisis. At its core, risk management is an exposure measurement and accounting system. The decision to take major risks is the responsibility of top management and the board of directors.[22]

Governance involves designing appropriate incentives and controls to ensure the alignment of potentially conflicting management and shareholder interests. This involves assigning decision rights, establishing performance metrics, and developing an appropriate rewards system. This is especially important to financial institutions that take opaque risk positions, which do not manifest themselves until later. Under these circumstances, high-powered incentive compensation arrangements coupled with information asymmetry create an incentive for management to game the system leading to Decisions at Risk (DAR)[23] in Exhibit 17.7. Bonuses tied to short-term performance and equity options misalign management and shareholder interests resulting in excessive risk taking.

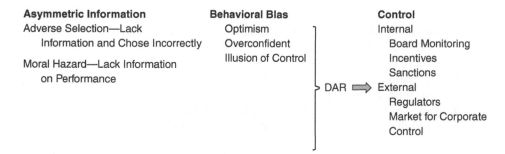

Asymmetric Information	Behavioral Bias	Control
Adverse Selection—Lack Information and Chose Incorrectly	Optimism	Internal
	Overconfident	Board Monitoring
Moral Hazard—Lack Information on Performance	Illusion of Control	Incentives
		Sanctions
	DAR ⟹	External
		Regulators
		Market for Corporate Control

Exhibit 17.7 DAR Control Framework

Management can exploit its information advantage to deceive the board of directors. Structured products have a high DAR because they involve complex accounting and valuation problems. This was the reason underlying Warren Buffett's charge that they constituted "weapons of mass destruction."[24] Furthermore, management may lack the capability to oversee and understand their risk positions. In these cases, senior management becomes a captive of middle managers whose incentives are to maximize their bonuses through increased risk taking. Arguably, this occurred at Bear Stearns where senior management did not understand its risk exposures.

Although we know how risk decisions should be made, less is known on how these decisions are actually made. Decision makers are subject to behavioral biases concerning how risk is perceived and managed. Behavioral finance examines how decision makers gather, interpret, and process information. These biases can corrupt the decision process, leading to suboptimal results.

Major behavioral biases include:

- Overconfidence: exaggerate skills and ignore the impact of change or external circumstances. It causes an underestimation of outcome variability; sometimes known as "confusing a bull market for skill."
- Availability bias: subjective probability depends on recent experience. Consequently, infrequent extreme events like market or firm collapse are overlooked creating a false sense of security.[25]
- Herding: individuals begin mimicking the decisions of others. Herding amplifies market cycles by overreliance on feedback loops.

No matter how good the data or how sophisticated the model, we can be fooled by randomness, confuse actions with outcomes, and fall prey to poor risk decisions.

This is especially important for certain types of difficult, rare decisions involving delayed feedback.[26] Major new investment programs are examples of this type of decision. This can lead to a tragedy of the commons (TOTC) situation when coupled with misaligned incentives. TOTC occurs when a finite resource is underpriced leading to its over-exploitation. Banks mispriced their capital by underestimating asset risk. This blinded them to the dangers of an increasing risk appetite.

Boards, suffering from DAR problems, became co-opted by management. They seldom questioned management unless forced by a market crisis. Symptoms of ineffective boards include:

- Large boards.
- Inexperienced directors.
- Retired CEOs predisposed to side with the CEO.
- Limited ownership: this curtails their commitment.

Boards need to understand the institution's strategy, risk appetite, and the impact of business plan assumptions. Otherwise, they will fail to notice risk appetite changes, the risk implications of strategy changes, required capital levels, and the incentive impact of compensation schemes and franchise bets.[27] Unfortunately, attempts to improve board performance can face challenges. This is similar to regulatory capture when mechanisms created to protect individuals end up acting in the interests of the regulated firms.

Internal control breakdowns usually lead to declining performance and shareholder pressure and changes in corporate control. The usual form of these actions involves proxy battles and hostile takeovers. In regulated industries, like banking, regulations make such actions difficult. The regulators become a replacement for the external market for control. Regulators are, however, an inefficient replacement. They are not necessarily aligned with shareholders, and face the same DAR problems as the board of directors. Furthermore, they are subject to being co-opted. The answer is not necessarily more regulation, but allowing for increased market discipline, which can be achieved in two areas.

First, large active shareholders with board representation, such as private equity firms, can counterbalance management. Unfortunately, bank holding company rules complicate this effort.[28] An alternative is based on contingent capital provided by private insurers in meaningful amounts.[29] The insurer will have a monetary incentive to challenge management and ensure appropriate risk management oversight. Another quasi-market approach is the requirement of banks to issue subordinated debt. Subordinated debt would act as the "canary in the coal mine" to provide an early warning of bank solvency issues.[30] We can expect further developments in this area. Absent such solutions, banks will suffer an information uncertainty discount, which will raise their cost of capital.[31] Thus, an institution's ownership structure and composition should be an important risk management consideration.

NEW DIRECTIONS

We need to move beyond risk measurement to risk management that integrates risk into strategic planning, capital management and governance. Enterprise risk management provides a framework to integrate these functions.

Enterprise Risk Management (ERM): The First Step

Risk management is a strategy and a means to an end, and not an end in itself. The focus is on linking the control aspects of governance with strategy and performance

Exhibit 17.8   Firm and Its Environment

in a holistic integrated fashion. Risk is viewed on a total firm portfolio basis linking both sides of the balance sheet. The firm, and consequently, risk management is more than the sum of the parts. The interactions among various units and risks, something ignored by silo-based risk management, is just as important as the units and risks themselves. ERM provides such a unifying mechanism. Its scope goes beyond traditional financial risks to include human resources, incentives, and governance matters as well.

ERM is a consolidated top-down cross-functional total risk management exercise, which cuts across all business units and risk types. The focus is strategic, not transactional. It seeks to improve decision making through a portfolio view of interrelated risks across the firm. This is accomplished by imbedding a risk culture within business units so risk considerations become an input versus a consequence of these strategies. This ensures that an organization in control, rather than a control organization, develops. This is especially important in a rapidly evolving financial services market with institutions struggling with declining core operations, and searching for replacement business models.

Risk management does not operate in a vacuum. It is context-dependent, and must take the external environment into account. ERM can become too inward-looking and fail to consider the firm's adaptability to changing unstable market conditions. A useful approach is referenced in Exhibit 17.8.

Industries are interactively complex. The relationships are nonlinear, meaning that small changes can have disproportionate impacts. Additionally, the system is tightly connected by feedback loops. Events spread quickly throughout the system in unpredictable ways. The current crisis represents a system failure and attempts to identify a single cause or assign blame are fruitless.

To ensure success, risk strategies must be flexible enough to change once environmental conditions change. Sophisticated systems that work in only one market state, that is, the current one, are of limited use in alternative states. Firms need enough resiliency to survive and adapt to unanticipated environmental changes.

Enterprise Resilience (ER): The Next Step?

Firms are part of a complex living market system. Crises within that system may be infrequent, but are inevitable. A firm's ability to adapt to unforeseen events—its resilience—becomes a critical success factor. The system is too complex to predict when and where accidents will occur. The key is the flexibility to sense and respond

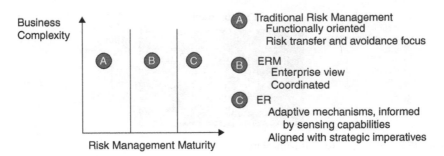

Exhibit 17.9   Adaptive Risk Management

to accidents. ER is a possible next step in the development of risk management as reflected in Exhibit 17.9.[32]

ER involves a focus on what can happen regardless of probability, and across multiple market states. Then the firm needs to build a risk management structure to withstand whatever category market storm fits its risk tolerance. Although not optimal in all market states, ER ensures survival over multiple market states.

CONCLUSION

The structured finance credit crisis illustrates the shortcomings of current risk management. Risk management lagged financial innovation. Risk at best was measured, but not managed adequately. Instead, it evolved as a ritualistic prediction activity. Conventional risk management became overconfident, a regulatory fiction behind which excessive risk taking occurred.

Risk management must include the risk return tradeoff facing the entire firm. This includes strategic risk and capital structure issues. There is nothing necessarily wrong about high-risk strategies, provided the firm is compensated, understands the risk, can withstand an adverse event, and stakeholder interests are aligned.

The risk from declining banking business models increases concerns for misalignment. ERM and ER offer the opportunity to bridge this gap by combining business and risk considerations into a single, whole-firm view of value creation over multiple market states. Next, governance issues, which are partly the source of the current problems, or may just not be adequate to control other sources of risk, must be addressed. Governance concerns the assignment of decision rights to identifying, addressing, and resolving conflicting stakeholder claims. Additionally, reporting transparency that reflects the risk appetite and the risk profile is needed. The most important component of risk management is management, not measurement. If successful, these developments will transform risk management into a strategic value enabler.

NOTES

1. Refer to Credit Suisse, "European Banks," June 22, 2008.
2. See F. Guerra, "Merrill's Recent Losses...," *Financial Times*, August 29, 2008, 1.

3. TARP is the Troubled Asset Relief Program enacted by the U.S. Treasury in October 2008.

4. See Credit Suisse, "European Banks," id.

5. Common off-balance sheet vehicles included, among other things, structured investment vehicles, and asset-backed commercial paper conduits. They functioned as de facto unregulated banks developed to arbitrage banking regulation.

6. Lehman Brothers increased its asset size by almost $300 billion in 2004–2007, on only a $6 billion capital increase. At the time of its bankruptcy, leverage levels exceeded 30 to 1. 2004 was the year in which the SEC enacted a new capital rule allowing major broker dealers to increase leverage levels based on internal risk models.

7. Sometimes known as "the Law of Small Numbers"; in other words, the exaggerated belief that a small sample resembles the population from which it is drawn. See M. Rabin, "Inferences by Believers in the Law of Small Numbers."

8. Warren Buffett referred to this as a self-graded exam.

9. Peso risk refers to the possibility an unprecedented or infrequent event affects asset prices. The extra, alpha, yield is an illusion based on the small sample size bias in expected returns defined here for first time. Peso risk was first raised in the early 1970s by M. Friedman.

10. This reflects the fundamental asymmetry in rewards between prevention and rescue. This was highlighted by large compensation awards granted to postcrisis risk managers brought in to rescue institutions like Merrill.

11. This is highlighted by the statement from Citigroup's CFO, Gary Crittenden, in October 2007. He stated they thought the risk in structured products was predominately market risk, when it fact, it was credit. Thus, they missed the real risk in their portfolio.

12. This was colorfully demonstrated by Per Bak's collapsing sand pile example.

13. See R. Kroszner, "Strategic Risk Management in an Interconnected World." RMA Speech, October 20, 2008.

14. Recent research by A. Kucitzkes at Oliver Wyman shows that firms that grew faster than 25 percent between 2004 and 2006 experienced trading and credit losses twice the level incurred at more stable firms during the period.

15. The October 23, 2008, congressional testimony of former Federal Reserve Chairman A. Greenspan highlights this probability neglect. He states that two decades of data caused him to commit a policy error concerning the ability of institutions to act in their self-interest.

16. The risk compensation concept was developed by J. Adams. He noticed that seat-belt laws did not reduce fatalities. Rather, drivers tended to drive faster. Pedestrian and cyclist deaths increased thereby offsetting the seat-belt benefits to drivers.

17. Mispricing hidden catastrophic event risk in structured products was illustrated in J. Coval, J. Jurek, and E. Stafford, "Economic Catastrophic Bonds," Harvard Business School Working Paper No. 07–102, April 2008. This showed that taking equivalent alternative exposures in the underlying assets yielded a significantly higher return. The mispricing is attributed to the increased demand for the less transparent structured securities, which can be used to exploit risk management systems.

18. Structured finance can be viewed as a compensation scheme masquerading as a business.

19. AAA-rated structured products received premium spreads over the nonstructured corporate AAA instruments, which further enhanced their demand by naive investors. This raises questions over the accuracy of the rating.

20. The shadow banking system of unregulated credit providers such as hedge funds greatly expanded endogenous liquidity. This led to a false sense of security concerning the continuing availability of such liquidity. The subsequent demise of this system has triggered a painful liquidity squeeze.

21. As R. Bookstabler noted in his June 19, 2008, Senate Testimony, in a crisis the key issues are who owns what, the pressure they are under to liquidate, and what else they own.

22. See R. Stulz, "Risk Management Failures: What Are They and When Do They Happen?" *Journal of Applied Corporate Finance* vol. 20 no. 4 (Fall 2008).

23. Information asymmetry is a condition where relevant information is not equally shared among participants. It underlies agency problems where management, the agent, can exploit shareholders, principals, because they know more.

24. See the 2002 annual report of Berkshire Hathaway.

25. The law of declining vigilance states that vigilance declines by the square of the time since the last event.

26. See R. Thaler and C. Sustein. *Nudge: Improving Decisions About Health, Wealth and Happiness.* (Yale University Press, 2008).

27. According to the *Wall Street Journal* April 16, 2008, Merrill Lynch in 2006 fired a risk officer who insisted on holding CDO exposures at $1–$2 billion. Afterward, CDO began growing at $5 billion per quarter—all without questions from the board. Just as you do not need a scale to know if someone is fat, you do not need a model to know the growth and size of such exposures is risky.

28. The Federal Reserve has recently relaxed some of the private equity restrictions. Yet control restrictions coupled with large losses of Texas Pacific Group and Corsair in their passive bank investments demonstrates the need to go further.

29. See A. Kashyar, R. Rajan, and J. Stein, "Rethinking Capital Regulation," unpublished paper prepared for the Federal Reserve Bank of Kansas City Symposium on "Maintaining Stability in a Changing Financial System." Jackson Hole, WY, August 21–23, 2008.

30. Large banks successfully lobbied against the imposition of this potential limitation on their risk taking when it was raised in the late 1990s.

31. Investors would apply an uncertainty discount against banks to reflect their mistrust in risk management.

32. Adopted from Booz Allen and Hamilton, "Redefining the Corporate Governance Agenda: From Risk Management to Enterprise Resilience," June 2003, available at www.boozallen.com.

REFERENCES

Adams, J. 1995. *Risk.* New York: Routledge.

Bak, P. 1996. *How nature works: The source of self-organized criticality.* New York: Copernicus Books.

Berkshire Hathaway. 2002. Annual report: Principles of insurance underwriting, 7.

Bookstabler, R. 2007. *Demons of own design.* New York: John Wiley & Sons.

Brealey, R., Myers, S., and Allen, R. 2008. *Principles of corporate finance,* 9th ed. New York: McGraw-Hill.

Buehler, K., Freeman, A. and Hulme, R. 2008. New arsenal of risk management. *Harvard Business Review* (September).

Credit Suisse, "European Banks" (June 11, 2008) 35.

Crouhy, M., Galai, D., and Marx, R. 2006. *The essentials of risk management*. New York: McGraw-Hill.

Doud J. 1998. *Beyond value at risk: New science of risk management*. New York: John Wiley & Sons.

Froot, K., and Stein, J. 1998. A new approach to capital budgeting for financial institutions. *Journal of Applied Corporate Finance*, vol. II, no. 2, (Summer) 59.

Goldman Sachs. 2005. Annual Report.

Hahn, A.H. 2008. Missing pieces. *CFO* (March) 51.

Kashyar, A., Rajan, R., and Stein, J. 2008. Rethinking capital regulation. Paper prepared for Federal Reserve Bank of Kansas City Symposium. Jackson Hole, Wyoming (August).

Kucitzkes, A. 2008. Risk governance: Seeing the forest for the trees. *MMC Journal*. Oliver Wyman, (October 14).

Jorion, P. 2000. Risk management lessons from long-term capital management. *European Financial Management* 6 (September) 277.

Lam J. 2003. *Enterprise risk management: From incentives to control*. New York: John Wiley & Sons.

Laurin, Pierre. 2006. OCCA presentation at Towers Perrin, December 6.

Merton, R. 1974. On the pricing of corporate debt: The risk structure of interests. *Journal of Finance* 29: 449.

Meulbrook, L. 2001. Total strategies for company-wide risk control. *Financial Times Mastering Risk* vol. 1: Pickford, J. (ed.) Harlow, UK: Pearson.

Miller, M., and Modigliani, F. 1961. Dividend policy, growth, and the valuation of shares. *Journal of Business* 34 (October) 411–433.

Nocco, B., and Stulz, R. 2006. Enterprise risk management: Theory and practice. *Journal of Applied Corporate Finance* 18: 4. Fall 2008.

Oliver Wyman. 2007. The new finance and risk agenda: What's your risk appetite.

Persaud, A. 2003. *Liquidity black holes*. London, UK: Risk Books.

Perrow, C. 2007. *The next catastrophe*. Princeton, NJ: Princeton University Press.

Petroski, H. 2006. *Success through failure: The paradox of design*. Princeton, NJ: Princeton University Press.

Pulliam, S., Serna, N., and Smith, R. 2008. Merrill Lynch will report up to $8 billion in write downs. *Wall Street Journal*, April 16.

Rabin, M. 2000. Inference by believers in the law of small numbers. *Quarterly Journal of Economics*.

Rizzi, J. 2007. The mismanagement of risk management. *American Banker* (September 28).

Rizzi, J. 2008. Why this crisis goes deeper than credit. *American Banker* (September 5).

Rosen, D., and Zenros, W. 2006. Enterprise-wide assets and liability management: Issues, institutions and models. *Handbook of Asset and Liability Management*, vol. I (ed. W. Zenios, and W. Zima. 2006 Elsevier R.V.) Chapter 1.

Sheffi Y. 2005. *The resilient enterprise: Overcoming vulnerability for competitive advantage*. Cambridge, MA: MIT Press.

Smithson, C., and Simkins, R. 2005. Does risk management add value: A survey of the evidence. *Journal of Applied Corporate Finance*, vol. 17, no. 3, 8 (Summer).

Stulz, R. 2008. Risk management failures: What are they and when do they happen? *Journal of Applied Corporate Finance*, vol. 20, no 4 (Fall).

Stulz, R. 1996. Rethinking risk management. *Journal of Applied Corporate Finance*, vol. 9, no. 3, p. 8 (Fall) 8. 1996

Thaler, R., and Sunstein, C. 2008. *Nudge: Improving decisions about health, wealth and happiness*. New Haven, CT: Yale University Press.

Tirole, J. 2006. *The theory of corporate finance*. Princeton, NJ: Princeton University Press.

Wruk, K. 2008. Private equity, corporate governance, and the reinvention of the market for corporate control. *Journal of Applied Corporate Finance* vol. 20, no. 3 (Summer).

ABOUT THE AUTHOR

For 24 years before joining CapGen, **Joe Rizzi** was a member of the ABN AMRO Group or its U.S. affiliate, LaSalle Bank. He most recently served as Managing Director of LaSalle Bank Corporation's Enterprise Risk Management unit for North America.

During his tenure with the ABN AMRO Group, Mr. Rizzi worked in several areas of the company. He began his career there with Secured Lending and Leasing and then joined the Corporate Banking group. From 1986 through 2000, he was a leading member of the Strategic Planning, Structured Finance or Leveraged Finance teams located in Chicago.

In 2001, he began his role as a group head in Amsterdam. Over the next five years, Mr. Rizzi alternated working at ABN AMRO in Amsterdam and New York City, focusing on Group Risk Management, Asset and Liability Management, as well as Country Management.

He is a widely published author and has lectured to various professional organizations in Europe and the United States. He taught regularly at the Amsterdam Institute of Finance and at the University of Notre Dame's Mendoza School of Business.

Mr. Rizzi graduated summa cum laude from DePaul University, earned an MBA from the University of Chicago, and received a JD magna cum laude from the University of Notre Dame Law School.

CHAPTER 18

Managing Financial Risk and Its Interaction with Enterprise Risk Management

DANIEL A. ROGERS
School of Business Administration, Portland State University

INTRODUCTION

Financial risk management encompasses corporate strategies of employing financial transactions to eliminate or reduce measurable risks. Most businesses face financial risks of some sort, such as currency price volatility, interest rate changes, commodity price fluctuations, or from some other source.

A key attribute of a financial risk is that it can be managed by entering into some form of contract that can be settled in cash. Classic forms of contracts with these characteristics include forward contracts privately arranged between two parties or futures contracts traded on exchanges located around the world. Exhibit 18.1 includes an overview of some of the types of contracts traded at several of the largest futures exchanges in the United States. As may be seen from the wide array of contract types and underlying assets, futures markets exist to manage risks as disparate as those arising from the stock market (i.e., S&P 500) to the amount of snowfall in Boston or New York City.

Financial risk management strategies, often called financial "hedging," can be considered as a predecessor in the evolution of enterprise risk management (ERM) programs. ERM addresses a far broader array of risks than those that can easily be hedged using financial contracts. However, hedging of financial risk by firms around the world has been sufficiently commonplace that this behavior has been well studied, especially over the last 15 years. Given the considerable amount of research that has been completed on the benefits of financial hedging, the findings are relevant to firms considering the implementation of broader risk management strategies such as ERM.

In this chapter the discussion first provides additional background on financial risk management, including possible definitions and examples of industry applications of financial hedging. The discussion then moves to a basic review of the theoretical rationales for managing (financial) risk and the related empirical findings. The potential for the interaction of financial hedging with other areas of risk management (such as operational and strategic) is then explored. Finally, there is a

Exhibit 18.1   Examples of Contracts Traded at Major U.S. Futures Exchanges

Contract Type	Exchange	Underlying Asset
Agricultural	Chicago Board of Trade	Corn
	Chicago Board of Trade	Wheat
	Chicago Mercantile Exchange	Cattle
	Chicago Mercantile Exchange	Milk
Energy	New York Mercantile Exchange	Crude oil
	New York Mercantile Exchange	Natural gas
	New York Mercantile Exchange	Gasoline
Metals	New York Mercantile Exchange	Gold
	New York Mercantile Exchange	Platinum
Equities	Chicago Mercantile Exchange	S&P 500 Index
	Chicago Board of Trade	Dow Jones Index
	Chicago Mercantile Exchange	Nasdaq Biotechnology Index
Foreign Exchange	Chicago Mercantile Exchange	Euro
	Chicago Mercantile Exchange	Japanese yen
Interest Rates	Chicago Mercantile Exchange	Eurodollar
	Chicago Mercantile Exchange	10-year Swap Rate
	Chicago Board of Trade	U.S. Treasury Bonds
Weather	Chicago Mercantile Exchange	Hurricane Index
	Chicago Mercantile Exchange	Snowfall Index

discussion regarding the lessons that can be applied to ERM from the knowledge base about financial hedging.

WHAT IS FINANCIAL RISK AND HOW IS IT MANAGED?

In the context of corporate risk management, financial risk has two necessary characteristics. The first characteristic of financial risk is that it is an exogenous event (i.e., outside the company's control) having the potential to affect a financial outcome. Any (or all) of the following are potential consequences of the realization of a corporate financial risk:

- Reduced cash flow.
- Reduced market value.
- Reduced accounting income.

The second characteristic of financial risk is that it can be reduced by entering into a financial contract with cash settlement. The most common means for corporations to manage financial risk is by using derivative financial instruments, such as forward or futures contracts, swap contracts, and/or option contracts. Derivative contracts used can be exchange-traded or over-the-counter (OTC) contracts that are privately negotiated.

In this section, there are straightforward examples of various types of financial risks that are commonly experienced by corporations. For each case, there is an example as to how the risk can be managed by using a specific derivative contract.

Case 1: Currency Price Risk: The Multinational Corporation

At the end of 2007, Coca-Cola Company generates revenues in more than 200 countries. Given the multinational flavor of its operations, it is natural to expect Coca-Cola to be significantly affected by currency fluctuations. Box 18.1 shows the general currency risk disclosure contained in Coca-Cola's 10-K filing for 2007.[1]

Box 18.1 Coca-Cola's Currency Risk Disclosure in SEC 10-K Filing

---

Fluctuations in foreign currency exchange could affect our financial results.

We earn revenues, pay expenses, own assets and incur liabilities in countries using currencies other than the U.S. dollar, including the euro, the Japanese yen, the Brazilian real and the Mexican peso. In 2007, we used 67 functional currencies in addition to the U.S. dollar and derived approximately 74 percent of our net operating revenues from operations outside of the United States. Because our consolidated financial statements are presented in U.S. dollars, we must translate revenues, income and expenses, as well as assets and liabilities, into U.S. dollars at exchange rates in effect during or at the end of each reporting period. Therefore, increases or decreases in the value of the U.S. dollar against other major currencies will affect our net operating revenues, operating income and the value of balance sheet items denominated in foreign currencies. Because of the geographic diversity of our operations, weaknesses in some currencies might be offset by strengths in others over time. We also use derivative financial instruments to further reduce our net exposure to currency exchange rate fluctuations. However, we cannot assure you that fluctuations in foreign currency exchange rates, particularly the strengthening of the U.S. dollar against major currencies, would not materially affect our financial results.

Source: SEC 10-K filing for calendar year 2007 by Coca-Cola Co. (filed on February 28, 2008), page 13 (see the following URL). www.sec.gov/Archives/edgar/data/21344/000119312508041768/d10k.htm.

Coca-Cola's operating revenues are flavored in 67 currencies other than the U.S. dollar, and 74 percent of its operating revenues are derived from outside the United States. Between 2006 and 2007, Coca-Cola's net operating revenues increased by 20 percent, of which one-fifth of the revenue gain was attributed to the weakening U.S. dollar (see page 47 of the 10-K filing). While the weaker U.S. dollar also contributed to increases in selling, general, and administrative expenses, the overall effect of the weaker dollar contributed positively to Coca-Cola's operating income (see page 51 of the 10-K filing). The implication from Coca-Cola's 2007 results is that, in the future, weaker foreign currencies could possibly reduce the company's reported earnings and cash flows.

How does Coca-Cola manage the risk of its currency fluctuations? In footnote 12 of its 10-K filing for 2007, the company discloses:

We enter into forward exchange contracts and purchase foreign currency options (principally euro and Japanese yen) and collars to hedge certain portions of forecasted cash flows denominated in foreign currencies.

In 2007, Coca-Cola reported no other material derivative contracts (such as interest rate or commodity). Its disclosures provide no detail as to the extent of exchange rate contracts traded during 2007 or held as of the end of 2007. However, it appears that the weakening U.S. dollar did not cause a great deal of derivative losses for Coca-Cola in 2007 (presuming that the company would hedge against a strengthening U.S. dollar). Coca-Cola discloses a $64 million net loss on derivatives in Accumulated Other Comprehensive Income during 2007 (see Coca-Cola's Statement of Shareowners' Equity on page 69 of its 10-K filing). Relative to its 2007 reported net income of almost $6 billion, this loss on foreign exchange derivatives is quite small (about 0.1 percent of net income).

Case 2: Interest Rate Risk: The "Heavy-Debt" Firm

Comcast Corporation had more than $31 billion of debt outstanding at the end of 2007.[2] Its debt load created $2.3 billion of interest expense during 2007. Meanwhile, the company generated approximately $5.6 billion in operating profits. Comcast regularly borrows additional funds to finance its operations with more than $11.2 billion of new debt during 2006 and 2007, while it repaid $3.4 billion of outstanding loans.

Although Comcast does not provide clear discussion in its 10-K filing as to the composition of its interest rate risk, the implication is that Comcast considers both cash flow and market value effects of interest rate fluctuations. In other words, some of its interest expense is variable over time (i.e., cash-flow risk), while debt with fixed interest expense will vary in market value as interest rates change (i.e., market-value risk).

At the end of 2007, Comcast managed its interest rate risk by entering into interest rate swap contracts by which the company pays a variable rate while receiving a fixed rate. Comcast holds interest rate swaps with combined notional values of $3.2 billion, and the contracts mature between 2008 and 2014. In essence, by converting approximately 10 percent of its overall debt to floating-rate debt, Comcast is reducing the market value risk of its existing debt. Over the course of the time span from 2006 year-end to 2007, the company's average pay rate on the swap has declined from 7.2 percent to 6.8 percent (while the average fixed "receive" rate is 5.9 percent). The market value of the swap contracts has increased by $120 million from ($103 million) at year-end 2006 to $17 million at the end of 2007. This market value increase in the swap offsets Comcast's opportunity loss on its fixed-rate debt as variable interest rates decline.

Case 3: Commodity Price Risk: The Firm with a Highly Volatile Input Cost

In 2007, jet fuel costs comprised 28 percent of Southwest Airline's operating expenses.[3] The spot price of jet fuel has approximately tripled between the end of

2002 and 2007, and this fact is only partially reflected by an increase in Southwest's average per gallon fuel cost from $0.72 during 2003 to $1.70 during 2007.[4] In other words, Southwest's average fuel cost has only increased by 2.36 times rather than the 3 times implied by the increase in spot jet fuel prices. How has Southwest limited growth in its fuel costs?

Southwest Airlines has managed to partially mitigate the effects of rising jet fuel prices by entering into hedging transactions that benefit from higher crude oil and refined products prices. During 2007, the company realized $727 million in cash settlements from derivative contracts previously entered into for the purpose of hedging jet fuel price risk. These gains are a critical element in Southwest's reported 2007 net income of $645 million.

THEORETICAL UNDERPINNINGS OF FINANCIAL HEDGING AND EMPIRICAL FINDINGS

In a perfect capital markets framework, firms have no reason to alter their risk profile. This statement follows directly from the capital structure analysis performed by Modigliani and Miller (1958).[5] However, the real-world violations of the perfect capital market assumptions create an environment in which firms have legitimate reasons for hedging financial risks. Furthermore, many of these reasons imply that hedging creates additional value for shareholders. In this section, I outline the basic arguments for risk management, discuss whether each theorized argument supports the notion that "hedging adds value," and provide a short review of empirical support for the arguments (i.e., whether the argument explains observed variations in financial hedging). I conclude the section by reviewing empirical findings that specifically address whether hedging adds value.

Hedging Reduces Expected Costs of Financial Distress and Underinvestment

One commonly cited benefit of an effective financial hedging program is that it should reduce the probability that the company encounters financial distress. This fundamental argument was first made formally by Smith and Stulz (1985). Fundamental business valuation principles such as discounted cash flow ignore the potential effects of distress because the onset of distress is not assumed to affect expected cash flows (rather it is just one potential outcome of the cash flow distribution), and distress is an idiosyncratic risk so the cost of capital does not incorporate the effects of distress. As such, an extended business valuation model reflects the present value of expected future cash flows minus expected distress costs. Although a firm can likely do little to change costs incurred if distress occurs, the firm can reduce expected distress costs by reducing the probability of encountering financial distress. Therefore, a firm that effectively reduces its probability of encountering financial distress by hedging financial risk should be awarded a higher valuation than if unhedged.

Financial distress costs are often interpreted as consisting of the costs associated with bankruptcy (such as legal and accounting fees, and management time directed toward dealing with bankruptcy procedures rather than toward managing the business). However, one of the most pervasive costs associated with financial distress is the value lost because of a firm's inability to take advantage of valuable investment opportunities. This type of problem is often referred to as the "underinvestment problem." Froot, Scharfstein, and Stein (1993) developed a formal model to illustrate how a firm's financial hedging decisions can help it avoid the potential for underinvestment. In particular, if the realization of a risk exposure causes a firm's operations to yield lower operating income, the firm may choose not to take a valuable investment opportunity because of a lack of internal capital and poorer access to outside capital. On the other hand, if the firm had previously entered into a financial hedge that offsets the risk exposure, then the profit on the hedging instrument provides additional cash flow to the firm. If this cash flow is then used to invest in a valuable investment opportunity, the underinvestment problem is solved and firm value reflects the positive value of the investment.

Empirical studies of corporate hedging are generally supportive of the financial distress cost hypotheses (including the underinvestment costs hypothesis); however, the findings are far from unanimous.[6] In general, there is sufficient evidence to believe that many firms find hedging to be beneficial in reducing expected costs associated with financial distress and underinvestment.

Hedging Creates More Debt Capacity

If hedging of financial risk reduces a firm's probability of distress, its optimal action might be to increase its debt. Leland (1998) theorizes that the primary benefits of reducing risk by hedging are the incremental tax benefits accruing from additional debt after the firm readjusts its capital structure. In general, this line of thought suggests that hedging creates value because extra debt allows for additional tax benefits or is used to finance valuable investment opportunities.

Graham and Rogers (2002) provide the first substantive evidence that the "debt capacity" argument for hedging financial risk is important on average. They find that an "average" user of interest rate and/or currency derivatives has a higher debt ratio than a nonhedger of financial risk, and that the higher debt ratio provides more than 1 percent extra value, on average, through tax benefits.

Hedging to enable greater debt capacity might be beneficial to a firm's shareholders beyond providing additional value through tax benefits. If additional debt is used to increase the firm's capital base and provide funds for pursuing valuable investment opportunities, then the added debt capacity reflects value-adding capital. Additionally, firms might benefit from a reduced cost of capital.

Hedging Reflects the Incentives of the Firm's Management and Board

A firm's financial risk management strategy may be a function of the incentives and characteristics of its senior management as well as of its board of directors. For example, Smith and Stulz (1985) argue that senior managers who hold significant amounts of wealth in options may have greater incentives to increase, rather than decrease, firm risk because the extra volatility makes the options more valuable. On the other hand, they show that managerial holdings of stock reinforce personal risk aversion, and, therefore, firms in which managers hold more shares of stock will be more likely to hedge. Tufano (1998) extends the model proposed by Froot et al. (1993), and shows that self-interested managers might engage in hedging to avoid the oversight of external capital market providers so that management can consume perquisites at the expense of internal equity providers. The board's role in risk management has not been modeled explicitly, but the fact that management has incentives to pursue self-interested policies (possibly at the expense of share-holders) suggests that the board might also play an oversight role in a company's hedging policy.

Other theoretic research, such as Hall and Murphy (2002) and Meulbroeck (2001), suggests that the Smith and Stulz (1985) framework does not account for the interaction of personal risk aversion and lack of diversification. A poorly diversified manager may not recognize the risk-increasing incentives of option compensation. In such a case, option holdings of management would lead to a desire to decrease risk by hedging. In general, the management incentives arguments are silent as to whether hedging adds value.

Tufano (1996) provides evidence that gold price hedging by mining firms is primarily determined by managerial characteristics, including option and stock holdings. Rogers (2002) shows that firms in which CEOs have more risk-taking incentives from options use fewer interest rate and currency derivatives, and finds evidence that these two choices (hedging and risk-taking incentives provided to management) are simultaneously determined.

As opposed to the firm's senior managers, a vast majority of its directors are unlikely to hold economically significant amounts of stock and/or options in the company on whose board they sit. Nevertheless, the monitoring role of directors suggests that they should have a keen understanding of the firm's significant risks and how these are being managed.

Borokhovich, Brunarski, Crutchley, and Simkins (2004) hypothesize that a firm with a bigger difference between the number of outsider and insider directors is more likely to be focused on maximizing wealth by effectively managing risk. They test their hypothesis by analyzing the interest rate derivatives usage by large non-financial firms in 1995, and find evidence suggesting that outside directors play an important role in the corporate risk management process. Furthermore, if outside directors are effective watchdogs for value maximization, then risk management is likely adding value. A possible extension of this argument is that effective boards will design equity-based compensation contracts that provide senior managers with proper incentives to manage risk.

Does Hedging Affect Firm Value?

Theories of risk management largely pose hedging as a corporate strategy that can increase firm value. Ultimately, the question posed by this section is an empirical one. Interestingly, financial research has not provided extensive direct study of this question. Allayannis and Weston (2001) is the first study to directly analyze the effect of corporate hedging decisions on corporate valuations. They conclude that firms with exposure to foreign currency fluctuations who choose to hedge their exposure with derivatives are, on average, about 5 percent more valuable relative to firms that do not hedge this exposure.

More recently, Carter, Rogers, and Simkins (2006a and 2006b) analyze the jet fuel hedging of U.S. airlines. They argue that an industry-specific sample improves the ability to understand the source of value improvements if these are apparent in the data. They find that median jet fuel hedgers (about 30 percent of the next year's fuel requirements) are valued approximately 5 percent to 10 percent higher than nonhedging counterparts. They conclude that this hedging premium is a result of the ability to use hedging profits in bad industry cycles to pursue valuable investment opportunities (either by buying assets from financially distressed airlines or by pursuing new routes as distressed competitors retrench).

However, hedging may not add value in all settings. Jin and Jorion (2006) study the hedging decisions of oil and gas producing firms. They show that hedging is not associated with higher firm value across their sample firms. Tufano (1996) concludes that the only factor that drives hedging decisions by gold-mining firms is managerial incentives. Although Tufano did not study the effect of hedging on value explicitly, his results are not particularly supportive that these firms considered value-maximizing rationales in making hedging decisions.

To summarize the key aspects of the discussion, hedging is often a value-maximizing strategy, but only if investors view it as providing tangible benefits. Firms that pursue financial risk management strategies should have clear understandings as to the benefits provided by hedging, and more specifically, if the benefits are economically significant enough to outweigh the costs associated with pursuing an ongoing hedging program.

INTERACTION OF FINANCIAL HEDGING WITH OTHER TYPES OF RISK MANAGEMENT

Financial risk management is only one strategy employed by companies to manage their risk exposures. One noteworthy feature of financial hedging is that it is, in most cases, a short-term risk management strategy. Guay and Kothari (2003) illustrate that the derivative positions held by most firms are too small to realize significant cash flows in the event of abnormally large shocks to the value of the underlying asset hedged. They argue that results such as Allayannis and Weston's (2001) hedging premium of 5 percent probably reflect effects beyond the use of derivatives. In particular, it might be inferred that significant derivatives use is indicative of broader risk management efforts. As a result, corporate hedging strategies using derivatives should complement (or at least not detract from) other types of risk management strategies. At this stage, I discuss potential interactions of financial hedging with other forms of corporate risk management.

Credit Risk Management

Credit risk is a potentially large source of risk for many companies. Notably, companies in financial industries often own receivables as their primary earning asset base. But even nonfinancial companies have a significant portion of their assets in receivables. For fiscal 2007 (covering years ending June 2007 through April 2008), the 395 nonfinancial companies in the S&P 500 had $994 billion in receivables on their balance sheets (in total) on aggregate sales of $7,132 billion, so approximately 14 percent of booked revenues reflect uncollected sales dollars.

Sales made on credit reflect short-term lending decisions by firms, and the inability to collect on such sales can have a damaging effect on a firm's overall profitability if its credit department underestimates the degree to which credit risk might be realized by nonpayment for goods and/or services supplied. To illustrate this with a simple example, suppose a company has $100 million in sales, $14 million in receivables, and its expected net profit margin is 5 percent, so its expected net income is $5 million. If 25 percent of its receivables become uncollectible unexpectedly, the company's actual net income is only $1.5 million (i.e., net income is $3.5 million less than expected).

In the last two decades, the derivatives market has expanded to include credit derivatives. This market is large and growing. At the end of 2007, the notional amount of credit default swaps was $58 trillion and these contracts were valued at $2 trillion according to the Bank of International Settlements (BIS).[7] At the end of 2005, credit default swaps in the amount of $14 trillion notional value and $243 billion in market value were outstanding. As such, it might be expected that credit risk management is included in the definition of financial hedging. As a contrast, OTC commodity contracts amount to $9 trillion in notional value (and $753 billion in market value) at the end of 2007. However, Smithson and Mengle (2006) note that nonfinancial corporations have not embraced credit derivatives as a hedging tool. He states that recent data from the British Bankers Association shows only 2 percent of credit protection buyers are nonfinancial corporations.

The major interaction between financial hedging and credit risk management stems mostly from the fact that many hedging strategies are used to manage the currency and/or commodity price risks associated with anticipated transactions. If the anticipated transactions are expected future sales, then the financial risk (i.e., currency and/or commodity risk) is typically recognized before the firm recognizes its credit risk to its customer (because the credit risk is initiated when the credit sale is actually recognized for accounting purposes). By managing financial risk in advance of credit risk, the firm is better able to manage its expected profit on future transactions, while credit risk management is used to ensure realization of the profit. Given the relative underutilization of credit derivatives by nonfinancial corporations, it appears that most companies employ other techniques to manage the risk of nonpayment by customers.

Operational Risk Management

A firm's operating choices expose it to many risks. A fundamental theory of financial economics is that a firm's investment choices reflect positive net present value (NPV) opportunities on a risk-adjusted basis. In other words, a company invests in risky assets in which it believes its people have the necessary expertise and knowledge to create value from these assets. The firm's operational risk management[8] strategy includes actions that reduce the risks associated with its operating choices.

Financial risk is often embedded in a company's operating choices. For example, a manufacturing firm faces choices as to where to locate its manufacturing facilities. Suppose the company chooses to build its manufacturing facility in a country with low labor costs, but the product is exported to other markets globally. The firm has exposed itself to currency risk, and this can be managed by using currency derivatives (i.e., a financial hedge). Suppose, on the other hand, that the manufacturing location is chosen based on its superior access to the ultimate markets in which the product is sold. In this case, the currency risk may be less than in the first case (but it still exists).

The choice of manufacturing location is an operating decision that changes the firm's risk profile depending on the choice of parameters used. From finance theory, the location with the highest expected value on a risk-adjusted basis is chosen, and this reflects the operating risk management decision. Financial risk management can be employed on a flexible basis to offset any hedgeable risks that are explicit functions of the company's operational risk management choice.

The company may periodically reevaluate its operating choices (i.e., consider selling an existing plant and buying or building a plant in another location). For example, the current weak U.S. dollar has created conditions under which U.S.-based companies with foreign manufacturing operations chosen previously because of lower costs relative to manufacturing domestically are considering moving some manufacturing capabilities to the U.S. As a recent example, FEI Corporation announced in its April 29, 2008, earnings release that it plans to transfer supply chain and manufacturing operations to "lower-cost alternatives that are primarily dollar-based."[9]

Strategic Risk Management

Strategic risk reflects the opportunities and threats faced by the firm given its competitive environment. Obviously, this type of risk is of paramount importance to businesses. Financial risk clearly constitutes risks that are not part of strategic risk. Nevertheless, financial risk management may assist firms in taking advantage of certain types of strategic risks.

One of the noted benefits of financial hedging is its ability to reduce underinvestment problems. An inability to capitalize on all valuable investment opportunities represents one source of strategic risk. Thus, financial risk management provides a potential avenue for firms to make value-enhancing investments during periods in which they might otherwise be unable to do so.

An excellent example of this type of interaction has occurred in the U.S. airline industry. Southwest Airlines has been, by far, the most active hedger of financial risk occurring from the uncertainty of future jet fuel prices. During this time frame, the company has grown considerably while other airlines have been forced to retrench. In a July 1, 2008, Associated Press article on jet fuel hedging in the airline industry, S&P airline analyst, Betsy Snyder, is quoted, "This (Southwest Airlines) is a company that has always taken advantage of others' misfortune."[10] The cash flows realized from its active program of hedging anticipated jet fuel costs have been instrumental in pursuing this strategy.

Reputation and Legal Risk Management

A company's failures in managing financial risk can affect its reputation and even its existence. In the mid-1990s, several high-profile cases of big risk management failures occurred. Chance and Brooks (2007) highlight the hedging debacles of Metallgesellschaft AG in 1993 ($1.3 billion lost on crude oil, heating oil, and gasoline futures contracts), Orange County, California, in 1994 ($1.6 billion lost on leveraged repurchase agreements), and Barings PLC in 1995 ($1.2 billion on stock index futures and options). These cases (as well as numerous other deriva-tive losses shown on pages 572–573 of Chance and Brooks 2007) are worth noting for all users of derivatives because of the risk of business failure that can occur if derivatives are used improperly. Additionally, poorly devised financial hedg-ing strategies could conceivably make a firm susceptible to legal actions filed by unhappy shareholders.

On the other hand, some firms have been held up as role models for successful financial hedging. Carter, Rogers, and Simkins (2006b) note that Southwest Airlines has realized significant cash flows from its jet fuel hedging strategies and that these cash flows are instrumental in helping the company take advantage of growth opportunities. Merck's currency hedging strategy has served to protect its ability to fund valuable research and development (R&D) spending, and is frequently cited by academics (for an example, see "University of Georgia Roundtable on Enterprise-Wide Risk Management" 2003).

Financial Reporting and Disclosure Risk Management

Financial hedging has caused additional financial reporting requirements associ-ated with using derivative financial instruments. In 2000, the U.S.-based accounting standards setter, the Financial Accounting Standards Board (FASB), implemented FAS 133, which sets the U.S. GAAP rules with respect to accounting for derivatives. Prior to the adoption of FAS 133, firms using derivatives were merely required to provide disclosures in financial statement footnotes about fair values of derivative contracts held at the end of the reporting period, notional value of these deriva-tives, and some additional qualitative disclosure regarding the strategies employed for using derivatives (including the firm's purpose). With the advent of FAS 133, market values of derivative contracts are now required to be disclosed as assets or liabilities, reflecting whether the contract is in a receivable or payable position. The fundamental accounting treatment of derivatives under FAS 133 is similar to those required under international accounting rules (i.e., IAS 39).

The most significant aspect of FAS 133 is the fact that firms must qualify their derivative contracts as being eligible for "hedge accounting." If a deriva-tive transaction qualifies for hedge accounting, then the derivative contract does not affect earnings until a realized gain or loss occurs. However, if a derivative transaction does not qualify for hedge accounting treatment, then unrealized mar-ket value changes in derivative contracts are required to be reflected in a firm's earnings.

If accounting regulations make qualification for hedge accounting difficult, financial hedging might add volatility to a company's reported earnings. If investors do not understand the requirements for hedge accounting (entirely possibly given that FAS 133 is widely considered the most complicated accounting standard ever written by FASB), it is quite feasible that firms employing eco-nomically meaningful financial hedging strategies could exhibit more volatile net income over time because of the effects of unrealized derivative gains and losses that are included in income.

As an example of how the accounting regulations can create more volatility in reported income, Southwest Airlines disclosed in its 2007 10-K filing that, in 2006, the company recognized $101 million in nonoperating losses because of its inability to qualify its fuel hedges for hedge accounting under FAS 133.[11]

On the other hand, Southwest recognized $110 million of nonoperating gains during 2005 for the same reason. By creating the potential for periodic shifts between nonoperating gains and losses associated with unrealized derivative value changes, FAS 133 creates an environment in which hedging firms may exhibit more volatility in net income than nonhedgers.

WHAT CAN WE LEARN ABOUT ERM GIVEN OUR KNOWLEDGE OF FINANCIAL HEDGING?

The answer is "plenty." The theory base used in studying financial hedging is directly applicable to better understanding the benefits of ERM. We have discussed the fact that risk management can add value to a business through different avenues. First, effective risk management reduces the probability of "bad" outcomes related to risk factors facing the company. Financial hedging focuses on reducing easily observed and measurable risk factors that can be offset by entering into financial contracts such as derivatives. An ERM program should be designed to identify, measure, and manage other significant risk factors beyond financial risks. Thus, in this sense, rigorous financial risk management should be a subset of a good ERM program for any business in which financial risks are significant.

Second, financial hedging has been argued to provide a mechanism for businesses to turn "bad" outcomes to their advantage. Earlier, I mentioned the fact that Southwest Airlines has used cash flows achieved from its jet fuel hedging program to benefit from rising oil prices to continue its market share gains in the U.S. domestic airline industry. In this sense, financial hedging becomes one element of strategic risk management (i.e., another risk factor addressed by an ERM program).

Third, financial hedging can affect a firm's leverage decisions. Prior research suggests that hedging firms may borrow more. Perhaps a reason underlying such a decision is that hedging firms are viewed as less risky, and can command lower default risk premiums on new borrowings. Credit rating agencies, such as Standard & Poor's, are studying the possibility of incorporating analysis of companies' ERM programs into credit ratings. Firms that can illustrate strong capabilities in managing financial risks may be better positioned to illustrate strong risk management credentials with respect to identifying, measuring, and managing other important risks in their conversations with the credit rating agencies.

Fourth, boards with a greater shareholder monitoring focus (and therefore, more of a value-creation mindset) are the governance norm at firms that are more active financial hedgers. Given that active board involvement and buy-in are critical to implementation of a successful ERM program, boards that better understand financial risks are likely to be more receptive to conversations about other significant risks that could negatively affect company performance.

Finally, the evidence suggesting that financial hedging is valued by the equity market should lend a level of comfort to senior managers and board members interested in pursuing ERM. If ERM programs can be effectively implemented to reduce significant risks of negative business outcomes, as well as identify potential opportunities to achieve strategic gains, then ERM is a potentially valuable new business strategy for corporate managers to pursue.

NOTES

1. Coca-Cola Company's SEC 10-K filing for calendar year 2007 (filed on February 28, 2008) is available at www.sec.gov/Archives/edgar/data/21344/000119312508041768/d10k.htm.

2. All of the information from this case is available in Comcast's 2008 SEC 10-K filing at www.sec.gov/Archives/edgar/data/1166691/000119312508034239/d10k.htm.

3. All information other than jet fuel price data is taken from Southwest Airline's 2008 SEC 10-K filing available at www.sec.gov/Archives/edgar/data/92380/000095013408001572/d53331e10vk.htm.

4. Spot prices for jet fuel are available at http://tonto.eia.doe.gov/dnav/pet/pet_pri_spt_s1_d.htm.

5. Given the assumptions of perfect capital markets, a firm's risk profile is completely transparent to investors. The firm's investors could trade in appropriate markets for financial hedging instruments to design their own preferred risk profile. This is essentially the same argument that Modigliani and Miller (1958) make for the irrelevance of capital structure.

6. Triki (2005) provides an excellent overview of the empirical research on corporate hedging up through 2005. She incorporates results from 29 published and unpublished papers into her discussion. Most of the papers discussed study the relation between debt ratios and hedging to test the financial distress cost hypothesis. Meanwhile, underinvestment costs are typically measured with measures of investment opportunities, such as market-to-book ratio, R&D expenditures, or some other investment variable (such as exploration expenditures by gold mining firms). Carter, Rogers, and Simkins (2006a) use the U.S. airline industry to argue that tests of the underinvestment hypothesis should consider the correlation between the availability of valuable investment opportunities and hedgeable risks.

7. The BIS survey data is available at www.bis.org/statistics/otcder/dt1920a.pdf.

8. "Operational risk" is a term in which a more consistent taxonomy would be useful in both industry and academics. I use the term generally to reflect the risk associated with a firm's operating choices. However, this is not a standard definition, by any means. A recent practitioner/academic roundtable discussion on ERM illustrates this lack of a consistent definition of operational risk (see Branson, et al. 2008).

9. The filing is available at www.sec.gov/Archives/edgar/data/914329/000119312508095083/dex991.htm.

10. See the Associated Press article by David Koenig dated July 1, 2008, entitled, "Airlines try to hedge against soaring fuel costs."

11. This information is from the "Fuel Contracts" discussion in footnote 10 (entitled, "Derivative and Financial Instruments") to the financial statements in Southwest Airline's 2007 SEC 10-K (dated February 1, 2007). The URL is www.sec.gov/Archives/edgar/data/92380/000095013407001724/d42975e10vk.htm.

REFERENCES

Allayannis, G., and J.P. Weston. 2001. The use of foreign currency derivatives and firm market value. *Review of Financial Studies* 14, 243–276.

Borokhovich, K.A., K.R. Brunarski, C.E. Crutchley, and B.J. Simkins. 2004. Board composition and corporate use of interest rate derivatives. *Journal of Financial Research* 27, 199–216.

Branson, B., P. Concessi, J.R.S. Fraser, M. Hofmann, R. Kolb, T. Perkins, et al. 2008. Enterprise risk management: Current initiatives and issues—Journal of Applied Finance roundtable. *Journal of Applied Finance* 18, no. 1 (Spring/Summer), 115–132.

Carter, D.A., D.A. Rogers, and B.J. Simkins. 2006a. Does hedging affect firm value? Evidence from the U.S. airline industry. *Financial Management* 35, 53–86.

Carter, D.A., D.A. Rogers, and B.J. Simkins. 2006b. Hedging and value in the U.S. airline industry. *Journal of Applied Corporate Finance* 18, 21–33.

Chance, D.M., and R. Brooks. 2007. *An introduction to derivatives and risk management*, 7th ed. Mason, OH: Thomson Southwestern.

Froot, K., D. Scharfstein, and J. Stein. 1993. Risk management: Coordinating investment and financing policies. *Journal of Finance* 48, 1629–1658.

Graham, J.R., and D.A. Rogers. 2002. Do firms hedge in response to tax incentives? *Journal of Finance* 57, 815–839.

Guay, W., and S.P. Kothari. 2003. How much do firms hedge with derivatives? *Journal of Financial Economics* 70, 423–461.

Hall, B.J., and K.J. Murphy. 2002. Stock options for undiversified executives. *Journal of Accounting and Economics* 33, 3–42.

Jin, Y., and P. Jorion. 2006. Firm value and hedging: Evidence from U.S. oil and gas producers. *Journal of Finance* 61, 893–919.

Leland, H.E. 1998. Agency costs, risk management, and capital structure. *Journal of Finance* 53, 1213–1243.

Modigliani, F., and M.H. Miller. 1958. The cost of capital, corporation finance and the theory of investment. *American Economic Review* 48, 261–297.

Meulbroeck, L.K. 2001. The efficiency of equity-linked compensation: Understanding the full cost of awarding executive stock options. *Financial Management* 30, 5–44.

Rogers, D.A. 2002. Does executive portfolio structure affect risk management? CEO risk-taking incentives and corporate derivatives usage. *Journal of Banking and Finance* 26, 271–295.

Smith, C.W. Jr., and R.M. Stulz. 1985. The determinants of firms' hedging policies. *Journal of Financial and Quantitative Analysis* 20, 391–405.

Smithson, C., and D. Mengle. 2006. The promise of credit derivatives in nonfinancial corporations (and why it's failed to materialize). *Journal of Applied Corporate Finance* 18, 54–60.

Triki, T. 2005. Research on corporate hedging theories: A critical review of the evidence to date. Unpublished working paper, HEC Montreal.

Tufano, P. 1996. Who manages risk? An empirical examination of risk management practices in the gold mining industry. *Journal of Finance* 51, 1097–1137.

Tufano, P. 1998. Agency costs of corporate risk management. *Financial Management* 27 (1), 67–77.

University of Georgia roundtable on enterprise-wide risk management. 2003. *Journal of Applied Corporate Finance* 15, 8–26.

ABOUT THE AUTHOR

Daniel A. Rogers, PhD, has taught courses in valuation (including real estate valuation), corporate finance, and derivative securities at Portland State University, Northeastern University, Massey University, and University of Utah. He has published research in the areas of corporate risk management and derivatives usage, managerial incentives arising from compensation, and stock option repricing. His published work includes articles in the *Journal of Finance, Journal of Banking and Finance, Financial Management, Journal of Applied Corporate Finance*, and *Journal of*

Futures Markets. His *Financial Management* article on the valuation effects of jet fuel hedging in the airline industry (co-authored with David Carter and Betty Simkins) was a co-winner of the Addison-Wesley Prize in 2006. Prior to his life as an academic, Dr. Rogers held management positions with a national airline and a petroleum products distributor during which he purchased jet and diesel fuel, and managed the price risk associated with these commodities. Dr. Rogers has a BA in Business Administration from Washington State University; MBA from Tulane University; PhD (Finance) from University of Utah.

CHAPTER 19

Bank Capital Regulation and Enterprise Risk Management

BENTON E. GUP, PhD
Chair of Banking, The University of Alabama

INTRODUCTION

Bankers and bank regulators throughout the world are facing the challenge of dealing with globalization and the changing risk profile of banks. One aspect of this challenge is that international bank regulators have undertaken major efforts to harmonize prudential regulatory standards. *Harmonization* refers to uniform regulations as well as stemming divergent standards that are applied to similar activities of different financial institutions. The Basel Committee on Banking Supervision, a committee of national bank supervisors, has led the effort to establish uniform standards. In 1988, the Basel Committee established risk-based capital standards for banks. In a competitive market system, equity capital cushions debt and equity holders from unexpected losses. In regulated banking systems, required capital is used to reduce the costs of financial distress, agency problems, and the reduction in market discipline caused by federal safety nets.[1]

Many countries throughout the world adopted the Basel I capital standards of holding capital of 8 percent or more of assets based on the risks of various types of assets. A study by Barth, Caprio, and Levine (2006) of more than 150 countries, revealed that minimum required capital ratios ranged from 4 percent to 20 percent of assets.

One particularly challenging problem for banks operating in multiple jurisdictions is different capital standards resulting in competitive advantages or disadvantages, that is, an uneven playing field. Another challenge is the allocation of capital for operational risk among the legal entities within and across jurisdictions.[2] Operational risk will be discussed shortly. It deals with failed processes, people, systems and events. Capital standards are evolving to take Enterprise Risk Management (ERM) and Economic Capital into account.

THE EVOLUTION OF BANK CAPITAL REQUIREMENTS

Banking used to be simple, local, and dominated by small banks, Today it is complex, global, and dominated by large banks. In the past, small banks made loans

Exhibit 19.1   U.S. Bank Equity/Asset Ratios

Date	U.S. Banks	Nonfinancial Corporations
1896	23.5%	
1900	17.9%	
1980	5.8%	69.1%
1988	6.2 % (Basel I)	
2000	8.5%	49.2%
2007	10.2%	35.4% (2005)

Sources: All-bank Statistics, United States, 1896–1955, Statistical Abstract of the United States 1989, 1993, 2008. Note that the latest data for Nonfinancial Corporations (Table 730 Corporations) is for 2005. The data will be published in the 2008 Statistical Abstract. FDIC Quarterly Banking Profile, (2008). Full Year 2007, Table III-A. FDIC-Insured Commercial Banks.

to local customers. Their major concern was their customer's ability to repay the loans. Today, large international banks buy and sell packaged loans and engage in other activities around the world. The personal link between lenders and borrowers has largely disappeared for these banks. And the risks associated with buying and selling loans and other banking activities has increased dramatically. Bank capital serves as a cushion against losses from loans and other activities. In the sections that follow, the evolution of bank capital requirements in the United States and internationally is examined.

Overview of U.S. Capital Ratios

The data shown in Exhibit 19.1 shows the ratio of equity capital to assets of U.S. banks during the 1896–2007 period. Equity capital, which is the book value of assets less the book value of liabilities, is different than regulatory capital that can include subordinated debt and some adjustments for off-balance sheet items. It also differs from economic capital, which is a statistical estimate of risk and capital that will be discussed shortly.

As shown in Exhibit 19.1, banks in the United States had equity/asset ratios of 23.5 percent in 1896. The ratios in 1896 and 1900 reflect a time when many banks were operating under the "real-bills doctrine"—borrowing short term and lending short term.

The equity/asset ratio gradually declined to less 5.8 percent in 1980. Over the years, bankers expanded their lending horizons and made longer-term loans, including real estate loans. They were still borrowing short term, but the longer-term loans increased their risk. During the 1985–1992 period, 1,373 banks that were insured by the Federal Deposit Insurance Corporation (FDIC) failed.[3] In addition 1,073 savings and loan associations and 1,707 credit unions failed. All were federally insured. Thus, there was pressure in the United States for increased regulations dealing with bank capital. The end result was the passage of the Federal Deposit Insurance Corporation Improvement Act of 1991 (FIDICIA), which increased bank capital requirements. FIDICA included Prompt Correct Action (PCA) rules of how to deal with undercapitalized banks that have risk-based capital ratios of 6 percent or less. Well-capitalized banks have risk-based capital ratios of 10 percent or more.

Two additional factors contributed to increased growth opportunities and risks for banks. The first factor is the laws that allowed simple commercial banks to form multibank holding companies, and then expand into underwriting securities, insurance, merchant banking, insurance, and other complementary activities.[4] This opened the door for banks to become Large Complex Banking Organizations (LCBOs). Second was the growth of securitization in mortgage lending. Securitization is the packaging and selling pools of mortgage loans to investors.[5] Securitization can involve complex structures such as Mortgage Backed Securities (MBS), Collateralized Debt Obligations (CDOs), and Structured Investment Vehicles (SIVs) backed by pools of MBS and CDO bonds.

Exhibit 19.1 also shows that nonfinancial corporations had equity/asset ratios that ranged from 69 percent to 35 percent. This is substantially greater than the banks' equity/asset ratios for several reasons. One reason why banks have lower equity/asset ratios is that they are regulated by federal and state agencies and subject to various laws such as the Federal Deposit Insurance Corporation Insurance Act or 1991 FIDICIA that requires bank regulators to take prompt corrective actions if a bank's risk-based capital falls below predetermined levels. Risk-based capital ratio refers to a percentage of a bank's risk-weighted assets (e.g., loans) to its capital accounts. Well-capitalized banks have risk-based capital ratios of 10 percent or more. Undercapitalized banks have ratios of 6 percent or less. Other reasons include access to the Federal Reserve's discount window, government intervention, and the Too-Big-To-Fail doctrine.[6]

Basel I

On the international scene, the Basel Committee on Banking Supervision was established in 1974. It focused on facilitating and enhancing information sharing and cooperation among bank regulators, and developing principles for the supervision of internationally active large banks. Following the large losses from the less-developed countries (LDC) in the late 1970s, the Basel Committee became increasingly concerned about the failure of large banks and cross-border contagion. In particular, they were concerned that large banks did not have adequate capital in relation to the risks they were assuming. In the 1980s, their concerns were directed at Japanese banks that were expanding globally. The end result was a uniform one-size-fits-all 8 percent capital requirement that became known as the 1988 Capital Accord, or Basel I.

Under Basel I, bank capital consisted of two tiers. Tier 1 includes shareholder equity and retained earnings, and it is 4 percent. Tier 2 includes additional internal and external funds available to the bank and also is 4 percent.[7] Thus, Basel I required 8 percent risk adjusted capital.

Basel I focused primarily on credit risk, and risk-weighted assets ranged from 0 percent weight for claims on Organization for Economic Cooperation and Development (OECD) central banks and governments to 100 percent weights for commercial and consumer loans and loans to non-OECD governments.

Along this line, banks were required to hold more capital against ordinary mortgages than against pools of mortgages that were securitized. Therefore, banks began to change the way they did business from holding the mortgage loans to securitizing them and selling them to other investors. While banks continued to make mortgages and other loans, the securitization process allowed them to shift the risk to the investors who bought the securitized loans.[8]

The 8 percent risk-based capital ratio is an arbitrary ratio that is used to monitor risk. The 8 percent "Minimum capital is a guidepost.... It was not and is not intended as a level toward which the firms should aim nor as a standard for internal risk management."[9] It does not measure risk. Equally important, a large number of failed banks had capital ratios in excess of 8 percent shortly before failure. According to a FDIC study, 26 percent of the 1,600 U.S. banks that failed between 1980 and 1994 had CAMEL ratings (capital, asset quality, management, earnings, and liquidity) of 1 or 2, one year before failure.[10] CAMEL ratings are used by bank regulators to evaluate banks. The ratings range from a high of 1 to a low of 5.[11] The study went on to say that "... bank capital positions are poor predictors of failure several years before the fact."[12]

In 2007, all FDIC insured commercial banks in the United States held an average of 12.23 percent risk-based capital, far in excess of the 8 percent regulatory capital required by Basel I.[13] The smallest banks (assets of less than $100 million) held 19.84 percent risk-based capital, while the largest banks (greater than $10 billion) held 11.86 percent. The holding of capital in excess of regulatory requirements is due in part to FIDICA, higher earnings, goodwill due to mergers, and to take advantage of growth opportunities.[14]

From 1980 to 1996, 133 of the International Monetary Fund's (IMF) 181 member countries experienced significant banking sector problems.[15] As a general rule, bank failures tend to be in large numbers, they are frequently associated with financial shocks (e.g., foreign exchange), and real estate defaults is the most common cause of bank failures.

In the early 1980s, Chile also experienced systemic banking problems. Falling copper prices, a severe recession, rising interest rates in the United States, and the 90 percent decline of the peso adversely affected foreign exchange–linked loans to domestic borrowers. The Central Bank in Chile took over 14 of the 26 commercial banks and 8 of the 17 domestic finance companies. Eight of the banks and all of the finance companies were liquidated.[16]

The bottom line about Basel I is that bank capital matters. However, a number of changes occurred that undermined Basel I. These changes include developments in derivatives, globalization, and the consolidation of LCBOs. Equally important, the basic business model of commercial banks has shifted from the real bills doctrine (borrowing short term and lending short term) to borrowing short term and lending long term (i.e., buy and hold), and more recently to borrowing short term and selling assets (i.e., originate and distribute to other investors through syndications, securitization, and credit derivatives).[17] Along this line, Federal Reserve Governor Susan Schmidt Bies (2007) said,

U.S. supervisors support the 2005 Basel/International Organization of Securities Commissions' (IOSCO) revisions to the 1996 Market Risk Amendment (MRA). Since adoption of the MRA, banks' trading activities have become more sophisticated and have given rise to a wider range of risks that are not easily captured in the existing value-at-risk (VaR) models used in many banks. For example, banks are now including more products related to credit risk, such as credit-default swaps and tranches of collateralized debt obligations, in their trading books. These products can create default risks that are not captured well by the methodologies required under the current MRA rule—which specifies a ten-day holding period and a 99 percent confidence interval—thereby creating potential arbitrage opportunities between the banking book and the trading book.

In a nutshell, former Federal Reserve Vice Chairman Ferguson (2003) said that "Basel I is too simplistic to address the activities of our most complex banking institutions." It is not sufficiently risk sensitive. Thus, Ferguson supported Basel II that was proposed by the Basel Committee on Banking Supervision in 2001.

Basel II

Basel II[18] is a work in progress. It is an attempt to align regulatory capital with the risks that banks face. There are two distinctly different but related aspects of Basel II. One involves the *three pillars*, and the other involves *enterprise risk management*. Each is discussed here.

> Pillar 1: **Minimum Capital Requirements**—The regulatory capital requirements are based on *credit risk* (defaults by counterparty), *market risk* (price changes—on- and off-balance sheet), and *operational risk* (failed processes, people, systems, events). The definition of total capital in Basel II is the same as in Basel I. Total capital divided by credit risk, market risk, and operational risk must be equal to or greater than 8 percent.

$$\frac{\text{Total Capital (definition unchanged)}}{\text{Credit risk} + \text{Market risk} + \text{Operational risk}} \geq 8\% \text{ minimum capital ratio}$$

$$(19.1)$$

> Pillar 2: **Supervisory review process**—Foster supervisor-bank dialogue on risk management.
> Pillar 3: **Market discipline**—Based on disclosure of information.
> Without going into details, banks quickly discovered that it is relatively easy to get around the Basel II capital requirements.[19] There are three ways to compute the capital requirements—(1) the Standardized Approach, (2) the Foundation internal rating based (IRB) Approach, and (3) the Advanced IRB Approach.

The data shown in Exhibit 19.2 shows that the minimum capital for a $100 commercial loan can vary from $1.81 to $41.65 depending on the credit risk and the approach used to calculate the required capital.

Exhibit 19.2 Basel II – Minimum Capital for a $100 Commercial Loan

	AAA Credit Risk	BBB–Credit Risk	B Credit Risk
Standardized Approach	$1.81	$8.21	$12.21
Foundation IRB	$1.41	$5.01	$18.53
Advanced IRB	$0.37 to $4.45	$1.01 to $14.13	$3.97 to $41.65

Source: Susan Burhouse, John Field, George French, and Keith Ligon, 2003, "Basel and the Evolution of Capital Regulation: Moving Forward and Looking Back," An Update on Emerging Issues In Banking, FDIC, February 13.

Exhibit 19.3   Regulatory Arbitrage: Two Loans for $1 Million Each

Expected Loss EL =	Probability of Default (PD) x	Loss Given Default (LD)
Loan 1 EL = 1%	5%	20%
Loan 2 EL = 1%	2%	50%
Capital charges $1 mil × 1%	= $10,000	= $10,000

In addition, Exhibit 19.3 illustrates regulatory arbitrage for two $1 million loans where the Expected Loss (EL) is equal to the Probability of Default (PD) times the Loss Given Default (LD). Although the PD and LD of the two loans vary widely, they both have the same capital charge.

Banks can avoid charge-offs by restructuring loans that may become nonperforming loans. Alternatively, they can make a second loan to the obligor that would cover the payments of the first loan and keep it from defaulting. Finally, they can securitize loans—get them off the balance sheet.

Several Quantitative Impact Studies (QIS) have been run in order to test various aspects of Basel II. The FDIC's View of the Fourth Quantitative Impact Study-QIS-4 said that "The results of QIS-4 show Basel II would most likely lead to an *unacceptably large decline in capital for the largest banks.* . . . Competing head to head with large banks, holding in some cases a fraction of the capital that non–Basel II banks hold on the same loan portfolio, would be a *daunting challenge for the nation's community banks.*"[20] There was a 31 percent (median) reduction in Tier 1 Capital.[21] This is not conducive to a level playing field for all banks in general, and community banks in particular. However, as previously noted, small community banks in the United States held capital far in excess of minimum required levels of regulatory capital, and it does not seem to have hurt their competitive positions.

Nevertheless, in July 2007, U.S. Federal Banking Agencies reached an agreement to implement Basel II.[22] It will be tested over a three-year transitional period, and it will allow a cumulative capital reduction of no more than 15 percent. The primary impact will be on the LCBOs and other large banks that choose to use "opt in." Smaller banks will be using the "standardized" approach. In June 2008, the FDIC approved the standardized approach for all banks except the largest, most complex banks that are subject to the advanced approaches.[23]

Federal Reserve Governor Kroszner (2007) observed that while Basel I is based on "rules," Basel II is based on "principles." He said that "Taking a more principles-based approach means that we must allow bankers some flexibility in meeting the requirements and permit a reasonable amount of diversity of practices across banking organizations." In other words, the capital requirements for the same loan may vary from bank to bank.

Another complicating factor is adoption of Fair Value Accounting for valuing bank assets, liabilities, and certain financial instruments.[24] Barth (2004), and Gup and Lutton (2008) point out that there is added volatility of assets and liabilities associated with fair value accounting. The volatility could have a positive or negative effect on bank capital adequacy.

FDIC Chairman Sheila Bair (2008) in a speech about Basel II and risk management said that there was a major lack of transparency in structured finance (i.e., Collateralized Debt Obligations, CDOs). She said that "The advanced approaches in general represent a heavy bet on the accuracy of models and quantitative risk metrics." The unintended consequence is that the Basel II framework results in lower capital requirements for most credit classes with a favorable loss history. "And this can encourage banks to lever up ... to boost their return on equity." Therefore, she says that the "advanced approaches can be far off the mark. Now (there is) widespread recognition that there is more to sound risk management than mathematical formulas...." She favors a simple "leverage ratio." In testimony before the U.S. Senate, she argued that "The leverage ratio complements the risk based capital requirements by ensuring a base level of capital exists to absorb losses ... even in situations where risk-based metrics erroneously indicate risk is minimal and little capital is needed. These safeguards, along with the Prompt Corrective Action framework ... will preserve capital and promote a safe and sound banking system ..."[25]

In July 2008, an interagency statement was issued concerning the "U.S. Implementation of Basel II Advanced Approaches" for selected banks and bank holding companies.[26] The statement said that banks and bank holding companies planning to operate under the advanced approaches must follow certain procedures that will lead to their implementation no later than April 1, 2011.

Enterprise Risk Management (ERM) and Economic Capital

Basel II must be considered in the context of enterprise risk management (ERM). The Committee on Sponsoring Organizations (COSO) defines ERM as "a process affected by an enterprise's board of directors, management, and other personnel that is applied across an enterprise that is used to identify, assess, and manage risks within its risk appetite, to provide reasonable assurance of achieving its objectives."[27]

Federal Reserve Governor Susan Schmidt Bies (2006) commented on the COSO definition of ERM, and she said that it can mean different things to different people, but "all banking organizations need good risk management. An enterprise-wide approach is appropriate for setting objectives across the organization, instilling an enterprise-wide culture, and ensuring that key activities and risks are being monitored regularly."

The key point here is that ERM is forward looking. It takes into account economic conditions and a wide range of risks and other factors affecting banks in the future. Regulatory capital is history—not the future.

ERM employs the concept of *economic capital*—a statistical concept that measures risk, and it reflects the bank's estimate of the amount of capital needed to support its risk-taking activities. It is not the amount of *regulatory* capital held.[28]

A study of Risk Based Capital by the Government Accountability Office (GAO) found that "although the advanced approaches of Basel II aim to more closely align regulatory and economic capital, the two differ in significant ways, including in their fundamental purpose, scope, and consideration of certain assumptions. Given these differences, regulatory and economic capital are not intended to be equivalent.... Economic capital models may explicitly measure a broader range of risks, while regulatory capital as proposed in Basel II will explicitly measure only credit, operational, and where relevant, market risks."[29] Thus, economic capital reflects the bank's estimate of the amount of capital (not book value capital or regulatory capital) needed to support its risk-taking activities. In statistical terms, it is a conditional random variable. In practical terms, some large banks use a Return on Risk Capital (RORC) that is related to Economic Capital in making lending and investment decisions throughout the organization.

In the context of ERM, risks for global banks go far beyond credit risk, market risk, and operational risk. They include, but are not limited to, breakdown of critical infrastructure, changing laws and regulations, changes in technology, defaults of sovereign debts, hurricanes, oil prices, terrorism, political instability, and other factors. Although some of these risks may seem remote, they have happened in the past and may happen again. For example, there have been sovereign defaults in Latin America/Caribbean dating back to the early 1800s. Chile, for example, defaulted on government debts in 1826, 1880, 1931, and 1983. The most recent sovereign default in that region was in Dominica in 2003.[30]

Risk is measured in terms of probability, expected impact, and standard errors. Thus, Economic Capital is the difference between a given percentile of a loss distribution and the expected loss. It is sometimes referred to as the unexpected loss at the 99.97 percent confidence level. That means a 3 in 10,000 probability of the bank becoming insolvent during the next 12 months. It is important to recognize that measures of economic capital will vary from bank to bank and over time as conditions change. Exhibit 19.4 illustrates the concept of economic capital.

In March 2007, the Basel Committee on Banking Supervision gave its Risk Management and Modeling Group the mandate to assess the range of practices for measuring economic capital.[31] The areas of potential emphasis include:

- New measurement approaches for credit risk.
- Diversification effects.
- Complex counterparty credit risks.
- Interest rate risk.
- Firms' approaches to validation of internal capital assessments.[32]

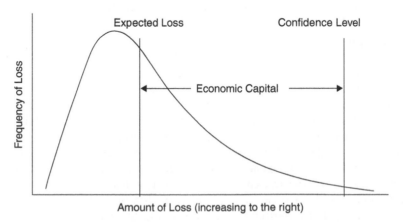

Exhibit 19.4   Economic Capital
Source: Robert L. Burns. (2004) "Economic Capital and the Assessment of Capital Adequacy," *Supervisory Insights*, FDIC, Winter.

In theory, economic capital sounds good. In practice,

> the Federal Reserve conducted a review across a number of large banking organizations to assess these firms' use of so-called "economic capital" practices, which are a means for firms to calculate, for internal purposes, their capital needs given their risk profile. Consistent with other findings, we found that some banks relied too extensively on the output of internal models, not viewing model output with appropriate skepticism. Models are dependent on the data used to construct them. When data histories are short or are drawn mostly from periods of benign economic conditions, model results may not be fully applicable to an institution's risk profile. We concluded that banks would generally benefit from better evaluation of inputs used in their internal capital models, stronger validation of their models, and broader use of stress testing and scenario analysis to supplement the inherent limitations of their models.[33]

CONCLUSION

Globalization in banking is here to stay and it raises issues for banks and bank regulators throughout the world. In order to have a level playing field for banks, the Basel Committee on Banking Supervision established Basel I with an 8 percent risk-based capital ratio. As previously noted, bank capital ratios in more than 150 countries had minimum required capital ratios ranged from 4 percent to 20 percent.[34] One has to question the value of an international capital standard that requires less capital than the banks are holding now. On the other side of the coin, one consequence of banks having to increase their capital ratios may be a reduction of lending. For example, U.S. banks trying to meet the Basel I standards contributed to the credit crunch of the early 1990s.[35]

As previously noted, Basel II is a work in progress and needs an increased emphasis on ERM. In June 2007, Nout Wellink, Chairman of the Basel Committee on Banking Supervision, said "One example is Basel II's *greater focus on firms' risk management infrastructure.* For instance, the Framework requires fundamental improvement in the data supporting PD (probability of default), LGD (loss given default), and EAD (estimated exposure at default) estimates that underpin economic and regulatory capital assessments over an economic cycle. This has spurred improvements in areas such as data collection and management information systems. These advances, along with the incentives to improve risk management practices, will support further innovation and improvement in risk management and *economic capital modelling.*"[36]

Generally speaking, regulators treat banking as a single line of business or a "silo" approach for capital adequacy where credit risk is the dominant concern. However, LCBOs have diverse lines of business such as asset management, data processing, investment banking, and life insurance, which all face distinctly different risks. Equally important, the basic business model of banking is changing for the larger banks from acquiring deposits and making loans to acquiring deposits and distributing loans via securitization.

ERM uses a "building block" approach to aggregate the risks from all lines of business. Along this line, ERM takes into account the benefits of diversification that are usually greatest when dealing with a single line of business, such as credit risk. It tends to diminish across different lines of business.[37]

Because of the complexity associated with ERM and economic capital for individual banks, it is difficult to align interests across countries and between institutions. Thus, estimating economic capital is an ongoing process because banks will have continuously changing levels of economic capital reflecting changing business cycles, differences in foreign exchange rates, and other factors.

Economic capital makes more sense than an arbitrary 8 percent regulatory capital—no matter how it is calculated. However, in the interest of having a level playing field globally, it is important that the amount of economic capital be equal to or greater than the regulatory capital required in Basel II. Economic capital must be "forward looking," and based on expected scenarios instead of recent history.

The recent subprime crisis makes it clear that our largest banks and financial institutions do not have adequate risk management as evidenced by problems with Citigroup and Bear Stearns. Along this line, unexpected losses at Citigroup, UBS, Barclays, and other large banks required large injections of equity capital. Equally important, models employing economic capital are subject to large errors. The headlines of an article in the *Wall Street Journal* (Hadas, April 7, 2008) read "Seduced by Moral hazard: Low rates, weak oversight lured bankers and traders, but many easily tempted." Similarly, the front page of *Fortune* magazine (April 14, 2008) said "Bankers fell victim to their love of risk, leverage, and high pay."[38] Stated otherwise, banks overvalued their financial rewards and underestimated the risks associated with complex debt obligations. Asset bubbles are hard to detect until after they have burst.

Finally, Standard & Poor's announced that the quality of ERM by large, internationally active corporations is one of the factors that it will take into account in assigning corporate ratings.[39] These ratings, in turn, will affect each bank's cost of capital, which is an important aspect of a bank's capital strategy.

NOTES

1. Berger et al. (1995).
2. Ferguson (December 2, 2003).
3. FDIC Annual Report, 2001, 86.
4. Bank Holding Company Act of 1956, Gramm-Leach Bliley Act of 1999.
5. Richard J. Rosen (2007), "The Role of Securitization in Mortgage Lending," *Chicago Fed Letter*, no. 244, November.
6. For information on Too-Big-To-Fail and government intervention see B. Gup, (2004). *Too Big To Fail, Policies and Practices in Government Bailouts* (Westport, CT: Praeger).
7. Tier 2 is limited to no more than 100 percent of Tier 1 capital.
8. Wessel (2007).
9. Estrella (1995).
10. History of the Eighties-Lessons for the Future (1998), Washington, DC, FDIC, vol. 1, 57.
11. In 1997, regulators added an "S" to CAMEL. "S" stands for sensitivity. For additional information about CAMEL, see Curry, et al., 2003.
12. History of the Eighties-Lessons for the Future (1998), op. cit., 80.
13. FDIC Quarterly Banking Profile (2008). Full Year 2007, Table III-A.
14. For further discussion of capital levels, see Berger et al., 2007, and Carlson, 2007, A47, A48.

15. Lindgren et al. (1996), Table 3, Gup (1998).

16. Dziobak (1988).

17. Wellink (February 2007).

18. For more information about Basel I, see B. Gup. (2004) *The New Basel Capital Accord* (New York: Thomson/Texere).

19. See B. Gup (2005).

20. FDIC (2005), "Supervisory Insights," Winter.

21. S. Bair (2007).

22. Board of Governors of the Federal Reserve System (2007).

23. FDIC Press Release (2008), "FDIC Board Approves Basel II-Based Standardized Approach Capital Proposal as an Alternative to the Current Rules," (June 26).

24. See Financial Accounting Standards Board (2007), "Summary of Statement No. 157. Fair Value Measurements," Financial Accounting Standards Board (2007), Summary of Statement No. 159, "The Fair Value Option for Financial Assets and Liabilities—including and amendment to FASB Statement No. 115."

25. Bair, S. (2008). Statement by Sheila C. Bair, Chairman, Federal Deposit Insurance Corporation on the State of the Banking Industry; Part II before the Committee on Banking, Housing and Urban Affairs, June 5.

26. FDIC Press Release (2008), "Interagency Statement—U.S. Implementation of Basel II Advanced Approaches," PR-55-208, July 7. The advanced approaches apply to banks with $250 billion or more consolidated assets, $10 billion or more on-balance sheet foreign exposure, or that are a parent or subsidiary of a bank using the advanced approaches.

27. "Enterprise Risk Management-Integrated Framework, Executive Summery," (2004) Committee of Sponsoring Organizations of the Treadway Commission.

28. For further discussion see R. Burns, (2004).

29. "Risk Based Capital," (2007).

30. Hatchondo, et al. (2007).

31. "Basel Committee Newsletter No. 11," (2007).

32. Ibid.

33. Kohn (2008).

34. Barth, Caprio, and Levine (2006).

35. Brealey (2006).

36. Wellink (June 27, 2007).

37. Kuritzkes, et al. (2002).

38. For the full article see Tully (2008).

39. "Standard & Poor's To Apply Enterprise Risk Analysis to Corporate Ratings," (2008).

REFERENCES

All-bank statistics, United States, 1896–1955 (1959). Washington, D.C., Board of Governors of the Federal Reserve System, Table B1, 53.

Bair, S. 2007. Remarks by Sheila C. Bair, Chairman, Federal Deposit Insurance Corporation, before the Global Association of Risk Professionals; New York City, February 26.

Bair, S. (2008). Remarks by Sheila C. Bair, Chairman, Federal Deposit Insurance Corporation, before the Global Association of Risk Professionals; New York City, February 25.

Bair, S. (2008). Statement by Sheila C. Bair, Chairman, Federal Deposit Insurance Corporation on the State of the Banking Industry; Part II before the Committee on Banking, Housing and Urban Affairs, June 5.

Barth, J. G., Caprio, Jr., and R. Levine. 2006. *Rethinking bank regulation, till angels govern.* New York: Cambridge University Press.

Barth, M. 2004. Fair values and financial statement volatility, appears in *The market discipline across countries and industries*, edited by C. Borio, W. Hunter, G. Kaufman, and K. Tsatsaronis. Cambridge, MA: MIT Press.

Basel Committee Newsletter No. 11. 2007. Progress on Basel II implementation, new workstreams and outreach. Bank for International Settlements, May.

Berger, A., R. Herring, and G. Szego. 1995. The role of capital in financial institutions. *Journal of Banking and Finance* 19, 393–440.

Berger, A., R. DeYoung, and M. Flannery. 2007. Why do large banking organizations hold so much capital? Presented at the Federal Reserve Bank of Chicago, Bank Structure Conference, May.

Bies, S. 2007. Remarks by Governor Susan Schmidt Bies. An update on Basel II implementation in the United States. Presented at the Global Association of Risk Professionals Basel II Summit, New York, February 26.

Bies, S. 2006. Remarks by Governor Susan Schmidt Bies—A supervisory perspective of enterprise risk management, October 17.

Board of Governors of the Federal Reserve System. 2007. Banking agencies reach agreement on Basel II implementation. Joint Press Release, July 20.

Brealey, R. 2006. Basel II: The route ahead or cul-de-sac? *Journal of Applied Corporate Finance,* Fall, 34–43.

Burhouse, S., J. Field, G. French, and K. Ligon. 2003. Basel and the evolution of capital regulation: Moving forward and looking back. An update on emerging issues in banking, FDIC, February 13.

Burns, R. 2004. Economic capital and the assessment of capital adequacy. *Supervisory Insights,* FDIC, Winter.

Carlson, M., and G. Weinbach. 2007. Profits and balance sheet developments at U.S. commercial banks in 2006. *Federal Reserve Bulletin,* July, A37–A71.

Curry, T., P. Elmer, and G. Fissel. 2003. Using market information to help identify distressed institutions: A regulatory perspective. *FDIC Banking Review,* September.

Dziobak, C. and C. Pazarbasioglu. 1988. Lessons from systemic bank restructuring. *Economic Issues,* no. 14. International Monetary Fund, May.

Enterprise risk management-integrated framework, executive summary. 2004. Committee of Sponsoring Organizations of the Treadway Commission.

Estrella, A. 1995. A prolegomenon to future capital requirements. *Economic Policy Review,* Federal Reserve Bank of New York, July, 1–12.

FDIC Annual Report, 2001. 2002. Washington, D.C., FDIC.

FDIC Press Release. 2008, FDIC board approves Basel II-based standardized approach capital proposal as an alternative to the current rules. June 26.

FDIC Press Release. 2008. Interagency statement—U.S. implementation of Basel II advanced approaches. PR-55–208, July 7.

FDIC Quarterly Banking Profile. 2008. Full Year 2007, Table III-A. FDIC-Insured Commercial Banks.

FDIC. 2005. Supervisory insights. *Winter.*

Ferguson, R. Jr. 2003. Remarks by Vice Chairman Roger W. Ferguson Jr., at the ICBI Risk Management Conference, Geneva, Switzerland, December 2.

Ferguson, R. Jr. 2003. Testimony of Vice Chairman Roger W. Ferguson Jr., Basel II, before the Committee on Banking, Housing, and Urban Affairs, U.S. Senate, June 18.

Financial Accounting Standards Board. 2007. Summary of statement No. 157. Fair value measurements.

Financial Accounting Standards Board. 2007. Summary of statement No. 159. The fair value option for financial assets and liabilities—including an amendment to FASB statement No. 115.

Gup, B. 1998. *Bank failures in the major trading countries of the world: Causes and remedies.* Westport, CT: Quorum Books.

Gup, B. 2004. *The new Basel capital accord.* New York: Thomson/Texere.

Gup, B. 2004. *Too big to fail: Policies and practices in government bailouts.* Westport, CT: Praeger.

Gup, B. 2005. Capital games. Appears in Benton E. Gup, *Capital markets, globalization, and economic development.* New York: Springer Science, Chapter 3.

Gup, B., and T. Lutton. 2008. Potential effects of fair value accounting on U.S. bank regulatory capital. Working Paper.

Hadas, E. 2008. Seduced by moral hazard: Low rates, weak oversight lured bankers and traders, but many easily tempted. *Wall Street Journal,* April 7, C12.

Hatchando, J., L. Martinez, and H. Sapriza. 2007. The economics of sovereign defaults. *Economic Quarterly,* Federal Reserve Bank of Richmond, Spring, 163–187.

History of the eighties—lessons for the future. 1998. Washington, D.C., FDIC, vol. 1.

Kohn, Donald L. 2008. Vice Chairman, Federal Reserve, Risk management and its implications for systemic risk. Before the Subcommittee on Securities, Insurance, and Investment, Committee on Banking, Housing, and Urban Affairs, U.S. Senate, June 19.

Kroszner, R. 2007. Remarks by Governor Randall S. Kroszner at the New York Bankers Association Annual Washington Visit, Washington, D.C. "Basel II Implementation in the United States," July 12.

Kuritzkes, A., T. Schuermann, and S. Weiner. 2002. Risk measurement, risk management and capital adequacy in financial conglomerates. Wharton School Center for Financial Institutions. Working Paper 03–02.

Lindgren, C., G. Garcia, and M. Saal. 1996. *Bank soundness and macroeconomic policy.* Washington, D.C., International Monetary Fund.

Risk based capital. 2007. United States Government Accountability Office, GAO-070253, February.

Rosen, Richard J. 2007. The role of securitization in mortgage lending. *Chicago Fed Letter,* no. 244. November.

Standard & Poor's to apply enterprise risk analysis to corporate ratings. 2008. Standard & Poor's Ratings Direct, May 7. www.standardandpoors.com/ratingsdirect.

Statistical Abstract of the United States 1989. 1990. Washington, D.C., U.S. Census Bureau.

Statistical Abstract of the United States 1993. 1994. Washington, D.C., U.S. Census Bureau.

Statistical Abstract of the United States 2001. 2002. Washington, D.C., U.S. Census Bureau.

Statistical Abstract of the United States 2008. 2009. Washington, D.C., U.S. Census Bureau (forthcoming).

Tully, S. 2008. What's wrong with Wall St., and how to fix it. *Fortune,* April 14, 71–76.

Wellink, N. 2007. Risk management & financial stability—Basel II & beyond. Remarks by Dr. Wellink, Chairman of the Basle Committee on Banking Supervision, at GARP 2007 8th Annual Risk Management Conference, New York, February 27.

Wellink, N. 2007. Basel II and financial institution resiliency. Remarks by Dr. Nout Wellink, President of the Netherlands Bank and Chairman of the Basel Committee on Banking Supervision, at the Risk Capital 2007 conference, Paris, June 27.

Wessel, D. 2007. Revised bank rules help spread woes *Wall Street Journal,* September 20, A7.

World's Best Banks. 2007. Annual Survey, Global Finance, October, 80.

ABOUT THE AUTHOR

Dr. Benton E. Gup has a broad background in finance. His undergraduate and graduate degrees are from the University of Cincinnati. After receiving his PhD in economics, he served as a staff economist for the Federal Reserve Bank of

Cleveland. He currently holds the Robert Hunt Cochrane/Alabama Bankers Association Chair of Banking at the University of Alabama, Tuscaloosa, Alabama. He also held banking chairs at the University of Virginia and the University of Tulsa. He worked in bank research for the Office of the Comptroller of the Currency while on sabbatical.

He is an internationally known lecturer in executive development and graduate programs in Australia (University of Melbourne, University of Technology, Sydney, Monash University, Melbourne), New Zealand (University of Auckland), Peru (University of Lima), and South Africa (Graduate School of Business Leadership). He has been a visiting researcher at the Bank of Japan, and at Macquarie University, Sydney, Australia. Finally, he lectured in Austria, Brazil, Greece, Morocco, and Tunisia on current economic topics for the U.S. Department of State, and served as a consultant to the IMF in Uruguay.

Dr. Gup is the author or editor of the following 28 books: *The Valuation Handbook: Valuation Techniques from Today's Top Practitioners* (with Rawley Thomas, Forthcoming), *Handbook for Directors of Financial Institutions* (2008); *Corporate Governance in Banking: A Global Perspective* (2007); *Money Laundering, Financing Terrorism, and Suspicious Activity* (2007), *Capital Market, Globalization, and Economic Development* (2005); *Commercial Banking: The Management of Risk*, 3rd. ed., (with J. Kolari, 2005); *The New Basel Capital Accord* (2004); *Too-Big-To-Fail: Policies and Practices in Government Bailouts* (2004); *Investing Online* (2003); *The Future of Banking* (2003); *Megamergers in a Global Economy—Causes and Consequences* (2002); *The New Financial Architecture: Banking Regulation in the 21st Century* (2000); *Commercial Bank Management*, 2nd ed. (with D. Fraser and J. Kolari); *International Banking Crises; Bank Failures in the Major Trading Countries of the World; The Bank Director's Handbook; Targeting Fraud; Interest Rate Risk Management* (with R. Brooks); *The Basics of Investing*, 5th ed.; *Bank Fraud: Exposing the Hidden Threat to Financial Institutions; Bank Mergers; Cases in Bank Management* (with C. Meiburg); *Principles of Financial Management; Financial Institutions; Financial Intermediaries; Personal Investing: A Complete Guide; Guide to Strategic Planning; and How to Ask for a Business Loan.*

Dr. Gup's articles on financial subjects have appeared in *The Journal of Finance, The Journal of Financial and Quantitative Analysis, The Journal of Money, Credit, and Banking, Financial Management, The Journal of Banking and Finance, Financial Analysts Journal*, and elsewhere.

CHAPTER 20

Legal Risk Post-SOX and the Subprime Fiasco

Back to the Drawing Board

STEVEN A. RAMIREZ
Director, Business & Corporate Governance Law Center, Loyola University Chicago

INTRODUCTION

Enterprise-wide risk management (ERM) views all risks to the firm as subject to management and control. Legal risk management is certainly no exception. Indeed, this chapter is premised on the principle that legal risk is simply one of many types of risk facing a firm. This necessarily means that like other risks legal risk should be managed in accordance with basic notions of risk management generally—that it should not exist within a risk "silo" but should be managed with a view toward the firm's overall risk tolerance and through coordinated efforts of senior management, including the board (Simkins and Ramirez 2008). Therefore, ERM includes consideration of the optimal means of managing legal risk.

After the revelation of widespread fraud and illegality within American public companies in late 2001 and 2002, leading to the failure of such major firms as Enron and WorldCom, Congress enacted the Sarbanes-Oxley Act of 2002 (SOX). SOX pre-empted state rules of professional responsibility governing attorneys and imposed federal standards for those representing public companies. SOX also prompted the SEC to create a new mechanism for the management of legal compliance (the Qualified Legal Compliance Committee or QLCC) within public corporations in the United States. SOX completely reworked the regulation of the audit function. It further encouraged firms to impose codes of conduct as a means of assuring ethical conduct. Finally, it promulgated new statutory provisions giving whistle-blowers expanded protections from retaliation. Thus, SOX paved the way for a more optimal legal and reputational risk management mechanism within the public company. In particular, the Commission's QLCC innovation may prove to be an "invaluable" corporate governance organ for the management and reduction of legal and reputational risk, if properly structured and managed (Volz and Tazian 2006).

The subprime mortgage fiasco posed the first major test of this new regime. Unfortunately, it does not appear that the SOX framework effectively reduced legal and reputational risk to an optimal level. Firms that originated subprime

mortgages like Countrywide Financial faced allegations of predatory lending leading to multibillion dollar settlements with state authorities. Firms that securitized
such mortgages like Goldman Sachs were sued for fraud in connection with the
packaging of mortgages to investors throughout the world. In testimony before
Congress, the rating agencies admitted that their ratings had a questionable basis
(text message records produced to Congress showed a ratings agency employee
stating: "we would rate a deal structured by a cow") and that the quest for revenue
outweighed the need to provide accurate information to the investors (Paletta and
Scannell 2009). Citigroup was forced to repurchase billions in subprime mortgage
instruments pursuant to contractual obligations that were not even disclosed to
senior management or the board, much less public shareholders, and Merrill Lynch
settled securities fraud claims for more than $500 million (S. Ramirez 2009). Ul-
timately each of these firms faced major restructurings and inflicted precipitous
losses upon their shareholders. As of the end of 2008, the macroeconomic consequences of this massive mismanagement of legal and reputational risk continued
to unwind, but had aggregated to a multitrillion dollar debacle.

Legal and reputational risk can take many forms, beyond losses from lawsuits
or criminal and regulatory penalties. Prior to the subprime fiasco, firms like Texaco
suffered huge shareholder losses and consumer boycotts as a result of disclosure of
apparent violations of antidiscrimination laws (S. Ramirez 2000). A large number
of firms used backdated options to illegally enhance the compensation of their executives that led to huge shareholder losses when this practice was disclosed to the
investing public (Ramirez 2007). In the lead up to the passage of Sarbanes-Oxley a
slew of firms suffered adverse financial consequences from disclosure of auditing
irregularities (S. Ramirez 2002). Finally, there is growing movement toward social
investing, which suggests that a firm's cost of capital may increase if its conduct
is found to be legal but morally questionable; assets under management in so-
called social investment funds grew 18 percent from 2005 to 2007 to $2.7 trillion
(Social Investment Forum 2007). Firms, therefore, face a myriad of risks from legal
noncompliance, and associated irregularities that can harm a firm's ability to inspire investor confidence, to protect shareholders from undisclosed legal liabilities,
to maximize consumer market penetration, and to avoid regulatory sanctions or
scrutiny.

This chapter reviews the legal and regulatory framework currently governing
the efforts of public corporations to control and mitigate legal and reputational risk.
Next, this chapter assesses the shortcomings of this regime, focusing on the recent
meltdown in global financial markets arising from subprime mortgages that too
often were originated, packaged, and sold to investors worldwide in illegal and inappropriate ways. Finally, this chapter articulates a more efficacious means of controlling reputational and legal risk, both at the firm level and in terms of a superior
legal framework. In short, the subprime fiasco sheds light on the nature of legal and
reputational risk, and provides lessons for the proper management of these risks.

THE LEGAL FRAMEWORK OF LEGAL AND
REPUTATIONAL RISK MANAGEMENT

Prior to SOX, there was little substance to the law governing legal and reputational
risk management. In general, the rules of professional responsibility governing

lawyers were flawed, corporate law was stunted, whistle-blowing was not encouraged, codes of conduct were wholly optional, and there was insufficient regulation of the audit function.

There were scattered legal provisions governing whistle-blower protection, but these protections were too complex and difficult to predict to encourage much whistle-blowing, and the best advice an attorney could give a putative whistleblower was to refrain from blowing the whistle. According to Professor Mary Ramirez:

> *Whistleblower protection has evolved in response to specific breakdowns in law enforcement over time. Instead of a tightly woven blanket, the evolution has yielded a porous net of protections that is complex and non-intuitive; under current protections, being a whistleblower requires bearing costs and risks. Two key considerations tend to arise for employees faced with this decision of stepping forward: First, will coming forward with the information change the status quo and fix the problem; and second, will they be protected from a destroyed career, financial ruin, and, perhaps, physical threat. Given the stakes, the only sound course of action for a putative whistleblower is to get a lawyer.[1]*

Naturally, this limits the universe of whistle-blowers to the ill-informed and those with enough money to make substantial expenditures, in order to enforce legal and ethical obligations upon firms.

Similarly, attorneys have few incentives to blow the whistle on their clients. The Model Rules of Professional Responsibility do not even mandate an attorney representing a corporation to alert its management that wrongdoing is afoot, unless they "know" there had been a violation of law. Of course, "[l]awyers never 'know' their client is committing a crime" (Koniak 2003). Furthermore, corporate illegality could not be disclosed to authorities unless it threatened "substantial bodily harm." However, "lawyers will have strong economic incentives to please the managers of their current or potential clients by refraining from reporting, even if their inaction allows questionable activity to go unchecked" (*Harvard Law Review* 2004). Thus, prior to SOX, much illegality was not detected, and even if an attorney had notice of possible illegal conduct that could prove harmful to a firm's shareholders, the attorney could remain silent rather than risk alienating important corporate agents.

No law required any corporate code of conduct for public companies. Professor Cynthia Williams argued in 1999 that the SEC was incorrect to maintain its position, heralding from the 1970s, that matters of social responsibility were not material to the business of the public corporation, and therefore did not require any disclosure in a firm's securities filings. She demonstrated the potential financial consequences of questionable corporate behavior and the increasing interest of investors in the approach of firms to questions of corporate ethics (Williams 1999). Nevertheless, it took the corporate corruption crises of the turn of the twenty-first century to prompt congress to change the SEC's position.

With respect to corporate governance law and regulation, Delaware law (the most influential jurisdiction in terms of corporate law) permits a high degree of flexibility in the structure of corporate governance with few legal mandates insofar as legal and reputational risk management is concerned. Given the excessive CEO influence over corporate governance constraints (such as autonomy over the selection of directors and control over the proxy machinery) that marks American corporate governance law (S. Ramirez 2007), it should come as no surprise that CEOs are risk silos for legal and reputational risk management. The CEO, however, is not institutionally suited for exclusive management of legal and reputation risk, just as the CEO really is not the optimal manager of the audit function. As will be discussed, SOX stripped the CEO of control over the audit. The same cannot be said of the legal function. Perhaps the prime lesson of the subprime fiasco is that incentives matter, and too often CEOs face compensation incentives that encourage the deferral of substantial risks in order maximize current profitability and thus compensation (Rajan 2007). Moreover, the CEO is not required to have any particular expertise in the management of legal and associated reputational risk, or in the communication of that risk to the board or to shareholders. The outcome of this regime is likely to be too much legal and reputational risk, with inadequate transparency to investors. Finally, Delaware law imposes little sanction on management for failure to detect and prevent illegal conduct, as it has effectively abolished duty of care liability for directors; directors will not be held liable so long as they exercise good faith (Sale 2007).

The federal securities laws (prior to SOX) required the disclosure of all material facts concerning a public firm, and mandated that the auditors of public firms build in measures to ferret out illegal conduct as part of their audit, at least to the extent illegal conduct could have a material effect on the firm's financial condition (Backer 2003). Nevertheless, private enforcement of the securities laws has been hopelessly restricted (S. Ramirez 1999), and the SEC generally has insufficient resources to enforce the securities laws effectively. Recent revelations regarding a massive Ponzi scheme operated within a firm regulated by the SEC have painfully illustrated once again the limits on public enforcement of the securities laws due to resource constraints. Further, not all illegal conduct will be detected within the audit process (Orol 2008). Consequently, the federal securities regime has not been effective in assuring that illegal conduct is detected and disclosed to shareholders.

SOX changed this regime, at least with respect to public companies, in four important ways: (1) SOX preempted state regulation of attorneys representing public firms (to a limited extent, at least) and mandated a new regime for reporting violations of certain laws to senior management as well as to the SEC; (2) SOX revamped audit regulation; (3) SOX expanded whistle-blower protections; (4) SOX encouraged firms to impose codes of conduct. Each of these changes means that the detection of wrongdoing is more likely, and that detection should be sooner than under the preexisting regime.

As such, SOX represented a revolution in the legal framework governing legal and reputational risk management. Unfortunately, this revolution has been incomplete if not aborted. SOX only applies to public firms. The most innovative elements of the SOX regime are optional and the vast majority of firms have declined to adopt its institutional reforms. One effort of the SEC to enhance reports of wrongdoing within the public firm never became law. Overall, the SOX initiative and the SEC's implementation of that initiative are suboptimal.

Nevertheless, this chapter attempts to articulate an optimized legal and reputational risk management regime within the context of U.S. corporate governance law, building upon the SOX framework, and the flaws within that framework as revealed by the subprime debacle.

The Federal Rules of Professional Responsibility for Attorneys

The most important element of SOX reform insofar as legal risk management is concerned relate to the exercise of federal power to govern the professional responsibility of certain counsel representing issuers of publicly traded securities. There has long been hope that corporate counsel could act to protect their client from the often severe financial losses accompanying illegal conduct. Historically counsel has been hobbled by their financial dependence on corporate managers who are often involved in wrongdoing and are always wary of having an attorney second-guess business judgment (Henning 2004). The SEC regulations promulgated under SOX create an important new innovation that may operate to enhance the ability of public companies to manage and reduce legal and reputational risk.

Overview and Introduction

Section 307 of SOX required the SEC to promulgate regulations applicable to attorneys "appearing or practicing before the Commission" on behalf of public companies. Congress specified that the SEC issue regulations providing that attorneys report certain "material violations" of certain laws to senior management and monitor the response of management. As such, congress has supplemented state regulation of counsel's obligations to report legal violations within the public corporation. This authority to regulate "minimum standards of professional conduct for attorneys" represented the first substantial federal regulation of the standards of professional conduct for attorneys.

The SEC issued Part 205 of its regulations to implement this congressional directive, and these regulations became effective on August 3, 2003. As a threshold matter, the SEC defined certain elements of the statute. For example, in Section 205.2 the Commission broadly defined attorneys "appearing or practicing before the commission" to include any attorney advising a public company with respect to filings pursuant to the federal securities laws or with respect to information that may be included in any public filing. The comments to the rules suggest that any attorney responding to an audit letter would be with the ambit of Part 205. Naturally, in the absence of judicial authority counsel for public firms should presume they are within the scope of the SEC's rules.

Attorneys within the scope of Part 205 are obliged to act when the attorney has "credible evidence, based upon which it would be unreasonable, under the circumstances for a prudent and competent attorney not to conclude that it is reasonably likely that a material violation has occurred." Stripped of the double negative, it appears that if the attorney has credible evidence that reasonably supports that a violation has occurred, the rules are triggered. Credible evidence means evidence that does not include gossip, hearsay, or innuendo, according to the SEC's comments accompanying the release of its rules.

Section 205.2 also defines "material violation" to include either a material violation of the federal securities laws or state securities law, or a material breach of fiduciary duty under state or federal law. The SEC also defined "similar" legal violations to be "material violations." There is no substantive means for determining when a legal or regulatory violation is similar to a securities law violation or a breach of federal or state fiduciary duty—presumably common law fraud, consumer fraud, and negligent misrepresentation would qualify as "similar" under the statute. The SEC did not define the term "material," but case law under the federal securities laws measures materiality by whether a reasonable investor would want such information in making an investment decision.

The ambiguity and uncertainty in the definition of "material violation" is troubling because the two primary obligations of attorneys under the SEC's rules (specifically delineated in Section 205.3) are triggered by an attorney having "credible evidence" that would lead a "prudent and competent attorney" to conclude that it is "reasonably likely" a material violation has occurred. The first obligation is to report material violations to the chief legal officer or to the chief legal officer and the chief executive officer. The second obligation is to monitor the response of those officers and if the response is found not to be "appropriate" then the attorney must notify the board of directors.

The SEC also authorized (under Section 205.3) attorneys practicing and appearing before the Commission to report material violations to the SEC, without violating state confidentiality standards, so long as the attorney reasonably believes that disclosure to the SEC is necessary to prevent a material violation that would harm the public corporation or the investing public; that disclosure is necessary to prevent perjury or fraud on the Commission; and that disclosure is necessary to rectify a material violation the attorney furthered. The regulation suggests such reporting to the SEC is optional; however, counsel should be aware that the failure to report a material violation that subsequently leads to losses to the public company could well form the basis of a malpractice claim. Counsel may assume that expert testimony would be available to support claims that if counsel fails to notify the SEC of a material violation that harms the corporate-client, the attorney has breached common law duties.

The Qualified Legal Compliance Committee

The new federal rules of professional responsibility imposed under SOX create two risks for counsel of public companies. First, the rules put counsel in the uncomfortable position of monitoring the response of senior management to any report of a material violation. Second, the rules authorize disclosures to the SEC whether or not counsel finds management's response to be appropriate, raising the specter of a potential malpractice claim. Both of these risks can be eliminated through an innovation of the SEC—the qualified legal compliance committee.

Under Section 205.2(k), a qualified legal compliance committee (QLCC) is a committee of the board, which includes at least one member of the audit committee and at least two members of the board not otherwise employed by the public company. The QLCC must be empowered to receive reports of material violations and to determine if an investigation of the report is warranted. The QLCC must be authorized to hire outside attorneys and experts to assist and reports its activities to the full board or the audit committee. The QLCC recommends an appropriate response to the report of material violation or its investigation, and to recommend any remedial measures based on its conclusions. The QLCC may also report its findings to the SEC if its recommendations are ignored.

The advantage of the QLCC is that under Section 205.3(c) a counsel working for a public firm need not monitor the firm's response to a report of evidence of a material violation. A report to the QLCC discharges the attorney's duties under the SEC's rules. Moreover, since the QLCC has the power to pursue any report and even report its findings to the SEC, it is difficult to imagine an attorney having exposure to malpractice liability for reporting to the QLCC instead of making a report to the SEC. Thus, firms with a QLCC can expect counsel to perceive less risk in representation versus firms without QLCCs because of these advantages.

The QLCC also remedies certain deficiencies within the SEC's rules of professional responsibility for lawyers. Early on commentators identified key weaknesses in the SEC's approach. For example, the SEC's approach did not create any true whistle-blowers because attorneys will rarely find it in their interest to blow the whistle on their corporate agents; indeed, it would be difficult to imagine that a whistle-blowing lawyer would find many future clients at all. Similarly, lawyers may well report violations up the ladder to corporate managers, but this will not usually disrupt illegal transactions where senior management or the board is complicit in wrongdoing or simply refuses to confront wrongdoing (*Harvard Law Review* 2004). The QLCC, on the other hand, has both the power to stop wrongdoing, by notifying either the full board or (in a worst-case scenario) the SEC. Additionally, the QLCC has the incentive to disrupt wrongdoing, in order to avoid director liability as well as SEC sanction. Therefore, the QLCC is a superior means of stemming legal and reputational risks. As will be discussed below, the QLCC can be further optimized by a public firm, so long as it meets the minimum requirements set forth by the SEC.

Yet, a QLCC remains optional. Surveys suggest that only a small percentage of public firms have opted for QLCCs. According to Rosen (2005), 96 percent of NYSE listed firms opted not to use a QLCC as of late 2005. Nonpublic firms are not even subject to the SEC's professional responsibility regulation, and are thus unlikely to have QLCCs. There seems to be sound arguments for concluding that QLCCs are a corporate governance best practice and that they are likely to enhance legal compliance and lower outside counsel fees (Lipman and Lipman 2006). It appears that firms resist the QLCC despite its clear benefits.

Whistle-Blower Protection Under Sox

Congress has long appreciated that sound law enforcement regimes encourage whistle-blowing. Thus, Section 806 of SOX grants employees of public firms limited whistle-blower protection from retaliation. An employee is protected if the employee provides information regarding conduct that the employee reasonably believes violates the federal securities laws (or wire fraud, mail fraud, or bank fraud prohibitions); to a supervisor, federal agency, or a congressional committee investigation; and the employee seeks relief (before the Department of Labor) within 90 days of the retaliation. If the employee prevails, the employee may seek reinstatement, back pay, and litigation costs. Section 1107 of SOX provides that anyone who interferes with a person providing truthful information to a federal law enforcement agent shall be subject to fine or imprisonment of not more than 10 years.

Far more employees seek protection under the SOX whistle-blower provisions than the number found to be within SOX protection. As of mid-2006, 702 petitioners sought protection and 499 claims for protection had been dismissed. In the first 27 months following the enactment of the SOX whistle-blower protection, the Department of Labor dismissed more than 95 percent of claims. Thus, it is clear that many employees expect to be protected but are not. It seems likely that the SOX whistle-blower provision protecting employees is not functioning to encourage employees to blow the whistle on wrongdoing; it almost certainly is insufficient to overcome the powerful social mores against being a "snitch" or "rat." One scholar has suggested that an omnibus statute is needed to grant broad protection to any person blowing the whistle on any wrongful conduct to any government authority or any authority within the corporation (M. Ramirez 2007). Another has suggested a system of monetary rewards for whistle-blowers (Dworkin 2007). Assuring anonymity also could encourage more whistle-blowing, and this will be addressed in the context of audit committee reform under SOX.

Audit Reform

Many commentators and policy makers identified audit failure as the prime cause of the corporate crises of 2001–2002. SOX consequently reconfigured the audit function of the public firm. In addition to an entirely new regulatory structure over the public audit industry (the Public Company Accounting Oversight Board), the SOX mandated an independent audit committee for every public firm; required each such committee to have at least one financial expert; vested power over the audit function in the audit committee (and removed that function from the scope of CEO authority); and required the audit committee to create procedures for the receipt and investigation of whistle-blowing complaints relating to audit and accounting matters (Section 301).

On this point SOX revolutionized corporate governance. For the first time federal law mandated a corporate governance structure—the independent audit committee—that no state law had ever required. Additionally, the relocation of the audit function from just another management issue under the control of the CEO to an independent board committee represented a breakthrough in rethinking the institutional structure of corporate governance; more specifically, SOX amounted to a determination that the CEO has no particular expertise in the management of the audit function, and is institutionally ill-suited to manage that function because of the incentives the CEO may have to corrupt the audit process. There is simply no reason for the law to permit unbridled CEO autonomy over the audit. This realization is important for thinking about optimal structure for the management of legal and reputational risk.

Codes of Conduct

Much conduct that may not be illegal can nevertheless cast a firm in a negative public light that impedes its ability to maximize shareholder wealth and financial performance. Corporate behavior viewed as unethical is not likely to be costless and there is evidence that there are close links between corporate financial performance and commitment to ethical behavior. Consumers, employees, and investors are not insensitive to ethical business conduct or unethical business conduct (Verschoor 1999). Thus, firms should consider how ethics can inspire consumer and employee loyalty as well as a lower cost of capital. Additionally, a robust culture of ethical behavior is apt to lead to enhanced legal compliance and lower costs in terms of legal sanctions.

Section 406 of SOX requires the SEC to enact regulations providing for the disclosure of whether a public firm has a code of ethics for its financial officers.

The SEC expanded this statutory directive to include executive officers. More importantly, the SEC approved listing requirement rules at both the NYSE and the Nasdaq Marketplace that require listed firms to have a code of ethics, to disclose these codes and to disclose any waivers from these codes. These codes must apply to all directors, officers, and employees (Barclift 2008). The vast majority of public firms have codes of conduct or ethics codes that are publicly disclosed. This disclosure obligation is content-neutral.

Backer (2008) suggests that mere disclosure of ethics codes is sufficient to assure that corporations operate in accordance with community norms as reflected in the decisions of important constituencies such as employees, consumers, suppliers, and investors. Since there is no objective consensus regarding ethical corporate behavior, Backer argues that the market is an appropriate mechanism for setting such standards as it permits economic actors to "effectively impose values upon themselves through their economic decisions." Certainly, Backer is correct that it is difficult to articulate an alternative basis for setting ethical norms, particularly in a globalized economy that spans multiple cultures. It is also difficult to argue that disclosure of corporate behavior and standards is not positive.

Nevertheless, there is clearly more to ethical behavior than that which is embodied in the norms of market decisions. Sometimes markets may find behavior acceptable that is found unacceptable by some authority that is not dominated merely by markets. For example, consider decisions made by German firms during World War II. In particular it is worth noting that 13 IG Farben executives were sentenced at Nuremberg to terms ranging from 18 months to 8 years for using slave labor. German steel magnate Friedrich Flick was sentenced to seven years in prison for seizing foreign factories and using slave labor. Alfried Krup was sentenced to 12 years for similar war crimes (Ehrenfreund 2007). Nuremberg should not be viewed as an aberration, as other firms have faced sanctions as a result of misconduct related to World War II. Indeed, Swiss banks, French banks, and even the Ford Motor Company faced substantial litigation risk and paid settlements that were well in excess of $1 billion, combined, more than 50 years after the conclusion of World War II (Bazyler and Alford 2007).

Perhaps Backer's market-based notion of corporate ethics is presumptively appropriate, so long as management comprehends the cost of short-term market signals being overridden over the long term. The best approach is probably to rely on the market with a strong moral compass to avoid market-based excesses.

AN ASSESSMENT OF THE SOX FRAMEWORK ON LEGAL AND REPUTATIONAL RISK

The SEC created the QLCC from whole cloth. By so doing, it essentially challenged the development of corporate governance law at the state level; the SEC's innovation amounted to an assertion that state corporate governance law was underdeveloped. Yet, as of 2005, Professor Rosen could find only one instance where a QLCC had ever been called into action (Rosen 2005). Moreover, it does not appear that for all the apparent wrongdoing arising from the subprime mortgage crisis, any whistles were blowing. Professor Peter J. Henning predicted that Sarbanes-Oxley would not be effective in encouraging counsel to blow the whistle, and the subprime mortgage shows he was correct (Henning 2004). This section will review the wrongdoing that is emerging in connection with the subprime fiasco and use that review to illustrate the shortcomings of SOX approach insofar as legal and reputational risk management is concerned.

The Subprime Fiasco

As of this writing, the full tale of the subprime crisis remains untold. Still, the picture emerging is one of pervasive illegality, and near illegality. Indeed, every key step in the subprime mortgage process, from origination to securitization, to investment and to the ratings game seems to have been corrupt. This corruption has resulted in billions of payouts already. More will no doubt follow. This section cannot at this date comprehensively summarize the toll of legal and reputational risk arising from the subprime debacle. Others have sought to write a first draft of that history (Bethel, Ferrell, and Hu 2008). Instead this section will simply provide a broad overview in an effort to illustrate the role of legal and reputational risk mismanagement.

The allegations leveled against Countrywide illustrate the kind of corruption present in the origination of subprime mortgages. Both the State of Illinois and the State of California sued Countrywide for predatory and deceptive lending. Ultimately Countrywide agreed with 11 states to modify 400,000 mortgages at a cost of $8.7 billion. Countrywide originated more mortgages than any other lender and originated more subprime mortgages than any other lender. Countrywide allegedly sought to saddle borrowers with unnecessarily costly and risky mortgages in order to enhance cash generated from the sale of those loans into the world's capital markets. Countrywide incentivized its loan officers to sell riskier, more expensive loans. Consequently, the subprime loans that Countrywide originated defaulted at a disproportionately high rate (*Illinois v. Countrywide* 2008). According to the attorney general of the State of Illinois, Lisa Madigan, the multibillion dollar settlement of these allegations: "holds the number-one mortgage lender in the country accountable for deceptively putting borrowers into loans they didn't understand, couldn't afford, and couldn't get out of. These are the very practices that have created the economic crisis we're currently experiencing" (Illinois Attorney General Lisa Madigan 2008). Countrywide essentially engaged in systematic predatory lending that contributed greatly to the crash of the nation's residential real estate market.

The securitization of mortgages has also spawned substantial legal and reputational risks for those selling mortgage-backed securities to investors. Private plaintiffs have already filed suits against investment banks such as Goldman Sachs for disclosure deficiencies under the federal securities laws. The allegations in these suits mirror the allegations against Countrywide, and involve many loans originated by Countrywide:

> *The underwriting, quality control, and due diligence practices and policies utilized in connection with the approval and funding of the mortgage loans were so weak that borrowers were being extended loans based on stated income that could not . . . possibly be reconciled with the jobs claims on the loan application or through a check of free "online" salary databases.*
>
> *—NECA-IBEW Health and Welfare Fund v. Goldman Sachs & Co.* 2008

The City of Cleveland sued 21 investment banks for creating public nuisance caused by massive foreclosures within the City of Cleveland leading to lost property tax revenues and increased costs in dealing with abandoned property (*City of Cleveland v. Deutsche Bank* 2008). It may be some time before the total losses from these kinds of claims is finally tallied, but in all events the risks that firms took with respect to subprime securitizations appear not to have been managed in any rational way. The securitization of mortgages also involved the pervasive mismanagement of legal and reputational risk.

The Congressional testimony and documents produced by representatives from the ratings industry also paints a bleak picture of short-term profits trumping sound legal and reputational risk management. For example, one document produced to the Committee on Oversight and Government Reform was a series of text messages between two representatives of a rating agency:

Official number one.   By the way, that deal is ridiculous.
Official number two.   I know, right, model definitely does not capture half the risk.
Official number one.   We should not be rating it.
Official number two.   We rate every deal. It could be structured by cows, and we would rate it.

Another former senior manager of a rating agency explained "we sold our soul to the devil for revenue" (Committee on Oversight and Government Reform 2008). The rating agencies apparently miscalculated the long-term damage that their cavalier attitude toward risk would inflict on their business. For example, on December 3, 2008, the SEC approved new regulations on the rating agencies; this is not likely to be the last regulatory initiative arising from the agencies' rather suboptimal performance in connection with the subprime fiasco.

Legal risk mismanagement also plagued the investment in subprime-related mortgages. For example, Citigroup, one of the most sophisticated banks in the world, offered investors in certain collateralized debt obligation funds a so-called liquidity put, which obligated Citigroup to repurchase the instruments at cost in the event of specified market disruptions. Citigroup thus ended up with $50 billion in subprime products on its balance sheet without disclosure of this risk to its shareholders or even its own senior management. Amazingly, Robert Rubin, the Chair of Citigroup's Executive Committee was unaware of the liquidity puts (Loomis 2007). AIG specifically told stock analysts in late 2007 that it had "minimal" exposure to subprime mortgages (Villagran 2007). Ultimately, the firm recognized $43 billion in such losses and required a government bailout of $150 billion (Son 2008). Apparently at the time AIG reassured the investing public that it had controlled its risk exposure on subprime assets, its operating subsidiaries were entering into long-term derivatives contracts that led to billions in subprime losses (Loomis 2008).

In sum, poor legal risk management infected all phases of the subprime fiasco, from origination, to securitization, to risk assessment, to investment. Indeed, the full range of legal and reputational risk management, from regulatory risk to litigation risk, proved defective.

The SOX Shortcomings

The SOX regime may have been a step in the right direction. The lesson of the massive mismanagement of legal and reputational risk underlying the subprime fiasco is that much more is needed. There is a strong case that congress should step in and remedy the deficiencies inherent in corporate risk management with respect to law and ethics. Firms wishing to manage these risks can undertake many of these suggestions even without congressional action. The following steps should be taken.

Step 1: The QLCC Should Become Mandatory

Perhaps the most compelling context for a mandatory QLCC for the purpose of managing and reducing legal and reputational risk is the financial services industry. Indeed, the Basel Core Principles for Bank Regulation specifically highlight legal and reputational risks for financial institutions. The Basel statement suggests that legal risk should be thought of as broader than the risk of legal or regulatory violations or outcomes in lawsuits, to include the "the risk that assets will turn out to be worth less or liabilities will turn out to be greater than expected because of inadequate or incorrect legal advice or documentation." This appears to be a perfect description of the risks Citigroup faced under so-called "liquidity puts" relating to subprime mortgage product, leading to that bank being forced to reacquire billions in questionable assets—a risk that not even the Chair of Citigroup's Executive Committee, Robert Rubin, understood. The Basel statement also asserts that banks are uniquely exposed to reputational risk, depending as they do on the confidence of their depositors for their viability.

The Core Principles therefore urge regulators to assure that banks have mechanisms to manage and reduce legal and reputational risk. The Basel statement suggests that policies be "comprehensive" and include "appropriate board and senior management oversight" (Basel Committee on Banking Supervision 1997). The QLCC accomplishes these aspirations by formally involving the board, for the first time in U.S. corporate governance law, in legal compliance across the full range of the public firm's business. In the author's opinion, the QLCC should become mandatory for all firms, particularly financial institutions.

Step 2: The Definition of a Violation Should Be Broader

A firm (and its shareholders) may be harmed by any material violation of law or governing regulation. Further, violations of ethical norms may harm the firm regardless of whether they are related to securities laws, fraud, or fiduciary duty. The public reaction and the market reaction to revelations of racism within the business culture of Texaco demonstrate this point. Countrywide paid $8.7 billion to settle claims of predatory lending. Consequently, there is little basis to limiting the SEC's rules of professional responsibility only to violations as defined; a definition limited to federal fraud and violations of securities laws. The QLCC should be empowered to investigate reports of all wrongdoing or illegality regardless of which laws or ethics standards are violated or suspected of being violated. Similarly, there is no reason to limit those reporting violations to lawyers; any corporate agent having information relating to a violation should be required to report to the QLCC. This would allow the QLCC to act with maximum effectiveness to protect the firm from legal and reputational risk from all potential legal and ethical violations.

Step 3: Broader Whistle-Blower Protection Is Needed

SOX's whistle-blower protection fails to secure whistle-blowing. Professor Mary Ramirez (2008) suggests a broad-based protection that shields whistle-blowers from retaliation as broadly as possible. The social pressures against whistle-blowing are so strong that the broadest protection is needed to facilitate the flow of information. If reports can be made to a QLCC composed of lawyers such communications would enjoy attorney-client privilege. Firms should make the privileged nature of such communications clear to their workers, and also contractually assure employees that retaliation for filing reports constitutes grounds for dismissal. This will maximize the flow of information to the appropriate corporate decision maker—presumably the QLCC.

Step 4: Anonymity

One further method of securing more reports is to allow anonymous reporting. Attorneys, for example, do not want to alienate client-representatives that sign the checks that pay the attorney's fees. Under these circumstances it is not rational for attorneys to make reports unless the evidence in support of the report is overwhelming. Optimal management of legal and reputational risk mandates that mere suspicions be weighed by the appropriate corporate authority (as previously shown the current best practice is the QLCC). That authority does not suffer from the inherent institutional infirmity as counsel who may understandably be preoccupied with payment of fees and maintaining functional relationships with the client-representative. The only means of assuring the proper flow of material legal and reputational risk is to maximize the confidentiality of any reports. This would effectively change the calculus counsel faces: risk of employment loss is minimized while malpractice liability for failure to report is maximized because anonymity renders reporting nearly costless. A nonreporting attorney would find decisions not to report difficult to justify, if such reports enjoyed both maximum anonymity as well as privileged status.

TOWARD OPTIMAL REPUTATIONAL AND LEGAL RISK MANAGEMENT

SOX innovations and the subprime experience teach much about the optimal means of managing and reducing legal and reputational risk, beyond legal reform. Empirical support is difficult to come by, because the vast majority of firms have historically and currently leave these issues in the hands of the CEO. Nevertheless, there are certain conclusions that seem reasonable.

First, there appears to be good reason for firms to embrace the QLCC and little reason to eschew that option. Susan Hackett, the General Counsel for the American Corporate Counsel Association has termed the QLCC a "very bright solution" to the problem facing lawyers after SOX—specifically the challenges of assessing when a client has responded appropriately to a report of a "violation" or determining when a report to the SEC is proper (*American University Law Review* 2003). Other commentators suggest QLCCs "threaten dominant hierarchal relations" within corporations and this is the reason for the lack of diffusion of QLCCs (Rosen 2005). Given the clear advantages of the QLCC, and the institutionally suspect nature of leaving legal and reputational risk in the hands of CEOs, the QLCC should be embraced by firms that are serious about managing legal and reputational risk. Additionally, in order to secure the benefits of institutional expertise, as well as maximizing the applicability of the attorney-client privilege, the QLCC should consist entirely of lawyers.

Second, the QLCC can be easily enhanced to address not just "violations" as defined by the Commission but to be a general mechanism for weighing and managing legal and reputational risk in a manner that reduces (but certainly does not eliminate) CEO control over this function, based on the same policy underlying the reconfiguration of the audit function under SOX. The QLCC is the logical locus for investigation and enforcement not just of violations as defined by the SEC but of all potential legal violations and violations of the firm's code of conduct. The charter of the QLCC should be as expansive as the firm's legal and reputational risk.

Third, corporations wishing to control legal and reputational risk should have an ethics code that is sensitive to its consumers, investors, suppliers, and regulatory context, as well as minimal notions of morally acceptable behavior. Under the approach of Professor Backer, as endorsed (in modified form) herein, there is little down side to managing reputational risk (and indirectly legal risk) through a code of conduct that is enforced and that reflects the moral sensibilities of key corporate constituencies. In fact, properly conceived, an ethics code should enhance corporate profitability over the long term.

Fourth, on optimized QLCC can create an anonymous means of reporting violations of law or regulation, conduct that violates the corporate code of conduct, or otherwise unacceptable behavior that shields the reporting individual from the adverse consequences of reporting. The social stigma associated with being a whistle-blower is too powerful to ignore. The only means of effectively countering this stigma is to eliminate to the maximum extent possible by maximizing the confidential nature of such whistle-blower communications. Anonymity protects reporters from retaliation.

Fifth, the structure of the QLCC should assure that it works closely with the audit committee. The audit committee is involved in all aspects of the firm's business. Unlike the QLCC, the audit committee will necessarily be testing financial data against actual evidence demonstrating the validity and accuracy of that data. This detailed analysis of the firm's business can no doubt facilitate investigations of the QLCC as well as corroborate reports of violations. Moreover, audit committee members are familiar with the firm's system of internal controls, as well as that system's limitations. Finally, audit-related personnel will also be a source of reports. Thus, the relationship between the QLCC and the audit committee should be as close as possible. The SEC's requirement that one member of the QLCC also be a member of the audit committee should be viewed as an absolute minimum, not the ideal.

Finally, firms should consider the utility of an annual legal audit. The QLCC as conceived by the SEC is a dormant committee until a report is made to it. This is in part a response to objections raised to the American Law Institute's proposal in the 1990s that the board assume responsibility for legal compliance (Rosen 2005). The expertise called for, however, in order for the QLCC to function properly, creates an expert committee of the board to act to guide the board with respect to issues of legal compliance and reputational risk. Thus, the corporation now has an institutionally competent board committee with legal expertise to assist the board in all facets of legal and reputational risk. The final step in optimizing the corporate governance structure for dealing with legal and reputational risk is to empower the QLCC to conduct annual legal and reputational risk assessments, with reporting to the chief risk officer as well as the chief legal officer. Note that the concept of a legal audit also highlights the role of the firm's chief legal officer. The QLCC would have no role other than to receive reports of potential violations. A legal audit function would expand its role only marginally—by means of annual analysis of the firm's legal and reputational risk profile. Other than receiving reports and the possibility of an audit the legal function of the firm remains under the control of management, as it has historically been.

CONCLUSION

This chapter reviewed the most developed legal framework governing legal and reputational risk—SOX. It then tested that framework against the legal and reputational risk manifest in the subprime mortgage fiasco. Overall, the SOX framework appears flawed. Legal and reputational risk was ill-managed, and these largely unabated risks contributed to the causes of subprime mortgage fiasco and exacerbated it. Nevertheless, SOX still forms the foundation for thinking about how best to control legal and reputational risk. The linchpin for managing legal and reputational risk is the QLCC (which probably should be mandated by law to a greater extent than is now the case). A robust QLCC, including the enhancements articulated, should be associated with superior financial performance over the long term, by removing legal and reputational risk from the exclusive control of the CEO to a more institutionally suited organ of corporate governance—the QLCC.

NOTE

1. M. Ramirez (2007) (internal citations omitted).

REFERENCES

Backer, Larry Cata. 2008. From Moral obligation to international law: Disclosure systems, markets and the regulation of multinational corporations, 39. *Georgetown Journal of International Law* 591.

Backer, Larry Cata. 2003. The duty to monitor: Emerging obligations of outside lawyers and auditors to detect and report corporate wrongdoing beyond the federal securities laws, 77. *St. John's Law Review* 919, 928–929.

Barclift, Jill. 2008. Codes of ethics and state fiduciary duties: Where is the line? 1. *Journal of Business, Entrepreneurship and the Law.* 237.

Basel Committee on Banking Supervision, Core Principles for Effective Banking Supervision, September 1997, available at www.bis.org/publ/bcbs30a.pdf?noframes=1.

Bazyler, Michael, and Roger P. Alford. 2007. *Holocaust restitution: Perspectives on the litigation and its legacy.* New York: New York University Press.

Bethel, Jennifer E., Allen Ferrell, and Gang Hu. 2008. Legal and economic issues in litigation arising from the 2007–2008 credit crisis. November 17. Available at http://papers.ssrn.com/sol3/papers.cfm?abstract_id=1096582&rec=1&srcabs=980025.

City of Cleveland v. Deutsche Bank Trust, et al., Court of Common Pleas, Cuyahoga County, No. CV 08 646970, available at www.pbs.org/moyers/journal/07182008/Foreclosure_Doc.pdf.

Committee on Oversight and Government Reform, U.S. House of Representatives, Credit Rating Agencies and the Financial Crisis, October 22, 2008, available at http://oversight.house.gov/documents/20081023162631.pdf.

Developments in the law: Corporations and society. 2004. 117 *Harvard Law Review* 2169, 2244–2248.

Dworkin, Terry M. 2007. SOX and whistleblowing, *Michigan Law Review* 1757–1780.

Ehrenfreund, Edmund. 2007. The Nuremberg legacy: How the Nazi war crime trials changed the course of history. New York: Palgrave MacMillan.

Henning, Peter J. 2004. Sarbanes-Oxley Act § 307 and Corporate Counsel: Who better to prevent corporate crime? 8 *Buffalo Criminal Law Review* 323.

Implementation of Standards of Professional Conduct for Attorneys, 67 Fed. Reg. 71, 670 (Dec. 2, 2002) (codified at 17 C.F.R. § 205) available at www.sec.gov/rules/final/33-8185.htm.

Koniak, Susan P. 2003. When the hurlyburly's done: The bar's struggle with the SEC, 103. *Columbia Law Review* 1236, 1271.

Lipman, Frederick D., and Keith Lipman. 2006. *Corporate governance best practices* 190–192. Hoboken, NJ: John Wiley & Sons.

Loomis, Carol J. 2008. AIG's rescue has a long way to go. CNNmoney.com, December 24, available at http://money.cnn.com/2008/12/23/news/companies/AIG_150bailout_Loomis.fortune/index.htm.

Loomis, Carol. 2007. Robert Rubin on the job he didn't want. November 11. CNNmoney.com available at http://money.cnn.com/2007/11/09/news/newsmakers/merrill_rubin.fortune/index.htm.

NECA-IBEW Health and Welfare Fund v. Goldman Sachs & Co., et al. 2008. U.S. District Court for the Southern District of New York. Available at http://securities.stanford.edu/1041/GS_01/20081211_f01c_.pdf.

Orol, Ronald D. 2008. Madoff arrest raises questions about SEC oversight, Marketwatch.com, December 8. Available at http://www.marketwatch.com/news/story/madoff-arrest-raises-questions-about/story.aspx?guid=%7BE2002EFA-C24D-453B-BF6C-EC67992A0A3C%7D&dist=msr_44.

Paletta, Damien, and Kara Scannell. 2009. Ten questions for those fixing the financial mess. WSJ.com, March 9. Available at http://online.wsj.com/article/SB123665023774979341.html.

People of the State of Illinois v. Countrywide Financial Corporation, et al. Circuit Court of Cook County, No. 08-22994. Available at www.illinoisattorneygeneral.gov/pressroom/2008_06/countrywide_complaint.pdf.

Rajan, Raghuram. 2008. Bankers pay is deeply flawed. *Financial Times* January 8. Available at www.ft.com/cms/s/0/18895dea-be06-11dc-8bc9-0000779fd2ac.html.

Ramirez, Mary Kreiner. 2007. Blowing the whistle on whistleblower protection: A tale of reform versus power, 76 University *Cincinnati Law Review* 183, 191.

Ramirez, Steven A. 2000. Diversity and the boardroom, 6 *Stanford Journal of Law, Business and Finance* 85, 108.

Ramirez, Steven A. 2007. The end of corporate governance law: Optimizing regulatory structures for a race to the top, 24 *Yale Journal on Regulation* 313.

Ramirez, Steven A. 2002. Fear and social capitalism: The law and macroeconomics of investor confidence, 42 *Washburn Law Journal* 31.

Ramirez, Steven A. 2009. Lessons from the subprime debacle: Stress testing CEO autonomy. March 18. Available at http://papers.ssrn.com/sol3/papers.cfm?abstract_id=1364146.

Rosen, Robert Eli 2005. Resistances to reforming corporate governance: The diffusion of QLCCs, 74 *Fordham Law Review* 1251, 1309.

Sale, Hillary A. 2007. Monitoring Caremark's good faith, 32 (3) *Delaware Journal of Corporate Law* 719–755.

Sarbanes-Oxley Act of 2002, Pub. L. No. 107-204, 116 Stat. 745 (codified in scattered sections of 11, 15, 18, 28, and 29 U.S.C.S. [2005]). Available at www.pcaobus.org/About_the_PCAOB/Sarbanes_Oxley_Act_of_2002.pdf.

Simkins, Betty J. and Steven A. Ramirez. 2008. Enterprise-wide risk management and corporate governance, 39 (3) *Loyola University Chicago Law Journal.*

Social Investment Forum, Press Release. 2008. Report: Socially Responsible Investing Assets In U.S Surged 18 Percent From 2005 To 2007, Outpacing Broader Managed Assets, March 8. Available at www.socialinvest.org/news/releases/pressrelease.cfm?id=108.

Son, Hugh. 2008. With fed's help, AIG unloads $16 billion in credit default swaps. *Washington Post*, December 25, at D-2. Available at www.washingtonpost.com/wp-dyn/content/article/2008/12/24/AR2008122402128.html.

Verschoor, Curtis C. 1999. Corporate performance is closely linked to a strong ethical commitment, 4. *Business and Society Review* 407.

Villagran, Lauren. 2007. AIG reassures investors on subprime, Washingtonpost.com, August 9. Available at www.washingtonpost.com/wp-dyn/content/article/2007/08/09/AR2007080901027.html.

Volz, William H., and Vahe Tazian. 2006. The role of attorneys under Sarbanes-Oxley: The qualified legal compliance committee as facilitator of corporate integrity. 43 *American Business Law Journal* 439.

Williams, Cynthia A. 1999. The securities and exchange commission and corporate social transparency. 112. *Harvard Law Review* 1197, 1294–1296.

ABOUT THE AUTHOR

Steven A. Ramirez is a Professor of Law at Loyola University Chicago, where he also directs the Business & Corporate Governance Law Center. Prior to entering the legal academy he practiced law for 10 years, including working as an Enforcement Attorney for the Securities and Exchange Commission and as a Senior Attorney with the FDIC/RTC, Professional Liability Section. He has served on a number of corporate boards.

CHAPTER 21

Financial Reporting and Disclosure Risk Management

SUSAN HUME
Assistant Professor of Finance and International Business, School of Business,
The College of NJ

There are some things you learn best in calm, and some in storm.
—Willa Sibert Cather

THE IMPORTANCE OF DISCLOSURE MANAGEMENT AND ERM

Enterprise risk management (ERM) is a discipline that allows management to judge total business risk. There are diverse audiences who are interested in monitoring the firm's enterprise risks. There are the internal audiences—the board of directors, management, and employees—and the external participants—investors, vendors, and rating agencies. The ERM process can help the firm avoid or weather a powerful category five storm if the appropriate quantitative modeling is in place and qualitative reasoning prevails by management.

ERM reporting and disclosure provides the forum to discuss the key vulnerabilities and risks of the firm and strengthens management accountability. It cannot provide management with good business sense, for executives need to determine what makes their business unique and establish comprehensive guidelines within which all in the firm operate. Transparency is important to ERM disclosure as business managers, senior managers, and the board of directors (referred to as board) need to track exposures and discuss these regularly. Without transparency and disclosure, a firm lacks the information to make important risk decisions.

Instituting full ERM systems can be costly and involve a significant resource of employees and a patchwork of vendor systems. Good disclosure management in a transparent organization will provide the communication of risks up and down the corporation. Downward risk policy is for the board and senior management to establish the key levels of acceptable risk exposure and to communicate these policies to managers and other employees. Implementation and reporting then flows up from the bottom to senior management and to the Risk Management Committee, which may be a subcommittee of the board in the ideal structure. Information is

369

also disclosed to the external auditors, regulators, credit rating agencies, investors, and vendors, as appropriate. Disclosure needs to be adequate and broad-based, providing quantitative and qualitative assessments for interest rates, market, credit quality, and operational risks. It considers specifics of measurement and limits on exposures. Overall, disclosure serves many audiences, but adequacy is important as it drives the quality.

FOUNDATIONS IN THE UNITED STATES

The current framework for disclosure risk management begins with the legislative and regulatory response to the corporate crises of 2001–2002. The collapse of Enron Corporation, WorldCom, Tyco, Global Crossing, Adelphia, HealthSouth, Parmalat, and the accounting firm Arthur Andersen represented failures of not only corporate disclosure, fraud, and lack of internal control, but also accounting conflicts of interest and weak oversight. See Exhibit 21.1.

Exhibit 21.1   Recent Firm Failures and Disclosure Management

Firm	Type of Failure	Impact
Enron	Accounting, Financial Fraud	$3 billion losses
WorldCom	Financial Reporting Fraud	$9 billion unreported expenses
Global Crossing	Financial Reporting Fraud	$12.4 billion overstated earnings
Tyco International	Corporate Governance Failure, Executive Fraud and Larceny	$7 billion income charges, $580 million executive fraud
Adelphia	Financial Reporting Fraud	$1.6 billion debt unreported, $350 million overstated equity
HealthSouth	Financial Reporting Fraud	$4 billion overstated profit from overbilling
Parmalat (Italy)	Financial Reporting Fraud	$4.98 billion fake bank deposits and unreported debt
Arthur Andersen	Corporate Governance Failure Obstruction of Justice	Firm collapses, $72.5 million settlement
Amaranth Advisors	Corporate Governance Failure, Market Manipulation	$5.85 billion fund losses
Fannie Mae	Corporate Governance Failure, Accounting Fraud	$10 billion hedging loss adjustments, insolvent Government Sponsored Enterprise (GSE)
Freddie Mac	Corporate Governance Failure, Accounting Fraud	$4.5 billion derivatives loss, earnings manipulation, insolvent GSE
Lehman Brothers	Enterprise Risk Management Failure	$4 billion mortgage exposure when bankrupt
Madoff Investments	Accounting Fraud	$50 billion Ponzi scheme
Satyam (India)	Corporate Governance Failure, Accounting Fraud	$1 billion overstated revenues

The government responded to the 2001 and 2002 failures with significant burdensome accounting and legislative requirements. The aim was to require management to better align their interests with shareholders. The purpose of this regulatory reform was to strengthen corporate governance through internal control policies. The initial U.S. reform was more rules-based rather than principles-based as in Europe.[1]

DISCLOSURE AND SARBANES-OXLEY

The Sarbanes-Oxley Act (SOX) of 2002 profoundly impacted the financial reporting and disclosure environment, particularly of U.S. corporations with SEC-registered securities, both large and small.[2] Two sections of SOX influenced reporting of internal control directly and ERM indirectly: (1) CEOs and CFOs of public corporations must assure the veracity of the firm's public statements, and (2) companies must establish and test internal financial controls, including those to protect against or detect fraud. The SOX Act established important requirements for external public accounting firms for their dealings with the firms that they audit, with the aim of improving independence and transparency of reporting.

Most importantly, SOX required management to take responsibility for the material in quarterly and annual publicly reported financial statements. These included all documentation, reviews of statements and internal controls systems. SOX required corporations to follow an accepted internal control framework such as the Committee of Sponsoring Organizations' (COSO) 1992 framework of internal controls. Subsequent to SOX, COSO 2 was released for enterprise risk management. While SOX focuses primarily on internal control, COSO introduced a more broad-based ERM philosophy in its integrated framework in 2004.

New Group for Reporting: Public Company Accounting Oversight Board

To govern financial reporting and internal control, SOX established the Public Company Accounting Oversight Board (PCAOB) under Section 101 of the Act. PCAOB, pronounced peek-a-boo, is a nonprofit organization under the authority of the SEC.[3]

PCAOB sets financial reporting and audit standards for public companies while monitoring public accounting firms. The SEC Board appoints the PCAOB members in consultation with the executive branches of the monetary authority of the Federal Reserve System, and the fiscal authority of the U.S. Treasury Secretary. Some contend that the SEC has too much control over the PCAOB, which should be more independent in setting audit and reporting standards. Further, there is legal controversy regarding whether appointment of PCAOB members should be made directly by the SEC or through a legislative confirmation process appointed by the U.S. President. Although the U.S. Appeals Court found in August 2008 that PCAOB board members are not officers under the U.S. Constitution and thus are not required to be appointed by the U.S. President, this process may change under appeal.

Since SOX's implementation in 2002, firms have devoted considerable internal and external talent and monies to achieving the SOX framework for internal control. The legislation required all U.S. firms with SEC-registered securities to comply on their periodic financial filings, including annual 10-K reports (with exceptions granted to non-U.S. firms). Many small firms felt overburdened by the scope of the reporting requirements, voicing protests that the costs of compliance outweighed the benefits and made them less competitive compared to international firms based outside the United States. Additionally, several U.S.-based multinational firms have switched to a principles-based focus with the adoption of international accounting standards prepared according to the International Financial Reporting Standards (IFRS). Current transition to IFRS is set for 2014, with some firms choosing early conversion by 2009. The global financial crisis necessitated further coordination between the U.S. FASB and the international accounting standard equivalent, International Accounting Standards Board (IASB). Some U.S. firms are discussing the postponement of adapting IFRS in the face of understanding new changes in disclosures that are expected.

IMPORTANT SOX SECTIONS

The overriding intention of the SOX framework is to install governance in financial reporting into the corporation. SOX's key provisions for internal control are Sections 103, 302, and 404. Section 103 stipulates the specific requirements that must be included in the auditor's report. Section 302 assigns corporate responsibility for financial reports to management. Top officers of a firm set the tone for attesting to the correctness of published reports that flow down to all corporate levels. Section 404 establishes comprehensive internal controls policies with an assessment by management and certification by the external auditors. These important provisions are discussed below by order of greatest impact.

Section 404: Internal Controls and Compliance Management

The post-Enron regulatory environment placed heavy emphasis on establishing internal controls and compliance by management. Section 404 required all firms to describe and document key internal controls, test and verify those controls, and disclose material weaknesses. External auditors are charged with the responsibility of reviewing, auditing, and independently assessing these internal controls documents and stating their opinion on the fairness of these controls. Management is charged with the responsibility of reporting on the quality and effectiveness of internal controls on a regular basis. This requires a comprehensive documentation process. The auditor is responsible for reviewing all of the control reports and inputs to certify that management has accurately described the internal control environment.

SOX implementation required U.S. firms to address internal control issues that some firms had not implemented previously in a control framework such as COSO.

Section 302: Who Is Responsible for Financial Reporting?

This section, referred to as the "signature clause," was initiated as a response to prior scandals where corporate executives denied involvement or knowledge of fraudulent filings. Its purpose was to charge senior management with accountability and to certify the reporting responsibility of financial statements.

Public quarterly and annual reports were now required to be certified by senior management. The buck stops at the top, as the CEO, CFO, and other senior executive officers responsible for signing and certifying the financial reports, could no longer claim ignorance on financial disclosures. The measures in Section 302 require firms to establish a control framework for internal controls and reporting. The penalties for noncompliance are substantial for the executive officer, with criminal charges, fines, and possible jail time if convicted. These penalties are fines of up to $1 million and 10 years in prison for the submission of a wrong certification, or if done willfully, a maximum penalty of $5 million with increased prison time of 20 years. This indicates the seriousness of the legislation and firms developed substantial risk monitoring and reporting processes to handle the internal controls. Companies can use a chain-of-command approach by requiring business managers and staff at lower levels to first sign off on the financial statements' compliance and adequacy.

At the heart of Section 302 are four specific requirements:

1. Establish the officers responsible for certifying the financial reports.
2. Require that the designated officers review the report and sign off on internal control.
3. Certify that statements do not contain misleading or materially untrue information.
4. Certify that the statements represent clearly the financial condition and results of operations of the firm.

Under Section 302, the signing officers will not only disclose these statements to external auditors and in periodic SEC filings, that is, 10-K and 8-Q, but also to internal stakeholders such as the audit committee and the board of directors. If there are deficiencies in internal controls, these are also to be disclosed to the external and internal participants. Along with this disclosure comes the responsibility for establishing and maintaining a framework for internal controls. The signing officer will evaluate the controls process 90 days prior to public release of the report and evaluate the effectiveness of those controls for the reporting date. See Box 21.1.

Box 21.1   Rule 13a-14(A) Certification of Chief Executive Officer

I, James A. Skinner, Vice Chairman and Chief Executive Officer of McDonald's Corporation, certify that:

(1) I have reviewed this annual report on Form 10-K of McDonald's Corporation;
(2) Based on my knowledge, this report does not contain any untrue statement of a material fact or omit to state a material fact necessary to make the statements made, in light of the circumstances under which such statements were made, not misleading with respect to the period covered by this report;

(3) Based on my knowledge, the financial statements, and other financial information included in this report, fairly present in all material respects the financial condition, results of operations and cash flows of the registrant as of, and for, the periods presented in this report;

(4) The registrant's other certifying officer(s) and I are responsible for establishing and maintaining disclosure controls and procedures (as defined in Exchange Act Rules 13a-15(e) and 15d-15(e)) and internal control over financial reporting (as defined in Exchange Act Rules 13a-15(f) and 15d-15(f)) for the registrant and have:

    (a) Designed such disclosure controls and procedures, or caused such disclosure controls and procedures to be designed under our supervision, to ensure that material information relating to the registrant, including its consolidated subsidiaries, is made known to us by others within those entities, particularly during the period in which this report is being prepared;

    (b) Designed such internal control over financial reporting, or caused such internal control over financial reporting to be designed under our supervision, to provide reasonable assurance regarding the reliability of financial reporting and the preparation of financial statements for external purposes in accordance with generally accepted accounting principles;

    (c) Evaluated the effectiveness of the registrant's disclosure controls and procedures and presented in this report our conclusions about the effectiveness of the disclosure controls and procedures, as of the end of the period covered by this report based on such evaluation; and

    (d) Disclosed in this report any change in the registrant's internal control over financial reporting that occurred during the registrant's most recent fiscal quarter (the registrant's fourth fiscal quarter in the case of an annual report) that has materially affected, or is reasonably likely to materially affect, the registrant's internal control over financial reporting; and

(5) The registrant's other certifying officer(s) and I have disclosed, based on our most recent evaluation of internal control over financial reporting, to the registrant's auditors and the audit committee of the registrant's board of directors (or persons performing the equivalent functions):

    (a) All significant deficiencies and material weaknesses in the design or operation of internal control over financial reporting which are reasonably likely to adversely affect the registrant's ability to record, process, summarize and report financial information; and

    (b) Any fraud, whether or not material, that involves management or other employees who have a significant role in the registrant's internal control over financial reporting.

Date: February 25, 2008
By James A. Skinner,
Vice Chairman, Chief Executive Officer and Director

Given the signing officer's personal stake in the disclosure process, SOX implementation created a high need for risk reporting and monitoring. Firms have established detailed electronic trails with procedures to support the sign off. Of concern is materiality of errors in financial statements where a misstatement would affect a reasonable investor's view of a company. Prior to SOX, external auditors often viewed a material weakness as when the misstatement caused an adjustment of 5 percent or more in pretax income. SOX dissolved any predefined quantitative threshold for materiality.

The ERM financial reporting component identifies internal control gaps or control weaknesses and senior management is held responsible for disclosing key deficiencies. Adding to the ambiguity in materiality is that if an internal weakness created a significant error, this would not be material if reported to the external auditors. But it would be material if discovered in the internal audit or risk assessment and not reported, thus exposing the signing officer to face criminal actions. An effective ERM plan would recognize this risk as significant and work with SOX compliance staff to integrate the gap into internal control compliance.[4]

OTHER FINANCIAL REPORTING

ERM disclosure today is also impacted by Accounting for Derivatives (FASB 133), the attempt to streamline SOX disclosures with Auditing Standard 5 (AS5) and Fair Value Accounting (FASB 157). These requirements and their implications are topics in our discussion.

Accounting for Derivatives—FASB 133

After 10 years of work initiated in response to significant derivatives losses that remained unreported by firms, the Accounting Standards Board implemented a new standard—Accounting for Derivatives Instruments and Hedging Activities FASB 133, effective in 2001.[5] Financial reporting for derivatives would now take a fair value approach. The objective was to measure a firm's derivatives value on a mark-to-market or fair value basis on the balance sheet, as an asset or liability, rather than in notes to financial statements.

Where firms use derivatives to hedge, the intent is that if an asset had a loss in value, the derivative should have a corresponding gain to offset the underlying asset's loss. Changes in fair value flow through as gains or losses and are recognized in current period income. The underlying asset or liability is also mark-to-market and adjustments similarly flow directly through to earnings. The new rules were designed to expose the underlying volatility of the derivatives contract to the hedged balance sheet item by reporting changes in corporate earnings. Shareholders would benefit from these changes with improved information as management would have less opportunity to smooth earnings. However, financial reporting is still anything but transparent for investors, creditors, and regulators, as accounting choices and conflicts still exist.

Firm Choice for FASB 133 and Disclosure Risk Management

FASB 133 is a mixed disclosure philosophy for firms as it does not fully require mark-to-market accounting for derivatives. This is referred to as a mixed attribute model for accounting treatment that is neither "fish nor fowl," but a combination of financial reporting based on both historic cost and mark-to-market. Firms can choose to designate a derivatives position as either not for hedging or as a hedging instrument. A firm can report three types of hedge accounting: (1) fair value hedges, (2) cash flow hedges, and (3) net investment hedges in a foreign operation.

A fair value hedge is the hedge of the fair value of an asset or liability at a market value. To qualify, the hedged item must be bought, sold, or committed at a definite price and date. The gain or loss on the derivative appears in current income in the same period, along with the gain or loss on the hedged item.

Cash-flow hedges are permitted on the forecasted risk of uncertain cash flows. Strict criteria for performance need to be met to qualify for a cash-flow hedge. The time frame for measuring these criteria commences when the hedge is instituted. The gain or loss of the hedged component is reserved in "other comprehensive income" (OCI) and moved into income during the appropriate recognition period. Examples of cash-flow hedges are interest rate exposure for variable or floating interest rates, planned purchases or sales of assets, planned issuance of debt or deposits, planned purchases or sales of foreign currency, and currency risk associated with proposed cash flows.

Net investment hedges relate to foreign currency hedging for foreign operations and allowed FASB 52 to effectively continue. Effective hedges are consolidated into OCI with translation adjustments. Any differences between total hedged results and translation adjustments flow through income directly.

Consider the difference between fair value and cash-flow hedges and the effect on disclosure. Firms with sales in foreign currencies may use forward contracts to hedge accounts receivables. Let's assume that the accounts receivable sale for a U.S.-based company is €1 million due in three months and the exchange rate when the sale made is $1.30 for €1. This represents a dollar sales value of $1.3 million. The company chooses to hedge immediately by selling euros forward in exchange for dollars at a price of $1.25. This reduces the uncertainty of being unhedged, but costs the firm $50,000 ($1.25–$1.30 times €1 million) as the accounts receivable exchange rate is more than the forward rate. The appeal of cash flow hedging is that the forward contract, which has a predetermined loss at the outset, is amortized over the period of the receivable. This contrasts with fair value accounting, which directly affects income during each accounting period while the receivable is still outstanding. Under fair value, the forward contract is marked-to-market at each reporting period at the market rate compared with the asset value. Thus, the fair value method increases variability even when costs are established upfront with the initiation of the forward contract.

Many corporations use a combination of all three methods, especially for derivatives that are not exchange-traded but traded privately in the over the counter market. This makes disclosure in financial reports nontransparent. The financial statement details show that the impact of derivatives is hidden and parked in OCI along with other nonhedging items, or pass directly into current income, again with other income items. It is impossible for an investor or creditor to gauge the impact of derivatives use because the information is buried in the financial statements and the financial footnotes. Firms contend that separate disclosure would damage their competitive position. Going forward from the global financial crisis, firms and investors will benefit from better disclosure with FASB

161. After November 2008, "Statement 161 requires companies with derivative instruments to disclose information for financial-statement users to understand the level of derivative activity entered into by the company." These disclosures require standardized tabular reports illustrating the derivatives instruments by their underlying risk exposure (interest rate, credit or foreign exchange, for example) and by hedge designation (fair value, cash flow, or net investment).[6]

RISK IDENTIFICATION, MONITORING, AND REPORTING

The following sets out a typical and suggested way of establishing methods of identifying, monitoring, and reporting risk.

ERM systems integration and sophistication varies widely among firms. Tracking activities for ERM systems ideally operate in real time and cover all major aspects of risk identified by senior management and the board. Reporting and monitoring provide management with an assessment of operational, compliance, and control risks across lines of business, legal entities, and processes. The framework should be based on COSO and also support SOX and other compliance needs. Monitoring and reporting should track potential and real losses of vendor and third-party exposures, and notify management automatically when risks exceeded company-specified thresholds. A wide variety of components of ERM systems include compliance solutions, predictive analytics, specific risk management systems, fraud solutions, business process management, data management, core systems, and dashboards. For example, predictive analytics model uncertainty to forecast the outcomes of key risk events and exposures. Risk management systems track credit and other financial risks.

Consider how a corporate treasurer and risk committee monitor external counterparty risk that arises from investments, bank facilities, and vendor needs. See Exhibit 21.2.

Reports take a "dashboard" platform and show risk exposures to other firms by maturity amounts and time buckets. Also reported are current and outlook bond ratings of counterparties. Color codes show risk levels provided by rating agencies with green for acceptable, yellow for cautionary, and red for higher risk.

Historically, rating agencies have been criticized for failing to adequately anticipate defaults and incorrectly assigning high ratings for firms that later become bankrupt. In this environment, companies use other methods to assess the potential for credit deterioration, such as statistical modeling or VAR, and may also make use of credit default swaps to mitigate the risk. A company tracks credit default swap prices for each counterparty to assess default risk perceived in the market.[7] Some firms purchase statistical packages to model the market value of a company's assets. For example, Moody's KMV model is an expected default frequency valuation that combines asset volatilities, equity price, and credit data history. Firms find it useful to have a counterparty monitoring system that combines changes in credit spreads, expected default frequency, changes in market capitalization, changes in rating agency ratings, rating outlook, VAR changes, changes in notional and fair value, and other measures. These are aggregated by the counterparty exposures

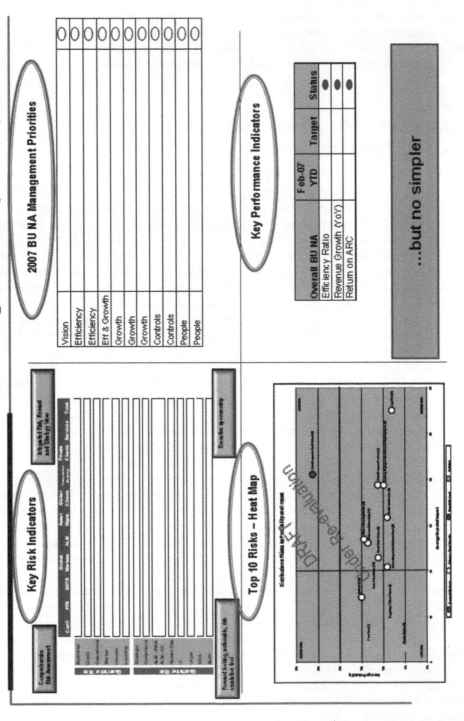

Exhibit 21.2 ERM Dashboard

unique to the firm and consider foreign exchange risk, derivatives use, and pension portfolio exposures.

FINANCIAL REPORTING CHALLENGES TODAY

What challenges face risk managers today? Let's investigate further the influence of important events and regulatory requirements on ERM disclosure.

Paring Down Internal Control: Auditing Standard 5 (AS5)

SEC issuers, especially smaller firms, were critical of Section 404, stating that it was unreasonably burdensome, expensive, and time-consuming. In response to the criticism, the PCAOB adopted a new standard, AS5, in July 2007, which still requires auditors to test the effectiveness of a company's internal controls, but allows a more principles-based approach, including relying on the work of others. The focus shifts internal controls reporting from bottom-up to top-down, as a risk-based ERM approach. Bottoms-up means instituting risk assessments unit by unit at local levels and then rolling the results upward. A bottoms-up approach incurs increased cost as it views controls at a detailed level rather than at the optimal corporate level. Top-down means looking at company-level risks first, with an assessment of where material risks could arise, and then focusing on key controls. Top-down requires that board members and senior management establish the strategies of risk management, then use internal control to aid in reporting and decision making.

AS5 streamlined reporting and required just one opinion from auditors on compliance for internal control for financial reporting. A survey of internal audit professionals in 2008 reported that many have decreased the time spent on compliance since AS5 was introduced.

Connie Whitecotton, Chief Risk and Compliance Officer at Alfa Corporation, slashed external audit hours by 60 percent, bringing total 404 compliance costs for Alfa way down. Her secret was to shift from simply achieving compliance on 404 to a 404 audit based on the ERM program she was implementing. The company identifies risks, but also assesses whether each risk is material, evaluates which risks require action, determines how to mitigate risk and then monitors the process of mitigation (*Treasury & Risk*, February 2008).

Global Financial Crisis and ERM

> *Risk managers need to be perceived like good goalkeepers, always in the game and occasionally at the heart of it, like in a penalty shoot-out.*
> —*The Economist*, 2008, Goals and goal keepers

Corporations in 2008, especially financial institutions, found disclosure risk management at the heart of a category five storm. This storm began quietly at the beginning of the century when low interest rates and several legislative changes allowed banks and investment banks to compromise standard lending practices on mortgage loans. Further, by securitizing assets in structured pools in traded credit products such as CDO tranches and other asset-backed securities, this risk was dispersed globally. Poor corporate governance by the firms, outright fraud on the creation of the underlying mortgages, faulty regulatory oversight, and rating agency conflicts of interest added to the storm.

The financial crisis exposed weaknesses in the disclosure processes of risk management at major global financial firms. Senior managers at many of these firms failed to identify and report the maximum exposure in trading positions, believing that securities were liquid and saleable to third parties. Further, they failed to reject risky new deals and establish adequate controls in the trading account. Consider the confessions of an anonymous risk manager at a large commercial bank:

> *Over time we accumulated a balance-sheet of traded assets which allowed for very little margin of error. We owned a large portfolio of "very low-risk" assets which turned out to be high-risk. A small price movement on billions of dollars' worth of securities would translate into large mark-to-market losses. We thought that we had focused correctly on the non-investment-grade paper, of which we held little. We had not paid enough attention to the ever-growing mountain of highly rated but potentially illiquid assets. We had not fully appreciated that 20 percent of a very large number can inflict far greater losses than 80 percent of a small number. ("Confessions of a risk manager," Spoilsport section, The Economist 2008)*

A study by Towers Perrin for insurance CFOs suggests that the vast majority lack the tools necessary to identify, prioritize, and measure risk at the enterprise level, yet these same firms are in the business of managing credit, market, interest, and operational risks. Federal Reserve Chairman Ben Bernanke posits that quantifying economic capital and market liquidity risks are essential to the well-being of financial institutions. He suggests that business managers had little incentive to compile this information. Better management of trading company positions as is done with "held to maturity" assets would have had management limiting exposures and perhaps limiting the level of mortgage assets issued during this housing asset bubble. Again, disclosure transparency can only aid the firm and its stakeholders in understanding its business.[8]

Reexamining Fair Value Accounting: FASB 157

In light of the 2008 financial crisis and U.S. government bailout package that purchased distressed bank assets and injected capital, the issue of fair value accounting for financial assets under FASB 157 returns to center stage. The underlying question is: When should assets that are marked to market in a trading portfolio currently based on "fair value" be reclassified to "held to maturity"? U.S. GAAP and IASB permit a firm to reclassify those trading assets, which originally were marked to market and would flow through the income statement, to be measured at amortized cost and subject to testing for impairment. In the United States, fair value relates principally to derivatives values, while IFRS applies to assets and liabilities in general.

Although IFRS has allowed companies the flexibility to reclassify fair-valued assets, the U.S. regulators have not been as consistent. In October 2008, the SEC released clarifications regarding fair value accounting under FASB 157. This statement established a framework for measuring fair value of an asset at a specific date between market participants. Level 1 assets are those that can be marked-to-market using a readily quoted price in an active market. Examples are stocks or futures contracts traded on an organized exchange, where bid-and-ask prices show the demand for securities and actual prices trade and can be observed impartially to mark to fair value. Level 2 assets are widely quoted and standardized, but not exchange traded. Level 3 are illiquid assets with values that are based entirely on management's best estimate and with underlying value that is derived from mathematical models. These assets use the mark-to-model and values are estimated based on unobservable market prices and management's assumptions using inputs for liquidity, credit risk, and market risk. Especially in the distressed mortgage market in the second half of 2008, firms had difficulty in measuring the fair value of these assets as these markets were inactive. In the words of the SEC, "the concept of a fair value measurement assumes an orderly transaction between market participants, where an orderly transaction is one that involves market participants that are willing to transact and allows for adequate exposure to the market." FASB subsequently issued clarification in early October, which gave management leeway in determining value, which may be based on factors such as internal models, recent market inputs, or broker quotes.

Academics and industry executives initially predicted that FASB 157 would increase a firm's earnings volatility. This was not borne out initially. A study by Andrew Alkon found that the financial services sector performed well when measured by earnings and that there was not a significant change in earnings volatility.[9] There are several possible reasons for this outcome. One possibility is that volatility was at a low level during this time and had not yet changed during the study period. However, financial risk was quite high. Noble Laureate Dr. Robert Engle suggests that volatility is mean reverting, and would increase to a much higher level. Historically, he posits that when volatility increases sharply, the equity markets will decline. The global credit crunch of 2007–2008 reflects this mean reverse to historic high volatility. Transparency continues to be a problem as much derivatives detail continues to be reflected in financial statement notes and not discernible on the balance sheet.[10]

Conflicts with International Standards: Rules versus Principles

On August 27, 2008, the SEC voted to consider whether adoption of the use of IFRS by U.S. firms should begin in 2014. IFRS reporting is more principles-based than rules-based as in the United States. This raises the following question for firms in an ERM context: Can the international standards be regarded as more effective considering that firms in Europe were also heavily involved in the global crisis? The fundamentals of IFRS are that public disclosure information has a qualitative component that is useful, understandable, relevant, and reliable. The expectation is that there will be a more meaningful dialogue between firms and auditors to disclose risks. The most important facets of IFRS in theory are transparency and reliability from period to period. But as the saying goes "good disclosure does not make up for good accounting and financial reporting." Moreover, the notion of fair value of assets and liabilities is subjective when criteria are not standardized, which can lower the reliability of the information publicly disclosed for investors. The capital markets of Brazil, Canada, China, India, Japan, and Korea will either convert to or have plans to converge to IFRS by year-end 2010. Not all U.S. companies are convinced that conversion will be beneficial overall, as some have suggested that there will be a negative accounting effect during the conversion, in addition to the conversion costs of implementation of new management philosophies, personnel, and systems. A global international advisory board with the two accounting standards boards is reviewing financial reporting issues related to the credit crisis, to consider these issues.

In the aftermath of the global financial crisis, IASB and FASB are deliberating substantive changes to the reporting and measurement of financial instruments. These changes will be as sweeping as SOX and FASB 133. This quickly moving environment highlights the importance of ERM managers and boards to work with senior executives and develop risk management policies that are evolutionary and adaptive. See Box 21.2.

Box 21.2   Is Fair Value Accounting Fair? Point and Counterpoint

Ideally financial statements of public companies should provide investors, creditors, and regulators with some of management's measures of a firm's significant enterprise risks. Theoretically, using fair value estimates allows these companies to adjust derivatives values to market levels compared with valuing an asset or liability at historic cost. Critics would argue that if the asset were held to maturity, then marking to market is not necessary unless that asset is impaired. So we are faced with this conflict: investors rely on management's assessment of fair value, while management can value balance sheet positions using market-traded securities if available, or else internal models with inputs that reflect judgments about loss outcomes using assigned probabilities.

Two contrary contemporary views are presented.

- Point: Harvey Pitt, former Chairman of the SEC
  "The concept is not the problem, the implementation is. The problem is that companies are valuing toxic assets at levels buyers don't want to buy them at. We should ask for independent assessment by economists to evaluate the methodologies and values and ask regulators to require greater disclosures. Fair value is not going to go away. It is not to blame for the problems."
- Counterpoint: William Isaac, former FDIC Chairman during the S&L real estate crisis of the 1980s
  "Fair value is highly pro-cyclical and has resulted in eliminating capital. During the S&L crisis (of the 1980s), fair value would have caused (an) additional $100 billion in losses. Further, fair value was suspended during the depression. We need to go back to the future. It makes no sense to destroy capital at the same time the Treasury is taking our money as taxpayers and putting it back into the system."

Source: October 6, 2008, Address at Yale Club.

Adding ERM to Company Credit Ratings

Standard & Poor's incorporates ERM practices into its credit rating process for financial firms and expects to also do so for nonfinancial firms. Standard and Poor's experience with ERM by insurance firms after Hurricane Katrina suggests that firms with strong ERM practices were able to quickly estimate losses within 25 percent of claims. Those with weak ERM practices were unable to quantify exposure and had greater losses than expected (Standard & Poor's 2007).

To meet the stated expectations of rating agencies, the implementation of ERM by nonfinancial firms with no previous exposure to the concept of ERM could be costly. Although this is a topic of discussion, there is not yet meaningful action by many nonfinancial firms, except on an ad-hoc basis. Firms may be frustrated with the additional requirements, as happened with SOX, but also may not understand ERM's importance except when a "storm" hits. One financial argument in favor of adopting ERM is that the firm will receive a better credit rating, which will reduce the cost of capital and improve profitability.

CONCLUSION

The firm with an effective ERM system that manages quantitative risks with additional qualitative business judgments, integrates communication between business managers and risk managers, and provides transparency of disclosures will be better prepared for not only business as usual, but business during stressful times. Lessons learned for the firm are to carefully consider the financial industry, which forgot the basic principles of ERM-exposure management to balance overall business risks and capabilities, in favor of sophisticated quantitative analytics and modeling devoid of good business deliberation.

NOTES

1. Canadian reform has been similar to that of the United States, based on rules, however, much slower and gentler, in other words, no requirement for external audit of controls.

2. Foreign firms with SEC-registered securities have less rigorous reporting requirements.

3. There are five members of the board, two of which are required to be certified public accountants. See the official web site www.pcaobus.org/ for current standards and discussion about financial oversight in the U.S.

4. A complete review of SOX sections and requirements are discussed in SOX PCAOB and SEC web sites. www.sec.gov/rules/pcaob.shtml and www.pcaobus.org.

5. FASB 133 was effective for large corporations in 2001 and a year later for smaller corporations.

6. The Basel Committee recommended that mark-to-market on debt and illiquid transactions be avoided as these are difficult to determine, verify, and audit. The committee suggested enhanced disclosure on fair value and the potential for overstating liabilities values when firms are financially distressed. Another idea to add transparency is to establish a clearinghouse or exchange traded derivatives contract so that hedges have a tradable market value.

7. Credit default swaps are private over-the-counter agreements that can be purchased to guarantee bond payments on specific firm bonds.

8. One measure to improve disclosure for financial institutions is rigorous stress tests of assets to identify aggregate market risks. Such disclosure would suggest which financial firms had adequate capital and which did not. The United States, recently instituted the disclosure of these tests to aid both investors with investment decisions and regulators for supervision and emergency lending.

9. Alkon (2006) studied 190 firms through 2005 and did not find any strong trend in volatility. Most (80 percent) showed a decrease in volatility with 41 percent registering significantly reduced market volatility. Of the total firms, only 2 percent had significant increases in standard deviation of returns.

10. See Dr. Engle's session on volatility and risk at www.ft.com/cms/a5dd621a-e39d-11dc-8799-0000779fd2ac.html?_i_referralObject=452409012&fromSearch=n.

REFERENCES

Alkon, Andrew. 2006. Result of FASB 133 on market volatility in the financial services sector, *MIT Undergraduate Research Journal*, vol. 13: 44–47.

Anonymous. 2008. A personal view of the crisis: Confessions of a risk manager. August 7. *The Economist* retrieved online at www.economist.com/finance/displaystory.cfm?story_id=11897037.

Desender, Kurt. 2007. The influence of board compensation on enterprise risk management implementation. Working paper. Universitat Autonoma de Barcelona, October.

Dreyer, Steven, and David Ingram. 2007. Criteria: Request for comment: Enterprise risk management analysis for credit ratings of nonfinancial companies. *Standard & Poor's*, retrieved online February 15, 2009, at www2.standardandpoors.com/portal/site/sp/en/us/page.article_print/3,1,1,0,1148449315878.html.

Pagach, Don, and Richard Warr. 2008. The effects of enterprise risk management on firm performance. Working paper. North Carolina State University, June.

Rosen, Robert. 2003. Risk management and corporate governance: The case of Enron. *Connecticut Law Review*, vol. 35: 1157–1184.

SEC web site www.sec.gov/rules/pcaob.shtml and the PCAOB web site www.pcaobus.org/ for rules and regulations related to PCAOB.

ABOUT THE AUTHOR

Susan Hume is an Assistant Professor of Finance in the Department of Finance and International Business at The College of New Jersey. She has teaching, research, and professional experience in international corporate finance and capital markets, banking, and derivatives securities. She has worked extensively in hedging, derivatives securities, bank lending, and bank regulations, often during periods of market crisis. Her research focus includes papers on derivatives hedging and the capital markets, corporate social responsibility, emerging market financing, and collaborative research with students. Prior to her recent appointment at TCNJ, she taught for Baruch College's Executive MBA Program in Taiwan and at Baruch College, Zicklin School of Business. She earned her doctorate at Baruch College, Zicklin School and City University of New York. She was inducted into Beta Gamma Sigma Honor Society, and is listed in various Who's Who publications (World, America, Finance and Education). She has an MBA from Rutgers University and a BA in American Studies from Douglass College.

PART V

Survey Evidence and Academic Research

CHAPTER 22

Who Reads What Most Often?

A Survey of Enterprise Risk Management Literature Read by Risk Executives

JOHN R.S. FRASER
Vice President, Internal Audit & Chief Risk Officer, Hydro One Networks Inc.

KAREN SCHOENING-THIESSEN
Senior Research Associate, The Conference Board of Canada

BETTY J. SIMKINS
Williams Companies Professor of Business and Professor of Finance,
Oklahoma State University

INTRODUCTION

Enterprise risk management (ERM) is an important discipline that is gaining popularity and recognition, both as a governance best practice and as "just good management." More and more risk executives in related roles are getting involved or are being assigned the challenging task to implement ERM.

So, what exactly is meant by "enterprise risk management?" Enterprise risk management has been defined by the Committee of Sponsoring Organizations of the Treadway Commission (COSO) as:

> "... a process, effected by an entity's board of directors, management and other personnel, applied in strategy setting and across the enterprise, designed to identify potential events that may affect the entity, and manage risk to be within its risk appetite, to provide reasonable assurance regarding the achievement of entity objectives."[1]

The first question many beginners ask, as well as those farther down the path, is: "What available research can I read to learn about this methodology or to increase my knowledge base?" There is general consensus that research and learning from others can shorten the learning curve and help avoid expensive mistakes or even the risk of failure in any project or change management initiative. Academics are entering this new field as well from a documentation and research perspective and are finding that unlike most other disciplines, there is little already written that they can use as reference material. Although a number of recent surveys have been conducted on ERM, to our knowledge no study has explored the literature that risk executives are reading or examined the perceptions of available literature.[2]

This paper provides the results of a survey conducted during the fall of 2007 by the Conference Board of Canada (CBoC)[3] to the member organizations of its Strategic Risk Council (SRC).[4] The survey served two purposes: (1) to determine how useful risk executives find published literature about enterprise risk management, and (2) to uncover weaknesses and needs in the current resources available on this critical topic. More specifically, we investigated what leading ERM practitioners used for their research materials with a view to answering a number of research objectives such as:

- Determining ERM tools and techniques most frequently used by respondents. Identifying the most widely read and highly evaluated materials in the eyes of ERM practitioners.
- Assessing whether there were potential gaps in knowledge due to the unavailability of sources of reference material (e.g., such as this paper).
- Investigating correlations between the experience of ERM practitioners or their organizations and the extent and types of research materials used.

Some of the results were indeed surprising. For example, more than one-third of survey respondents had not referred to the Australian/New Zealand Risk Management Standard 4360, which had, since 1994, been generally considered the simplest, most convenient document on risk management. Many Canadian ERM practitioners were seemingly not using the Canadian Risk Management Standard either.[5]

Based on the results of the survey, we identified the top 10 articles, the top 10 books, and the top 10 research reports available on ERM. Furthermore, we uncovered an important need for more information on ERM, especially detailed information on integrating risks, the impact of corporate culture, and actual case studies. For example, several respondents stated the following:

—There was a distinct lack of information on how to bring all the silos together—other than to say that a common reporting system and language are important.
—It was difficult to find true life examples of how the information was gathered and presented to show a greater risk picture.
—The impact of corporate culture on ERM implementation and practices is not well addressed in the literature.

Boards of directors want a risk culture that supports business growth.[6] According to the results of this survey, risk executives also want more information on developing the desired risk culture, particularly on maximizing opportunities and on how culture impacts the ERM process. As director David Yule stated in the report, "Risk, Governance and Corporate Performance,"[7] "Culture is an organization's most important risk management strategy." What is not a surprise, given the role of boards and the responsibilities of risk executives, is that boards do not want to be bogged down in the details of ERM, whereas risk executives are very much interested in knowing the "how to" of implementing ERM.

Of interest to risk executives is the evolution of the role of the chief risk officer (CRO). This is evident from the ratings of the top 10 articles and research that risk executives have read. Boards look to their chief executive officer (CEO) as having ultimate responsibility for managing risks; however, CEOs rely on their CRO for the necessary risk information and for coordinating the ERM process.[8] This is one of the main reasons why CROs are interested in learning how their roles, responsibilities, and skills are leveraged within an organizational structure where ERM is a key governing tool for corporate performance.

Overall, we present key findings from our survey, which are discussed in detail in this chapter. The results of this study help highlight excellent opportunities for academics to closely collaborate with practitioners to conduct research in these key areas of need.

The second section of this chapter describes the survey methodology and how we selected the literature to include in the survey. The third section summarizes the survey results, highlights critical areas where additional information is needed about ERM, and describes our key findings. A conclusion is provided in the final section.

SURVEY METHODOLOGY

This survey was developed using input from several risk professionals experienced in ERM. The survey was Web-based using the latest technology and was "pretested" with corporate risk executives for clarity and ease of use. In September 2007, e-mail invitations were sent to 87 risk executives asking them to participate in the survey: 52 members of the Strategic Risk Council at the CBoC, and 35 members of the Strategic Risk Council of the U.S. Conference Board.[9] Only professionals with ERM experience were asked to participate and most had a high level of expertise in ERM. After a second e-mail in October and follow-up telephone calls in October and November, 44 survey responses (37 Canadian and 7 U.S. organizations) had been received. Overall, the response rate was 50.6 percent.

Regarding the survey questions, each respondent was asked to provide the following background information: organization, industry, title, area of expertise, years of experience with ERM, years organization has been implementing ERM, organization size, number of employees, scope of operations, benefits executive management stated as reasons to implement ERM, respondent's area of expertise, use of consultants, and use and benefit of COSO and other sources of ERM knowledge.

When selecting the literature to include, we conducted an extensive and exhaustive review of published material as of summer 2007 on the subject of ERM. To our knowledge, we considered all leading sources of published information before selecting the final set of 88 publications to include in the survey.[10] Appendix 22.A lists these publications. In the survey, we asked respondents to rate ERM literature by responding to the following two questions:

1. Did you read this book/research paper/article and if so to what extent? (Note: Response choices were: 1=never heard of it, 2=heard of it, but not really read it, 3=read less than 10 percent of it, 4=read between 10 percent and 80 percent, and 5=read more than 80 percent.)

2. In terms of adding value to your knowledge of ERM, how would you rate this book/research paper/article according to methodologies, tools, techniques, and leading practices for ERM? (Note: Response choices were: 1=not really relevant to ERM, 2=some value but not a lot, 3=reasonably useful, 4=very good in ERM, and 5=a must read for ERM.)

Additional questions were also asked in the survey. The next section summarizes our results and highlights top needs for more relevant and useful literature on ERM.

SURVEY RESULTS

In this section, we first discuss background characteristics and related questions on ERM answered by the survey respondents before presenting the main objective of our survey, to determine the most useful literature read by risk executives. We wrap up the section by discussing critical areas of need in the ERM literature and highlighting the key findings of our survey.

Survey Respondent Profile

A broad range of industries were represented in the survey as shown in Exhibit 22.1: 32 percent in financial services, 18 percent in the utility sector, 9 percent in telecommunications, 9 percent in the public sector, 7 percent in energy, 5 percent in manufacturing, 5 percent in health care, and 15 percent in other industries. See Appendix 22.B for a list of companies that responded to the survey and gave

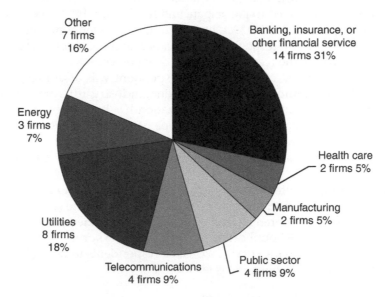

Exhibit 22.1 Industry Affiliation of Survey Respondents
This graphic lists the number of firms and the percentage of total firms by industry that responded to the survey.

Exhibit 22.2 Experience with Enterprise Risk Management

	For how many years have you been practicing ERM?	Number of years your organization has implementing ERM
0 years	0%	2.3%
>0 to 1 year	7.0%	9.3%
>1 to 3 years	37.2%	25.6%
>3 to 5 years	16.3%	39.5%
>5 years	39.5%	23.3%
Average	5.3 years	3.8 years

This table summarizes the experience survey respondents and companies have with ERM. The responses are listed as a percentage of total responses.

us permission to be identified. Since the survey was given through the CBoC, most respondents were from Canada but 16 percent were from the United States. Although 78 percent of the companies' operations were primarily in the United States and Canada, 28 percent of the respondents worked for companies that had operations in at least one international country (and almost all had global operations). Most organizations that participated in the survey were large and the average size was approximately $27 billion in total assets and 18,000 employees. The largest participating organization was General Motors. However, a few small businesses participated in the survey: approximately 10 percent of the survey respondents had fewer than 100 employees but only one organization had assets less than $1 million.

Exhibit 22.2 lists the numbers of years of experience that survey respondents and companies have had with ERM. As shown, all respondents had some experience, and 95 percent listed risk management as their primary area of expertise. The mean ERM experience was 5.3 years and approximately 40 percent of the respondents have more than 5 years of experience. Only one respondent had less than one year of experience with ERM and 11 percent had less than two years of experience. The respondents had more years of ERM experience on average than their organizations (5.3 years versus 3.8 years). Most companies that responded have implemented ERM to a certain extent. Approximately 88 percent of companies had more than one year of experience and more than 60 percent had at least three years of experience. These results are consistent with other surveys indicating that companies are moving toward more advanced stages of ERM as external stakeholders, rating agencies, and analysts expect more information on risk management techniques being employed.[11]

Most survey respondents held high positions within the organization: more than one-half (52.3 percent) held positions at the chief risk officer level or higher. The largest group in the survey held the title of director (31.8 percent) while 9.1 percent were chief officers (not risk). Most respondents reported to top officials of the organization: 31 percent to the chief financial officer and 26.2 percent to the chief executive officer.[12] It is interesting to note that 24 percent stated they also reported functionally to the audit committee.

Exhibit 22.3   Drivers for Implementing Enterprise Risk Management

Benefits of Enterprise Risk Management	% of Firms Responding (38)
Better understanding and management of risk (including integrated view)	44.7
Improve corporate governance or meet board requirements	18.4
Assist in allocation of resources	15.8
Effective decision making	15.8
Minimize surprises	13.2
Improve risk reporting and risk controls	10.5
Achieve financial stability or better risk-adjusted returns	10.5
Improve credit rating	10.5
Compliance	10.5
Enhance shareholder or firm value	7.9
Create a risk-aware culture	7.9
Best practices or achieve excellence	5.3
Support business or strategic plan	5.3

This table lists the most frequently cited responses to the open-ended question: What benefits has executive management stated as reasons to implement ERM?

Exhibit 22.3 lists the most frequently cited benefits by executive management of implementing ERM. Respondents were allowed to list multiple benefits. As shown, the most cited benefit is "Better understanding and management of risk (including an integrated view)."[13] This benefit, cited by 44.7 percent of respondents, shows a high level of acceptance of ERM and suggests that companies genuinely understand the importance of this advanced risk process. The second most cited reason (18.4 percent), "Improve corporate governance or meet board requirements," reflects recent regulatory changes and the increased emphasis on corporate governance. Another survey by Gates (2006) has found a higher percent (66 percent) listing this benefit.[14] Given that 84 percent of the organizations in our study are Canadian and are less likely to be required to comply with Sarbanes-Oxley (SOX), the second-place ranking is not surprising.[15] It is interesting to note that 10.5 percent listed improving their credit rating as a benefit of ERM. We expect this percentage to increase over time given that ratings agencies are now including ERM as part of their ratings process for nonfinancials.[16]

ERM Tools and Techniques Used by Respondents

Do risk executives follow COSO's ERM recommended tools and techniques? Exhibit 22.4 summarizes the survey responses. Surprisingly, 19 organizations (48.7 percent) responded they seldom do this, 20.5 percent responded "sometimes," and only 30.8 percent responded "to a large extent." No organization responded "as much as possible." While COSO is the most read resource (see later discussion on this), it does not appear to be the most useful for actual practice at this time. Anecdotal input from informal surveys and roundtables indicate that COSO is

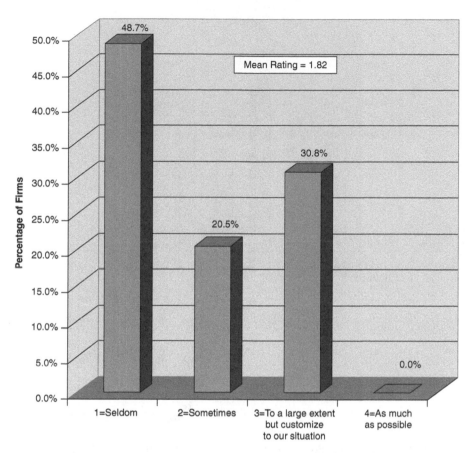

Exhibit 22.4 Extent of Following COSO's ERM Recommended Tools and Techniques
This graph lists the responses to the question: To what extent do you follow COSO's ERM recommended tools and techniques?

written in a style that is hard to read and to absorb. It is our belief that many readers give up partway through and therefore do not refer to COSO or use its ideas in practice. However, this means that there is an important opportunity for COSO to be rewritten in the future. Protiviti's (2006) "Guide to Enterprise Risk Management: Frequently Asked Questions" seems to have garnered greater readership and to be an easier document to read and understand.

So how useful are other sources of best practices and methodology for ERM? Exhibit 22.5 answers this question for the following sources: COSO, public accounting firms and consultants, professional associations (RIMS, PRIMIA, SOA, etc.), newspapers and magazines, academic journals and papers, and literature in general. Response choices were: 1=seldom; 2=fair/occasional; 3=good/frequent, and 4=as much as possible. As shown in Exhibit 22.5, risk executives rated knowledge of the literature as the highest source of guidance on ERM practices and methodology (mean rating of 3.08), followed by professional associations as the next most useful source of information (mean rating of 2.52). Consistent with Exhibit 22.4, COSO received the lowest rating of 1.81.

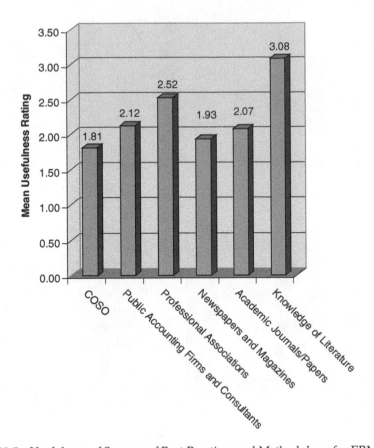

Exhibit 22.5 Usefulness of Sources of Best Practices and Methodology for ERM
This graph lists the mean response rating to the question: How useful are the following sources of best practices and methodology for ERM? Ratings response categories were: 1=Seldom, 2=Fair/Occasional, 3=Good/Frequent, and 4=As much as Possible.

How useful are consultants to the implementation of ERM? Fifty-nine percent of the organizations have used consultants to help with their journey in ERM. In response to the question "Do you feel you have learned more from reading and researching ERM than from consultants?" it appears respondents find the literature more helpful: 53 percent responded "yes," 39 percent responded "somewhat," and 8 percent responded "no." Respondents were allowed to comment regarding their responses. The following comments illustrate three of the key concerns executives face with consultants:

1. Consultants have no choice but to provide generic/academic frameworks and tools. Only in-house management can implement a true ERM approach for their own company because they know their business, processes, culture, and just what makes sense for them that no outside party can truly know. It becomes inefficient to educate an outside party on your business just so they can try to tell you what you should be doing (from generic models) to manage it better.

2. Consultants generally advocate a single perspective—often a COSO view—which we find too restrictive and compliance-based. Some consultants advocate the use of Basel but it is not a good fit for our industry. An ERM program needs to be developed from within. We have used the Australian Standard 4360 to help build our program.
3. Some articles (if current) are sometimes more pragmatic and "out of the box" versus consultants. Consultants seem to have capabilities around risk assessment, but less so for robust ERM framework/implementation efforts.

Although it is clear that risk executives as a group find ERM literature more helpful, several respondents indicated the benefits of consultants, too:

- My belief is that consultants are helpful in the "getting started" phase and also for specific tasks, such as facilitating a risk profiling process with an executive group.
- Consultants can be useful but I want to know the theory and practice myself so that I can direct and check the recommendations of consultants.
- The consultants were useful in the implementation of what we had decided we wanted as a framework. However, they provided good value in benchmarking best practices that we would not have been able to do.

And one must be careful with the literature, as one survey respondent points out,

The problem is sorting out the good readings from the bad (or even harmful).

We also investigated the relationship between risk executives experience and their familiarity with ERM literature using the categories shown in Exhibit 22.5. Experience was measured as the number of years the respondent had with ERM. Although we find no significant relationship between risk executives' experience and their ratings on the benefits of COSO and other major sources of ERM information, we do find that more experienced risk executives had a greater knowledge of the literature than their less experienced counterparts (Pearson correlation coefficient of 51 percent; significant at the 1 percent level). We discuss the relation between experience and the most frequently read literature in more detail in the next section.

Risk executives in higher positions had read significantly more than those in lower positions (Pearson correlation coefficient of 28 percent; significant at the 10 percent level).[17] We also found that risk executives in higher positions rated academic papers less useful (Pearson correlation coefficient of −19 percent but insignificant at the 10 percent level). Although the result is not significant at conventional levels, it is worth noting and in contrast to the finding of almost no relationship between years of experience and usefulness of academic papers. Given that few academic papers have been published on ERM, one should not draw any strong conclusions from this result other than the indication that there is a crucial need for academics to publish more useful research on ERM.

Most Frequently Read Literature on ERM

Now to the main objective of our study: to uncover the most useful literature read by risk executives. As discussed in the previous section, we asked respondents to rate each reading by answering the following two questions: (1) Did you read this book/research paper/article and if so to what extent?; and (2) in terms of adding value to your knowledge of ERM, how would you rate this book/research paper/article according to methodologies, tools, techniques, and leading practices for ERM? (Note: For discussion purposes, we refer to the Question 1 response as "read" and the Question 2 response as "value.")

We classified the 88 readings according to articles (24 total, which includes surveys, academic studies, and practitioner articles), books (32 total), and research reports (32 total). Exhibit 22.6 summarizes the mean ratings of the readings for all publications and by type (i.e., articles, books, and research reports). Panel A summarizes the "read" and "value" ratings and Panel B analyzes the ratings based on the respondents experience with ERM. In Panel B, risk executives with five years or more experience were classified as having "high experience" and those with less than five years experience were classified as "low experience." (Note: The mean level of experience of all risk executives was 5.3 years.) As shown in Panel A, the mean ratings for "read" and "value" do not differ greatly according to publication type. However, in Panel B, risk executives with greater experience were more familiar with all publication types (difference of means t-test significant at the one percent level in all groups). There was no significant difference in the "value" rating based on experience.

To select the "top readings" individually, we first ranked the readings by type (i.e., articles, books, and research reports) using a weighting scheme based on the responses to the two questions. We then sorted the ranked categories into quartiles and the readings, which were ranked in the top quartiles based on both questions that were first considered as "top readings." Only literature rated by at least six respondents was considered in the final rankings.[18] A few articles with second quartile rankings still made the top 10 lists. The results of our "Top 10" readings are presented in Exhibits 22.7, 22.8, and 22.9 for the articles, books, and research reports, respectively. Our survey participants may not represent all ERM executives' familiarity with the literature, but, to our knowledge, we present the first survey evidence on this important topic. Anyone wishing to learn more about ERM should consider placing these publications on their "must read" list.

Exhibit 22.7 lists the top 10 articles on ERM sorted according to the year of publication. As mentioned earlier, we include surveys, academic studies, and practitioner articles in this category. Although not indicated in the table, the highest ranked study in this category is "Risk Management Reports" by H. Felix Kloman (later Beaumont Vance), followed by "Enterprise Risk Management at Hydro One Inc." by Fraser, Quail, and Kirienko (2001).[19]

The top 10 books on ERM are listed in Exhibit 22.8.[20] The books receiving the highest overall rating are 20 Questions Directors Should Ask about Risk by Lindsay, Fraser, Goodfellow, and Toledano (2006) and the COSO publication, "Enterprise Risk Management: Integrated Framework: Executive Summary" (2004). This COSO publication was the most well read in our survey (mean "read" rating of 4.13; read by 74 percent of survey respondents) but received a mean "value" rating of 2.45,

Exhibit 22.6 Mean Ratings of Publications Used in Survey

Publication Type	N	"Read" Mean Rating	"Value" Mean Rating
Panel A. Ratings of Publications by Type			
All	88	1.68	2.69
Articles	23	1.42	2.68
Books	33	1.71	2.71
Research Reports	32	1.84	2.88

Panel B. Ratings of Publications by Type and Level of ERM Experience

Publication Type	"Read" Mean Rating			"Value" Mean Rating		
	Low Experience N=24	High Experience N=20	t-statistic (p-value)	Low Experience	High Experience	t-statistic (p-value)
All	1.38	1.92	−3.55 (0.001)***	2.78	2.68	1.22 (0.233)
Articles	1.25	1.67	−2.73 (0.009)***	2.68	2.70	−0.08 (0.935)
Books	1.45	2.09	−3.82 (0.001)***	2.89	2.65	0.96 (0.359)
Research Reports	1.59	2.22	−3.24 (0.003)***	3.03	2.67	1.17 (0.260)

This table reports summary ratings of ERM literature based on the following two survey questions: (1) Did you read this book/research paper/article and if so to what extent? Response choices were: 1=never heard of it, 2=heard of it, but not really read it, 3=read less than 10% of it, 4=read between 10%–80%, and 5=read more than 80%), and (2) in terms of adding value to your knowledge of ERM, how would you rate this book/research paper/article according to methodologies, tools, techniques and leading practices for ERM? Response choices were: 1=not really relevant to ERM, 2=some value but not a lot, 3=reasonably useful, 4=very good in ERM, and 5=a must read for ERM. The Question 1 and Question 2 responses are reported in this table as "Read" and "Value," respectively. Panel B reports the results of ratings based on the respondents experience with ERM. Respondents with 5 years or more were classified as having "high experience" and those with less than 5 years were classified as "low experience." The panel also presents univariate tests of the differences in mean values between ratings for the high and low experience groups. The t-statistic provides a test of the null hypothesis that the mean value does not differ between the two groups. Significance levels are indicated as follows: ***1%, **5%, *10%.

which can be viewed as an average rating. This is consistent with our findings discussed earlier regarding the COSO publications.

Exhibit 22.9 lists the top 11 research reports. Eleven reports are listed due to a tie for 10th place. Three research reports received significantly higher ratings than other reports and are as follows (listed in order of ranking): "Risk Management" by AS/NZS 4360 (1995, 1999, and 2005), "Guide to Enterprise Risk Management: Frequently Asked Questions" by Protiviti (2006), and "ERM: Inside and Out" by Thiessen (2005).

Exhibit 22.7   Top 10 Articles

Journal/Source	Date	Authors	Title
Seawack Press Inc.	1974+	Kloman, later Vance	*Risk Management* Reports (a monthly publication)
Conference Board of Canada	2001	Fraser, Quail and Kirienko	Enterprise Risk Management at Hydro One Inc.
Risk Management	2001	Lam	The CRO is Here to Stay
Journal of Applied Corporate Finance	2002	Harrington, Niehaus, and Risko	Enterprise Risk Management: The Case of United Grain Growers
Risk Management and Insurance Review	2003	Dleffner, Lee, and McGannon	The Effect of Corporate Governance on the Use of Enterprise Risk Management: Evidence from Canada
Journal of Applied Corporate Finance	2005	Aabo, Fraser, and Simkins	The Rise and Evolution of the Chief Risk Officer: Enterprise Risk Management at Hydro One
Journal of Accounting and Public Policy	2005	Beasley, Cluen, Hermanson	Enterprise Risk Management: An Empirical Analysis of Factors Associated with the Extent of Implementation
FT Partnership Publications	2006	London Financial Times and Ernst & Young	*Mastering Uncertainty*
James Lam & Associates	2006	James Lam & Associates	Emerging Best Practices in Developing Key Risk Indicators and ERM Reporting
Journal of Applied Corporate Finance	2006	Gates	Incorporating Strategic Risk into Enterprise Risk Management: A Survey of Current Corporate Practice

This chart lists the top 10 articles based on the survey responses. The articles are listed by year of publication. Refer to the references for complete citation information.

Are there other useful readings we omitted from our study? We asked respondents to identify literature they found useful in early stages and advanced stages of ERM that we had omitted from our list. The most frequently mentioned publications are listed in Exhibit 22.10. Panel A lists studies useful in early stages and Panel B lists ones useful in more advanced stages. Interestingly, respondents indicated that some of the best literature they have read does not necessarily mention ERM, but simply addresses various aspects of risk. The variety of risk literature fits with the fact that the respondents come from diverse lines of businesses, industries, and corporate structures, not to mention representing a large range of individual interests. It should be noted that only one publication was mentioned by more than one respondent (i.e., Black Swan); all others were only mentioned once. This supported the validity of our original survey lists that there were no major omissions. The Black Swan was omitted from our survey list as it was published in April 2007 during the compilation of our survey list.

Exhibit 22.8 Top 10 Books

Publisher	Date	Authors	Title
Currency/Doubleday	1991 & 1996	Schwartz	The Art of the Long View
John Wiley & Sons	1996	Bernstein	Against The Gods: The Remarkable Story of Risk
Prentice Hall/FT	2000	DeLoach	Enterprise-wide Risk Management: Strategies for Linking Risk and Opportunity
Texere LLC	2001	Taleb	Fooled by Randomness
IIA Research Foundation	2001	Miccolis, Hively, and Merkley	Enterprise Risk Management: Trends and Emerging Practices
IIA Research Foundation	2002	Barton, Shenkir, and Walker	Enterprise Risk Management: Putting it All Together
Prentice Hall & FT Foundation	2002	Barton, Shenkir, and Walker	Making Enterprise Risk Management Pay Off
Committee of Sponsoring Organizations (COSO)	2004	COSO	Enterprise Risk Management— Integrated Framework: Application Techniques
Committee of Sponsoring Organizations (COSO)	2004	COSO	Enterprise Risk Management: Integrated Framework: Executive Summary
Canadian Institute of Chartered Accountants (CICA)	2006	Lindsay (Fraser, Goodfellow, Toledano)	20 Questions Directors Should Ask about Risk
Risk Insurance Management Society	2007	Vance and Makomaski	Enterprise Risk Management for Dummies

This table lists the top 10 books based on the survey responses. The books are listed by year of publication. Refer to the references for complete citation information.

Critical Areas of Need

Answers provided to open-ended questions in the survey suggest that there is a critical need for more detailed "real-world" applications on ERM. In response to the question, "What problems/challenges have you encountered in implementing ERM that were not addressed in the literature?" the following quotes by risk executives summarize key areas of need:

- In addition, virtually all literature is silent on how to deal with the myriad cultural, logistical, historical challenges that exist and are unique to all organizations. These (and other) challenges create significant (and sometimes insurmountable) barriers that must be addressed if an organization hopes to manage risk on an integrated basis.

Exhibit 22.9 Top 11 Research Reports

Source	Date	Authors	Title
Austraila (AS) and New Zealand (NZS)	1995, 1999 & 2005	AS/NZS	Risk Management
Enterprise Risk Management	2000	Tillinghast-Towers Perrin	An Analytical Approach
Conference Board of Canada	2001	Thiessen, Hoyt, and Merkley	A Composite Sketch of a Chief Risk Officer
Standards Australia	2002	Standards Australia	Organizational Experiences in Implementing Risk Management Practices
John Wiley & Sons	2003	Lam	Enterprise Risk Management: From Incentives to Controls
Conference Board of Canada	2005	Thiessen	Enterprise Risk Management: Inside and Out
Standard & Poors	2005	Standard & Poors	Enterprise Risk Management for Financial Institutions
Guide to Enterprise Risk Management	2006	Protiviti	Frequently Asked Questions
Standard & Poor's	2006	Standard & Poor's	Criteria: Assessing Enterprise Risk Management Practices of Financial Institutions: Rating Criteria & Best Practices
The Conference Board	2006	Brancato	The Role of U.S. Corporate Boards in Enterprise Risk Management
Committee of Chief Risk Officers (CCRO)	2007	CCRO	Enterprise Risk Management and Supporting Metrics

This table lists the top 11 research reports based on the survey responses. Eleven reports are listed due to a tie for 10th place. The reports are listed by year of publication. Refer to the references for complete citation information.

- Many of the articles describe what the process should look like and how it should function but there are few that provide details of how to get to that step. Many of the articles use great overarching statements that seem very much like motherhood statements. There was a distinct lack of information on how to bring all the silos together—other than to say that a common reporting system and language are important. It was difficult to find true life examples of how the information was gathered and presented to show a greater risk picture.
- The impact of corporate culture on ERM implementation and practices is not well addressed in the literature.

Key Findings of Our Survey

To summarize the most important results of our survey, we identify the following five findings. Our results help illuminate areas of need in the practice of ERM. We

Exhibit 22.10 Other Useful Literature for the Implementation of ERM Not Included in the Survey

Panel A: At Early Stages

Source	Date	Authors	Title
UCL Press	1995	Adams	Risk
Harper and Rowe	2002	Knight	Risk, Uncertainty and Profit
Simon and Schuster	2002	Gigerenzer	Calculated Risks: How to Know When Numbers Deceive You
IRMIC, ALARM, IRM	2002	IRMIC, ALARM, IRM	A Risk Management Standard
McGraw/Hill	2004	Dallas	Governance and Risk
Deloitte and Touche	2004	Bailey, Bloom, and Hida	Assessing the Value of Enterprise Risk Management
The Conference Board	2005	Subramaniam	Keep It Simple: Getting Your Arms Around Enterprise Risk Management
Protiviti	2006	Protiviti	Enterprise Risk Management: Practical Implementation Advice
Harvard Business School Press	2006	Apgar	Risk Intelligence: Learning to Manage What We Don't Know
RMA Journal	2007	Dev and Rao	ERM: A New Way to Manage a Financial Institution
Random House	2007	Taleb	The Black Swan: The Impact of Highly Improbable Events

Panel B: At More Advanced Stages

Source	Date	Authors	Title
Vintage Books	1996	Tenner	Why Things Bite Back: Technology and the Revenge of Unintended Consequences
Princeton University Press	2000	Shiller	Irrational Exhuberance
IIA Research Foundation	2000	Hubbard	Control Self-Assessment: A Practical Guide
Oxford University Press	2003	Koen	Discussion of the Method
KPMG	2003	KPMG	Enterprise Risk Management: An Emerging Model for Building Shareholder Value
KPMG	2003	Hashagen	Basel II—A Closer Look: Managing Operational Risk
John Wiley & Sons	2005	Dowd	Measuring Market Risk
Risk Center	2005	Banfield	Creating a Risk Inventory and Gap Analysis, and Dealing with Obstacles to Enterprise-Wide Risk
The Conference Board	2007	Hexter	Risk Business: Is Enterprise Risk Management Losing Ground?
MIT Sloan Management Review	2007	Bonabeau	Understanding and Managing Complexity Risk

This table includes the responses from risk executives about the literature they found useful in early stages and advanced stages of ERM that we excluded from our survey list. Panel A lists studies useful in early stages and Panel B lists ones useful at more advanced stages. Refer to the references for complete citation information.

hope that our results are useful to practitioners wanting to learn more about enterprise risk management and also to academics interested in conducting research in this crucial area.

1. Surprisingly, COSO was not being considered and used as the key source of information and guidance.
2. Challenges remain for new implementers, especially as to specific guidance on what to do in their cultural context.
3. Much more work is needed in the areas of research and case studies so that risk executives can learn from the experiences of others who have successfully implemented ERM. More specifically, risk executives are looking for more practical "how to's," sharing of experiences, impacts of different corporate culture, and best practices at the different stages of ERM implementation. This is an excellent opportunity for academics to closely collaborate with practitioners to conduct research in these key areas of need. (Note: What was read in the top 10 articles, books, and research was mostly about the "how to" aspects of ERM.)
4. Despite the wealth of practical experience of survey respondents, most of whom are from large companies, there clearly remain many areas to explore and discuss before a common understanding or methodology for ERM could be considered to be in place.
5. Experienced risk executives are more familiar with the literature and also find publications about "risk in general" very useful at early and advanced stages of enterprise risk management implementation.

CONCLUSION

Our study presents the first survey evidence of risk executives working in the area of ERM about the literature they find most effective in assisting and facilitating the successful implementation of ERM. This is the first of a planned periodic survey on this topic by the Conference Board of Canada.

Without a doubt, ERM is a paramount topic for business enterprises desiring to survive and succeed in the future. ERM is not a fad—it is here to stay and is the natural evolution of risk management to view risk at the enterprise-wide level. New external drivers are pushing risk executives to find out more about ERM and the level of interest in this topic is increasing with time. Some of the drivers for ERM are as follows: boards are being held more accountable for risk management; stakeholders are becoming more vocal about corporate activities and demanding better management of risk; corporate disasters such as Société Générale, Enron, WorldCom, and the subprime crisis are making board members and corporate executives more aware of the consequences of ineffective risk management; ratings agencies are including this in their credit-rating analyses not only for financial firms, but also for nonfinancial firms as of 2008; globalization of corporations including increased outsourcing, supply chain management, and other factors, affects the risks and management of them; and many companies have reported significant benefits from ERM programs.

To summarize, the most important findings of our study are as follows: first, surprisingly, COSO was not considered a key source of information and guidance. Second, organizations new to ERM are still facing hurdles, despite all the resources at hand. Third, clearly, much more work is needed in the areas of research and case studies so that risk executives can learn from the experiences of others who have successfully implemented ERM. Fourth, many areas still need to be explored and discussed before a common understanding or methodology for ERM could be considered to be in place; and fifth, experienced risk executives are not only much more familiar with the literature, but they also find publications about "risk in general" useful at both early and advanced stages of enterprise risk management implementation.

To help facilitate progress on the global practice of ERM, we would like to encourage academics to collaborate closely with practitioners to conduct research and develop case studies.[21] We also encourage interested parties to contact the Conference Board of Canada about the Strategic Risk Council and its evolving work in ERM. This study highlights crucial areas of need on ERM, and we hope will help be a starting point to encourage and stimulate more advances in the research and practice of ERM. As Leonardo da Vinci noted more than 500 years ago about the importance of knowledge in both theory and practice: "He who loves practice without theory is like the sailor who boards ship without a rudder and compass and never knows where he may cast."

APPENDIX 22.A: PUBLICATIONS INCLUDED IN THE SURVEY

The following is a list of the literature included, sorted by year of publication, in the survey including the source, author(s), year published, title, and type (i.e., articles, books, and research reports). Refer to the references for complete citation information. Publication types are indicated as follows: Articles (which include surveys, academic studies, and practitioner articles) are indicated by a "1," books by a "2," and research reports by a "3."

Source	Date	Authors	Title	Type
Seawack Press, Inc.	1974+	Kloman and Vance	Risk Management Reports	1
Omega Systems Group	1987	Grose	Managing Risk: Systematic Loss Prevention for Executives	2
Currency/ Doubleday	1991, 1996	Schwartz	The Art of the Long View	2
Committee of Sponsoring Organizations (COSO)	1992	COSO	Internal Control: Integrated Framework	2

Source	Date	Authors	Title	Type
Austraila (AS)/New Zealand (NZS)	1995, 1999, and 2004	AS/NZS 4360	Risk Management	3
Toronto Stock Exchange (TSE) Committee on Corp. Gov. in Canada	1994	TSE Committee on Corp. Gov. in Canada	Where Were the Directors: Guidelines for Improved Corporate Governance in Canada	3
Economic Intelligence Unit	1995	Arthur Anderson	Managing Business Risks: An Integrated Approach	3
John Wiley & Sons	1996	Bernstein	Against The Gods: The Remarkable Story of Risk	2
Standards Council of Canada	1997	Standards Council of Canada	Risk Management: Guideline for Decision-Makers	3
Conference Board of Canada	1997	Nottingham	A Conceptual Framework for Integrated Risk Management	3
Conference Board of Canada	1998	Birkbeck	Realizing the Rewards: How Integrated Risk Management Can Benefit Your Organization	3
Canadian Institute of Chartered Accountants (CICA)	1998	Bradshaw and Willis	Learning About Risk: Choices, Connections and Competencies	2
Risk Mgmt and Insurance Review	1999	Colquitt, Hoyt, and Lee	Integrated Risk Management and the Role of the Risk Manager	1
Conference Board of Canada	1999	Birkbeck	Forewarned if Forearmed: Identification and Measurement in Integrated Risk Management	3
Tillinghast-Towers Perrin	2000	Tillinghast-Towers Perrin	Enterprise Risk Management—An Analytical Approach	3
Canadian Institute of Chartered Accountants (CICA)	2000	CICA	Guidance for Directors Dealing with Risk in the Boardroom	2

Source	Date	Authors	Title	Type
American Institute of Certified Public Accountants (AICPA) and CICA	2000	Lindsay	Managing Risks in the New Economy	2
Prentice Hall/Financial Times	2000	DeLoach	Enterprise-wide Risk Management: Strategies for Linking Risk and Opportunity	2
Journal of Risk Mgmt of Korea	2001	D'Arcy and Brogan	Enterprise Risk Management	1
Conference Board of Canada	2001	Thiessen, Hoyt, and Merkley	A Composite Sketch of a Chief Risk Officer	3
Canadian Centre of Mgmt Development	2001	Canadian Centre of Mgmt Devel.	A Foundation for Developing Risk Management Learning Strategies in the Public Sector: CCMD Roundtable on Risk Management	3
Treasury Board of Canada Secretariat	2001	Treasury Board of Canada Secretariat	Integrated Risk Management Framework	3
Conference Board of Canada	2001	Fraser, Quail, and Kirienko	Enterprise Risk Management at Hydro One Inc.	1
McGraw-Hill	2001	Grouhy, Galai, and Mark	Risk Management	2
Random House Trade Paperbacks	2001	Lowenstein	When Genius Failed: The Rise and Fall of Long-Term Capital Management	2
IIA Research Foundation	2001	Miccolis, Hively, and Merkley	Enterprise Risk Management: Trends and Emerging Practices	2
Conference Board of Canada	2001	Thiessen	Integrating Risk Management Through a Change Management Process	3
International Risk Mgmt Institute	2001	Miccolis	ERM and September 11	1
Jossey-Bass Wiley	2001	Weick and Sutcliffe	Managing the Unexpected	2
Risk Mgmt Magazine	2001	Lam	The CRO is Here to Stay	1
Texere LLC	2001	Taleb	Fooled by Randomness	2
Standards Australia	2002	Standards Australia	Organizational Experiences in Implementing Risk Management Practices	3

Source	Date	Authors	Title	Type
The Strategy Unit: Cabinet Office Britain	2002	Strategy Unit: Cabinet Office Britain	Risk: Improving Government's Capability to Handle Risk and Uncertainty	3
The Non Profit Risk Mgmt Center	2002	The Non Profit Risk Mgmt Center	Enlightened Risk-Taking: A Guide and Workbook to Strategic Risk Management for Nonprofits	2
IIA Research Foundation	2002	Barton, Shenkir, and Walker	Enterprise Risk Management: Putting It All Together	2
CPA Australia	2002	CPA Australia	Enterprise-Wide Risk Management: Better Practice Guide for the Public Sector	3
CPA Australia	2002	CPA Australia	Case Studies in Public Sector Risk Management	3
National Association of Corporate Directors (NACD)	2002	NACD	Report of the NACD Blue Ribbon Commission on Risk Oversight: Board Lessons for Turbulent Times	3
Prentice Hall & FT Foundation	2002	Barton, Shenkir, and Walker	Making Enterprise Risk Management Pay Off	2
Journal of Applied Corporate Finance	2002	Meulbroek	A Senior Manager's Guide to Integrated Risk Management	1
Journal of Applied Corporate Finance	2002	Harrington, Niehaus, and Risko	Enterprise Risk Management: The Case of United Grain Growers	1
IFAC and Chartered Institute of Mgmt Acct (CIMA)	2002	IFAC and CIMA	Managing Risk to Enhance Stakeholder Value	3
John Wiley & Sons	2003	Lam	Enterprise Risk Management: From Incentives to Controls	3
Casualty Actuarial Society	2003	Casualty Actuarial Society	Overview of Enterprise Risk Management	3
Journal of Applied Corporate Finance	2003	Chew, et. al.	University of Georgia Roundtable on Enterprise-Wide Risk Management	1
Internal Auditor	2003	Walker	ERM in Practice	1

Source	Date	Authors	Title	Type
Risk Management and Insurance Review	2003	Liebenberg and Hoyt	The Determinants of Enterprise Risk Management: Evidence from the Appointment of Chief Risk Officers	1
Risk Management and Insurance Review	2003	Kleffner, Lee, and McGannon	The Effect of Corporate Governance on the Use of Enterprise Risk Management: Evidence from Canada	1
Committee of Sponsoring Organizations (COSO)	2004	COSO	Enterprise Risk Management: Integrated Framework: Executive Summary	2
Age of Risk Management (AORM)	2004	Thompson	Risk in Perspective: Insight and Humor in the Age of Risk Management	2
HM Treasury	2004	HM Treasury	The Orange Book: Management of Risk—Principles and Concepts	2
Committee of Sponsoring Organizations (COSO)	2004	COSO	Enterprise Risk Management—Integrated Framework: Application Techniques	2
Canadian Institute of Chartered Accountants (CICA)	2005	Sabia and Goodfellow	Integrity in the Spotlight: Audit Committees in a High Risk World	2
IIA Research Foundation	2005	Sobel	Auditor's Risk Management Guide: Integrating Auditing & ERM	2
John Wiley & Sons	2005	Pickett	Auditing the Risk Management Process	2
Viking Books	2005	Diamond	Collapse: How Societies Choose to Fail or Succeed	2
Conference Board of Canada	2005	Thiessen	ERM: Inside and Out	3
Lloyds and The Economist Intelligence Unit (EIU)	2005	Lloyds and EIU	Taking Risk on Board	3
Journal of Applied Corporate Finance	2005	Aabo, Fraser, and Simkins	The Rise and Evolution of the Chief Risk Officer: Enterprise Risk Management at Hydro One	1

Source	Date	Authors	Title	Type
Harper-Collins Publishers Ltd	2005	Rosenthal	Struck by Lightning: The Curious World of Probabilities	2
Strategic Finance	2005	Stroh	Enterprise Risk Management at United Healthcare	1
Standard & Poor's	2005	Standard & Poor's	Enterprise Risk Management for Financial Institutions	3
The Economist Intelligence Unit (EIU)	2005	EIU	The Evolving Role of the CRO	3
Journal of Accounting and Public Policy	2005	Beasley, Clune, and Hermanson	Enterprise Risk Management: An Empirical Analysis of Factors Associated with the Extent of Implementation	1
Journal of Applied Corporate Finance	2005	Chew, et al.	Morgan Stanley Roundtable on Enterprise Risk Management and Corporate Strategy	1
SMACP/AICPA	2005	Epstein and Rejc	Identifying, Measuring and Managing Organizational Risks for Improved Performance	3
Oxford University Press	2006	Coffee	Gatekeepers: The Professions and Corporate Governance	2
Conference Board (U.S.)	2006	Brancato	The Role of U.S. Corporate Boards in Enterprise Risk Management	3
John Wiley & Sons	2006	Pickett	Enterprise Risk Management—A Manager's Journey	1
James Lam & Associates	2006	James Lam & Associates	Emerging Best Practices in Developing Key Risk Indicators and ERM Reporting	1
Risk Mgmt Magazine	2006	Vance	Zen, Five Steps and ERM	1
Standard & Poor's	2006	Standard & Poor's	Criteria: Assessing Enterprise Risk Management Practices of Financial Institutions: Rating Criteria & Best Practices	3
Guide to Risk Management	2006	Protiviti	Frequently Asked Questions	3
Institute of Management Accountants	2006	Shenkir and Walker	Enterprise Risk Management: Frameworks, Elements, and Integration	3
Journal of Cost Management	2006	Shenkir and Walker	Enterprise Risk Management and the Strategy-Risk-Focused Organization	2

Source	Date	Authors	Title	Type
Canadian Institute of Chartered Accountants (CICA)	2006	Lindsay (Fraser, Goodfellow, Toledano)	20 Questions Directors Should Ask about Risk—Second Edition	2
FT Partnership Publications	2006	London Financial Times with Ernst & Young	Mastering Uncertainty	1
Financial Times and Prentice Hall	2001	Financial Times and Prentice Hall	Mastering Risk Volume 1: Concepts	2
The Geneva Papers on Risk and Insurance: Issues and Practice	2006	Acharuya and Johnson	Investigating the Development of ERM in the Insurance Industry: An Empirical Study of Four Major European Insurers	1
Journal of Applied Corporate Finance	2006	Nocco	Enterprise Risk Management: Theory and Practice	1
Journal of Applied Corporate Finance	2006	Gates	Incorporating Strategic Risk into Enterprise Risk Management: A Survey of Current Corporate Practice	1
Conference Board (U.S.)	2007	Tonello	Emerging Governance Practices in Enterprise Risk Management	3
IIA Research Foundation	2007	Roth and Sobel	Four Approaches to Enterprise Risk Management and Opportunities in Sarbanes-Oxley Compliance	2
AWWA Research Foundation	2007	Pollard	Risk Analysis Strategies for Credible and Defensible Utility Decisions	1
Institute of Management Accountants	2007	Shenkir and Walker	Enterprise Risk Management: Tools and Techniques for Effective Implementation	3
Committee of Chief Risk Officers (CCRO)	2007	CCRO	ERM and Supporting Metrics	3
Risk Insurance Mgmt Society	2007	Vance and Makomaski	ERM for Dummies	2
American Bankers Association	2007	Oberg and Skinner	The Bank Executive's Guide to Enterprise Risk Management	2

APPENDIX 22.B: SURVEY RESPONDENTS WHO GAVE PERMISSION TO BE IDENTIFIED

This appendix only lists survey respondents who gave us permission to be identified. As a result, this is not a complete list of members of the Strategic Risk Councils for the Conference Board of Canada and the Conference Board, Inc.

Alberta Environment
Aon Reed Stenhouse Inc.
Bell Aliant Regional Communications
Business Development Bank of Canada
Cameco Corporation
Canada Deposit Insurance Corporation
Canada Revenue Agency
Canadian Blood Services
Canadian Broadcasting Corporation
Canada Mortgage and Housing Corporation (CMHC)
Coast Capital Savings Credit Union
Concentra Financial
EPCOR Utilities Inc.
Equitable Life Insurance Company of Canada
General Motors Corporation
The Great-West Life Assurance Company
Hydro One Inc.
Independent Electricity System Operator
L'Alliance des Caisses Populaires de l'Ontario Limitée
Ontario Power Generation Inc.
Pason Systems Inc.
Petro-Canada
Seawrack Press, Inc.
The Standard Life Assurance Company
Suncor Energy Inc.
TELUS Communications, Inc.

NOTES

1. See page 2 of Enterprise Risk Management—Integrated Framework, Executive Summary, by COSO, September 2004.
2. Recent surveys on enterprise risk management include PRMIA (2008), Tonello (2007), Gates (2006), and Thiessen (2005), among others.
3. The Conference Board of Canada is the foremost independent, not-for-profit applied research organization in Canada. The Conference Board of Canada helps build leadership capacity for a better Canada by creating and sharing insights on economic trends, public policy issues, and organizational performance. Its members include a broad range of Canadian organizations from the public and private sectors.
4. The Strategic Risk Council (SRC) of the Conference Board of Canada helps organizations develop, implement, and sustain an enterprise-wide risk management process that is appropriate to their organization's unique set of goals, strengths, weaknesses,

and structures. It provides strategic and operational insights into how organizations can establish risk management capabilities by integrating successful board and senior management governance principles with strategic planning processes.

5. See the *Risk Management: Guideline for Decision-Makers—A National Standard of Canada. Canadian Standards Association* (1997 reaffirmed 2002) CAN/CSA-Q850–97.

6. See Risk, "Governance and Corporate Performance," May 2008, the Conference Board of Canada by Karen Schoening-Thiessen. This briefing captures the observations and concerns of 16 of Canada's most experienced directors of publicly held and public sector organizations. The directors were asked for their thoughts on the relationships between good governance, effective risk management, and strategic planning. The interview process produced a series of candid discussions and revealed common themes underlying a range of experiences and approaches.

7. Ibid.

8. Ibid.

9. The Strategic Risk Council of the Conference Board of Canada has grown in memberships by more than 50 percent in the last two years. Clearly, interest in the application of ERM is growing rapidly in Canada, and most likely elsewhere.

10. We also included a few books in the survey on the topic of risk, such as *Art of the Long View* and *Fooled by Randomness* that did not specifically mention ERM.

11. See Tonello (2007), 26.

12. In the report "ERM: Inside and Out," 2005, by the Conference Board of Canada, (pp. 8–9), there were 28 percent of CROs who reported directly to the CEO and 21 percent to the CFO. What is interesting to note is that the "ERM: Inside and Out" report had close to double the number of respondents (86 in total versus 44 for this survey), thereby showing significant involvement of the CFO in ERM and an increase of reporting to the CFO as well. The statistics also prove that ERM is on the rise as risk executives report directly to the CEO.

13. We also analyzed the response to this question by industry but do not report the results separately. At least one firm in each major industry listed this response, but all utilities that responded, except for one, listed this benefit.

14. Gates (2006) finds the most cited reason is "Corporate governance requirements" and the second most cited reason as "Great understanding of strategic and operating risks." He points out that Canadian respondents put "Greater understanding of strategic and operating risks" at the top of their list and notes (see page 85): ". . . . perhaps reflecting their longer experience with regulatory requirements for risk management that started in the 1990s." In *Risk, Governance and Corporate Performance* (2005), boards acknowledged that they predominantly view risks in two main categories: strategic and operational.

15. Some Canadian companies in the sample are listed on the New York Stock Exchange and are required to comply with SOX.

16. See Standard & Poor's "Enterprise Risk Management: Standard & Poor's To Apply Enterprise Risk Analysis to Corporate Ratings," May 7, 2008.

17. Respondents were classified into the following six categories from entry level to the highest level positions as follows: advisor or analyst, manager or senior manager, director, chief officer (other), chief risk officer, and vice president level or higher.

18. It was necessary to relax this restriction when selecting 2 of the top 10 articles read by respondents. However, both of these articles received high ratings based on value.

19. It should be noted that "Risk Management Reports" was published monthly until recently, so this ranking is based on a series of reports, not one specific publication.

20. Actually, 11 books are listed in this table. The two COSO publications were rated separately, but can be viewed as part of the same overall publication.

21. For academics and practitioners interested in conducting collaborative research, please refer to the Financial Management Association's (FMA) initiative, Practitioner Demand Driven Academic Research Initiative (PDDARI), which was started in 2007. More information can be obtained from the FMA's web site (www.fma.org) or in the *Journal of Applied Finance*.

REFERENCES

Aabo, T., J.R.S. Fraser, and B.J. Simkins. 2005. The rise and evolution of the chief risk officer: Enterprise risk management at Hydro One. *Journal of Applied Corporate Finance* 17 (3), 62–75.

Acharuya, M., and J.E.V. Johnson. 2006. Investigating the development of ERM in the insurance industry: An empirical study of four major European insurers. *The Geneva Papers on Risk and Insurance: Issues and Practice* 55–80.

Adams, J. 1995. *Risk*. London: UCL Press.

Apgar, D. 2006. *Risk intelligence: Learning to manage what we don't know*. Boston, MA: Harvard Business School Press.

Arthur Anderson. 1995. *Managing business risks: An integrated approach*. The Economist Intelligence Unit (EIU).

Bailey, M.A., L. Bloom, and E.T. Hida. 2004. *Assessing the value of enterprise risk management*. New York: Deloitte & Touche.

Banfield, E. 2005. Enterprise risk: Fighting risk measurement myopia, creating a risk inventory and gap analysis, and dealing with obstacles to enterprise-wide risk management. Risk Center (December).

Barton, T.L., W.G. Shenkir, and P.L. Walker. 2002. *Making enterprise risk management pay off*. Upper Saddle River, NJ: Financial Times/Prentice Hall and Financial Executives Research Foundation.

Barton, T.L., W.G. Shenkir, and P.L. Walker. 2002. *Enterprise risk management: Pulling it all together*. Altamonte Springs, FL: Institute of Internal Auditors (IIA) Research Foundation.

Beasley, M.S., R. Clune, and D.R. Hermanson. 2005. Enterprise risk management: An empirical analysis of factors associated with the extent of implementation. *Journal of Accounting and Public Policy* 24 (6), 521–531.

Bernstein, P.L. 1996. *Against the gods: The remarkable story of risk*. New York: John Wiley & Sons.

Birkbeck, K. 1998. Realizing the rewards: How integrated risk management can benefit your organization. The Conference Board of Canada.

Birkbeck, K. 1999. Forewarned is forearmed: Identification and measurement in integrated risk management. The Conference Board of Canada.

Bonabeau, E. 2007. Understanding and managing complexity risk. *MIT Sloan Management Review* 48 (4), 62–68.

Bradshaw, W.A., and A. Willis. 1998. *Learning about risk: Choices, connections and competencies*. Toronto: Canadian Institute of Chartered Accountants.

Brancato, C.K. 2006. The role of U.S. corporate boards in enterprise risk management. The Conference Board Inc.

Cabinet Office Britain. 2002. Risk: Improving government's capability to handle risk and uncertainty. The Strategy Unit: Cabinet Office Britain.

Canadian Institute of Chartered Accountants. 2000. Guidance for directors dealing with risk in the boardroom. CICA.

Canadian Standards Association. 1997 (reaffirmed 2002). Risk management: Guideline for decision-makers—A national standard of Canada. CAN/CSA-Q850–97.

Casualty Actuarial Society. 2003. Overview of enterprise risk management.

Chew, D., G. Niehaus, C. Briscow, W. Coleman, K. Lawder, S. Ramamurtie, and C. Smith. 2003. University of Georgia roundtable on enterprise-wide risk management. *Journal of Applied Corporate Finance* 15 (4), 8–26.

Chew, D., B. Anderson, T. Copeland, T. Harris, and J.H. Kapitan. 2005. Morgan Stanley roundtable on enterprise risk management and corporate strategy. *Journal of Applied Corporate Finance* 17, (3), 32–61.

Coffee, J.C. Jr. 2006. *Gatekeepers: The professions and corporate governance.* United Kingdom: Oxford University Press.

Colquitt, L., R.E. Hoyt, and R.B. Lee. 1999. Integrated risk management and the role of the risk manager. *Risk Management and Insurance Review* 2: 43–61.

Committee of Chief Risk Officers, 2007, " Enterprise Risk Management and Supporting Metrics," Committee of Chief Risk Officers (CCRO).

Committee of Sponsoring Organizations of the Treadway Commission. 2004. Enterprise risk management—integrated framework: Application techniques. Committee of Sponsoring Organizations of the Treadway Commission (COSO).

Committee of Sponsoring Organizations of the Treadway Commission. 2004. Enterprise risk management: Integrated framework: Executive summary. Committee of Sponsoring Organizations of the Treadway Commission (COSO) (September). Committee of Sponsoring Organizations of the Treadway Commission. 1992. Internal control: Integrated framework. COSO.

Crouhy, M., R. Mark, and D. Galai. 2001. *Risk management.* New York: McGraw-Hill.

Dallas, G.S. 2004. *Governance and risk.* New York: McGraw-Hill.

D'Arcy, S.P., and Brogan, J.C. 2001. Enterprise risk management. *Journal of Risk Management of Korea* (12), 207–228.

DeLoach, J.W. 2000. *Enterprise-wide risk management: Strategies for linking risk and opportunity.* London, UK: Prentice Hall and Financial Times.

Dev, A., and V. Rao. 2007. ERM: A new way to manage a financial institution. *Risk Management Association (RMA) Journal* (February).

Diamond, J. 2005. *Collapse: How societies choose to fail or succeed.* New York: Viking Books.

Dowd, K. 2005. *Measuring market risk.* Hoboken, NJ: John Wiley & Sons.

Economist Intelligence Unit. 2005. *The Evolving Role of the CRO.* London.

Epstein, M.J., and A. Rejc. 2005. Identifying, measuring, and managing organizational risks for improved performance. Society of Management Accountants of Canada and American Institute of Certified Public Accountants.

Financial Management Accounting Committee. 2002. Managing risk to enhance stakeholder value. International Federation of Accountants (IFAC) and Chartered Institute of Management Accountants.

Fraser, J.R.S., R. Quail, and N. Kirienko. 2001. Enterprise risk management at Hydro One Inc. The Conference Board of Canada.

Gates, S. 2006. Incorporating strategic risk into enterprise risk management: A survey of current corporate practice. *Journal of Applied Corporate Finance* 18 (4), 81–90.

Gigerenzer, G. 2002. *Calculated risks: How to know when numbers deceive you.* New York: Simon & Schuster.

Grose, V.L. 1987. Managing risk: Systematic loss prevention for executives. Arlington, VA: Omega Systems Group.

Harrington, S., G. Niehaus, and K. Risko. 2002. Enterprise risk management: The case of United Grain Growers. *Journal of Applied Corporate Finance* 14 (4), 71–81.

Hashagen, J. 2003. " Basel II: A closer look—Managing operational risk." KPMG Germany.

Head, G.L., and M.L. Herman. 2002. *Enlightened risk taking, a guide to strategic risk management for nonprofits*. Washington, DC: Nonprofit Risk Management Center.

Her Majesty's Treasury. 2004. *The orange book: Management of risk—Principles and concepts*. Controller of Her Majesty's Stationery Office.

Hexter, E. 2007. Risk business: Is enterprise risk management losing ground? The Conference Board Inc.

Hills, S., and G. Dinsdale. 2001. A foundation for building risk management learning strategies in the public service. Ottawa: Canadian Centre for Management Development.

Hively, K., B.W. Merkley, and J.A. Miccolis. 2001. Enterprise risk management: Trends and emerging practices. Altamonte Springs, FL: The Institute of Internal Auditors (IIA) Research Foundation.

Hubbard, L. 2000. *Control self-assessment: A practical guide*. Altamonte Springs, FL: The Institute of Internal Auditors (IIA) Research Foundation.

Institute of Risk Management (IRM). 2002. The Association of Insurance and Risk Managers (AIRMIC) and ALARM (The National Forum for Risk Management in the Public Sector). *The Risk Management Standard*, IRM, AIRMIC, and ALARM.

James Lam and Associates. 2006. Emerging best practices in developing key risk indicators and ERM reporting.

Kleffner, A.E., R.B. Lee, and B. McGannon. 2003. The effect of corporate governance on the use of enterprise risk management: Evidence from Canada. *Risk Management and Insurance Review* 6 (1), 53–73.

Kloman, H.F., and V. Beaumont. 1974. *Risk Management Reports*. Lyme, CT: Seawack Press Inc.

Knight, F.H. 2002. *Risk, uncertainty, and profit*. Washington, DC: Beard Books.

Koen, B.V. 2003. *Discussion of the method: Conducting the engineer's approach to problem solving*. United Kingdom: Oxford University Press.

KPMG. 2003. *Enterprise risk management*. Australia: KPMG.

Lam, J. 2001. The CRO is here to stay. *Risk Management*, 48 (4), 16–22.

Lam, J. 2003. *Enterprise risk management: From incentives to controls*. New York: John Wiley & Sons.

Liebenberg, A., and R. Hoyt. 2003. The determinants of enterprise risk management: Evidence from the appointment of chief risk officers. *Risk Management and Insurance Review* 6 (1), 37–52.

Lindsay, H. 2000. Managing risks in the new economy. American Institute of Certified Public Accountants (AICPA) and Canadian Institute of Chartered Accountants (CICA).

Lindsay, H., J.R.S. Fraser, J. Goodfellow, and J. Toledano. 2006. *20 questions directors should ask about risk*—2nd ed., Canadian Institute of Chartered Accountants (CICA).

Lloyd's. 2005. Taking risk on board. Lloyd's and the Economist Intelligence Unit (EIU).

Lockwood, B. 2002. Case studies in public sector risk management. CPA Australia and Public Sector Centre of Excellence.

Lockwood, B. 2002. *Enterprise-wide risk management: Better practice guide for the public sector*. CPA Australia.

London Financial Times. 2006. *Mastering uncertainty*. London: Financial Times Partnership Publications (with Ernst & Young).

Lowenstein, R. 2001. *When genius failed: The rise and fall of long-term capital management*. New York: Random House Trade Paperbacks.

Meulbroek, L. 2002. A senior manager's guide to integrated risk management. *Journal of Applied Corporate Finance* 14 (4), 56–70.

Miccolis, J. 2001. *ERM and September 11*. International Risk Management Institute (IRMI).

National Association of Corporate Directors. 2002., *Report of the NACD Blue Ribbon Commission on Risk Oversight: Board lessons for turbulent times*. NACD.

Nocco, B.W., and R. M. Stulz. 2006. Enterprise risk management: Theory and practice. *Journal of Applied Corporate Finance* 18 (4), 8–20.

Nottingham, L. 1997. *A conceptual framework for integrated risk management*. The Conference Board of Canada.

Oberg, R., and T. Skinner. 2007. *The bank executive's guide to enterprise risk management*. The American Bankers Association, 1.

Pickett, K.H.S. 2006. *Enterprise risk management—A manager's journey*. New York: John Wiley & Sons.

Pickett, K.H.S. 2005. *Auditing the risk management process*. Hoboken, NJ: John Wiley & Sons.

Pickford, J. 2001. *Mastering risk volume 1: Concepts*, London: Financial Times and Prentice Hall.

Pollard, S. 2007. Risk analysis strategies for credible and defensible utility decisions. AWWA Research Foundation.

Professional Risk Managers' International Association. 2008. Enterprise risk management (ERM): A status check on global best practices. www.prmia.org.

Protiviti. 2006. Guide to enterprise risk management: Frequently asked questions. Robert Half International.

Protiviti. 2006. Enterprise risk management: Practical implementation advice. Robert Half International.

Rosenthal, J. S. 2005. *Struck by lightning: The curious world of probabilities*. Canada: HarperCollins.

Roth, J., and P. Sobel. 2007. Four approaches to enterprise risk management and opportunities in Sarbanes-Oxley compliance. Altamonte Springs, FL: Institute of Internal Auditors (IIA) Research Foundation.

Sabia, M.J., and J.L. Goodfellow. 2005. *Integrity in the spotlight: Audit committees in a high risk world*. Canadian Institute of Chartered Accountants (CICA).

Schoening-Thiessen, K. 2008. Risk, governance and corporate performance. The Conference Board of Canada, Conference Board of Canada. (May).

Schwartz, P. 1991. *The art of the long view*. New York: Currency/Doubleday.

Shenkir, W.G., and P.L. Walker. 2006. Enterprise risk management and the strategy-risk-focused organization. *Journal of Cost Management* 20 (3), 32–38.

Shiller, R.J. 2000. *Irrational exuberance*. Princeton, NJ: Prince University Press: Broadway Books.

Shenkir, W.G., and P.L. Walker. 2006. *Enterprise risk management: Frameworks, elements, and integration*. Institute of Management Accountants.

Shenkir, W.G., and P.L. Walker. 2007. *Enterprise risk management: Tools and techniques for effective implementation*. Institute of Management Accountants.

Sobel, P. 2005. *Auditor's risk management guide: Integrating auditing & ERM*. Institute of Internal Auditors (IIA) Research Foundation.

Standard & Poor's. 2005. Enterprise risk management for financial institutions.

Standard & Poor's. 2006. Criteria: Assessing enterprise risk management practices of financial institutions: Rating criteria & best practices.

Standard & Poor's. 2008. Enterprise risk management: Standard & Poor's to apply enterprise risk analysis to corporate ratings. *RatingsDirect* May 7, 1–7.

Standards Australia. 1995, 1999, and 2004. AS/NZS 4360 risk management. Standards Australia, Sydney.

Standards Australia. 2000. HB 250—Organisational experiences in implementing risk management practices. Standards Australia, Sydney.

Stroh, P.J. 2005. Enterprise risk management at United Healthcare. *Strategic Finance* July, 27–35.

Subramaniam, R. 2005. Keep it simple: Getting your arms around enterprise risk management. The Conference Board, Inc.

Taleb, N.N. 2001. *Fooled by Randomness* Texere LLC.

Taleb, N.N. 2007. *The Black Swan, The impact of the highly improbable events.* New York: Random House.

Tenner, E. 1996. *Why things bite back: Technology and the revenge of unintended consequences.* New York: Knopf, Vintage Books.

Thiessen, K. 2005. Enterprise risk management: Inside and out. The Conference Board of Canada.

Thiessen, K. 2001. Integrating risk management through a change management process. The Conference Board of Canada.

Thiessen, K., R.E. Hoyt, and B.M. Merkley. 2001. A composite sketch of a chief risk officer. The Conference Board of Canada.

Thompson, K. 2004. *Risk in perspective: Insight and humor in the age of risk management.* Age of Risk Management (AORM): Harvard University School of Public Health.

Tillinghast-Towers Perrin. 2000. Enterprise risk management, an analytical approach. (January), 1–38.

Tonello, M. 2007. Emerging governance practices in enterprise risk management. The Conference Board Inc.

Toronto Stock Exchange Committee. 1994. Where were the directors: Guidelines for improved corporate governance in Canada. Toronto Stock Exchange Committee on Corporate Governance in Canada (Report of the Dey Committee).

Treasury Board of Canada Secretariat. 2001. *Integrated risk management framework.* www.tbs-sct.gc.ca.

Vance, B. 2006. Zen, five steps and ERM. *Risk Management Magazine,* 54 (April).

Vance, B., and J. Makomaski. 2007. *Enterprise risk management for dummies.* Risk Insurance Management Society (RIMS). Hoboken, NJ: John Wiley & Sons.

Walker, P.L., W.G. Shenkir, and T.L. Barton. 2003. ERM in practice. *Internal Auditor,* 60 (4), 51–5.

Weick, K.E., and K.M. Sutcliffe. 2001. *Managing the unexpected: Assuring high performance in an age of complexity.* San Francisco: Jossey-Bass Wiley.

ABOUT THE AUTHORS

John Fraser is the Vice President, Internal Audit & Chief Risk Officer of Hydro One Networks Inc, one of North America's largest electricity transmission and distribution companies. He is an Ontario and Canadian Chartered Accountant, a Fellow of the Association of Chartered Certified Accountants (U.K.), a Certified Internal Auditor, and a Certified Information Systems Auditor. He has more than 30 years' experience in the risk and control field mostly in the financial services sector, including areas such as finance, fraud, derivatives, safety, environmental, computers, and operations. He is currently the Chair of the Advisory Committee of the Conference Board of Canada's Strategic Risk Council, a Practitioner Associate Editor of the *Journal of Applied Finance,* and a past member of the Risk Management and Governance Board of the Canadian Institute of Chartered Accountants. He is a recognized authority on Enterprise Risk Management and has co-authored three academic papers on ERM—published in the *Journal of Applied Corporate Finance* and the *Journal of Applied Finance.*

Betty J. Simkins is Williams Companies Professor of Business and Professor of Finance at Oklahoma State University (OSU). She received her BS in Chemical Engineering from the University of Arkansas, her MBA from OSU, and her PhD from Case Western Reserve University. Betty is also very active in the finance profession and currently serves as Vice-Chairman of the Trustees (previously President) of the Eastern Finance Association, on the Board of Directors for the Financial Management Association (FMA), as co-editor of the *Journal of Applied Finance*, and as Executive Editor of FMA Online (the online journal for the FMA). She has co-authored more than 30 journal articles in publications including the *Journal of Finance, Financial Management, Financial Review, Journal of International Business Studies, Journal of Futures Markets, Journal of Applied Corporate Finance*, and *the Journal of Financial Research* and has won a number of best paper awards at academic conferences.

Karen Schoening-Thiessen is a Senior Research Associate with the Conference Board of Canada. She currently manages the Strategic Risk Council, which focuses on the tactical and strategic development, implementation and sustainability issues of an enterprise risk management (ERM) program. Her research is based primarily on what is happening in the world of ERM, strategy and corporate performance. Some of her studies included:

- *Who Reads What Most Often? A Survey of Enterprise Risk Management Literature* read by risk executives, Spring/Summer issue of the *Journal of Applied Finance* 2008 (in conjunction with Betty J. Simkins, Oklahoma University and John Fraser, VP of Internal Audit and CRO at Hydro One)
- *A Board's Eye View:Risk, Strategy and Corporate Performance*, May 2007
- *ERM Inside and Out*, 2005
- *Know and Tell: A Business Perspective on the Risk of Disclosure*, July 2005
- *Risk-based Reporting: Delivering Results in a New World of Reporting*, June 2004
- *Integrated Risk management through a Change Management Process*, October 2001
- *A Composite Sketch of a Chief Risk Officer*, September 2001 (in conjunction with Tillinghast-Towers Perrin and the University of Georgia)

Prior to joining the Conference Board, Karen's career has crossed various industry sectors, including public stock, Crown Corporation, and provincial government. She served in various corporate management functions, conducting financial, operational, and loss control audits; managing legal and liability risks, overseeing medical and rehabilitation cases, and ensuring implementation of compliance, prevention and health and safety initiatives.

© The Financial Management Association, International, University of South Florida, COBA, 4202 E. Fowler Avenue, Ste #3331, Tampa, FL 33620-5500 www.fma.org.

CHAPTER 23

Academic Research on Enterprise Risk Management

SUBRAMANIAN R. IYER
Student in Finance, The Spears School of Business, Oklahoma State University

DANIEL A. ROGERS
Associate Professor of Finance, Portland State University

BETTY J. SIMKINS
Williams Companies Professor of Business and Professor of Finance,
Oklahoma State University

INTRODUCTION

Despite the growing interest of practitioners in enterprise risk management (ERM) and numerous surveys by providers of ERM "solutions" (such as governance, risk, and compliance [GRC] software), very little academic research has been conducted to provide a better understanding of ERM. For example, researchers study topics such as what ERM is (or is not), practical measurement of the degree to which ERM is implemented within different industries, factors determining ERM's implementation (or lack thereof), the effect of ERM implementation on business market values, and the interaction of ERM with overall business objectives.

The purpose of this chapter is to provide a review of academic research to date on ERM. To conduct the review, we searched academic journals and other databases of academic research (such as the Social Science Research Network) for papers written on ERM. We limit our focus to papers that can be classified as either academic research or case studies that would be appropriate for a classroom setting. To qualify as academic research, the paper had to be published in a peer-reviewed academic journal, be under review at a peer-reviewed academic journal, and/or appear to be written for an academic audience (i.e., focus of the paper is on statistical testing of one or more academically motivated hypotheses). Because ERM solution providers often provide white papers or case studies that are more of a marketing effort, we restrict case studies to those published in outlets that would be marketed to academics. After a thorough search of ERM literature, we located 10 research studies and 5 case studies that are appropriate to our purpose.[1]

Not surprisingly, we conclude that there is significant scope for further academic research on ERM. The pace of research has principally been hindered by difficulties in measuring ERM for individual businesses. Researchers who have studied ERM to date have utilized primarily two differing approaches. One approach used thus far to create variables measuring ERM has been to conduct surveys of risk managers of businesses. The survey approach is flexible because researchers can address different questions of interest to organizations and potentially follow up with more detailed questions. Unfortunately, response rates are typically low, and it may be difficult to identify the best individual within an organization to address the survey's questions. Additionally, individual biases may affect respondents' answers, thus adding noise to subsequent statistical analysis conducted by the researchers. A second (and more recent) approach has been to gather data from publicly available data sources. The majority of ERM research using public data has been to proxy for ERM by identifying firms that appoint a chief risk officer (CRO). Although this data approach may eventually allow for larger data samples to be analyzed, there are still relatively few companies (at least in the United States) that have appointed a CRO. An additional weakness in the "appointment of CRO" approach is that this appointment may come at differing stages of ERM implementation. In other words, this (like the survey responses) may produce a noisy variable. One additional issue with CRO appointments is that they are heavily clustered in finance-related industries. Thus, this approach does little to help researchers understand ERM in nonfinancial companies.

Our review of existing research uncovers no clearly consistent findings about ERM. Very little of the existing research seems to be clearly motivated by earlier studies of risk management. Rather, researchers seem to be addressing fairly specific questions about ERM. We classify much of the existing ERM research as descriptive with hypotheses being formed without guidance from an existing theoretical framework. The quality of corporate governance appears to be frequently a hypothesized factor that influences the decision to implement ERM. Recently, research efforts have been made to use theories of hedging as the framework for understanding the determinants of ERM.

ERM research does not seem to have a natural "disciplinary home." Published papers to date have appeared in peer-reviewed insurance and accounting journals. Although no ERM papers have yet been published in peer-reviewed finance journals, several of the recent working papers test hypotheses that should be of interest to corporate finance researchers. This interdisciplinary appeal suggests that, depending on the hypotheses, ERM is a topic that can be studied from various business lenses. It is conceivable that future work on ERM could have management or operations management appeal.

This chapter proceeds as follows. We first provide a chronological discussion of the academic research on ERM to date. For each paper reviewed, we focus on providing a clear distinction of the approach used to identify and measure ERM, and the major hypotheses tested. We then offer an overview of lessons from case studies for students of ERM. Finally, we conclude with a call to action for continued research of ERM.

ACADEMIC RESEARCH ON ENTERPRISE RISK MANAGEMENT

In this section, we examine the academic research studies on enterprise risk management. After examining all publications in academic research journals, we uncovered 10 academic studies on enterprise risk management that include empirical results of actual companies. Refer to Exhibit 23.1 for a summary of these studies. More than 50 percent of the articles (six) are written within the last three years. Four of the studies are unpublished working papers. ERM is clearly a relatively new area of academic research, as the first academic study on ERM was published about 10 years ago (in 1999).[2]

Early empirical work on ERM investigated why companies adopted ERM and most studies utilized survey data. The first study by Colquitt, Hoyt, and Lee (1999) investigated the characteristics and extent of integrated risk management by surveying 397 risk managers. They found that political risk, exchange rate risk, and interest rate risk were the three most common nonoperational risks handled by the risk management department. Another study Kleffner, Lee, and McGannon (2003b) surveyed Canadian Risk and Insurance Management Society members about ERM adoption. They found that 31 percent had adopted ERM and that the primary reasons for adoption were risk manager influence, board encouragement, and stock exchange guidelines.

Other early work on ERM included a focus on the determinants of ERM. One of the first papers in this area, Liebenberg and Hoyt (2003), compared firms that appointed a chief risk officer to a matched sample. They found that firms that appoint a chief risk officer are more likely to be financially leveraged.[3] They concluded that further research is necessary to understand ERM determinants. A related but more recent investigation was done by Pagach and Warr (2007). They also studied the announcements of senior risk officer appointments and found that such appointments are positively associated with size, leverage, volatility, and the number of business segments.

More recent work on ERM has examined additional determinants of ERM adoption. Desender (2007) studied 100 pharmaceutical companies and coded their ERM efforts based on public filings from 2004. He found an association between a separate chairman and CEO and the degree of ERM implemented by the company. Another paper related to ERM determinants was Beasley, Clune, and Hermanson (2005). They surveyed internal auditors and their views on factors associated with ERM implementation. They found that ERM implementation is positively associated with board independence, requests from the CEO or CFO to have internal audit involved, the presence of a CRO, the company's auditor being a Big Four audit firm, size, and industry group (banking, education, and insurance). It is interesting to note that they also found U.S.-based companies are not as advanced in ERM implementation.

These earlier studies make it clear that ERM adoption may be related to various firm characteristics. Two of the most recent studies on ERM, Beasley, Pagach, and Warr (2008) and Gates, Nicolas, and Walker (2009) extend the ERM literature by moving beyond the ERM adoption question and examine aspects of whether ERM adds value.[4] Beasley, Pagach, and Warr (2008) examined market reactions to the announcement of officers overseeing an ERM process. Given the limited research in this area, this paper is an important step in the direction of assessing value related to ERM adoption. The more recent of the two studies on ERM and value, Gates, Nicolas, and Walker (2009), extends the early work by examining the value seen inside the company as measured by better decision making and increased profitability.

In summary, academic research to date on ERM includes studies that focus on various determinants of ERM (including the hiring of CROs and firm

Exhibit 23.1 Academic Research on Enterprise Risk Management—Research Articles

Journal/Source	Date	Authors	What Was Examined?	Findings
Risk Management and Insurance Review	1999	Colquitt, Hoyt, and Lee	The objective of the study was to assess the characteristics and extent of integrated risk management. Survey results obtained from 379 risk managers and was conducted in 1997.	Results given on the background and training of risk managers. Political risk, exchange rate risk, and interest rate risk are the three most common nonoperational risks handled by the risk management department. Role of risk manager is evolving and covering a wider spectrum of risks.
Risk Management and Insurance Review	2003	Kleffner, Lee, and McGannon	Survey of 118 Canadian Risk and Insurance Management Societies on the impact of the Toronto Stock Exchange (TSE) guidelines on risk management strategy and evolution of risk management discipline.	37% of respondents said that TSE guidelines were a driving force behind the ERM decision and 51% said that it was due to encouragement by directors. 61% of respondents said having a risk manager influenced the decision to implement ERM. Factors impeding implementation of ERM were an organizational culture that discouraged ERM, an overall resistance to change, and the lack of qualified personnel to implement ERM.
Risk Management and Insurance Review	2003	Liebenberg and Hoyt	Sample consists of U.S. firms that announced appointment of a chief risk officer. Objective to investigate the differences between firms that have appointed CRO and matched sample.	Find there is no systematic difference between firms that signal their use of ERM by the appointment of a CRO and matched sample. Study assumes that the appointment of a chief risk officer also means the company has an ERM process. Large firms and highly leveraged firms are more likely to appoint a CRO.

Internal Auditor	2005a	Beasley, Clune, and Hermanson	Survey of members of Institute of Internal Auditors (IIA) Global Auditing Information Network (GAIN) on internal auditing's involvement in ERM. 90% of the 175 respondents were chief audit executives.	Survey reveals wide diversity in the adoption of ERM and in internal auditing department's role in ERM. There was optimism regarding ERM's impact on the company and on internal auditing.
Journal of Accounting and Public Policy	2005b	Beasley, Clune, and Hermanson	Survey responses from 175 members of Global Audit Information Network (GAIN) to investigate factors associated with extent of ERM implementation.	Results show that CRO presence, more independent BOD, explicit calls from CEO or CFO for internal audit involvement in ERM, are positively associated with extent of ERM deployment. Results indicate that U.S. firms are not advanced in their ERM implementations.
Working Paper	2007	Desender	The objective of the study was to explore the link between ERM implementation and board composition. One hundred randomly selected firms from the pharmaceutical industry in 2004 were studied.	Results suggest that board independence in isolation has no significant relation with ERM quality. Firms that have separate chairmen and CEOs favor more elaborate ERM and show the highest level of ERM implementation.
Journal of Accounting, Auditing and Finance	2008	Beasley, Pagach, and Warr	Study provides empirical evidence on the value of corporate actions such as the hiring of senior risk executives. The study measures the equity market response to the hiring announcements of senior executives in charge or risk management.	Findings indicate that shareholders of firms with little financial slack welcome ERM. Shareholders of large nonfinancial firms with volatile earnings, greater amounts of intangible assets, low leverage, and low amounts of slack also react positively toward ERM.

(Continued)

Exhibit 23.1 *(Continued)*

Journal/Source	Date	Authors	What Was Examined?	Findings
Working Paper	2008a	Pagach and Warr	Study explores the link between ERM implementation and characteristics of firms that implement ERM. Appointment of a CRO is used as a proxy for ERM implementation. Data was based on the announcements of the hiring of 138 senior risk officers.	Results show that larger firms and those with higher leverage tend to hire CROs. Firms that have growth options are less likely to hire a CRO and conversely firms that hire CROs tend to have fewer growth options. A negative relation is found between CRO hiring and change in the size of the firm.
Working Paper	2008b	Pagach and Warr	Study examines the impact of ERM implementation on financial, asset, and market characteristics. Data was based on the announcements of the hiring of 138 senior risk officers.	Results suggest that there is no support for the position that ERM is value creating. Firms hiring CRO, when compared to non-CRO firms, exhibited increased asset opacity, a decreased market to book ratio, and decreased earnings volatility.
Working Paper	2009	Gates, Nicolas, and Walker	Research questions examined include which components of ERM frameworks lead to better decisions and which components of the ERM frameworks lead to increased profitability.	Results show that the ERM stage, a good ERM environment, better communication of ERM missions, and explicit risk tolerance levels, positively influenced better decision making. A better ERM environment, explicit risk tolerance levels along with the number of employees devoted to ERM process appear to have an impact on profitability.

characteristics) and, more recently, research has investigated the potential value associated with ERM adoption. Each of the 10 research studies is discussed in more detail below.

Colquitt, Hoyt, and Lee (1999)

The objective of this study was to assess the characteristics and extent of integrated risk management. The aspects of risk management that were evaluated are:

- The extent to which risk managers are involved in managing pure financial risks facing their firms.
- The nonoperational types of risks handled by risk managers and techniques being used to handle a broader set of risks.
- The effect of factors such as firm size, the industry characteristics, and the background and training of the risk manager have on participation in integrated risk management activities.

The data was collected from a questionnaire sent in October 1997 to firms found in the *Business Insurance 1995-96 Directory of Insurance Buyers of Insurance, Benefit Plans & Risk Management Services*. Only those firms with a dedicated employee in charge of risk management were included in the sample. As a result, many smaller firms were not included in the sample. A sample of 1,780 questionnaires was sent and 379 responses (21 percent response rate) were received. Fifty percent of the responses came from the manufacturing industry and only 9 percent of the responses came from the finance, insurance, and real estate industries.

Regarding the background and training of the risk manager, some of the key findings are: the number of risk managers without a college degree was minimal; the majority of risk managers reported that they hold an undergraduate degree; 40 percent of the risk managers held a master's degree; the Associate in Risk Management (ARM) is the most favored professional designation obtained by risk managers; risk management is the most common background (66 percent of respondents); risk managers with a legal background interacted more frequently with the finance or treasury department, which suggests that risk managers with a legal background relied heavily on financially trained employees; risk managers in smaller firms and those with finance, accounting, or legal backgrounds are likely to be involved in the decision to use derivatives as a risk management tool; lack of qualified personnel, educating management, and resistance from the board of directors are the most cited barriers to integrated risk management.

Regarding the structure and operation of risk management within the company, the authors found that risk management formed part of the finance and/or treasury department, with 36 percent of respondents and 29 percent of companies having separate risk management departments. For 22 percent of companies, the operational risk management function was handled entirely by the finance and treasury department. Political risk, exchange rate risk, and interest rate risk were the three most common nonoperational risks handled by the risk management department. Among derivative instruments used for risk management, swaps and forwards were the most common. Options and futures were used by 45.8 percent and 39.5 percent of the respondents, respectively. Finally, the authors found that multiyear contracts were the favorite alternative risk management, with captives coming in at a distant second.

The study concluded by saying that the role of the risk manager was evolving and that the risk manager was getting involved in the management of a wider spectrum of risks faced by the firm. The trend toward integrated risk management was expected to continue.

Kleffner, Lee, and McGannon (2003)

The authors motivate their study by pointing out that public companies world-wide are facing ever-increasing scrutiny of their corporate governance policies and practices. ERM evolved as a result of this scrutiny, and also as a fallout of the accounting debacles such as Enron and WorldCom. According to a 2001 study by Economist Intelligence Unit (EIU), only 41 percent of companies in Europe, North America, and Asia had implemented ERM, but when U.S. and Canadian companies are analyzed, the number of firms that had implemented ERM drops to 34 percent. The researchers hypothesize that increased scrutiny of companies by various agencies, and the Toronto Stock Exchange (TSE) guidelines, will urge more companies to adopt ERM.

The researchers pose the following questions:

- To what extent do companies in Canada use ERM?
- What are the characteristics associated with ERM?
- What obstacles do companies face in implementing ERM?
- What role have corporate governance guidelines played in the decision to adopt ERM?

The data was obtained through a survey to the members of the Canadian Risk and Insurance Management Society as well as telephone interviews with 19 of those respondents.

The results indicate that of the 118 firms in the sample, only 37 used an ERM approach, 34 were investigating an ERM approach, and 47 companies were not considering ERM. Of those companies that implemented ERM, 37 percent said that TSE guidelines were a driving force behind the decision, 51 percent said that it was due to the encouragement of the directors, 28 percent said concern for directors' and officers' liability was important, and 61 percent said that the presence of a risk manager influenced the decision to implement ERM.

Other factors that deterred the implementation of ERM were an organizational culture that discouraged ERM, an overall resistance to change, and the lack of qualified personnel to implement ERM. The overall results indicate that an increasing number of companies were aware of the importance of ERM and more companies were moving in the direction of implementing ERM as a result of TSE guidelines and other agencies.

Liebenberg and Hoyt (2003)

Liebenberg and Hoyt state that the appointment of a chief risk officer (CRO) signals to the world the importance attached to ERM by a company and assume that the appointment of a CRO also says that the company is ready to reap the benefits associated with ERM.

The objective of the research was to investigate the differences between a sample of firms that have signaled the appointment of CROs and a closely matched control sample that have not appointed a CRO. The authors highlight the difficulty in obtaining data, since public companies are not mandated to disclose the presence of an ERM system or the appointment of a CRO.

The authors investigate the following research hypotheses:

- Firms with higher volatility in terms of earnings and stock price are likely to appoint a CRO.
- Highly leveraged firms are more likely to appoint a CRO.
- Growing firms are more likely to appoint a CRO.
- Financially opaque firms are more likely to appoint a CRO.[5]
- Firms that have a higher percentage of institutional holding are more likely to appoint a CRO.
- Firms that have subsidiaries in Canada or the United Kingdom are more likely to appoint a CRO.

The sampling population is defined as those U.S. firms that announced the appointment of a CRO between 1997 and 2001. The article concludes that there is no systematic difference between firms that signal their use of ERM by the appointment of a CRO and similar firms. However, the research did find that large firms and highly leveraged firms are more likely to appoint a CRO.

Beasley, Clune, and Hermanson (2005a)

By the time of this study and the following study (Beasley, Clune, and Hermanson 2005b), there had been a rising interest in ERM and added interest in ERM by many internal auditors. The data used in both of these studies was funded by the IIA Research Foundation to examine internal auditing's involvement in ERM. A survey was administered to more than 1,170 Institute of Internal Auditors (IIA) who were members of the Global Auditing Information Network (GAIN) service. Completed survey responses were received by 175 respondents (response rate of 10.3 percent) and approximately 90 percent of those respondents were chief audit executives (CAEs). The CAEs were the primary intended targets for the survey.

Most of the respondents were from the United States, with representation from other countries including Canada, the United Kingdom, and Australia. No one industry represented more than 15 percent of the respondents. A majority of the respondents were from government, manufacturing, financial, and education industries. Most of the responding companies were large, with median 2003 revenues of $1.3 billion. The respondents were familiar with Committee of Sponsoring Organizations (COSO) guidelines. Eleven percent of the surveyed firms have a complete ERM framework, 37 percent of the responding firms have a partial ERM framework, and 17 percent of the firms have no plans to implement ERM.

As an indicator of the organization's commitment to risk management, respondents were asked about the existence and nature of the CRO. Of the responding firms, 33 percent have a formally designated CRO and 15 percent believe they have someone fulfilling the role of CRO. In companies with a formally designated CRO, they found that there is a great deal of interaction between the CRO and CAE. Among firms with partial ERM implementation, there is significant interaction between the audit department and the risk management department.

The survey reveals wide diversity in the adoption of ERM and in the internal auditing department's role in ERM. There was optimism regarding ERM's impact on the company and on internal auditing. The authors state that ERM adoption is likely to gain traction and will demand more involvement with internal auditing.

Beasley, Clune, and Hermanson (2005b)

This study is the second in a series that the authors conduct. The first study summarized above (see Beasley, Clune, and Hermanson 2005a) describes the survey results. This second article is a more advanced analysis employing regression analysis to more deeply explore factors associated with the extent of implementation of ERM. The authors note that there is little research on what factors affect the stages of ERM implementation, including board of director characteristics. Stages of ERM, which form the dependent variable of this research paper, refer to the level of ERM implementation in an organization. ERM 1 suggests that no plans exist to implement ERM and ERM 5 suggests that a complete ERM is in place.

As described above, the data for this research was collected in 2004 through survey responses from members of GAIN. Responses were received by 175 respondents but 52 observations had to be dropped because applicable data was not available for the regression analysis. The final sample consisted of 123 organizations.

The researchers probed the following research questions:

- Is the presence of a Chief Risk Officer positively associated with an enterprise's stage of ERM deployment?
- Is a higher percentage of board of director (BOD) members who are independent positively associated with enterprise's stage of ERM deployment?
- Are explicit calls from the chief executive officer (CEO) or chief financial officer (CFO) for internal audit involvement in ERM positively associated with an enterprise's stage of ERM deployment?
- Is the presence of a Big Four auditor positively associated with an enterprise's stage of ERM deployment?
- Are larger firms more likely to have further-developed ERM deployments?
- Are entities in the banking, education, or insurance industries more likely to have further-developed ERM deployments?
- Are non-U.S. enterprises more likely to have further-developed ERM deployments?

The results show that variables such as CRO presence, more independent BOD, explicit calls from CEO or CFO for internal audit involvement in ERM, are positively associated with a company's extent of ERM deployment. Large firms and those audited by Big Four audit firms are further into their ERM deployment stage. Also, firms in the banking, education, and insurance fields are found to be further into their ERM deployment stages. Finally, the results indicate that U.S. firms are not advanced in their ERM implementations.

Desender (2007)

Desender points out that given the increased attention and scrutiny on risk management practices, little research has been performed to explore why some firms adopt ERM and why some do not. The paper explores the link between ERM implementation and board composition. The author claims that the paper makes significant contributions to corporate governance research by establishing a relationship between board composition and ERM.

The hypotheses tested are as follows:

- There is a positive relation between the percentage of outside directors on the board and degree of ERM.
- There is a positive relation between the separation of CEO and chairman, and ERM.
- The relationship between board independence and ERM is stronger when there is a separation of CEO and chairman.

One hundred randomly selected firms from the pharmaceutical industry in 2004 were chosen for the study. To assess the degree of ERM, the author uses publicly available information such as 10-K reports, proxy statements related to fiscal year 2004, and the company web site. All other data was collected through Worldscope. One unique aspect of this study is that the author coded the ERM efforts by the COSO ERM component.

The pharmaceutical industry was chosen for the following three reasons: (1) this industry has been used in previous corporate governance research; (2) this industry is competitive and has been known to take shortcuts to perform; and (3) the pharmaceutical industry is faced with multiple risks and should display sufficient variation in the implementation of ERM.

The results suggest that board independence in isolation has no significant relation with ERM quality. Firms that have a different chairman and CEO favor more elaborate ERM and show the highest level of ERM implementation. The author takes a bold step to postulate that CEOs do not favor ERM implementation and, therefore, withstand pressure from the board to adopt ERM when the CEO is also the chairman of the company.

Beasley, Pagach, Warr (2008)

At the time of this study, there has been little empirical research on the costs and benefits of ERM adoption. Proponents of portfolio theory would argue against ERM because it is costly and idiosyncratic risks can be diversified away by investors at a low cost. On the other hand, it can be argued that markets are never perfect and there are benefits to the adoption of ERM by firms with certain characteristics, whereas ERM adoption by firms with certain other characteristics might destroy value.

This study aims to provide empirical evidence on the value of hiring a senior risk executive. The authors measure the equity market response to the hiring announcements of senior executives in charge of risk management.

The research hypotheses are that the market reaction to firm announcements of appointments of CROs will be positively associated with the firm's:

- Growth options.
- Amount of intangible assets.
- Financial slack.
- Variance in earnings per share (EPS).
- Leverage.
- Size.

The data was obtained through the keyword search of terms such as "announced," "named," or "appointed" in conjunction with position descriptions of "chief risk officer" or "risk management" through Lexis-Nexis during 1992 to 2003. The final sample consisted of 126 observations. The data was split into two groups—financial firms and nonfinancial firms. Multivariate analysis on separated samples indicate that among the financial firms, only the slack variable is found to be significantly associated with the market reaction to announcements of appointments of senior executive officers supervising risk. For nonfinancial firms, there is no statistical association between the announcement period returns and growth. However, announcement period returns are positively associated with a firm's extent of intangible assets, prior EPS volatility, and size (while negatively associated with the slack and leverage).

The overall results of the study indicate that the shareholders of firms with little financial slack welcome ERM. Shareholders of large nonfinancial firms with volatile earnings, greater amounts of intangible assets, low leverage, and low amounts of slack also act positively toward ERM. The authors conclude that a well-implemented ERM program can create value when it restricts the likelihood of significant downside risks such as financial distress.

Pagach and Warr (2008a)

At the time of this study, published research has focused on the benefits accrued as a result of ERM implementation but few studies have investigated the characteristics of the firms that adopt ERM. This working paper explores the link between ERM implementation and firm characteristics. Appointment of a chief risk officer (CRO) is used as a proxy for ERM implementation. The objectives of this paper follow closely from Liebenberg and Hoyt (2003), the differences being in the sample size, methodology, and the use of a larger set of variables, including the stock options of managers.

The research hypotheses are:

- Firms with more leverage and less financial slack will more likely implement ERM.
- Firms with more opaque assets, greater R&D expense, and more growth options are more likely to benefit from ERM.
- Firms with relatively more volatile stock prices are likely to benefit from ERM.

The data was collected by performing a search for key terms in the Lexis-Nexis library. For a period between 1992 and 2005 there were 138 announcements of senior risk officers. Data was also collected from Compustat and CRSP.

The results corroborate previous findings regarding firm size and leverage. Firms that are larger and those with higher leverage tend to hire CROs. Firms that have growth options are less likely to hire a CRO and conversely firms that hire CROs tend to have fewer growth options. (Note: A plausible explanation for the result is that stable firms tend to favor the adoption of ERM as a means to boost their bottom lines.) A negative relation is found between CRO hiring and change in the size of the firm. Higher CEO risk-taking incentives increase the likelihood of ERM adoption. When financial firms are considered in isolation, banks with lower Tier 1 Capital are more likely to hire a CRO.

Pagach and Warr (2008b)

The authors point out that the introduction of ERM in the rating process by Standard & Poor's is a source of motivation for companies to implement ERM. However, the cost associated with ERM adoption is nontrivial; hence, ERM should be value enhancing in some manner. The working paper focuses on the impact of ERM implementation on financial, asset, and market characteristics.

The research hypotheses are:

- Do firms experience a change in earnings volatility around ERM adoption?
- Do firms adopting ERM improve financial performance relative to past performance and after controlling for industry performance?
- Do firm financial characteristics, such as leverage, growth, and asset opacity change after ERM implementation?

CRO appointment is used as a proxy for ERM implementation. The business library of Lexis-Nexis was searched for search words such as "announced," "named," or "appointed," in conjunction with words such as "chief risk officer" or "director of risk management." The search produced 138 announcements of senior risk officer between the 1992 and 2004 period. The appointment of a CRO is assumed to be the commencement of an ERM program.

The results suggest that there is no support for the position that ERM is value-creating. Firms hiring a CRO, when compared to non-CRO firms, exhibited increased asset opacity, a decreased market to book ratio, and decreased earnings volatility. The authors find a negative relationship between the change in the firm's market to book ratio and earnings volatility. The study also notes that banks increased leverage after ERM adoption and that firms adopting ERM exhibit reduced stock price volatility.

Gates, Nicolas, and Walker (2009)

Up until this point, previous work on ERM has looked at the determinants of ERM adoption and those factors that explain the appointment of a chief risk officer, which some studies have used as a proxy for ERM implementation. This working paper attempts to extend the work performed earlier by examining ERM's value inside the company, measured by better decision making and increased profitability.

The COSO framework on ERM provides a list of components that should be in place to help a company manage risk and provide reasonable assurance about meeting its objectives. However, it is not clear whether these components add value or which of these components add the most value. The authors surveyed audit and risk management executives to obtain data related to ERM deployment and organizational characteristics.

The research questions the authors pose are:

- Which components of the ERM framework lead to better decisions?
- Which component of the ERM framework leads to increased profitability?

The study finds that the ERM stage, a good ERM environment, better top-down and bottom-up communication of ERM missions, and explicit risk tolerance levels, positively influenced better decision making. A better ERM environment, explicit risk tolerance levels along with the number of employees devoted to ERM process appear to have an impact on profitability. Although companies perceive they are making better decisions, the results may not necessarily show up as increased profitability, which highlights the difficulty in bridging the value of ERM and internal control, and financial reports.

CASE STUDIES ON ERM

Exhibit 23.2 summarizes the five case studies published or co-authored by academics on ERM and published in academic journals. As noted earlier, only case studies published in journals (not books) are examined. Three of the case studies are published in the *Journal of Applied Corporate Finance*, one is published in *Strategic Finance*, and one is published in the *Geneva Papers on Risk and Insurance*. It is useful to note that Fraser, Schoening-Thiessen, and Simkins (2008) find that there is a lack of case studies on ERM and practitioners are requesting that more be written on the topic.

Each case study is described in more detail next.

Harrington, Niehaus, and Risko (2002)

United Grain Growers (UGG), a Winnipeg, Manitoba–based agricultural company was one of the first companies in Canada to embrace ERM. Although UGG managed risk by hedging currency and commodity exposures as well as purchasing insurance against potential losses, the company's earnings continued to exhibit significant volatility.

UGG is comprised of four main business segments: (1) Grain Handling Services, (2) Crop Production Services, (3) Live-stock Services, and (4) Business Communications. Increased disclosure requirements, Toronto Stock Exchange (TSE) guidelines, the emphasis placed on risk management by credit rating agencies, and UGG's perception that equity analysts' views were based on earnings results were some of the reasons that prompted UGG to explore ERM.

UGG started by forming a risk committee, which consisted of the CEO, CFO, risk manager, treasurer, compliance manager, and manager of corporate audit

Exhibit 23.2   Academic Research on Enterprise Risk Management—Case Studies

Journal/Source	Date	Authors	What Was Examined?
Journal of Applied Corporate Finance	2002	Harrington, Niehaus, and Risko	The implementation of enterprise risk management at United Grain Growers including the benefits and insights gained.
Journal of Applied Corporate Finance	2005	Aabo, Fraser, and Simkins	The implementation of enterprise risk management at Hydro One including the rise and evolution of the chief risk officer.
Strategic Finance	2005	Stroh	The implementation of enterprise risk management and business risk management at United Health Group.
Journal of Applied Corporate Finance	2006	Nocco and Stulz	A discussion of the theory and practice of enterprise risk management with some extensions to Nationwide Insurance.
The Geneva Papers on Risk and Insurance: Issues and Practice	2006	Acharyya and Johnson	The development of enterprise risk management of four major European insurance companies.

services. The committee appointed a major insurance company to analyze the risks faced by UGG. They established a relationship between weather and UGG's gross profit by linking weather to crop yields, crop yields to grain volume, and grain volume to profit.

UGG's business is a low-margin, high-volume business with heavy fixed costs. If anything goes wrong with the volume, then profits are deeply affected. UGG focused on hedging its grain risk and bundled other risks such as property and liability risks along with the hedging strategy.

The benefits accrued to UGG by embracing ERM were:

- The risk costs did not increase significantly, even when a comprehensive risk strategy was put in place.
- Provided a better understanding of ERM and improved communications about risk.
- Improved cooperation from top management and better coordination between different departments.

Insights for other firms:

- Companies in high-volume low-margin industries such as retailing and stock broking are prime targets for implementation of ERM.
- ERM does not increase the overall cost of managing risk.
- ERM is time-consuming, yet a learning experience.

- Technical expertise in the form of statistical and financial knowledge is important for successful implementation of ERM.

Aabo, Fraser, and Simkins (2005)

This case study is published in Chapter 28 of this book and is titled: "The Rise and Evolution of the Chief Risk Officer: Enterprise Risk Management at Hydro One." Please refer to this chapter for a full discussion on this case.

This case describes the successful implementation of ERM at Hydro One Inc. over a five-year period. Hydro One is a Canadian electric utility company that has experienced significant changes in its industry and business. The company is the largest electricity delivery company in Ontario, Canada, and one of the 10 largest such companies in North America. Hydro One has been at the forefront of ERM for many years, especially in utilizing a holistic approach to managing risks, and provides a best practices case study for other firms to follow.

This case describes the process of implementation ERM at Hydro One beginning with the creation of the chief risk officer position, the deployment of a pilot workshop, and the various tools and techniques critical to ERM (e.g., the Delphi Method, risk trends, risk maps, risk tolerances, risk profiles, and risk rankings).

The case presents the following key benefits of ERM at Hydro One:

- Achieve lower cost of debt.
- Focus capital expenditures process on managing/allocating capital based on greatest mitigation of risk per dollar spent.
- Avoid "land mines" and other surprises.
- Reassure stakeholders that the business is well managed—with stakeholders defined to include investors, analysts, rating agencies, regulators, and the press.
- Improve corporate governance via best practices guidelines.
- Implement a formalized system of risk management that includes an ERM system (a required component of the 1995/1999/2004 Australian Standard for Risk Management).
- Identify which risks the company can pursue better than its peers.

The authors conclude by stating that: "As a result, the management of Hydro One feels that the company is much better positioned today than five years ago to respond to new developments in the business environment, favorable as well as unfavorable."

Stroh (2005)

The article describes the implementation of ERM at UnitedHealth Group and the success factors. The author states that ERM is quickly becoming the minimum expected of any corporation and is also the key to survival for many companies.

The following definition for ERM, used by the author, is one among many definitions provided for ERM: "ERM is meant to identify risk factors in a business, then assess their severity, quantify the magnitude, and mitigate the downside exposures while capitalizing on the upside opportunities." The author notes that

ERM approaches differ by industry and that ERM is quantifiable in highly regulated industries such as banking and energy.

At UnitedHealth Group, Business Risk Management (BRM) precedes the ERM and BRM evolves into ERM. BRM is a corporate-driven process that is expected to achieve the following objectives:

- Consistently achieve business objectives and improve shareholder value.
- Enable confidence in decision making.
- Avoid operational and financial surprises.

After implementing BRM, the managers at UnitedHealth Group turned their attention to enterprise portfolio views and aggregations. The BRM philosophy evolved into ERM and resulted in more business risk transparency and value creation.

The critical success factors identified in the implementation of BRM are as follows:

- Strong top management support.
- A planned and staged implementation methodology.
- Clear and established accountabilities.
- Facilitating and administering reconciliation of views.
- Diverse team.
- Culture accustomed approach.
- Integration of internal audit and BRM discipline.
- Continuous persistence for improvement.

The author calls for the move beyond Sarbanes-Oxley and external compliance activity to promote more value-added services.

Acharyya and Johnson (2006)

The article is based on a study of four major European insurers. The authors investigate the understanding, evolution, design, and performance of ERM in these organizations, and the challenges they faced while implementing ERM.

The researchers conducted face-to-face interviews with the respondents in two insurance companies, while a structured survey was administered to the other two companies. Although theoretical literature calls for a holistic approach and implementation of ERM, the reality is far from expectation. These four companies approach ERM in parts, adopting no holistic view.

Sixty-two face-to-face interviews were conducted and through these interviews data was collected using semi-structured interviews. However, for the other two companies a highly structured questionnaire was administered. The questionnaire involved a series of "Yes" or "No" questions. To bring comparability, the researchers used judgment in filing the responses of the face-to-face interviews.

The research questions are:

- What is the understanding of the nature of ERM within the insurance industry?
- What motivates insurance companies to develop ERM?

- How do they structure ERM?
- What challenges do they face in implementing ERM?
- How do they measure the performance of ERM?

The results revealed that there exists an inconsistent understanding of ERM within insurance companies. CEO leadership and regulations appear to be the most important motivating factors for developing ERM. The design of ERM is customized and it depends on many factors such as the business model and geographical presence. Communication and cultural barriers are found to be the most important challenges to implementing ERM. There is no effective ERM performance measurement matrix. Overall, the case studies revealed that there are numerous differences between the models of ERM suggested by theory and those in place at leading insurance companies.

Nocco and Stulz (2006)

In this article,[6] Nocco and Stulz discuss the theory and practice of ERM and a few examples for Nationwide Insurance. The authors explain how ERM can give companies a competitive advantage and add value for shareholders. The article discusses the process and challenges involved in implementing ERM such as how a company should assess its risk appetite, how companies should measure their risks, ways to lay off "noncore" risks, and the major difficulties that arise in practice when implementing ERM.

The authors discuss the following main challenges involved in implementing ERM:

- Inventory of risks.
- Economic value versus accounting performance.
- Aggregating risks.
- Measuring risks.
- Regulatory versus economic capital.
- Using economic capital to make decisions.
- Governance of ERM.

The authors conclude that more academic research is needed to help companies to have a better understanding of risks and how to quantify them reliably. They point out that: "Companies find that some of their most troubling risks—notably, reputation and strategic risks—are the most difficult to quantify. At this point, there is little research that helps practitioners in assessing these risks, but much to gain from having a better understanding of these risks even if they cannot be quantified reliably."

CONCLUSION

Enterprise risk management (ERM) is being adopted by an increasing number of firms and is viewed as a paramount topic for business enterprises desiring to survive and succeed in the future. As Fraser, Schoening-Thiessen, and Simkins

(2008) state: "ERM is not a fad—it is here to stay and is the natural evolution of risk management to view risk at the enterprise-wide level. New external drivers are pushing risk executives to find out more about ERM and the level of interest in this topic is increasing with time."

Unfortunately, the pace of academic research does not seem to be keeping pace with corporate interest in the topic. A primary hindrance to research of ERM is a lack of well-defined variables that measure either company-level implementation of ERM or the degree of implementation. However, recent research has focused on the appointment of a chief risk officer (CRO) as a proxy variable, and this variable may have promise for research purposes as more firms see value in having a C-level executive who oversees the corporate risk management process. On the other hand, given that one of the goals of ERM is to make risk management a pervasive part of a company's culture, there is the possibility that very successful implementers of ERM may eventually not need a CRO.

Our study finds little in the way of consistent results about ERM. This lack of consistency is primarily a function of the fact that existing research in ERM has lacked a foundational framework, and, therefore, many of the studies we examine do not build from prior research in ERM. This trend may be changing as the research increasingly utilizes the CRO appointment as a key variable measuring ERM. However, we also note that ERM lends itself to research utilizing several business disciplines, including accounting, finance, insurance, and perhaps management, and operations management. Additionally, ERM should be interesting from a legal perspective. In fact, one of the areas that several of the existing research studies seem to focus on is the potential link between good corporate governance and ERM. Given that corporate governance is a field in which numerous business and legal researchers are interested, we believe that there are research opportunities. Finally, more case studies are needed so that risk executives can learn from the experiences of others who have successfully implemented ERM. Providers of ERM solutions should consider collaboration with academicians interested in ERM to provide case studies of ERM implementation that are written more for teaching purposes (as opposed to marketing purposes).

We hope that by summarizing academic research on ERM, this chapter will help to encourage and stimulate more advances in the research on ERM.

NOTES

1. Early field-based research on enterprise risk management is published in books by Barton, Shenkir, and Walker (2002) and Walker, Shenkir, and Barton (2002). These books also include several case studies on ERM.

2. James Lam coined the term "enterprise risk management" in the mid-1990s.

3. Their paper assumes that the appointment of a chief risk officer also means the company has an ERM process.

4. One of the difficulties of conducting research on ERM is the limited amount of data available. One constraint is that companies in the U.S. are required to disclose the effectiveness of internal control over financial reporting, but they are not required to disclose an effective or ineffective ERM process. As a result, many companies with ERM programs do not mention this in their annual financial statements.

5. Financial opaqueness is measured as a dummy variable that equals 1 if there is a difference between S&P's and Moody's ratings for debt issued in the year prior to CRO appointment.

6. This article is not actually a case study but does include some discussion about ERM at Nationwide Insurance in parts of the paper. For this reason, we include it in our chapter.

REFERENCES

Aabo, T., J.R.S. Fraser, and B.J. Simkins. 2005. The rise and evolution of the chief risk officer: Enterprise risk management at Hydro One. *Journal of Applied Corporate Finance*, 17 (3): 62–75.

Acharuya, M., and J.E.V. Johnson. 2006. Investigating the development of ERM in the insurance industry: An empirical study of four major European insurers. *The Geneva Papers on Risk and Insurance: Issues and Practice*, 55–80.

Barton, T.L., W.G. Shenkir, and P.L. Walker. 2002. *Making enterprise risk management pay off*, Upper Saddle River, NJ: Financial Times/Prentice Hall and Financial Executives Research Foundation.

Beasley, M. S., R. Clune, and D.R. Hermanson. 2005a. ERM: A status report. *Internal Auditor* 62 (1): 67–72.

Beasley, M.S., R. Clune, and D.R. Hermanson. 2005b. Enterprise risk management: An empirical analysis of factors associated with the extent of implementation. *Journal of Accounting and Public Policy*, 24 (6): 521–531.

Beasley, M., D. Pagach, and Warr. 2008. Information conveyed in hiring announcements of senior executives overseeing enterprise-wide risk management processes. *Journal of Accounting, Auditing & Finance*, 23 (3): 311–332.

Colquitt, L., R.E. Hoyt, and R.B. Lee. 1999. Integrated risk management and the role of the risk manager. *Risk Management and Insurance Review*, 2, 43–61.

Desender, K.A. 2007. The influence of board composition on enterprise risk management implementation. Working Paper. Available at SSRN http://papers.ssrn.com/sol3/papers.cfm?abstract_id=1025982.

Fraser, J.R.S., K. Schoening-Thiessen, and B.J. Simkins. 2008. Who reads what most often? A survey of enterprise risk management literature read by risk executives. *Journal of Applied Finance* vol. 18 (1): 73–91.

Gates, S., J.L. Nicolas, and P.L. Walker. 2009. Perceived value of enterprise risk management. University of Virginia Working Paper.

Harrington, S., G. Niehaus, and K. Risko. 2002. Enterprise risk management: The case of United Grain Growers. *Journal of Applied Corporate Finance* 14 (4): 71–81.

Kleffner, A.E., R.B. Lee, and B. McGannon. 2003a. Stronger corporate governance and its implications on risk management. *Ivey Business Journal* 67 (5): 1.

Kleffner, A.E., R.B. Lee, and B. McGannon. 2003b. The effect of corporate governance on the use of enterprise risk management: Evidence from Canada. *Risk Management and Insurance Review* 6 (1): 53–73.

Liebenberg, A., and R. Hoyt. 2003. The determinants of enterprise risk management: Evidence from the appointment of chief risk officers. *Risk Management and Insurance Review* 6 (1): 37–52.

Nocco, B.W., and R.M. Stulz. 2006. Enterprise risk management: Theory and practice. *Journal of Applied Corporate Finance* 18 (4): 8–20.

Pagach, D., and R. Warr. 2008a. The characteristics of firms that hire chief risk officers. North Carolina State University Working Paper.

Pagach, D., and R. Warr. 2008b. The effects of enterprise risk management on firm performance. North Carolina State University Working Paper.

Stroh, P.J. 2005. Enterprise risk management at United Healthcare. *Strategic Finance*, July, 27–35.

Walker, P.L., T.L. Barton, and W.G. Shenkir. 2002. *Enterprise risk management: Pulling it all together*. Altamonte Springs, FL: Institute of Internal Auditors (IIA) Research Foundation.

ABOUT THE AUTHORS

Subramanian Rama Iyer is a PhD student in Finance in the Spears School of Business at Oklahoma State University (OSU). He also holds an MBA from OSU and an undergraduate degree in Chemistry from Mahatma Gandhi University, India. While pursuing his MBA, he was awarded many scholarships. He has published in *Expert Systems with Applications* and in the *International Journal of Knowledge Management*. He has worked in India for the banking industry. He has also served as an Adjunct Faculty in the Institute of Management Studies (IMS), India.

Daniel A. Rogers is Associate Professor of Finance at Portland State University. He holds a BA in Business Administration from Washington State University; MBA from Tulane University; and PhD (Finance) from University of Utah. Dr. Rogers has taught courses in valuation (including real estate valuation), corporate finance, and derivative securities at Portland State University, Northeastern University, Massey University, and University of Utah. He has published research in the areas of corporate risk management and derivatives usage, managerial incentives arising from compensation, and stock option repricing. His published work includes articles in the *Journal of Finance, Journal of Banking and Finance, Financial Management, Journal of Applied Corporate Finance,* and *Journal of Futures Markets*. His *Financial Management* article on the valuation effects of jet fuel hedging in the airline industry (co-authored with David Carter and Betty Simkins) was a co-winner of the Addison-Wesley Prize in 2006. Prior to his life as an academic, Dr. Rogers held management positions with a national airline and a petroleum products distributor, during which he purchased jet and diesel fuel, and managed the price risk associated with these commodities.

Betty J. Simkins is Williams Companies Professor of Business and Professor of Finance at Oklahoma State University. She received her BS in Chemical Engineering from the University of Arkansas, her MBA from OSU, and her PhD from Case Western Reserve University. Betty is also active in the finance profession and currently serves as President of the Eastern Finance Association, on the Board of Directors for the Financial Management Association (FMA), as co-editor of the *Journal of Applied Finance*, and as Executive Editor of *FMA Online* (the online journal for the FMA). She has co-authored more than 30 journal articles in publications including the *Journal of Finance, Financial Management, Financial Review, Journal of International Business Studies, Journal of Futures Markets, Journal of Applied Corporate Finance,* and the *Journal of Financial Research* and has won a number of best paper awards at academic conferences.

CHAPTER 24

Enterprise Risk Management

Lessons from the Field

WILLIAM G. SHENKIR
William Stamps Farish Professor Emeritus, University of Virginia's McIntire
School of Commerce

THOMAS L. BARTON
Kathryn and Richard Kip Professor of Accounting, University of North Florida

PAUL L. WALKER
Associate Professor of Accounting, University of Virginia

> *You can resist an invading army; you cannot resist an idea whose time has come.*
>
> —Victor Hugo

INTRODUCTION

As this is being written, the U.S. economy is currently reeling from what many
describe as the worst financial crisis since the Great Depression. Analysts of the
current crisis have been asking: "How could so many capable executives, regulators, the congress, and the administration have underestimated the enormous
risk in the subprime mortgage market and related areas such as securitized subprime loans and credit default swaps." The current crisis seems to indicate that
the drive for profits by some organizations was accompanied by questionable risk
management practices.

Before the current financial crisis, some leading opinion-making organizations
recognized that enterprise risk management (ERM) was an idea whose time had
come. In 1999, a blue ribbon commission of the National Association of Corporate
Directors (NACD) concluded that audit committees should "define and use timely,
focused information that is responsive to important performance measures and to
the key risks they oversee" (National Association of Corporate Directors 1999,
2). Additionally, the commission stated that audit committees should develop an
agenda that includes "a periodic review of risk by each significant business unit"
(National Association of Corporate Directors 1999, 3). As further evidence of this

risk awareness, a survey of chief financial officers and controllers in 2000 by the Financial Executives Institute ranked "key areas of business and financial risk" as the number one area of importance for audit committee oversight (Financial Executives Institute January 12, 2000).

ERM is a fairly new management discipline, but some companies have been implementing it for several years and have matured in their ERM efforts. This chapter highlights some key lessons that can be learned from these companies.[1]

LESSONS FROM THE ERM PROCESS

ERM is an iterative and disciplined process that can take many forms and designations but typically includes these key steps: clarifying strategies and objectives, identifying risks, assessing risks, acting upon those assessments, and monitoring risks. At the outset in ERM implementation, it is critical to the success of the initiative that C-level (CEO, CFO, chief audit executive) support is unwavering. Without that level of commitment, a project as important and overarching as ERM will not obtain the needed support and resources, or even survive.

Clarifying Strategies and Objectives

Organizations must clarify their strategy and related objectives before they identify their risks. These can be the company's strategic objectives if ERM is being applied to the company as a whole. Alternatively, they can be a department's objectives or the objectives for a new project if ERM is being applied at those levels. For example, an energy company used ERM to identify and manage risks around a new e-business initiative, as well as to identify and manage risks of the entire organization (Walker, Shenkir, and Barton 2002, 63).

Without this initial focus on strategy and objectives, managers have no way of knowing how their daily efforts and risk management processes relate to the organization's goals. They would also have no way of knowing if they are managing the relevant risks. One of the early lessons companies glean from ERM is that many layers of the company including senior management, operating managers, and regular employees do not know or understand the strategies and objectives of the organization and how these, in turn, relate to their daily job and tasks. ERM compels companies to identify and focus on the organization's strategies and objectives. Indeed, some companies have had to call a temporary halt in the ERM implementation process and spend time clarifying and interpreting the strategies and objectives with their associates before proceeding to the next step. One major retailer appropriately starts its ERM process with a focus on vision, strategy, and objectives (Walker, Shenkir, and Barton 2002, 129).

In the typical ERM process, risks are defined broadly to include any event or action that will prevent the organization from achieving its objectives. ERM reinforces priorities to everyone involved, and ultimately creates a focus on the risks surrounding those priorities. Knowing the priorities and the risks is essential to creating value for the stakeholders and to managing the company successfully. As one general auditor who served as the ERM process owner, noted: "An organization cannot shrink its way to greatness—it must grow and one of the keys to successful growth is excellent risk management" (Walker, Shenkir, and Barton 2002, 87).

Identifying Risks

Companies identify their risks by using a variety of methods as shown in Box 24.1. In studying how companies have approached risk identification, it is clear that one technique cannot fit all organizations. Below we contrast the approaches of four companies to risk identification:

1. Company A decided that it would not prescribe any particular technique to its business units but let them select the one that would work best for them.
2. Company B, in focusing on the risks embedded in the organization's strategies, used a facilitated workshop method with senior executives as participants. They were asked to brainstorm as a group on the possible risks. Using senior executives from across the business units greatly increased the value of the process because it helped the group learn how risks and objectives are correlated and how they can impact each of the business units differently. The sessions also allowed participants to rank the risks in terms of impact by using group software to vote anonymously on the risks. The company believed that the anonymity increased the reliability of the results.

Box 24.1   Risk Identification Techniques

Internal interviewing and discussion:
- Interviews
- Questionnaires
- Brainstorming
- Self-assessment and other facilitated workshops
- SWOT analysis (strengths, weaknesses, opportunities, and threats)

External sources:
- Comparison with other organizations
- Discussion with peers
- Benchmarking
- Risk consultants

Tools, diagnostics and processes:
- Checklists
- Flowcharts
- Scenario analysis
- Value chain analysis
- Business process analysis
- Systems engineering
- Process mapping

Source: AICPA 2000, 9.

3. Company C used a combination of techniques. Initially, a questionnaire was sent to the operating units, which asked them to list not more than 10 of their strategies and objectives, identify the risks impacting those strategies and objectives, list the factors that contribute to the risks, state the management activities or controls that were in place to mitigate the risks, and finally to assess their readiness to seize opportunities and manage risks. After receiving the completed questionnaires, the internal audit unit (which operated the ERM process but did not own the risks) followed up with interviews to clarify the information received and then summarized the results. Workshops conducted by internal audit staff, who had been specially trained in facilitation skills, were used to rank the risks in terms of impact and likelihood.

4. Company D instructed its units not to use questionnaires but to engage in face-to-face discussions in facilitated workshops to identify risks.

The risk identification process yields a risk language for the organization. Companies either develop their own risk frameworks or modify the frameworks of others to fit the unique qualities of their own organizations. Exhibit 24.1 provides an example of a generic risk template applicable to any company. It can be used to seed the discussion using techniques shown in Box 24.1. Exhibit 24.2 is an example of a general risk template that could be used by specific operating units in an organization as they focus their specific risks. Both templates are useful in helping participants consider the spectrum of risks and for seeding the risk identification process. Risk templates are also a valuable method for categorizing risks, allowing organizations to aggregate risks for upstream reporting to senior management and the board, and to better integrate risks.

Assessing Risk

The next step in the ERM process is to assess risk. Exhibit 24.3 shows an array of informal and formal, qualitative and quantitative approaches that are used by various organizations (Shenkir and Walker 2007a and 2007b). Some companies believe it is a necessary step to validate empirically a risk's effect on the company using a traditional metric. As an example, one company quantifies all risks in terms of net operating profit (NOP) because not knowing the significance of the risk could lead to wasting valuable resources such as time and capital. The operating units at Microsoft are able to access "quantification resources" within the organization's treasury group to assist "the business units in modeling a specific risk" (Barton, Shenkir, and Walker 2001, 128).

Many companies plot their assessments on risk maps (see Exhibit 24.4), which are constructive because they can summarize all of the significant risks in one visual display. Risk maps embody the 80/20 rule in that 80 percent of risk management focuses on 20 percent of the risks (Barton, Shenkir, Walker 2001, 136). The maps allow others such as senior executives and board members to review the identified risks and related rankings, thus enabling sharper focus and management of the key risks.

As shown in Exhibit 24.3, a number of techniques are available for measuring the impact of a specific risk in order to place it on a risk map. Some organizations

Exhibit 24.1 Business Risk Model—A Common Language

Environment Risk

Competitor	Sensitivity	Shareholder Relations	Capital Availability
Catastrophic Loss	Sovereign/Political	Legal Regulatory	Industry Financial Markets

Process Risk

Operations Risk	Empowerment Risk	Financial Risk	Information Processing/ Technology Risk	Integrity Risk
Customer Satisfaction	Leadership	Currency	Access	Management Fraud
Human Resources	Authority	Interest Rate	Integrity	Employee Fraud
Product Development	Limit	Liquidity	Relevance	Illegal Acts
Efficiency	Performance Incentives	Cash Transfer Velocity	Availability	Unauthorized Use
Capacity	Communications	Derivative		Reputation
Performance Gap		Settlement		
Cycle Time		Reinvestment/Rollover		
Sourcing		Credit		
Commodity Pricing		Collateral		
Obsolescence/Shrinkage		Counterparty		
Compliance				
Business Interruption				
Product/Service Failure				
Environmental				
Health and Safety				
Trademark/Brand Name Erosion				

Information for Decision-Making Risk

Operational	Financial	Strategic
Pricing	Budget and Planning	Environmental Scan
Contract Commitment	Completeness and Accuracy	Business Portfolio
Measurement	Accounting Information	Valuation
Alignment	Financial Reporting Evaluation	Measurement
Completeness and Accuracy	Taxation	Organization Structure
Regulatory Reporting	Pension Fund	Resource Allocation
	Investment Evaluation	Planning
	Regulatory Reporting	Life Cycle

Source: Economist Intelligence Unit 1995, 15.

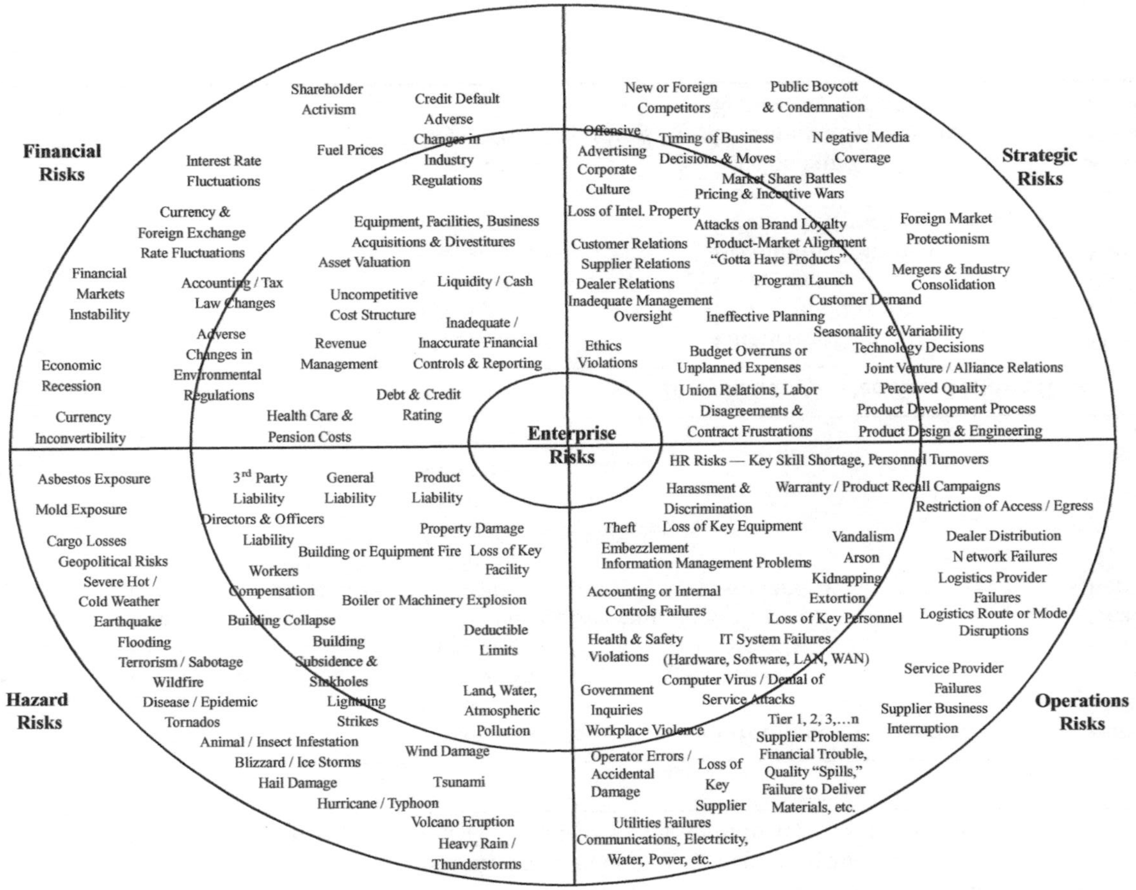

Exhibit 24.2 Industry Risk Portfolio

Source: Elkins 2006. Permission granted to use.

Qualitative	Qualitative/ Quantitative	Quantitative
Risk identification	Validation of risk impact	
Risk rankings	Validation of risk likelihood	
Risk maps	Validation of correlations	Probabilistic techniques:
Risk maps with impact	Risk corrected revenues	cash flow at risk
and likelihood	Gain/loss curves	earnings at risk
Risks mapped to objectives	Tornado charts	earnings distributions
or divisions	Scenario analysis	eps distributions
Identification of risk	Benchmarking	
correlations	Net present value	
	Traditional measures	

Level of Difficulty and Amount of Data Required →

Exhibit 24.3 Qualitative and Quantitative Approaches to Assessment and Measurement
Source: Shenkir and Walker 2007a, B-1401; Shenkir and Walker 2007b, 12.

tend to give more attention to quantification of impact and, as previously noted, will use a metric such as one based on net operating profit to that end. The determination of likelihood, on the other hand, might be based more on a consensus judgment among the participants in the specific area responsible for managing and monitoring the risk. Organizations whose cultures are measurement-oriented have

	Dollars		Probability of Occurrence				
Critical	> $15 M	5					
High	$10–$15 M	4					
Moderate	$5–$10 M	3					
Low	$1–$5 M	2					
Not Significant	< $1 M	1					
Annualized impact measured in terms of NOP			1	2	3	4	5
			< 10%	10%–30%	30%–60%	60%–90%	> 90%
Probability measured over a one-year time horizon			Slight	Not Likely	Likely	Highly Likely	Expected

Exhibit 24.4 Risk Map

found that ERM is more readily accepted by people in the organization when efforts are made to measure the impact of risks. As an example, one organization that implemented ERM is also committed to the Six Sigma problem-solving process: define, measure, analyze, improve, and control (DMAIC). When ERM was introduced, the director of ERM observed that management recognized a relationship between the Six Sigma process and ERM and as a result, ERM was more readily accepted into the culture.

Acting on the Risks

Once the risks surrounding the organization's objectives are identified and assessed, the next step is to isolate the risks and then take appropriate actions on those risks. Possible actions related to the risk include accepting, avoiding, reducing, and sharing the risk. The goal is for the organization to make conscious decisions about risk even though that may mean choosing to accept the risk over the other actions. In Exhibit 24.5, the risks map shows that 12 risks have been identified, and risks one and eight are critical—high impact and high likelihood. The 12 risks were plotted on the risk map in their inherent state, which is before any further mitigation action. Taking some mitigation action moves risks one and eight in the direction of the arrows to their residual risk level, a position after mitigation action. The remaining question is: Can management accept the residual risks? To answer this question involves analyzing the costs of additional mitigation action against the benefits of operating with further reduced risks. Another issue in mitigation is to recognize if some risks are correlated. As an example, United Grain Growers (UGG), now part of Viterra, found highly correlated business risks that they had not been aware of before they embarked on their enterprise risk process. Subsequently, they transferred and reduced some of the risks in a bundled

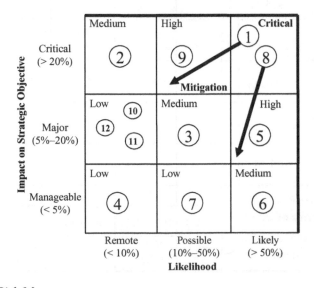

Exhibit 24.5   Risk Map

financing package and lowered their overall costs of managing the combined risks (Barton, Shenkir, Walker 2001, 161).

Monitoring Risks

Once the process and actions are underway, the final step includes monitoring the risk. Monitoring involves communication both upstream and downstream and across the organization. It also includes periodic reporting and follow-up on the risks by various levels of management, risk committees, and internal auditors. Additionally, monitoring should include board oversight and review. One monitoring approach that is evolving in ERM is the use of key (target) performance indicators (KPIs) or metrics as part of a risk scorecard.[2] A KPI might also be used as a key risk indicator (KRI) or the two might be separate metrics. These risk-related metrics can be a valuable way to monitor the improvement of key risks and to link the improvement back to improved cash flow and earnings. As an example, Wal-Mart develops metrics incorporated into a scorecard to track performance on risks and to determine the company's progress in managing the risk. They also use these metrics to determine the value added by the ERM process (Walker, Shenkir, and Barton 2002, 134). The discussion on metrics is continued below under the balanced scorecard discussion.

LESSONS FROM INTEGRATING ERM WITH ONGOING MANAGEMENT INITIATIVES

A director of ERM at a major company recently stated that his company's goal is to "embed ERM in the rhythm of the business." Some of the opportunities for integrating ERM into the rhythm of the business are: strategic planning, balanced scorecard (BSC), budgeting, internal auditing, business continuity planning and crisis preparedness, and corporate governance (Shenkir and Walker 2006a and 2006b; Shenkir and Walker 2007a).

Strategic Planning and ERM

The relationship among strategic planning, the balanced scorecard, and budgeting is depicted in Exhibit 24.6. The COSO view of ERM is specific in stating that implementation begins with strategic planning (COSO 2004a, 4). Although it is tempting to view ERM and strategy formulation as independent of each other, they are properly seen as complementary activities. A strategy is in danger of failure if it is devised without identifying the attendant risks, and without an assessment and management of the risks. Along these lines, ERM implementation must commence with a holistic identification of risks tied to the company's strategy if it is to be complete (Nagumo 2005).

Observers have pointed to the mismanagement of strategic risks as a source of major declines in shareholder value. Two important studies support this claim. For the period 1993–1998, Mercer Management Consulting analyzed value destruction in the *Fortune* 1000 and found that 10 percent of these companies lost 25 percent of shareholder value within a one-month period. Mercer was able to track the

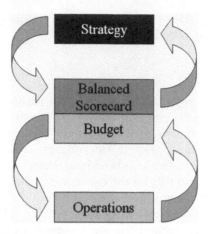

Exhibit 24.6 Strategy, the Balanced Scorecard, and the Budget
Source: Adapted from Kaplan and Norton, *The Strategy Focused Organization*, 275.

losses back to their root causes and determined that 58 percent were triggered by strategic risk, 31 percent by operational risk, 6 percent by financial risk, and none by hazard risk (Economist Intelligence Unit 2001, 8). Booz Allen Hamilton analyzed 1,200 large firms (market capitalizations exceeding $1 billion) during the period of 1999 through 2003. The lowest-performing index for that period, the S&P 500, was set as a benchmark. Then the weakest performing companies were identified as those that trailed the S&P 500. The study concluded that strategic and operational failures were the prime triggers for losses of shareholder value. For the 360 worst performing companies, 87 percent of their value destruction was tied to mismanagement of strategic and operational risks (Kocourek et al. 2004).

In the process of formulating the company's strategy, top management analyzes its strategic opportunities and identifies factors that could threaten their attainment. The risks embedded in each strategic opportunity are plotted on a risk map, and alternatives can be evaluated against the organization's capabilities in both people skills and capital. Risks can also be checked for how they align with the company's risk appetite.

The concept of risk appetite is central to ERM and strategic planning, and is the overall level of risk that an organization is willing to accept given its capabilities and the expectations of its stakeholders. What we see in the financial crisis of 2008 is that some boards and the executive management team did not clearly articulate and communicate the organization's risk appetite and/or did not understand the risks they were assuming. Also, in some of the companies, risks were managed in silos as if they were independent of each other and without executive management and the board requiring information that provided an integrated perspective on all the potential, interconnected risks facing the organization (Morgenson 2008a and 2008b).

In considering strategic opportunities, companies can build their risk appetites into their decision making processes. Presented below are examples:

- *Avoid the risk.* Some strategic opportunities might be outside the risk appetite of the company and a conscious decision is made not to pursue them.

- *Accept the risk.* Other strategies may be risky but can be managed and monitored carefully and thus will be pursued (e.g., operating in a high risk country).
- *Share the risk.* Another strategy may be risky but the decision is made to pursue it through a joint venture.
- *Reduce the risk.* Still another alternative strategy with considerable risk embedded in it might be pursued incrementally.

ERM improves strategy formulation because risks are identified, and the strategic opportunities are assessed given the company's risk appetite. For example, the front end of the strategy formulation process is typically an environmental scan, which reveals risks and opportunities when performed *comprehensively.* ERM will lack the proper foundation otherwise. Integrating ERM with strategic planning forms the basis for a strategy-risk-focused organization (Shenkir and Walker 2006a).

A company's strategic planning process may involve decisions regarding growth through acquisitions and mergers. ERM can be integrated effectively into the initial decision-making process to acquire a company, the integration with the acquired company, and the post-merger evaluation. As an example, the BOC group, now part of Linde Group, (Gates and Hexter 2005, 18) is a British company that supplies a variety of gases to a broad spectrum of industrial users and has integrated risk assessment into its merger and acquisition process (see Exhibit 24.7). The BOC risk management team focuses on these key areas in assessing the target company: people issues, financial risks, and the overall impact of the acquisition on the company. In addressing these issues, the case discussion on the target

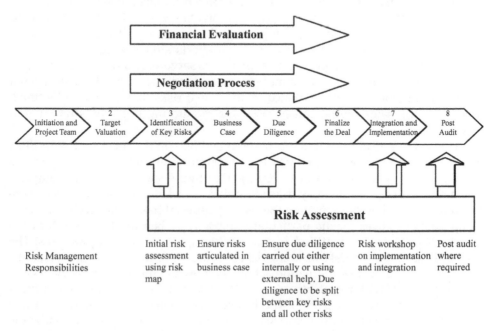

Exhibit 24.7 Risk Management in Acquisitions
Source: Gates and Hexter 2005, 20.

company highlights risks related to the target company in its business environment, the likely impact of the target company on BOC, its financial health, the future of the target company beyond the acquisition, and its operational complexity.

The business case for the acquisition given to BOC's senior management and the board contains the initial risk assessment for the target company. Once the acquisition is approved by the board, the risk management team coordinates the due diligence activity, classifying the risks identified as key risks versus all other risks. When the merger is finalized, the risk management team leads the effort to discuss the integration of the key risks with the target firm's employees. Finally, the risk management team is involved in the post-merger evaluation process, asking a question such as: "Were there any risks that should have been picked up?" (Gates and Hexter 2005, 20).

The Balanced Scorecard and ERM

The balanced scorecard (BSC) is a tool for communicating and cascading the company's strategy throughout the organization. The conventional BSC captures the company's strategy in four key perspectives: (1) customer, (2) internal processes, (3) innovation and learning, and (4) financial. Variations on these four perspectives exist in practice.

The BSC was launched in the early 1990s (Kaplan and Norton, 1992) and as ERM has evolved, some organizations have integrated their BSC system with ERM to enhance performance management. In the BSC, objectives are identified for each of the perspectives; ERM begins with an understanding of objectives. For each BSC perspective, metrics (KPIs) are selected and stretch targets are established. ERM adds value to the BSC through the identification of events (risks) that could stand in the way of achieving the targets in each of the four perspectives. Management can assess how effectively the risk mitigation efforts are working by monitoring the KPIs. The KPIs for each perspective, then, also serve as KRIs although that was not their original purpose. For example, if a target for customer satisfaction is not achieved, this points to the existence of additional risks that must be identified. Effectively, the same metric can be used for monitoring both the strategy and the risk.

As shown in Exhibit 24.8, the conventional BSC can be integrated with ERM to manage and monitor risks related to the objectives in each of the perspectives (Shenkir and Walker 2006a and b, 2007a). This figure shows how one company used a risk scorecard for the key risks identified in each of the BSC perspectives to assign responsibility for managing the risk. The special risk scorecard begins with the specific objectives for the particular perspective. Then the key risks for each of those objectives are identified as well as the suggested control processes. The focus area specifies the risks as strategic, operational, or financial. Management's self-assessment of its risk mitigation actions is shown in the worksheet by asking: "Is it in place? If so, how effective is it?" The last column focuses on identifying the owner of the risk—the person who is held accountable for managing it. A risk scorecard maintained on the company's intranet allows managers to review the scorecard at any time, adding strength to the accountability for the management of the risk.

No.	Objective	Risk Number	Risk	Suggested Control Processes	Focus Area	In Place	Effectiveness*	Comments	Owner of Corrective Action
Learning and Growth Objectives						Mitigation Process			

Exhibit 24.8 Balanced Scorecard and Strategic Risk Assessment

*Effectiveness Rating: 1 to 10, with 10 being very effective.

Budgeting and ERM

A company's budget shows its financial commitment in the current year to achieve the organization's long-term strategy. The annual budget can be integrated with ERM to provide insights on what the strategic business unit's leadership sees as the risks to meeting its financial plan and other strategic objectives. In the conventional budgeting process, the leadership of the strategic business unit presents its profit plan to senior management, who then probe and ask questions to uncover the risks implicit in the numbers. A company that has progressed in its ERM implementation will ask each operating unit to include a risk map for the unit when it submits its budget

These risk maps (as shown in Exhibit 24.4 and 24.5) provide information to senior management as to the major risks associated with meeting the financial plan and other strategic objectives for the year. A risk map gives senior management critical insight in the budget review process without having to waste time uncovering the implicit budget risks separately. It is clear that operating units should be knowledgeable about their risks to meet their budget targets. An added benefit of risk maps for the budget is this: senior management can compare the risks they have identified in the strategic plan with those identified by the operating units in the budgets. Any disparities between the two can be further analyzed.

When a risk map accompanies the budget, senior management can ask questions about the costs in the budget that relate to risk mitigation decisions for the high impact/high likelihood risks such as risks one and eight in Exhibit 24.5. Also, if a decision was made not to mitigate certain risks such as five and nine in this figure, it is important to understand the potential impact on the unit's cost structure by making that decision. Another relevant issue is to understand to what extent the cost of mitigating or accepting a risk has been built into the price of the product or service sold by that operating unit. ERM coupled with the budget review process can enrich a discussion and lead to a better understanding of the risks standing in the way of achieving budget targets, KPIs, and other strategic objectives. Combining ERM and budgeting can also lead to further risk identification. One company's budgetary pressure was so tight that management realized that it was leading to missed strategic opportunities to develop new products and areas of business.

Internal Auditing and ERM

Internal auditing and the chief audit executive can have an important role in implementing and integrating ERM across an organization, especially in organizations in which internal auditing has undergone a paradigm shift (McNamee and Selim 1998). The shift could include a movement from an internal control approach to a business risk approach, and from testing important internal controls to examining important business risks. To reflect this paradigm shift, the Institute of Internal Auditors (IIA) even changed the definition of internal auditing as follows: "Internal auditing is an independent, objective assurance and consulting activity designed to add value and improve an organization's operations. It helps an organization accomplish its objectives by bringing a systematic, disciplined approach to evaluate and improve the effectiveness of *risk management,* control and governance processes" (IIA, emphasis added). This shift in thinking by internal auditors and chief audit executives is valuable to senior level managers who need assistance in changing how an entire organization manages risk. However, it is important to remember that ERM is not exclusively an internal audit activity. For real efficacy, ERM must involve multiple levels of management and employees and be integrated in all aspects of the business including strategy, operations, accounting, information technology, and human resources.

One organization that has strongly embraced ERM is Canada Post Corporation (CPC) (Walker, Shenkir, and Barton 2002). The CPC's chief audit executive is required by the board to provide an annual assessment of the greatest risks facing the organization and an evaluation of the control effectiveness surrounding those risks. To provide the required risk and control assessments, CPC developed an integrated risk management process called Dynamic Assessment of Risk and Enablers (D.A.R.E.) that is designed to answer three questions:

1. Is CPC likely to achieve its objectives?
2. Is CPC managing the organization's significant risks?
3. Is CPC recognizing opportunities and acting on them?

It seems obvious that these are questions that all organizations in the twenty-first century should be asking.

The D.A.R.E. process was developed by the internal audit unit and ties into CPC's overall risk process. The risks CPC is trying to manage are broadly defined as anything that will keep it from achieving its objectives. CPC has developed its own risk framework that is unique to its activities. In accord with normal ERM practice, CPC ranks risks to determine their potential impact on the organization. For any risk that is ranked as exceeding a certain level, an action plan by the risk owner is required. Internal audit also follows up on those action plans and reports to the board of directors on outstanding action plans and progress on those plans. This process strongly enhances the corporate governance process at CPC.

Business Continuity Planning, Crisis Preparedness, and ERM

Some unknown risks will remain unknown at the end of the process regardless of how robust the effort to identify risks. A company can prepare for these unknown risks through its business continuity and crisis management plan, which is an essential element of the ERM process. It is not unusual for the owner of the ERM process, not of the specific risks, to also have oversight over business continuity (Walker, Shenkir, and Barton 2002, 99).

Chat rooms, bloggers, message boards, e-mail lists, independent news web sites, and other Internet-based new media have changed the informational landscape. A company must be prepared to recognize a crisis and respond swiftly and decisively to contain it before severe damage is done to its reputation and brands. A company needs to "play war games" to test the crisis management plan and to ensure that all the key employees know their roles. In addition, communication with the entire work force about the plan in advance of a crisis is an essential part of the preparation.

When a crisis occurs, it does not generally evolve in a linear way. This is because a series of reactions and events in other areas either within and/or outside the organization may be triggered if the crisis is not recognized and dealt with quickly (Walker, Shenkir, and Barton 2002, 100). In effect, without quick containment, the initial event may have a ballooning impact and may develop exponentially. To illustrate, a major company sold contaminated product in two countries and some purchasers fell ill. The company failed to acknowledge the crisis quickly and as a result, the governments of the two countries removed the product from store shelves. After some delay, the CEO traveled from the United States to the countries and eventually made a public apology. By then, though, the damage had been done—the company's stock price fell precipitously and eventually the CEO was replaced.

Corporate Governance and ERM

Corporate governance is receiving much attention today, and ERM strengthens corporate governance in a number of ways (Walker, Shenkir, and Barton 2002, 26–28). An individual who serves on several boards has noted to the authors that if a company on whose board he has been asked to serve has not adopted an ERM process and identified its key business risks, he requests that external consultants come in and perform a risk assessment. He does not feel comfortable joining a board without ERM as a part of the corporate governance structure.

As noted previously, the National Association of Corporate Directors has suggested that audit committees develop an agenda that includes a periodic review of risk "by each significant business unit." Additionally, failure to manage risk can lead to missed opportunities and loss of shareholder value, adding pressure (both internal and external) to improve corporate governance.

As depicted in Exhibit 24.9, reporting to the board and audit committee on the key risks facing the organization is one way ERM can improve corporate governance. An arrangement often adopted is this: the chief audit executive owns the ERM process and he or she reports directly to the board's audit committee.[3] The chief audit executive might also survey the audit committee and ask whether "the internal audit function has provided a reliable, overall assessment of risks and internal control effectiveness" (Walker, Shenkir, and Barton 2002, 50).

ERM results in enhanced upstream reporting to the board and audit committee and the type, volume, and frequency of information changes with ERM. Canada Post's chief audit executive is required to report annually on all major business risks to the audit committee. Wal-Mart reported that it is not just the reporting that is helpful, but also the quantity of information available to the board. Wal-Mart's board is interested in risks and often asks questions on how management is addressing risks. As a result, the chief audit executive at Wal-Mart reports to the board on the top risks, presents risk maps, and discusses the action plans and linkage to shareholder value (Walker, Shenkir, and Barton 2002, 125).

Other forms of corporate governance improvement show up in the appointment of chief risk officers, ERM committees, and risk champions. For example, Wal-Mart appointed a risk committee and that committee reports to the board on progress toward targeted risks. Some organizations have designated risk champions for the ERM process while others appointed champions for a specific risk.

The previously mentioned changes that occur in internal auditing also improve corporate governance. Internal auditors now take a more business-oriented

Exhibit 24.9   Corporate Governance and ERM
Source: Walker, Shenkir, and Barton 2002, 27.

approach, develop greater knowledge of the business and its risks, and change their audit approach to focus on those business risks, resulting in greater risk coverage and efficiency for their organizations. Furthermore, internal auditing can now perform more effective follow-ups on outstanding ERM scorecards and metrics. These same scorecards and metrics can also be used to increase management accountability and follow-up, especially when management knows that there is upstream risk reporting to the board and audit committee. Corporate governance is enhanced when an operating unit, as a result of process risk management, develops an action plan listing improvements that must be made with specific people assigned the responsibility to follow up. In addition, the action plans can be stored on a centralized database to facilitate management review and monitoring.

SOME KEY VALUE LESSONS FROM ERM

A key lesson from ERM case studies (Barton, Shenkir, and Walker 2001; Walker, Shenkir, and Barton 2002) is the belief on the part of each company that ERM was adding value (see Box 24.2). But the sources of the value tended to be unique across the companies. Some saw the value as reduced revenue volatility and a more predictable earnings stream. Other companies saw value in the risk identification step. That is, these companies admitted that, prior to implementing ERM, they did not know or understand all of their risks. It is somewhat surprising to consider that large organizations are operating in an environment in which they do not know their major risks. Other companies mentioned the value in just increasing the probability that they were helping to avoid potential debacles by knowing their risks.

Box 24.2   Some Key Value Lessons

- A focus on value added.
- Effective risk management necessitates that companies identify all business risks using a formal and dedicated process.
- Risks must be identified and understood from an enterprise-wide perspective.
- A one-size-fits-all approach is not feasible because of the influence of company culture and the change agents who lead the effort; thus ERM infrastructures vary.
- Ownership of ERM process versus ownership of specific risks.
- Risk identification should be dynamic.
- Risks must be assessed on some scale of impact and likelihood.
- Although some risks can be measured with sophisticated tools, these measurements must be understandable by management.
- The risk appetite of stakeholders (management, shareholders, and others) must be considered.
- ERM requires both a risk champion and C-level support and commitment.
- Integrating risk and risk responses can offer additional insights and value.
- Making risk consideration part of normal and regular decision making is a valuable benefit derived from ERM.
- ERM leads to changes in internal audit.
- ERM enhances corporate governance.

Sources: Barton, Shenkir, Walker 2001, 11–33; Walker, Shenkir, Barton 2002, 11–28.

Still other companies took great pride in the value gained from integrating the risks—that is, from understanding how actions in one area (such as the CFO or controller's office) affect the actions of other areas (such as the company's strategic planning group). Some companies noted that they found that they were overmanaging some risks and undermanaging other, more significant risks. As a result, these companies believed that ERM helped them better evaluate management and allocate resources. Although some companies were satisfied with risk maps and qualitative rankings, others took risk measurement to a new level and attempted to quantify what they could; and they were not overly concerned if they did not capture everything in their measurements. One company learned from their risk measurement that certain divisions have financial risks that appear to exceed the relative profits they bring in to the overall organization. Peter Cox, former Chief Financial Officer of United Grain Growers (now Viterra) appropriately stated at the time, "I think the point to risk management is not to try and operate your business in a risk-free environment. It is to tip the scale to your advantage. So it becomes strategic rather than just defensive" (Barton, Shenkir, Walker 2001, 143). Several other value lessons learned from the companies are highlighted in Box 24.2. These lessons include the dynamic nature of risk identification, understanding the risk appetite of stakeholders, making risk assessment a normal part of decision making, and establishing risk infrastructures.

One company also emphasized that value was added through the ERM process itself. In fact, Wal-Mart's chief financial officer required the ERM team to link the risk process to value added in the organization. Additionally, while the role of internal audit was critical to these organizations, most of the chief audit executives interviewed in the study mentioned that internal auditing itself greatly benefited from being involved. They noted how it forced their audit team to think "like managers" rather than internal auditors, and how their audit team gained a broader knowledge of business risk (Walker, Shenkir, and Barton 2002).

One of the major value statements of an ERM effort was improvement in corporate governance. This was accomplished through the emergence of risk champions, risk committees, and in some cases, chief risk officers. That is, by designating employees and teams to identify and assess the risk, the organizations learned more about themselves and their risks than they had ever realized. This information alone—knowing the key risks facing the business—can make the process worth the effort. Armed with information about the key risks, management can better evaluate risks taken, profits made, merger prices, hedged risks, more efficiently allocate resources, and even increase the chances that their organization will meet earnings, revenue, and cash flow targets. Furthermore, this information can be reported upstream to audit committees and boards of directors so that improved corporate governance can occur. What board or audit committee member, for example, does not want to know the major risks facing the organization and what management is currently doing to manage those risks?

CONCLUSION

In the perilous economic times of today, enterprise risk management is a necessity, not a luxury. Effective business management requires that firms understand all of their risks and have plans in place to manage those risks in a unified, integrated manner. Failure to do so may result in a modest decline in shareholder value all the way to the complete financial destruction of the firm. Recent events demonstrate that this latter result is not at all far-fetched, even for large, mature organizations that dominate their industries.

Over the years, ERM has been implemented effectively in a number of organizations of varying sizes. Many of these organizations have generously shared their accumulated knowledge and insights—their lessons from the field. They believe that ERM has been a worthwhile undertaking, creating significant added value for stakeholders. ERM is the wave of the future, and organizations that refuse to recognize this do so at their own peril.

NOTES

1. The authors have been involved in the area of ERM since 1996 teaching ERM at the undergraduate and graduate levels and for businesses and executives worldwide as well as consulting on ERM implementation. As noted in the references, the authors have co-authored books and articles on ERM. It is with that background that this chapter has

been written. Where permission has been granted, company names are used in the text. Otherwise, reference is to "a company."

2. Some view a KRI as a future indicator and KPI as historical. Of course, targeted KPIs are futuristic as well. Refer to Chapter 8 in this book, which has more information on KRI.

3. It is important to note the distinction between owning the process and owning the risk. Some companies choose to have internal auditing own the process, while others do not.

REFERENCES

American Institute of Certified Public Accountants and Canadian Institute of Chartered Accountants. 2000. *Managing risk in the new economy*. New York: AICPA.

Barton, T.L., W.G. Shenkir, and P.L. Walker. 2001. *Making enterprise risk management pay off*. Upper Saddle River, NJ: Financial Executives Research Foundation.

Committee of Sponsoring Organizations of the Treadway Commission (COSO). 1992. *Internal control—Integrated framework: Executive summary framework*. New York: AICPA.

———. 2004a. *Enterprise risk management—Integrated framework: Executive Summary framework*. New York: AICPA.

———. 2004b. Enterprise Risk Management—Integrated Framework: Application Techniques. New York: AICPA.

Economist Intelligence Unit. 1995. *Managing business risks—An integrated approach*. New York: The Economist Intelligent Unit.

———. 2001. *Enterprise risk management—Implementing new solutions*. New York: The Economist Intelligent Unit.

Elkins, D. 2006. Managing risks in global automotive manufacturing operations. Presentation at the University of Virginia (January 23).

Financial Executives Institute. 2000. Survey: Audit committees should focus on key business risks. FEI Press Release (January 12).

Gates, S., and E. Hexter. 2005. *From risk management to risk strategy*. New York: The Conference Board.

Kaplan, R.S., and D.P. Norton. 1992. The balanced scorecard—Measures that drive performance. *Harvard Business Review* (January–February): 71–79.

——— and ———. 2001. The strategy-focused organization. Boston, MA: Harvard Business School Press.

Kocourek, P., R.V. Lee, C. Kelly, and J. Newfrock. 2004. Too much SOX can kill you. *Strategy+Business* (Reprint, January): 1–5.

McNamee, D., and G.M. Selim. 1998. *Risk management: Changing the internal auditor's paradigm*. Altamonte Springs, FL: The Institute of Internal Auditors Research Foundation.

Morgenson, G. 2008a. Behind biggest insurer's crisis, a blind eye to a web of risk. *New York Times* (September 28): 1 and 18.

——— 2008b. How the thundering herd faltered and fell. *New York Times* (November 9): BU 1 and 9.

Nagumo, T. 2005. Aligning enterprise risk management with strategy through the BSC: The Bank of Tokyo-Mitsubishi approach. Balanced Scorecard Report (Harvard Business School Publishing, Reprint No. B0509D, September–October): 1–6.

National Association of Corporate Directors. 1999. *Report of the NACD blue ribbon commission of audit committees—A practical guide*. National Association of Corporate Directors.

Shenkir, W., and P.L. Walker. 2006a. Enterprise risk management and the strategy-risk-focused organization. *Cost Management* (May–June): 32–38.

———, and ———. 2006b. *Enterprise risk management: Framework, elements, and implementation*. Montvale, NJ: IMA.

————, and ————. 2007a. *Enterprise risk management.* Washington, DC: BNA.

————, and ————. 2007b. *Enterprise risk management: Tools and techniques for effective implementation.* Montvale, NJ: IMA.

Walker, P.L., W.G. Shenkir, and T.L. Barton. 2002. *Enterprise risk management: Pulling it all together.* Altamonte Springs, FL: The Institute of Internal Auditors Research Foundation.

FURTHER READING

Augustine, N.R. "Managing the Crisis You Tried to Prevent." *Harvard Business Review* (November–December 1995): 147–158.

Barton, T.L., W.G. Shenkir, and P.L. Walker. "Managing Risk: An Enterprise-wide approach." *Financial Executive* (March–April 2001): 48–51.

————, ————, and ————. "Managing the Unthinkable Event." *Financial Executive* (December 2008): 24–29.

Bernstein, P.L. *Against the Gods—The Remarkable Story of Risk.* New York: John Wiley & Sons, 1996.

Bodine, S., A. Pugliese, and P. Walker. "A Road Map to Risk Management." *Journal of Accountancy* (December 2001).

Corporate Executive Board. *Confronting Operational Risk—Toward an Integrated Management Approach.* Washington, DC: Corporate Executive Board, 2000.

DeLoach, J.W. *Enterprise-wide Risk Management: Strategies for Linking Risk and Opportunity.* London: Financial Times, 2000.

Deloitte & Touche LLP. *Perspectives on Risk for Boards of Directors, Audit Committees, and Management.* Deloitte Touche Tohmatsu International, 1997.

Epstein, M.J., and A. Rejc. *Identifying, Measuring, and Managing Organizational Risks for Improved Performance.* Society of Management Accountants of Canada and AICPA, 2005.

Gibbs, E., and J. DeLoach. "Which Comes First . . . Managing Risk or Strategy-Setting? Both." *Financial Executive* (February 2006): 35–39.

King Committee on Corporate Governance. *King Report on Corporate Governance for South-Africa.* Institute of Directors in Southern Africa, 2002.

"Joint Standards Australia/ Standards New Zealand Committee." *Risk Management.* Standards Australia/Standards New Zealand, 2004.

————. *Risk Management Guidelines.* Standards Australia/Standards New Zealand, 2004.

Kaplan, R.S., and D.P. Norton. "Putting the Balanced Scorecard to Work." *Harvard Business Review* (September–October 1993): 134–147.

Kaplan, Robert S., and David P. Norton. *The Balanced Scorecard.* Boston, MA: Harvard Business School Press, 1996.

"Living Dangerously: A Survey of Risk. *The Economist* (January 24, 2004): 1–15.

Miccolis, J.A., K. Hively, and B.W. Merkley. *Enterprise Risk Management: Trends and Emerging Practices.* Altamonte Springs, FL: The Institute of Internal Auditors Research Foundation, 2001.

Nagumo, T., and B.S. Donlon. "Integrating the Balanced Scorecard and COSO ERM Framework." *Cost Management* (July/August 2006): 20–30.

New York Stock Exchange. *Final NYSE Corporate Governance Rules.* (November 4, 2003).

Nottingham, L. *A Conceptual Framework for Integrated Risk Management.* The Conference Board of Canada, 1997.

Schwartz, P. *The Art of the Long View.* New York: Currency Doubleday, 1991.

Shenkir, W.G., and P.L. Walker. "Ensemble Performance." *Business Officer* (December 2008): 14–20.

Simons, R.L. "How Risky Is Your Company?" *Harvard Business Review* (May–June 1999): 85–94.

Smith, Wendy K. "James Burke: A Career in American Business (A) (B). "Harvard Business School Case 9-389-177 and 9-390-030. Harvard Business School Publishing, 1989.

Slywotzky, A.J., and J. Drzik. "Countering the Biggest Risk of All." *Harvard Business Review* (Reprint R0504E, April 2005): 1–12.

Stroh, P. "Enterprise Risk Management at United Health Group." *Strategic Finance* (July 2005): 27–35.

Thornton, E. "A Yardstick for Corporate Risk." *Business Week* (August 26, 2002): 106–108.

Walker, P.L., W.G. Shenkir, and T.L. Barton.. "ERM in Practice." *Internal Auditor* (August 2003): 51–55.

Walker, P.L., W.G. Shenkir, and S. Hunn. "Developing Risk Skills: An Investigation of Business Risks and Controls at Prudential Insurance Company of America." *Issues in Accounting Education* (May 2001): 291–304.

———, and ———. "Teaching a Risk Assessment Course." *Advances in Accounting Education,* 2000: 33–56.

ABOUT THE AUTHORS

William G. Shenkir, PhD, CPA, is the William Stamps Farish Professor Emeritus at the University of Virginia's McIntire School of Commerce, where he served on the faculty for almost 40 years and as the dean from 1977 to 1992. He has co-authored three books on enterprise risk management and continues to consult in the area.

He has produced more than 60 professional publications in leading academic and practitioner journals, made more than 100 presentations before professional and academic organizations, and edited or co-authored eight books, From 1973 to 1976, he served on the staff of the FASB. Shenkir has served as President of the Association to Advance Collegiate Schools of Business International (AACSB) and as a Vice President of the American Accounting Association. He has served on numerous professional committees and on the board of directors of three corporations.

In 1995 he received the Virginia Outstanding Educator Award from the Carman Blough Chapter of the IMA, and in 1997 he was recognized as one of the 10 University of Virginia Distinguished Professors in the students' yearbook, *Corks and Curls.*

Thomas L. Barton, PhD, CPA is Kathryn and Richard Kip Professor of Accounting at the University of North Florida. He holds a PhD in accounting from the University of Florida and is a certified public accountant (CPA). Dr. Barton has more than 50 professional publications, including research articles in *Barron's, Decision Sciences, Abacus, Advances in Accounting, Financial Executive, CPA Journal,* and *Management Accounting;* and five books and one audio book. He received the Lybrand Silver Medal for his article, "A System is Born: Management Control at American Transtech." Dr. Barton is the creator of the Minimum Total Propensity to Disrupt method of allocating gains from cooperative ventures. This method has been the subject of several articles in *Decision Sciences.* He is also a recognized expert in the application of management controls to highly creative activities.

Dr. Barton has taught more than 150 professional development seminars and has extensive consulting experience with a wide cross section of organizations in the public and private sectors. Dr. Barton is the recipient of several teaching awards for his undergraduate and graduate work. He was a winner of the State University

System of Florida's prestigious Teacher Incentive Program award in the program's inaugural year.

Paul L. Walker, PhD, CPA, is an accounting professor at the University of Virginia. Professor Walker co-developed one of the first courses on enterprise risk management in the world. He has taught ERM at the University of Virginia, to numerous executives groups, and to boards. Professor Walker has also served as a visiting fellow at the London School of Economics Centre for the Analysis of Risk.

Professor Walker was one of the original consultants to COSO on their enterprise risk management process and framework and has served as an advisor to both small and large organizations on enterprise risk management (including the Federal Reserve Bank, several Fortune 500 companies, a leading university, and international companies). Additionally, he has been invited to train international audiences on ERM, including companies with operations in South Korea, Japan, and Belgium.

Professor Walker has visited the headquarters of some major companies (e.g., Wal-Mart, Microsoft, and DuPont) to study their ERM processes. Professor Walker has co-authored numerous manuscripts on enterprise risk management including the books *Making Enterprise Risk Management Pay Off* and *Enterprise Risk Management: Pulling it All Together.* He has also co-authored several articles on ERM including: "Managing Risk: An Enterprise-Wide Approach," "A Road Map to ERM" and "ERM and the Strategy-Risk Focused Organization."

Special Topics and Case Studies

CHAPTER 25

Rating Agencies' Impact on Enterprise Risk Management

MICHAEL J. MOODY
ARM, MBA, Strategic Risk Financing, Inc.

INTRODUCTION

There are many important stakeholders that have had an impact on the acceptance of enterprise risk management (ERM). However, one critically important stakeholder group within the financial services sector that has had a profound impact on ERM over the past few years is the rating agencies. Rating agencies have historically assessed the financial strength of a variety of corporate and governmental entities. In essence, they determine the entities' ability to meet the interest and principal payments of bonds and other debt obligations. The agencies provide the ratings after studying the terms and conditions of each specific debt instrument, as well as the entities' overall financial condition. As a result, the assigned rating then reflects the agency's degree of confidence about the specific borrower's ability to meet the interest and principal payment, as scheduled.

Credit ratings can be used by bankers, brokers, governments, and other interested parties to help determine the creditworthiness of a borrower. For investors, rating agencies can increase the range of investment alternatives by providing easy-to-use measurements of the relative credit risks. In general, this increases the efficiency of the market by lowering the costs to both borrowers and lenders. The key point to the rating provided by the agency is that it will ultimately determine the cost of capital for the entity. So, the better the rating, the lower the cost of capital; obviously, it is extremely important for any borrower to obtain the highest rating possible.

Over the past several years, however, rating agencies have been subject to some criticism for their ratings assignments. In fact, it was a response to this type of criticism following the fall of Enron, et al. that led President Bush to sign into law the "Rating Reform Act of 2006," on September 29, 2006. As part of revising their rating methodology, the agencies began a more robust risk management regime, such as considering enterprise risk management, and started providing additional assessments on a selective basis.

Today, there are three U.S. general rating agencies, Standards & Poor's (S&P), Moody's Investors Service (Moody's), and Fitch Rating (Fitch). In addition, there is one specialty agency, A.M. Best (Best), which is only active in rating insurance companies. Rating agencies have been actively involved with defining an ERM methodology in the banking industry, but it was only when they turned to using the methodology in conjunction with rating insurance companies that they began to fine-tune their approach. As a result, the agencies began to take a broader, holistic view of risk management, and the effect that would have on the company seeking the ratings.

One of the primary reasons for the aggressive movement into ERM is that the rating agencies believe that companies with an enterprise-wide view of risks, such as that offered by ERM, are better managed. Several of the agencies have also noted that ERM provides an objective view of hard-to-measure aspects such as management capabilities, strategic rigor, and ability to manage in changing circumstances. In addition, some agencies, such as S&P, believe that positive or negative changes in ERM programs are leading indicators that will show up long before they could be seen in a company's published financial data.[1]

The following sections summarize the rating agencies ERM rating practices by industry segments of banking, insurance, energy, and nonfinancial entities.

BANKING: GENERAL

Some of the rating agencies have been working with enterprise risk management within the banking industry for a number of years. In Moody's July 2004 "Risk Management Assessments" publication,[2] they emphasized the importance of developing a holistic review of both risk philosophy and risk practices in banks. Moody's pointed out that they would be moving away from the traditional, discrete risk sectors such as market risk, credit risks, and so on, to a more holistic view of risk management. They further commented on their desire to begin risk reviews on a more holistic basis in their October 2004 paper titled "Governance in the United States and Canada—August 2003–September 2004."[3] Moody's noted that more organizations continued to move toward an enterprise approach to risk management. The other major rating agencies also signaled an increased interest in ERM. Most of the rating agencies indicated that they would be developing criteria for formally assessing ERM. The major agencies indicated an interest in ERM, but initially it appeared that Standard & Poor's (S&P) was one of the first to provide specific information regarding their plans for ERM.

INSURANCE: S&P

One of the leaders in promoting the enterprise approach to risk management has been S&P. They completed their first review on the ERM program of an insurer in 2006. S&P noted that when evaluating insurers they look at not only how management defines their risk tolerance, but also how they ensure that it is kept within that level. Further, they also consider the degree that risk management is involved in setting the insurer's direction and strategic decision making. They also look to see if the ERM practices are being completed in a systemic and consistent way and that an optimal risk/reward structure is achieved. This information is then compared with other peer group organizations.

More specifically, S&P developed an ERM review that evaluates five distinct areas:

1. Risk management culture: S&P determines if risk and risk management are considerations in the everyday aspects of corporate decision making. Reviewing the effectiveness of the organizational and governance structures, as well as the effectiveness of the risk management communications, is another important part of the corporate culture. This includes an examination of how clearly articulated the risk tolerances are as well.

2. Risk control: The rater determines if risk control measures have been achieved via identification, measuring, and monitoring of risks. As part of this determination, S&P evaluates the risk control processes for each important risk.

3. Emerging risk management: Consideration is also given for those risks that either do not currently exist or are not currently recognized. Frequently, these are the risks that are associated with changes in the political, legal, market, or environment, such as nanotechnology or climate change that could become a major problem area for insurers.

4. Risk and economic capital models: Another important aspect of the review is the flow of relevant information from the insurer's risk models in relation to its risks. S&P analyzes not only the information, but how the information is used by management. Accordingly, the insurer needs to provide information that is sufficiently accurate, up-to-date, and timely in order to facilitate appropriate risk management decisions and actions.

5. Strategic risk management: The rating agency examines this key area because it deals with risks, risk return, and how they are incorporated into decision making. Key data is reviewed regarding the insurer's overall risk profile, as well as other important data concerning capital budgeting, asset allocation, performance measurements, and incentive compensation. This is an important review because other aspects of ERM focus on limiting the downside; however, the strategic risk management focuses more on the upside or reward aspects.

S&P makes an evaluation of the five separate areas as noted above. Once they have concluded this evaluation, they combine the evaluations into a single classification, which is an indication of the agency's overall rating for the insurer's ERM program. This assignment of a single classification is determined by S&P by providing a weighted average for each of the five factors according to the specific situation each insurer faces. Thus, according to S&P, the weighting is dependent on the insurer's individual risks as well as their capacity to absorb losses.[4]

S&P uses a four classification system of ERM programs with regard to their insurance company ratings. A summary of the four classifications is:

1. Excellent: Insurers who are awarded this classification must show that they have advanced capabilities to identify, measure, and manage risk exposures and losses within the company's predetermined risk tolerances. Additionally, they must demonstrate advanced implementation, development, and execution of ERM parameters. The insurer must also consistently optimize risk adjustment returns in their corporate decision making.

2. Strong: Those insurers who qualify for this classification have both a clear vision of risk tolerance as well as their overall risk profile, but can periodically experience unexpected losses that are outside their tolerance level. They will have a robust process for identifying risks and preparing for emerging risks. And they usually incorporate risk management into their decision making to optimize their risk adjusted returns.

3. Adequate: The insurer has adequate capabilities to identify, measure, and manage most major risk exposures and losses; however, they lack a comprehensive process needed to extend this to all significant risks. The execution of their risk management program is sufficient, but less comprehensive than strong or excellent ERM practices. As a result, unexpected losses are more likely to occur. Although risk management is often important to the insurer's decision making process, they may fail to prepare for emerging risks.

4. Weak: Insurers' risk management programs are considered weak when they have inconsistent or limited capacity to indentify, measure, and manage their risk exposures. Their risk management execution is sporadic and as a result losses cannot be expected to be limited to predetermined risk tolerances. Corporate decision making sometimes considers risk management, but frequently business unit managers have yet to adopt an enterprise approach to risk management. As a result, these insurers have incomplete control processes for one or more major risks.

According to S&P, they completed 274 ERM evaluations during 2007 for insurance companies, including property/casualty insurers, health insurers, life insurers, and reinsurers worldwide. Of that number, the majority (83 percent) were rated "adequate." In addition, 10 percent were rated "strong" and 3 percent were rated "excellent," but only 4 percent were rated as "weak." It should be noted that S&P has started to increase some insurers' overall credit ratings, due in large part to either their "strong" or "excellent" ERM ratings. The reverse is also true, since they have lowered overall ratings on some insurers with "weak" ratings. Since an ERM rating is used as an explicated component in their overall rating methodology, much more attention is being paid to their ERM ratings.[5]

INSURANCE: MOODY'S

Moody's Investors Services (Moody's) has been the least public with regard to how they view ERM. They have indicated that they view their risk management assessment as a portion of a broader program referred to as "Enhanced Analysis Initiative" (EAI). They have further noted that their EAI analysis is designed to bring additional scrutiny to the creditworthiness evaluation of a company and encompasses five separate areas:

1. Quality of financial reports—Financial reporting assessment.
2. Quality of corporate governance—Corporate governance assessment.
3. Vulnerability to an abrupt loss of market—Liquidity risk assessment.
4. Existence of material off-balance sheet risks—Off-balance sheet risk assessment.
5. Quality of risk management practices—Risk management assessment.

Moody's increased level of interest in the above five areas is the result of recent events that have "demonstrated that high-profile credit defaults, or severe credit deteriorations were often preceded by instances of poor financial reporting, weak governance practices, inadequate risk or liquidity management, or abusive uses of off-balance sheet structures."[6] Of the five areas noted above, Moody's major emphasis will be on the risk management assessment, because these assessments are much more closely aligned with their fundamental rating process. As a result of this increased emphasis on the risk management assessment, Moody's indicates that the impact of the assessment will be significant on their rating framework.

As Moody's began to reexamine their rating methodology, they found that risk management was a much more important aspect than they first believed. They indicated that a corporation's risk management practices essentially form the company's first line of defense against potentially devastating effects from various financial risks. They also point out that both risk control practices and risk measurement techniques have been making progress in recent years. Further, Moody's believes that additional innovation is on the horizon. However, they voice a concern about a lack of risk management uniformity across various industries.

In essence, Moody's is attempting to "assess the relationship between the firm's risk appetite and its risk control capacity."[7] As a result, Moody's ratings would be reflective of their determination on the relative creditworthiness of the issuer. And, as Moody's points out, their approach emphasizes a holistic view of risk philosophy and practices. Among other things, the risk management assessment will consider such things as the rigor of the process, the buy-in of management, the appropriateness of the measurements, as well as the issue of technical competence. Initially, Moody's states that they were going to apply their risk management assessment to the financial service sector, but they also note that they would be attending to the nonfinancial issuers at a later date.

INSURANCE: FITCH

According to Fitch, they do not think that ERM is new, and "there is no reason to create another component to Fitch's rating methodology."[8] As a result, there is no separate or explicate consideration of ERM within Fitch's rating matrix. They indicate that risk management is just part of their overall review of an insurance company, which would normally include such things as industry, operational, and organizational management as well as financial opinions of the company. Fitch does, however, believe that the improvements that result from ERM have allowed insurers to better control their risks. Further, they have stated that these improvements (i.e., ERM) will begin to affect the competitive landscape of the insurance industry and they think that insurers that have not embraced ERM may be at a disadvantage in the market.

NOTE: Information regarding Moody's position on ERM was taken from two documents; "Risk Management Assessments" and "Moody's Findings on Corporate Governance in the United States and Canada: August 2003-September 2004," both issued in 2004. Since that time, Moody's has not provided much additional data in the way of publicly released information. And despite numerous attempts to secure more current information directly and indirectly, none was forthcoming at this time.

Fitch's current rating methodology and categories already encompass the essence of ERM, so they saw no reason to develop a new "pillar" or consider ERM as a separate review area or stand-alone category. ERM does allow Fitch to investigate its traditional areas of analysis with a new perspective, which is based on modern risk management practices. Among the key areas of ERM that Fitch will begin to analyze are:

- Risk governance.
- Risk tolerance, monitoring, and reporting.
- Risk assessment—economic capital modeling and catastrophe risk management.
- Operational risk analysis—including planning for the unknown.
- Risk optimization.

In mid-2006, Fitch introduced a new economic capital model known as Prism. They believe that economic capital results are an important aspect of ERM since it analyzes an insurer's capital quality. As such, involvement with the Prism model will become a critical aspect of their ERM analysis since it can measure and aggregate risk. Fitch feels that the Prism mode can help them assess ERM in several ways, by providing a benchmark in-house economic capital calculation, by aiding in an understanding of the in-house model, as well as by measuring the effects of strategic actions carried out by management. A major portion of Fitch's ERM analysis will incorporate its Prism model. In the final analysis, Fitch says that "those insurers who significantly improve risk management, could experience future rating increases as the benefits of their strong ERM become evident."[9]

INSURANCE: A.M. BEST

A.M. Best (Best) is a specialty rating organization that limits their rating to the insurance industry. According to their published reports, Best believes that the two primary objectives of a sound risk management program are:

1. "To manage the organization's exposure to potential earnings and capital volatility."[10]
2. "To maximize value to the organization's various stakeholders."[11]

However, Best goes on to point out, that the objective is not to eliminate risks and volatility, but rather to understand risk and manage it. Best believes that if risk management is done correctly, it "fosters an operating environment that supports strong financial controls and risk mitigation, as well as prudent risk taking to seize market opportunities."[12]

According to Best, this has been their position for quite some time; however, the introduction of ERM has resulted in a major change in their view regarding risk management. As they say, "What's new about ERM, is the 'E,' which represents the development of an enterprise-wide view of risk,"[13] which allows insurers to consistently identify, quantify and manage risk on a holistic basis.

Thanks in large part to the movement to ERM, Best can now assign an interactive rating that encompasses an in-depth evaluation of an insurer's balance sheet strength, operating performance, and business profile. This is in sharp contrast to the traditional quantitative and qualitative standards they previously used. As a result, Best's new view of risk management (i.e., ERM) shows that risk management is the common thread that links balance sheet strength, operating performance, and business profile. A key consideration for Best is the insurer's "corporate DNA,"[14] which is the embedding of risk management into corporate business lines and functional area objectives. In order for this to be correct, the risk-return measures are incorporated into the financial planning and budgeting, strategic planning, performance measurements, and incentive compensation.

One of the major components to Best's rating review is the "Best's Capital Adequacy Ratio (BCAR)." This has become an important tool in Best's rating matrix where they can differentiate between companies since it will indicate whether the insurer's "capitalization is appropriate for a particular rating level."[15]

U.S. ENERGY COMPANIES: S&P

Since April 2006, S&P has expanded its ERM analysis to nonfinancial organizations, when it began assessing the trading risk management practices of U.S. energy companies. They focused on select energy companies' risk management policies, infrastructure, and methodology (PIM). This allowed S&P to include the PIM analysis along with their established liquidity survey and their capital adequacy methodology.

As explained in S&P's RatingsDirect "S&P Completes Initial 'PIM' Risk Management Review for Selected U.S. Energy Firms," dated May 29, 2007, the rater is moving from a passive perspective to a more enhanced analytic framework. They point out that the "policies" aspect of the review focuses on the stature of risk management, as well as an assessment of risk appetite, the risk control process, and risk information dissemination. The "infrastructure" portion of the analysis centers around the capture and management of risk data and an assessment of the back office functions. The "methodology" aspect deals with the technology of risk management such as the quality and variety of valuation techniques.

Originally, S&P used 10 energy trading companies to introduce their PIM approach; however, they now continue to expand their analysis to other energy organizations. The PIM analysis has become one of the centerpieces to S&P's ERM methodology.[16]

NONFINANCIAL COMPANIES: S&P

Given S&P's success with ERM analysis within the insurance sector, rumors during 2007 that they would extend ERM reviews to nonfinancial companies continued to persist during the year. Then in November 2007, they finally published their "Request for Comment: Enterprise Risk Management Analysis for Credit Ratings of Nonfinancial Companies," (RFC) which outlined their approach to introduce ERM scoring for this target group.[17] S&P proposed to revise its current corporate credit rating process to include ERM. In essence, S&P noted that the rationale for this change was due in large part that they "expect that deterioration or improvement in a company's ERM quality would potentially drive rating and outlook changes before the consequences are apparent in published financial results."[18] It should be noted that it is this one key belief that has accounted for much of S&P's commitment to ERM.

S&P requested comments on their overall ERM analytical approach, as well as the value of adding ERM analysis and the particulars of the proposed methodology. They indicated that their "principal interest in evaluating ERM is to implement steps that will limit the frequency and severity of losses that could potentially affect ratings."[19] According to the RFC, S&P proposed to use a similar rating plan as they had done with the insurance industry. As such, the scoring would utilize the four-level ratings approach that includes weak, adequate, strong, and excellent. S&P's ERM ratings within the financial sector produced two key types of information: (1) the degree to which a firm has comprehensively mastered the risks it faces, and (2) the extent that the firm's management optimizes revenue for the risks it is willing and able to take. Accordingly, they believe that "ERM could significantly enhance our assessment of a non-financial service sector company's ability to anticipate and manage risks."[20]

On May 7, 2008, S&P finally reported on the results of their RFC. In their report titled "Standard & Poor's to Apply Enterprise Risk Analysis to Corporate Ratings,"[21] they indicated that they would begin including discussions with rated companies during the third quarter of 2008 and would include commentary during the fourth quarter. They also provided a discussion of several other ERM-related timelines as related to their implementation schedule.

However, in the May 7, 2008, report S&P noted that they would be modifying their proposed ERM review, based on the feedback of more than 60 respondents. One of the biggest changes was the abandonment of S&P's five-pillar approach to ERM that had worked so well with the insurance industry. As a result, S&P's focus for nonfinancial rated companies will be only on two key areas, risk management culture and strategic risk management, which they believe are universally applicable aspects of ERM.

1. Risk management culture—As part of their review, S&P will analyze the risk management framework or structure that the organization is currently using. Additionally, as part of this area, they will evaluate the roles of the risk management staff as well as the reporting relationship of those staff members. S&P's guidelines suggest a strong expectation of a highly qualified and effective risk management department. Other items examined will be internal and external risk management communication including the risk management policies, and the effect of risk management on both budgetary and compensation management.
2. Strategic risk management—This will include an assessment of management's view of the most consequential risks, their likelihood, and the potential effect on the organization's credit. An examination of the method for updating risk exposure and the influence of risk management within the organization including the role of risk management in strategic decision making. In general, this aspect represents the upside of risk management from S&P's standpoint.

Furthermore, S&P also indicated that they would modify their original planned implementation schedule by deferring formal scoring of ERM capability, which they limited to three optional scores, strong, adequate, and weak, until sufficient data is collected to determine that proper evaluation criteria exists. Until that point, projected to be sometime in mid- to late 2009, they plan to withhold changes in credit ratings and/or rating outlooks.

The other major modification to S&P's proposed analysis is the recognition of generally accepted risk management standards. They indicated that accepted standards, such as the Committee of Sponsoring Organizations of the Treadway Commission (COSO) or the Joint Standards Australia/Standards of New Zealand Committee OB/7 (AS/NZS 4360) could be used as a foundation for ERM by the rated companies. However, S&P stated that neither of the above noted standards will be a prerequisite for, nor sufficient evidence of, effective risk management.[22] This recognition of generally accepted standards is significant. Movement to a COSO framework by organizations has, for the most part, been slow in catching on since it was introduced in 2004. However, with S&P's blessing, interest in the COSO Framework and the AZ/NZS standard, should increase significantly (see Box 25.1).

Box 25.1   Discussion Question for S&P Management Meetings

A number of questions have arisen regarding S&P's approach to ERM analysis for nonfinancial organizations. In an attempt to assist organizations better prepare for their management meetings, S&P has provided a sample of discussion topics and questions that are expected to be addressed. Among the questions noted by S&P are:

- What are the company's top risks, how big are they, and how often are they likely to occur? How often is the list of top risks updated?
- What is management doing about top risks?
- What size quarterly operating or cash loss has management and the board agreed is tolerable?
- Describe the staff responsible for risk management programs and their place in the organization chart. How do you measure success of risk management activities?
- How would a loss from a key risk impact incentive compensation of top management and on planning/budgeting?
- Tell us about discussions about risk management that have taken place at the board level or among top management when making strategic decisions.
- Give an example of how your company responded to a recent "surprise" in your industry and describe whether the surprise affected your company and others differently.*

---

*"Discussion Questions for Management Meetings," Non-Financial Issuers Rated to Enterprise Risk Management Reviews. (Standard & Poor's).

As noted above, movement into the nonfinancial market by S&P has slowed down from their original proposal. The agency has indicated that they would begin with a staggered implementation schedule. Their timeline points to ERM discussions that would be incorporated into regular review meetings during the third quarter of 2008. This schedule would give S&P one year to conclude their initial discussions with the organizations. During this period, they will begin to develop appropriate industry specific benchmarking information. They also note that they will begin to include analysis of emerging risk management and risk control processes as they gain better benchmarking insight.

Both Moody's and Fitch have also indicated a willingness to extend their ERM analysis to nonfinancial service organizations. However, unlike S&P, neither firm has provided specifics as to their approach for these additional organizations.

A FLY IN THE OINTMENT

Although each rating agency has made significant advancements with their ERM analysis and with the exception of A.M. Best (insurance company specific), they have plans to move aggressively into the nonfinancial service sectors. However, despite their best efforts, the rating agencies have become embroiled with congress, other regulatory agencies and investors, over their role in the financial mess caused by the subprime home loan meltdown. As a result, it would appear that all rating agencies could end up with significantly more regulations and oversight than they previously had. Additionally, major changes in their business model may be required or legislated, since there has been significant concern about the current approach to their method of compensation for services provided. Currently, the rated companies pay the rating agency for assigning a rate; however, the "conflict of interest" allegations may require a change in this arrangement, along with several other operational requirements.

As we have seen, S&P has taken the most aggressive approach by including the ERM analysis explicitly into their rating methodology. S&P evaluates eight specific areas as part of their rating process. These areas include management strategy, financial flexibility, earnings, liquidity, market position, investments, capital adequacy, and more recently, ERM. However, the other rating firms have "embedded" their ERM approach into their existing methodology. So, the rated company may have to make a choice regarding which rating agencies' ERM approach they wish to follow. Although many may feel that the S&P approach is the most robust and thus the most appropriate, it is still just one view of how the goal of effective risk management can be achieved. And for some, it may not even be the most obvious choice. For example, in the insurance industry, no insurance company would want to endanger their Best rating, so they may choose the Best approach. In the long term, it would be helpful to all stakeholders to have more alignment between the rating organizations regarding their ERM requirements, and identifying industry best practices.

CONCLUSION

Without question, the rating agencies have been a major driver in the increasing interest in ERM over the past three or four years. Most corporations realize the importance that a credit rating can bring. Not only is an increased credit rating good in and of itself, an increase in a rating can reduce the long-term cost of capital for most organizations. And, in the case of an insurance company, it can also affect the amount of surplus they would be required to maintain. Obviously, there are significant financial consequences that are associated with this new rating landscape. All of the agencies have voiced a commitment to their ERM programs, but their current regulatory and reputational woes may require a change in their implementation schedules.

NOTES

1. "Nonfinancial Corporations, ERM and the Rating Agencies" (White Paper, Towers Perrin, (November 2007) 2–4.
2. "Risk Management Assessments," Research Methodology (Moody's Investors Service, July 2004) 4.
3. "Moody's Findings on Corporate Governance in the United States and Canada: August 2003-September 2004," Special Comment (Moody's Investors Service, October 2004) 13.
4. "Criteria: Summary of Standard & Poor's Enterprise Risk Management Evaluation Process for Insurers" (Standard & Poor's, November 2007) 2–5.
5. "Enterprise Risk Management: ERM Development in the Insurance Sector Could Gain Strength in 2008," (Standard & Poor's, March 2008) 1.
6. "Risk Management Assessments," 2.
7. "Risk Management Assessments," 4.
8. "Enterprise Risk Management for Insurers and Prism's Role," Special Report (Fitch Ratings, September 2006) 2.
9. "Enterprise Risk Management for Insurers and Prism's Role," 10.
10. "Risk Management and the Rating Process for Insurance Companies," Rating Methodology, (A.M. Best, January 2008) 1.
11. "Risk Management and the Rating Process for Insurance Companies," 1.
12. "Risk Management and the Rating Process for Insurance Companies," 1.
13. "Risk Management and the Rating Process for Insurance Companies," 2.
14. "Risk Management and the Rating Process for Insurance Companies," 3.
15. "Risk Management and the Rating Process for Insurance Companies," 3.
16. "Taking The 'PIM' Approach When Assessing U. S. Energy Companies' Risk Management," Commentary Report, (Standard & Poor's, April 2006) 4.
17. "Request For Comment: Enterprise Risk Management Analysis For Credit Ratings Of Nonfinancial Companies," RatingsDirect, (Standard & Poor's, November 2007) 2.
18. "Request For Comment: Enterprise Risk Management Analysis For Credit Ratings Of Nonfinancial Companies," 2.
19. "Request For Comment: Enterprise Risk Management Analysis For Credit Ratings Of Nonfinancial Companies," 3.
20. "Request For Comment: Enterprise Risk Management Analysis For Credit Ratings Of Nonfinancial Companies," 5.
21. "Standard & Poor's To Apply Enterprise Risk Analysis To Corporate Ratings," Rating Direct (Standard & Poor's, May 2008) 2.
22. "Standard & Poor's To Apply Enterprise Risk Analysis To Corporate Ratings," 2.

FURTHER READING

"Assessing Enterprise Risk Management Practices of Financial Institutions." *Financial Institutions*, Standard & Poor's (September 2006).

"Enterprise Risk Management for Ratings of Nonfinancial Corporations," *RatingsDirect*, Standards & Poor's (June 2008).

"ERM, the Rating Agencies and You." ERM Road Map, Towers Perrin (November 2008).

"Evaluating Risk Appetite: A Fundamental Process of Enterprise Risk Management." Standard & Poor's. (October 2006).

Goldfarb, Richard. " ERM Practices and the Rating Agencies." *Contingencies*, (September/October 2005).

Maxwell, James. " Ratings Agencies Eye ERM for All Industries." *Financial Executive*, (March 2008).

"Progress Report: Integrating Enterprise Risk Management Analysis into Corporate Credit Ratings." Standard & Poor's (July 2009).

Protiviti. "Credit Rating Analysis of Enterprise Risk Management at Nonfinancial Companies: Are You Ready? *The Bulletin*, vol. 3, issue 2, (2008).

"Raising the Bar." Benfield Group (October 2006).

"S&P Completes Initial 'PIM' Risk Management Review For Selected U. S. Energy Firms." *RatingsDirect*, Standard & Poor's (May 2007).

"Winners & Losers: How the S&P ERM Decision Changes the Rating Game." *Insurance Day* (November 2005).

ABOUT THE AUTHOR

Mike Moody is the Managing Director of Strategic Risk Financing, Inc., an independent management consulting firm providing advice and counsel on risk management and enterprise risk management matters. Clients have ranged from a variety of public and private organizations to governmental agencies. He has an MBA with concentration in finance, as well as an Associate in Risk Management (ARM) designation. He has 25-plus years of experience in risk management, including as a corporate risk manager for a Fortune 500 corporation. He has also been employed by an international management consulting firm as well as worked for several international insurance brokers. He has been active in the Risk and Insurance Management Society (RIMS) having served both as a local and national officer. He has spoken at numerous risk management and risk financing presentations. He is also a recognized authority and author on the subject of risk management related issues, including enterprise risk management, where he has a monthly column on ERM in *Rough Notes* magazine. Currently, his project work is centered on assisting mid-size corporations in designing and implementing enterprise risk management programs.

CHAPTER 26

Enterprise Risk Management

Current Initiatives and Issues

JOURNAL OF APPLIED FINANCE ROUNDTABLE[1]
Financial Management Association International, October 2007, Annual
Meeting held in Orlando, Florida

PANELISTS
Bruce Branson, Pat Concessi, John R.S. Fraser, Michael Hofmann,
Robert (Bob) Kolb, Todd Perkins, and Joe Rizzi[2]

MODERATOR
Betty J. Simkins

Betty Simkins: Good afternoon. I'm Betty Simkins, co-editor of the *Journal of Applied Finance* and moderator of this roundtable. In this session, we will talk about the current initiatives and issues in Enterprise Risk Management (ERM). I view ERM as a natural evolution of risk management that looks at all risks across the organization, not just narrow "silos" of risk as viewed in the past. ERM is an important discipline that is gaining popularity and recognition with many companies and also in the educational process with universities.

Let's first begin with a definition of ERM to set the stage for our roundtable discussion. A good place to start is with the Committee of Sponsoring Organizations of the Treadway Commission (COSO)'s definition, which defines ERM:

> "...as a process, effected by an entity's board of directors, management and other personnel, applied in strategy setting and across the enterprise, designed to identify potential events that may affect the entity, and manage risk to be within its risk appetite, to provide reasonable assurance regarding the achievement of entity objectives."[3]

Surveys show the number of U.S. firms saying they have fully implemented enterprise risk management (ERM) tripled to 12 percent in 2007 from 4 percent in 2006.[4] Some companies have had little or no success while others have had extensive success with ERM. Several universities through education, research, and executive programs are active in the enterprise risk management initiative.

In our roundtable discussion, we will start off with a general introduction to enterprise risk management including how and why it is important to companies and education; the benefits, value, and education initiatives; and key organization structures, designs, processes, and best practices. To summarize, we will discuss the following six questions in this session:

Question 1: How do you define ERM?

Question 2: Where is your company or university in the ERM process?

Question 3: Let's talk about the taxonomy of risk, particularly operational risk. It seems that too many diverse risks get classified into this category (i.e., human frailties to unethical board members and corporate officers). How does your firm or university deal with these issues?

Question 4: What can universities do better in educating students on ERM? What would firms like to see their new employees know about ERM? What specific skills are most desirable?

Question 5: (For the corporate panelists) Do you think ERM contributes to shareholder value at your firm? If so, how?

Question 6: Are there organizational structures, designs, processes, or best practices that you believe are key for effective ERM implementation?

Question 7: How do you make ERM actionable and keep your ERM program dynamic?

Question 8: Do you have research ideas for academics? What is your forecast of how ERM will evolve over the next 10 years?

To address these questions, we've assembled a very distinguished panel consisting of five ERM executives and two ERM faculty experts. Let me introduce each of them now, beginning with the ERM executives.

Pat Concessi is a Partner in Deloitte & Touche's Global Energy Markets practice. She has been responsible for projects involving control infrastructure assessment and development, enterprise risk management, implementation of energy transacting and risk management policies, selection of risk measurement methodologies, and the selection and implementation of energy risk management systems. Her knowledge of power system operations provides valuable insight into the application of risk management practices in electricity markets. Pat also serves as the leader of Deloitte's global Climate Change and Sustainable Resources group. She has consulted for many energy companies with respect to management of commodity risk and this increasingly includes emission allowances, renewable energy, bio fuels, and other topics.

John Fraser is Chief Risk Officer and Vice President, Internal Audit, at Hydro One in Toronto, Ontario. John has worked at Hydro One since April 1999 and began implementing enterprise risk management at the company in 2000. He has over 30 years experience in the risk and control field, primarily in financial institutions, in public accounting and internal audit roles in publicly traded companies. John is a member of the Strategic Risk Council for the Conference Board of Canada. John has co-authored a number of books and articles on the topic of enterprise risk management and related issues. I'm a co-author with John on two articles on ERM that are published in the *Journal of Applied Corporate Finance*. John is a frequent speaker on enterprise risk management and has been interviewed by companies from around the world about his expertise in ERM.

Michael Hofmann is Vice President and Chief Risk Officer at Koch Industries in Wichita, Kansas. Koch Industries consists of a diverse group of companies in refining and chemicals; process and pollution control equipment and technologies; minerals and fertilizers; fibers and polymers; commodity and financial trading and services; and forest and consumer products. Koch companies have a presence in nearly 60 countries and employ about 80,000 people. Michael is responsible for ERM and oversees all global market, credit, and hazard risk management activities. He began his career with Koch Industries in 1991, was chief market risk officer from 1999 to 2000, led the development of trading operations, and assisted in the start-up of new trading ventures. Michael actively supports the advancement of risk management and serves on the Board of Trustees and Executive Committee of the Global Association of Risk Professionals (GARP).

Todd Perkins is the Director of Enterprise Risk Management for Southern Company. Southern Company owns electric utilities, a growing competitive generation company, as well as fiber optics and wireless communications. Southern Company has more than 42,000 megawatts of electric generating capacity and serves 4.3 million customers. Todd joined Southern Company in 1997 in its Treasury department where he had responsibility for credit and risk management policy development for the Company's energy trading and marketing activities. He also established and managed the Company's interest rate and currency risk management programs. In 2004, Todd became manager of the Risk Control group for the energy trading and marketing activities of Southern Company. In July of this year, he assumed his current position leading the ERM efforts of the entire company.

Joe Rizzi has been a member of the ABN AMRO Group or its U.S. affiliate, LaSalle Bank, for 24 years. He currently is Managing Director of LaSalle Bank Corporation's Enterprise Risk Management unit for North America.[5] During his tenure with the ABN AMRO Group, Joe has been part of several activities. For the past five years, Joe has alternated working at ABN AMRO in Amsterdam and New York City, focusing on Group Risk Management, Asset and Liability Management as well as Country Management. He is a widely published author and has lectured to various professional organizations in Europe and the United States. He teaches regularly at the Amsterdam Institute of Finance and is also an adjunct professor at the University of Notre Dame's Mendoza School of Business.

Next, let me introduce the two faculty panelists, both of whom represent universities with ERM centers: North Carolina State University's ERM Initiative is further along and Loyola University Chicago's ERM program is in the early stages.

Bruce Branson is Professor of Accounting in the Jenkins Graduate School of Management at North Carolina State University (NC State) and he also serves as the Associate Director of the College of Management's Enterprise Risk Management (ERM) Initiative. NC State's ERM Initiative is advanced in this area and began its outreach activities in 2004. In his role as Associate Director of the ERM Initiative, Bruce is responsible for administering research and curriculum grants to develop an ongoing research stream and graduate-level coursework focusing on ERM practices. Bruce has published many articles, a number of which are on ERM and related topics.

Robert (Bob) Kolb is the Frank W. Considine Chair in Applied Ethics and Professor of Finance at Loyola University Chicago. From 2003 to 2006, Kolb served at the University of Colorado in Boulder as a Professor of Finance and as Assistant Dean for Business and Society, where he led the school's program in business ethics. During his career, he published more than 50 academic research articles and more than 20 books, most focusing on financial derivatives and their applications to risk management. It is interesting to note that Bob holds, not one, but two PhDs: one in finance and one in philosophy.

As I mentioned earlier, I am **Betty Simkins** and am co-editor of the *Journal of Applied Finance* in which this roundtable article will be published. I am the Williams Companies Professor of Business and an Associate Professor of Finance in the Spears School of Business at Oklahoma State University in Stillwater, Oklahoma. I have published a number of papers on risk management and more recently in the area of enterprise risk management. So this is one of my favorite topics to discuss and I am honored to moderate this roundtable with this distinguished panel of experts.

Let's now get to the questions and we will start with Question 1: How do you define ERM? Joe, I would like you to get us started.

QUESTION 1

Joe Rizzi: I think of enterprise risk management as basically being a consolidating risk view from the top down that cuts across all the business units and all the risks in the organization.

Todd Perkins: To add to what Joe said, I will read a few sentences from our ERM framework that we use at Southern Company:

> *ERM at Southern Company is an ongoing and evolving effort by which the company attempts to enhance the value of the firm by efficiently and effectively managing risk across the Southern Company system. ERM recognizes that risk management occurs throughout the company and either explicitly or implicitly is part of virtually every decision. The goal of ERM is to ensure that structures, processes, and communications are in place to promote the achievement of the following three critical elements of ERM: Risk governance oversight and leadership; risk identification assessment, mitigation and monitoring; and risk quantification and reporting.*

Enterprise risk management broadly encompasses a large number of processes, controls, decision tools, governance, and oversight structures, as well as behaviors and corporate culture. As such, risk governance and oversight is largely embedded in existing organizational and control structures such as normal management oversight, project review processes, internal auditing, legal and regulatory compliance programs, and Sarbanes-Oxley compliance. The ERM governance structure is meant to provide a structure to bring together these efforts in order to facilitate communications across the entities and functions, promote consistency, and the use of best practices, creating a unified view of risk, and helping incorporate risk in strategy considerations.

Pat Concessi: I'd like to build upon your comment that ERM should integrate the strategy consideration, and emphasize that it is important for enterprise risk management to be related to the strategic objectives of the company. With that, I think we have a comprehensive definition.

Robert Kolb: I think of enterprise risk management as both a process and also a commitment. The process part being: developing techniques for looking at risk throughout the firm, and not focusing on just those kinds of risks that are highly quantifiable; realizing that some of the most important risks that a firm faces really are not so amenable to quantification; and bringing all of that into a unified framework. The commitment part is committing to treat risk seriously even if it's not so easy to quantify it because so much of the risk that a firm faces really isn't quantifiable—at least not with the precision of financial risks.

Bruce Branson: I agree that it's a process, although that word sometimes gives me a little bit of discomfort. In some sense, ERM is a mindset, a culture that permeates your entire organization. With the goal ultimately of having your employees, your managers, your executives, your board of directors, all risk aware, risk intelligent, looking for both opportunities and threats that add greater value to the enterprise.

Michael Hofmann: To me, ERM is also a mindset, a way of thinking to improve decisions. Yes, it is supported by processes, governance, effective communication, et cetera, but it is really an attempt to, as objectively as possible, incorporate uncertainty into decision making. It starts with clarifying a firm's risk tolerance, which can be challenging, and then creates a focus to identify, estimate, and communicate risks to effect behavior. Different risks require different capabilities but the aim of ERM is to create a common vision, risk understanding, and approach to risk-adjusted decision making.

John Fraser: I'd like to add two aspects of ERM that make it especially valuable: the first is the fact that it is forward looking at what uncertainties could impact the organization's business objectives, for example two to three years hence; and secondly, the process of prioritizing such risks to meeting the objectives and ensuring that resources are allocated on a prioritized basis to mitigate such risks.

QUESTION 2

Simkins: Now that we've established a view of what ERM is, let's discuss where your company or university is in the ERM process, including discussing challenges encountered such as difficulty with risks that are hard to be quantified. Pat, we will start with you.

Concessi: In general, we would say that the application of ERM within the energy sector should really be considered a work in process. Some risk categories like price risk and credit risk have been the focus of risk management activities for some time. Many companies have developed a clear quantitative view of their exposures and of mitigation strategies, such as hedging or insuring risks. Other risk categories have not received the same level of attention. So reputational risks and operational risks lag considerably behind in the application of risk management techniques. With this unevenness in the quantification of risks, it is hard for companies to aggregate the different risk types together.

We observe that some companies begin to implement ERM and then for some reason stop part way. There are interesting statistics on the number of companies that have completed the implementation of ERM versus the number of companies that have tried. Some of the reasons would be that implementing ERM takes a champion from senior management—somebody who cares about it, who is going to protect funding, and who will keep a focus on it. At the same time, implementing ERM can be a multiyear process, so if there are changes in the senior management roles, if the champion moves into a different area or if there are substantial funding cuts, ERM might get truncated part way through. The second reason is perhaps taking on too big a scope by trying to integrate all risk types across all business units. Rather, companies should identify the big risks and get those under control. This shows ERM's value early so that value is delivered before pressing further.

Perkins: I agree completely with Pat. At Southern Company, ERM started about 10 years ago through unrelated activities. We started by looking at some of the smaller noncore businesses and did risk assessments and risk profiles for those businesses. At the same time, we started developing risk policies and risk oversight structures primarily for our energy trading and marketing activities. There were no big changes or big efforts to create a consolidated ERM effort for about five years. Around 2003 there was a dedicated effort to create an ERM program. We have come a long way since then and we have faced some of the challenges mentioned earlier. In terms of quantification of risks, there has been a tremendous amount of work with trading, marketing, and related risks. The focus since we started this effort in 2003 has really been trying to get our arms around some of those other risk areas. I'll mention a few of them, which shows where we are today.

We formed a dedicated ERM group in the finance organization and it is very tightly integrated with our strategic planning group. We've implemented a company-wide risk assessment and risk profile process for all of our subsidiaries, business units, and functions. ERM has actually been pushed down within the organization to the point now where we actually do risk assessments and profiles at our power plants. Ultimately, what comes out of those processes feeds up into our consolidated view. There have been significant enhancements in our board reporting and the involvement of our board. The risk profile is reviewed by our full board at least annually. Our finance committee is very involved every quarter. They are updated with a financial plan risk assessment where we assess the risk associated with our financial plan for the next five years. The audit committee is also very involved, specifically related to ensuring our ERM process is in place and is working.

We've also done a lot in terms of reworking our risk governance and oversight structures so that the risk committees at the highest level of the company are in line with the top strategic decision makers at the company. We've formed a quantitative risk analysis group, which has brought together risk modeling expertise that lived in different parts of the company. We have integrated and created links among the various risk related functions as part of ERM. This includes: my group (the ERM group), internal auditing, legal and regulatory compliance, Sarbanes-Oxley, and business assurance.

Something relatively new for us is that we are beginning to become heavily involved in the disclosure process for the company. We want to ensure that we are disclosing the right risks, disclosing them appropriately, and communicating to investors what our risk profile is and why.

One of the biggest challenges we have faced is the natural reluctance of people to share a lot of information about the risks they face. I guess it is human nature and it has taken a lot of communication to get employees to share this information and not fear that it will be used against them.

One of the biggest challenges we face going forward is what I refer to as *ERM fatigue*. As ERM becomes more and more ingrained across our normal processes,

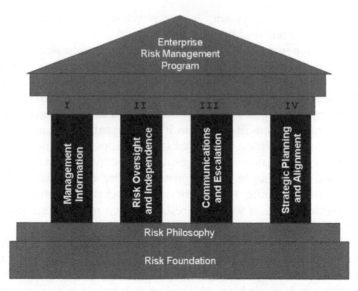

Exhibit 26.1   The Four Pillars of BU NA's ERM Program

I'm afraid that some of the things will be seen as routine and less value-added. This is something that we will fight—*how to avoid ERM fatigue and keep the process fresh and new.*

Rizzi: In our organization, we're both blessed and cursed. Regulators and rating agencies are very interested. To follow up on your point, I think you can use enterprise risk management as Velcro to pick up everything. Unless you keep it focused as to what you're trying to do and the value of that, you will you lose the freshness.

We try to develop enterprise risk management based upon four pillars as shown in Exhibit 26.1. The first one is the information pillar, which is like a dashboard of knowledge that allows senior management of our organization to get a consolidated view. Exhibit 21.2 in Chapter 21 of this book provides an example of the dashboard. It's an evolving document and not cast in stone. It has to do with narrowing down the reports that people have to read by simplifying it down to one smaller report.

The second pillar is to complete a governance report, to make sure decision rights are where they are supposed to be. Also, there is accountability so if people screw up, it wasn't necessarily a surprise; it was a risk that we accepted.

The third pillar that we tried to do was to enact a communications program that was addressing the cultural change. The motto that we use is basically that "everyone is a risk manager." We want people to think that risk management is just as much a part of their job as going out and selling to the customers and making a profit.

The fourth pillar is to make enterprise risk management, or risk management, real. You have to get ERM into the budgets and the bonuses. If you don't get it linked to the compensation system, you go nowhere. Once you do this, people start to say "ah this is real" and then it takes traction.

Concessi: When a number of us were thinking about our definitions of ERM, we talked about the requirement to integrate what would otherwise be treated as silos. So rather than measuring market or price risk separately from credit risk and operational risk, we really haven't finished the job without looking at the correlation between those risk types. If it's important to measure market risk and it's important to measure credit risk, then it's important to look at the interaction between those two risks. When really bad things happen to companies, it's often not because of risks in just one silo but because of the interaction between two.

Simkins: Yes, for example a joint survey by the Economist and Lloyds of London found that very thing: that many unexpected risks a company had faced that had the greatest impacts were the results of two unexpected and unrelated events occurring simultaneously.[6]

Fraser: We launched our version of ERM in 2000 following the principles in the Australian/New Zealand Risk Management Standard 4360. We did a literature review of available thinking on the topic and commenced doing semi-annual risk profiles and some risk workshops. A year or two later we introduced our risk methodologies into business planning, whereby all expenditures are prioritized based on mitigating risks to achieving our business objectives. Our board and management team cautioned us to focus on the big picture and not get caught up in detailed data analysis and number crunching (note that detailed analysis tends to be done in the various operating departments such as engineering or customer operations). After four years of ingraining these methods we decided to just stay in a maintenance mode as we were achieving our objectives of aligning board, executive, and management thinking and priorities about risk. Our ERM processes are now so ingrained that we all take it for granted that this is how risks should be managed and resources prioritized. It's hard to imagine managing any other way.

Hofmann: Our approach also evolved over more than 10 years and is based on our culture and management approach, Market Based Management. We started by developing a vision and realized that we had to clarify our risk tolerance. We developed our risk mentality to clarify which risks are unacceptable and which we are willing to absorb. We developed a common language and a framework to aid decision making based on a risk-adjusted economic capital concept. We also developed the capability to better identify, estimate, and communicate risks. In addition to a Koch Industries team we established risk teams in our various businesses based on the unique risk profiles of each business and invested in the necessary tools and systems. By far the most important progress came when we combined all of the components and tied them to decision rights and our incentive system. We have made good progress but will of course never be finished; market conditions and risks change, our businesses evolve, we continue to learn, and we can always get better.

Branson: At NC State, our ERM Initiative has hosted over two dozen ERM roundtable presentations that typically involve bringing in senior executives who have been tapped with the responsibility to develop ERM programs in their various organizations. Issues we frequently hear about include how companies have been inundated over the years with various change initiatives and that ERM is not yet particularly well-developed for many. A challenge for ERM is that it may be perceived as just another management fad (as total quality management has been often derided). A common issue for ERM program managers is in convincing others in the organization to invest time and effort on ERM implementation without fear that it's going to fade away in the not too distant future.

A key to successful buy-in is the alignment of incentives and program goals such as Joe mentions. This reminds me of a story told by David Whatley, one of our ERM roundtable speakers. This story illustrates how traditional corporate organizations have a series of compartmentalized silos with individuals and business units essentially managing risks in their various areas of responsibility but perhaps without sufficient regard to the risks they might be lobbing elsewhere within the business. David had recently stepped down from running the ERM program for Home Depot. One of Home Depot's important strategic objectives was to increase market share through an expansion of their geographic footprint. Home Depot was trying to move very aggressively into West Coast markets, and, in particular, into the San Francisco Bay Area. They tried for a period of four years to gain zoning variances that would allow them to build stores in these markets. The reason they were getting pushback was due to a history of stores failing to comply with local ordinances related to marketing product out in their parking lots.

From an individual store perspective, think about how a store manager is typically compensated. They typically have a tremendous incentive to drive sales revenue. For example, most of us have seen lawn tractors out in the parking lots of Home Depot stores (or competitors). For an individual store this is an easy decision—they can pay a $250 fine and generate $15,000 in sales that weekend. Of course, they are going to absorb the $250 fine without really thinking about how that decision may affect overall corporate objectives. This behavior hurt Home Depot because it prevented opportunities to expand in some new markets. David Whatley's point with this story was to show a real need to adjust store managers thinking (via a revised compensation package) to ensure that a more robust consideration of enterprise-level risk took place.

Simkins: Thank you Bruce. The Home Depot story is an excellent example of the importance of aligning incentives with ERM.

Bruce, since you brought up the topic of management fads, I am going to be the devil's advocate and say: "I think ERM is just another management fad." So what I would like to hear from panelists is a counterpoint to convince somebody with this attitude. Or if you think it's a fad, tell us.

Rizzi: I think that enterprise risk management is a step to get risk management back to corporate finance. The point I'm trying to make is that at least within financial organizations, we have seen the development of risk managers in white coats that do all sorts of interesting things. But basically they are historically focused on loss containment. Senior management is basically more future value and market oriented. And you can't get these to talk—so you see things like we just discussed where people are not looking at the correlation or interaction. Where I hope ERM is going to help is to develop a risk strategy for the organization. What risk do we want to take? What risk do we want to get rid of? What should our capital structure be? All of this is very important to risk management and is a step in the right direction. If it becomes the specialist function where guys in white coats are walking around, it will be just another fad.

Simkins: Joe, your comments remind me of a term that John Fraser and I like to use to describe one of the problems with ERM: *The Tower of Babble*—where everyone is speaking different risk languages and they don't communicate.

Kolb: Well, I'll play a little bit of a devil's advocate. I'm personally not so sure that enterprise risk management won't turn out to be a fad and that is sad. I don't think there is a single corporation that is finished with the implementation of enterprise risk management and has it all set up and running. On the other hand, as opposed to things that did turn out to be only fads, enterprise risk management has a lot of institutional support from regulatory bodies. This wasn't present in cases of other fads. I have made a personal commitment to enterprise risk management, so I believe in it. But on the other hand, I think the jury is out as to where it will be achieved.

Concessi: I agree with your point, but perhaps for a different reason. ERM often turns out to be a bigger challenge than companies anticipate at the outset. And the reason relates to data management challenges. We've already discussed the need to integrate market risk with credit risk. And then for electric utilities another significant source of risk is weather uncertainty, which drives demand, and of course that's correlated with price uncertainty. The risk assessment is based on the output of simulation systems that were developed independently and that work quite well on that basis. Normally, these systems work at a very granular level, so every single transaction and generating plant is modeled every hour of the year. These systems need to be integrated, and that is really hard to do. What can happen at this point is recognition that all of the data needs to be put into a common data warehouse, and companies may stop and say wait a minute, how long is this going to take, and how many millions is it going to cost. People rarely anticipated it being so data intensive.

Hofmann: If we define ERM as a mindset rather than a function, the ideal evolution would be for distinct risk organizations to no longer be necessary because risk understanding and risk-adjusted decision making would be fully integrated. I think that is an excellent goal to strive for but I also think that we will continue to benefit from risk professionals and specific ERM ownership. Not only because of technical skills but because as human beings, we are all subject to biases and can never be fully objective. We need to seek and share knowledge and challenge our thinking. We need other perspectives and benefit from the focus and challenge process provided by effective risk teams. And, because risks are often interrelated but not necessarily cumulative, most organizations should benefit from an aggregate perspective.

Simkins: Thank you everyone. We will drill down deeper into some of these issues later in the panel discussion. Recent surveys indicate that about 10 percent of companies say they've fully implemented the various stages of ERM—which means that 90 percent have not or are in the process of implementing ERM.

Let's hear from the university panelists next about Question 2.

Kolb: ERM is a new addition at Loyola and there are three major components. First, we have a center for integrated risk management and corporate governance, which is headed up by Don Schwartz. Don directs our center and he recently secured a $1 million grant from the Chicago Mercantile Exchange. Some key things that the center is going to do: running annual seminars, having a series of interviews with prominent people in risk management, and allocating funds to stimulate research in this area.

Second, we have a new program: a Master's of Science in Finance with a specialization in risk management. ERM is a key element in that program. The third major component is the position I've been lucky enough to be chosen to occupy—the Considine chair. As Betty mentioned, a lot of my work has been in derivatives. Part of the charge for this chair is to bring a broader perspective, such as ethics, into enterprise risk management. These are the three main elements of our program and we are in their formative stage on each.

Branson: The Enterprise Risk Management Initiative at NC State has been operating for approximately four years. Mark Beasley, our Director, served on the COSO task force that developed the ERM framework that was publicly released in 2004. That document has been widely embraced as a blueprint for developing ERM programs here in the U.S. After his COSO role, Mark began the process of establishing our initiative program within the College of Management as an inter-disciplinary center to provide outreach, research, and education on this emerging discipline. We also were very fortunate to receive significant funding by the Bank of America Foundation that has helped us get started.

NC State is a land grant university so outreach to the business and professional community is an integral component of our mission. We have been engaged in several activities in the ERM area, most notably the development of our ERM Roundtable series over the last four years. We hosted our 25th ERM Roundtable this past September. These are opportunities for business professionals in our area and from Charlotte, Atlanta, Richmond, and other cities. We typically hear from a speaker that has been charged with some facet of enterprise risk management within their organization. These events have become very popular and we have as many as 200 individuals attend early on a Friday morning. In the last year we have also developed a variety of executive education opportunities including an ERM fundamentals open enrollment workshop. We have partnered with the North Carolina State Banking Commission to do bank director training on enterprise risk management issues. We are also working closely with the AICPA to develop a program for audit committee directors so that they may better understand their risk oversight responsibilities.

We have also developed an extensive set of resources covering ERM that is available on the Web at www.mgt.ncsu.edu/erm/. We have assembled various materials that both academic researchers interested in the topic as well as practitioners can go to and learn more about this topic. For example, various frameworks for ERM program development, summaries of our past ERM roundtable presentations, PowerPoint slides from speakers, and synopses of business press and academic articles are available.

We are going to talk later in the panel about curriculum development and research. These are two additional areas of emphasis for us. We offered our first ERM course at the graduate level last fall as an overview on enterprise risk management.

QUESTION 3

Simkins: In answering this question, we will start with the corporate panelists first and then the university panelists.

Concessi: Taxonomy is a good example of Betty's comment on the Tower of Babble. It is really important to get a consistent taxonomy accepted through the organization. Operational risk is a good example for energy companies. In energy companies "operations" has traditionally related to the reliability of physical assets. Did your power generating unit start in the morning or did your gas pipeline compressor start when it needed to?

The ERM definition of operational risk relates to a middle office function associated with proper capture of transactions. This difference in definitions can lead to a lot of confusion in the energy industry. As a result, the Committee of Chief Risk Officers redefined the term for energy companies. They coined a new term, *operative risk*, which includes both operational and operations risk. Operational risk is defined as the possibility of human frailties and failure to properly capture transactions, whereas operations risk is the risk associated with operating physical facilities. The two terms are similar and easily confused. It is more important for an organization to get a taxonomy that is broadly understood across its own organization, in which case I might use the term "administrative risk." To summarize, the most important thing is that the taxonomy of ERM used is well understood across the organization because it is important to the acceptance of the entire ERM initiative.

Perkins: We have really resisted efforts to force things into really broad buckets like an operational risk. We do look at each individual risk and we categorize to bring those together into buckets such as governance risk or environmental items. We have not tried the categorization of risks into buckets as large as operational.

Rizzi: I have concerns about operational risk. I know how it is defined and it just is too broad. It is something we are working with to come up with numbers point of view.

Fraser: We don't use the term "operational risk" as it too broad to be meaningful or helpful. If you are going to address risks in a holistic way you need to avoid artificial groupings. Banks like this term as it allows credit and market risk managers to maintain their silos. The question I have is when a loan goes bad because the collateral loses market value and the collection department does not move fast enough—was that loss due to credit risk, market risk, or operational risk and does it really matter? I do agree that this is an area that begs for further study not only as to the categorizations being used but also the purposes of those categorizations.

Hofmann: I agree with John. Using a common language is very helpful as long as we don't lose sight of the objectives. Risks have traditionally been categorized to take advantage of specialized skills/expertise but organizations formed around these categorizations tended to work in silos. The ERM concept evolved to break these silos down, coordinate, influence, and apply a common thought process and risk tolerance. In addition, the most significant risks are often either unknown or combinations. The challenge is to benefit both from specialized expertise and the broader perspective.

Kolb: This is one area where I think academics might be able to make some kind of contribution. If we look at the way risks are classified, there is no standard taxonomy. Consider the four risks: market, financial, credit, and operational. Now think about the different risks that a firm faces if ERM is going to provide a totalizing framework. Let's look at climate change, which poses great risk to companies. It's not financial risk, not really market risk, not exactly credit risk, so it must be operational risk. From my point of view, the operational risk bucket has become "catch-all" for all sorts of different kinds of risks that are not at all commensurable. A challenge for people to work in ERM especially on the academic side is to work on improving the taxonomy so that it becomes meaningful and is a standard taxonomy that works for every firm.

Branson: I agree with Bob's point of view that this certainly is an area where academics can contribute. Regarding Todd's point, it is critical that within your organization, they understand a common language or taxonomy so that at a minimum, you are all speaking the same language within your group. A common pitfall to ERM implementation success is the failure to first establish this common risk language and definitions of such risk terms as frequency and impact.

QUESTION 4

Simkins: First, this question will be discussed by the corporate panelists.

Rizzi: I would like to see the view taught that risk management is not just a specialist sector. Second, I would like to see the human element. You are not just dealing with numbers. The way you pay people also impacts behavior. The other thing that I would ask for is to try and integrate the CFO functions and CRO functions.

Fraser: ERM requires a wide range of skills and many of these are being taught currently, the useful thing would be to see these put in the context of an organization as a whole. Currently, a number of the professions who have highly quantitative skills (actuaries, market risk, and insurance) are struggling with how to move from being a technician to being a risk manager or chief risk officer. A knowledge of quantitative analysis is good (essential?) but also a knowledge of bias and how human error can creep in to decision making is important (e.g., Long Term Capital Management). I remember reviewing the actuarial liabilities of an insurance company in the late 1970s and noted they were calculating actuarial liabilities to 17 decimal places with great pride for accuracy while using 3 percent interest rate assumptions at a time when prime rate was around 15 percent and this reality was not being reflected in the models. ERM is a contact sport and requires a high level of knowledge about human behavior, politics, marketing, and other business processes. Management methods such as management by objectives, governance principles, and the "Delphi" method all play a role in constructing an overarching holistic approach to risk management.

Perkins: Since ERM really is all encompassing, all employees in the entire culture should accept it. What I am going to say may sound pretty obvious to the finance folks but it may not be so obvious to nonfinance people. More than anything, all employees need to have a very solid understanding of the relationship between risk and return and to understand that risk is not always the bad thing. A thorough understanding of risk and communication of risk can actually lead to better decisions and better allocation of capital. I think there is also need for a basic understanding of the statistical concepts of probability of risk. Everyone needs to understand that a good outcome is not necessarily the result of a good decision and that a bad outcome is not necessarily the result of bad decision. Generally, all employees across the organization need to understand that risk decisions are implicit or explicit in virtually every decision they make.

Concessi: I will speak specifically from the viewpoint of a consulting firm that provides ERM services to clients and what they look for in employees. I agree with the things that Todd and Joe have listed. What consulting firms need is people with strong quantitative capabilities. We probably have one of the largest groups of energy transacting quants in North America. But somewhat surprisingly to me (because I am a simple engineer), quants are not all the same. Some of them are financial engineers, quants who know how to value a transaction, and some of them are specialists in risk measurement. The ones we need for ERM are the quants who understand *risk engines*—the mathematics of how risks are correlated and the ability to build systems and understand the mathematics behind those systems.

Simkins: What do you mean by risk engines?

Concessi: We frequently implement what we call high-end risk engines that don't just look at market risk or credit risk, but they are able to look at risks that are correlated across risk types. Examples are systems like Algorithmics, SAS, and QuIC. You really need a risk engine quantitative expert in order to get those risks modeled properly. It goes beyond common sense. I think it is something like stress analysis in Monte Carlo analysis where you build a correlation structure to get interactions among different kinds of risks.

Hofmann: In our experience, the most effective risk teams include professionals from multiple disciplines. We have individuals with engineering, mathematics, finance, accounting, economics, physics, and other backgrounds. Some of the modeling can be complex but critical thinking, economic analysis, understanding probabilities versus uncertainty, and the ability to communicate effectively form the core. In addition, it is very helpful to be aware of how human biases such as recency, risk aversion, framing, and anchoring influence decisions. I am encouraged by efforts to design cross discipline programs and encourage you to leverage faculty from different disciplines including business, mathematics, engineering, and so on when designing risk management curricula.

Kolb: Betty asked me to bring a sample syllabus. ERM is such a new field there are so few courses on it. This is our stab at the course and this course is elective for the MBA program. It is also our first course in the MS in Finance concentration in Risk Management.[7]

Branson: As mentioned earlier, this fall we have launched a curriculum on ERM education through our Jenkins Graduate School of Management. The course provides an overview of ERM to expose both MBA and Master of Accounting program students to ERM concepts and practices. In spring 2008, we will offer two more courses—one focusing on risk measurement tools that will investigate both quantitative and qualitative risk assessment, as well as a corporate risk management and derivatives course.

We offer an ERM concentration in our Masters in Accounting program to meet the needs of professional services firms that are rapidly moving into the ERM space. I am not sure we can satisfy Pat's needs mentioned earlier. Our program is not focused on the quantitative side of risk measurement and management. We are much more focused toward strategic planning and corporate governance and how ERM can contribute to those endeavors.

Kolb: As I mentioned, I am in finance and Bruce is in accounting so risk management in general and ERM in particular finds academic homes in different departments. At Loyola, risk management and ERM are housed mainly in the finance area. By contrast, at NC State, I gather that risk management is lodged more in the accounting area. It would not be at all surprising if other universities have management departments handling risk management. So it is not at all clear where the natural home is going to be in terms of academic organizations.

QUESTION 5

Simkins: In your response, I would like you to discuss whether you think ERM contributes to shareholder value. For example, can it reduce the cost of capital at your firm? We know that the ratings agencies incorporate whether a firm has ERM into the ratings methodology. This is well documented for the banking, financial institutions industry, and insurance. Both Moody's and Standard & Poor's are now refining guidelines for nonfinancial firms, too.

Rizzi: When people zero in on those types of things it only looks at one side of the question. You need to also consider "What is the cost to get the higher credit rating?" Did you forego some activity, which you could have earned more money or could have created more shareholder value? I would just caution people that when they look at those trying to justify ERM that they cover both sides— because lowering the cost of capital does not necessarily create value.

Simkins: Yes, I used the cost of capital as just one example. Please discuss any way it can create value. Earlier in our discussion, we all agreed ERM is a value-adding activity.

Rizzi: The basic problem comes down with risk management trying to add value. They don't have any statues in the park for people who prevented a crisis. For me, I look at risk management as to whether or not your firm is successful. Risk management at the end of the day has to make sure that the company has access to markets to fund a plan under all market conditions. In other words, not just perfect market conditions that we have had for the last three to four years but bear market conditions, too. If we do that, I think we are successful as risk managers. If it worked only under one particular environment and when the environment shifted, the value went down the drain, then we are unsuccessful.

Perkins: Because we are a large highly regulated company, we view managing and maintaining our risk profile as one of the most critical aspects of our strategy. Our strategy is based on maintaining a low-risk profile: delivering regular, sustainable, predictable earnings growth, and achieving the best risk adjusted return in our industry. Our strategy is predicated on risk management and our risk profile. So ERM certainly adds value to the degree that it helps us with our risk profile and to maintain that risk profile.

Concessi: I certainly believe that ERM contributes to shareholder value and in two ways: first in determining capital adequacy, and second in being the driver for capital allocation. But I come back to the point Joe made about "no statues in the park." It is a really interesting image to create here. If you have done a really good job of risk management, people won't notice that nothing went wrong. We run into this challenge fairly frequently when clients want to do a cost-benefit study for implementing ERM. This presents a challenge because you don't necessarily put a risk management program in place to earn more profit. Your focus is rather on reducing the probability of an unanticipated loss.

It's interesting to look at related incidents such as one I saw last winter when working in Europe. Europe had a really warm fall last year and many utilities had hedged their gas demand. They knew how much gas they needed on a historic basis to produce the power they had already sold. To hedge this, they purchased gas to match the power they had sold. However, the weather was substantially warmer than normal, reducing power demand and they ended up selling their over hedged gas position into a market of falling prices. The effective hedge would be to not just look at your expected gas demand but also the relationship between weather, electricity demand, and price. That's where ERM gets complex because you need to bring together these two separate functions that don't often have to talk to each other. The market risk hedging function needs to start talking to the demand forecasting function. A really sophisticated hedging operation requires you to bring those circles together to increase shareholder value.

Branson: An example with rating agencies is in regulated industries including financial services, insurance, and the energy sector. Standard & Poor's (S&P) is now explicitly incorporating an assessment of ERM programs when they conduct their evaluations. Just recently, S&P has announced that they will begin to incorporate ERM evaluations across a broad spectrum of new industry sectors. Findings of material deficiencies in ERM can lead to material changes in corporate credit ratings.

There are some other pressure points as well. The NYSE now requires members of the audit committee to explicitly engage in discussions on risk and risk management policies across the organizations they serve. The recent Disney case also is an example. The Delaware Court's findings can be interpreted as placing expanded responsibility on corporate directors to be aware of best practices in risk management so that they may be fully protected by the "business judgment" rule. ERM is arguably an emerging best practice for the management of corporate risks.

Fraser: I find it useful to think about organizations that do not have ERM (but should) and then ask if those that appear to be doing well are due to skill or luck. Imagine an organization where the board has one view of risks, while executive management another and line managers each have their own. Imagine a board that does not clearly understand the major risks to achieving its stated objectives. Imagine an organization where on the largest projects, or for the largest risks and or within each division there is no common discussion, agreement, and prioritization of the risks and how resources should be allocated fairly. If you can imagine organizations with these characteristics then you have an organization without ERM. However, when ERM is implemented successfully then you have the opposite—which we believe adds value: fewer surprises, and a common understanding and alignment of goals, risks, and mitigants. Measures would include reduced cost of capital due to meeting rating agency expectations, better comfort for shareholders and the investment community that the business is well managed, and better morale among staff in knowing that resources are allocated fairly across the organization based on agreed risk tolerances.

ERM is of greatest value to organizations in a rapidly changing industry, or for an organization undergoing great change or where the management team is new or changing. For a stable management team within a stable organization within a stable industry there is little need for ERM as there is less uncertainty and a greater common understanding of the business risks.

Hofmann: Understanding how we add value is not always easy but helps us adjust and prioritize. I am very fortunate to work for a private company and regularly review progress with our owners. Their perspective has been that effective risk management helps protect our capital but that is not sufficient without also helping improve risk-adjusted decision making. We therefore start with a "no surprises" (versus no loss) goal and also evaluate how we have helped improve decisions. Fortunately, we have specific measurable examples of profitable behavior changes and are confident that applying our economic capital framework adds significant value. I think the challenge for all of us is to develop good measures without falling into the trap of focusing too much on what is easy to measure. For example, it is easy for a credit person to measure losses and become risk averse. Measuring the lost opportunity of this risk aversion is much more challenging but may actually be more important.

QUESTION 6

Simkins: As part of Question 6, I would like panelists to discuss, if applicable, the following topics which are all related to the question: Do you think a separate ERM group is necessary in the organizational structure or what organizational structure is best? What skill sets do you think a chief risk officer should have? What is the role of the board of directors in this process and committees such as the audit committee? What role does resource allocation and culture change play in ERM? If possible, discuss the disclosure process in ERM and if this process is audited in your company. Joe, let's begin with you first.

Rizzi: One of the things that we struggled with is: Where does the ERM function best fit in the organizational structure? What we decided is that there was no one structure but a series of options. The structure that we ended up using is the one reporting directly to RISK. Let me give you the reasons why. You do not really need a separate ERM group as that just adds another layer of bureaucracy. What you need is an ERM-type function that is composed of the risk people and the business people and is embedded with management. We want a real ERM-type function. What we tried to do is move into the implementation phase and this is the dashboard I mentioned earlier (see Exhibit 21.2 again). The reason why I think this so important is that it really allows you to take positions. People have to comment on what's right and what's wrong with it; it's a report that comes out every month. Our senior management used it. In addition, six to seven reports from internal audit used it. Basically it was about 20-page report that drilled down to each of these areas.

Fraser: I'd like to pick up on Joe's comment regarding ERM adding a layer of bureaucracy. While that happens in some models it is not the only way of doing things. Our model for ERM has the CRO's role as a facilitator and to develop and implement the ERM methodology. Line managers manage their risks and make the risk decisions. Our role is to help ensure transparency and a common understanding. There certainly are models like in many financial institutions where the centralized risk group makes or vetoes key decisions. Our ERM group is seen as an enabler and not as a threat to management's independence.

Perkins: In order for ERM to be effective, I believe first and foremost it requires a commitment from the very top levels of management including the board of directors. Also, it requires a certain level of risk awareness throughout the organization and a culture that is structured and allows open communication of risk issues. In addition, it is important to have a very engaged board of directors both in terms of ensuring that the ERM process is in place and also a board that is actively overseeing the major risks that are identified through the ERM process. Different organizational structures can achieve this, perhaps even some that do not have an ERM dedicated group. At Southern Company, we have a very small ERM group that draws upon resources and people across the organization. Having an ERM group is really just a place where it comes together and is a coordination function. However ERM is structured in the organization, it is critical it integrate it with strategic planning and governance. At Southern Company, ERM has been structured in the same organization as strategic planning but also works closely with our legal organization.

Branson: Does your board have a risk management committee?

Perkins: Our board does not but this is something that we are currently moving toward. Although it's not fully implemented, we are assigning our major risks to various committees of the board. While we don't have a risk management committee, we do believe that the other committees—the finance committee, the audit committee, and governance committee—can effectively address major risks.

Branson: Certainly one of the things that we see in many of the companies that we talk to is that often it's the audit committee of the board that ends up with chief oversight responsibility for the ERM program. The reality is that the audit committee is swamped with other responsibilities as a function of the Sarbanes-Oxley legislation. There seems to be an emerging best practice leading to the development of a dedicated risk management committee that can sit on top of the ERM function and led by a chief risk officer with a direct reporting line to the board. This helps the board understand and oversee the ERM process.

Simkins: How many companies are you aware that have risk committees of the board?

Branson: I see it as an emerging best practice but not something that we see regularly.

Concessi: I would strongly recommend that during the implementation phase of ERM, there should be at least a small group of people who are dedicated to it full time. I have worked in implementations where the organization assigned responsibility to a number of people on a part-time basis. Implementation is just too time-intensive to get it done that way. The implementation phase is often more prolonged than people anticipate. I think there needs to have a dedicated small team in place.

The next question is whether those resources should be centralized or decentralized and there are pros and cons. If you focus on a centralized team, you will be emphasizing the bringing together of the risk measures and the consolidation. On the other hand, with a decentralized process, you are saying that people in the business units, who are closer to the risks, are better able to identify the risks and decide what the most appropriate measures are to address those risks. A critical topic is "whose risk measure are you going to use?" because business units will probably have their own risk measures.

In the most comprehensive ERM project that I worked on, a small centralized group was dedicated during the implementation. These people were in the corporate strategy group and once the implementation was finished, they returned to corporate strategy.

Hofmann: I think the specifics are dependent on the management approach and culture of the individual firm. In our case, we invest in a lot of different businesses and use a mostly decentralized approach but with very hands-on oversight. We considered both centralized and decentralized risk management approaches and concluded that we needed both. The business risk teams are responsible for understanding their business and helping improve decisions at that level. The Koch Industries team ensures needed capabilities exist, serve as a resource, aggregate all risks, support investment decisions, and provide governance and oversight. We focus a lot of our time on driving our vision, risk mentality, and economic capital approach while also trying to understand aggregate performance drivers and broader economic and strategic risks.

Fraser: What I'd like to add is that there are different types of skill required to make ERM successful. First, there has to be a real driving force, or champion at the right level. This often has more to do with their credibility than status. Secondly, there has to be some staff with the charisma and approachable personality that managers are going to feel comfortable with and who will be good at facilitating discussions, workshops, and the like. Lastly, there needs to be the analytical type(s) who manage large volumes of data and metrics and can produce the quantitative information required. These personality types are rarely to be found in one person and care has to be given to having this eclectic skill set working as a team.

QUESTION 7

Simkins: This is an important area companies actively pursuing ERM are facing. Todd brought up the term "ERM fatigue" earlier, which I think applies to this. When responding to this question, please mention, where relevant, your comments related to the authority process, asset allocation process, compensation, risk adjusted economic capital, or corporate strategy.

Perkins: To keep ERM actionable, you need specific, well-defined board of directors' responsibilities. At Southern Company, the board committees have specific risk-related responsibilities defined in their charters. Taking it down a level, specific, well-defined management accountabilities and reporting requirements are needed. Similar to our board, members of senior management are in risk committees and groups that have charters with clear accountabilities and responsibilities. We have a company-wide framework that lays out those responsibilities. In fact, the framework uses language similar to what Joe mentioned earlier such as defining everyone as a risk manager and making ERM part of their goals. We do that explicitly at the senior management level and discuss how to integrate with strategic planning. It is very important for our ERM group to deliver specific value-added services to the company and not be seen as just another group.

Rizzi: I will follow up on a few of the things you mentioned. I think the way to keep ERM actionable is getting it into the planning process and into the compensation process. If you do that, people will take it seriously. To bring in the element of strategic risk, it was brought home to me this year rather clearly. My current organization was relatively good at the technical aspects of risk management, but missed the strategic element of risk and ended up getting involved in a rather messy takeover battle. At the end of the day, what managers are focusing on is not so much the shareholder risk as much as their job risk.

Fraser: Some of the ways we keep ERM actionable are ensuring that out of every risk workshop there are champions identified and specific actions to address the risks that are considered intolerable. We also find that doing corporate risk profiles every six moths is about right for us and keeps the key business objectives and risks on the table for discussion and assessment. In terms of funding, in our business planning process, all capital and operating funding is based on mitigating risks that are intolerable according to our corporate risk tolerances, thus forcing managers to articulate their funding needs in terms of meeting business objectives and dealing with the related risks, that is, no risk means no funds. This was a major part of the culture change management required in implementing ERM.

Simkins: This is a good point to talk about the subprime crisis, specifically the structured finance risk management failure that happened this past summer. Many of these companies had enterprise risk management programs in place. Were their ERM programs flawed?

Rizzi: This topic has been bothering me the most. I'm trying to figure out whether I should wear a bag over my head because we spent billions of dollars on risk management and as a financial organization or industry, we missed it. And how did we miss it? I think it came down again to the issue of how people were compensated. If you have an annual bonus situation and if you can play around with the options which are imbedded in these products, you can create a nice steady stream of income and also increase it if you want. The tail risk is open. You will make a nice bonus for four years in a row and eventually you get caught, but then you're on to your next job. That is where I think enterprise risk and risk management as a profession has got to pick up the human element. It's not just numbers and when you miss that, all heck breaks loose. You could replicate that by just taking a position in the index and have exposure—you'd be liquid and could diversify. But you can't get a bonus for doing that. So you can take all these illiquid products that can be value-based upon a model, again which brings in the human element. That's why I say we must bring in people, human behavior, into the equation to correct this problem.

Simkins: If they could go back in time and change the ERM process for these companies, what should they have done different to catch this?

Rizzi: Well, here's the problem that I'm struggling with. The chief executive officer is getting paid based upon options. He's going to roll the dice as well and this makes his options more valuable. The subordinates are lining up to a bonus schedule so they will roll the dice as well. So let's fix that. Well, Warren Buffett tried to do that with Salomon Brothers. You lose all the bankers. If you're the first player to move toward a more rational payment program for your employees, you lose all your talent.

Academics are going to have fun with this. With the 1980s crash, you look back at it and say that it wasn't supposed to happen. This wasn't supposed to happen either. Okay—but it did.

Fraser: I'd like to point out that ERM does not guarantee that people will do their jobs and therefore that specific risks will not hurt you. I do not view the subprime crises as a failure of ERM. I am sure that there are many companies who avoided these losses either through ERM or just good management. This was a failure of "credit or market risk management" depending at the stage of the product chain (e.g., relying on debt insurance from companies lacking adequate resources). Poor credit risk management is due to those credit managers and boards who believed that lending money to people without jobs or collateral was a safe bet, and poor market risk was evidenced from those trading the product who believed that overheated rising markets go on forever. More needs to be studied about the smart companies who avoided this risky business and what made them smarter (or luckier), as well as the relationship between the size of losses and the general quality of management of the companies with losses.

Hofmann: I think this is a good example of how difficult it is to actually maintain effective risk management. It is not just the identification and modeling but even more importantly how we influence decision making and behavior. Do we really have a clear vision and risk mentality? Do we maintain the discipline to stay within that tolerance without getting caught up in euphoria or rationalization? Are we too busy with details to think about the big bets and core and often only implied assumptions? At Koch, we start with the premise that the future is unknown and unknowable. We consider a lot of scenarios but because we cannot know the future focus on maintaining discipline, communicating effectively, and balancing our business profiles. Most of all, we assume that we will be wrong and try to ensure that no matter what happens we protect our ability to survive and have options to continue our growth strategy.

Simkins: Pat, would you like to talk about the climate change initiative?

Concessi: Climate change is an emerging risk for a broad range of companies. Certainly it is a significant risk for electricity generators and oil and gas companies that have significant CO_2 emissions. And it is also a risk for financial institutions that may be trading carbon instruments, as well as lending to companies that emit large volumes of CO_2. In the U.S., the topic of carbon regulation has become a matter of "when" not "if," as both presidential candidates support creation of carbon markets, and regional markets are being developed in the northeast, California, the western states, and the mid-west. So carbon will become a potentially significant financial risk for large emitters. We are working with a number of companies to help them develop scenarios for future carbon legislation, to address their regulatory risk.

The risks associated with climate change are broader than just the risks associated with CO_2 emission. Companies should also be looking at their risk from the changing climate on the demand for their products and on their physical assets. These are termed their "climate change adaptation" risks. Risks related to climate change arise across the organization, are significantly correlated, and include all risk types. This makes them well suited to treatment with an ERM approach. The first step is to do risk identification, specifically on the climate change topic, to ensure that these new risks are included in your ERM process.

QUESTION 8

Simkins: Let's move to the final question. There are two parts to this question and let's just start with the first part. We're always looking for new research ideas. I would like to start with Bruce.

Branson: We've heard several ideas in our conversations today that could benefit from academic investigation. I will also add a few comments from the handout that is available. In this document, I've listed a number of research questions that the ERM initiative has identified as opportunities for more research.[8] An approach we have taken is to pull together a group of faculty at NC State interested in ERM and provide funding for them to conduct research that integrates with their existing research interests and skills. It's difficult to ask researchers that have invested a lot of time and effort into developing a skill set to think about engaging in a line of research where it's not clear where that research may ultimately be published. What we have tried to do is to encourage faculty to leverage their areas of expertise but to try and address the risk management question that would logically fit in within our focus on ERM. To do that, we floated requests for papers and requests for curriculum development. We had a group of faculty in the college respond to that call and they are engaged in six different projects, several of which have produced working papers and published papers.

What accompanied that call for papers was a list of questions that we thought were logical areas of inquiry. The questions span the gamut of various disciplines within traditional business schools. From this group, I think clearly one of the things we've heard today is maybe a real need to better understand ways that we might quantify some of these risks that fall in the operations area or operational risk. Another area where research is needed is to better understand correlations across these various risk categories or silos.

I mentioned the ERM initiative web site earlier, www.erm.ncsu.edu, and I encourage anyone interested in ERM and research on this topic to visit our web site. We have assembled significant resources such as a variety of funded projects underway by our NC State faculty and links to other research. We also have partnered with a group of faculty around the country and internationally that we refer to as our ERM Initiative Research Fellows. We've engaged with them to help us as additional eyes and ears—to help us be aware of ERM research or business press articles that they run across.

Simkins: Bob would you like to comment about the academic research?

Kolb: Well three things. First, and this is something we've already talked about: "How do you square finance theory with enterprise risk management?" Or does finance theory ultimately oppose enterprise risk management? Second, I think there are going to be more outlets for research in this area and we're offering one. We're going to have an annual risk management conference that will result in a published monogram. Finally, I think the field is wide open for research and it's now just becoming ripe for research. Let me explain what I mean by that. If you look at what's been written along the lines of research today, it's largely anecdotal or case studies. And the reason for that of course is because there's not much data available yet. And I think we're right on the cusp of having enough experience with corporations such that one can start doing such empirical studies with sample sizes that are sufficient to give validity. In fact, one of the papers on the program at this conference, a paper authored by Richard Warr and Don Pagach, investigates financial results from enterprise risk management and finds the event that divides the non-ERM and the ERM is the appointment of a chief risk officer.[9] So I think we're right on the verge of actually being able to do a lot of research in this area across the full range of issues.

Simkins: Would any of our industry speakers like to comment on research ideas?

Rizzi: Just to follow up on what I said before, I was focusing on bringing some of the behavioral finance elements into risk management. It's not just the number crunching. Does the structured finance debacle of the summer represent a failure of quantitative risk management? There are going to be a lot of people answering a lot of questions.

Hofmann: I agree and would also encourage more work in the area of decision making under uncertainty and when to apply and not apply common estimation methodologies.

Fraser: I think the research opportunities for enterprise risk management are endless. Little has been written to date in academia on ERM, despite the vast numbers of people and organizations now attempting it. Much of what has been written outside of academia has been by consulting firms with their own agenda and marketing motives. It is still an evolving science and therefore case studies and identifying "best practices" is needed, just like in the early days of exploration when new countries were first discovered (e.g., Darwin). What is succeeding? Why do so many fail? There is still mass confusion (Tower of Babble) where there is not even a semblance of alignment among the disciplines (even those present in this discussion) as to what ERM is. Comparative analysis studies of areas such as risk tolerances, risk profiles, and ERM policies would be of great benefit to the next generation of implementers and students. To produce someone who really understands and can deliver ERM requires a mixture of skills not currently found in any given discipline. Therefore, the challenge will be teaching methods and skills that may be outside of the academics area of comfort, for example, controls, workshop facilitation, risk tolerance bias, opinion bias, organizational behavior, nonfinancial risks like safety and environmental and reputation, governance, strategic planning, performance measurement, and so forth. I get calls from people asking where they can get trained and to date North Carolina State U is the only real ERM course of which I am aware.

Kolb: I think we really don't know much about the intricacies of the recent failure. But let me give you an example of where there is perhaps a parallel opportunity for disaster that hasn't occurred yet, and that is in the "carry trade."[10] The carry trade essentially bets against the interest rate parity theorem. And it is successful, and apparently continues to be successful year after year even though it shouldn't be working. But it has been working—lots and lots of people are doing it. It's kind of a lemming effect. And I think maybe that was the case with the mess this summer and going all the way back to Long-Term Capital Management. You have a kind of herd behavior. People act in a certain way that's maybe not a failure to perceive the risk according to the models, but a failure of management to abstain from doing those things that are against the models and contrary to our understanding, just because they seem to be working presently.

Simkins: Next, get out your crystal ball and I would like you to give your forecast of what you think is going to happen over the next decade in ERM. And you're going to go down in print on this, so we're going to hold you to your forecast.

Concessi: I think we need to develop more sophisticated risk measurement applications. The ability to meaningfully quantify risk is impeding a lot of implementation right now. We also need to get better at identifying and addressing the really big risks that we are currently not capturing. If companies keep having losses that result from things that aren't captured by the ERM program, and if those losses are relatively significant or larger than the risks that are captured, I think that would frustrate the whole development of ERM.

Kolb: I think certain kind of risks all get lumped into operational risks, but these risks are really very different. For example, in many classifications of risk we find the ethical failure of people at a high level in the organization, such as CEOs and directors, getting lumped together with completely different risks, such as natural catastrophes. Unless there is some work done at sorting those out and dealing with those really complex issues, say the differences between ethical failures and natural catastrophes, I think ERM can't fully succeed.

Perkins: I guess to really just piggyback on that, I think we'll see development down both of those paths. I think the quantification is critical that we do move forward on that but there are the qualitative aspects that have a long way to go. As we move forward, ERM is going to more and more become not a program, but part of a company's culture. I think it has to be viewed that way to be successful. One last thing, the ERM process needs to ultimately feed into the disclosure process and be effectively communicated to investors and stakeholders.

Rizzi: I guess my three observations going forward would be: First, if the culture shift takes place and everyone becomes a risk manager, ERM's function will basically disappear. It will be pushed into the business units just like strategic planning for the most part. Second, I think we will see happen in the financial organizations—the CRO and the CFO function are going to merge. They have to merge because right now it is just dysfunctional the way they work.

Branson: I think it's possible that we may not hear the term "enterprise risk management" specifically but it will be there; it's been successful; it's become simply the way certain companies do business. It will be embedded in their culture and an important part of the regular strategic planning activity of the board and in the development of business plans. We just won't be calling it ERM (perhaps). It's there and it's just good business at that point.

Simkins: We are now at the end of the roundtable discussion. Time will tell as to how ERM will evolve over time. ERM holds great promise and in my opinion, it is the natural evolution of risk management—whether we refer to it by name or it just becomes embedded in the culture.

In our discussion, we have covered many important aspects and highlighted excellent research opportunities on ERM. I would like to encourage academics to closely collaborate with practitioners to conduct research in these key areas of need. One way to do this is through PDDARI, which stands for Practitioner Demand Driven Academic Research Initiative. The FMA has established this research initiative to facilitate applied research, such as what we discuss in this roundtable, between academics and practitioners.[11]

Please join me in thanking our panelists for sharing their expertise with us in this thought provoking discussion.

NOTES

1. © The Financial Management Association, International, University of South Florida, COBA, 4202 E. Fowler Avenue, Suite #3331, Tampa, FL 33620-5500 www.fma.org.

2. Bruce Branson is an Associate Director of the Enterprise Risk Management Initiative and Professor in the Department of Accounting at North Carolina State University in Raleigh, North Carolina. Pat Concessi is a Partner in Global Energy Markets with Deloitte and Touche, LLC, Toronto, Canada. John R.S. Fraser is the Chief Risk Officer and the Vice President of Internal Audit at Hydro One Inc. in Toronto, Ontario, Canada. Michael Hofmann is a Vice President and the Chief Risk Officer at Koch Industries, Inc. in Wichita, Kansas. Robert (Bob) Kolb is the Frank W. Considine Chair in Applied Ethics at Loyola University Chicago in Chicago, Illinois. Todd Perkins is the Director of Enterprise Risk at Southern Company, Inc. in Atlanta, Georgia. Joe Rizzi is now the Senior Investment Strategist at CapGen Financial in New York, New York. At the time of the roundtable discussion, he was the Managing Director of Enterprise Risk Management at Bank of America and La Salle Bank in Chicago, Illinois. Betty J. Simkins, the moderator, is the Williams Companies Professor of Business and an Associate Professor of Finance in the Spears School of Business at Oklahoma State University in Stillwater, Oklahoma.

3. See page 2 of "Enterprise Risk Management—Integrated Framework, Executive Summary," by COSO, September 2004.

4. See "The 360° View of Risk: Excellence in Risk Management IV," by the Risk and Insurance Management Society (RIMS) and Marsh, New York, 2007.

5. Joe Rizzi is now the Senior Investment Strategist at CapGen Financial in New York.

6. See Lloyd's, 2005, "Taking Risk on Board," Lloyd's and the Economist Intelligence Unit (EIU), London.

7. Contact the panelist, Bob Kolb, for a copy of the current syllabus on enterprise risk management.

8. Copies of the handout, or an update, are available from Bruce Branson, upon request.

9. See "An Empirical Investigation of the Characteristics of Firms Adopting Enterprise Risk Management," by Richard S. Warr and Don Pagach, North Carolina State University working paper, available at www.fma.org/Orlando/Papers/warr_pagach _CRO_hazard.pdf.

10. The "carry trade" is the practice of borrowing funds in a country with a low nominal rate of interest and reinvesting those funds in another country with a higher nominal interest rate, with the intention of profiting on the differential in the two interest rates. Of course, the interest rate parity theorem asserts that the differential between the two rates is mediated by the difference between the spot exchange rate and the forward exchange rate between the two currencies, such that one cannot succeed in capturing this differential with certainty. In other words, the interest rate parity theorem rules out arbitrage. Therefore, the carry trade is a risky trade, subject to the risk that exchange rates will change in an adverse manner over the investment horizon and prevent the investor from capturing the differential between the two nominal rates of interest.

11. For more information about PDDARI, please see www.fma.org/PDDARI/PDDARI .htm.

CHAPTER 27

Establishing ERM Systems in Emerging Countries

DEMIR YENER, PhD
Senior Finance and Governance Advisor, Deloitte Consulting, LLP.

INTRODUCTION

The purpose of this chapter is to discuss enterprise risk management (ERM) in the context of corporate governance in emerging market corporations. There is a growing interest in improving corporate governance practices in emerging markets following the 1997–1998 financial crises in the Far East and Russia. With the contagion effects of the crisis in many other emerging markets, there was a realization that corporate governance practices had to be improved along with the financial sector infrastructure. This was the genesis for establishing a globally appealing set of principles or rules of good corporate governance.

Upon the initiation of international donors and G7 countries, the Financial Stability Forum was convened. The Principles of Corporate Governance were developed by the Organization for Economic Cooperation and Development (OECD) in 1999[1] and were later revised in 2004. During this period, other standards of business conduct were also introduced to provide guidance in a number of critical areas of global cooperation for business and finance among nations. Many emerging countries have since adopted the OECD principles and developed their own corporate governance codes.

Improving corporate governance is understood to improve the chances of accessing the various sources of finance. In most emerging market countries, the crucial pillars of transparency and disclosure are still considered off-limits due to concerns about business confidentiality. Effective regulatory enforcement has finally forced many exchange-listed firms to become more transparent thanks to improved disclosure requirements. Disclosure has helped make material and timely corporate information available to the investors. While this availability has helped to provide greater information about the firms' business prospects, it has also educated boards to help them improve their supervision of management actions.

Since the early 2000s, most listed companies in emerging countries have become more aware of the need to improve corporate governance practices, thereby helping to resolve the perceived risks related to firms. Improving corporate governance across the board in an emerging country setting will translate into improving shareholder value, by providing more assurance to investors of a better rate of return on their investment. This is especially true of the privately held small- and medium-sized enterprise companies, as it helps them gain better access to the sources of financing.

In the following sections, we offer a discussion of enterprise risk management by emerging market firms. We take a holistic approach to enterprise risk management as prescribed in the COSO definition.[2] Refer to the Appendix for a summary of the COSO approach to ERM.

ENTERPRISE RISK MANAGEMENT AND ITS BENEFITS IN EMERGING MARKETS

Enterprise risk management can be defined as the intelligent use of risk to promote business opportunities and gain competitive advantages for the firm. In this context, ERM encompasses a holistic culture, processes, and tools used throughout the firm to identify strategic opportunities and reduce uncertainty for a firm. ERM allows the comprehensive view of risk from both operational and strategic perspectives. It is a process that supports the reduction of uncertainty and promotes the exploitation of opportunities.

ERM is important for all successful companies managing the random and often interrelated types of risks that a business encounters during its existence. ERM offers companies strategically more effective risk management at "potentially lower" costs. From time to time, there are major events in finance that affect many stockholders and related stakeholders in many parts of the world. A well-known example is the demise of the Barings Group in the 1990s, a large British investment management company that lost many billions due to unscrupulous futures trading by a trader named Nick Leeson, who took unhedged positions without proper risk oversight. There are many other examples. Currently, the financial sector troubles and the economic meltdown have magnified the effects of excessive leverage that firms had accumulated in anticipation of high returns in a growth environment. Unfortunately, many firms grossly neglected the downside of the risks they had exposed themselves to, without much protection.

For example, many Asian exporting corporations have borrowed heavily from their domestic or international banks in anticipation that their foreign exchange earnings will continue for a foreseeable period of time. Unfortunately, the global economic meltdown has negatively affected their revenues, and therefore their ability to service their debts. The final outcome is still uncertain at this time. The current period is that of a crisis management mode and involves crisis risk management.

There are many benefits to ERM if applied properly. The key is that the firm must adopt ERM as a holistic process, and the firm should be involved in ERM at all levels from the board all the way down to the business units. ERM requires that management be responsible for the implementation of the policies, while the board monitors and provides guidance to the CEO. In the ongoing globalization process, and with the pressures to become more transparent, the financial services industry, along with utility companies and the airline industry, have increasingly adopted these practices.

Let's consider the airline industry in emerging markets: IATA, the International Air Travel Association, reports that civil aviation markets in Poland, China, Czech Republic, Qatar, and Turkey, will have a steady growth rate of 5 percent to 8 percent per year in terms of passenger and cargo volume through the first decade of this century. Given this expected growth in the aviation sector, a recent survey conducted among the 14 Turkish Airline companies reports that survey respondents generally agree that by developing an ERM policy, the airlines could implement a structured and disciplined approach in risk management. Respondents further understand that ERM aligns the organization's strategies, processes, technology, and knowledge with the purpose of improving its ability to develop a strategy and manage more effectively.[3]

The survey results, however, do not support the hypothesis that Turkish airline managements are interested in risk management as a holistic concept and want to implement ERM in their organizations. The findings suggest that while there is an increasing awareness of nonoperational risks (e.g., security, safety, and financial risk management), companies are just beginning to move toward an enterprise-wide view of risk. At the present time, the study finds that the airline managements still see risk management very narrowly, which is quite different from what ERM concepts require. The airlines perceive risk and ERM within the narrow framework of their corporate culture and management style and there is no uniformity in these risk perceptions. Airline executives care most about the *security, safety and financial* risks that they face, which may vary according to each company's market niche. We think that even this much awareness is a major step forward in an emerging country. However, more needs to be done to establish ERM techniques among the Turkish Airline companies. The very recent crash of a Turkish Airlines passenger jet in Amsterdam, the Netherlands, ought to be a wake-up call.[4]

In a recent study conducted by Ernst and Young to explore risk management in emerging markets, about 900 companies were surveyed regarding the leading risk management practices in Brazil, Russia, India, China, and Turkey as well as in 12 developed market countries.[5] The main finding of the study is that establishing a risk culture, improving communications, and aligning organizational structure and risk management processes can ultimately set a strong foundation for better risk management. See Box 27.1 for key findings.

ERM also involves understanding the risk in dealing with companies that are not transparent. A recent example from India may be cited here: In early January 2009, Satyam Computer Services, one of India's biggest software and services companies, revealed some alarming truths. The company's founder and chairman, B. Ramalinga Raju, confessed to a $1.47 billion fraud on its balance sheet, which he and his brother, Satyam's managing director, had disguised from the company's board, senior managers, and auditors for several years. As the business opportunities for Satyam grew, this fraud went mostly unnoticed by the shareholders of the company. As the markets began to contract, the deficit had to be covered, and thus, the scandal broke. This is a problem of abuse of shareholder trust.

Box 27.1   Example: ERM at Indian Companies

Because of globalization and the international growth of Indian companies, it is now more critical than ever that Indian firms pay attention to the most recent global developments regarding risk management elsewhere. Among the key findings and trends now emerging in India with regard to Enterprise Risk Management (ERM) are the following:[6]

- Strategic risks have not typically been considered in the early stages of building ERM at Indian companies.
- Most of the risks continue to be managed in silos, whether in business units or in functions. This approach does not take advantage of the holistic approach that ERM can bring to risks that cross businesses.
- Other than financial institutions, few Indian companies have developed sophisticated risk metrics. Even at financial institutions, risks are usually managed and monitored by class of risk such as credit or market risk, rather than holistically across the institution.
- Much of the focus on ERM in Indian companies to date has been on the downside risk, not the opportunity side of the equation. ERM may bring the necessary cultural change to identify opportunities and their associated risks and rewards.
- ERM has created greater transparency both internally and externally at those companies that have embraced it. Communication within the company has improved by adding a new perspective on risk and sharing risk information. Communication with shareholders and other external stakeholders has also improved through more thorough disclosure.
- The value proposition for ERM is not yet evident for most Indian companies since most companies and boards that have begun ERM are doing so more as a compliance exercise than a strategic one.
- Evolving legal standards make it prudent for business organizations operating in the Indian financial market to strengthen their ERM processes.

The risks in Satyam case are due to bad management decisions, and fraudulent action on the part of the chairman. Good corporate governance practices strongly discourage the chairman from also holding the role of the CEO. This is a common practice in all emerging market countries. Due to the power these two roles provide, management responsibility and accountability suffer along with transparency, oftentimes leading to potentially disastrous results. The risk to the investors is large in a thinly capitalized emerging market.[7] See Box 27.2.

Box 27.2 Findings of Survey on Risk Management in Emerging Markets

According to a survey conducted by Ernst and Young, the key "risk management lessons" taken from executives' experience across emerging and developed markets reveal the following findings:

- The main goal in emerging markets is growth. Companies have moved on from the traditional view that the primary objective of investment in emerging markets is cost saving.
- Risk priorities differ by location. Developed markets focus on political, operational, and supply chain risk. Emerging markets are more likely to focus on market, competitive, and pricing risk.
- There is a consensus that boards are not giving enough attention to risk in these markets. Only 41% of developed market companies have a risk strategy for emerging markets.
- Opinion differs on risk communication. While 71% of emerging market subsidiaries feel they provide sufficiently regular and robust information on risk, only 44% of the parent companies would say the same.
- Opinion also differs on internal audit. Developed market companies have less confidence in the quality of the internal audit testing of their subsidiaries than the emerging market subsidiaries themselves do.

Source: Ernst & Young. "Risk Management in Emerging Markets," 2007.

Evolution of Risk Management in Emerging Markets

Recent debacles such as misunderstanding the forces of globalization, frequent product recalls, fraudulent securities trading and accounting practices, major shifts in financial and commodity markets, or the failure of monetary and regulatory responses to financial crises, and the contagion effects of financial crises, have led to many lessons learned about the systemic risk inherent in the global marketplace.

International cooperation has tried to find solutions to the global implications of the financial crises. Further exacerbating the problems are the increasingly complex environmental or business changes that were not effectively recognized by management and which have underscored the need for enterprise risk management at the corporate level.

Risk management evolved as a result of a combination of issues. Box 27.3 provides a brief description of the risks that any business must consider in conducting its business. The items presented here are a select sample of the typical issues that may be raised when managing risk in a holistic manner.

Box 27.3   Types of Risk

The total risk of a firm consists of a combination of risk factors as depicted in the following.

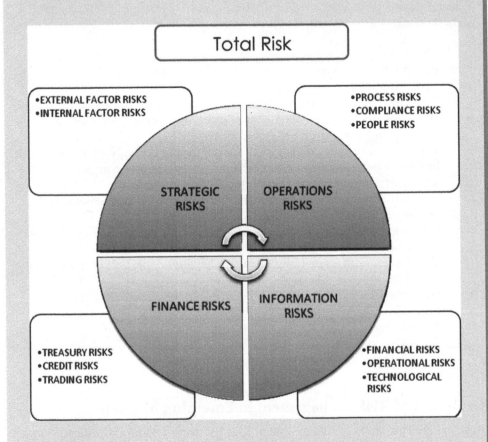

- *Strategic risks* group includes external and internal factor risks. The external factors essentially refer to the likelihood that industry, economy, legal, and regulatory changes and competitors will cause the breakdown of operations or variability in the firm's earnings. The internal factor risks relate to the likelihood that the firm's reputation, strategic focus, patent, and trademark types of company-specific factors will cause variability in the revenues or net earnings of the firm.
- *Operational risks* are the cause-effect related pressures on the revenues and net earnings of the firm resulting from the supply-chain discontinuities, customer satisfaction, cycle time, and manufacturing processes (process risks); while others may be caused by environment, regulations, policy and procedures, and litigations (compliance risks); and yet others may be caused by factors such as human resources, employee turnover, performance incentives, and training factors (people risk).

- *Finance risks* group includes the variability in earnings due to interest rate fluctuations, foreign exchange risks, and access to capital (treasury risks); while other factors include the capacity, collateral, concentration of debt, default risk related to credit (credit risks); and other pressures on the financing policies of the firm due to commodity prices, duration (trading risk).
- *Information risks* group includes issues that put pressure on the financial and investment policies of the firm due to accounting standards, budgeting, financial reporting, taxation, and regulatory reporting requirements (financial risks); while others such as pricing, performance measurement and employee safety (operational risks) risk; and, risks due to technological innovations such as information access, business sustainability, availability and infrastructure risks (technological risks) that may cause fluctuations in the earnings of the firm.

Source: Adapted from Robert Moeller. (2007) COSO Enterprise Risk Management: Understanding the New Integrated ERM Framework. Hoboken, NJ: John Wiley & Sons.

As globalization in world trade progressed during the last two decades, many emerging countries experienced the collapse of their financial systems. Excessive operating or financial risks undertaken by the corporate sectors were generally identified as the main culprit leading to the serious financial and economic meltdowns. Further, the inability of the international financial institutions to intervene in a timely fashion in order to help the countries' central banks and financial regulatory bodies to prevent this from happening has sent shock waves across the global landscape.

For instance, in a systemic crisis, such as the one the world markets face at this time, the large shocks to foreign exchange and interest rates, and a general economic slowdown cause the corporate and financial sectors to experience a number of defaults and difficulties to service their debt obligations on time. During these periods, nonperforming loans and the inability to service debt will increase sharply, causing the securities markets to decline precipitously. This situation is often accompanied by generally depressed asset prices, such as in equity and real estate prices. In emerging countries with chronic financial distress and other structural problems that reach large proportions, a systemic crisis may have different implications. Exhibit 27.1 presents some key variables for a sample of systemic crisis countries during the 1990s.[8]

The lessons learned from this experience were that globalization can have overreaching implications on all countries, and that financial sectors must be better regulated under internationally accepted principles. When a systemic crisis occurs, the future of an individual corporation, and its course of actions to deal with crisis management, will depend on the actions of many other corporations and financial institutions, and the general economic outlook. This is in essence a part of the risk management policies of the firm. The financial and the corporate sectors are almost always closely related and they will both need restructuring in this case. Corporate liquidity and solvency will be of the utmost importance. Governments

Exhibit 27.1 Patterns of Systemic Banking Crises

Country	Crisis year	Fiscal cost (% of GDP)	Peak NPL (% of loans)	Real GDP growth	Change in exchange rate	Peak in real interest rates	Decline in real asset prices
Finland	1992	11.0	13	−4.6%	−5.5%	14.3%	−34.6%
Indonesia	1998	50.0	65–75	−15.4%	−57.5%	3.3%	−78.5%
Korea	1998	37.0	30–40	−10.6%	−28.8%	21.6%	−45.9%
Malaysia	1998	16.4	25–35	−12.7%	−13.9%	5.3%	−79.9%
Mexico	1995	19.3	29.8	−6.2%	−39.8%	24.7%	−53.3%
Philippines	1998	0.5	20	−0.8%	−13.0%	6.3%	−67.2%
Sweden	1992	4.0	18	−3.3%	+1.0%	79.2%	−6.8%
Thailand	1998	32.8	33	−5.4%	−13.7%	17.2%	−77.4%

Source: Claessens, Stijn, Daniela Klingebiel and Luc Leaven. (2001). "Financial Restructuring in Banking and Corporate Sector Crises: What Policies to Pursue?" NBER Working Paper W8386. www.nber.org./papers/w8386.

will be expected to play a significant role in these circumstances, even though the final arbiters are the corporations themselves.

As a result of the financial crises of the 1990s, the leading nations convened various task forces to develop new ground rules to be set as guiding principles for operating financial markets in all countries. Some of these rules include the OECD Principles of Corporate Governance, IOSCO Principles of Securities Markets Regulations, International Accounting and Auditing standards, and a list of others.[9]

Financial Crises and Remedies

Most of the financial sector problems that caused the financial crisis of 1997–1998 were related to the excessive lending on the one hand, and excessive borrowing by the private sector firms on the other hand in emerging nations. One factor causing the financial crisis was the excessive exposure to international currencies that changed drastically, thus causing the firms with excessive exposures to those risks to collapse due to an inability to service their debts.

The causes of the financial crisis of 2008 were somewhat different and these will be discussed for a long time as there was a combination of factors that contributed to the crisis. The market participants, by and large, sought higher yields in a low-interest rate, low inflation rate environment, without adequate appreciation of the risks and failed to exercise proper due diligence. Box 27.4 lists the emerging sets of standards in market conduct. More detail is available in Box 27.5.

One major failure was that the policy makers and the regulatory institutions did not adequately address critical market issues as they were unfolding and they did not adequately appreciate the risks building up in the financial markets. Many financial companies' boards also failed to appreciate risks they were facing until the firms ran out of liquidity and faced bankruptcy. Now the issue of government bailout is a part of the solution. However, at the core, the solution lies in the board rooms to control the "infectious greed" of CEOs from taking over the whole institution due to the short-term profit motives.[10]

Box 27.4   Emerging Global Standards of Business Conduct

- Corporate Governance (OECD Principles).
- Accounting (IAS) and Auditing (ISA).
- Banking Supervision (BIS Standards).
- Securities (IOSCO).
- International Trade (WTO).
- Anticorruption.
- Insurance Supervision.
- Insolvency and Bankruptcy.
- Monetary and Fiscal Policy Transparency.

Box 27.5   The 12 Key Standards for Sound Financial Systems

The 12 standard areas highlighted here have been designated by the Financial Stability Forum as key for sound financial systems and deserving of priority implementation depending on country circumstances. While the key standards vary in terms of their degree of international endorsement, they are broadly accepted as representing minimum requirements for good practice. Some of the key standards are relevant for more than one policy area, for example, sections of the Code of Good Practices on Transparency in Monetary and Financial Policies have relevance for aspects of payment and settlement as well as financial regulation and supervision.

Policy Area	Title of the Standards	Implementer
Macroeconomic Policy and Data Transparency		
Monetary and financial policy transparency	Code of Good Practices on Transparency in Monetary and Financial Policies	IMF
Fiscal policy transparency	Code of Good Practices on Fiscal Transparency	IMF
Data dissemination	Special Data Dissemination Standard/ General Data Dissemination System*	IMF
Institutional and Market Infrastructure		
Insolvency	Guidelines on Insolvency Regimes**	World Bank
Corporate governance	Principles of Corporate Governance	OECD

Policy Area	Title of the Standards	Implementer
Accounting	International Accounting Standards (IAS)	IASB
Auditing	International Standards on Auditing (ISA)	IFAC
Payment and settlement	Core Principles for Systemically Important Payment Systems Recommendations for Securities Settlement Systems	CPSS/CPSS/ IOSCO
Market integrity	The Forty Recommendations of the Financial Action Task Force/ 9 Special Recommendations Against Terrorist Financing	FATF
Financial Regulation and Supervision		
Banking supervision	Core Principles for Effective Banking Supervision	BCBS
Securities regulation	Objectives and Principles of Securities Regulation	IOSCO
Insurance supervision	Insurance Core Principles	IAIS

*Economies with access to international capital markets are encouraged to subscribe to the more stringent SDDS and all other economies are encouraged to adopt the GDDS.
**The World Bank is coordinating a broad-based effort to develop a set of principles and guidelines on insolvency regimes. The United Nations Commission on International Trade Law (UNCITRAL), which adopted the Model Law on Cross-Border Insolvency in 1997, will help facilitate implementation.
Source: http://www.financialstabilityboard.org/cos/key_standards.htm.

Boxes 27.5 and 27.6 summarize some of the Financial Stability Forum recommendations made to the G7 ministers and central bank governors for enhancing the resilience of markets and financial institutions in reaction to the ongoing crises. The recommended actions are in five major areas, as shown in Box 27.6: (1) strengthening prudential oversight of capital; liquidity and risk management; (2) enhancing transparency and valuation; (3) changes in the role and uses of credit ratings; (4) strengthening the authorities' responsiveness to risks; and, (5) robust arrangements for dealing with stress in the financial system. These are all policy recommendations to deal with crises—in other words, risk management.

It is unclear as to what extent any of these recommendations were heeded since they were issued. Given the date of the report in April 2008, they came very close to predicting the financial crisis and warned the world of the dangers.

Globalization, liberalization of trade and financial markets, privatization, and the development of new financial market trading patterns have had a profound impact on the ways in which private enterprises conduct their investment and business decisions. New standards of doing business, and convergence in global

---

Box 27.6 Enhancing Market and Institutional Resilience

On April 11, 2008, the Financial Stability Forum (FSF) presented to the G7 finance ministers and central bank governors a report making recommendations for enhancing the resilience of markets and financial institutions. The recommended actions are in five areas:

1. Strengthened prudential oversight of capital, liquidity and risk management.
2. Enhancing transparency and valuation.
3. Changes in the role and uses of credit ratings.
4. Strengthening the authorities' responsiveness to risks.
5. Robust arrangements for dealing with stress in the financial system.

Public sector and private sector initiatives are underway in these areas. The FSF will facilitate coordination of these initiatives and oversee their timely implementation, thus preserving the advantages of integrated global financial markets and a level playing field across countries.

The interim report by the FSF's Working Group on Market and Institutional Resilience, setting out policy directions, was issued in February 2008. The preliminary report by the Working Group, setting out its work plan, was issued in October 2007, a copy of which can be obtained from the web site below.

Source: Financial Stability Forum, www.fsforum.org/.

---

financial and trading regulations have made doing business a lot more competitive. While opening up the venues for competitiveness, this has also caused vulnerabilities for the firms.

Even though these new measures were introduced around the turn of the new millennium to protect the global business environment from new crises, there will always be factors in free market economies that will cause distress and crises from time to time. These issues have made enterprise risk management all the more crucial for the long-term competitiveness and survival of any business.

The Rationale for Effective Risk Management in Emerging Markets

ERM is now more important than ever at all levels. Recognizing this, firms need to manage risk and consider the following six areas:[11] (1) tax considerations, (2) stakeholder considerations, (3) conflict of interest between shareholders and management, (4) management compensation, (5) financing and investment policy, and (6) dividend policy. Effective risk management requires an optimal combination of these considerations in order to keep the interests of the shareholders as a priority. In an emerging country environment, erratic dividend policies, an unbridled fast pace of growth, under capitalization, and riskier market environments have caused most companies to look at risk management as an approach too alien for their needs. In addition, many emerging market firms experience tough market pressures and corruption, which increases the cost of doing business. Weak accounting procedures have also had a large impact on the lack of transparency and inability of the firms to price their goods and services properly against competition.

Management compensation is not a major issue, even though good professional managers are hard to find. When they are recruited, they enjoy company perks more than large cash salaries or bonuses. One main reason is that controlling family ownership and the lack of understanding of global competitive forces has caused these firms not to pay too much attention to the need for paying competitive salaries.

Most firms have a small float in the stock markets, that is, between 5 percent and 30 percent, and this minimizes the perceived need of a satisfactory ERM approach in order to satisfy stakeholders. (Note: This will be discussed later in Exhibit 27.2.)

The Responsibility of the Board in Risk Management and Extensions to Emerging Markets

Boards of directors strengthen the corporate governance of a company when they first set a risk management policy that will address the risks that the company may face; second, understand and execute their oversight role, including understanding the company's risk profile and determine a risk/return profile for the firm; and last, approve the business strategy of the company, including approval of the overall risk tolerances and risk management procedures.

The duty of the board is to act on behalf of the shareholders by devising strategies in order to protect shareholders' investment in the firm from the overall risk exposures faced by the firm. Even if management may sometimes act on its own behalf, effective ERM should help protect the interests of the shareholders by aligning the interests of management with those of the shareholders. Box 27.7 provides a set of questions from a board perspective regarding the risks a company faces and its risk management processes.

The crucial issue has to do with the strategic management of a company. When the firm is first established and subsequently at various intervals, it determines a vision, a mission statement, and a set of objectives and targets to achieve the mission objectives. Targeted activities must pay attention to the overall risks faced by the firm.

Whether the firm is generating sufficient value for the given level of risks it has taken is a difficult question. Academic studies have shown that risk management can increase the market value of the firm, lower the cost of equity, and lower the volatility of earnings.

In their recent study, Smithson and Simkins conclude that interest rate, exchange rate, and commodity price risks are reflected in stock price movements. They find that the stock returns of financial firms are clearly sensitive to interest rate changes. In addition, they note that the corporate use of derivatives to hedge

> ## Box 27.7   How Risk Aware Is Your Board?
>
> *Questions Directors Should Ask!*
> - Is the board taking on the appropriate risks?
> - Are the risks taken closely related to the strategies, objectives and performance measures of the firm?
> - How relevant are the risks?
> - Is there a competitive advantage for the firm as a result of these risks?
> - Will the risks taken create value for the shareholders?
> - How closely does the board understand that risk taking is a part of business?
> - Are the risks taken well understood by each board member?
> - Will the risks defined in the risk appetite determination relevant to the overall level of risk?
> - Is the organizational risk appetite swell defined?
> - Has the risk appetite been properly quantified in aggregate and per occurrence?
> - How does our firm adequately manage the risks taken?
> - Is our risk management process coordinated and consistent across the entire enterprise?
> - How is the risk defined in our organization?
> - Are there any gaps and/or overlaps in our risk coverage?
> - Is the risk management process cost-effective?

interest rate and currency exposures appears to be associated with lower sensitivity of stock returns to interest rate and FX changes.[12] The findings of this study reinforce the preceding arguments of how the U.S. financial firms have both benefited during the growth periods, then encountered extreme consequences during market downturns.

In terms of risk management, the board must follow a structural approach in bringing its policies down to the level of business units.[13] The important thing for the board is that it ought to have a firm philosophy toward all types of risks the firm may face in its sector. The board members must understand the financial instruments the company uses or owns, especially the derivatives that the firm may use to hedge some risks, like currency, interest rates, and so on.

One important building block of an effective ERM program is to identify who formulates the firm's guidelines and policies on the use of financial instruments. Another question is whether or not the board has approved these policies. The board must determine the best way to foster a risk management culture throughout the firm. Once determined, the board must ensure the integrity of the risk management system.

Another important question is whether there is separation of duties between those who generate financial risks and those who manage and control these financial risks. The types of instruments to be used must be evaluated, their risks must

Exhibit 27.2 Comparative Review of Risk Management Applications Using COSO Model in Select Emerging Countries

	Egypt	Jordan	Mongolia	Serbia	Turkey	Ukraine
Internal Environment The internal environment encompasses the tone of an organization, and sets the basis for how risk is viewed and addressed by an organization's people, including risk management philosophy and risk appetite, integrity and ethical values, and the environment in which they operate.	Banks and some export oriented firms have embraced ERM. Risk appetite is determined to the degree the family owners deem it necessary. Banks focus on IT and financial risk appetite.	Most of the banks that follow Basel II criteria have determined rational methods of risk management. Risk appetite is mostly a matter that seems to concern the majority owners. Trading firms mainly focus on financial and business risk appetite. Due to a lack of corporate capacity and skills, no further application beyond this.	Especially the banks have developed ERM strategies and have been able to develop capacity to implement them. However, skills and capacity of the management and the board have been inadequate to successfully implement a coherent ERM program.	Given the business sector, risk appetite depends on the owners' perception rather than a rational system. Capacity is lacking.	Each business sector has a different risk appetite. But most family-owned firms treat risk as a necessary evil. Larger firms like airlines have focused mainly on security, safety, and financial risks. Not much in IT. Banks care more about IT. Most other firms do not treat risk management in a rational program. Capacity is lacking.	Most private sector firms do not have a systematic approach to risk. Banks that are following the Basel II criteria have determined risk appetite levels, such as IT, financial, and market risks. However, due to capacity not much beyond that is practiced.
Objective Setting Objectives must exist before management can identify potential events affecting their achievement. Enterprise risk management ensures that management has in place a process to set objectives and that the chosen objectives support and align with the organization's mission and are consistent with its risk appetite.	Banks and a few key listed companies have determined their risk management objectives. Most others do not have a set of risk management objectives.	Other than the top two to three banks and a couple of leading industrial companies no major risk management objective setting practices are observed.	Other than the few leading banks, no major risk management objective setting observed.	The boards are aware of the requirements, and the regulatory organizations have made this mandatory for all listed companies. However, other than the banks, in most cases no objective setting activity has been observed.	Mostly in banks following Basel II principles, and some in larger corporations, including top airline companies, objective-setting efforts are not a main activity at the boards of directors.	Only banks have addressed the objective setting for risk management.

Component						
Event Identification Internal and external events affecting the achievement of an organization's objectives must be identified, distinguishing between risks and opportunities. Opportunities are channeled back to management's strategy or objective-setting processes.	A couple of banks apply event identification methods. Industrial firms have looked into this phenomenon. A leading, large family-dominated firm has devised methods to tackle the potentially risky events.	A couple of leading banks have determined events that can be considered as risky for them as part of risk appetite determination.	Leading banks with international partners have attempted to determine events that may be considered risky. Industrials have not practiced this.	With a few exceptions, not much of an activity. Possibly due to lack of adequate capacity.	Some leading banks and industrials have followed programs to identify risky events. Capacities are newly developing.	Other than a few banks, not much.
Risk Assessment Risks are analyzed, considering likelihood and impact, as a basis for determining how they should be managed. Risks are assessed on an inherent and a residual basis.	This is not a regularly applied activity. Leading banks have performed risk assessment techniques but not all of the industries due to lack of capacity.	Some leading banks have done this under Central Bank of Jordan CG requirements. Industrials have not attempted this as yet.	Other than three top banks, no other listed company has attempted this.	Some narrow approach applied.	An increasing understanding of the ERM concept helps financial and industries to make serious assessments.	Banks have applied risk assessment techniques to ERM; industrials have not experienced this due to lack of interest.

(Continued)

Exhibit 27.2 *(Continued)*

	Egypt	Jordan	Mongolia	Serbia	Turkey	Ukraine
Risk Response Management selects risk responses—avoiding, accepting, reducing, or sharing risk—developing a set of actions to align risks with the entity's risk tolerances and risk appetite.	No specific application observed.	Other than a few specific actions, not too widespread.	Banks have been more active in this sense. However, no specific application can be cited.	No specific application other than the few banks.	With some exceptions, risk response rationale and planned actions are not widespread activities.	No specific applications.
Control Activities Policies and procedures are established and implemented to help ensure the risk responses are effectively carried out.	Banking sector firms under the Central Bank Basel II-based guidelines have begun to develop control mechanisms at all levels. Not too developed as yet.	Banking sector firms with Basel II guidelines have been more actively involved in establishing control activities. Listed firms in most cases have not begun. Recent Corporate Governance Code may cause acceleration of the development of control mechanisms by many firms, not too many. Audit capacity inadequate.	Leading three Mongolian banks with international institutional investors have been more actively engaged in developing control mechanisms. Corporations have not been able to begin the process.	Mostly banks have begun to comply with the Central Bank of Serbia guidelines by determining risk control policies. No further application information is available.	Most banks and larger holding companies have begun elaborate enterprise risk control initiatives. Varying degrees of success has been reported. Major obstacle is the lack of the general capacity to implement these policies, due to top down management style in most cases. Experience suggests corporate culture needs to develop further to embrace more professional attitudes.	Ukrainian banks have recently begun to apply the risk control measures in their operations. ERM in its full sense is not well understood as yet. Central Bank set some guidelines but the local banks have largely been unable to absorb the new approach. Other banks with foreign control have their HQ based risk management approach, which is largely working. A couple of listed firms have attempted to bring a rationale for risk control. This is an evolving area.

Component						
Information and Communication Relevant information is identified, captured, and communicated in a form and timeframe that enables people to carry out their responsibilities. Effective communication also occurs in a broader sense, flowing down, across, and up the entity.	Communication from the Board is by and large regarded as a new and additional responsibility, rather than a living ongoing process to prepare the organization to potentially manage detrimental risks.	Mostly banks try to apply risk management. However, local banks are still under the family ownership and control. This is a new challenge at most banks, and a paternalistic approach is still the order of the day.	Bank boards have adopted new approaches to manage risks, and this issue is communicated. However, there is still a lot of room for full evolution of this area. Generally top management "tells" the divisions about the new measures. In some banks there are specific Risk Management departments.	Information and communication is still considered a proprietary asset, and thus banks are reluctant to communicate complete information. Some training programs occur. Not too effective as yet. There is room for growth.	Remarkably, Turkish banks and leading industrial holding companies have developed ERM programs and have established open and clear communications. Majority of listed companies and banks have a way to go forward.	Some Ukrainian banks embraced modern management approaches and have established open and clear channels of communications inside the firm. Some larger firms have begun to improve internal communications.
Monitoring The entirety of enterprise risk management is monitored and modifications made as necessary. Monitoring is accomplished through ongoing management activities, separate evaluations, or both.	Some leading banks have established risk management committees that apply monitoring of the ERM activities. Egyptian Capital Markets Authority and the Central bank apply the risk management requirements and enforce the corporate governance codes. Capacity still lacking in effective monitoring and necessary modifications on a timely basis.	Only at the leading banks there are efforts to develop bank risk management methods. Boards do not have the committee structure unless it is required by law. New company law and the corporate governance codes require the establishment of ERM practices in all listed companies, banks, and corporates alike. Weakness is in the implementation.	Newly developing Financial Regulator Services board in collaboration with the Central Bank has been championing ERM to be applied at all levels and all corporations. This is marred by the inadequacy of skills and capacity. However, the necessary steps have been taken in most cases to apply the law in banks and leading corporates. This is a challenge and it is still evolving.	The concept is currently evolving in most banking and some industrial corporations. Further guidance from regulatory organizations would help these institutions greatly in establishing well-functioning and effective ERM. Currently the board structures are inadequate and directors are not well qualified to pursue the regulatory requirements. Outside talent is not easy to come by and it is costly.	Turkish banking and leading holding companies have developed adequate skills and capacity for effective monitoring of risk management activities within the firms. However, the majority of firms need to evolve the capacities in order to be able to effectively pursue ERM. The concept is still not yet well understood.	Leading banks and a few industrial firms have been able to develop monitoring activities to increase the effectiveness of ERM. However skills need to be developed.

be calculable, a value assessment approach must be in place, and policies on how these are entered into company records and monitored must be determined. Last, shareholders must be kept abreast of the risks that they could reasonably expect from their investment in the firm. This is a process that is holistic, because it affects all units and all levels of the firm.

Boards are increasingly more active in risk management. In general, emerging market corporate boards have increased their attention to risk matters especially since the financial crises have eroded much of the shareholders' capital and the firms had to take quite some time to readjust their capital base to regain the values lost. Although the interest in risk management is genuine, and most boards in emerging countries are paying more attention to risk than the other areas, there still is a lack of adequate understanding of how to best manage the risks. For instance, most companies in India and China manage risk in silos, and at department levels, rather than at the holistic level.

Boards in emerging markets are slowly realizing that it is within their duties to discuss market potential and expanding the firm. In addition, boards may need to consider forming risk advisory committees, or getting more directly involved in assessing market risks.[14]

Once the board has defined the level of loss it is prepared to tolerate across its businesses, in addition to the policy level deliberations, it must define the "risk appetite" of the firm. Other countries' regulatory agencies provide guidance to companies that wish to incorporate ERM into their Board practices.[15]

Regulatory pressures from such international bodies as the Basel Committee on Banking Supervision and a greater focus on corporate governance have been a stimulus for many changes in the financial industry—one of these has been the recognition of the need to articulate risk appetite more clearly. These factors have led the firms to determine a proactive risk culture for the firms. Box 27.8

Box 27.8   Proactive Risk Culture

Risk Perception and Behavior
- Risk management is on everyone's job description.
- Viewing risk as a positive, not a negative issue.
- Business Units, Risk Management, and Internal Audit share common view.
- Learning from mistakes, not conducting witch hunts.

Business Unit Activities
- Business units managing their own risks.
- Business units regularly analyze current, emerging, or potential risks.
- Staff across business units understand the unit's risk profile.
- Staff receive appropriate risk management training.
- Business units seek risk management's input to their plans.

Efficient Risk Management
- Establishing and monitoring key risk indicators.

summarizes the risk appetite determination approach used in Egypt, Jordan, Ukraine, and Russia. On the face of it, this may seem easy to do. After all, is it not simply a combination of an institution's desired credit rating, regulatory capital structure, and the relevant solvency needs that set the ability of the institution to withstand shocks and therefore represent its risk appetite?

For some smaller firms this approach may well be enough, but for others risk appetite is a more complicated affair at the heart of risk management strategy and indeed the business strategy.

Risk, Reward, and Risk Appetite in Emerging Markets

Finance theory defines the relationship between risk and reward such that for a given level of expected risk, a certain level of return is expected from an investment. In a business scenario, returns from various investments by different business units in the firm may be different. For some of the business units, the returns could be lower despite the higher expected risks.

It is also important to look at other aspects of risk. For example, it is essential to discuss risk in the context of a company's desired levels of return and growth. At the corporate level in a publicly traded company, this might involve a targeted Total Shareholder Return (TSR). Many companies set targets for these and publicize them—usually in terms of outperforming a peer group. If we turn this around and look at it from the risk perspective, it could be interpreted that management wishes to outperform its peers in assuming risk! We have yet to see a company in emerging markets set risk-adjusted TSR targets.

Many risk management failures have been caused by focusing on profits without clearly defining risk levels. Many times management makes the mistake of focusing on satisfying the risk appetite of one group of stakeholders without giving sufficient weight to the appetites of others.

In the Ernst & Young survey on risk management in emerging markets, it was determined that for most emerging country businesses, market risk or the competitive environment are the sources of most risks.[16] Other risks reported were: currency risk (when they operate in international markets), political risk, regulations, and the workforce issue.

The risk appetite of a firm is largely affected by the corporate culture. Perceptions, behavior, business unit activities, and the risk management approach must all converge for successful ERM. One of the more interesting internal challenges in financial services organizations, which often tend to be risk averse and conservative, is to ensure that business unit management is assuming sufficient risk. Commercial banks in emerging markets must rise to this challenge as they strive to find new growth opportunities. Incumbent management teams, who are often very good at maintaining the status quo, find they need new skills to tune up the engine and go faster.

Without a change in risk appetite, many companies may find themselves underperforming in terms of returns. Culture, strategy, and competitive position all influence risk appetite. Different firms will have different tolerances for different risk types. Furthermore, within a firm, appetite may differ between business units.

A bank's appetite for credit risk in consumer lending might be quite different to its appetite for market risk in its investment banking operation. Management's appetite for risk will differ in a start-up operation in a new market compared to maintaining an established business in a mature market—and so on. With ERM, all of these elements will eventually need to be aligned with the corporate appetite and tolerances. A major benefit of defining risk appetite is that it forces the debate and helps ensure that risks are managed explicitly. To change behavior in relation to risk, interventions through additional training or changing personnel may be needed, but in most organizations the tone set by senior management tends to have by far the greatest impact.

OBSERVATIONS OF ERM PRACTICES IN EMERGING COUNTRIES

In Exhibit 27.2, we summarize our comparative observations of the ERM practices in Egypt, Jordan, Mongolia, Serbia, Turkey, and Ukraine based on the COSO outline. These summary points represent our years of observation made relative to the development of effective corporate governance practices in a larger population of 30 countries since 1995. Our overall conclusion on this issue is that ERM is still considered a new phenomenon in the format provided by COSO and applied by the regulatory bodies in these respective countries.

Although everyone agrees that it is time to improve on risk management, it is difficult to launch an effective ERM practice without the guidance and support of boards of directors in emerging markets. This is mainly due to the lack of technical knowledge at the top levels, even though there are capacity and skills deficiencies at all levels to establish an ERM program. We think that there will eventually be an improved capacity developed to fully practice ERM programs; however, emerging market regulatory bodies need to issue guidance and direction in order for this to be effective.

Regulators must play a guidance role if the overall corporate governance effectiveness is to be enhanced. Full compliance with all corporate governance regulations will certainly help many companies to gain better access to finance, to improve internal management capabilities, improve board effectiveness, and make the firms more competitive in the global arena.

CONCLUSION

New corporate governance codes have become the driving force for organizations to implement enterprise risk management. An ERM framework has been provided through COSO in 2004. ERM is a process that begins with the definition of a risk appetite for the firm. Firms must manage risks in order to ensure shareholders a return on their investment leading to value creation.

Risk management is a continuous process, involving the board, management, and all individual employees at all business unit levels. ERM must achieve a broad "buy-in" at all levels in the firm to succeed. The benefits of ERM are yet to be proven, however, evidence suggests that ERM is closely correlated with increased shareholder value in many cases. The needs and focus of ERM varies between sectors. Not all risks should or can be intensively quantified and overly sophisticated solutions should be avoided.

In the select emerging countries that were observed for this purpose, ERM is still an evolving topic of concern. In all of the emerging countries in our sample, we looked at the leading listed companies' ERM applications. These countries include Egypt, Jordan, Mongolia, Serbia, Turkey, and Ukraine. In most countries, none of the objectives of enterprise risk management are fully practiced.

In terms of the *strategic objectives,* where the firm's high-level goals are aligned with and support the mission of an enterprise, few organizations have accomplished this objective in full. Second, in terms of the *operational objective* of ERM, where the firm utilizes its resources efficiently and effectively, our observations in the six countries have found that the lack of resources has been a major obstacle in most cases. Third, for the *reporting objective,* where the firm's reporting practices are reliable, relevant, timely, and replicable, the inadequacy of the accounting practices has been a major cause for concern in developing a fully effective ERM. Finally, in terms of the *compliance objective,* where the enterprise risk management framework is in compliance with applicable laws and regulations, despite the proliferation of legal and regulatory frameworks to enhance corporate governance through a number of ways including the risk management, we observe major weaknesses in full compliance.

At this time, corporate governance codes and regulations, and banking sector regulations have not been fully implemented in most banks or in listed corporations to the fullest degree to reach the desired objectives. It is most likely that in time many of these weaknesses and obstacles will be overcome and ERM will be fully practiced.

Our final observation is that the ERM concept is still a new concept and is likely to take a while to get the emerging country firms to reach the desirable level of risk management practices for sound business reasons rather than as a new responsibility that needs to be practiced because of the law.

APPENDIX: COSO APPROACH TO ENTERPRISE RISK MANAGEMENT

In the current global financial and product market environment, emerging country companies must generally undertake greater risks than companies from better established economies in order to gain market share. We argue that these firms are generally more risk prone in many aspects. We discuss these in the order defined by the COSO approach to risk management.

The goal of enterprise development projects undertaken by international financial institutions is to improve the business environment for increased investment and access to finance, thus focused on the creation of *safety, stability* and *transparency.* Safety and stability in the financial markets are of paramount importance for the foundation of any viable financial system, so that trust and confidence of market participants can be built in the system. In developing the system, appropriate institutions and legal and regulatory frameworks are built to ensure the integrity and sustainability of the financial system with the global markets.

ERM entails the efforts of risk management at the corporate level in a holistic manner. The COSO approach looks at enterprise risk management at four levels:

1. Strategic—whereby the firm's high level goals are aligned with and support the mission of an enterprise.
2. Operations—whereby the firm utilizes its resources efficiently and effectively.
3. Reporting—whereby the firm's reporting practices are reliable, relevant, timely, and replicable.
4. Compliance—whereby the enterprise risk management framework helps ensure compliance with applicable laws and regulations.

We think it is important to briefly review the COSO's approach to enterprise risk management, which encompasses the following:[17]

- Aligning risk appetite and strategy—The firm's risk appetite is determined in assessing strategic investments, then objectives are set and methodologies to manage those perceived risks are developed.
- Enhancing risk response decisions—Managing risk allows the firm to determine and develop alternatives in responding to the risks, such as avoiding, reducing, sharing, or accepting the perceived risks.
- Reducing operational surprises and losses—By reducing operational surprises and potential for losses, firms gain enhanced capability to identify potential events. The firm determines its responses to risks that help reduce the surprises to be encountered in time, and help determine approaches in dealing with the associated costs of these surprises that may lead to unexpected losses.
- Identifying and managing multiple and cross-enterprise risks—Every company will one way or another face risks that affect different parts of the organization. Risk management thus will facilitate the effective responses to these unexpected events and reduce the interrelated impact of unexpected, multiple risks on the firm.
- Seizing opportunities—Management is proactive in taking advantage of opportunities that may present themselves as a result of considering the possibilities.
- Improving deployment of capital—By collecting reliable risk information the firm is enabled to make effective use of the investment opportunities that are available in the financial markets, and make optimal allocation of capital that it is able to obtain.

The above COSO framework will provide guidance in reviewing the practices employed by emerging markets companies in this chapter.

NOTES

1. Please see Box 27.5 for further details on the Financial Stability Forum (www.fsf.org). OECD is the 30- member Organization for Economic Cooperation and Development, headquartered in Paris, France. (www.oecd.org). It brings together the governments of countries committed to democracy and the market economy from around the world to support sustainable economic growth, boost employment, raise living standards, maintain financial stability, assist other countries' economic development, and to contribute to growth in world trade.

2. COSO (Committee of Sponsoring Organizations of the Treadway Commission) issued the framework in 2004 for enterprise risk management (ERM) following the U.S. Sarbanes-Oxley Act of 2002. The Sarbanes-Oxley Act of 2002 extends the long-standing requirement for public companies to maintain systems of internal control, requiring management to certify and the independent auditor to attest to the effectiveness of those systems. The COSO framework helps incorporate the existing internal control mechanisms used by firms both to satisfy their internal control needs and to move toward a fuller risk management process.

3. Kucukyilmaz, Aysegul, and Guven Sevil. "Enterprise Risk Management Perceptions in Airlines of Turkey." Anatolia University, Faculty of Civil Aviation. Turkey. (2006). akucukyilmaz@anadolu.edu.tr.

4. "Nine killed as Turkish plane crashes near Amsterdam airport." CNN. February 25, 2009—Updated 2019 GMT. http://edition.cnn.com/2009/WORLD/europe/02/25/turkish.plane.amsterdam/index.html.

5. "Risk Management in Emerging Markets." Ernst and Young. (2007). www.ey.com.

6. Hexter, Ellen, Matteo Tonello, Sumon Bhaumik. (2008). "Assessing the Climate for Enterprise Risk Management in India." The Conference Board. The study looks into the ERM practices under COSO principles in four leading Indian companies, including, Tata Motors, ICICI Bank, Tata Chemicals Ltd and Dr. Reddy's.

7. See the *Economist*, January 8, 2009. Also, *Wall Street Journal* and *New York Times*, January 6–10, 2009.

8. Claessens, Stijn, Daniela Klingebiel, and Luc Leaven. (2001). "Financial Restructuring in Banking and Corporate Sector Crises: What Policies to Pursue?" NBER Working Paper W8386. www.nber.org./papers/w8386.

9. For further information, see the attached table in Box 27.6.

10. See *New York Times*, dated November 16, 2008, for a good discussion of the G-20 summit and its proceedings.

11. Fred Kaen. "Risk Management, Corporate Governance and the Public Corporation." Unpublished working paper. University of New Hampshire. 2004.

12. Smithson, Charles, and Betty J. Simkins. "Does Risk Management Add Value? A Survey of the Evidence." Lead article, *Journal of Applied Corporate Finance* Vol. 17 (No. 3), 2005, 8–17.

13. This discussion is based on 2009 Directors Training Program Lecture Notes by Demir Yener.

14. See the Ernst and Young Survey for a detailed discussion.

15. The approach has been adopted by the respective countries' securities regulatory agencies as part of a model introduced by this author.

16. Ernst & Young. "Risk Management in Emerging Markets Survey." (2007).

17. COSO Enterprise Risk Management—Integrated Framework Executive Summary, September 2004.

REFERENCES

Cassidy, John. 2008. Anatomy of a meltdown: Ben Bernanke and the financial crisis. *New Yorker*. December 1.

Claessens, Stijn, Daniela Klingebiel, and Luc Leaven. 2001. Financial restructuring in banking and corporate sector crises: What policies to pursue? NBER Working Paper W8386. www.nber.org./papers/w8386.

COSO, Enterprise risk management—Integrated framework. 2004. COSO (Committee of Sponsoring Organizations of the Treadway Commission), September. www.coso.org/.

Ernst & Young. 2007. Risk management in emerging markets: A survey. www.Ey.com.

Financial Stability Forum, www.fsforum.org/.

Hexter, Ellen, Matteo Tonello, and Sumon Bhaumik. 2008. Assessing the climate for enterprise risk management in India. Research Report. E-0016–08-RR.

Kaen, Fred R. 2004. Risk management, corporate governance and the public corporation. Unpublished note. University of New Hampshire, International Private Enterprise Center.

Kucukyilmaz, Aysegul, and Guven Sevil. 2006. Enterprise risk management perceptions in airlines of Turkey. Anatolia University, Faculty of Civil Aviation. Eskisehir, Turkey.

Meulbroek, Lisa K. 2002. Integrated risk management for the firm: A senior manager's guide. Working Paper. Harvard Business School, Boston, MA.

Moeller, Robert R. 2007. COSO enterprise risk management: Understanding the new integrated ERM framework. Hoboken, NJ: John Wiley & Sons.

The G-20 summit proceedings on the financial markets. 2008. *New York Times*. November 16.

Nocco, Brian W., and Stulz, Rene M. 2006. Enterprise risk management: Theory and practice. Available at SSRN: http://ssrn.com/abstract=921402.

OECD. 2004. OECD Principles of Corporate Governance.

Smithson, Charles, and Betty J. Simkins. 2005. Does risk management add value? A survey of the evidence. Lead article, *Journal of Applied Corporate Finance* vol. 17, no. 3, 8–17.

ABOUT THE AUTHOR

Demir Yener, PhD is a financial economist and has held various responsibilities as a professor of finance, educator, trainer, and senior financial and private sector consultant on international economic development projects, including capital markets development, corporate governance, entrepreneurship, and executive development in over 30 emerging market countries, such as Russia, Ukraine, Central Asian Republics, Caucasus, Poland, Hungary, former Yugoslavia, Western Africa, the Middle East, South Korea, Thailand, Mongolia, and other East Asian nations on behalf of the World Bank and USAID. He currently works as senior corporate governance and finance advisor at Deloitte Consulting. He has designed, developed and managed technical assistance projects in private sector development, enterprise restructuring, financial sector reform, capital markets, nonbank financial institutions development, and corporate governance with a strong emphasis on executive training and development, and has worked with policy makers, high-level government officials, academics, and business leaders. He also held the academic position of professor of finance at Babson College, and taught as visiting professor at various institutions, including Harvard University, Bocconi University (Italy), Maastricht School of Management and Utrecht Business School (Netherlands), the American University (France), Sabanci University (Turkey), and Cairo University, Faculty of Commerce (Egypt).

CHAPTER 28

The Rise and Evolution of the Chief Risk Officer

Enterprise Risk Management at Hydro One

TOM AABO
Associate Professor, Aarhus School of Business (Denmark)

JOHN R.S. FRASER
Chief Risk Officer, Hydro One, Inc.

BETTY J. SIMKINS
Professor of Finance, Oklahoma State University

危機

The Chinese symbols for risk shown here capture a key aspect of enterprise risk management. The first symbol represents "danger" and the second "opportunity." Taken together, they suggest that risk is a strategic combination of vulnerability and opportunity. Viewed in this light, enterprise risk management represents a tool for managing risk in a way that enables the corporation to take advantage of value-enhancing opportunities. A missed strategic opportunity can result in a greater loss of (potential) value than an unfortunate incident or adverse change in prices or markets.

As in the past, many organizations continue to address risk in "silos," with the management of insurance, foreign exchange risk, operational risk, credit risk, and commodity risks each conducted as narrowly focused and fragmented activities. Under the new enterprise risk management (ERM) approach, all would function as parts of an integrated, strategic, and enterprise-wide system.[1] And while risk management is coordinated with senior-level oversight, employees at all levels of the organization are encouraged to view risk management as an integral and ongoing part of their jobs.

Although there are theoretical arguments for corporate risk management,[2] the main drivers for the implementation of ERM systems have been studies such as the Joint Australian/New Zealand Standard for Risk Management, Committee of Sponsoring Organizations of the Treadway Commission (COSO) in the United States (in response to the control problems in the S&L industry), the Group of Thirty Report in the United States (following derivatives disasters in the early 1990s), CoCo (the Criteria of Control model developed by the Canadian Institute of Chartered Accountants), the Toronto Stock Exchange Dey Report in Canada following major bankruptcies, and the Cadbury report in the United Kingdom.[3] In addition, large pension funds have become more vocal about the need for improved corporate governance, including risk management, and have stated their willingness to pay premiums for stocks of firms with strong independent board governance.[4] These studies point out that boards of directors need to have a thorough understanding of the key risks in the organization and what is being done to manage such risks.

What's more, security rating agencies such as Moody's and Standard & Poor's have recently begun to take account of ERM systems in their ratings methodology. As reported in a recent study by Moody's:

> *Increasing numbers of companies are undertaking enterprise-level approaches to risk—a more encompassing and systematic review of potential risks and their mitigation than most companies have undertaken in the past. Business units are tasked with identifying risks and, where possible, quantifying and determining how to mitigate them. These assessments typically are rolled up to a corporate level, sometimes with direct input from the board or audit committee. These assessments have often been relatively broad, focusing on reputation, litigation, product development, and health and safety risks, rather than focusing solely on financial risks. Where we have seen these assessments implemented we have commented favorably, particularly when the board or the audit committee is actively involved.[5]*

Given the overwhelming incentives and pressures to employ an enterprise-wide approach to risk management, we are surprised that more firms are not doing so. One deterrent is the scarcity of case studies describing successful implementations of ERM. A recent study by the Association of Financial Professionals noted that although most senior financial professionals see their activities evolving into a more strategic role, most also feel that more education and training are needed to meet these future challenges.[6] The Joint Australian/New Zealand Standard for Risk Management provides the first practical prescription for implementation of ERM using generic examples. Some articles and reports provide examples and insights into the potential benefits of ERM, but most lack a useful framework and sufficient practical detail to guide other firms.[7] One case study published in this journal in 2002 by Scott Harrington, Greg Niehaus, and Kenneth Risko describes how United Grain Growers combined protection against financial (such as currency and interest rate) risk and conventional insurance risk using an integrated risk management policy provided by Swiss Re.[8] However, there is a crucial need for case studies that help firms to better understand the totality of risks faced—that is, a more holistic view of ERM—and not just those that are easier to quantify.[9]

Although there is no "one size fits all" approach to ERM, companies can benefit by following the best practices of successful firms. The purpose of this case study is to fill this gap in the literature by providing the process by which one firm, Hydro One Inc., has successfully implemented ERM. This firm is at the forefront of ERM, especially in the comprehensive management of risks faced. Risk managers from the World Bank, the Auditor General of Canada, Fluor Corporation, Toronto General Hospital/Universal Health Network, and other firms from various economic sectors have visited Hydro One in order to learn from its experiences.

This case study examines the implementation of ERM at Hydro One by describing the process the firm followed, beginning with the creation of the chief risk officer position (the rise of the CRO). We describe the steps of implementation, which started with a pilot study involving workshops conducted with one of the subsidiaries. The purpose of the pilot study was to determine if ERM should be deployed throughout the firm. We next analyze the ERM process and describe various tools and techniques such as the "Delphi" method, risk trends, risk maps, risk tolerances, risk profiles, and risk ranking as it relates to the capital expenditure process. Finally, we note that ERM has become such an integral part of the workplace that the corporate chief risk officer is now becoming a low-maintenance position (the evolution of the CRO) within the company.

HYDRO ONE

Hydro One Inc. is the largest electricity delivery company in Ontario, Canada, and one of the 10 largest such companies in North America. Its predecessor, Ontario Hydro, was founded nearly a century ago, principally to build transmission lines to supply municipal utilities with power generated at Niagara Falls. Hydro One came into being in 1999 after legislation divided Ontario Hydro's delivery and generation functions into two separate companies. Hydro One today consists of three businesses—(1) transmission, (2) distribution, and (3) telecom. Its main business (contributing 99 percent of revenue) is the transportation of electricity through the high-voltage provincial grid and low-voltage distribution system to municipal utilities, large industrial customers, and 1.2 million end-use customers.

Hydro One has total revenues of CAD 4.1 billion,[10] total assets of CAD 11.3 billion, and approximately 4,000 employees. Total equity is CAD 4.3 billion, or 38 percent of total assets, and all the shares are owned by the Ontario government. In 2001, the Ontario government announced its intention to proceed with an initial public offering (IPO). However, special interest groups successfully challenged the IPO in the Supreme Court of Ontario, and the prospectus was withdrawn. Long-term financing for Hydro One is provided by access to the debt markets, including a medium-term note program. Short-term liquidity is provided through a commercial paper program. The company's long-term debt is rated A2 by Moody's and A by Standard & Poor's, and its commercial paper is rated Prime-1 and A-2.

GETTING STARTED WITH ERM

Enterprise risk management was established at Hydro One in 1999. As part of the firm's spinoff from the previous Ontario Hydro, the management and board of Hydro One set high goals for being a best-practices organization with superior corporate governance and business conduct. Hydro One wanted to look at risks and opportunities in an integrated way that would lead to a better overall allocation of corporate resources. At the same time, the scheduled deregulation of the electricity markets posed a new external challenge that had to be addressed.

Finally, the increased scrutiny on corporate governance called for a comprehensive risk management program.

Corporate Risk Management Group

At first, the attempts to implement ERM were led by external consultants, but no lasting benefits or transfer of knowledge appeared to result from those initiatives. Then, in late 1999, the head of internal audit, John Fraser (one of the authors of this article), was asked to take on the additional role of chief risk officer (CRO). The Corporate Risk Management Group was established consisting of the CRO (part-time) and two full-time professionals, one with a degree in industrial engineering and one with an MBA in process reengineering and organizational effectiveness. The group was given six months to prove its worth. If it failed to demonstrate its value during this period, the idea of implementing ERM would be abandoned and the Corporate Risk Management Group dissolved.

In early 2000, the Corporate Risk Management Group prepared two documents with the help of experienced consultants: (1) an ERM policy (Box 28.1) and (2) an ERM framework (Exhibit 28.1). The ERM policy set forth the governing principles and who was responsible for specific aspects of risk management activities, and the ERM framework set out the procedures for ERM in greater detail. The Corporate Risk Management Group took the ERM policy and ERM framework to the Executive Risk Committee for discussion and approval. The committee, which consisted of the CEO and the most senior executives, suggested that a pilot study be undertaken with one of the small subsidiaries before formal approval of the policy and framework was sought from the audit and finance committee of the board.

Pilot Study

With some consulting assistance, the Corporate Risk Management Group planned the first ERM workshop in the subsidiary. Using its own staff, the group executed the first ERM workshop in spring 2000.

The workshop followed a conventional format. Prior to the workshop, a list of some 80 potential risks or threats to the business was developed and e-mailed to the management team of the subsidiary. Each member of the team was asked to choose the 10 most critical risks facing the company—and based on these choices, a list of the top eight was prepared. Then, at the workshop, these eight risks were discussed one at a time and their relative importance voted upon by the management team. Voting was accomplished using the Delphi method,[11] which involves a combination of facilitated discussions and iterative anonymous voting technology designed to quickly identify and prioritize risks based on magnitude and probability and to evaluate the quality of controls.

The first vote on the perceived magnitude of a particular risk—with risk defined on a five-point scale: Minor, Moderate, Major, Severe, and Worst Case—often showed wide dispersion. In each case, the initial vote was followed by discussion of the definition of the particular risk, and of its causes and consequences. Depending on the dispersion of votes in the first voting session, the discussion could be long or short. A second vote was then taken; and until a clear alignment or a clearly defined cause of disagreement was established, this sequence of discussion

Box 28.1   Hydro One Inc.: Enterprise Risk Management Policy

Hydro One Inc.
Enterprise Risk Management Policy

Hydro One Inc. and its subsidiaries use an enterprise-wide portfolio approach for the management of key business risks. Enterprise risk management provides uniform processes to identify, measure, treat and report on key risks*. It supports the Board's corporate governance needs and the due diligence responsibilities of senior management. It also helps to strengthen our management practices in a manner demonstrable to external stakeholders.

Management Principles

To fulfil this commitment, we abide by the following seven principles:

1. Risk management is everyone's responsibility, from the Board of Directors to individual employees. Each is expected to understand the risks that fall within the limits of their accountabilities and is expected to manage these risks within approved risk tolerances.

2. Hydro One will manage its significant risks through a portfolio approach that optimizes the trade-offs between risk and return across all business functions. Optimization ensures that the Corporation accepts the appropriate level of risk to meet its business objectives.

3. Each subsidiary or line of business is expected to undertake risk assessments on no less than an annual basis for the business as a whole, and as determined locally for elements below the subsidiary level.

4. Enterprise Risk Management will be integrated with major business processes such as strategic planning, business planning, operational management, and investment decisions to ensure consistent consideration of risks in all decision-making.

5. Enterprise Risk Management is a comprehensive, disciplined, and continuous process in which risks are identified, analyzed, and consciously accepted or mitigated within approved risk tolerances.

6. Enterprise Risk Management will continue to evolve to reflect industry best practices and Hydro One Inc.'s needs. This policy will be reviewed annually by the Senior Management Team and the Audit & Finance Committee of the Board.

7. Local risk management policies and processes will be consistent with this corporate policy and its companion Framework. Additionally, all local policies and processes will facilitate the upward consolidation and review of all significant business risks.

Responsibilities and Accountabilities (Governance Structure)

❖ The *Audit & Finance Committee* of the Board reviews annually with the officers of the Corporation: the Corporation's risk profile; the risk retention philosophy/risk tolerances of the Corporation; and the risk management policies, processes and accountabilities within the Corporation.

❖ The *President* has ultimate accountability for managing the Corporation's risks. The *Chief Financial Officer* has specific accountability for ensuring that enterprise risk management processes are established, properly documented and maintained by the Corporation.

❖ The *Senior Management Team* provides management oversight of the Hydro One risk portfolio and the Corporation's risk management processes. It provides direction on the evolution of these processes and identifies priority areas of focus for risk assessment and mitigation planning.

---

* *Details on these processes are available in the companion Enterprise Risk Management Framework.*

❖ Each of the *President's Direct Reports* has specific accountabilities for managing risks in their subsidiary or function. Each will establish specific risk tolerances for their lines of business that do not exceed the limits of corporate risk tolerances. On an annual basis, each is also expected to formally attest that the unit's risk management process is in place, operating effectively and is consistent with this policy.

❖ *Line and Functional Managers* are responsible for managing risks within the scope of their authority and accountability. Risk acceptance or mitigation decisions will be made explicitly and within the risk tolerances specified by the head of the subsidiary or function.

❖ The *Chief Risk Officer* provides support to the President, CFO, Senior Management Team and key managers within the Corporation. This support includes developing risk management policies, frameworks and processes, introducing and promoting new techniques, preparing annual corporate risk profiles, maintaining a registry of key business risks, and facilitating risk assessments across the Corporation.

Definitions

Risk: The potential that an event, action or inaction will threaten Hydro One's ability to achieve its business objectives. Risk is described in terms of its likelihood of occurrence and potential impact or magnitude. Broad categories of risk in Hydro One include strategic, regulatory, financial, and operational risks.

Risk Assessment: The systematic identification and measurement of business risks, on a project, line of business or corporate basis. It also includes the review or establishment of risk tolerances, the evaluation of existing mitigation/controls and conscious acceptance or treatment of residual risk.

Risk Mitigation/Treatment: Actions or decisions by management that will change the status of a risk. Options include retaining the risk (either completely or partially), increasing the risk (where mitigation is not cost-effective), avoiding the risk (by withdrawing from or ceasing the activity), reducing the likelihood (by increasing preventive controls), reducing the consequences (by emergency or crisis response), and/or transferring the risk (by outsourcing, insurance, etc.).

Risk Profile: The results of any risk assessment, assembled into a consolidated view of the significant strategic, regulatory, financial and operational risks at play in a project, line of business or across the Corporation.

Risk Tolerances: Guidelines that establish levels of acceptable and unacceptable exposure from any risk. Tolerances define the range of possible impacts (from minor to catastrophic) that risks might have on business objectives. Risk tolerances are established for the Corporation and reviewed annually. Each project, function or line of business assessing its risks is expected to use or develop a set of risk tolerances that does not exceed established corporate limits.

References

- Hydro One Inc. Board of Directors, Audit & Finance Committee, Terms of Reference, 2002
- Hydro One Corporate Policy on Internal Control, Dec. 2001
- Joint Australian/New Zealand Standard for Risk Management (AS/NZS 4360:1999)
- Conference Board of Canada, A Conceptual Framework for Integrated Risk Management, Sept.1997

_____			_____
President						Date
Hydro One Inc.

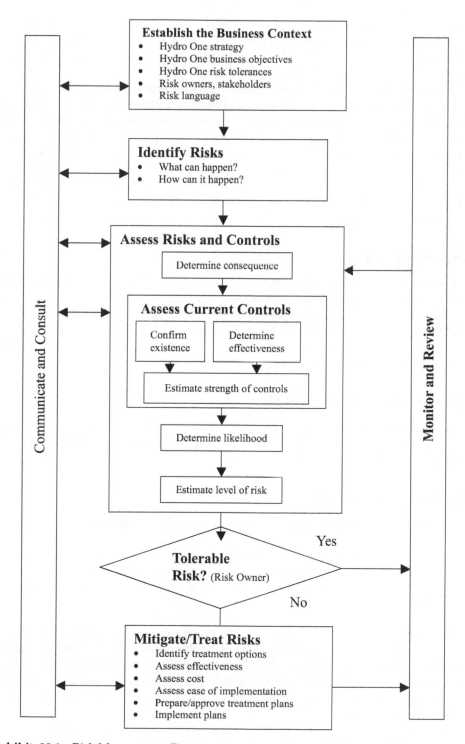

Exhibit 28.1   Risk Management Process

and voting might be repeated (usually no more than three votes were needed in practice). Then, with the voting and prioritization of risks completed, preliminary action plans were discussed and managers identified as "Champions" with the responsibility of developing more concrete action plans.

The discussions proved to be valuable. Issues that managers had thought about but never openly discussed were addressed. Concerns about some risks were allayed and new risks were identified; but in any case there was the beginning of a common understanding of risks and of a corporate plan for prioritizing action and resources to manage such risks. Since this was a pilot study for the Corporate Risk Management Group, the participants were asked to evaluate the quality and benefits of each workshop. The programs received high ratings and the managers of the subsidiary requested a follow-up session to discuss and rank the next eight risks that had been identified.

Final Approval

Following the pilot study in the subsidiary, the Corporate Risk Management Group returned to the Executive Risk Committee for debriefing. The pilot study was considered a success, and the chief risk officer presented the ERM policy and the ERM framework to the audit and finance committee of the board for approval. In the summer of 2000, the audit and finance committee approved the documents, and a roadmap for implementing ERM at Hydro One was established.

PROCESSES AND TOOLS

The overall aim of Hydro One's ERM framework (Exhibit 28.1) is not risk elimination or risk reduction per se, but rather attainment of an optimal balance between business risks and business returns.

The Business Context

The ERM Policy of Hydro One in Box 28.1 defines risk as follows:

> *The potential that an event, action, or inaction will threaten Hydro One's ability to achieve its business objectives. Risk is described in terms of its likelihood of occurrence and potential impact or magnitude. Broad categories of risk in Hydro One include strategic, regulatory, financial, and operational risks.*

Since risk is defined by its potential to threaten the achievement of business objectives, it is imperative to clearly state these objectives and how they contribute to Hydro One's overall strategy. The Corporate Risk Management Group found that objectives were not always clearly articulated, and that the workshop process from the pilot study helped in achieving clarity of business objectives needed to achieve the corporate mission.

The same was true of risk tolerances. Risk tolerances are guidelines that establish levels of acceptable and unacceptable exposures to any given risk (Exhibit 28.2 shows risk tolerances for 3 categories of risk out of 16). Tolerances define the range of possible impacts (on a five-point scale from Minor to Worst Case) of specific

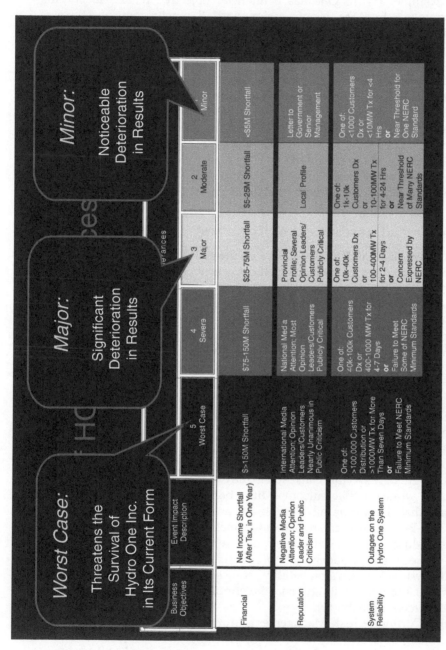

Definition of Risk Tolerances: (1) Minor: Noticeable disruption to results; manageable; (2) Moderate: Material deterioration in results; a concern; may not be acceptable; management response would be considered; (3) Major: Significant deterioration in results; not acceptable; management response required; (4) Severe: Fundamental threat to operating results; immediate senior management attention; (5) Worst Case: Results threaten survival of company in current form, potentially full-time senior management response until resolved.

Exhibit 28.2 Risk Tolerances

risks on business objectives. Through the workshops, a common understanding was developed as to how to categorize impacts from a particular risk on the firm's ability to accomplish key business objectives.[12]

As an example, Hydro One has a financial objective related to earnings stability—namely, to limit the risk of a major shortfall in net income and the associated possibility of financial distress costs. One source of the risk to net income is loss of competitiveness; another is the volatility of financial markets.

A second important corporate objective of Hydro One is maintaining its reputation and public profile. One potential source of reputational risk is pollution damage; another is inappropriate employment contracts. In this case, the magnitude of the risk is not measured in dollar terms, but in terms of the extent of public criticism both on a local as well as an international basis.

Although the ERM policy of Hydro One states that "risk management is everyone's responsibility, from the Board of Directors to individual employees," the risk facing a specific project or line of business will typically fall under the accountability of a primary risk "owner," typically the project manager or the business's CEO.

Identification and Assessment of Risks and Controls

The approach to risk identification depends on the depth and breadth of the activities under review and the extent to which these activities are "new" to Hydro One. As described above, however, the process typically involves the identification of 50 to 70 business risks, which are then narrowed down to the 10 most significant risks through interviews and focus groups. In assessing risks, the aim is to understand both the size of the potential losses as well as the associated probability of occurrence. In theory, the correct way to portray the estimated effect of a risk is to use a probability curve that reflects the potential outcomes and associated probabilities. But given the practical difficulties of "building" such a curve, Hydro One has instead chosen to focus on the "worst credible" outcome within a given time frame and its associated probability of occurrence. This has proven to be a practical and efficient way to focus on major risks while avoiding excessive detail and complex calculations.

For all risks deemed to be "major," Hydro One defines the "worst credible" outcome as the greatest loss that can result in the event that certain key controls fail. (As so defined, worst credible outcomes differ both from "inherent magnitudes," which assume that all controls fail or are absent, and "residual magnitudes," which assume that all key controls are in place and functioning.) The probability of such outcomes is evaluated for a specific time frame, generally two to five years, though for special projects the period is as short as six or nine months. As shown in Exhibit 28.3, Hydro One uses a probability rating scale from "Remote" (a 5 percent probability that the event will occur in the stipulated time frame) to "Virtually Certain" (95 percent probability).

After the Corporate Risk Management Group has helped management estimate the "worst credible" outcome, the impact on various objectives, and the associated probabilities for each risk (by workshops and the Delphi method), the next step is to produce a "risk map" like the one presented in Exhibit 28.4. The bubbles in the figure represent the expected effect of the risk on a certain objective in terms of its estimated impact (reflected on the horizontal axis) and the

Score	Rating	Description
5	*Virtually Certain*	95% probability that the event will occur in the next five years
4	Very Likely	75% probability that the event will occur in the next five years
3	Even Odds	50% probability that the event will occur in the next five years
2	Unlikely	25% probability that the event will occur in the next five years
1	Remote	5% probability that the event will occur in the next five years

Exhibit 28.3 Probability Rating Scale

estimated probability that the impact materializes (on the vertical axis). In the case of each risk, the estimated probabilities represent the relevant experts' best guess that the "worst credible" outcome will materialize. Management also uses the risk map to track the historical development of particular risks and to project expected future developments.[13]

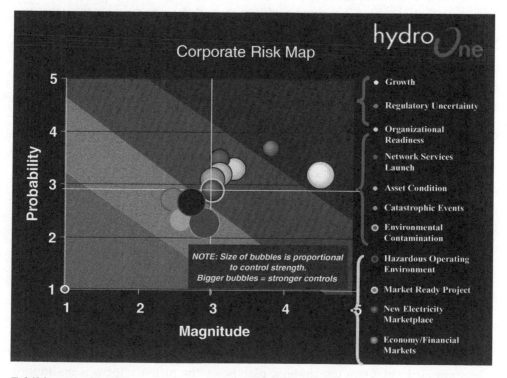

Exhibit 28.4 Risk Map

The size of the bubbles in the figure indicates the extent of management's confidence in the effectiveness of the company's controls and efforts to limit individual exposures. Control assessment involves the strength of existing organizations, processes, systems, and feedback loops that are in place to manage the risk. The company has developed a "control strength" model that is designed to complement its risk tolerances. For any given magnitude of risk (from Minor to Worst Case), there is a corresponding strength of control, with "1" representing few controls and "5" representing full prescriptive controls with executive oversight.

Tolerability of Risk—and Risk Mitigation

Once risks and controls are assessed, a rank-ordered list of "residual risks" is assembled. The risk owner (for example, the subsidiary CEO or the project manager) then determines the firm's tolerance for each risk. Within the limits of the risk owner's accountability, the risk owner decides either to accept the risk as is or to take (further) steps to mitigate it. If the risk owner accepts the risk as is, the risk is monitored and reviewed in the normal future course of risk management processes. If the risk owner decides to mitigate the risk, the process of risk mitigation is defined.

Risk owners thus have seven possible ways of dealing with significant risks:

1. **Retain:** Risk exposure is accepted as is without further mitigation, since the potential return is viewed as desirable and the downside exposure is not significant.
2. **Retain, but change mitigation:** A partially mitigated exposure is maintained, but a change in mitigation reduces the cost of control.
3. **Increase:** Risk exposure is increased, either because the potential return is viewed as desirable or the controls in place are not cost-effective.
4. **Avoid:** Risk exposure will be eliminated entirely (perhaps by withdrawal from a business area or ceasing the activity), since the potential return does not offset the downside exposure.
5. **Reduce the likelihood:** Risk exposure will be reduced cost-effectively through new or enhanced preventive controls.
6. **Reduce the consequences:** The impact of any risk that materializes will be reduced through emergency preparedness or crisis response.
7. **Transfer:** Risk exposure will be transferred to others (perhaps through an insurance policy or an outsourcing arrangement).

As can be seen from the list, risk mitigation is not necessarily the same as risk elimination or risk reduction. As previously mentioned, the purpose of strategic risk management at Hydro One is to balance business risks and business returns by taking into account the potential upside as well as the downside associated with a particular risk. Thus, a balancing act may involve an *increase* in risk. In practical terms, however, an increase in risk at Hydro One is most likely to be decided at the strategic level. Once the strategic plan is set, the primary focus is on limiting the downside risk of failure to achieve stated business objectives.

Monitor and Review

Risks do not remain static. The magnitude and probability of a certain risk is affected by internal controls (mitigation) as well as external changes in the environment. Monitoring and reporting are fundamental to effective management of business risks. Furthermore, risks may not always be categorized correctly in the first place. Risks are notoriously hard to predict, and assessing risks is to a large extent a matter of qualitative guesswork. As physicist Niels Bohr observed, "Prediction is very difficult, especially about the future."

An example of changing risk tolerances is Hydro One's decision to issue shares on the New York Stock Exchange. During the period leading up to the scheduled offering, one of management's greatest fears was the possibility of an unfavorable news story in the international press. As things turned out, however, the IPO was shelved. Then, in October 2003, the company had an oil spill that overflowed into a small stream and received a lot of press in Ontario.[14] When this got the attention of both the Ontario Government (Hydro One's shareholder) and the company's board of directors, the Corporate Risk Management Group quickly realized that their greatest reputational exposure was not to the international press, but to the local press and its power to inflame the sensitivities of Hydro One's primary stakeholders. As a consequence, negative provincial press stories are now identified as a worst-case scenario—considerably worse than their international counterparts—and strong measures are taken to avoid them.

CORPORATE RISK PROFILE

The risk management process described in the previous section serves as the basic framework for managing risks at Hydro One. The framework can be used in the normal conduct of business or for new projects.

To aggregate the information from these processes in a form suitable for the senior management and board of directors, the Risk Management Group prepares a Corporate Risk Profile twice a year. Exhibit 28.5 provides an illustration of the risk profile using the same risk sources contained in the risk map in Exhibit 28.4.

The purpose of the Corporate Risk Profile is to ensure that the senior management team shares a common understanding of the principal risks facing the organization and to provide a basis for allocating resources to address risks based on their priority. The Corporate Risk Profile is based on structured interviews with the top 40 to 50 executives together with databases from other sources (such as annual business plans and workshops). The profile reflects the executives' assessments of both previously identified risks and risks that may have been identified since the last profile in workshops, media scans, or other sources.

Description of Risk Sources

The June 2000 Corporate Risk Profile in Exhibit 28.5 shows the list of the top risks ranked as "Very High," "High," and "Medium." As of June 2000, 11 key risks had been identified. The figure also shows how these risks were rated in the previous profile and the estimated trend. And as the changes and trends suggest, the Corporate Risk Profile is by no means a static document. New risks arise

Mid-Year 2000 Corporate Risk Profile

Risk Source	Risk Rating Dec. 1999	Risk Rating June 2000	Risk Trend
Growth	Very High	Very High	↑
Regulatory Uncertainty	Very High	Very High	↑
Organizational Readiness	High	High	↑
Network Services Launch	N/A	High	New
Asset Condition	High	High	→
Catastrophic Events	High	High	↓
Environmental Contamination	High	High	→
Hazardous Operating Environment	Medium	Medium	↑
Market Ready Project	Medium	Medium	→
New Electricity Marketplace	Medium	Medium	→
Economy/Financial Markets	Medium	Medium	↓

Exhibit 28.5 Corporate Risk Profile

with legislation or new initiatives. The severity of some risks can be reduced by mitigation efforts or changes in external factors. And the estimated severity of some risks can also change because the risks (and the consequences of mitigation) are better understood.

In addition to the major sources of risk and their trends, the Corporate Risk Profile also describes the corporate objectives that are likely to be most affected by such risks and the corporate controls being used to mitigate such risks. Below we describe each of the 11 major risks as evaluated in June 2000 and the corporate measures to manage such risks.

1. **Growth:** Hydro One has plans for significant growth through acquisitions of both existing and related businesses within and beyond Ontario. This is a major risk source because there are many substantial barriers to the achievement of the planned growth. Business development and financial results are the objectives most likely to be affected. The actions of the government (as owner) create the largest part of this risk because the degree of owner support for the acquisition strategy is not always clear and firm. Hydro One has limited experience in identifying, negotiating, and integrating significant acquisitions. The exposure to government actions is mitigated by senior management participation in government review processes and a proactive government relations function. Acquisition risks are mitigated by various

means, including careful planning and analysis, staff skill development, and external advisors.

2. **Regulatory uncertainty:** The objectives of Hydro One are greatly influenced by the actions of regulators. The rules under which regulators operate will likely change as experience in the restructured industry is gained. Also, other stakeholder groups will influence regulatory decisions. The objectives most likely affected are financial results, legal/regulatory status, and reputation. Methods for mitigating this risk include increased and more effective interactions with the government and the Ontario Energy Board, increased priority and profile for regulatory matters within the company, and restoration of the company's regulatory staff capability through the addition of senior regulatory staff.

3. **Organizational readiness:** Organizational readiness reflects the ability of the company to provide effective services to customers and to improve operating efficiency in the new business environment. Many systems and processes are recognized to be less than optimally efficient and some inefficiencies are amenable to IT solutions. Readiness has been both helped and made more complex by the departure of 1,400 of the most seasoned employees through the recent voluntary retirement program (see Box 28.2). This risk source impacts competitiveness and customer service. Methods being used to mitigate this risk source include performance contracting, compensation programs, labor relations strategies, and improved technology prioritization processes.

4. **Network services launch:** The risks associated with the creation of a separate subsidiary to provide wire network services in the open market are many and varied, including uncertainty about the form of the future competitive market, the ability of the business to achieve a competitive cost structure, and the regulatory treatment of the business's reorganization costs. Possible consequences of such risks are reductions in competitiveness, reliability of customer service, and financial results. Mitigating this risk source involves a carefully crafted strategy and transition plan.

5. **Asset conditions:** The aging of asset wires and the possibility of under-funded maintenance and incomplete information about the condition of assets represent risks to customer service and reputation. Ways to mitigate this risk include redundancy on the transmission system, emergency response capability, and increased attention to this issue through higher planning priority.

6. **Catastrophic events:** Hydro One has assets covering a large geographical area, and the firm thus faces some exposure to destructive natural events such as tornadoes, which damage facilities every year, and ice storms, which are less frequent but can cause widespread damage and disruption of service. These events affect customer service, reputation, and financial results. Methods used to mitigate this risk include those listed under asset conditions (see above), as well as emergency preparedness plans and rehearsals, weather forecasting, and insurance.

7. **Environmental contamination:** This risk is largely driven by lands owned by the company that are contaminated with arsenic trioxide. Other contaminants are penta poles, transformer oils, and PCBs. To mitigate such

risks to the firm's reputation and financial results, as well as to the environment itself, the firm uses a combination of limited insurance coverage with initiatives designed to prevent such contamination.

8. **Hazardous operating environment:** Essentially all Hydro One facilities are electrically energized and so represent a threat to employees, contractors, and the public. In order to protect the firm's reputation as well as ensure employee and public safety, risk mitigation is accomplished through facilities design, asset maintenance, safe work practices, and employee training and supervision.

9. **Market Ready Project:** The Market Ready Project is a major complex undertaking with uncertain requirements and has the potential to cause Hydro One to delay the province's market opening, to cause significant customer or regulator dissatisfaction, or to well exceed its projected budget. Mitigation is provided by giving the project a high priority and profile. The recently announced delay in market opening reduces this risk, although it does not eliminate it, as even the delayed schedule is seen as tight.

10. **New electricity market:** The evolving electricity market exposes Hydro One to a wide range of unpredictable actions by competitors, customers, generators, and regulators. Any one of these parties may be able to erode the company's market position or increase its costs, thereby harming financial results. To limit this risk, the company's management is active on the IMO Board (the Independent electricity Market Operator) and is negotiating a comprehensive operating agreement with the IMO.

11. **Economy/financial markets:** Changes in commodity prices, exchange rates, or interest rates can have adverse effects on net income and cash flows. Hydro One has no commodity risk and does not trade in energy derivatives. The direct effect of fluctuations in exchange rates is considered insignificant, although this may change in the future if the company issues foreign currency debt. (All debt is currently denominated in local currency.) The company is, however, exposed to fluctuations in interest rates through its floating-rate debt (though corporate policy specifies that at most 15 percent of total debt can have floating rates) and through the refinancing of its maturing longer-term debt. Besides limiting its use of floating-rate debt, the company also periodically uses interest rate swap agreements to manage interest rate risk. Management estimates that a 100-basis-point increase in interest rates would reduce net income by roughly CAD 25 million—a risk deemed to be "Minor" or "Moderate" on the risk tolerance scale. All prudent expenses, including interest, are part of the rate base and recoverable through billing rates, so that any interest rate increase would eventually be recovered, but it would not be regarded as good management by the board and would show up as a reduction of profits in the current year.

Hydro One has some exposure to credit risk, both from its customers and from the possibility of counterparty default on its interest rate swaps. The credit risk associated with customers is effectively managed through a broadly diversified customer base. The counterparty default risk is limited by the company's policy of transacting only with highly rated counterparties, limiting total exposure levels with individual counterparties, and entering into master agreements that allow "net settlement."

Box 28.2   Strategic Risk Management Analysis of Voluntary Retirement Package

In the early summer of 2000, the Risk Management Group was asked to perform an enterprise risk management analysis of the risks related to a Voluntary Retirement Package (VRP) that was offered to employees at Hydro One. The purpose of the Voluntary Retirement Package was to reduce staff and related costs in preparation for an IPO. However, the Voluntary Retirement Package turned out to be almost too much of a success. Hydro One lost 1,300 employees out of a total of more than 6,000 employees—far more than the 800 that were expected to take the package. And the 1,300 employees were in most cases senior and experienced personnel. The senior management of Hydro One feared that without a rigorous analysis, some unjustified requests for personnel to replace those who had left would eradicate the economic benefits of the program. In risk map terms, the purpose of the enterprise risk analysis was to address the bubbles in the far right-hand corner and move these bubbles toward the lower left-hand corner as cost effectively as possible. (See Exhibit 28.4 for an illustration of this concept.)

The Corporate Risk Management Group discussed business objectives and related risk tolerances with about 40 managers whose groups had experienced material VRP losses. The group asked the managers what actions they had taken or planned to compensate for VRP losses (such as efficiency improvements or dropping activities) and where they felt they still had a resource gap that could impact corporate objectives. The interviews allowed the Corporate Risk Management Group to identify units where the VRP losses resulted in material risk and what the impacts of those risks might be. The group vetted this feedback through a series of interviews with senior management responsible for each major functional area (finance, regulatory, and so on) to validate middle management's assessment of both the gap and the impacts. For areas of material risk ("Major" or higher), the group asked managers what could be done in order to reduce risk to a "Moderate" level or lower.

The managers indicated that they had taken actions or had plans underway to compensate for the loss of some of the employees. The most important mitigating technique was from planned efficiency gains, but the possibility of hiring contract/temporary workers was also planned. Overall, managers estimated that they could compensate for 1,100 employees out of the 1,300 employees lost, thus leaving a gap of some 200 employees to mitigate excessive levels of risks.

The Corporate Risk Management Group developed a draft list of VRP risk sources, which the senior management team assessed and ranked at a two-hour facilitated workshop, using electronic voting technology and the Delphi method. The result was a list of 11 risk sources ranked according to their significance. "Customer Relations" and "Network Services" topped the list with a risk score of 3.9 and 3.8 on a five-point scale integrating both magnitude and probability. For example, "Customer Relations" was voted as having a magnitude of 3.8 and a probability of 4.1, which gave an ultimate risk score of 3.9.

Some of the risk sources pertained to specific organization units while other risk sources were generic (organization-wide). For the unit-specific risks, the Corporate Risk Management Group calculated on the basis of input from managers that a mitigation process that reduced all risks to a "Moderate" level or lower (1 or 2 on a five-point scale—see Exhibit 28.2) would require 126 full-time employees and CAD 4.4 million. For the generic risks, a combination of monitoring, planning, and risk assessment programs was proposed. The mitigation as to unit-specific risks as well as generic risks was not intended to eliminate the VRP as a source of risk but to reduce the risks to acceptable levels in a cost-effective way.

QUANTIFYING THE UNQUANTIFIABLE

The final step of the ERM process at Hydro One is to prioritize the use of resources for investment planning based on the risks identified. Hydro One is inherently an asset management company in the sense that most of its assets have a life expectancy of 30 to 70 years. The Investment Planning Department of Hydro One collaborated with the Corporate Risk Management Group to develop a risk-based approach for allocating resources. Using this approach, the company has managed to find an innovative way of "quantifying the unquantifiable."

The approach rests on three pillars:

1. The five-point risk tolerance scale (from Minor to Worst Case) for assessing the estimated impact of a given risk on a given corporate objective (illustrated earlier in Exhibits 28.2 and 28.4).
2. The five-point probability rating scale (from Remote to Virtually Certain) for evaluating the probability that a given impact will materialize (shown in Exhibit 28.3 and 28.4).
3. The quality of controls (or other risk management mechanisms) designed to reduce the residual risks.

Exhibit 28.6 illustrates this risk-based approach for determining capital expenditures. Each class of asset or type of expenditure is categorized into different levels as follows:[15]

- Highest Risk Exposure: an unacceptable level of risk that must be funded as a priority (and shown in color in Exhibit 28.6).
- Minimum Funding Level: the level of service at which the risk to the company's business objectives is considered barely tolerable.
- Level 1: at this level of funding, the risk to business objectives is materially lower than at the Minimum Funding Level.
- Levels 2 and 3 (not illustrated in the figure): At these levels of funding, the risk to business objectives is materially lower than at Level 1. A description

Program	Level	Cost	Cuml. Cost	Risk If Not Done	Bang for the Buck
Tree Trim	Red	$2	$2	4.6	
Lines	Red	$6	$8	4.5	Intolerable Risk
Poles	Red	$1	$9	3.9	
Tree Trim	Minimum Level	$1	$10	2.8	2.80
Lines	Level 1	$3	$13	3.0	1.00
Tree Trim	Level 1	$2	$15	1.9	0.95
Lines	Minimum Level	$5	$20	3.2	0.64 "Bang for the Buck"
Poles	Minimum Level	$12	$32	2.3	0.19

This illustrates Hydro One's risk-based structural approach for determining capital expenditures. The three projects in the box have the highest risk exposure measure and will have the top priority for resource allocation. This type of ranking of projects across work programs is very useful for resource allocation prioritization in the capital expenditures process. "Bang for the Buck" equals "Risk if not done" divided by dollar cost.

Exhibit 28.6   A Risk-Based Structural Approach to Investment Planning at Hydro One

of the expenditures and associated risks is provided for each level. The investment levels are associated with specific accomplishments—for example, numbers of kilometers of line cleared, or numbers of calls answered within 30 seconds.

As also shown in Exhibit 28.6, all investment levels for each asset class are risk-rated based on magnitude and probability for the major corporate objectives using a grid. This grid defines intolerable combined levels of magnitude and probability (shown as Highest Risk in Exhibit 28.6), and assigns a risk rating based on a scale for the combined rating. Each class of asset is stratified into different levels of risk (Highest Risk, Minimum Funding Level, Level 1, and so on). As an example, "Tree Trim" is broken down into several categories, each with its own risk rating. Highest Risk might be minimum clearance near urban centers, while Level 2 might correspond to a deeper clearance on small lines with lower risk.

Hydro One has applied a method named "Bang for the Buck" to be used in prioritizing expenditures for non–Highest Risk risks. The Bang for the Buck index prioritizes by calculating the risk reduction per dollar spent. For example, at the top of the Bang for the Buck index in Exhibit 28.6 is "Tree Trim" (Minimum Level), which shows 2.8 risk units ("Risk if not done") eliminated by spending one dollar ("Cost"). This gives a Bang for the Buck value of 2.8. At the other end of the scale, the elimination of 2.3 risk units in relation to Poles (Minimum Level) by spending $12 gives a more modest Bang for the Buck value of 0.18.

At the point where the cumulative expenditures reach the level of the available resources, the planned work for the year is determined. The documented prioritization of planned investments in assets is then the subject of a formal two-day meeting between the senior asset managers and the executives that is designed to probe and validate assumptions before the investment plan is presented to the board of directors as part of the annual business planning process.

Using this approach to enterprise risk management, the company then attempts to combine the qualitative, imaginative strengths of scenario planning with the quantitative rigor associated with real options analysis.[16] Scenario planning is a well-established approach (the origins of which are generally traced to practices at Royal Dutch/Shell)[17] for thinking about major sources of corporate uncertainty. Real options, on the other hand, is a more scientific, finance-oriented approach that, at least in well-defined cases, can be used to quantify possible outcomes and the value of different strategies for dealing with such outcomes. In the case of an oil exploration company, for example, scenario planning might be used to help management anticipate the set of political and economic events that could lead to $100 per barrel oil prices. Real options could be used to estimate how much the firm would be worth while also providing management with a value-maximizing schedule for developing its reserves.

BENEFITS OF ERM AND OUTCOMES AT HYDRO ONE

Hydro One's 2003 Annual Report summarizes the benefits of ERM as follows: "An enterprise-wide approach enables regulatory, strategic, operational, and financial risks to be managed and aligned with our strategic business objectives." Exhibit 28.7 reflects our attempt to list and elaborate on some of the key benefits. Although most are qualitative and difficult to quantify, all are perceived as valuable.

From a finance perspective, the most direct evidence of a benefit from ERM is the positive reaction of the credit rating agencies and the resulting reduction in the company's cost of debt.[18] In 2000, Hydro One issued $1 billion of debt, its first issue as a new company after the split-up of Ontario Hydro. According to recent conversations with senior ratings analysts at Moody's, ERM was then (and continues to be) a significant factor in the ratings process for the company.[19] The firm reportedly received a higher rating on this initial issue (AA− from S&P and A+ from Moody's) than initially anticipated, and the issue was oversubscribed by approximately 50 percent. To quantify the potential yield savings, consider that since 2000, the long-term mean yield spread between AA and A has averaged approximately 20 basis points. And if we conservatively credit ERM with reducing the company's debt costs by, say, 10 basis points, this translates into annual savings in interest costs of $1 million on the $1 billion in new debt.

Another clearly important benefit is the improvement of Hydro One's capital expenditure process using the risk mitigation prioritization index. As described in the previous section, this process takes into account the benefit of risk reduction in all major risk categories (that is, regulatory, financial, reliability, safety, reputation, and so on) by allocating capital expenditures according to the greatest overall risk reduction per dollar spent. While the system is complex and involves extensive computer modeling, the result is a capital allocation process that is much more likely to lead the firm toward the optimal (viewed on a risk-adjusted basis) portfolio of capital projects.

In addition to a lower cost of capital and improved capital allocation, our discussions with Hydro One's management also suggest a number of less tangible benefits, some of which are described in Exhibit 28.7. Perhaps most important, top management seems convinced that employees at all levels of the organization now have a much better understanding of the firm's risks and what they can do to

Exhibit 28.7   Benefits of ERM and Outcomes at Hydro One

Examples of ERM Benefits	Hydro One Experiences
Achieve lower cost of debt	Realized higher debt rating and lower interest costs than expected on $1 billion debt issue, which was the first issue as a new company. Issue was heavily oversubscribed. Ratings analysts stated ERM was a significant factor in the ratings process for Hydro One.
Focus capital expenditures process on managing/ allocating capital based on greatest mitigation of risk per $ spent	Capital expenditures are allocated and prioritized based on a risk-based structural approach. An "optimal portfolio" of capital investments is achieved providing the greatest risk reduction per $ spent. Also, ERM has been used in the management of major projects such as the 88 corporate utility acquisitions during 2000 and the potential building of an underground cable to the USA.
Avoid "land mines" and other surprises	Since starting ERM, there have been many unusual occurrences at the company. Two significant ones were spelled out in the Corporate Risk Tolerances ahead of time: the dismissal of the Board of Directors and the reaction to a large oil spill.
Reassure stakeholders that the business is well managed with—stakeholders defined to include investors, analysts, rating agencies, regulators, and the press	During the IPO road shows, the Corporate Risk Management Group was told that the ERM workshops had greatly assisted the executive team in articulating the risks they faced and what was being done about them. There are many other examples.
Improve corporate governance via best practices guidelines	Hydro One has moved from the Board Committees asking why these risk summaries were being brought to them to a point at which they now routinely expect this information. Directors recognize that Hydro One is ahead of other companies on whose boards they sit.
Implement a formalized system of risk management that includes an ERM system (a required component of the 1995/1999/2004 Australian Standard for Risk Management)	Hydro One has a formalized system that drives periodic assessment, documentation, and reporting of all risks.
Identify which risks the company can pursue better than its peers	Although not necessarily attributable solely to ERM: • A subsidiary involved in marketing electricity was sold due to high commodity risks. • Several processing and administrative functions were outsourced to transfer labor union and labor cost risks.

manage them. And, as described in the next section, this process appears to have led to an impressive change in the company's corporate culture.

Current Status

Instead of the title "Current Status," we could have substituted "The Evolution of the CRO." At the outset of the ERM initiative, the Corporate Risk Management Group consisted of the CRO (part-time) and two full-time professionals. To date, the group has conducted more than 180 workshops and authored numerous internal reports on strategic risk management. Some of these reports were prepared in the normal conduct of business and were issued regularly. Other reports were requested ad hoc, such as the strategic risk management analysis of a voluntary retirement program at Hydro One that is summarized in the box insert.

From the end of 2003 until the present, there have been no full-time members of the Corporate Risk Management Group. The CRO devotes 20 percent of his time to this role, and his previous staff have been reassigned to other jobs, although they are occasionally "borrowed back" for certain specific high-risk ERM projects. This reduction in personnel is not a sign of failure, but rather of two notable accomplishments:

1. The transfer and generation of knowledge on strategic risk management throughout the organization has been so effective that strategic risk management is considered to be embedded in the various subsidiaries and divisions to such an extent that the need for extensive central planning, implementation, and monitoring is significantly reduced. As evidence of Hydro One's success in making "risk management everyone's responsibility," in 2002 the Corporate Risk Management Group received the firm's "Sir Graham Day Award for Excellence in Culture Change."[20] In the words of the then CEO and President of the company,
   Thanks to this team, Hydro One is becoming a leader in enterprise risk management—a key best-practice in the energy industry, and a critical element of good corporate governance . . . This group's progress to date has also garnered attention from other organizations. In fact, the risk managers from the World Bank and Toronto General Hospital have visited Hydro One to learn about our methods.
2. Hydro One has become a well-established company both internally and externally. In 1999 it was a "new" company operating in a market that was to be deregulated and it was scheduled for privatization through an IPO. Today Hydro One has more than five years of experience as an independent company. It has demonstrated its ability to compete in a market that *had been* deregulated (but is now moving toward more regulation), and its ownership structure is now considered stable. Thus, the extent to which Hydro One faces internal and external changes has been markedly reduced.

The CRO continues to provide support for senior managers and develop risk management policies, frameworks, processes, and other analyses as needed. But thanks to the success of the program, the demand for hosting numerous workshops and establishing a risk management culture is greatly diminished. In short, risk management and awareness has become a mature operation at Hydro One.[21]

CONCLUSION

This chapter describes the implementation over a five-year period of enterprise risk management at Hydro One, a Canadian electric utility company that has experienced significant changes in its industry and business. Starting with the creation of the position of chief risk officer and the deployment of a pilot study involving one of the firm's subsidiaries, the ERM implementation process has made use of a variety of tools and techniques, including the "Delphi Method," risk trends, risk maps, risk tolerances, risk profiles, and risk rankings.

Among the most tangible benefits of ERM at Hydro One are a more rational and better-coordinated process for allocating capital and the favorable reaction of Moody's and Standard & Poor's, which has arguably led to an increase in its credit rating and a reduction of its cost of capital. But perhaps just as important is the company's progress in realizing the first principle of its ERM policy—namely, that "risk management is everyone's responsibility, from the board of directors to individual employees. Each is expected to understand the risks that fall within the limits of his or her accountabilities and is expected to manage these risks within approved risk tolerances." The implementation process itself has helped make risk awareness an important part of the corporate culture.

As a result, the management of Hydro One feels that the company is much better positioned today than five years ago to respond to new developments in the business environment, favorable as well as unfavorable. Indeed, ERM can be viewed as an integral part of the company's current business model. As Charles Darwin noted more than 150 years ago, in a world where mutability is the only permanent feature of the landscape, "It's not the strongest of the species that survive, nor the most intelligent, but those that are the most responsive to change."

NOTES

1. We view the terms "integrated," "strategic," and "enterprise-wide" as interchangeable in what we call enterprise risk management.

2. In the hypothetical Modigliani and Miller world of corporate finance, risk management does not add value. However, in the nonfrictionless environment of the real world, risk management by the firm can create value in one or more of the following ways that investors cannot duplicate for themselves: (1) facilitate the risk management efforts of the firm's equity holders; (2) decrease financial distress costs; (3) lower the risk faced by important nondiversified investors (such as managers and employees); (4) reduce taxes; (5) reduce the firm's capital costs through better performance evaluation and reduced monitoring costs; and (6) provide internal funding for investment projects and facilitate capital planning. Refer to "A Senior Manager's Guide to Integrated Risk Management" by Lisa Meulbroek, *Journal of Applied Corporate Finance*, vol. 14, no. 4 (Winter 2002) for more information on these benefits. Another view of how risk management can maximize firm value is that risk management should eliminate costly "lower-tail outcomes," while preserving as much of the upside as possible; see R. Stulz, "Rethinking Risk Management," *Journal of Applied Corporate Finance*, vol. 9, no. 3 (Fall 1996). Corporate risk management should include choosing the optimal mixture of securities and risk

management products and solutions to give the company access to capital at the lowest possible cost; see Christopher Culp, "The Revolution in Corporate Risk Management: A Decade of Innovations in Process and Products," *Journal of Applied Corporate Finance,* vol. 14, no. 4 (Winter 2002).

3. The Joint Australian/New Zealand Standard for Risk Management (AS/NSZ 4360: 1999), first edition published in 1995, provides the first articulation of practical enterprise risk management. This guide covers the establishment and implementation of the risk management process involving the identification, analysis, evaluation, treatment, and ongoing monitoring of risks. Committee of Sponsoring Organizations of the Treadway Commission (COSO) (September 1992); Group of Thirty, Derivatives: Practices and Principles (Washington, DC, 1993); "Where Were the Directors"—Guidelines for Improved Corporate Governance in Canada, Report of the Toronto Stock Exchange Committee on Corporate Governance in Canada (December 1994); CoCo (Criteria of Control Board of the Canadian Institute of Chartered Accountants); and Committee on the Financial Aspects of Corporate Governance (Cadbury Committee, final report and Code of Best Practices issued December 1, 2002).

4. In McKinsey & Company and Institutional Investor, "Corporate Boards: New Strategies for Adding Value at the Top," a 1996 study of 50 money managers.

5. Refer to Moody's "Findings on Corporate Governance in the United States and Canada: August 2003–September 2004." (New York: Moody's Investors Service, October 2004).

6. See the Association for Financial Professionals, "The Evolving Role of Treasury: Report of Survey Results," (November 2003).

7. See, for example, "University of Georgia Roundtable on Enterprise-Wide Risk Management," *Journal of Applied Corporate Finance,* vol. 15, no. 4 (Fall 2003); "Strategic Risk Management: New Disciplines, New Opportunities," CFO Publishing Corporation (2002); Marie Hollein, "Measuring Risk: A Strategic Review and Step-by-Step Approach," *AFP Exchange,* vol. 23, no. 6 (Nov./Dec. 2003); and James C. Lam and Brian M. Kawamoto, "Emergence of the Chief Risk Officer," *Risk Management* (September 1997); and similar articles in *CFO* magazine (www.cfo.com).

8. See S. Harrington, G. Niehaus, and K. Risko, "Enterprise Risk Management: The Case of United Grain Growers," *Journal of Applied Corporate Finance,* vol. 14, no. 4 (Winter 2002), and Chapter 6 of T.L. Barton, W.G. Shenkir, and P.L. Walker, "Making Enterprise Risk Management Pay Off," Financial Executives Research Foundation, Inc. (2002).

9. As reported in a recent survey, companies indicated that quantifiable risks are still absorbing too much of their attention and that they need to better understand the totality of the risks their firm faces. See "Uncertainty Tamed? The Evolution of Risk Management in the Financial Services Industry," a joint project by PricewaterhouseCoopers and the Economist Intelligence Unit (2004).

10. CAD = Canadian dollars.

11. The Delphi method, originally developed by the RAND Corporation in 1964 for technological forecasting, is a way of estimating future measures by asking a group of experts to make estimates, recirculating the estimates back to the group, and repeating the process until the numbers converge. It is a formal method used to generate expert collective decisions. The Delphi method recognizes human judgment as legitimate and useful inputs in generating forecasts. Single experts sometimes suffer biases and group meetings may suffer from "follow the leader" syndromes and/or reluctance to abandon previously stated opinions. The Delphi method is characterized by anonymity, controlled feedback, and statistical response. The Rand report is still interesting to read and contains many innovations that are used in the analysis and describes Delphi results. For instance, the report presents arguments for using median values rather than the mean values of the

group's responses and also illustrates how ranges of opinions can be presented graphically (see T.J. Gordon and Olaf Helmer, "Report on a Long Range Forecasting Study,"
R-2982, Rand Corporation, 1964). For a broad review of the literature on Delphi and
references to the method and past studies, refer to Fred Woudenberg, "An Evaluation
of Delphi," Technological Forecasting and Social Change (September 1991). For further
information on practical applications, see Michael Adler and Erio Ziglio (eds.), *Gazing
into the Oracle: The Delphi Method and its Application to Social Policy and Public Health*
(Jessica Kingsley Publishers, 1996).

12. The two scales (risk tolerance and probability rating) form the backbone of the quan-
    tification of risks at Hydro One and make comparisons possible between impacts that
    are easily quantifiable in monetary terms (e.g., shortfall in net income) with impacts
    that are more qualitative in nature (e.g., extent of criticism). For example, a risk that has
    an impact of 3 in relation to objective A and an impact of 2 in relation to objective B
    is a more serious threat to Hydro One in relation to objective A than it is in relation to
    objective B.

13. For another example of how a firm uses risk maps in enterprise risk management, refer
    to Chapter 5 on Microsoft Corporation, in T.L. Barton, W.G. Shenkir, and P.L. Walker
    (2002), cited earlier.

14. Refer to Hydro One news releases on October 1 and 2, 2003, about the oil spill in
    Pickering. Initially, the city of Pickering was upset about the oil spill from a station, the
    largest single transformer station in North America, in a residential community (see
    "Hydro Plant Oil Spill Riles Mayor of Pickering" in *Bell Globemedia*, October 2, 2003).
    Later, the mayor praised Hydro One's quick response to the clean up (see "Hydro One
    Picks Up Tab for Oil Spill," *Electricity Forum News*, October 2003).

15. A useful analogy for this methodology is to consider in a typical household that each
    asset (e.g., house, car, kids' education) has certain expenditure requirements that are
    broken down into levels of expenditure; for example, the car has levels defined as Red
    Zone = fixing brakes (impacts safety objectives), Minimum Funding Level = changing
    oil to lengthen life (long-term financial objective; could also be viewed as Level 1),
    Level 3 = paint job (improve the family's social image).

16. See, for example, Kent D. Miller and H. Gregory Waller, "Scenarios, Real Options and
    Integrated Risk Management," *Long Range Planning*, vol. 36 (2003) 93–107, for a good
    general discussion.

17. See, for example, Paul J. H. Schoemaker and Cornelius A.J.M. van der Heijden, "Inte-
    grating Scenarios into Strategic Planning at Royal Dutch/Shell," *Planning Review*, vol. 20,
    no. 3 (May–June 1992) 41–46.

18. For additional discussion and examples of ERM and its effect on the cost of capital, see
    "University of Georgia Roundtable on Enterprise-Wide Risk Management," *Journal of
    Applied Corporate Finance*, vol. 15, no. 4 (Fall 2003) 18–20.

19. On September 13, 2004, telephone interviews were conducted with senior ratings ana-
    lysts at Moody's to verify the importance of Hydro One's ERM program in the credit
    rating process on their long-term debt. Moreover, as part of Moody's Enhanced Analy-
    sis Initiative, ratings methodologies measuring the quality of corporate governance and
    risk management include specific questions related to enterprise risk management. See,
    for example, Questions 16, 17, and 18 of Moody's Corporate Governance Assessment
    and Moody's research methodology.

20. See Hydro One Inc.'s 2002 President's Awards.

21. Interestingly, the outcome of ERM at Hydro One is consistent with the predictions of
    a survey by the Conference Board of Canada in which respondents felt that the need

for a specific risk officer may decline as it is more widely implemented in organizations and the CRO's responsibilities would then be distributed to the operating units or assimilated into the CFO's duties; see the Conference Board of Canada, "A Composite Sketch of a Chief Risk Officer" (2001).

ABOUT THE AUTHORS

Tom Aabo is an Associate Professor at the Aarhus School of Business in Denmark. He has taught courses in corporate finance, international business finance, foreign direct investment, and internationalization of the firm at the Aarhus School of Business. His areas of research are strategic risk management, exchange rate exposure management, real options analysis, and international corporate finance. He is published in the *Journal of Applied Corporate Finance, International Journal of Managerial Finance, European Financial Management*, and *Review of Financial Economics* (among others). Tom also serves on the editorial board of the *Asian Journal of Finance and Accounting*. Prior to getting his PhD, Tom worked in industry for Amersk and Gudme Raaschou. Tom received a BA in Business Administration from Aarhus School of Business (Denmark), a MS in Business Administration, and PhD from Aarhus School of Business.

John Fraser is the Vice President, Internal Audit & Chief Risk Officer of Hydro One Networks Inc., one of North America's largest electricity transmission and distribution companies. He is an Ontario and Canadian Chartered Accountant, a Fellow of the Association of Chartered Certified Accountants (U.K.), a Certified Internal Auditor, and a Certified Information Systems Auditor. He has more than 30 years experience in the risk and control field mostly in the financial services sector, including areas such as finance, fraud, derivatives, safety, environmental, computers and operations. He is currently the Chair of the Advisory Committee of the Conference Board of Canada's Strategic Risk Council, a Practitioner Associate Editor of the Journal of Applied Finance, and a past member of the Risk Management and Governance Board of the Canadian Institute of Chartered Accountants. He is a recognized authority on Enterprise Risk Management and has co-authored three academic papers on ERM—published in the *Journal of Applied Corporate Finance* and the *Journal of Applied Finance*.

Betty J. Simkins is Williams Companies Professor of Business and Professor of Finance at Oklahoma State University (OSU). She received her BS in Chemical Engineering from the University of Arkansas, her MBA from OSU, and her PhD from Case Western Reserve University. Betty is also very active in the finance profession and currently serves as Vice-Chairman of the Trustees (previously President) of the Eastern Finance Association, on the Board of Directors for the Financial Management Association (FMA), as co-editor of the *Journal of Applied Finance*, and as Executive Editor of FMA Online (the online journal for the FMA). She has coauthored more than 30 journal articles in publications including the *Journal of Finance, Financial Management, Financial Review, Journal of International Business Studies, Journal of Futures Markets, Journal of Applied Corporate Finance*, and the *Journal of Financial Research* and has won a number of best paper awards at academic conferences.

Index